CLB 2205
This edition published 1991 by Colour Library Books Ltd, Godalming, Surrey
© 1988 Colour Library Books Ltd
Printed and bound in Italy by New Interlitho, SpA
All rights reserved ISBN 0 86283 613 1

The recipes for Chocolate Orange Cake, Loganberry Torte, Strawberry Box, Chocolate Terrine with Cherry Sauce, Chocolate Rum Fool, Chocolate Rum Sauce, Mocha Ice Cream, Truffles, Zigzag Shortbread and Peppermint Sauce are the copyright of Jennie Reekie, and are reproduced by kind permission of Ward Lock Limited.

Compiled by
Anne D. Ager
Lalita Ahmed
Judith Ferguson
Denise Jarret-Macauley
Maureen McCall
Beverley Piper

Designed by
Philip Clucas and Sara Cooper

THE COMPLETE
COOKBOOK

COLOUR LIBRARY BOOKS

Contents

VEGETARIAN CUISINE

Introduction to Vegetarian Meals

It is amazing how rigid we are when it comes to the subject of food and what we eat. In all other aspects of life virtually anything goes: people walk the streets with pink hair; sail the Atlantic single-handed or jog around the houses for two hours every morning and yet if we prefer beans and lentils to beef and chicken we are considered as being rather odd.

Vegetarians are not cranks, and there is nothing weird and wonderful about a pattern of vegetarian eating; they just prefer to eat dishes which do not contain meat, poultry, game and, quite often, fish. 'Why don't they become ill?' you hear people say; 'Where do they get their energy from if they don't eat meat?'; 'How boring to live on just vegetables and those little dried peas!' As vegetarians will happily tell you, they feel perfectly healthy, have quite sufficient energy to cope with day-to-day activities and, above all, *they really enjoy their food.*

A vegetarian diet can be just as varied and interesting as one based on meat and fish. Meat is much the same the world over, which cannot be said of the wide and wonderful range of fresh fruits and vegetables. And it is variety which is very much the keynote of vegetarian eating: different pastas, rices, cheeses, nuts and pulses are just a selection of the varied ingredients of a vegetarian diet. Most important of all, vegetarian dishes are every bit as nutritious as their meat-rich counterparts. The main difference lies with the types of food which provide us with the necessary nutrients. In a typical vegetarian dish, the protein usually comes from pulses, nuts or cheese, or a combination of these ingredients. Minerals, vitamins, fats and carbohydrates come from all the other basic foods, such as those already mentioned.

Eating 'the vegetarian way' has all sorts of advantages in its favour. A meatless diet is a very healthy one since it is nutritious, low in fat and high in bulk and fibre. Vegetarians rarely need to watch their weight as a diet that is high in natural fibre and low in fat is comparatively low in calories. The traditional pattern of Western eating is relatively expensive to follow, whereas vegetarian dishes are more economical to prepare and cook. In fact, meatless meals can simply make a nice change from the traditional pattern of eating. Vegetarian cooking is fun, and eating vegetarian meals is healthy and good for you.

Vegetarian food really can be exciting and delicious, and even if you are not a committed vegetarian many of the following ideas are well worth trying. The dishes combine unusual tastes with an imaginative use of spices and fresh herbs for extra flavour. If you served many of the recipes to your family and friends they probably wouldn't even realise that their meal was meatless.

Soups

Cucumber Soup

PREPARATION TIME:	15 minutes
COOKING TIME:	8-10 minutes
SERVES:	4 people

1 large cucumber
250ml (8 fl oz) water
600ml (1 pint) vegetable stock
15ml (1 tblsp) white wine vinegar
30ml (2 tblsp) cornflour mixed with
30ml (2 tblsp) water
30ml (2 tblsp) soured cream
30ml (2 tblsp) natural yogurt
Salt and ground white pepper to taste
15ml (1 tblsp) chopped chives or
   green spring onion tops
Chilli powder

Cut ¼ of the cucumber into wafer thin rounds and keep aside for garnishing. Puree the rest of the cucumber with the water in a liquidiser. Put the vegetable stock and the pureed cucumber into a saucepan and bring to the boil over a medium heat. Add the vinegar and cook for 1 minute. Add the cornflour mixture gradually. Stir well until the soup starts to thicken. Simmer for 2-3 minutes. Remove from the heat and cool slightly. Blend in the liquidiser and add the soured cream and yogurt. Return to the saucepan and season with salt and pepper. Heat through gently to serve hot or chill to serve cold. Serve garnished with sliced cucumber and chopped chives or spring onion tops. Sprinkle with chilli powder.

Daal Soup

This is a thick and hearty soup, made from lentils. The lentils most often used for making soup are red lentils, or yellow lentils which are called Toor daal. The recipe below can be made with either variety.

PREPARATION TIME:	15-20 minutes
COOKING TIME:	15 minutes
SERVES:	4-6 people

350g (12oz) red lentils (see above)
900ml (1½ pints) water
4 canned tomatoes, drained and
   crushed
1 green chilli, sliced lengthways and
   seeded
30ml (2 tblsp) natural yogurt or
   soured cream
15g (½oz) butter
1 medium onion, peeled and chopped
salt and freshly ground black pepper
   to taste
1-2 sprigs fresh green coriander
   leaves, chopped

Wash the lentils in 4-5 changes of water. Drain the lentils and put them into a pan with the water. Cover the pan and bring to the boil; simmer for 10 minutes. Beat until smooth with an egg whisk. Add the crushed tomatoes and green chilli and simmer gently for 2 minutes. Stir in the yogurt or soured cream. Melt the butter in a small pan and fry the onion until golden. Season the hot soup with salt and pepper and pour into a serving bowl; sprinkle with the fried onion and chopped coriander. Serve immediately with buttered brown bread, crisp rolls or croutons.

Tomato Saar

This is a thin tomato soup from the South of India. It makes a refreshing and interesting starter.

PREPARATION TIME:	15 minutes
COOKING TIME:	17-18 minutes
SERVES:	4-6 people

10ml (2 tsp) butter
1 small onion, peeled and chopped
225g (½lb) tomatoes, skinned and
   chopped
1 litre (1¾ pints) water
15ml (1 tblsp) tomato puree
4-6 green curry leaves
Salt and freshly ground black pepper
   to taste
3 cloves of garlic, peeled and crushed

Garnish
1-2 sprigs fresh green coriander or
   parsley leaves, chopped
1 green chilli, chopped (optional)

Melt half of the butter and fry the onion for 3-4 minutes. Add the skinned and chopped tomatoes and cook for 5 minutes. Blend the water and tomato puree and add to the onion and tomatoes. Add curry leaves. Season with salt and pepper. Cover and simmer for 5-7 minutes. Heat the remaining butter and fry the crushed cloves of garlic until dark brown. Pour the mixture over the simmering tomato soup. Remove from the heat. Sprinkle over the chopped coriander and chilli. Discard green chilli before eating. Serve piping hot either with French bread or with a little plain boiled rice. Alternatively: blend the skinned tomatoes to give a smooth textured soup.

Mixed Vegetable Soup

This Indian recipe can include a wide variety of vegetables. One creates one's own dish by adding or subtracting one or more vegetables.

PREPARATION TIME:	15 minutes
COOKING TIME:	about 20 minutes
SERVES:	6 people

10ml (2 tsp) butter
1 medium onion, peeled and chopped
6 cloves
2.5cm (1 inch) piece cinnamon stick
4 small green cardamoms
1 small bayleaf
1 medium potato, peeled and
   chopped
2 carrots, peeled and chopped
1 banana, peeled and chopped
6 florets of cauliflower
50g (2oz) shelled fresh or frozen peas
1 leek, washed and chopped
1 stick celery, chopped
50g (2oz) green beans (sliced or
   chopped)
1 litre (1¾ pints) water
Salt and freshly ground black pepper
   to taste

Garnish
1-2 sprigs fresh green coriander
1-2 green chillies chopped

Melt the butter in a large saucepan and fry the onion for 3 minutes. Add the cloves, cinnamon, cardamom, bayleaf and fry for 1 minute. Add the potato, carrots, banana and cauliflower. Fry for 3 minutes. Add the remaining vegetables and cook for 2-3 minutes. Add water and salt and pepper to taste. Cover and simmer gently for 8-13 minutes until vegetables are cooked. Adjust seasoning. Garnish with chopped coriander leaves and green chillies. Discard green chillies before eating. The vegetables should float in the clear soup; do not blend.

Carrot Soup

PREPARATION TIME:	12 minutes
COOKING TIME:	20-25 minutes
SERVES:	4 people

4-6 carrots, peeled and cut into thick
   slices
1 medium onion, peeled and
   quartered
1 medium turnip, peeled and cut into
   wedges
2 cloves garlic, peeled
750ml (1¼ pints) water or
   vegetable stock
2.5ml (½ tsp) dried thyme
Salt and ground white pepper to taste
Hot pepper sauce to taste

Garnish
25g (1oz) toasted sunflower seeds,
   flaked almonds and pistachio nuts
   (mixed together)

Put the carrots, onion, turnip, garlic and water into a large saucepan. Cover and simmer for 15 minutes. Add thyme and salt and pepper to taste and simmer for a further 5 minutes. Cool slightly and blend in a liquidiser. Return to the saucepan and heat the soup through. Ladle the soup into bowls. Add hot pepper sauce to taste. Serve garnished with toasted nuts.

Facing page: Tomato Saar (top right), Daal Soup (centre left) and Mixed Vegetable Soup (bottom).

Minestrone Soup

This famous vegetable and pasta soup from Italy can be made in many different ways. The recipe below is a simple, but delicious one – served with bread, it is a complete meal in itself.

PREPARATION TIME: 20 minutes

COOKING TIME: 30 minutes

SERVES: 4-6 people

45ml (3 tblsp) olive oil
1 medium onion, peeled and chopped
2 cloves of garlic, peeled and crushed
2 medium potatoes, peeled and diced
3 carrots, peeled and diced
2 stems celery, chopped
175g (6oz) shredded cabbage
4-5 skinned or canned tomatoes, chopped
900ml (1½ pints) water or vegetable stock
1 bouquet garni

Quick Tomato Soup (above right), Minestrone Soup (right) and Onion Soup (far right).

175g (6oz) shelled fresh, or frozen
   peas
50g (2oz) boiled and cooked red
   kidney beans
100g (4oz) macaroni or any shaped
   pasta
Salt and freshly ground black pepper
   to taste
50g (2oz) grated Parmesan cheese

Heat the olive oil in a saucepan and fry the onion and garlic until the onion is soft, 2-3 minutes. Stir in the potatoes, carrots and celery and fry for 3 minutes; add the cabbage and tomatoes. Cook for 5-6 minutes. Add water or stock and bouquet garni. Add peas, kidney beans, pasta and simmer gently, covered, for 10-15 minutes, or until the pasta is just tender. Season with salt and pepper and ladle into bowls. Sprinkle generously with grated Parmesan cheese before serving. Serve Minestrone soup with crusty bread.

Quick Tomato Soup

This is quite an exotic soup and is made within a few minutes. It is ideal for a hot summer's day.

PREPARATION TIME: 10 minutes plus chilling time

SERVES: 4-6 people

600ml (1 pint) chilled tomato juice
50g (2oz) fresh or canned tomato
   puree, chilled
2.5ml (½ tsp) hot red pepper sauce
2.5ml (½ tsp) grated lemon peel
2.5ml (½ tsp) grated orange peel
45-60ml (3-4 tblsp) dry white wine
Salt and ground white pepper to taste
Little iced water
45ml (3 tblsp) natural yogurt
60ml (4 tblsp) soured cream
6 balls of honeydew melon
6 balls of water melon
6 balls of ripe pear

Garnish
Mint leaves

Mix the tomato juice, tomato puree, pepper sauce, fruit peels and wine together. Season with salt and pepper, cover and refrigerate for 3-4 hours. Thin the soup with a little iced water if necessary. Whisk the yogurt and cream together until smooth and light. Divide the soup amongst 4-6 bowls. Spoon the yogurt and cream mixture into the centre of each portion and float the fruit balls on top. Garnish with mint leaves and serve.

Rice and Mushroom Soup

Ideal for a party or for summer afternoons.

PREPARATION TIME: 10 minutes

COOKING TIME: 40-50 minutes

SERVES: 6-8 people

125g (4oz) wild rice or brown rice
250ml (8 fl oz) water
25g (1oz) butter
1 medium onion, peeled and finely chopped
1 stem celery, chopped
100g (4oz) mushrooms, chopped
2.5ml (½ tsp) powdered garam masala
2.5ml (½ tsp) ground mustard seed
Salt and freshly ground black pepper to taste
1 litre (1¾ pints) water or stock
22ml (1½ tblsp) cornflour blended with
30ml (2 tblsp) water
75ml (5 tblsp) single cream

Garnish
1-2 sprigs fresh green coriander or parsley, chopped

Wash the rice in 3-4 changes of water; cook covered in 250ml (8 fl oz) water for 25-30 minutes, or until rice is tender. Keep on one side. Melt the butter in a large saucepan; saute the onion until tender for 3-5 minutes. Add the celery and mushrooms. Cook for 1-2 minutes. Stir in the powdered garam masala, mustard and salt and pepper to taste. Add the water or stock. Simmer for 5 minutes. Add the cornflour mixture and simmer for a further 3 minutes. Add the cooked rice and cream. Gently stir over a low heat for 2 minutes to heat through. Ladle the soup into bowls and garnish with coriander or parsley.

Onion Soup

Onion soup has been made famous by the French. Here is a delicious recipe based on the French style.

PREPARATION TIME: 20 minutes

COOKING TIME: 1 hour

SERVES: 4-6 people

75g (3oz) butter
3-4 large onions, peeled and sliced into rings
30ml (2 tblsp) flour
900ml (1½ pints) vegetable stock

Salt and ground white pepper to taste
6 slices of French bread 1½cm (¾ inch) thick
2 cloves of garlic, peeled and bruised
75g (3oz) grated Parmesan cheese

Melt the butter in a saucepan and fry the onions briskly on a very low heat. Cover and simmer the onions in their own juices for 25-30 minutes, stirring occasionally until golden brown. Remove from the heat. Stir in the flour and add the stock gradually. Season with salt and pepper and return to heat. Bring to the boil quickly; reduce the heat and simmer covered for 15-20 minutes. Rub the bread pieces each side with the bruised garlic. Float the bread rounds in the soup and sprinkle grated Parmesan cheese generously over the top. Put under the grill and cook for 2-3 minutes or until the top is golden. Serve at once. Alternatively – fry the bread rounds or bread slices in butter prior to rubbing with garlic.

Carrot Soup (top), Rice and Mushroom Soup (centre right) and Cucumber Soup (bottom left).

VEGETARIAN CUISINE

Snacks and Starters

Flour Pancake

This is a favourite pancake from the southern part of India and it is really worth making; good, wholesome and nutritious.

PREPARATION TIME:	10 minutes
COOKING TIME:	20 minutes
SERVES:	6 people

275g (10oz) wholemeal flour
2.5ml (½ tsp) salt
150ml (¼ pint) natural yogurt
1 egg, beaten
1 small onion, peeled and chopped
1-2 green chillies, chopped
2 sprigs fresh green coriander leaves, chopped
15ml (1 tblsp) grated fresh coconut, or desiccated coconut
10ml (2 tsp) sugar
Olive oil

Sieve the flour and salt and add the yogurt and egg. Mix in sufficient water to make a thickish batter of pouring consistency. Beat the mixture well and add the onion, chilli, coriander, coconut and sugar. Mix well. Allow to stand for 2-3 minutes. Heat 15ml (1 tblsp) oil in a small frying pan or omelette pan. Spoon in a little of the batter to give a depth of 5mm (1¼ inch). Cover with a lid and cook over a low heat for 3-5 minutes. Turn the pancake over and pour a little oil around the edge; cover and cook until the pancake is set and brown on both sides. Repeat with the remaining batter until you have several pancakes. Serve piping hot.

Dosas

Dosas can be eaten plain or with a filling. Eat them as a snack, for breakfast, or as a main meal with a filling and accompanied by chutney and daal (lentil dish).

PREPARATION TIME:	overnight, plus 20 minutes
COOKING TIME:	30-45 minutes
SERVES:	6 people

450g (1lb) rice
225g (½lb) white lentils (urid daal)
1.25ml (¼ tsp) fenugreek seeds
5ml (1 tsp) dried yeast
5ml (1 tsp) sugar
2.5ml (½ tsp) salt
15ml (1 tblsp) natural yogurt
Olive oil

Wash the rice and white lentils separately in 3-4 changes of water. Soak in fresh water for 1 hour. Grind the rice with a little water to a thick, coarse paste. Grind the white lentils with fenugreek seeds and a little water into a fine paste. (Use a food processor, food liquidiser or food grinder). Mix the dried yeast with 15ml (1 tblsp) tepid water and the sugar. Mix well and leave to stand for 10 minutes until frothy. Mix the ground rice and lentils with the salt, yeast and yogurt and mix well. Cover with a cloth and leave in a dark, warm place overnight. Next day mix well with sufficient water to give a smooth, thickish batter. Heat a medium non-stick frying pan and grease well with 5ml (1 tsp) oil. Pour in 30-45ml (2-3 tblsp) of the

Baisen Omelette (top right), Flour Pancake (centre left) and Dosas (bottom).

rice batter, spread it around to make a thin pancake. Cover with a lid. Cook for 3-4 minutes; spoon a little oil around the edge of the frying pan and turn the dosa over.

Cook for a further 2-3 minutes and serve hot. make the remaining dosa in the same way. Dosas can be made as large as 30-35cm (12-14 inches) in diameter.

Vegetable Filling

45ml (3 tblsp) olive oil
2 large onions, peeled and thinly sliced
5ml (1 tsp) white lentils (urid daal), washed and soaked in water for 5-10 minutes
2.5ml (½ tsp) mustard seed
8-10 fresh curry leaves
2 green chillies, cut into quarters
750g (1½lb) potatoes, boiled in their skins, peeled and cubed
Salt to taste

Heat oil and fry the onions for 4-5 minutes or until light brown. Add the drained lentils and mustard seed. Fry for ½ minute; add the curry leaves and green chillies. Add the potatoes and salt to taste. Cover and cook for 8-10 minutes, stirring occasionally. To serve: make the dosa as above and place 30ml (2 tblsp) of the potato filling in the centre; fold the dosa over like an omelette.

Samosa

These crispy triangles with a vegetable filling can be eaten hot or cold.

PREPARATION TIME:	40 minutes
COOKING TIME:	25 minutes
SERVES:	4-6 people

Pastry

275g (10oz) plain flour, sieved
1.25ml (¼ tsp) salt
1.25ml (¼ tsp) baking powder
Water

Make the dough by adding water, a little at a time, to the sieved flour, salt and baking powder. Mix to a soft pliable dough. Cover and allow to stand.

Filling

45ml (3 tblsp) oil
1 medium onion, peeled and chopped
450g (1lb) potatoes, peeled and cubed
2 carrots, peeled and grated
50g (2oz) shelled green peas
50g (2oz) green beans, chopped
5ml (1 tsp) chilli powder
5ml (1 tsp) salt
5ml (1 tsp) garam masala powder
2.5ml (½ tsp) ground turmeric
15ml (1 tblsp) dry mango powder, or lemon juice
Oil for deep frying

Heat the oil and fry the onions for 2-3 minutes. Add the potatoes and carrots and cook for 3 minutes. Add peas and beans and cook for 2-3 minutes. Sprinkle chilli, salt, garam masala, turmeric and mango powder. Mix well, cover and cook till potatoes are tender. Remove from heat and allow to cool. Divide the dough into 12-14 equal sized balls; roll each one out on a floured surface to a thin circle, 6-7cm (2½-3 inch) in diameter. Cut each circle in half. Apply the flour paste on the straight edge of each half. bring the edges together, overlapping them so as to make a cone. Fill the cone with the filling. Apply a little flour paste on the open edge and seal by pressing both the edges together. This will make a

triangular shape. Make all the samosas in the same way. Heat the oil for deep frying. When the oil is hot, reduce the heat and fry the samosas, a few at a time, until golden brown on either side (about 4-5 minutes). Drain on kitchen paper and serve with chutney or tomato sauce.

Curry Puffs

Like sausage rolls, curried vegetable puffs make an ideal dish for snacks and cocktails. The size can be varied to suit the occasion.

PREPARATION TIME:	1 hour
COOKING TIME:	20 minutes
SERVES:	4-6

450g (1lb) ready-made puff pastry

Filling

45ml (3 tblsp) oil
1 large onion, peeled and chopped
5ml (1 tsp) cumin seeds
450g (1lb) potatoes, peeled and diced
2 carrots, peeled and shredded
100g (4oz) shelled peas
5ml (1 tsp) salt
5ml (1 tsp) freshly ground black pepper
2-3 sprigs fresh green coriander leaves, chopped
5ml (1 tsp) garam masala powder

Flour paste: mix together 10ml (2 tsp) flour with water to make a sticky paste.

Heat the oil and fry the onion for 2 minutes. Add cumin seeds and allow to crackle, then add the diced potatoes. Stir fry over a medium heat for 5-6 minutes. Add the carrots and stir fry for 2 minutes. Add the peas and season with salt, pepper and chopped coriander leaves. Stir well. Cover and cook for 5-6 minutes or until the potatoes are tender. Sprinkle with the garam masala and lemon juice. Mix well. Remove from the heat and allow to cool. Roll out the puff pastry thinly. Cut into 7.5cm (3 inch) by 15cm (6 inch) rectangles. Place 15ml (1 tblsp) filling at one end and roll up the pastry like a swiss roll. Secure the ends with the

Potato Cutlets (top), Samosa (above left) and Curry Puffs (left).

flour and water paste. Preheat the oven to 190°C, 375°F Gas Mark 5. Arrange the curry puffs on greased baking sheets and bake for 10-15 minutes or until golden. Serve hot with tomato sauce.

Potato Cutlets

PREPARATION TIME:	30 minutes
COOKING TIME:	30 minutes
SERVES:	6 people

15ml (1 tblsp) oil
1 medium onion, peeled and chopped
175g (6oz) shelled peas
750g (1½lb) potatoes, boiled in their skins, peeled and mashed
5ml (1 tsp) salt
5ml (1 tsp) freshly ground black pepper
30ml (2 tblsp) lemon juice
2 eggs, beaten
Breadcrumbs
Oil for shallow frying

Heat 15ml (1 tblsp) oil in a frying pan and fry the onion for 3 minutes; add the peas and fry for 2 minutes. Mix the onion and peas with the mashed potatoes. Add salt and pepper to taste and the lemon juice. Mix well. Divide mixture into 24-30 small even-sized cakes. Dip firstly into beaten egg and then coat evenly with breadcrumbs. Heat sufficient oil in a frying pan for shallow frying. Shallow fry the potato cutlets for 3-4 minutes or until golden. Serve hot or cold with chutney or tomato sauce.

Baisen Omelettes

These vegetarian omelettes are made with chickpea (baisen) flour and can be eaten as a quick snack. Easy to make and quick to prepare, they are ideal for unexpected friends or late night guests.

PREPARATION TIME:	10 minutes
COOKING TIME:	20 minutes
MAKES:	12

275g (10oz) sieved baisen flour
1 small onion, peeled and finely chopped
1-2 green chillies, chopped (optional)
2 sprigs fresh green coriander, chopped
2 tomatoes, seeded and diced
50g (2oz) shelled peas
2.5ml (½ tsp) salt
Pinch chilli powder
Olive oil

Mix the baisen flour with the onion, chillies, coriander, tomatoes and peas. Add sufficient water to made a thick batter, about 450ml (¾ pint). Season with salt and chilli powder, Mix well and allow to stand for 5 minutes. Heat a solid based frying pan or griddle pan and brush with oil. Ladle in sufficient batter to cover the base of the pan. Cover and cook over a low heat for 4-5 minutes. Turn the omelette over and cook for 3-4 minutes. Both sides should be browned evenly. Make the rest of the omelettes in the same way. Serve hot with tomato sauce.

Stuffed Marrow

Marrows can be stuffed with a vegetable or meat filling. Here is a delectable recipe for a vegetable stuffed marrow.

PREPARATION TIME:	15 minutes
COOKING TIME:	45 minutes
SERVES:	4-6 people

1 marrow 25-30cm (10-12 inches) in length

Filling
45ml (3 tblsp) oil
1 large onion, peeled and chopped
450g (1lb) potatoes, peeled and diced
5ml (1 tsp) crushed fresh root ginger
5ml (1 tsp) crushed garlic
5ml (1 tsp) chilli powder
2.5ml (½ tsp) turmeric powder
5ml (1 tsp) garam masala powder
100g (4oz) shelled peas
4 tomatoes, chopped
2.5ml (½ tsp) salt
2.5ml (½ tsp) freshly ground black pepper
1 green chilli, chopped
10ml (2 tsp) melted butter

Heat the oil in a wok or large frying pan and fry the onion for 2 minutes. Add the potatoes and stir-fry for 3-4 minutes. Add the ginger, garlic, chilli powder, turmeric and garam masala powder. Mix well and add the peas, tomatoes, salt and pepper and the green chilli; cover and cook until the potatoes are tender, about 6-8 minutes. Add the lemon juice. Remove a thin slice from each end of the marrow. Scoop out the centre pith leaving a 2cm (¾ inch) shell. Remove the skin in alternate strips to give it firmness. Fill the hollowed marrow with the prepared potato filling. Place the stuffed marrow on a rectangle of foil and brush with melted butter; season with salt and pepper. Wrap the foil around the marrow; bake at 180°C, 350°F Gas Mark 4 for 40-45 minutes. Remove the foil from to time and brush with the juices. Serve hot.

Vegetable Kebabs

This Turkish/Greek recipe makes an ideal side dish for barbecue parties.

PREPARATION TIME:	30 minutes
COOKING TIME:	30 minutes
SERVES:	4-6 people

1 aubergine cut into 2.5cm (1 inch) pieces
1 large green pepper, seeded and cut into 2.5cm (1 inch) pieces
12-14 small cherry tomatoes (or 6-8 tomatoes, halved)
12-14 small pickling onions, peeled and blanched for 5 minutes
12-14 large button mushrooms
2 medium potatoes, boiled in their skins, peeled and cut into 2.5cm (1 inch) cubes
Olive oil
30ml (2 tblsp) lemon juice
1.25ml (¼ tsp) salt
2.5ml (½ tsp) freshly ground black pepper

Put all the vegetables into a large bowl and add 60ml (4 tblsp) olive oil, lemon juice and salt and pepper. Mix together and leave to stand for 10-15 minutes, turning the vegetables once or twice. Thread the vegetables alternately onto skewers. Brush with the marinade. Grill for 3-4 minutes, until evenly browned. Brush the vegetables with oil or marinade during grilling. Serve piping hot.

Stuffed Peppers

PREPARATION TIME:	30 minutes
COOKING TIME:	30-40 minutes
SERVES:	6 people

6 even sized peppers (green or red)
45ml (3 tblsp) oil
1 medium onion, peeled and chopped
2 cloves garlic, peeled and chopped
2 tomatoes, chopped
1 green chilli, chopped
100g (4oz) plain boiled rice
1 medium potato, peeled and diced
1.25ml (¼ tsp) salt
2.5ml (½ tsp) freshly ground black pepper
50g (2oz) shelled peas
15ml (1 tblsp) lemon juice
15ml (1 tblsp) chopped parsley or coriander leaves
30ml (2 tblsp) water or vegetable stock

Cut a slice from the top of each pepper; scoop out the centre seeds. Heat the oil and fry the onion for 1-2 minutes. Add the garlic, tomatoes and green chilli and stir fry for 2-3 minutes. Add the rice, potato, salt and pepper, peas and lemon juice and parsley. Cover and cook for 2-4 minutes. Arrange the peppers in an ovenproof dish and stuff the peppers with the rice mixture. Pour the stock around the peppers. Bake at 195°C, 375°F, Gas Mark 5, for 20-30 minutes, basting occasionally with the juices. Serve hot.

Stuffed Tomatoes

Tomatoes stuffed with a vegetable filling and served with a tangy sauce make a good starter.

PREPARATION TIME:	20 minutes
COOKING TIME:	15-18 minutes
SERVES:	6 people

12 medium size firm tomatoes
30ml (2 tblsp) oil
10-12 spring onions (only the white part), chopped
10ml (2 tsp) chopped parsley or coriander leaves
100g (4oz) cooked rice
10ml (2 tsp) pine kernels, or skinned hazelnuts, chopped
10ml (2tsp) roasted sesame seeds
2.5ml (½ tsp) salt
1.25ml (¼ tsp) freshly ground black pepper
1.25ml (¼ tsp) ground mixed spice
250ml (8 fl oz) vegetable stock
10ml (2 tsp) cornflour
30ml (2 tblsp) lemon juice
1 egg, well beaten

Stuffed Marrow (top), Vegetable Kebabs (centre right) and Stuffed Peppers (bottom).

Slice the tops off the tomatoes and scoop out the centre pulp, leaving a 2cm (¾ inch) "shell". Reserve the tomato pulp. Heat the oil in the frying pan and fry the onions for 2-3 minutes. Add the parsley, cooked rice, nuts, sesame seeds, salt and pepper and allspice. Add the tomato pulp and any juice which may have formed. Cook, uncovered, for 3-4 minutes, until most of the moisture has evaporated. Stuff the hollowed tomatoes with the rice mixture and arrange in a large frying pan. Add the stock and cook for 4 minutes. Remove the tomatoes. Bring the liquid back to the boil and add the blended cornflour and lemon juice. Remove from the heat. Add the beaten egg a little at a time. Return the mixture to the heat and cook until thickened. Add the stuffed tomatoes and cook over a low heat for 5 minutes, spooning the sauce over the tomatoes from time to time.

Fritters
(TEMPURA)

PREPARATION TIME: 10 minutes

COOKING TIME: 10-15 minutes

SERVES: 4 people

Batter
225g (8oz) plain flour
15ml (1 tblsp) cornflour
1.25ml (¼ tsp) salt
250ml (8 fl oz) chilled water
1 egg yolk
2 egg whites, stiffly beaten

Oil for deep frying
225g (8oz) fresh green beans, cut into 5cm (2 inch) pieces
10-12 fresh asparagus spears, cut in 5cm (2 inch) lengths
1 aubergine, cut into 2.5cm (1 inch) cubes
1 large potato, peeled and sliced 5mm (¼ inch) thick
10-12 fresh mushrooms, halved
6-8 cauliflower florets, halved

Tempura sauce: A
250ml (8 fl oz) water
60ml (2 fl oz) sherry
60ml (2 fl oz) soya sauce
5ml (1 tsp) sugar
½ a vegetable stock cube

Mix the ingredients together and bring to the boil. Stir until dissolved.

Tempura sauce: B
2.5cm (1 inch) fresh root ginger, peeled and grated
30ml (2 tblsp) grated turnip
30ml (2 tblsp) grated radish
45ml (3 tblsp) prepared mustard
45ml (3 tblsp) soya sauce

Mix the ingredients together and keep covered.

To make the batter: mix together the flour, cornflour and salt. Make a well in the centre. Mix the chilled water and egg yolk together and pour into the centre of the flour. Stir in the flour and blend lightly. Fold in the whisked egg whites.

Heat oil for deep frying. Dip the vegetables into the batter and fry in hot oil for 2-3 minutes until golden. Drain on kitchen paper and serve hot with the Tempura sauces. Use the batter within a few minutes of making. Do not allow it to stand for long.

Cheese and Lentil Rissoles

PREPARATION TIME: 30 minutes

COOKING TIME: 1 hour

SERVES: 4 people

175g (6oz) red lentils
400ml (⅔ pint) water
100g (4oz) grated cheese
1 medium onion, peeled and chopped
2 large eggs
50g (2oz) fresh breadcrumbs
5ml (1 tsp) mixed dried herbs
15ml (1 tblsp) lemon juice
Salt to taste
2.5ml (½ tsp) freshly ground black pepper
Oil for shallow frying

Wash the lentils in 3-4 changes of water. Drain the lentils and put them into a pan with the water. Cook until the lentils are tender and the water has been absorbed. Remove from heat and allow to cool. Mix the cooked lentils with the cheese, onion, egg, breadcrumbs, herbs, salt and pepper and the lemon juice. Mix well and shape into rissoles. Shallow fry the rissoles for 4-5 minutes on each side until golden brown. Drain on absorbent paper and serve immediately.

Mixed Nut Rissoles

PREPARATION TIME: 15 minutes

COOKING TIME: 20-25 minutes

SERVES: 4 people

25g (1oz) hazelnuts, chopped
50g (2oz) shelled peanuts, chopped
50g (2oz) cashew nuts, chopped
25g (1oz) pistachio nuts, chopped
1 onion, peeled and chopped
75g (3oz) fresh breadcrumbs
3 eggs, beaten
Salt and freshly ground black pepper to taste
2.5ml (½ tsp) dried, chopped marjoram
1 carrot, peeled and grated
15ml (1 tblsp) lemon juice
Little milk
Oil for shallow frying

Mix the chopped nuts with the onion, breadcrumbs, eggs, salt and pepper, marjoram, carrot and lemon juice. Add a little milk to bind the mixture, if necessary. Shape into rissoles. Shallow fry the rissoles in oil, for 4-5 minutes on each side, until golden brown. Drain well on absorbent paper and serve immediately. Alternatively, brush the rissoles generously with oil, put them onto a baking tray and bake in the oven at 220°C, 425°F, Gas Mark 7 for 15 minutes. Turn the rissoles halfway through cooking and brush with extra oil.

Cashew Nut Pie

PREPARATION TIME: 20-25 minutes

COOKING TIME: 30-40 minutes

SERVES: 4 people

Filling
2 medium onions, peeled and chopped
30ml (2 tblsp) oil
225g (8oz) shredded cabbage
50g (2oz) carrots, peeled and grated

Pie Crust
100g (4oz) crushed cornflakes
50g (2oz) cashew nuts, coarsely ground
175g (6oz) grated cheese
5ml (1 tsp) mixed dried herbs
Salt and freshly ground black pepper to taste
2 large eggs
100g (4oz) fresh breadcrumbs
15ml (1 tblsp) oil
50g (2oz) butter

To make the filling: fry the onions in the oil for 2 minutes; add the cabbage and carrots and fry for a further 4-5 minutes. Remove from the heat and allow to cool.

To make the pie crust: mix all the ingredients together in a bowl, apart from the oil, butter and 50g (2oz) of the grated cheese. Grease a baking tray with the oil. Press half the pie crust ingredients out to form an even base. Spread the filling mixture on top, and then press over the remaining pie crust ingredients. Sprinkle with the remaining grated cheese and dot with butter. Bake in oven at 200°C, 400°F, Gas Mark 6, for 25-30 minutes.

Tomato, Onion and Mushroom Flan

PREPARATION TIME: 20 minutes

COOKING TIME: 40-45 minutes

SERVES: 6 people

225g (8oz) shortcrust pastry
225g (8oz) grated Cheddar cheese
4 tomatoes, skinned and chopped
15ml (1 tblsp) chopped chives or parsley
100g (4oz) mushrooms, sliced
10ml (2 tsp) corn oil
1 large onion, peeled and chopped
3 eggs, beaten
150ml (¼ pint) milk
2.5ml (½ tsp) salt
1.25ml (¼ tsp) freshly ground black pepper

Roll out the pastry and use to line a 20-23cm (8-9 inch) flan dish. Put 50g (2oz) of the grated cheese into the pastry case followed by the tomatoes, chives or parsley and the mushrooms. Heat the corn oil and fry the onion for 2-3 minutes. Mix the beaten eggs with the milk, salt and pepper and fried onion. Pour into the flan case and top with the remaining grated cheese. Bake at 200°C, 400°F Gas Mark 6 for 35-40 minutes, or until set. Serve hot or cold.

Mixed Nut Rissoles (left),
Cheese and Lentil Rissoles
(below) and Cashew Nut Pie
(bottom).

Pakora

This is the Indian version of vegetable fritters. Fried with or without batter, they make an interesting starter or snack.

PREPARATION TIME: 15 minutes
COOKING TIME: 15-20 minutes
SERVES: 4-6 people

1 large potato, or
2 medium potatoes, peeled and cut into 5mm (¼ inch) thick slices
8-10 cauliflower florets, halved lengthways
6 carrots, cut into 5cm (2 inch) lengths and halved
1 aubergine, cut into 5cm (2 inch) cubes
6 courgettes, trimmed and cut into 5cm (2 inch) pieces and then quartered
1-2 green peppers, seeded and cut into 5mm (¼ inch) thick rounds or 2.5cm (1 inch) pieces
5ml (1 tsp) salt
5ml (1 tsp) red chilli powder
2.5ml (½ tsp) turmeric powder
Oil for deep frying
6 lemon wedges

Sprinkle the vegetables with the spices and rub well in. Keep on one side. Heat the oil for deep frying. When it is beginning to smoke, reduce the heat. Fry the vegetables a few at a time, in batches. Fry for 2-3 minutes and drain on kitchen paper. Serve piping hot with wedges of lemon and a sweet and sour chutney or tomato ketchup. (These uncoated fritters are called Bhaja).

Batter
275g (10oz) baisen flour, sieved
5ml (1 tsp) salt
5ml (1 tsp) chilli powder
5ml (1 tsp) ground cumin
15ml (1 tblsp) lemon juice
300ml (½ pint) water

Mix the sieved flour with the salt, chilli powder, cumin and lemon juice. Make a well in the centre and add the water; stir in the baisen flour until all the flour has been incorporated. Beat well to give a smooth batter. Adjust seasoning. Allow the batter to stand for a few minutes. Heat the oil as above. Dip the vegetables into the batter and then fry for 2-3 minutes. Drain on kitchen paper and serve piping hot with tomato sauce. Other vegetables which may be used: onions rings, raw banana slices, green tomato slices, spinach leaves.

Stuffed Mushrooms

PREPARATION TIME: 20 minutes
COOKING TIME: 10-15 minutes
SERVES: 4-6 people

Filling
1 small onion, peeled and finely chopped
10ml (2 tsp) oil
1cm (½ inch) fresh root ginger, peeled and crushed
2 cloves garlic, peeled and crushed
225g (8oz) boiled, peeled and mashed potatoes
Salt and freshly ground black pepper to taste
15ml (1 tblsp) lemon juice
10ml (2 tsp) chopped chives or parsley
20-24 large button mushrooms
175g (6oz) grated Cheddar cheese
Oil for brushing

Fry the onion in the 10ml (2 tsp) oil for 2 minutes; add the ginger and garlic. Fry for 1 minute and mix with the mashed potatoes. Season to taste with salt, pepper, lemon juice and chopped parsley. Mix well. Remove the stalks from the mushrooms; stuff the hollows with the potato filling and top with a little Cheddar cheese. Brush the mushrooms with a little oil and arrange them on a baking tray. Bake the mushrooms in a moderately hot oven, 190°C, 375°F, Gas Mark 5, for 10 minutes until the cheese is brown.

Aloo Bonda

This is an Indian potato fritter recipe made in the shape of spicy balls. Eaten hot or cold, they are ideal for parties, snacks and picnics.

PREPARATION TIME: 25 minutes
COOKING TIME: 30 minutes
SERVES: 4-6 people

Batter
225g (8oz) baisen flour, sieved
1.25ml (¼ tsp) salt
1.25ml (¼ tsp) baking powder
300ml (½ pint) water

450g (1lb) potatoes, boiled in their skins and peeled
1 large or 2 medium onions, peeled and chopped
2.5cm (1 inch) fresh root ginger, peeled and finely chopped
2-3 green chillies, chopped
4-5 sprigs fresh green coriander leaves, chopped
2.5ml (½ tsp) salt
1.25ml (¼ tsp) freshly ground black pepper
15ml (1 tblsp) lemon juice
Oil for deep frying

Mix the sieved flour with the salt and baking powder. Make a well in the centre and add the water. Beat well to give a smooth batter. Chop the boiled potatoes into tiny cubes; add the chopped onions, ginger, chillies, coriander leaves, salt and pepper to taste and lemon juice. Mix well and adjust seasoning to taste. Mould into even-sized balls with dampened hands. Heat the oil for deep frying. When hot, dip the vegetable balls into the batter and then fry for 3-4 minutes over a gentle heat until golden brown. Drain on kitchen paper and serve with tomato sauce.

This page: Aloo Bonda (top), Fritters (Tempura) (centre right) and Pakora (bottom left).

Facing page: Stuffed Tomatoes (top right), Stuffed Mushrooms (centre left) and Tomato, Onion and Mushroom Flan (bottom).

Salads

Onion Salad

This salad is usually served as an accompaniment to kebabs. Onion salad goes very well with a variety of main courses, as a side salad.

PREPARATION TIME: 5-7 minutes
SERVES: 4 people

2 large Spanish onions, peeled and thinly sliced
2-3 sprigs fresh green coriander, chopped
1 green chilli, sliced
Juice of 1 lemon
2.5ml (½ tsp) salt
Pinch paprika

Combine the onion rings, coriander leaves and chilli in a bowl. Add the lemon juice and salt and mix well. Put the onion salad onto a serving plate and sprinkle with paprika.

Tabbouleh

This is a Lebanese salad and it is very good for parties and picnics.

PREPARATION TIME: 2 hours 30 minutes
SERVES: 6 people

225g (8oz) bulgar or pourgouri (precooked, cracked wheat)
250ml (8 fl oz) boiling water
8-10 spring onions, chopped
1 green pepper, seeded and chopped
120ml (8 tblsp) chopped parsley
30ml (2 tblsp) chopped mint leaves

Dressing
45ml (3 tblsp) lemon juice
175ml (6 fl oz) olive oil
5ml (1 tsp) grated lemon peel
5ml (1 tsp) ground mixed spice
2.5ml (½ tsp) ground cumin
5ml (1 tsp) salt
1.25ml (¼ tsp) freshly ground black pepper
1 small iceberg lettuce, shredded
2 large firm tomatoes, cut into wedges
10-15 pitted black olives, halved
2-3 sprigs mint
1-2 sprigs fresh green coriander

Place the pourgouri or bulgar into a bowl and add boiling water. Cover and stand for 1½-2 hours. Drain the bulgar by squeezing out the excess water. Mix the spring onions, green pepper, parsley and mint with the bulgar. Combine all the dressing ingredients in a screw top jar and shake well. Pour the dressing over the bulgar mixture and mix lightly. Line a platter with shredded lettuce. Place the prepared bulgar in the centre. Garnish with tomato, olives, mint and coriander leaves.

Sweet and Sour Coleslaw

A variation on the usual theme, but a definite winner.

PREPARATION TIME: 20 minutes
SERVES: 6 people

½ small red cabbage, shredded
1 small green cabbage, shredded
1 large sweet carrot, peeled and shredded
3 spring onions, finely chopped
75ml (5 tblsp) cider vinegar
45ml (3 tblsp) brown sugar
2.5ml (½ tsp) salt
1.25ml (¼ tsp) freshly ground black pepper
75ml (5 tblsp) soured cream
5ml (1 tsp) French mustard

Combine the red and green cabbage, carrots and spring onions in a mixing bowl. Mix the vinegar, sugar and salt and pepper in a small saucepan and stir over the heat to dissolve the sugar. Pour the hot vinegar sauce over the cabbage mixture and mix well. Stir the soured cream and mustard together in a separate bowl; stir this mixture into the vegetables. Mix well and serve.

Mixed Bean Salad

This nutritious salad is made from a medley of beans and is very good for health conscious and athletic people. Either cook the dried beans at home or buy ready-cooked ones. Soak the beans separately overnight, and then boil them separately until tender. Drain well.

PREPARATION TIME: 15 minutes
SERVES: 4-6 people

175g (6oz) cooked red kidney beans
175g (6oz) cooked black eyed beans (Lobia)
175g (6oz) cooked chick peas
175g (6oz) cooked butter beans
100g (4oz) shelled broad beans
225g (8oz) sliced green beans, blanched

Dressing
30ml (2 tblsp) brown sugar
120ml (4 fl oz) white wine vinegar
2.5ml (½ tsp) salt
1.25ml (¼ tsp) freshly ground black pepper
120ml (4 fl oz) olive oil
2.5ml (½ tsp) dry mustard powder
2.5ml (½ tsp) dried basil leaves
1 large Spanish or red onion, peeled and thinly sliced into rings
30ml (2 tblsp) chopped parsley

Mix all the beans together in a large bowl. Mix the sugar and vinegar together with salt and pepper to taste. Stir in the oil, mustard and basil. Pour this vinegar mixture over the beans. Mix thoroughly. Refrigerate until ready to serve. Before serving, mix in the onion rings and parsley.

Nutty Salad

PREPARATION TIME: 20 minutes
SERVES: 4 people

450g (1lb) boiled potatoes, diced
175g (6oz) shelled green peas
100g (4oz) cooked carrots, diced
1 medium onion, peeled and chopped
1 small green pepper, seeded and chopped
8-10 radishes, chopped
2 stems celery, chopped
¼ cucumber, chopped
50g (2oz) roasted peanuts, coarsely chopped
50g (2oz) grated fresh coconut
15ml (1 tblsp) sunflower seeds
2-3 sprigs fresh green coriander leaves or parsley, chopped

Dressing
30ml (2 tblsp) lemon juice
60ml (4 tblsp) olive oil
5ml (1 tsp) salt

2.5ml (½ tsp) freshly ground black pepper
2.5ml (½ tsp) brown sugar

Mix all the vegetables together, except the nuts and sunflower seeds, in a large bowl. Mix the dressing ingredients together in a screw top jar and shake well. Add the dressing to the salad and mix throughly. Sprinkle with the nuts and sunflower seeds before serving.

Rice and Nut Salad

This salad has a very refreshing taste. The main ingredients are nuts, raisins, carrots and rice.

PREPARATION TIME: 15 minutes
SERVES: 4 people

30ml (2 tblsp) olive oil
30ml (2 tblsp) lemon juice
Salt and freshly ground black pepper to taste
100g (4oz) sultanas
50g (2oz) currants
275g (10oz) cooked long grain rice, well drained
75g (3oz) chopped blanched almonds
50g (2oz) cashew nuts, chopped
50g (2oz) shelled walnuts, chopped
425g (15oz) can peach slices, drained and chopped
¼ cucumber, cubed
100g (4oz) cooked red kidney beans
15ml (1 tblsp) chopped pitted olives

Mix the olive oil, lemon juice and salt and freshly ground black pepper in a screw top jar; shake vigorously. Soak the sultanas and

Facing page: Onion Salad (top), Nutty Salad (centre) and Tabbouleh (bottom).

currants in sufficient boiling water to cover, for 10 minutes. Drain the fruits. Mix the rice, nuts and soaked sultanas and currants. Add the chopped peaches, cucumber, red kidney beans and olives. Pour the dressing over the salad and toss lightly together. Serve on a bed of chopped lettuce.

Cheese Salad

This cheese salad originates from Greece and has many variations; it is popularly known as Horiatiki.

PREPARATION TIME: 10-12 minutes

SERVES: 4 people

½ a head of endive
½ iceberg lettuce
1 cucumber, peeled and sliced
3-4 large tomatoes, cut into wedges, or
15-20 cherry tomatoes, halved
8-10 pitted green or black olives, halved
1 medium Spanish or red onion, peeled and chopped
125g (4oz) Feta cheese, cut into 1cm (½ inch) pieces

Dressing

75ml (5 tblsp) olive oil
30ml (2 tblsp) red wine vinegar
5ml (1 tsp) chopped fresh oregano or
1.25ml (¼ tsp) dried oregano
2.5ml (½ tsp) salt
1.25ml (¼ tsp) freshly ground black pepper
2.5ml (½ tsp) brown sugar

Wash and dry the endive and lettuce leaves; tear into bite size pieces. Place the endive and lettuce in a large bowl and add the cucumber, tomatoes, olives, onion and cheese. Shake the dressing

Cheese Salad (bottom left), Mixed Bean Salad (below) and Rice and Nut Salad (bottom right).

ingredients together in a screw top jar. Pour the dressing over the salad. Toss lightly and serve.

Mixed Fresh Vegetable Salad

This salad can be prepared with any combination of vegetables, in any proportion. Add or subtract according to personal taste.

PREPARATION TIME: 20 minutes

SERVES: 6 people

1 large spring onion, peeled and chopped
½ cucumber, diced
3 carrots, peeled and diced
6 large tomatoes, diced, or
8 cherry tomatoes, halved
10 button mushrooms, diced
3 stems celery, diced
1 green pepper, seeded and diced
15-20 tiny cauliflower florets
15-20 radishes, quartered
15ml (1 tblsp) chopped watercress or mustard and cress
2 sprigs fresh green coriander leaves or parsley, chopped

Dressing
2.5ml (½ tsp) salt
2.5ml (½ tsp) freshly ground black pepper
5ml (1 tsp) brown sugar
30ml (2 tblsp) cider vinegar
15ml (1 tblsp) lemon juice
15ml (1 tblsp) honey
60ml (4 tblsp) olive oil
Pinch mustard powder
8 lettuce leaves

Combine all the vegetables in a large bowl. Mix together all the dressing ingredients. Pour the dressing over the vegetables and serve on a bed of lettuce leaves.

Pasta Salad

This is a popular salad from America. It can be eaten as a main dish or as a side salad – it is a wonderful combination of vegetables, pasta and kidney beans.

PREPARATION TIME: 15-20 minutes

SERVES: 6 people

450g (1lb) cooked red kidney beans, drained
350g (12oz) pasta shells or spirals, cooked
1 large green pepper, seeded and sliced into 2.5cm (1 inch) long pieces
1 large red pepper, seeded and sliced into 2.5cm (1 inch) long pieces
20-30 pitted black olives, sliced in half
15ml (1 tblsp) capers
4-5 sprigs fresh parsley, chopped

Dressing

200ml (⅓ pint) olive oil
45ml (3 tblsp) lemon juice
10ml (2 tsp) finely chopped fresh basil leaves
5ml (1 tsp) salt
1.25ml (¼ tsp) freshly ground black pepper
2 cloves garlic, peeled and minced
1 small head curly endive

Combine the beans, pasta, peppers, olives, capers and parsley in a large bowl. Mix all the dressing ingredients together; add to the salad ingredients and toss together. Line the serving platter or bowl with endive leaves; place the pasta salad in the centre. Alternatively: add 225g (½lb) of thinly sliced salami or Italian sausages or can sausages in brine cut into bite size pieces.

This page: Sweet and Sour Coleslaw (top left), Mixed Fresh Vegetable Salad (top right) and Pasta Salad (bottom).

Facing page: Kedgeree (top left), Sweet Savoury Rice (centre right) and Vegetable Pulao Rice (bottom).

VEGETARIAN CUISINE
Rice and Pulses

Kedgeree

PREPARATION TIME: 15 minutes, plus soaking time

COOKING TIME: 30 minutes

SERVES: 4-6 people

225g (8oz) long grain rice
225g (8oz) red lentils
750ml (1¼ pints) tepid water
100g (4oz) butter (or an equivalent
   amount of olive oil)
1 medium onion, peeled and chopped
2.5ml (½ tsp) crushed fresh root
   ginger
2.5ml (½ tsp) crushed garlic
2.5cm (1 inch) piece cinnamon stick
6 cloves
1 bayleaf
5ml (1 tsp) ground coriander
1.25ml (¼ tsp) ground turmeric
2.5ml (½ tsp) salt
2 green chillies, sliced in half
   lengthways

Wash the rice and the lentils in 4 to 5 changes of water; soak them in the 750ml (1¼ pints) tepid water for 30 minutes. Heat the butter or oil in a large pan; add the onion and fry for 2-3 minutes. Add the ginger, garlic, cinnamon stick, cloves and bayleaf, and fry for 1 minute. Drain the water from the rice and lentils; reserve the water. Add the rice and lentils to the fried onion, together with the coriander, turmeric, slt and green chillies. Stir over the heat for 2-3 minutes, until the rice and lentils are evenly coated with fat. Add the reserved water and bring to the boil; reduce the heat and simmer covered for 8-10 minutes, without stirring, until the water has been absorbed and the rice and lentils are tender. Serve with a vegetable curry.

Vegetable Pulao Rice

PREPARATION TIME: 30 minutes

COOKING TIME: 30 minutes

SERVES: 4-6 people

450g (1lb) long grain rice (Basmati)
750-900ml (1¼-1½ pints) water
1 medium onion, peeled and diced
2.5cm (1 inch) piece cinnamon stick
1 bayleaf

6 cloves
5ml (1 tsp) black cumin (shah-zeera)
6 small cardamoms
2.5ml (½ tsp) crushed fresh root ginger
2.5ml (½ tsp) crushed garlic
1 medium potato, peeled and diced
1 carrot, peeled and diced
100g (4oz) shelled peas
75g (3oz) sliced green beans
5ml (1 tsp) garam masala powder
2.5ml (½ tsp) chilli powder
5ml (1 tsp) ground coriander
5ml (1 tsp) ground cumin
5ml (1 tsp) salt
30ml (2 tblsp) lemon juice
100g (4oz) butter (or an equivalent amount of olive oil)

Wash the rice in 4-5 changes of water and soak in the 750-900ml (1¼-1½ pints) water for 30 minutes. Melt the butter in a pan and fry the onion for 2-3 minutes. Add the cinnamon, bayleaf, cloves, black cumin, cardamoms, ginger and garlic. Fry for 1 minute, stirring, and add the potato, carrot, peas, green beans, garam masala, chilli, coriander, cumin and salt. Mix well. Drain the soaked rice, retaining the water and add the rice to the onion and spices. Stir the mixture gently and add the reserved water. Bring to the boil and then reduce the heat; cover and simmer gently for 10-15 minutes, until the rice is tender and the water has been absorbed. Do not stir during cooking. Sprinkle with the lemon juice and serve. To colour pulao: dissolve a pinch of saffron in 15ml (1 tblsp) warm milk; pour over the rice and allow to stand over a very low heat for 5 minutes.

Mixed Daal

This is a mixed lentil stew, using 3 or 4 varieties of daal. Add a few vegetables of your choice to turn it into a substantial meal.

PREPARATION TIME: 15 minutes	
COOKING TIME: 30 minutes	
SERVES: 4 people	

75g (3oz) split Bengal grain (Channa)
50g (2oz) yellow lentils (Toor Daal)
100g (4oz) red lentils (Masoor)
50g (2oz) dehusked split mung (Moong), or any other daal
2.5ml (½ tsp) ground turmeric
7.5ml (1½ tsp) ground coriander
4 canned tomatoes, chopped
2 green chillies

3 sprigs fresh green coriander leaves
Salt to taste
100g (4oz) butter
1cm (½ inch) fresh root ginger, peeled and chopped
1 onion, chopped
1 clove garlic, chopped

As some of these pulses have different cooking times, wash each pulse separately in 3-4 changes of water. Drain. Soak separately in water for 5 minutes. Bring 600ml (1 pint) water to the boil; add the drained channa daal. Boil for 15-20 minutes or until the pulses are tender. Add the remaining pulses well drained, and simmer gently with the turmeric and ground coriander for 15-20 minutes, or until all the pulses are soft. Beat with an egg whisk. Add the tomatoes, green chillies and coriander leaves. Simmer for a further 5-6 minutes. Pour into a serving bowl and keep warm. Melt the butter in a frying pan and fry the ginger for 2 minutes. Add the onion and garlic and fry until golden brown. Pour this mixture over the mixed daal and serve immediately.

Sweet Savoury Rice

PREPARATION TIME: 20 minutes	
COOKING TIME: 30 minutes	
SERVES: 4-6 people	

450g (1lb) rice (Basmati or long grain)
750-900ml (1¼-1½ pints) water
50g (2oz) raisins
75g (3oz) cashew nuts, chopped
50g (2oz) blanched almonds, split
50g (2oz) pistachio nuts, split
100g (4oz) butter (or an equivalent amount of olive oil)
2.5cm (1 inch) piece cinnamon stick
6 cloves
6 small cardamoms
1 bayleaf
2.5cm (½ tsp) black cumin seed (shah-zeera)
100g (4oz) sultanas
5ml (1 tsp) salt
5ml (1 tsp) sugar
Pinch of saffron

Wash the rice in 4-5 changes of water and soak in the 750-900ml (1¼-1½ pints) water for 30 minutes. Soak the raisins and nuts in a little water for 10 minutes. Drain the raisins and nuts. Melt the butter in a large pan and fry the cinnamon, cloves, small

cardamoms, bayleaf and black cumin for 1-2 minutes. Add the nuts, raisins and sultanas. Drain the soaked rice retaining the water; add the rice to the saucepan. Fry for 1 minute. Add salt, sugar and the reserved water. Bring to the boil. Reduce the heat and add a pinch of saffron. Stir once gently. Cover and simmer gently for 10-15 minutes, without stirring, until the rice is tender and the water has been absorbed. Serve with curries.

Red Kidney Bean Curry

A popular dish from the Punjab province of India. It is similar to Chilli Con-Carne and makes a hearty meal with bread or rice.

PREPARATION TIME: overnight, plus 15 minutes	
COOKING TIME: 20-45 minutes	
SERVES: 4 people	

225g (8oz) dried red kidney beans, washed and soaked overnight in sufficient water to cover
2 medium onions, chopped
45ml (3 tblsp) oil
1 bayleaf
2.5cm (1 inch) piece cinnamon stick
6 cloves
6 small green cardamoms
2 green chillies, quartered
3 cloves garlic, peeled and finely chopped
2.5cm (1 inch) fresh root ginger, peeled and finely chopped
2.5ml (½ tsp) chilli powder
1.25ml (¼ tsp) ground turmeric
7.5ml (1½ tsp) ground coriander
5ml (1 tsp) ground cumin
5ml (1 tsp) garam masala powder
425g (15oz) can peeled tomatoes, chopped
2.5ml (½ tsp) salt
2-3 sprigs fresh green coriander, chopped

Either pressure cook the red kidney beans for 5-6 minutes, or cook them in their soaking water for 15-20 minutes until soft. Remove from the heat; allow to stand, covered. Fry the onions in the oil in a large saucepan over a moderate heat until tender. Add the bayleaf, cinnamon, cloves and cardamoms and fry for 1 minute. Add the chillies, garlic and ginger and fry until golden. Sprinkle with the chilli powder, turmeric, ground coriander, ground cumin and garam masala. Avoid burning the mixture. Stir the mixture to blend the spices. Add the tomatoes and

season with salt. Cover and simmer for 2-3 minutes. Drain the cooked beans and collect the thick red liquid. Add the beans to the spiced tomato mixture. Stir gently and cook for 1 minute. Add the red liquid and chopped coriander; cover and simmer for 3-5 minutes. Serve with bread or boiled rice.

Red Lentil Daal

There is an abundance of natural protein in pulses and there is a great variety of pulses now available.

PREPARATION TIME: 10 minutes	
COOKING TIME: 30 minutes	
SERVES: 4 people	

225g (8oz) red lentils
350ml (12 fl oz) water
1.25ml (¼ tsp) ground turmeric
5ml (1 tsp) ground coriander
1 green chilli, cut in half
Salt to taste
4-6 canned tomatoes, chopped
2 sprigs fresh green coriander leaves, chopped
50g (2oz) butter
1 small onion, peeled and finely chopped

Wash the lentils in 3-5 changes of water. Put the lentils into a pan with the 350ml (12 fl oz) water; cover and cook over a low heat for 10-15 minutes. Remove any froth with a spoon. Once the lentils are tender and yellow, blend until smooth with an egg whisk. Add the turmeric, ground coriander, chilli, salt to taste and chopped tomatoes. Cover and simmer for 10 minutes. Add the coriander leaves and pour into a dish. Keep warm. Melt the butter in a frying pan and saute the onion until golden brown. Pour the onions and butter juices over the daal. Serve with rice or bread.

Facing page: Mixed Daal (top left), Red Kidney Bean Curry (centre) and Red Lentil Daal (bottom).

Bread and Pizza

Puri

These deep-fried breads are simple to make once the art has been mastered.

PREPARATION TIME: 10-15 minutes

COOKING TIME: 20 minutes

MAKES: 30-32

450g (1lb) wholemeal flour
2.5ml (½ tsp) salt
250-300ml (8-12 fl oz) water
Oil for deep frying

Sieve the flour and salt into a mixing bowl. Mix to a soft dough with water. Knead well and leave to relax for 5 minutes, covered with a damp cloth. Divide the dough into 30-32 small even sized balls; roll out each ball into a small round about 6-7cm (2½-3 inch) in diameter. Heat the oil for deep frying and drop in a small piece of dough. If it rises to the top instantly then the correct temperature for frying has been reached. Place one puri at a time into the hot oil, taking care not to splash the oil. Gently stir the puri and it will begin to swell. Turn over and cook on the underside until golden brown – about ½-1 minute. The flip side is always the thick side and it needs extra cooking time. Drain the puris on the side of the frying pan, and place them on

Puri (above), Roti (right) and Paratha (far right).

kitchen paper to drain, before serving. Puris are best when served piping hot. Puris can be served cold and they can also be reheated under the grill.

Paratha

These shallow-fried breads can either be made plain, or stuffed with a favourite filling, such as cheese, potato etc.

PREPARATION TIME: 15-20 minutes	
COOKING TIME: 20-30 minutes	
MAKES: 16-18	

450g (1lb) wholemeal flour
2.5ml (½ tsp) salt
250-300ml (8-12 fl oz) water
Melted butter or oil

Sieve the flour and salt into a mixing bowl. Mix to a soft dough with water. Knead the dough well; leave to relax, covered, for 5 minutes. Divide the dough into 16-18 even-sized balls. Roll each ball into a small round about 5cm (2 inches) in diameter. Brush each round of dough with oil or melted butter and fold in half. Brush the upper folded surface with oil or butter and fold in half to form a small triangle. On a well floured surface roll out these triangles thinly. Heat a solid based frying pan or a griddle. Put the paratha onto the heated frying pan and cook for ½-1 minute or until small brown specks appear. Cook the other side in the same way. Brush a little oil or butter over the paratha and turn over. Fry for 1 minute and then brush the second side with oil or butter. Fry on both sides until the paratha is golden and crisp. Make the rest of the paratha in the same way. Keep them soft and warm, well wrapped in a clean tea towel or foil.

Roti

Roti is best made with wholemeal flour; any variety may be used.

PREPARATION TIME: 20 minutes

COOKING TIME: 20-30 minutes

MAKES: about 24

450g (1lb) wholemeal flour
2.5ml (½ tsp) salt
250-300ml (8-12 fl oz) water

Sieve the flour and salt into a mixing bowl. Mix to a soft dough with water. Knead the dough for 2-3 minutes. Cover and allow to relax for 5-6 minutes before shaping the bread. Divide the dough into 25g (1oz) balls. Roll each ball into a thin round about 13-15cm (5-6 inches) in diameter. Place a solid based frying pan or a griddle over a medium heat; when the pan is hot, place the shaped roti onto it. Cook for ½ minute on each side and then place under a preheated grill to bloat (little brown specks will appear on the surface). The first 2 rotis do not usually bloat, so do not be alarmed. Make all the rotis and stack them one on top of each other. Keep them covered with a clean tea towel or foil. Serve hot with any curry or spicy savoury dish.

Banana and Nut Bread

PREPARATION TIME: 30 minutes

COOKING TIME: 1 hour

MAKES: 1 loaf

100g (4oz) butter
225g (8oz) brown sugar
1 egg, well beaten
225g (8oz) wholemeal flour
2.5ml (½ tsp) salt
7.5ml (1½ tsp) baking powder
60ml (4 tblsp) natural yogurt
2 ripe bananas, peeled and mashed
50g (2oz) raisins
100g (4oz) mixed nuts, chopped

Preheat the oven to 180°C, 350°F, Gas Mark 4. Cream the butter and sugar until light and fluffy and gradually beat in the egg. Sieve the flour, salt and baking powder

together. Add half the yogurt to the butter and sugar mixture and then mix in half the sieved dry ingredients. Beat in the remaining yogurt, flour, mashed banana, raisins and chopped nuts. Mix well. Put the mixture into a greased loaf tin. Bake at 180°C, 350°F, Gas Mark 4, for 1 hour.

Crusty Loaf

PREPARATION TIME: 3 hours 40 minutes

COOKING TIME: 45 minutes-1 hour

MAKES: 2 loaves

300ml (½ pint) tepid water
15g (½oz) fresh yeast or 10ml (2 tsp) dried yeast
2.5ml (½ tsp) salt
15g (½oz) butter
15ml (1 tblsp) sugar
400g (14oz) sieved plain flour
15ml (1 tblsp) melted butter
25g (1oz) caraway, sesame or poppy seeds for topping (optional)

Sprinkle or crumble the yeast into the tepid water; stir to dissolve. Leave for a few minutes until frothy. Mix the salt, butter, sugar and flour together; stir in the yeast liquid and mix to a dough. Knead the dough for 10 minutes on a lightly floured surface. Place the dough in a greased bowl and brush the top lightly with melted butter; cover with a damp cloth and leave it to rise in a warm place (free from draught), until doubled in bulk (about 40-45 minutes). Punch the dough down and let it rise again until almost double its original size about (30 minutes). Punch down once again and turn out onto a floured surface, cut into two equal portions. Roll each one into an oblong about 20-25cm (8-10 inches) in length. Beginning with the wide side, roll up each oblong tightly. Seal the edges by pinching together. Holding each end of the roll, roll it gently backwards and forwards to lengthen the loaf and shape the ends. Place the loaves on a greased baking sheet lightly sprinkled with plain flour. Brush the loaves either with milk, or with cornflour glaze, and leave to rise for 1½ hours, uncovered. With a sharp knife, make 5mm (¼ inch) slashes at regular intervals. Bake in a hot oven, 200°C, 400°F, Gas Mark 6, for 10 minutes. Brush once again with milk or cornflour glaze and sprinkle with poppy seeds

(or other seeds). Return to the oven and bake for 25-30 minutes or until golden brown.

To make cornflour glaze: mix 5ml (1 tsp) cornflour with 5ml (1 tsp) cold water. Add 120ml (4oz) boiling water and cook for 1-2 minutes until smooth. Cool slightly before use.

Wholemeal Bread

PREPARATION TIME: 2 hours 30 minutes

COOKING TIME: 50 minutes

MAKES: 1 large loaf

750g (1½lbs) wholemeal flour
2.5ml (½ tsp) salt
50g (2oz) margarine
25g (1oz) fresh yeast, or
15ml (1 tblsp) dried yeast (see below)
15ml (1 tblsp) granulated or brown sugar
300ml (½ pint) tepid water
150ml (¼ pint) tepid milk
15ml (1 tblsp) melted butter

Sieve the flour and salt into a warm bowl and rub in the margarine. Cream the fresh yeast with the sugar and stir in the warm water and milk. (If using dried yeast, sprinkle it onto the warm water and milk, with the sugar, and leave to stand for 10 minutes until thick and frothy). Make a well in the centre of the flour and pour in the yeast liquid; gradually mix in the flour to form a dough. Knead the dough well. Cover it with a damp cloth and leave to rise until double in bulk (about 1¼ hours). Grease a loaf tin, 23cm by 13cm by 7.5cm (9 inches by 5 inches by 3 inches). Turn the risen dough onto a floured surface and knead well; place in the loaf tin. Leave in a warm place to rise for 40 minutes. Brush the loaf with melted butter and bake at 200°C, 400°F, Gas Mark 6, for about 50 minutes.

Wholemeal Pizza Dough

PREPARATION TIME: 50-60 minutes

200ml (⅓ pint) tepid water
7.5ml (1½ tsp) dried yeast
2.5ml (½ tsp) salt
5ml (1 tsp) sugar

5ml (1 tsp) olive oil
100g (4oz) wholemeal flour
150g (5oz) plain flour

Mix the dried yeast with the tepid water. Add the salt, sugar and oil. Mix in the flours a little at a time, to make a dough. Use extra water if needed. Turn the dough onto a lightly floured surface and knead until smooth (about 5-8 minutes). Cover the dough with a clean damp tea towel and leave to stand for 15-20 minutes. Knead once more for 1-2 minutes. You can make either one large pizza base or several smaller ones. Grease one 35cm (14 inch) pizza pan and roll out the dough to make a round large enough to fit the pizza pan. Shape the pizza dough with the hands to fit the pan. Top with the chosen topping and bake.

Basic Pizza Dough

This is the basic recipe for pizza dough and although there are many variations, the making of the dough is very important. Pizza originated in Italy, around the Naples area, but it is now eaten and enjoyed worldwide. Once the basic dough is perfected, toppings can be adjusted to one's taste. In fact, on one single pizza, each slice can have a different taste (i.e. with a different topping). See Taco Pizza Topping and Mixed Vegetable Pizza Topping recipes.

PREPARATION TIME: about 1 hour 30 minutes

1.25ml (¼ tsp) sugar
15ml (1 tblsp) dried yeast
120ml (4 fl oz) tepid water
5ml (1 tsp) salt
225g (8oz) plain flour, sieved

Mix the dried yeast with 30ml (2 tblsp) of the tepid water and the sugar. Stir until dissolved. Leave to stand for 10-15 minutes until frothy. Put the flour and salt into a

Facing page: Crusty Loaf (top), Banana and Nut Bread (centre) and Wholemeal Bread (bottom).

bowl and make a well in the centre. Add the yeast liquid and the remaining tepid water; mix to form a dough. Kneed the dough on a floured surface for 8-10 minutes. Cover with a damp cloth and leave to rise in a warm place for 40-45 minutes, until double its original size. Knead once again on a lightly floured surface for 3-5 minutes until soft and elastic. You can make either one large pizza base, or several smaller ones. Grease one 35cm (14 inch) pizza pan and roll out the dough. Shape the pizza dough with the hands to fit the pan. Top with the chosen topping and bake.

Taco Pizza

This idea is taken from the taco (a Mexican pancake). The pizza base is made with a mixture of cornmeal and flour and some of the topping ingredients are the same as those used in a taco filling.

PREPARATION TIME: 30-40 minutes
COOKING TIME: 30-35 minutes
SERVES: 6 people

Dough
175g (6oz) plain flour
75g (3oz) fine yellow commeal
10ml (2 tsp) baking powder
5ml (1 tsp) salt
100g (4oz) margarine
120ml (4 fl oz) milk

Sieve the flour, cornmeal, salt and baking powder into a mixing bowl. Rub in the margarine. Add the milk, gradually, to form a medium soft dough. Knead the dough on a well floured surface for 4-5 minutes, until smooth. Roll into a circle to cover a 33-35cm (13-14 inch) pizza pan, with a 2.5cm (1 inch) high rim. Grease the pizza pan and cover with the dough. Shape the pizza dough to fit the pan. Pinch the edges to form a deep rim. Keep on one side until the topping is ready.

Topping
30ml (2 tblsp) olive oil
1 clove garlic, peeled and crushed
1 small onion, peeled and chopped
½ green pepper, seeded and coarsely chopped
4-6 mushrooms, sliced
225g (8oz) cooked red kidney beans (or drained canned ones)
2 spring onions, chopped
3 large tomatoes, chopped
6-8 pitted black olives, halved
3-4 pickled Mexican chillies, chopped
225g (8oz) Mozzarella, Cheddar or Monterey Jack cheese, cut into slivers
1 carrot, peeled and grated
150ml (¼ pint) soured cream
Bottled taco sauce

Heat the oil and fry the garlic, chopped onion, pepper and mushrooms for 2 minutes; add the kidney beans and stir fry for 1-2 minutes. Remove from the heat and stir in the spring onions. Spread the above topping mixture over the pizza base. Arrange the tomatoes evenly on top. Add the olives, Mexican chillies and slivers of cheese. Bake at 200°C, 400°F, Gas mark 6, for 15-20 minutes until the edges turn golden brown and crusty. Serve with grated carrots, whipped soured cream and taco sauce.

Mixed Vegetable Pizza Topping

PREPARATION TIME: 30 minutes
COOKING TIME: 20 minutes
SERVES: 4-6 people

30ml (2 tblsp) olive oil
1 small onion, peeled and chopped
2 spring onions, chopped
1 medium courgette, trimmed and thinly sliced
4 mushrooms, sliced
Salt and freshly ground black pepper to taste
6-8 canned tomatoes, chopped
10ml (2 tsp) tomato puree

8 pitted black olives
2 tomatoes, thinly sliced
1 green pepper, seeded and chopped
1 green chilli, chopped
5ml (1 tsp) dried oregano
175g (6oz) Mozzarella cheese, Cheddar cheese or a mixture of the two, cut into thin slivers
30ml (2 tblsp) grated Parmesan cheese

Heat the olive oil in a large frying pan; add the onions and sauté for 1-2 minutes. Add the courgette and sauté for 2 minutes. Add the mushrooms and salt and pepper to taste and stir fry for 1 minute to glaze the vegetables. Remove from the heat and cool. Mix the chopped tomato with the tomato puree and spread evenly over the pizza base. Spoon the vegetable mixture over the pizza and arrange the olives, sliced tomatoes, green pepper and green chilli on top. Sprinkle with the oregano, the slivers of cheese and the grated Parmesan cheese. Bake at 230°C, 450°F, Gas mark 8 for 12-15 minutes, or until the edge of the pizza is golden brown and crusty.

Taco Pizza (top right) and Mixed Vegetable Pizza Topping (bottom right).

VEGETARIAN CUISINE
Main Meals

Okra Curry

A dry vegetable curry made with okra and potato.

PREPARATION TIME:	10-15 minutes
COOKING TIME:	30 minutes
SERVES:	4 people

45ml (3 tblsp) oil
1 onion, peeled and chopped
2 medium sized potatoes, peeled and
   cut into 2.5cm (1 inch) pieces
450g (1lb) okra, topped and tailed,
   and chopped into 1cm (½ inch)
   pieces
Salt to taste
2.5ml (½ tsp) ground turmeric
5ml (1 tsp) chilli powder
7.5ml (1½ tsp) ground coriander
2-3 sprigs fresh green coriander
   leaves, chopped

Heat the oil in a wok or solid based frying pan and fry the onion for 3-4 minutes. Stir in the cubed potatoes; cover and cook for 3-4 minutes. Add the okra, and stir fry for 2 minutes. Sprinkle with salt to taste, turmeric, chilli and ground coriander. Mix gently; cover and cook for 8-10 minutes. Stir occasionally and continue cooking until the potatoes are tender. Sprinkle with the chopped coriander leaves. Mix well and serve.

Okra Fry

This is a dry "curry" – no spices are added; the okra supplies the hotness.

PREPARATION TIME:	15 minutes
COOKING TIME:	20-30 minutes
SERVES:	4 people

450-750g (1-1½lb) okra
Oil for deep frying
15ml (1 tblsp) oil
1 large onion, peeled and chopped
Salt and freshly ground black pepper
   to taste

Top and tail the okra; chop them into 5mm (¼ inch) even-sized pieces. Heat the oil for deep frying; add the chopped okra, a little at a time, and deep fry until brown and crisp. Drain on absorbent paper and keep warm in a dish. Heat the 15ml (1 tblsp) oil and fry the onion until tender about 4-5 minutes. Remove the onion and mix with the fried okra. Sprinkle with salt and pepper to taste. Serve with chapati, or as a side dish.

Aubergine Bake

PREPARATION TIME:	30 minutes
COOKING TIME:	30-40 minutes
SERVES:	6 people

3 large Dutch aubergines
10ml (2 tsp) salt
Malt vinegar
30ml (2 tblsp) oil
2 large onions, peeled and sliced
2 green chillies, chopped
425g (15oz) can peeled tomatoes,
   chopped
2.5ml (½ tsp) chilli powder
5ml (1 tsp) crushed garlic
2.5ml (½ tsp) ground turmeric
Oil for deep frying
60ml (4 tblsp) natural yogurt
5ml (1 tsp) freshly ground black
   pepper
4 tomatoes, sliced
225g (½lb) Cheddar cheese, grated

Cut the aubergines into 5mm (¼ inch) thick slices. Lay in a shallow dish. Sprinkle with 5ml (1 tsp) salt and add sufficient malt vinegar to cover. Allow to marinate for 20-30 minutes. Drain well. Heat 30ml (2 tblsp) oil in a frying pan and fry the onions until golden brown. Add the chillies, chopped tomatoes, remaining salt, chilli powder, garlic and turmeric. Mix well and simmer for 5-7 minutes. Remove from the heat. Cool and blend to a smooth sauce in the liquidiser. Keep the sauce on one side. Heat the oil for deep frying and deep fry the drained, marinated aubergine until brown on both sides (2-3 minutes each side). Drain well on kitchen paper. Grease a large deep baking tray. Arrange half the fried aubergine rounds closely together in the tray. Spoon over half the tomato sauce and beaten yogurt. Season with pepper. Add the remaining aubergine rounds and the rest of the tomato sauce and yogurt. Cover with slices of tomatoes and grated cheese. Bake at 180°C, 350°F, Gas Mark 4, for 10-15 minutes, or until the cheese melts and turns brown. Serve hot as a side dish, or as a main course with brown bread or pitta bread.

Stuffed Courgettes

This is a delightful dish from Southern Italy.

PREPARATION TIME:	30 minutes
COOKING TIME:	30-40 minutes
SERVES:	4 people

50g (2oz) fresh coarse breadcrumbs
60ml (4 tblsp) milk
8 medium sized courgettes, trimmed
1 onion, peeled and finely chopped
2 tomatoes, chopped
6-8 mushrooms, sliced
1 clove garlic, peeled and chopped
60ml (4 tblsp) olive oil
10ml (2 tsp) dried oregano
Salt and freshly ground black pepper
   to taste
1 egg, beaten
75g (3oz) Mozzarella cheese (or
   Cheddar), cut into thin slivers
75g (3oz) grated Parmesan cheese

Soak the breadcrumbs in the milk for 15-20 minutes. Cook the courgettes in boiling water for 5 minutes. Drain and cool. Slice them in half lengthways and scoop out the flesh, leaving a thick shell at least 5mm (¼ inch). Take care not to break or crack the courgettes.

This page: Aubergine Bake (top left), Okra Curry (centre right) and Okra Fry (right).

Overleaf: Courgette Bake (left), Stuffed Courgettes (centre) and Spicy Corn (right).

Keep the scooped flesh on one side. Squeeze out the excess milk from the breadcrumbs and put them into a bowl. Fry the scooped courgette flesh, chopped onion, tomatoes, mushrooms and chopped garlic in half the olive oil for 5 minutes. Mix with the breadcrumbs, oregano, salt and pepper to taste, the beaten egg and half the cheeses. Spoon the mixture evenly into all the courgette shells. Arrange the stuffed courgettes on a lightly greased baking tray. Sprinkle the remaining cheese over them and brush with the rest of the oil. Bake for 18-20 minutes at 200°C, 400°F, Gas Mark 6, or until the cheese has melted and turned golden brown. Serve at once.

Spicy Corn

This dish originates from East Africa, it makes a tasty hot snack or supper dish.

PREPARATION TIME: 15 minutes

COOKING TIME: 35-40 minutes

SERVES: 6 people

45ml (3 tblsp) oil
1 large onion, peeled and chopped
2 medium potatoes, peeled and cubed
8 fresh curry leaves (optional)
2.5ml (½ tsp) cumin seed
2.5ml (½ tsp) mustard seed
5ml (1 tsp) crushed fresh root ginger
5ml (1 tsp) crushed garlic
750g (1½lb) frozen sweetcorn kernels
5ml (1 tsp) salt
5ml (1 tsp) chilli powder
5ml (1 tsp) ground coriander
2.5ml (½ tsp) ground turmeric
425g (15oz) can peeled tomatoes, chopped
15ml (1 tblsp) tomato puree
1-2 green chillies, chopped
2 green peppers, seeded and cut into 2.5cm (1 inch) pieces
3 sprigs fresh green coriander, chopped
15ml (1 tblsp) thick tamarind pulp, or
30ml (2 tblsp) lemon juice

Heat the oil and fry the onion for 3 minutes; add the potatoes and fry for 5 minutes. Add the curry leaves, cumin and mustard seed and stir fry for 1-2 minutes. Add ginger and garlic and stir fry for 1-2 minutes. Add the sweetcorn, salt, chilli powder, ground coriander and turmeric. Mix well and cook for 2-3 minutes. Add the chopped tomatoes, tomato puree, chopped chillies, green peppers and coriander leaves. Stir in the tamarind pulp and mix well adding a little water if the mixture seems too dry. Cover and cook over a low heat until the potatoes are tender about 10-15 minutes. The spicy corn should be thick but moist. Serve hot or cold.

Spiced Peas

PREPARATION TIME: 10 minutes

COOKING TIME: 15 minutes

SERVES: 6 people

30ml (2 tblsp) oil
1 large onion, peeled and chopped
2 green chillies, sliced in half lengthways
1kg (2lb) shelled peas (fresh or frozen)
Salt and freshly ground black pepper to taste
15ml (1 tblsp) lemon juice
Lemon wedges

Heat the oil in a wok or solid based frying pan and fry the onion until tender. Add the chillies and fry for 1 minute. Add the peas and salt and pepper to taste; stir fry for 5-10 minutes, or until well coloured and "dry". Put into a serving dish and sprinkle with lemon juice. Garnish with lemon wedges. Serve as a side dish, or as a snack.

Spinach with Paneer

Paneer is a home-made cheese; it is made by separating milk into curds and whey by means of a souring agent such as lemon juice. It is eaten extensively in northern parts of India and is a good source of protein.

PREPARATION TIME: 15 minutes, plus time for making paneer

COOKING TIME: 20-30 minutes

SERVES: 4 people

To make paneer: (This is an overnight process)
1.2 litres (2 pints) milk
30ml (2 tblsp) lemon juice

Bring the milk to the boil. Reduce the heat and sprinkle with the lemon juice. The milk will separate into pale watery whey and thick white paneer (or curds). Remove from the heat and allow the paneer to coagulate (if the milk has not separated properly, add a few more drops of lemon juice. The whey should be a clear, pale, yellow liquid. Pour the paneer and liquid through a muslin-lined sieve. Discard the liquid whey and tie the muslin over the paneer. Flatten the paneer to 1cm (½ inch) thick; place it on a tray and rest it in a tilted position. Place more muslin over the top and weight it down. The pressure will drag out the remaining moisture and the tilted position will channel the liquid away from the paneer. Leave to drain overnight. Next day, cut the firm paneer into 2.5cm (1 inch) cubes.

75g (3oz) butter
1 medium onion, peeled and finely chopped
2.5cm (1 inch) piece cinnamon stick
1 bayleaf
450g (1lb) frozen spinach puree, or fresh leaf spinach, cooked and pureed
5ml (1 tsp) chilli powder
2.5ml (½ tsp) salt
120g (4½oz) natural yogurt
3 sprigs fresh green coriander leaves, chopped
5ml (1 tsp) garam masala powder
Oil for deep frying

Heat the butter in a pan and fry the onion until golden brown. Add the cinnamon and bayleaf and fry for 1 minute. Add the spinach and stir to mix. Sprinkle with the chilli powder and salt and stir in the yogurt, coriander leaves and garam masala. Cover and cook for 2-3 minutes. Simmer gently. Meanwhile, deep-fry the drained paneer cubes until golden. Add the paneer cubes to the spinach and simmer together for 4-5 minutes. Serve hot with chapati or pulao rice.

New Potato Fry

This Oriental dish is very versatile; it can be served as a side dish, as a snack, or as a main curry. It is also a wonderful way of serving potatoes with traditional roast meats.

PREPARATION TIME: 20 minutes

COOKING TIME: 10-12 minutes

SERVES: 3-4 people

45ml (3 tblsp) oil
5ml (1 tsp) mustard seed
450g (1lb) small, even sized new potatoes, boiled in their skins and peeled
5ml (1 tsp) red chilli powder
7.5ml (1½ tsp) ground coriander
1.25ml (¼ tsp) ground turmeric
2.5ml (½ tsp) salt
3 sprigs fresh green coriander leaves, chopped (optional)
Lemon juice to taste

Heat the oil in a wok or solid based frying pan and add the mustard seed and the whole, peeled potatoes. Stir fry over a low heat until they are lightly browned. Sprinkle with the spices, salt and chopped coriander leaves. Stir fry over a low heat for 5-6 minutes until golden brown. Remove from heat. Put into a dish and sprinkle with the lemon juice. Serve hot or cold.

Courgette Bake

Serve this dish as a main course with fried rice, or as a side dish.

PREPARATION TIME: 20-30 minutes

COOKING TIME: 35 minutes

SERVES: 4-6 people

1kg (2lbs) courgettes, trimmed and coarsely grated
5ml (1 tsp) salt
30ml (2 tblsp) melted unsalted butter (or oil)
3-4 eggs, well beaten
175-200g (6-7oz) grated mild cheese (Edam, Samso, etc)
1 medium onion, peeled and finely chopped
2 cloves garlic, peeled and finely chopped
30ml (2 tblsp) chopped parsley
5ml (1 tsp) dried basil
2.5ml (½ tsp) freshly ground black pepper
30-40g (1-1½oz) grated Parmesan cheese

Put the grated courgettes into a colander and sprinkle with salt. Leave to drain for 10 minutes. Squeeze the moisture out of the

Facing page: Spiced Peas (top), Spinach with Paneer (centre right) and New Potato Fry (bottom).

courgettes until quite dry. Lightly grease a baking dish (size approx. 25cm x 18cm (10 inches x 7 inches). Heat the butter in a non-stick frying pan and fry the courgettes for 3-4 minutes until tender. Mix the beaten eggs, grated cheese, chopped onion, garlic, parsley, basil and pepper. Place the sauteed courgettes in the baking dish and pour egg mixture over the top. Sprinkle with the Parmesan cheese and bake at 180°C, 350°F, Gas mark 4, for 25-30 minutes until set. Serve cut into squares or diamond shapes. Can be eaten hot or cold.

Vegetable Stir Fry with Tofu

This is a Chinese stir fry dish with Tofu which makes a filling main course.

PREPARATION TIME: 30 minutes

COOKING TIME: 10 minutes

SERVES: 4 people

10ml (2 tsp) soya sauce
10ml (2 tsp) Worcestershire sauce
2.5cm (1 inch) fresh root ginger, peeled and thinly sliced
3 cloves garlic, peeled and crushed
225g (8oz) Tofu, cut into 1cm (½ inch) pieces
10ml (2 tsp) cornflour
200ml (⅓ pint) water
45ml (3 tblsp) oil
3 stems celery, sliced thinly
2 carrots, peeled and cut into thin diagonal slices
2-3 courgettes, trimmed, and cut into thin diagonal slices
1 green pepper, quartered, seeded and sliced thinly
8 mushrooms, thinly sliced
1-2 tomatoes, cut into wedges
50g (2oz) mange tout, or thinly sliced green beans

Mix the soya sauce with the Worcestershire sauce, ginger and garlic. Add the Tofu cubes and marinate for 8 minutes. Pick out the Tofu and keep on a plate. Stir the cornflour into the soya sauce mixture and blend in the water. Heat the oil in a wok over a medium heat. Add the celery and carrots and stir fry for 2 minutes. Add the courgettes and green pepper and stir fry for 2 minutes. Add the tomatoes and mange tout or green beans. Stir fry for 2 minutes. Add the mushrooms and stir fry for 1 minute. Stir in the water and soya sauce mixture. Cook until thickened, stirring for 1-2 minutes. Add the Tofu. Heat through and serve immediately.

Cheese Bourag

PREPARATION TIME: 30-40 minutes

COOKING TIME: 20-25 minutes

SERVES: 4 people

225g (8oz) plain flour
Salt
7.5ml (3 tsp) baking powder
40g (1½oz) unsalted butter
120-150ml (4-5 fl oz) milk
225g (8oz) strong Cheddar cheese, grated
45ml (3 tblsp) chopped parsley
Oil for deep frying

Sieve the flour, 1.25ml (¼ tsp) salt and baking powder into a bowl; rub in the butter. Add the milk, a little at a time, and mix to a dough with a palette knife. Cover the dough and leave in a cool place to relax. Mix the grated cheese with the chopped parsley and a little salt to taste. Roll the dough out very thinly on a floured board and cut into 5cm (2 inch) squares. Brush the edges of half the squares with a dampened pastry brush. Place a little filling in the centre of each one and cover with the remaining squares. Seal the edges well by pinching with the fingers or notching with the prongs of a fork. Heat the oil for deep frying. Fry the bourags a few at a time in hot oil until golden and crisp. Drain on kitchen paper and serve hot with sweet and sour sauce.

Avial

This is a mixed vegetable dish made with coconut.

PREPARATION TIME: 30 minutes

COOKING TIME: 20 minutes

SERVES: 4 people

2 medium sized potatoes, peeled and cut into 2.5cm (1 inch) cubes
175g (6oz) lobia beans, trimmed and cut into 5cm (2 inch) pieces
50g (2oz) green beans, trimmed and sliced
4 drumstick or yard long beans, strung and cut into 2.5cm (1 inch) pieces
175g (6oz) squash, peeled and cut into 2.5cm (1 inch) cubes
1 green unripe banana, peeled and cut into 2.5cm (1 inch) pieces
1 aubergine, trimmed and cut into 2.5cm (1 inch) chunks
100g (4oz) shelled peas
½ fresh coconut, shelled, skin removed and thinly sliced
7.5ml (1½ tsp) cumin seeds
2 green chillies, chopped
120ml (4 fl oz) water
150ml (5oz) natural yogurt
45ml (3 tblsp) coconut oil for cooking

Steam all the vegetables for 10-15 minutes until almost tender, but still slightly crisp. Grind the spices with the water in a liquidiser until smooth. Mix the spice liquid with the coconut. Heat the coconut oil in a saucepan and add the vegetables, spice mixture and yogurt. Bring to the boil and simmer with the lid on for 5 minutes. Serve with rice.

Garlic Hash Brown

This is a favourite dish in America, where it is eaten with steak and burgers.

PREPARATION TIME: 20 minutes

COOKING TIME: 30 minutes

SERVES: 4 people

60ml (4 tblsp) oil
4 cloves of garlic, peeled and quartered lengthways
3 whole red chillies
Salt
450-750g (1-1½lb) potatoes, peeled and coarsely grated

Heat the oil in a wok or a large non-stick frying pan. Fry the garlic until lightly browned. Add the red chillies and fry for 30 seconds. Sprinkle with salt to taste and add the grated potato. Stir fry for 5 minutes. Cover and cook for a further 8-10 minutes. The potatoes should be crisp and golden brown. Cook until the potatoes are tender. Serve as a side dish or for breakfast.

Vegetable Stir Fry with Tofu (top), Avial (centre left) and Cheese Bourag (bottom right).

Spiced Chick Peas

This dryish curry is a "must" on any Punjabi menu. It is usually served with milk bread or pitta bread and an onion salad.

PREPARATION TIME: overnight overnight for soaking, plus 15 minutes

COOKING TIME: 40-50 minutes

SERVES: 4-6 people

450g (1lb) chick peas
5ml (1 tsp) baking powder
4 cloves
5ml (1 tsp) cumin seed
4 large black cardamoms, ground
4 small cardamoms, ground
1 large onion, peeled and chopped
45ml (3 tblsp) oil
2 bayleaves
2.5cm (1 inch) piece cinnamon stick
2 green chillies, sliced in half lengthways
2.5cm (1 inch) fresh root ginger, peeled and finely chopped
4 cloves garlic, peeled and crushed
7.5ml (1½ tsp) ground coriander
250-300ml (8-10 fl oz) canned tomatoes, chopped
2.5ml (½ tp) freshly ground black pepper
2.5ml (½ tsp) salt
5-6 sprigs fresh green coriander leaves, chopped

Wash the chick peas and soak them overnight in 1.2 litres (2 pints) water and the baking powder. The following day, cook the chick peas in their soaking liquid in a pressure cooker for 10-15 minutes. If a lot of liquid has been absorbed during soaking, add a little more. Dry roast the cloves and cumin seed in a frying pan. Grind the cloves, cumin, large and small cardamons into a fine powder. Fry the onion in the oil for 2-3 minutes. Add the bayleaves, cinnamon, chillies, ginger and garlic. Fry for 1 minute, add the ground coriander and tomatoes. Fry for 2-3 minutes. Strain the chick peas, retaining any liquid. Add the chick peas to the tomato mixture and add black pepper, salt and the dry roasted spices. Mix well and add 250ml (8 fl oz) of the strained chick pea liquid. Sprinkle with chopped coriander; cover and cook for 8-10 minutes. Add a little extra liquid if necessary. Serve with bread or rice.

Vegetable Pancakes (far left) and Spiced Chick Peas (left).

Vegetable Pancakes

A combination of shredded vegetables makes a delicious pancake, when added to the batter before cooking.

PREPARATION TIME: 15 minutes

COOKING TIME: 15 minutes

SERVES: 4-6 people

100g (4oz) butter
225g (8oz) shredded or coarsely grated carrots
225g (8oz) shredded or coarsely grated courgettes
450g (1lb) shredded or coarsely grated potatoes
1 medium onion, thinly sliced
3 eggs, well beaten
200ml (1/3 pint) soured cream
60ml (4 tblsp) cornflour
2.5ml (1/2 tsp) salt
2.5ml (1/2 tsp) freshly ground black pepper
Oil for frying
Wedges of lemon

Melt the butter in a frying pan; add the carrots, courgettes, potatoes and onion. Saute for 3-4 minutes, stirring continuously. Beat the eggs together with the soured cream, cornflour and salt and pepper. Mix well. Stir in the semi-cooked vegetables. Mix together gently. Heat a large non-stick frying pan and brush with 10ml (2 tsp) oil; add 15ml (1 tblsp) batter. Cook until light brown; turn the small pancake over and cook until the other side is also brown. Make 3 or 4 at a time. The size of the pancakes can be increased by using more batter for each pancake. Serve with salads or with tomato sauce as a light meal or snack.

Green Beans with Coconut

PREPARATION TIME: 10 minutes

COOKING TIME: 20 minutes

SERVES: 3-4 people

30ml (2 tblsp) oil
2 cloves garlic, peeled and crushed
2 green or red dried chillies
450g (1lb) green beans, sliced
1.25ml (1/4 tsp) salt
30ml (2 tblsp) desiccated coconut, or grated fresh coconut

Heat the oil in a wok or frying pan. Add the garlic and fry until golden brown. Add the chillies and stir fry for 30 seconds. Add the green beans and sprinkle with salt. Stir fry for 8-10 minutes until the beans are tender but still crisp. Sprinkle with the coconut and stir fry for a further 2-3 minutes. Serve as a side dish.

Mixed Vegetable Raita

Raitas are yogurt-based Indian dishes served as accompaniments to curries etc. Natural yogurt is usually mixed with fruits, vegetables, and herbs such as coriander or mint.

PREPARATION TIME: 10 minutes

SERVES: 4-6 people

300ml (1/2 pint) natural yogurt
1/2 cucumber, chopped
1 small onion, peeled and chopped
2 tomatoes, chopped
2 stems celery, chopped
1 small apple, cored and chopped
2 boiled potatoes, peeled and chopped
1.25ml (1/4 tsp) salt
1.25ml (1/4 tsp) freshly ground black pepper
1 sprig fresh green coriander, chopped

Beat the yogurt in a bowl. Add all the remaining ingredients, seasoning well with salt and pepper. Chill before serving.

Cannelloni with Spinach and Ricotta

PREPARATION TIME: 20 minutes

COOKING TIME: 1 hour 20 minutes

SERVES: 4 people

30ml (2 tblsp) olive oil or melted butter
1 large onion, peeled and finely chopped
2 large cloves garlic, peeled and crushed
425g (15oz) can peeled tomatoes, chopped
15ml (1 tblsp) tomato puree
Salt and freshly ground black pepper to taste
7.5ml (1 1/2 tsp) dried basil
2.5ml (1/2 tsp) dried oregano
350g (12oz) cannelloni tubes
60ml (4 tblsp) thick spinach puree
225g (8oz) Ricotta cheese
30ml (2 tblsp) grated Parmesan cheese

To make the sauce: heat the oil or butter and fry the onion and garlic for 2-3 minutes. Add the tomatoes and tomato puree and mix well. Simmer for 2 minutes. Add the salt and pepper, basil and oregano. Cover and simmer for 10-15 minutes until thick.

Bring a large pan of salted water to the boil; cook the cannelloni tubes for 10 minutes until just tender. Do not overboil. Lift out the cannelloni tubes and put them into a bowl of cold water to cool quickly. Drain well. Mix together the spinach, ricotta and salt and pepper to taste. Fill the cannelloni tubes with the spinach mixture and arrange them in a greased shallow ovenproof dish. Pour the tomato sauce over the cannelloni; sprinkle with the Parmesan cheese. Bake for 20-30 minutes at 180°C, 350°F, Gas Mark 4 or until the top is browned and bubbling. Serve at once.

Ginger Cauliflower

This is a very simple and extremely subtle vegetable dish spiced with ginger.

PREPARATION TIME: 15 minutes

COOKING TIME: 15 minutes

SERVES: 4 people

45ml (3 tblsp) oil
1 medium onion, peeled and chopped
2.5cm (1 inch) fresh root ginger, peeled and sliced
1-2 green chillies, cut in half lengthways
1 medium cauliflower, cut into 2.5cm (1 inch) florets, along with tender leaves and stalk
Salt to taste
2-3 sprigs fresh green coriander leaves, chopped
Juice of 1 lemon

Heat the oil in a wok or solid based saucepan; fry the onion, ginger and chillies for 2-3 minutes. Add the cauliflower and salt to taste. Stir to

Noodles with Vegetables (top left), Green Beans with Coconut (centre right) and Garlic Hash Brown (bottom).

mix well. Cover and cook over a low heat for 5-6 minutes. Add the coriander leaves and cook for a further 2-3 minutes, or until the florets of cauliflower are tender. Sprinkle with lemon juice, mix well and serve immediately. Serve with pitta bread.

Mung Fritters

These tiny marble-sized fritters are made with mung pulse. They can be eaten as a cocktail snack or made into a curry with a well-flavoured sauce.

PREPARATION TIME: 1 hour 30 minutes

COOKING TIME: 30 minutes

SERVES: 4 people

225g (8oz) split mung pulse
1 small onion, peeled and chopped
5ml (1 tsp) chilli powder
7.5ml (1½ tsp) garam masala powder
2.5ml (½ tsp) cumin seed
4-5 sprigs fresh green coriander leaves, chopped
2.5ml (½ tsp) salt
Oil for deep frying

Wash and soak the mung pulse for 1 hour in sufficient cold water to cover. Drain and then grind into a thick coarse paste, adding 120-250ml (4-8 fl oz) water as you go. It should be the consistency of peanut butter. Mix the mung paste with the onion, chilli powder, garam masala, cumin seed, coriander leaves and salt. Mix well and adjust seasoning if necessary. Heat the oil for deep frying. Using a teaspoon, shape the paste into small "marbles" and fry in the hot oil until golden brown. Drain on kitchen paper and serve piping hot with chutney, a chilli sauce or a dip. To turn into a curry, add the Mung Fritters to the following curry sauce.

Sauce
10ml (2 tsp) oil
1 small onion, finely chopped
2.5ml (½ tsp) chilli powder
5ml (1 tsp) ground coriander
5ml (1 tsp) ground cumin
4-6 canned tomatoes, chopped
Salt to taste
3-4 sprigs fresh green coriander leaves, chopped

Heat the oil in a saucepan and fry the onion for 3 minutes. Stir in all the above ingredients; cover and

simmer for 5-8 minutes. Add a little water to make a thickish sauce. Add ready-fried Mung Fritters and simmer for 3-5 minutes.

Noodles with Vegetables

This exotic noodle dish can be served hot or cold, as a main course, as a side dish or as a snack.

PREPARATION TIME: 20 minutes

COOKING TIME: 30 minutes

SERVES: 4 people

Salt to taste
450g (1lb) egg noodles, or broken spaghetti
45ml (3 tblsp) oil
2.5cm (1 inch) fresh root ginger, peeled and thinly sliced
1 large or 2 medium onions, peeled and sliced
75g (3oz) green beans, sliced
75g (3oz) carrots, peeled and cut into matchstick strips
100g (4oz) white cabbage, or Chinese leaves, shredded
50g (2oz) shelled peas
75g (3oz) sprouting mung beans
1 green pepper, seeded and cut into 2.5cm (1 inch) pieces
1-2 stems celery, chopped
1-2 green chillies, split lengthways
2.5ml (½ tsp) monosodium glutamate (optional)
30ml (2 tblsp) soya sauce
15ml (1 tblsp) lemon juice
5-10ml (1-2 tsp) Chinese red pepper sauce
60ml (4 tblsp) vegetable stock

Bring a large pan of water to the boil and add 5ml (1 tsp) salt. Add the noodles or spaghetti and boil gently for 5-6 minutes. Drain the noodles. Rinse the noodles in cold water and drain once again. Heat the oil in a wok or large frying pan. Fry the ginger for 1-2 minutes. Add the onions and fry for 2-3 minutes.

Add the beans and carrots and fry for 2 minutes. Add the remaining vegetables and the chillies and stir fry for 3-4 minutes. Add salt to taste and the noodles. Stir lightly with two forks. Dissolve the monosodium glutamate in the soya sauce and sprinkle over the noodle mixture; stir in the lemon juice, Chinese sauce and stock. Heat through for 2-3 minutes. Serve hot.

This page: Mung Fritters.

Facing page: Ginger Cauliflower (top left), Mixed Vegetable Raita (top right) and Cannelloni with Spinach and Ricotta (bottom).

Sauces, Dips and Chutney

Plum Chutney

Any variety of plum can be used; either singly or in a mixture of one or more varieties.

PREPARATION TIME: 10 minutes

COOKING TIME: 40 minutes

MAKES: about 3kg (6lbs)

2kg (4½lb) plums, pitted
2.5cm (1 inch) fresh root ginger, peeled and finely chopped
10ml (2 tsp) salt
1.5kg (3lb) brown sugar
5ml (1 tsp) cumin seed
5ml (1 tsp) coriander seed
4 dried red chillies
5ml (1 tsp) onion seed
30ml (2 tblsp) malt vinegar
50g (2oz) chopped blanched almonds
50g (2oz) chopped cashew nuts or hazelnuts
100g (4oz) raisins
100g (4oz) sultanas

Put the plums, ginger, salt and sugar into a saucepan, preferably a non-stick pan. Cover and cook gently until the plums are soft (about 15-20 minutes). Dry roast the cumin seed, coriander seed and red chillies in a frying pan for 1-2 minutes. Remove the red chillies and coarsely grind the cumin and coriander seeds. Add the roasted red chillies, ground spices and onion seed to the cooked plums. Add the malt vinegar, nuts, raisins and sultanas and simmer gently for 5-6 minutes. Allow to cool slightly. Pour into clean, warm glass jars and seal.

Guacamole
(AVOCADO DIP)

This is a popular Mexican dip, usually eaten with crisps, salty biscuits or sticks of raw vegetable, such as cucumber, celery etc.

PREPARATION TIME: 5 minutes

SERVES: 6-8 people

1 avocado, peeled, stoned and mashed
1 large clove garlic, peeled and crushed
5ml (1 tsp) salt

1.25ml (¼ tsp) freshly ground black pepper
1 large tomato, skinned and chopped
5ml (1 tsp) olive oil
15ml (1 tblsp) lemon juice
2-3 sprigs fresh green coriander leaves, finely chopped
1 small onion, peeled and grated

Blend the avocado pulp in the liquidiser with the salt, pepper, tomato, olive oil, lemon juice and coriander leaves. Put into a small bowl and mix with the onion. Serve with savoury biscuits, crisps or sticks of raw vegetables.

Tamarind Dip

PREPARATION TIME: 20 minutes

MAKES: about 400ml (⅔ pint)

75g (3oz) tamarind pods
250ml (8 fl oz) boiling water
2.5ml (½ tsp) salt
75-90g (3-3½oz) brown sugar
1 green chilli, chopped
1.25ml (¼ tsp) chilli powder

Soak the tamarind pods in boiling water for 5-6 minutes, or until soft. Rub the pods in the water to separate the dried pulp around the seeds. Squeeze out the seeds and skins of the pods. (Do not discard as a second extract can be obtained for future use). Add the salt and sugar to the tamarind pulp. Mix in the chilli and chilli powder and leave to stand for 5 minutes before using. Salt and sugar can be adjusted according to personal taste.

Savoury Coconut Chutney

PREPARATION TIME: 15 minutes

MAKES: about 450ml (¾ pint)

1-2 fresh coconuts, shell removed, outer skin peeled and cut into pieces
1cm (½ inch) fresh root ginger, peeled and chopped
2 green chillies, chopped
5ml (1 tsp) cumin seed

1-2 bunches fresh green coriander leaves, chopped
45ml (3 tblsp) thick tamarind pulp or
60ml (4 tblsp) lemon juice
5ml (1 tsp) sugar
2.5ml (½ tsp) salt

Put all the ingredients into the liquidiser and blend until smooth and creamy. If the mixture is too thick, add a little water. Serve with hot snacks, such as toasted chicken sandwiches.

Mixed Fruit Chutney

This sweet-sour chutney goes particularly well with pork dishes, such as spareribs.

PREPARATION TIME: 30 minutes

COOKING TIME: 40 minutes

MAKES: about 2¼kg (5¼lb)

3 firm pears, cored and sliced
4 apples, cored and chopped
4 peaches, skinned, stoned and sliced or
425g (15oz) can peach slices, drained
450g (1lb) plums, halved and stoned
6 rings canned pineapple, cut into cubes
100g (4oz) dates, stoned and chopped
225g (8oz) dried prunes, soaked overnight
100g (4oz) dried apricots, soaked overnight
1kg (2¼lb) brown sugar
10ml (2 tsp) salt
2.5cm (1 inch) fresh root ginger, peeled and thinly sliced
100g (4oz) chopped blanched almonds
100g (4oz) cashew nuts, chopped
60ml (4 tblsp) malt vinegar
8 cloves, coarsely ground
5ml (1 tsp) chilli powder
5cm (2 inch) piece cinnamon stick
2 bananas, peeled and sliced

Put all the fruit into a saucepan (apart from the bananas) with the sugar, salt and ginger. Cover and cook for 15-20 minutes. Add the nuts, vinegar, cloves, chilli powder and cinnamon stick. Stir well and cook for 6-8 minutes. Simmer gently, stirring occasionally, until

most of the liquid has evaporated. The chutney should be thick and sticky. Add the sliced bananas and stir over the heat for 1 minute. Cool slightly. Pour into clean, warm glass jars and seal.

Green Tomato Relish

Use the last crop of tomatoes to make this relish. Serve with any grilled meat, barbecued chicken, etc.

PREPARATION TIME: 4 hours

COOKING TIME: about 20 minutes

MAKES: about 1½kg (3lb)

1kg (2lb) green tomatoes, seeded and chopped
75g (6oz) shredded white cabbage
2 red peppers, seeded and chopped
1 onion, peeled and chopped
15ml (1 tblsp) salt
225g (8oz) brown sugar
300ml (½ pint) distilled white vinegar
10ml (2 tsp) mustard seed
10ml (2 tsp) celery seed
15ml (1 tblsp) prepared horseradish sauce

Mix the tomatoes, cabbage, peppers and onion together. Sprinkle with the salt and mix well. Leave to stand for 2-3 hours. Drain well and then rinse under cold running water. Drain and gently squeeze out the excess moisture. Mix the sugar, vinegar, mustard seed, celery seed and horseradish

Facing page: Plum Chutney (top right), Mixed Fruit Chutney (centre) and Green Tomato Relish (bottom).

Tamarind Dip (far left),
Savoury Coconut Chutney
(centre) and Guacamole
(Avocado Dip) (above).

Blend the parsley, garlic and vinegar in the liquidiser. Pour the parsley sauce into a small bowl and mix with the capers, olive oil, spring onions and salt and pepper. Mix well. Cover and chill for 10-15 minutes. The sauce can be thinned to the desired consistency with a little olive oil or chicken stock.

Chilli Sauce

This classic piquant sauce is perfect for those who love hot, spicy food.

PREPARATION TIME: 20 minutes	
COOKING TIME: 2 hours	30 minutes
MAKES: about 600ml (1 pint)	

8 large ripe tomatoes, skinned and
   chopped
2-3 small green peppers, seeded and
   chopped
2 medium onions, peeled and finely
   chopped
4 stems celery, chopped
10-15ml (2-3 tsp) salt
250g (9oz) granulated sugar
350ml (12 fl oz) cider vinegar
2-3 bay leaves
5ml (1 tsp) coriander seeds
5ml (1 tsp) freshly ground black
   pepper
1.25ml (¼ tsp) ground cloves
2.5ml (½ tsp) ground cinnamon
5ml (1 tsp) ground ginger
5ml (1 tsp) mustard seed

Mix all the ingredients together in a pan and bring to the boil. Cover and simmer for about 2 hours over a low heat, until thick. Stir once to mix and simmer again for 10 minutes. Remove from the heat and cool slightly. Pour into clean, warm glass jars and seal.

sauce together in a large solid based pan. Bring to the boil over a medium heat. Add the vegetables, cover and simmer gently for another 16-18 minutes until the relish is sticky. Remove from the heat and cool slightly. Pour into clean, warm glass jars and seal. Will keep for up to 2 months.

Mexican Salsa

This is a beautiful fresh sauce which goes well with barbecued meats, curries and, of course, burritos and tacos.

PREPARATION TIME: 10 minutes
MAKES: about 150ml (¼ pint)

5 tomatoes, skinned and chopped
1 small onion, chopped
1-2 pickled or canned Mexican
   chillies, chopped
2 cloves garlic, peeled and crushed
10ml (2 tsp) malt vinegar
2.5ml (½ tsp) salt
2.5ml (½ tsp) sugar
2-3 sprigs fresh green coriander,
   chopped
5ml (1 tsp) bottled chilli sauce

Mix all the ingredients together in a bowl. Chill for 2 to 3 hours before serving.

Salsa Verde

A perfect Italian sauce to serve with any pasta, or with veal.

PREPARATION TIME: 15 minutes
MAKES: about 200ml (⅓ pint)

75ml (5 tblsp) chopped fresh parsley
30ml (2 tblsp) white wine vinegar
3 cloves garlic, peeled and sliced
30ml (2 tblsp) capers, finely chopped
30ml (2 tblsp) olive oil
2-3 spring onions, chopped
Salt and freshly ground black pepper
   to taste

This page: Chilli Sauce (top left), Salsa Verdi (centre) and Mexican Salsa (bottom).

Facing page: Rice Pudding (top), Potato Pudding (centre) and Cabbage Pudding (bottom).

Sweets

Carrotella

PREPARATION TIME: 15 minutes

COOKING TIME: 35-40 minutes

SERVES: 4-6 people

1.2 litre (2 pints) milk
450g (1lb) carrots, peeled and
  shredded
200ml (⅓ pint) canned evaporated
  milk
100g (4oz) granulated sugar
50g (2oz) raisins
Seeds of 8 small cardamoms, crushed
2 drops rose-water or vanilla essence
50g (2oz) chopped blanched almonds
50g (2oz) pistachio nuts, chopped

Put the milk into a pan and simmer over a low heat until reduced to 900ml (1½ pints). Add the carrots; cover and cook over a medium heat for 15 minutes. Add the evaporated milk, sugar and raisins. Cover and simmer gently for another 5 minutes. Remove from the heat. Stir in the crushed cardamom seeds and essence and pour into a serving dish. Allow to cool slightly. Sprinkle nuts on the top and serve. On hot summer days, the Carrotella is best chilled.

Carrot Cake

PREPARATION TIME: 30 minutes

COOKING TIME: 45-50 minutes

MAKES: 25cm (10 inch) loaf

175g (6oz) butter or margarine
175g (6oz) brown sugar
100g (4oz) granulated sugar
2 eggs, well beaten
225g (8oz) plain flour
7.5ml (1½ tsp) bicarbonate of soda
2.5ml (½ tsp) baking powder
1.25ml (¼ tsp) ground cinnamon
2.5ml (½ tsp) salt
225g (8oz) peeled carrots, shredded
75g (3oz) raisins
50g (2oz) chopped walnuts
1.25ml (¼ tsp) small cardamom
  seeds, crushed
Icing sugar for dredging

Cream the butter and sugars together. Add the eggs, a little at a time, beating well after each addition. Sieve the flour, bicarbonate of soda, baking powder, cinnamon and salt together. Fold the dry ingredients into the egg mixture. Add the carrots, raisins, nuts and crushed cardamom. Mix well and pour the mixture into a well buttered 25cm (10 inch) loaf tin. Bake at 180°C, 350°F, Gas Mark 4, for 45-50 minutes, or until a fine metal skewer comes out clean when inserted into the centre of the cake. Cool in the tin for 10-15 minutes, before turning out. Dredge with icing sugar before serving.

Rice Pudding

There are many ways of making a rice pudding, but this is definitely one of the best. It is suitable for serving on any occasion, from everyday meals to smart dinner parties.

PREPARATION TIME: 10 minutes

COOKING TIME: 1 hour
             30 minutes

SERVES: 6 people

50g (2oz) unsalted butter
1 bayleaf, crumbled
2.5cm (1 inch) piece cinnamon stick,
  crushed
175g (6oz) pudding rice, washed
  and drained
1.2 litre (2 pints) milk
400ml (⅔ pint) canned evaporated
  milk
175g (6oz) granulated sugar
50g (2oz) raisins
50g (2oz) chopped blanched almonds
50g (2oz) pistachio nuts, chopped or
  cut into slivers
Seeds of 8 small cardamoms, crushed

Melt the butter in a saucepan and fry the bayleaf and cinnamon for 1 minute. Add the rice and stir well. Add the milk and bring to the boil. Reduce the heat and simmer for 40-50 minutes, stirring occasionally to prevent the rice from sticking to the pan. Add the sugar and evaporated milk, and simmer for a further 20-30 minutes, stirring frequently. Thin layers of light brown skin form on the base of the pan, this is what gives the pudding its rich reddish tinge and flavour. Add the raisins and half the chopped almonds. Mix well and simmer for a further 5-10 minutes, or until the pudding is really thick. Mix in the crushed cardamom seeds and pour into a serving dish. Decorate with the remaining chopped almonds and pistachio nuts. Serve hot or cold.

Carrot Halva

A delightful sweet from the mysterious East. Serve it hot or cold, with or without cream.

PREPARATION TIME: 20 minutes

COOKING TIME: 50 minutes

SERVES: 8-10 people

2kg (4lb) large sweet carrots, peeled
  and shredded
900ml (1½ pints) canned
  evaporated milk
750g (1½lbs) granulated sugar
175g (6oz) unsalted butter
75g (3oz) raisins
Seeds of 10 small cardamoms,
  crushed
100g (4oz) chopped mixed nuts
  (blanched and chopped almonds,
  cashews, pistachios etc.)
Single cream

Put the carrots, evaporated milk and sugar into a large solid based pan and bring to the boil. Reduce the heat and cook the carrots gently for 30-40 minutes, or until the milk has evaporated. Add the butter and raisins and stir over a gentle heat for 8-10 minutes, until the Halva is dark and leaves the sides of the pan clean. Add the cardamom seeds and mix well. Pour into a flat shallow dish about 2.5cm (1 inch) deep. Flatten the Halva evenly with a spatula. Sprinkle with the chopped nuts. Serve hot or cold, cut into squares, with single cream.

Potato Pudding

This old-fashioned Oriental pudding has a rich and lovely flavour. It keeps for weeks and can be frozen.

PREPARATION TIME: 15 minutes

COOKING TIME: 1 hour
             15 minutes

SERVES: 6 people

1kg (2lb) potatoes, peeled and
  shredded
225g (8oz) unsalted butter
750ml (1¼ pints) canned
  evaporated milk
350g (12oz) granulated sugar
100g (4oz) ground almonds
1.25ml (¼ tsp) saffron
50g (2oz) chopped almonds and
  pistachios

Wash the potatoes thoroughly and drain them well. Squeeze the potatoes to remove all excess moisture. Put the potatoes, butter and evaporated milk into a large solid based saucepan and cook slowly until mushy. The potatoes will disintegrate into a mashed state as they cook. Add the sugar and stir to dissolve. The mixture will bubble and splatter like bubbling mud from hot springs. Wrap a damp tea towel around your hand and stir the mixture for 20-30 minutes over a gentle heat. Add the ground almonds and saffron. Continue stirring over the heat until the pudding becomes thick, sticky and oily on the surface. Pour the pudding into a shallow dish and decorate with the chopped nuts.

Cabbage Pudding

PREPARATION TIME: 10 minutes

COOKING TIME: 40 minutes

SERVES: 4-6 people

175g (6oz) finely shredded white
  cabbage
30ml (2 tblsp) pudding rice
1.2 litre (2 pints) milk

**Facing page: Carrot Cake
(top), Carrot Halva (centre)
and Carrotella (bottom).**

200ml (⅓ pint) canned evaporated
  milk
2.5cm (1 inch) piece cinnamon stick
1 bayleaf
100-175g (4-6 oz) granulated sugar
50g (2oz) raisins
50g (2oz) chopped blanched almonds
50g (2oz) pistachio nuts, chopped
Seeds of 6 small cardamoms, crushed

Put the cabbage, rice, both milks,
cinnamon and bayleaf into a pan.
Bring to the boil and simmer gently
for 15-20 minutes, stirring
occasionally to prevent the mixture
from sticking to the pan. Add the
sugar and simmer gently until the
mixture is thick. Add the raisins
and nuts. Remove from the heat
when the rice is tender and the
milk has been reduced to approx.
600ml (1 pint). Pour into a serving
dish and sprinkle with the crushed
cardamom seeds. Mix well and
serve.

Frozen Lemon Yogurt Souffle

PREPARATION TIME: 20 minutes

SERVES: 4-6 people

900ml (1½ pints) natural yogurt
225g (8oz) caster sugar
Juice and finely grated rind of 2
  lemons
5ml (1 tsp) vanilla essence
2 egg whites
1.25ml (¼ tsp) salt
1.25ml (¼ tsp) cream of tartar
120ml (4 fl oz) double cream,
  whipped
Few thin lemon slices for decoration

Mix the yogurt, sugar, lemon juice,
lemon rind and vanilla essence
together. Whisk the egg whites, salt
and cream of tartar until stiff but
not dry. Fold the egg whites gently
into the yogurt mixture, and then
fold in the whipped cream. Pour
the mixture into a souffle dish and
freeze overnight. Garnish with
lemon slices before serving. Serve
either frozen or partially thawed.

Mango Fool

This delicious sweet can be made
with fresh or canned mangoes;
crushed cardamom seeds give it a
characteristic flavour.

PREPARATION TIME: 10 minutes

SERVES: 4-6 people

450g (1lb) canned mango slices or
  the equivalent amount of fresh
  mango, stoned and peeled
200ml (⅓ pint) canned evaporated
  milk
Seeds of 6 cardamoms, crushed
Sugar to taste
Whipped cream

Put the mango, evaporated milk
and cardamoms into a liquidiser
and blend until smooth. Add a
little sugar if necessary. Pour into a
serving bowl and chill for 20
minutes before serving. Serve with
whipped cream.

Tropical Fruit Dessert

An exotic sweet dish to finish any
special meal. A delightful dessert
from nature's fruit garden.

PREPARATION TIME: 30 minutes

SERVES: 8-10 people

4 bananas, cut into 5mm (¼ inch)
  thick slices
5 rings pineapple, cut into chunks
  (fresh or canned)
2 semi-ripe pears, peeled, cored and
  cut into chunks
2 medium red-skinned apples, cored
  and cut into chunks
8 peach slices, chopped
225g (8oz) red cherries, pitted
45ml (3 tbsp) grated fresh coconut
1 honeydew melon, peeled and cut
  into chunks
450g (1lb) marshmallows
6-8 slices mango, cut into chunks
  (fresh or canned)
2 kiwi fruit, peeled and cut into
  chunks
20-25 strawberries, halved
Few seedless white and black grapes,
  halved
15ml (1 tbsp) icing sugar
100g (4oz) cottage cheese
Few drops vanilla essence

Mix all the ingredients together in
a large bowl. Cover and chill for 1
hour.

Tropical Fruit Salad

This medley of fruits is very
colourful and it offers a variety of
tastes and textures.

PREPARATION TIME: 40 minutes

2 bananas, sliced
4 kiwi fruit, peeled and sliced
10 dates, stoned and sliced in half

2 guavas, halved and then sliced into
  wedges
1 pawpaw, cut into thin crescent
  shapes
450g (1lb) canned lychees, drained
225g (8oz) canned pineapple
  chunks, drained (or pieces of fresh
  pineapple)
2 fresh mangoes, peeled and sliced
Few seedless grapes, white and black,
  halved
1 small melon, cut into chunks
¼ water-melon, cut into chunks
4 fresh figs, halved

Dressing
30ml (2 tblsp) lemon juice
Pinch salt
50g (2oz) chopped toasted walnut or
  pine kernels

Prepare the fruits as suggested and
arrange in a large glass bowl, in
layers. Spoon over the lemon juice
and sprinkle with salt. Sprinkle
over the chopped nuts.

Semolina and Coconut Slices

PREPARATION TIME: 10 minutes

COOKING TIME: 30 minutes

SERVES: 6 people

175g (6oz) unsalted butter
175g (6oz) coarse semolina
225g (8oz) desiccated coconut
350g (12oz) granulated sugar
250ml (8 fl oz) canned evaporated
  milk
250ml (8 fl oz) water
100g (4oz) chopped mixed nuts:
  blanched almonds, cashews,
  walnuts, hazelnuts and pistachios
75g (3oz) raisins
Seeds of 6 cardamoms, crushed

Melt the butter in a frying pan and
add the semolina. Dry roast the
semolina by stirring it until it turns
lightly golden. Spoon onto a plate.
Dry roast the coconut in the same
pan until lightly golden. Add the

**Tropical Fruit Dessert (top
right), Frozen Lemon Yogurt
Souffle (top left) and Tropical
Fruit Salad (bottom).**

semolina, sugar, milk and water to the coconut. Stir the mixture over the heat for 5-8 minutes. Add the chopped nuts, raisins and crushed cardamom seeds. Mix well and stir over a gentle heat for 5-6 minutes, until the mixture is thick and the oil begins to separate. Pour into a shallow dish, smooth with a spatula and allow to cool. Cut into diamond shapes or squares.

Mint Barley Sherbet

PREPARATION TIME:	10 minutes
COOKING TIME:	20 minutes
SERVES:	4-6 people

100g (4oz) whole barley
900ml (1½ pints) water
25g (1oz) mint leaves, minced
Pinch salt

75g (3oz) granulated sugar
Juice of 3 lemons
1-2 drops green food colouring
Grated rind of 1 lemon
Few mint leaves and lemon slices to decorate

Wash the barley in 2-3 changes of water. Soak the barley in the measured water for a few minutes; add the minced mint leaves and

This page: Yogurt, Almond and Saffron Sherbet (top centre), Mango Sherbet (left), Maori Shake (centre) and Tropical Blizzard (right).

Facing page: Mint Barley Sherbet (top left), Spiced Tea (top right) and Rich Coffee (bottom).

bring to the boil. Simmer gently for 10-15 minutes. Remove from the heat and strain; discard the barley grains. Dissolve the salt and sugar in the barley liquid; add the lemon juice, colouring and lemon rind. Mix well and make up to 900ml (1½ pints) with water. Pour into glasses and add crushed ice. To make clear sherbet; allow the barley water to stand for 10 minutes, so that the starch settles. Pour off the clear liquid and serve with a twist of lemon and mint leaves floating on the top.

Yogurt Dessert

This yogurt dessert is a light, delicious way of ending a rich meal; it is also simple and easy to make.

PREPARATION TIME: 15 minutes, plus setting time

COOKING TIME: 15 minutes

SERVES: 4-6 people

2¼ litres (4 pints) milk
100-125g (4-5oz) granulated sugar or to taste
50g (2oz) finely chopped blanched almonds
50g (2oz) raisins
Seeds of 8 small cardamoms, crushed
2-3 drops rose water or vanilla essence
30ml (2 tblsp) natural yogurt
25g (1oz) pistachio nuts, chopped

Simmer the milk in a large pan until it is reduced by half. Add the sugar to the milk and stir until dissolved. Add half the almonds, the raisins and cardamom seeds. Allow to cool until the milk is just tepid. Add the essence and beaten yogurt to the milk and stir well. Pour into a large, shallow serving dish. Cover and leave in a warm place, such as an airing cupboard, until the yogurt has set (about 5-6 hours). Sprinkle with the chopped pistachio nuts and remaining chopped almonds. Chill for 1 hour before serving. Will keep for up to 15 days in the refrigerator.

Tropical Blizzard

PREPARATION TIME: 3-4 minutes

SERVES: 4 people

250ml (8 fl oz) pineapple juice or orange juice
300ml (10 fl oz) natural yogurt
6 slices mango (canned or fresh)
15ml (1 tblsp) sugar
Soda water
Ice cubes

Put the fruit juice, yogurt, mango and sugar into the liquidiser; blend for ½ minute. Pour into 4 glasses and dilute with soda water. Serve with ice cubes.

Maori Shake

A new taste experience; kiwi fruit blended with lemon yogurt.

PREPARATION TIME: 5 minutes

SERVES: 4-6 people

250ml (8 fl oz) pineapple juice
2 kiwi fruits, peeled and chopped
300ml (10 fl oz) lemon yogurt
Ice cubes
Lemonade
1 kiwi fruit, peeled and thinly sliced for decoration

Put the pineapple juice, chopped kiwi fruit and lemon yogurt into the liquidiser; blend for 30 seconds-1 minute, until smooth. Pour into 4-6 tall glasses; add ice cubes and top up with lemonade. Stir to mix. Serve with slices of kiwi fruit on top.

Mango Sherbet

This is a pretty green mango sherbet made from unripe mangoes. Windfallen mangoes are usually used for making this refreshing drink in India.

PREPARATION TIME: 20 minutes

COOKING TIME: 5-6 minutes

SERVES: 6 people

2 medium size unripe mangoes
1.25ml (¼ tsp) salt
1 litre (1¾ pints) water
Sugar to taste
Crushed ice

Boil the mangoes in sufficient water to cover for 5-6 minutes. Remove and allow to cool under cold running water. Peel off the skins. Put the water and salt into a punch bowl. Scrape all the mango flesh away from the stones and add to the punch bowl. Discard the stones. Whisk the sherbet until well blended. Pour into tall glasses; add sugar to taste and crushed ice.

Yogurt, Almond and Saffron Sherbet

A good healthy drink, which can be given a sweet or salty flavour.

PREPARATION TIME: 5 minutes

SERVES: 5-6 people

1 litre (1¾ pints) water
450ml (¾ pint) natural yogurt
10ml (2 tsp) lemon juice
12 blanched almonds
1.25ml (¼ tsp) saffron
2 drops vanilla essence or rose water
Salt or sugar to taste

Put 400ml (⅔ pint) water into the liquidiser with the yogurt, lemon juice, almonds, saffron and essence; blend until smooth. Mix in the remaining water. Pour into tall glasses over crushed ice. To make sweet sherbet, stir 10-15ml (2-3 tsp) sugar into each glass; and to make a salty sherbet, sprinkle on a pinch of salt.

Rich Coffee

This is an old and traditional method of making coffee from the Orient.

PREPARATION TIME: 8 minutes

SERVES: 6-8 people

1 litre (1¾ pints) water
450ml (¾ pint) milk
30ml (2 tblsp) freshly ground
  medium roast coffee
Seeds of 4 small cardamoms, crushed
Sugar to taste

Put the water and milk into a stainless steel pan and bring to the boil. Add the coffee and crushed cardamoms. Cover the pan and remove from the heat. Allow to brew for 2-3 minutes. Stir once. When the coffee grains settle to the bottom, strain off the coffee into cups and add sugar to taste.

Spiced Tea

This is a very different and interesting way of serving tea; it is refreshing served hot or cold.

PREPARATION TIME: 5 minutes

SERVES: 6 people

1 litre (1¾ pints) water
450ml (¾ pint) milk
1.25cm (½ inch) piece cinnamon
  stick
4 cloves
Seeds of 4 small cardamoms, crushed
6 teabags
or 30ml (2 tblsp) tea leaves
Sugar to taste

Put the water, milk, cinnamon, cloves and cardamom seeds into a stainless steel pan. Bring to the boil and add the tea. Cover the pan and remove from the heat. Allow to brew for 2 minutes. Stir well. Add sugar to taste. Strain into cups and serve. Alternatively, allow the tea to cool and then chill and serve with ice.

Yogurt Dessert (top left), Mango Fool (left) and Semolina and Coconut Slices (bottom left).

HOME FARE

Smoked Haddock in
French Mustard Sauce (top),
Chicken Curry (left) and
Poussin in White Sauce (right).

Meals for Two

Poussin in White Sauce

1 pkt sage and onion stuffing
2 poussins
Fat
300ml (½ pint) milk
25g (1oz) plain flour
25g (1oz) soft margarine
Salt and pepper

Make the stuffing as directed on the packet and use to stuff the poussins. Place the poussins in a roasting tin with melted fat, and cook in the oven for 30-40 minutes at 180°C, 350°F, Gas Mark 4, until tender. Put the milk, flour, margarine and seasoning into a pan and bring gradually to the boil, whisking all the time. Cook gently for 3 minutes, stirring. Serve with baked potatoes and sweet corn with red peppers.
Serves two.

Smoked Haddock in French Mustard Sauce

350g (¾lb) smoked haddock fillet, skinned and cut into two
A little milk
Salt and pepper
15g (½oz) butter
15g (½oz) flour
150ml (¼ pint) milk
15ml (1 tblsp) French mustard
Chopped chives (optional)

Place the fish in an ovenproof serving dish. Pour a little milk over the fish and season. Cover and

cook in the oven for 15-20 minutes at 160°C, 325°F, Gas Mark 3. Heat the butter in a pan, stir in the flour and cook for 2 minutes. Allow to cool, then pour in the milk gradually. Bring to the boil, stirring. Season and stir in the French mustard. Spoon the sauce over the fish and garnish with chopped chives if desired. Serve with potato croquettes and broccoli.
Serves two.

Mixed Grill

2 sausages
Liver
2 pork chops
Tomatoes
Mushrooms, sliced if flat

Grill the sausages, liver, pork chop and tomatoes until tender. Boil mushrooms until soft. Serve with baby new potatoes.
Serves two.

Chicken Curry

25g (1oz) butter
1 small chicken, jointed
1 small onion, peeled and chopped
1 small apple, peeled and chopped
5ml (1 tsp) curry powder
10g (¼oz) flour
2.5ml (½ tsp) curry paste
300ml (½ pint) chicken stock
1 chilli (optional)
Pinch of powdered ginger
Pinch of powdered turmeric
5ml (1 tsp) chutney
Squeeze of lemon juice
Salt and pepper
25g (1oz) desiccated coconut
15g (½oz) sultanas

Garnish
Thin onion rings, lightly fried
Thin green pepper rings, lightly fried
Lemon rind, lightly fried

Heat the butter and fry the chicken pieces. Remove and drain on paper towels. Fry the onion and apple for 2-3 minutes, then add the curry powder, flour and curry paste. Cook briefly, then carefully blend in most of the stock, reserving 50ml (2 fl oz). Bring to the boil and cook for a few minutes until a thin sauce. Add the remaining spices, chutney, lemon juice and seasoning. Return the chicken pieces to the pan. Pour the remaining stock over the coconut

and allow to stand for a few minutes, then add the strained liquid to the curry. If preferred, fresh coconut or coconut milk can be used instead. Add the sultanas then cover and simmer for 2-3 hours. Garnish with onion, pepper and lemon rind to serve.
Serves two.

Plaited Lamb

450g (1lb) minced lamb
2 onions, peeled and chopped
25g (1oz) breadcrumbs
15g (1 tsp) dried rosemary
15ml (1 tblsp) tomato purée
15ml (1 tblsp) Worcestershire sauce
2 eggs, beaten
Salt and pepper
225g (8oz) puff pastry

Mix together the minced lamb, onions, breadcrumbs, rosemary, tomato purée, Worcestershire sauce and one of the eggs. Add salt and pepper. Roll out the pastry on a floured surface into an oblong. Place the lamb mixture in the centre, cut diagonal strips from the centre to the edges along both sides. Brush all four sides with a little beaten egg. Fold the pastry at each end and then fold the strips over alternately so they meet in the centre. Place the plaited lamb on a greased baking tray and brush with the remaining beaten egg. Cook in the oven for 15-20 minutes at 220°C, 425°F, Gas Mark 7. Then reduce the heat to 180°C, 350°F, Gas Mark 4 and cook for a further 30 minutes. Serve with new potatoes and a green vegetable.
Serves two.

Pasta Fish Pie

40g (1½oz) macaroni
Salt
225g (8oz) white fish

Cheese Sauce
15g (½oz) butter or margarine
15g (½oz) flour
150ml (¼ pint) milk
Salt and pepper
Pinch of dry mustard
40g (1½oz) Cheddar cheese, grated

Break the macaroni into small pieces (if using long macaroni) and cook in 2 pints of boiling, salted water until tender. Meanwhile, simmer the fish in a little salted water until tender. Lift the fish out

and flake with a fork. Heat the butter or margarine in a pan, stir in the flour, and cook the 'roux' for 2-3 minutes over a low heat. Remove the pan from the heat and gradually add the milk, seasoning and mustard. Bring to the boil, cook until thickened, then add the grated cheese. Put the drained macaroni and fish into a hot dish and top with the cheese sauce. Place for 2-3 minutes under a hot grill until the cheese topping bubbles. Serve with runner beans and sweet corn.
Serves two.

Braised Beef

15g (½oz) fat
350g (12oz) of brisket or topside of beef cut into pieces
1 carrot, peeled and sliced
1 onion, peeled and sliced
1 turnip, peeled and sliced
1 leek, trimmed and sliced
2 sticks celery, trimmed and sliced
25g (1oz) fat bacon, diced
Bouquet garni (mixture of fresh herbs, i.e. parsley, thyme, sage, in muslin bag)
Salt and pepper
150ml (¼ pint) beef stock
60ml (2 fl oz) red wine

Heat the fat in a flameproof casserole or large saucepan and brown the meat for 3 minutes. Lift the meat onto a plate. Brown the vegetables in the fat together with the diced bacon. Add the bouquet garni, seasoning, stock and wine then return the meat on top of the mixture. Cover tightly and cook very slowly for about 1 hour. Lift the lid from time to time and add more stock if the mixture appears to be running dry. Remove the bouquet garni. Sieve the vegetables and stock to make a sauce or use a blender and reheat with the meat. Serve with boiled potatoes.
Serves two.

Stuffed Mushrooms

Two large, flat mushrooms
15g (½oz) butter
1 rasher of streaky bacon, rinded and chopped
15g (½oz) fresh breadcrumbs
5ml (1 tsp) chopped parsley
Grated rind of ¼ lemon
2.5ml (½ tsp) lemon juice
25g (1oz) Cheddar cheese, grated
Salt and pepper
Cress

Remove the stalks from the mushrooms and chop finely. Heat the butter and fry the mushroom stalks and the bacon for a few minutes. Remove from the heat and stir in the breadcrumbs, parsley, lemon rind and juice, and cheese. Season well. Place the mushroom caps on a greased baking sheet, divide the filling between each cap and cook for 15-20 minutes at 170°C, 325°F, Gas Mark 3. Sprinkle with cress. Serve with sweet corn and sauté potatoes.
Serves two.

Veal Cutlets Bonne Femme

2x225g (two 8oz) veal cutlets
Salt and pepper
25g (1oz) flour
50g (2oz) clarified butter or butter and oil mixed
100g (4oz) boiled, cold potatoes, thinly sliced
50g (2oz) button onions
50ml (2 fl oz) sherry
150ml (¼ pint) demi-glacé sauce
15ml (1 tblsp) chopped parsley

Sprinkle the veal cutlets with salt and pepper and dredge with flour. Heat the butter or butter and oil, in a frying pan and gently fry the cutlets on both sides for a few minutes. Place the cutlets in an ovenproof dish and cook in the oven for 15-20 minutes at 180°C, 350°F, Gas Mark 4 until tender. Fry the potatoes in the same pan until golden brown, remove and keep warm. Fry the onions for two minutes. Transfer the onions to a saucepan of water and boil until soft. Drain off the butter and pour the sherry into the pan. Add the demi-glacé sauce and bring to the boil, stirring continuously. Arrange the cutlets on a serving dish, surrounded by the fried potatoes and onions. Cover with the demi-glacé sauce and decorate with chopped parsley.
Serves two.

Facing page: Plaited Lamb (top left), Pasta Fish Pie (top right) and Veal Cutlets Bonne Femme (bottom).

Bacon and Chestnuts

450g (1lb) joint of bacon, boned and
  rolled
25g (1oz) butter
1 small onion, peeled and chopped
50g (2oz) chestnut purée
1.25ml (¼ tsp) mixed herbs
1.25ml (¼ tsp) mixed spice
5ml (1 tsp) soft brown sugar
1 beaten egg
450g (1lb) puff pastry

Place the bacon in a saucepan,
cover with cold water, bring to the
boil then simmer for 1 hour.
Remove the bacon from the pan
and trim off any excess fat, leave
until cold. Melt the butter and fry
the onion until soft. Mix with the
chestnut purée, herbs, spice and
sugar, and half the beaten egg to
bind the mixture. Roll out the
pastry to a circle large enough to
wrap around the bacon joint.
Spread the mixture over the top of
the bacon. Fold the pastry up over
the joint and seal with a little of the
beaten egg. Place on a baking sheet.
Brush with beaten egg. Cook in the
oven for 30-35 minutes at 220°C,
425°F, Gas Mark 7. Serve with
carrots and broad beans.
Serves two.

Demi-Glacé Sauce

25g (1oz) dripping or butter
25g (1oz) peeled and chopped onion
25g (1oz) peeled and chopped carrot
25g (1oz) flour
1 rasher bacon, rinded and diced
600ml (1 pint) brown stock
5ml (1 tsp) tomato purée
5ml (1 tsp) mixed herbs
Salt and pepper

Heat the dripping or butter, fry the
onion, bacon and carrot until very
lightly browned. Do not overcook
at this stage as burnt onion gives a
bitter taste to the sauce. Add the
flour and continue cooking slowly
until a rich chestnut colour. Draw

Pork Fillets and Apricots

225g (8oz) pork fillet, cut into
  small pieces
15ml (1 tblsp) seasoned flour
25g (1oz) butter
200g (7oz) can of apricot halves
15ml (1 tblsp) Worcestershire
  sauce
15ml (1 tblsp) soft brown sugar
10ml (2 tsp) wine vinegar
5ml (1 tsp) lemon juice

2.5ml (½ tsp) powdered cinnamon
60ml (4 tblsp) water
100g (4oz) long grain rice

Toss the pork pieces in the
seasoned flour. Heat the butter in a
flameproof casserole and fry the
pork until lightly browned. Chop
all but three of the apricot halves.
Mix 4 tablespoons of the apricot
syrup with the Worcestershire
sauce, sugar, vinegar, lemon juice,
cinnamon and water. Pour the

apricot sauce and chopped fruit
over the pork. Bring to the boil,
stirring continuously. Reduce the
heat, cover and simmer for 15
minutes. Meanwhile, cook the rice
in boiling, salted water. Spoon the
pork and sauce onto a serving dish
and spoon the drained rice around
the meat. Decorate with the
reserved apricots. If required serve
with a green vegetable.
Serves two.

**This page: Braised Beef (top
left), Mixed Grill (centre) and
Stuffed Mushrooms (bottom).**

**Facing page: Filled Jacket
Potatoes (top left), Sausage and
Mushroom Pie (top right),
Bacon and Chestnuts (bottom
right) and Stuffed Aubergines
(bottom left).**

the pan aside, add the stock and when all the liquid has been incorporated, add the purée, herbs and seasoning to taste. Bring to the boil, skim thoroughly and simmer, covered, for 30 minutes. Strain through a fine-meshed strainer, pressing as much as possible of the vegetables through.
Makes 1 pint.

Sausage and Mushroom Pie

225g (8oz) pork sausages
25g (1oz) butter
1 onion, peeled and sliced
20g (¾oz) flour
150ml (¼ pint) milk
150ml (¼ pint) brown stock
Salt and pepper
Pinch of mixed herbs
100g (4oz) sliced button mushrooms
225g (8oz) puff pastry
1 egg, beaten

Prick the sausages and grill them until golden. Heat the butter in a pan and fry the onion for 5 minutes. Stir in the flour and cook for a further minute. Gradually add the milk and stock and bring to boil. Stir until thickened then add the seasoning, herbs and mushrooms. Place the sausages in a pie dish and pour over the mushroom sauce. Roll out the puff pastry, and use to cover the dish. Trim off any excess pastry. Glaze the top of the pie with the beaten egg and cook in the oven for 40 minutes at 200°C, 390°F, Gas Mark 6. Serve with new or boiled potatoes and a green vegetable.
Serves two.

Stuffed Aubergines

3 medium aubergines, washed and stalks removed
Salt
275g (10oz) butter
1 medium onion, peeled and finely chopped
1 clove garlic, peeled and crushed
175g (6oz) minced beef
400g (14oz) can of tomatoes
15ml (1 tblsp) chopped parsley
5ml (1 tsp) dried marjoram
10ml (2 tsp) tomato purée
Pepper
10ml (2 tsp) cornflour
100g (4oz) Cheddar cheese, grated

Slice the aubergines in half lengthways. Scoop out the flesh carefully and chop finely. Put the flesh on a large plate, sprinkle with salt and leave for 30 minutes. Blanch the aubergine skins in boiling water for 5 minutes. Remove and place on a serving dish. Heat the butter, add the onion and garlic and cook until soft. Stir in the minced beef and cook until brown. Add the tomatoes, parsley, marjoram and tomato purée. Season with pepper and bring to the boil. Blend the cornflour with a little cold water and add to the beef and tomato mixture. Return to the boil, then remove from the heat. Drain the aubergine flesh in a sieve and rinse in cold water. Stir half the flesh into the beef and tomato mixture and use to stuff the aubergine halves. Top each one with grated cheese and cook in the oven for about 30 minutes at 180°C, 350°F, Gas Mark 4. (Use the left-over aubergine flesh in a bolognese sauce or as a vegetable covered with a cheese sauce.) Serve the stuffed aubergines hot with a tossed green salad.
Serves two.

Hearts and Stuffing

2 lambs' hearts
Seasoned flour
20g (¾oz) unsalted butter
300ml (½ pint) brown stock
1 small onion
100g (4oz) carrots
1 celery heart

Stuffing
2 shallots
1 stick celery
25g (1oz) belly pork
25g (1oz) fresh breadcrumbs
1 rounded tblsp parsley
5ml (1 tsp) curry powder
Salt and pepper
20g (¾oz) melted butter

First make the stuffing. Peel and chop the shallots. Scrub and dice the celery stick. Mince or finely chop the pork. Place these ingredients in a bowl with the breadcrumbs, parsley, curry powder and seasoning. Bind together with the melted butter. Rinse the hearts. Cut out any tubes and discard, and fill the hearts with the stuffing. Sew up the openings and coat the hearts with seasoned flour. Melt the butter in a heavy pan and fry the hearts over a

high heat until brown. Lift the hearts into a casserole dish. Stir in enough seasoned flour to absorb the fat. Cook for 2-3 minutes then add the stock and bring to the boil. Pour over the hearts. Cover the casserole and cook in the oven at 170°C, 325°F, Gas Mark 3 for 2 hours. After 2 hours peel and chop the onion, carrot and celery heart. Add to the casserole and continue to cook for a further 1 hour. Serve with boiled potatoes and green vegetables.
Serves two.

Filled Jacket Potatoes

2 medium-sized potatoes
25g (1oz) butter
Salt and pepper

Cheddar Cheese Filling
75g (3oz) Cheddar cheese, grated
25g (1oz) butter
A little milk
Salt and pepper
15ml (1 tblsp) Parmesan cheese

Bacon Filling
75g (3oz) bacon, rind removed, chopped and fried
25g (1oz) butter
A little milk
Salt and pepper
1 small green pepper, cored, seeded and finely chopped

Sausage and Onion Filling
2 small pork sausages, chopped and grilled
25g (1oz) butter
A little milk
Salt and pepper
1 small onion, peeled, chopped and fried

Liver and Courgette Filling
75g (3oz) lamb's liver, chopped and fried
25g (1oz) butter
A little milk
Salt and pepper
2 small courgettes, diced and fried

Scrub the potatoes well. Prick them and dot their skins with butter. Sprinkle lightly with salt and pepper. Cook in the oven for 1-1¼ hours at 200°C, 400°F, Gas Mark 6. When cooked, cut in half lengthways and scoop out the centres, keeping the skins intact. Mash the potato in a basin, adding one of the filling mixtures. Return the mixture to the potato skins. Cook for a further 15-20 minutes.
Serves two.

Lasagne

150g (5oz) margarine
1 small onion, peeled and sliced
100g (4oz) minced beef
200g (7oz) can of tomatoes
5ml (1 tsp) tomato purée
150ml (¼ pint) beef stock
5ml (1 tsp) dried marjoram
5ml (1 tsp) mixed herbs
Pinch garlic salt
Salt and pepper
5ml (1 tsp) cornflour
75g (3oz) lasagne
10g (¼oz) butter
100g (4oz) margarine
150g (5oz) flour
150ml (¼ pint) milk
75g (3oz) Cheddar cheese, grated

Heat the margarine and fry the onion until soft. Stir in the minced beef and cook until browned. Add the tomatoes, tomato purée, stock, herbs and garlic. Season well, cover and simmer for 30 minutes. Meanwhile, mix the cornflour to a paste with a little cold water, stir into the meat sauce and bring to the boil, stirring continuously. Cook the lasagne in boiling, salted water, adding the 10g (¼oz) butter, for 10-15 minutes. Drain carefully. Heat the margarine, stir in the flour and cook for a few minutes. Allow to cool and gradually add the milk. Return to the heat and bring to the boil, stirring continuously. Stir in two-thirds of the cheese. Cover the base of a greased ovenproof dish with half the lasagne. Spoon over half the meat and tomato sauce. Cover with the remaining lasagne and spoon over remaining tomato sauce. Pour on the cheese sauce, sprinkle the Cheddar cheese on top and cook in the oven at 190°C, 375°F, Gas Mark 5 for 30-35 minutes.
Serves two.

Facing page: Lasagne (top left), Hearts and Stuffing (top right) and Pork Fillets and Apricots (bottom).

HOME FARE
The Family Roast

Lamb

ROASTING TIME: 25 minutes per 450g (1lb) + 25 minutes, at 160°C, 325°F, Gas Mark 3.

Place in the centre of a preheated oven. If a covered roasting tin is used basting is not necessary, but if the joint is uncovered or pot-roasted, the meat should be basted every 20-30 minutes. The meat should be turned over, using 2 metal spoons, halfway through the cooking. Transfer the meat from the tin to a hot, flat dish large enough to allow for carving. Keep hot. As accompaniments: medium brown, thickened gravy, mint or cranberry sauce. Serve with new potatoes, peas, French or runner beans.

Veal

ROASTING TIME: 25 minutes per 450g (1lb) + 25 minutes at 160°C, 325°F, Gas Mark 3.

Place in the centre of a preheated oven. If a covered roasting tin is used basting is not necessary, but if the joint is uncovered or pot-roasted, the meat should be basted every 20-30 minutes. The meat should be turned over, using 2 metal spoons, halfway through cooking. Transfer the meat from the tin onto a large, flat carving dish. Keep hot. As accompaniments: medium brown, thickened gravy, veal forcemeat stuffing, squeeze of lemon, bacon rolls. Serve with green vegetables, onions, tomatoes, baked or boiled potatoes.

Turkey

ROASTING TIME: For a 2.75-3.5kg (6-8lb) turkey cook for 15 minutes at 200°C, 400°F, Gas Mark 6, then reduce temperature to 180°C, 350°F, Gas Mark 4 and allow 15 minutes per 450g (1lb) + 15 minutes.

If the bird is frozen it must be allowed to thaw out completely before cooking. Stuff the bird, sprinkle with salt and place in a roasting tin. Brush the bird with melted dripping, butter or oil. The bird may be wrapped in foil, but the cover should be removed for the last 20-30 minutes to brown the skin. If left unwrapped, the bird should be basted frequently. Transfer to a large carving dish when cooked. As accompaniments: sausages, chestnut, sausage meat or veal forcemeat stuffing, bacon rolls, cranberry or celery sauce, thickened gravy. Serve with roast, fried or boiled potatoes, onions, peas or Brussels sprouts.

This page: Turkey (top), Pork (centre right) and Lamb (bottom).

Facing page: Mutton (top), Steak (centre left), Veal (centre right) and Duck (bottom).

Beef

ROASTING TIME: 15 minutes per 450g (1lb) + 15 minutes, at 180°C, 350°F, Gas Mark 4.

Place in the centre of a preheated oven. If a covered roasting tin is used basting is not necessary, but if the joint is uncovered or pot-roasted, the meat should be basted every 20-30 minutes. The meat should be turned over, using 2 metal spoons, halfway through the cooking. Transfer the meat from the tin to a hot, flat dish large enough to allow for carving. Keep hot. As accompaniments: thin, dark brown gravy, Yorkshire pudding, horseradish sauce, roast parsnips. Serve with baked or boiled potatoes and any vegetable.

Baked Whole Gammon

ROASTING TIME: 30 minutes per 450g (1lb) + 30 minutes at 180°C, 350°F, Gas Mark 4.

Spread gammon with a little melted butter or margarine and wrap in foil. Place in a roasting tin in the centre of a preheated oven. Transfer the meat from the tin when cooked, remove the foil and put the gammon onto a large, flat carving dish. Keep hot. As accompaniments: dark brown, thin gravy, sage and onion stuffing, apple sauce. Serve with baked or boiled potatoes, cabbage, celery, Brussels sprouts or cauliflower.

Pork

ROASTING TIME: 30 minutes per 450g (1lb) + 30 minutes, at 180°C, 350°F, Gas Mark 4.

Place in the centre of a preheated oven. If a covered roasting tin is used basting is not necessary, but if the joint is uncovered or pot-roasted, the meat should be basted every 20-30 minutes. The meat should be turned over, using 2 metal spoons, halfway through the cooking. Transfer the meat from the tin to a hot, flat dish large enough to allow for carving. Keep hot. As accompaniments: dark brown, thin gravy, sage and onion stuffing, apple sauce. Serve with boiled potatoes, cabbage, cauliflower, celery, onion, spinach or Brussels sprouts.

Duck

ROASTING TIME: For a 1-1.5kg (2-3lb) duck cook for 15 minutes per 450g (1lb) + 15 minutes at 180-190°C, 350-375°F, Gas Mark 4-5.

If the bird is frozen it must be thawed out completely before cooking. Stuff the bird with sage and onion stuffing, and place in a roasting tin. Brush the bird with melted dripping, butter or oil. Duck must be well pricked all over the breast to allow the fat to run out and leave the breast skin crisp and succulent. Transfer to a large carving dish when cooked. As accompaniments: apple sauce; thin gravy, flavoured with orange juice if liked. Serve with roast potatoes, peas, carrots and any green vegetable.

Steak

Season steak before cooking. Steak can be grilled, fried or roasted until tender and cooked to one's liking. Serve with baked or boiled potatoes and any vegetable.

Mutton

ROASTING TIME: 25 minutes per 450g (1lb) + 25 minutes, at 160°C, 325°F, Gas Mark 3.

Place in the centre of a preheated oven. If a covered roasting tin is used basting is not necessary, but if the joint is uncovered or pot-roasted, the meat should be basted every 20-30 minutes. The meat should be turned over, using 2 metal spoons, halfway through the cooking. Transfer the meat from the tin onto a large, flat carving dish. Keep hot. As accompaniments: medium brown, thickened gravy, redcurrant, cranberry or mint sauce. Serve with baked or boiled potatoes and any vegetable.

Chicken

ROASTING TIME: 15 minutes per 450g (1lb) + 15 minutes at 200°C, 400°F, Gas Mark 6.

If the bird is frozen it must be allowed to thaw out completely before cooking. Stuff the bird, sprinkle with salt and place in a roasting tin. Brush the bird with melted dripping, butter or oil. The bird may be wrapped in foil, but the cover should be removed for the last 20-30 minutes to brown the skin. If left unwrapped, the bird should be basted frequently. Transfer the bird to a large carving dish. As accompaniments: veal forcemeat, bread sauce, bacon rolls and thin gravy. Serve with baked, fried or boiled new potatoes, and green vegetables.

Beef (top), Chicken (far left) and Baked Whole Gammon (left).

Meals for Special Occasions

Remove from the oven, allow to cool in the tin for 30 minutes, then turn out and leave to cool completely. Drain the apricots, reserving the juice. Garnish the loaf with apricot halves and the stuffed olives. Mix the cornflour with a little of the apricot juice, then add the rest of the juice and the wine. Heat, stirring, until thickened. Cool, then brush over the meat loaf and serve the rest separately in a jug. Serve the meat loaf on a bed of lettuce leaves, with potato croquettes and vegetables. Serves eight-ten.

Boeuf en Croûte

15ml (1 tblsp) oil
1.5kg (3lb) beef topside
25g (1oz) butter
1 onion, peeled and chopped
100g (4oz) button mushrooms, chopped
30ml (2 tblsp) freshly chopped parsley
Salt and pepper
275g (10oz) bought or home-made rough puff pastry
A little milk
Few sprigs of watercress to garnish

Heat the oil in a large pan and fry the meat quickly on all sides to seal the juices. Transfer the oil and the meat to a roasting dish. Cook in the oven for 45 minutes at 200°C, 400°F, Gas Mark 6. Leave to cool. Melt the butter in a pan and fry the onions until soft. Add the mushrooms, parsley and seasoning. Cover and fry for 5 minutes. Roll out the pastry to make a rectangle large enough to cover the meat. Spread ⅓ of the stuffing over the

Turkey and Apricot Loaf

675g (1½lb) uncooked turkey meat, minced
175g (6oz) fresh white breadcrumbs
1 onion, peeled and finely chopped
15ml (1 tblsp) Worcestershire sauce
1 egg, beaten
Pinch of mixed herbs
Pinch of allspice
Salt and pepper
425g (15oz) can apricot halves
100g (4oz) stuffed, green olives, sliced
10ml (2 tsp) cornflour
150ml (¼ pint) dry white wine

Grease a 450g (1lb) loaf tin and set aside. In a large bowl, mix together the turkey, breadcrumbs, onion, Worcestershire sauce, egg, herbs, allspice and seasoning, and combine well. Spoon the mixture into the loaf tin, making sure the corners are well filled, smooth over the top and bang the tin on a flat surface to release any air bubbles. Cook in the oven for about 90 minutes at 180°C, 350°F, Gas Mark 4, or until the meat loaf is cooked through. The juices will run clear when a skewer is inserted.

This page: Sweet and Spicy Noisettes (top), Veal in Orange (centre left) and Peppered Steak (bottom right).

Facing Page: Boeuf en Croûte (top), Turkey and Apricot Loaf (centre left) and Stuffed Trout with Almonds (bottom).

centre of the pastry and place the meat on top. Spread the rest of the stuffing over the meat. Dampen the edges of the pastry and fold them over the meat like a parcel. Trim as necessary. Place the meat, joins downwards, in a roasting pan. Roll out any pastry trimmings and cut into leaf shapes, to decorate the top. Brush the top with a little milk. Increase the oven temperature to 220°C, 425°F, Gas Mark 7, and cook the beef for about 40-45 minutes until the pastry is golden. Place the meat on a serving dish and garnish with watercress. Serve with baked potatoes, Brussels sprouts and carrots.
Serves six-eight.

Veal in Orange

750g-1kg (1½-2lb) veal fillet
1 onion
600ml (1 pint) white stock
Salt and pepper
2 oranges
4 small, young carrots
225g (8oz) long grain rice
50g (2oz) butter
40g (1½oz) flour
Pinch of powdered saffron
150ml (¼ pint) double cream
Parsley to garnish

Dice the veal. Peel the onion and keep it whole. Put the veal, onion, stock and seasoning into a pan. Bring to the boil. Lower the heat and simmer for 40 minutes until the meat is tender. Remove the onion. Cut away the peel from 1 orange, remove the white pith, then cut the orange flesh into narrow strips. Soak in 150ml (¼ pint) water for 30 minutes. Peel the carrots, cut into neat matchsticks, put with the orange rind and a little seasoning and simmer in a covered pan for 20 minutes. Remove the carrots and orange rind and cook the rice in remaining salted water. Heat the butter in a pan, stir in the flour and cook for several minutes. Add the strained veal stock and bring to the boil. Cook until thickened. Add the orange rind, carrots, cooked rice and any liquid left, together with the pinch of saffron powder and the cream. Stir over a low heat until smooth. Add the cooked veal and mix thoroughly. Arrange a border of rice with the remaining orange cut into slices on a serving dish. Spoon the veal mixture in the centre of the dish and sprinkle with parsley. Serve with potatoes and vegetables of your own choice.
Serves six.

Veal with Cucumber

225-350g (8-12oz) fillet veal, cubed
Salt and pepper
15ml (1 tblsp) cornflour
50g (2oz) butter
100g (4oz) button mushrooms
2 eating apples, peeled, cored and sliced
1 cucumber, peeled and diced
1 green pepper, cored, deseeded and sliced
1 red pepper, cored, deseeded and sliced
100g (4oz) cooked rice

Sweet and Sour Sauce
15ml (1 tblsp) cornflour
30ml (2 tblsp) sugar
10ml (2 tsp) soy sauce
45ml (3 tblsp) vinegar
150ml (¼ pint) chicken stock

Toss the veal in seasoned cornflour and fry in the butter until golden. Remove and keep warm. Fry the mushrooms, apple slices and cucumber. Fry the peppers. Return the meat to the pan. Cover and cook for 10 minutes until the meat is tender. Stir in the cooked rice. Transfer to a serving dish and keep hot. Mix the sweet and sour sauce ingredients together, add to the pan and, stirring gently, boil for 2-3 minutes, until the sauce is transparent. Pour the sauce over the veal and cucumber mixture. This can be served as a meal in its own right, or served with a vegetable if required.
Serves four.

Sweet and Spicy Noisettes

5ml (1 tsp) honey
5ml (1 tsp) dry mustard
Salt and pepper
1 garlic clove, peeled and crushed
10ml (2 tsp) lemon juice
6 noisettes of lamb
3 canned pineapple rings with juice
15g (1oz) butter
20ml (1½ tblsp) chopped mint
1 tomato, quartered
3 glacé cherries

Combine the honey, mustard, seasoning, garlic and lemon juice and spread the noisettes with the mixture. Leave to stand for 20 minutes. Place 50ml (2 fl oz) of the pineapple juice in a pan, add the butter and bring to the boil. Boil until reduced by half and add the mint. Keep warm. Grill the noisettes, basting them occasionally with the pineapple mixture. When the meat is cooked, arrange it on a warmed serving dish and decorate with the tomatoes and the pineapple rings. Garnish with the glacé cherries. Serve with fried mushroom rings and bird's nest potatoes.
Serves three.

Stuffed Trout with Almonds

Salt and pepper
2 medium trout, filleted
100-150g (4-5oz) butter
50g (2oz) blanched almonds

Stuffing
175g (6oz) fresh, white breadcrumbs
30ml (2 tblsp) chopped fresh parsley
1 medium onion, peeled and finely chopped
Salt and pepper
10ml (2 tsp) mixed dried herbs
1 cooking apple, peeled and finely chopped
1 small egg, beaten
A little water

Season the fish lightly and fry for about 10 minutes in the butter, until tender. Transfer to a hot dish. For the stuffing mix together the breadcrumbs, parsley, onion, seasoning, herbs and apple. Stir in the beaten egg, and water if necessary, to give a soft consistency. Stuff the fish with this mixture. Fry the almonds for about 5 minutes, adding extra butter if necessary. Scatter the almonds over the fish. Garnish with parsley, and serve with sauté potatoes and a vegetable.

Three Ring Rice

1 red pepper
100g (4oz) butter or margarine
225g (8oz) cooked rice
2 medium onions, peeled and chopped
½ green pepper, cored, deseeded and chopped
1 small garlic clove, peeled and crushed
225g (8oz) minced beef
175g (6oz) can of concentrated tomato purée
5ml (1 tsp) salt
2.5ml (½ tsp) chilli powder
100g (4oz) packet of frozen peas

Core, deseed and cut the red pepper into strips. Arrange at intervals in the bottom of a ring mould. Melt half the butter or margarine. Stir in the rice and spoon into the mould over the pepper. Fry the onion and green pepper together with the garlic in the remaining butter until soft. Add the minced beef and cook until brown. Stir in the tomato purée, salt and chilli powder. Cook the peas, strain, put on top of the rice, then cover with the beef mixture. Press down each layer firmly. Place the mould in a shallow pan of hot water. Cook in the oven for about 20 minutes at 180°C, 350°F, Gas Mark 4, or until firm to the touch. Turn out onto a hot dish. Serve with sweet corn or a side salad.

Veal with Cucumber (above right) and Three Ring Rice (below right).

layers. Season each layer and add herbs. Pour over the juice from the tomatoes and finish with a layer of potato slices. Pour water in to come halfway up the dish and dot the butter over the top. Cover tightly and cook in oven for 90 minutes at 180°C, 350°F, Gas Mark 4. Remove the lid and cook for a further 30 minutes to brown the potatoes. Serve with boiled carrots tossed in butter and chopped parsley.
Serves six.

Gammon with Mixed Fruit

1.75-2.25kg (4-5lb) gammon hock
30ml (2 tblsp) apricot jam
30ml (2 tblsp) made mustard
Cloves for decoration
1 small, fresh pineapple, peeled
15ml (1 tblsp) chutney
60ml (2¼ fl oz) unsweetened pineapple juice
1kg (2lb) canned apricot halves, drained

Cover the gammon with cold water and soak for 4 hours. Drain the gammon and wrap in foil. Place in a roasting pan and cook in the oven for 2 hours at 190°C, 375°F, Gas Mark 5. Remove the rind from the gammon and score the surface of the meat. Mix half the apricot jam with the mustard and spread the mixture over the gammon. Stud the meat with the cloves in a decorative pattern and return the meat to the oven for about 30 minutes. Cut the pineapple into slices and remove the core from each slice. Heat the remaining apricot jam with the chutney and pineapple juice in a wide pan. Glaze the pineapple slices and the apricot halves in this mixture. Place the finished gammon joint in a serving dish and garnish with the glazed pineapple slices and apricot halves. Serve with an exotic salad.
Serves ten.

This page: Pork Provençal (top) and Turkey Roast with Fruit Sauce (bottom).

Facing page: Crown Roast of Lamb (top), Egg and Melon Salad (bottom left) and Gammon with Mixed Fruit (bottom right).

Crown Roast of Lamb

2 best ends of lamb, chined
10ml (2 tsp) butter
1 cooking apple, peeled, cored and chopped
225g (8oz) pork sausage meat
30ml (2 tblsp) fresh breadcrumbs
15ml (1 tblsp) chopped fresh parsley
15ml (1 tblsp) finely chopped mint
Glacé cherries

Trim the skin and fat from the ends of the rib bones so that 2.5cm (1 inch) of the bone protrudes. Place the two joints back-to-back with the bones curving upwards and outwards. Secure with kitchen thread. Heat the butter and sauté the apple, add the sausage meat, cook for 2-3 minutes then stir in the rest of the ingredients. Place the stuffing in the cavity of the crown. Cover the tips of the bones with foil and roast in the oven for 30 minutes per 450g (1lb) plus 30 minutes at 180°C, 350°F, Gas Mark 4. Decorate the bone ends with cutlet frills and glacé cherries and serve with roast potatoes and a green vegetable.
Serves six-eight.

Pork Provençal

1kg (2lb) pork fillets
425g (15oz) can tomatoes
750g (1½lb) potatoes, peeled and thinly sliced
350g (12oz) onions, peeled and thinly sliced
Salt and pepper
1.25ml (¼ tsp) dried mixed herbs
25g (1oz) butter

Slice the meat and trim off any surplus fat. Butter an ovenproof dish then arrange the tomatoes, meat, onions and potatoes in

Egg and Melon Salad

1 small cabbage
1 firm, ripe melon
1 orange
Salt and pepper
2 carrots, peeled and grated
4 hard-boiled eggs
Few sprigs of watercress
Few leaves of chicory
8 radishes

Cooked Salad Dressing
5ml (1 tsp) flour
15ml (1 tblsp) sugar
Salt and pepper
2.5ml (½ tsp) mustard powder
1 large egg, beaten
30ml (2 tblsp) water
30ml (2 tblsp) vinegar
5ml (1 tsp) butter

To prepare the dressing, combine the flour, sugar, mustard and seasoning in a heavy-based saucepan. Mix in the egg to form a smooth paste. Add the water, vinegar and butter and stir over a low heat until the sauce begins to thicken. Remove from the heat, stir thoroughly and, if necessary, strain to remove any lumps. Cool in the refrigerator. Chop the cabbage very finely. Cube the melon. Peel the orange and cut the segments into pieces. Combine these ingredients with the grated carrots in a mixing bowl. Season as required. Pour over the cooled dressing and spoon the salad mixture onto a large salad dish. Shell and slice the hard-boiled eggs and arrange them with the watercress and chicory leaves round the salad. Cut the radishes into floral shapes and garnish the salad and serve.
Serves four.

Barbados Turkey

25g (1oz) flour
5ml (1 tsp) powdered ginger
5ml (1 tsp) curry powder
100g (4oz) turkey escalopes
75g (3oz) butter
50ml (2 fl oz) rum
50g (2oz) desiccated coconut
45ml (3 tblsp) pineapple juice
70ml (2½ fl oz) chicken stock
50ml (2 fl oz) double cream
Salt and pepper
Few sprigs of parsley
6-8 slices canned pineapple

Mix together the flour, ginger and curry powder and use to coat the turkey. Heat the butter and fry the escalopes for about 10 minutes each side until cooked and golden. Add the rum and set alight. When the flames subside, remove the escalopes and keep hot. Add the coconut to the pan and brown quickly. Then stir in the pineapple juice and stock. Boil for 5 minutes, reduce the heat and stir in the cream and seasoning. Arrange the escalopes in a serving dish and cover with the sauce. Garnish with the parsley and pineapple. Serve with boiled rice and green vegetables.
Serves four.

Crown of Chicken

Salt and pepper
25g (1oz) flour
1kg (2lb) potatoes
45ml (3 tblsp) milk
25-50g (1-2oz) butter
6 or 8 chicken legs
60ml (4 tblsp) olive oil
1 can cherry fruit pie filling
Watercress to garnish

Coat the chicken legs in seasoned flour. Peel the potatoes and cook in boiling, salted water. Drain and mash the potatoes with the milk and butter and keep hot. Meanwhile, fry the chicken in the olive oil until cooked and golden brown. Drain on paper towels and keep hot. Drain excess oil from the frying pan, add the cherry pie filling and heat gently. Place the creamed potatoes in centre of a hot serving dish, stand the chicken legs round the edges. Pour over the hot cherry sauce. Garnish with watercress and serve with a green salad.

Duck with Orange Sauce

1 large duck, e.g. 1.5kg (3lb)
1 orange
300ml (½ pint) bought Espagnole
    sauce
15ml (1 tblsp) lemon juice
30ml (2 tblsp) white wine
150ml (¼ pint) water
Orange segments to garnish

Place the duck in an open roasting tin. No fat is necessary. Cook in the oven at 150°C, 300°F, Gas Mark 2. Cook for 25 minutes for every 450g (1lb) in weight and 30 minutes over. Prick the breast skin after 30 minutes with a fine skewer. Pare the rind from the orange, cut into wafer-thin strips and simmer in water for about 10 minutes. Strain the Espagnole sauce carefully, reheat with the orange rind, orange juice, lemon juice and wine. Garnish the duck with orange segments and serve with the orange sauce. Serve with potato croquettes, broccoli and roast turnips.
Serves four.

Peppered Steak

Steak, as required
A little oil or butter
Peppercorns

Brush the steak with oil or melted butter and grill until tender, or as required. When the steak is cooked, place on a serving dish and sprinkle with the peppercorns. Tap with a steak hammer to crush the peppercorns into the steak. Serve with French fries, potato croquettes, onion rings or broccoli, or a mixed side salad.

Turkey Roast with Fruit Sauce

25g (1oz) butter
2.5kg (5½lb) white turkey roast
1 red pepper
1 small green pepper
1 onion
225g (8oz) can mandarin oranges
225g (8oz) canned sweet corn

For the Sauce
10ml (2 tsp) cornflour
15ml (1 tblsp) vinegar
5ml (1 tsp) sugar
5ml (1 tsp) Worcestershire sauce
15-30ml (1-2 tblsp) sherry

Spread the butter over the turkey roast then wrap in foil to make a parcel. Place in a roasting pan and roast in the oven for 90 minutes at 190°C, 375°F, Gas Mark 5. Core, deseed and chop the peppers. Peel and chop the onion. Drain the mandarins and sweet corn, reserving the juices. Mix the mandarins, sweet corn, peppers and onion together. To make the sauce, mix the cornflour with a little water to make a smooth paste. Blend the juices from the mandarins and sweet corn with the vinegar, sugar, Worcestershire sauce, sherry and cornflour and heat until thickened, stirring well. Add the fruit and vegetables. Remove the turkey roast from the oven and unwrap the foil. Pour a little of the sauce all over and round the turkey and cover again with the foil. Cook the turkey for a further 1-1½ hours or until the turkey is tender and cooked through. Unwrap the turkey and place on a serving dish. Surround with fruit sauce and serve the rest of the sauce separately. Serve with roast potatoes and vegetables of your own choice.
Serves six-eight.

Crown of Chicken (right),
Duck and Orange Sauce
(below) and Barbados
Turkey (bottom).

83

MICROWAVE COOKING

Introducing the Microwave

The microwave oven is one of the most exciting kitchen appliances available. It may be used to defrost, reheat, and cook foods, and is therefore more versatile than a conventional oven; in fact it can cope with 75% of your normal cooking chores.

The theory behind microwave cooking must be learned and fully understood before a microwave oven can be used to its full extent. It is a very different method of cooking, which is clean, quick, efficient, labour saving and economical.

The Principles of Microwave Cookery

The oven is plugged in by means of a 13 amp plug to a normal electrical socket and it is usually positioned on the kitchen work top. Electricity is converted into microwave energy inside the oven by the magnetron. The 'microwaves' are transferred into the oven cavity where they bounce off the metal interior and penetrate the outer 2-4cm (1"-1½") of the food. They pass through non-metal containers as though they were not there, and simply cause the molecules in the food to vibrate very fast indeed. The heat that is created passes by conduction through to the centre of the food and the food is cooked by friction heat. As a rough guide, cooking times by the microwave method are about ⅓ to ¼ of the conventional times.

Different Types of Microwave Ovens

A microwave oven may be either free standing or built-in. If built-in, it is placed in a housing unit, with a conventional oven situated above or below the microwave.

Convected Hot Air and Microwave Combined

These ovens are now widely available. They are more expensive than an ordinary microwave oven as they combine two units in one. The most common criticism of food cooked in a microwave is that it does not appear 'brown'. This is because there is no dry heat available to caramelise or 'brown' the food. Some people prefer to buy the combination ovens, which use traditional cooking methods and microwave cooking combined. In some models both cooking methods may be used simultaneously, whilst in others the microwave and the hot air ovens are used one after the other.

Grills
Some microwave ovens offer a browning grill.

Safety
All microwave ovens offered for sale in this country pass rigorous safety tests. Choose one which has the British Standard kite mark.

The Output of the Microwave
The cooking time for each dish/recipe is governed by the electrical output of the microwave oven, and the output also controls the running costs of the appliance. The output is measured in watts. A 700w microwave oven (the most powerful available on the domestic market) consumes about 1.3k per hour and is, therefore, a most economical method of cooking. Microwave ovens are available with maximum power ratings of 700w, 650w, 600w and 500w. The cooking, re-heating and defrosting times vary according to the output. A 1.5kg (3lb) chicken takes 21 minutes in a 700w microwave and 28 minutes in a 500w. There is no pre-heating before use, and no cooling down after cooking.

Versatility
A microwave oven may be used to defrost, cook and reheat food. It is also well suited to the many different methods of cooking – a microwave oven can poach, shallow fat fry, braise, roast, boil and bake. It will even dry herbs for winter use, and may be used to sterilise jam jars. The oven and cooking containers stay cool, and microwave ovens are, therefore, perfectly safe for elderly people to use, and for households where there are children.

Cleaning

As the oven cabinet does not get very hot, all that is necessary is a wipe with a clean dish cloth. Should smells cling e.g. curry or fish, simply squeeze a lemon into 450ml (¾ pint) water and bring to the boil. Wipe the oven with the acidulated water. Food does not bake onto the containers so they are easier to wash up.

Turntables

Manufacturers choose different methods of ensuring that the food cooks evenly. Go by personal recommendation wherever possible. Hidden turntables are popular as they do not restrict the shape of dish used. Some ovens offer stirrer fans and turntables.

Standing Times

Standing, or equalising, time is simply the time that the food takes to finish cooking. The heat is passed from the outside to the centre by conduction. The standing time will vary according to the size and density of the food. Standing time may take place either inside or outside the microwave oven; it is an important part of microwave cookery which must be used. It is just as important after defrosting.

Containers for Use in the Microwave Oven

Special containers are available for microwave cookery, but they are not essential. The heat is localised in the food, and not in the container, so the dish itself does not usually become hot. Some plastics, Pyrex, china, glass, and even paper and basketware, may be used. Be guided by the length of time the food is to be in the microwave, and by the temperature that it will reach.

Plastic cling film is a boon to the microwave owner, as it may be used in place of a lid to cover foods and prevent splashing. Do remember to pierce cling film and roasta bags to allow steam to escape.

Metal – including tin foil – may damage the heart of the microwave oven, the magnetron, and should not be used unless specifically directed by the manufacturer.

Browning Dish or Skillet

A browning dish is a special dish which, when preheated in the microwave oven, will become very hot over the base. Several shapes and sizes are available, either with a lid or without. The dish is used to brown such foods as chops, sausages, hamburgers, bacon, eggs etc. The food must be turned to brown on the other side. The deep

Herby Roast Chicken (left), Devilled Pork Chops (below) and Chicken Breasts in Garlic Cream Sauce (right).

Variable Power Chart

MICROWAVE POWER LEVEL	DESCRIPTION AND SUGGESTED USE
10 or Full–High	Microwave energy constant at full wattage. For cooking vegetables, poultry, fish and some sauces, start joints.
8 or Roast	Power on for 13 seconds, auto cut-out for 2 seconds. Repeated continually for time selected, for reheating some joints.
7 and 6 – Medium	Power is on for about 10 seconds, off for 5 seconds, for chops, meat balls, chicken pieces, cakes.
4 and 5 – Simmer	Power is on for 6 seconds, off for 9 seconds, for completing casseroles, defrosting large joints, egg and cheese dishes.
3 – Defrost	Generally for defrosting (allow a standing time afterwards), for melting chocolate, and for delicate sauces.
2 – Very Low	Power is on for 3 seconds, off for 12 seconds. Keep cooked food warm for up to ½ hour. Soften butter and cream cheese from refrigerator.

Please note that this chart is given only as a guide. The variable power dial differs slightly from manufacturer to manufacturer.

Cooked food reheats remarkably quickly without drying out. A chart is provided to give some of the most common foods. Allow a few minutes standing time, after reheating, and before serving.

GENERAL RULES FOR REHEATING.
1. Cover food, allowing steam to escape, unless told specifically not to cover.
2. Stir foods such as casseroles, baked beans, stewed fruits, halfway through reheating.
3. Allow a short standing time – 3-5 minutes before removing covering and serving.
4. Reheat small items, such as sausage rolls or sausages, arranged in ring fashion on outside edge of plate. Reheat on Power 4, or Simmer.

Re-heating Chart

TYPE OF FOOD & WEIGHT	COVER	STIRRING	POWER LEVEL	TIME
1 Plated Meal	Cling Film	–	Full	3-4 minutes
1 Large Macaroni Cheese	Cling Film	Yes, once	Power 7 or Roast	10 minutes
2 Bowls Soup	–	Yes, once	Full	5 minutes
Baked Beans 100g (4ozs)	–	–	Power 7 or Roast	2 minutes
Baked Beans 450g (16ozs)	Yes	Yes, twice	Power 7 or Roast	7 minutes
Chicken Pieces 2 x 225g (8ozs)	Yes	–	Full	3-4 minutes
Beef Casserole for 4	Yes	Yes, twice	Full	10-12 minutes
Cooked Vegetables 100g (4ozs)	Yes	–	Full	45 seconds
Cooked Vegetables 450g (1lb)	Yes	Yes, once	Full	2 minutes
1 Family Meat Pie	No	No	4 or Simmer	7-8 minutes
6 Mince Pies	No	No	4 or Simmer	4 minutes
4 Bread Rolls	Kitchen Roll	No	4 or Simmer	2 minutes
Christmas Pudding 750g (1½lb)	Cling Film	No	Power 7 or Roast	3 minutes
Sauce 300ml (½ pt)	Cling Film	Yes, twice	Full	2 minutes
Fish 350g (12ozs)	Cling Film	–	Full	2 minutes

Defrosting Chart

FOOD TO BE DEFROSTED AND WEIGHT	POWER LEVEL	MICROWAVE TIME	STANDING TIME
Mince 450g (1lb)	4 or Defrost	6 minutes	15 minutes
Chicken 1½kg (3lb)	4 or Defrost	30 minutes	30 minutes
Joint of Beef 1½kg (3lb)	4 or Defrost	20 minutes	30 minutes
Shepherd's Pie 450g (1lb)	4 or Defrost	8 minutes	10 minutes
Large Lasagne	6 or Simmer	20 minutes	15 minutes
Chops 450g (1lb)	4 or Defrost	6 minutes	10 minutes
Sausages 450g (1lb)	4 or Defrost	6 minutes	10 minutes
Cod 225g (8ozs)	4 or Defrost	6 minutes	10 minutes
Raspberries 225g (8ozs)	4 or Defrost	4 minutes	15 minutes
1 Victoria Sandwich (2 egg)	4 or Defrost	2-3 minutes	15 minutes
Large Sliced Loaf	4 or Defrost	7 minutes	10 minutes
Cheese Sauce 300ml (½ Pint)	4 or Defrost	7 minutes	7 minutes
Chicken in Sauce for 4	Simmer	12 minutes	10 minutes
Family Apple Pie	4 or Defrost	8 minutes	5 minutes
Family Meat Pie or Quiche Lorraine	4 or Defrost	6-7 minutes	10 minutes

The microwave oven makes a perfect partner for your freezer as it enables you to defrost frozen foods in a fraction of the time that it would normally take. Remember to turn or stir the foods, for more even defrosting, and remember that a standing time is very important.

ALTERING TIMINGS

The recipes given in this book can be cooked in any model of variable power microwave oven that is available today. Each of these recipes was tested in a 700W microwave oven. Convert the timings in the following way, if the output of your oven is other than 700W:–

If using an oven of 500W, add 40 seconds for each minute stated in the recipe.

If using an oven of 600W, add 20 seconds for each minute stated in the recipe.

If using an oven of 650W plus, you will only need to allow a slight increase in the overall time.

browning dishes with lids are also used as casserole dishes. **These containers must not be used in conventional ovens.**

Stirring and Turning

Stirring and turning are methods used to equalise the heat in the food, i.e. the cooking of the food. The amount of stirring or turning will be governed by the type of food to be cooked, the cooking time and the even distribution of energy in the microwave oven. The recipes in this section give you a guide as to when to stir and turn. Adjust, if necessary, according to your own particular oven. Arrange foods such as baked apples or jacket potatoes in a ring fashion, leaving a space in the centre.

Starting Temperature of Food

The starting temperature of food will alter the cooking time. It may be at average room temperature, at cold room temperature or taken from the refrigerator or cold larder. Please note that the timings in this section are calculated for food at average room temperature, unless otherwise stated.

Can You Cook a Complete Meal by Microwave?

The easiest way to use a microwave oven is to employ stage cookery. The microwave oven cooks according to weight and time, not by temperature, and different types of food require different cooking times. During the standing time of the denser foods, such as joints and jacket potatoes, the less dense items, such as vegetables and sauces, are completely cooked. Foods of similar density may be cooked together, e.g. potatoes and carrots, but remember that the total energy available in the microwave oven must be shared between the foods introduced. If carrots and potatoes are cooked simultaneously, the resulting weight must be checked, and the cooking time calculated accordingly.

Some Things Cannot be Done

Do not try to cook Yorkshire puddings or other batter recipes, boil eggs, deep fat fry, or produce really crisp foods such as roast potatoes, as none of these will be successful. **Pastry** – baking blind, suet crust and some puff pastry recipes work beautifully, but do not try to cook the top of an apple pie. Baked pies may be reheated successfully on Simmer, or Power 4 – see chart.

Soups and Starters

Vegetable Soup

PREPARATION TIME: 10 minutes
MICROWAVE TIME: 21-26 minutes
SERVES: 4 people

25g (1oz) butter
450g (1lb) young leeks, cleaned and sliced
1 medium onion, peeled and sliced
175g (6oz) potato, peeled and diced
1 carrot, peeled and diced
Salt and freshly ground black pepper to taste
15ml (1 tblsp) chopped fresh parsley
450ml (¾ pint) homemade chicken stock
300ml (½ pint) milk

Melt the butter in a 2¼ litre (4 pint) casserole dish. Microwave on Full Power for 1 minute. Stir in all the prepared vegetables, salt and pepper, parsley and 45ml (3 tblsp) of the stock. Cover the dish, piercing the cling film if used. Microwave on Full Power for 12 minutes. Stir. Set aside, covered, for 5 minutes. Transfer the vegetables into the food processor bowl or liquidizer goblet; add the milk and liquidize or process until smooth. Return to the casserole and stir in the remaining stock. Microwave on Full Power, covered, for 3-5 minutes. Stir well before serving.

Asparagus with Mayonnaise

PREPARATION TIME: 10 minutes
MICROWAVE TIME: 10-12 minutes
SERVES: 4 people

450g (1lb) frozen asparagus spears
250ml (8 fl oz) corn oil
25g (1oz) butter
1 egg
1 egg yolk
150ml (¼ pint) olive oil
Salt and freshly ground black pepper to taste
30ml (2 tblsp) lemon juice
Chopped fresh parsley

Arrange the asparagus in a roasta bag in a suitable dish. Add 45ml (3 tblsp) water to the bag, with the butter. Seal the bag with a rubber band. Pierce the bag once at the base. Microwave on Full Power for 10-12 minutes, turning the bag over once halfway through cooking time. Set aside. Put the egg and egg yolk into the goblet of a food processor or liquidizer with the salt and pepper. Blend on maximum. Add the oil, in a steady trickle, blending to a smooth mayonnaise. Add the lemon juice. Carefully drain the asparagus and arrange on a heated serving dish. Sprinkle with the parsley and serve accompanied by the mayonnaise. Serve immediately.

Soured Cream Prawns

PREPARATION TIME: 5 minutes
MICROWAVE TIME: 7-8 minutes
SERVES: 4 people

50g (2oz) butter
225g (8oz) peeled shrimps
Freshly ground black pepper to taste
1 egg yolk
150ml (¼ pint) soured cream
Paprika

Butter 4 ramekin dishes and divide the shrimps amongst them. Season well with black pepper. Combine the egg yolk and soured cream and spoon over the shrimps. Dot with the remaining butter. Microwave all 4 ramekins together on Power 4, or Simmer, for 7-8 minutes. (The dishes should be arranged in a ring, leaving a space in the centre.) Serve immediately sprinkled with paprika.

Sweetcorn Starter

PREPARATION TIME: 5 minutes
MICROWAVE TIME: 15 minutes
SERVES: 4 people

4 corn cobs
Sprigs of fresh savory
Salt and freshly ground black pepper to taste
100g (4oz) butter

Arrange the cobs in a suitable dish. Add 2-3 tblsp cold water and a few sprigs of savory. Season. Cover with cling film and pierce. Microwave on Full Power for 6 minutes. Turn each cob over. Re-cover and microwave on Full Power for 6 minutes. Set aside. Put the butter into a 600ml (1 pint) jug and microwave on Power 4 or Simmer for about 3 minutes or until melted. Transfer the cooked cobs to a serving dish. Pour over the butter and sprinkle with extra chopped savory before serving.

Individual Frozen Pizzas

PREPARATION TIME: 2 minutes
MICROWAVE TIME: 6½-8½ minutes
SERVES: 1 person

Preheat a browning dish, without the lid, for 5-7 minutes. Put 15ml (1 tblsp) of oil and 1 individual pizza onto the dish. Microwave uncovered for approximately 1½ minutes on Full Power. Allow to stand for 1 minute before serving. As many pizzas as will fit onto your dish may be microwaved at the same time; increase the microwave time accordingly. Pizzas may be heated directly from the freezer, without the browning dish, on an ordinary non-metallic plate but the base will not be as crisp.

Chestnut Soup

PREPARATION TIME: 15 minutes
MICROWAVE TIME: 34 minutes
SERVES: 4 people

25g (1oz) butter
1 stem celery, chopped
2 large onions, chopped
900ml (1½ pint) homemade chicken stock (hot)
225g (8oz) unsweetened chestnut puree
Salt and freshly ground black pepper to taste
4 rashers streaky bacon, de-rinded

Put the butter, celery and onions into a 2¼ litre (4 pint) casserole dish; cover with a lid and microwave on Full Power for 4 minutes. Stir. Mix 300ml (½ pint) stock with the chestnut puree, in a 1.2 litre (2 pint) mixing bowl. Stir into the onion mixture. Season with salt and black pepper; cover and microwave on Full Power for 7 minutes. Stir in the remaining stock and microwave on Full Power for 20 minutes. Allow to stand whilst preparing the bacon. Arrange the bacon on a microwave roasting rack, or on 2 sheets of absorbent kitchen paper. Microwave, uncovered, on Full Power, for about 3 minutes. Serve the soup sprinkled with the crumbled crispy bacon.

Tomato Baskets

PREPARATION TIME: 5 minutes
MICROWAVE TIME: 5½-6½ minutes
SERVES: 6 people

6 large firm tomatoes
225g (8oz) packet frozen mixed vegetables
50g (2oz) butter
Salt and freshly ground black pepper to taste
Few sprigs of fresh mint

Cut the top off each tomato and reserve. Using a grapefruit knife or a teaspoon, carefully scoop out the centre flesh. (Use in a soup or sauce recipe). Pierce the pouch of frozen vegetables once and place in a dish. Microwave on Full Power for 3½ minutes, turning the bag once halfway through the cooking time. Set aside. Stand the prepared tomatoes upright on a serving dish,

Asparagus with Mayonnaise (top), Vegetable Soup (centre) and Soured Cream Prawns (bottom).

in a ring. Dot with half the butter. Microwave on Full Power for about 2-3 minutes until very hot. Mix the drained, cooked vegetables with the remaining butter and salt and pepper and spoon into the tomato shells. Top with the reserved lids, and garnish with sprigs of mint. Serve immediately.

Quick Bap Pizzas

PREPARATION TIME: 10 minutes

MICROWAVE TIME: 6½-7½ minutes

SERVES: 4 as a main meal, 8 as a snack

4 baps
1 medium onion, finely chopped
5ml (1 tsp) tomato puree
5ml (1 tsp) dried oregano
225g (8oz) can tomatoes, chopped
5ml (1 tsp) French mustard
Salt and freshly ground black pepper to taste
150g (5oz) Cheddar cheese, thinly sliced or grated
Stuffed olives, sliced

Tomato Baskets (right), Quick Bap Pizzas (below) and Individual Frozen Pizza (far right).

Cut the baps in half and arrange in a ring on a suitable baking sheet. Place the onion in a 1.2 litre (2 pint) mixing bowl; cover and microwave for 1½ minutes on Full Power. Stir in the tomato puree, oregano, chopped tomatoes and the mustard. Season with salt and pepper. Divide amongst the baps, and cover with the cheese. Decorate with the sliced olives. Microwave on Power 4 for 5-6 minutes, until the cheese has melted. Serve immediately.

Garlic Prawn Starter

PREPARATION TIME: 30 minutes	
MICROWAVE TIME: 20 minutes	
SERVES: 4 people	

750g (1½lb) courgettes, cleaned, topped and tailed
Salt and freshly ground black pepper to taste
350g (12oz) peeled prawns
15ml (1 tblsp) chopped chives
30ml (2 tblsp) dry white wine

2 cloves garlic, crushed
15ml (1 tblsp) lemon juice
50g (2oz) butter

Garnish
Unpeeled prawns

Slice the courgettes thinly into a colander, sprinkling them generously with salt. Cover with a plate and weigh down; leave to stand for 20 minutes. Rinse well under cold running water. Drain thoroughly. Arrange the courgettes in a vegetable dish. Season with salt and pepper. Cover and microwave on Full Power for 12 minutes. Stir. Set aside, covered. Put the peeled prawns, chives, wine, garlic, lemon juice and butter into a 1.2 litre (2 pint) casserole. Cover with a lid. Microwave on Power 4, or Simmer, for 8 minutes. Stir once halfway through cooking time. Drain the excess liquid from the courgettes. Top with the heated prawns and their juices. Garnish with the unpeeled prawns and serve immediately.

Egg and Tuna Starter

PREPARATION TIME:	10 minutes
MICROWAVE TIME:	10 minutes
SERVES:	4 people

200g (7oz) can tuna fish in oil, drained
2 hard boiled eggs, cooked conventionally and chopped
300ml (½ pint) milk
25g (1oz) butter
Salt and freshly ground black pepper to taste
25g (1oz) plain flour
5ml (1 tsp) made mustard
50g (2oz) grated Cheddar cheese

Garnish
Stuffed olives, sliced

Flake the tuna fish and divide between 4 ramekin dishes. Top with the egg. Melt the butter in a 1 litre (1¾ pint) jug for 1 minute on Full Power, or until very hot. Stir in the flour and gradually stir in the milk. Microwave on Full Power for 2 minutes. Beat well with a balloon whisk. Microwave on Full Power for 2 minutes. Beat well with a balloon whisk. Beat in salt and pepper and cheese. Divide the sauce amongst the ramekins. Garnish with sliced olives. Microwave all 4 ramekins together for 5 minutes on Power 4 or Simmer. Serve immediately.

Mackerel Pate

PREPARATION TIME:	10 minutes plus chilling
MICROWAVE TIME:	3 minutes
SERVES:	6 people

1 onion, finely chopped
50g (2oz) butter
225g (8oz) cream cheese
30ml (2 tblsp) lemon juice
30ml (2 tblsp) chopped fresh parsley

350g (12oz) smoked mackerel fillets
5ml (1 tsp) coarse French mustard
Freshly ground black pepper to taste
45ml (3 tblsp) soured cream
10ml (2 tsp) tomato puree

Garnish
Lemon wedges
Fresh parsley and cucumber slices

Put the onion into a soup bowl. Cover with cling film and pierce. Microwave on Full Power for 1 minute. Set aside. Flake the fish into the food processor or liquidizer goblet, discarding skin and bones. Add the onion. Place the butter in the bowl used for the onion and microwave on Power 4, or Simmer, for 2 minutes. Add to the processor or liquidizer with all the remaining ingredients. Process or liquidize until smooth. Pour into a dampened loaf tin; smooth the surface. Chill until firm. Turn out onto a serving dish and garnish with wedges of lemon, crimped cucumber slices and parsley.

This page: Sweetcorn Starter (top), Garlic Prawn Starter (bottom).

Vegetables

All types of vegetables, both frozen and fresh, microwave exceptionally well. They keep their colour, flavour and shape. Follow a few simple rules and use the charts to help you.

Helpful Hints
1. If you want to add salt, dissolve it in a little water beforehand. Adding salt can cause some vegetables to dry; to be on the safe side season with salt after cooking.
2. Always cover vegetables – roasta or freezer bags are very useful, but remember to pierce them.
3. Stir at least once during the cooking time or, if using a bag, turn it over.
4. Add only the amount of water necessary.
5. Cut the vegetables into even sized pieces.
6. Allow a standing time after cooking and before serving.
7. Cook frozen vegetables from frozen, do not defrost them first.

Fresh Vegetable Chart

VEGETABLE AND WEIGHT	ADDITION	MICROWAVE TIME	STANDING TIME
Sliced Green Beans 450g (1lb)	45ml (3 tblsp) water	8 minutes	5 minutes
Broad Beans 450g (1lb)	45ml (3 tblsp) water	8 minutes	5 minutes
Broccoli Spears 225g (8ozs)	45ml (3 tblsp) water	7 minutes	4 minutes
Sliced Carrots 450g (1lb)	30ml (2 tblsp) water	7-8 minutes	4 minutes
Cauliflower Florets 450g (1lb)	45ml (3 tblsp) water	7-8 minutes	5 minutes
Chopped Celery 225g (8ozs)	45ml (3 tblsp) water	7 minutes	4 minutes
Courgettes 450g (1lb)	25g (1oz) butter	10 minutes	3 minutes
Leeks 450g (1lb)	30ml (2 tblsp) water	7-8 minutes	3 minutes
Mushrooms (Sliced) 225g (8ozs)	25g (1oz) butter	2 minutes	2 minutes
Sliced Marrow 450g (1lb)	25g (1oz) butter	7 minutes	3 minutes
New Potatoes 450g (1lb)	30ml (2 tblsp) water	7 minutes	4 minutes
Old Potatoes 450g (1lb)	45ml (3 tblsp) water	9 minutes	5 minutes
Sliced Onions 450g (1lb)	30ml (2 tblsp) water	8-9 minutes	4 minutes
Brussels Sprouts 450g (1lb)	30ml (2 tblsp) water	6-7 minutes	4 minutes
Diced Swede 450g (1lb)	30ml (2 tblsp) water	13 minutes	6 minutes

Baked Stuffed Marrow

PREPARATION TIME: 20 minutes
MICROWAVE TIME: 22 minutes
SERVES: 4 people

1 medium size marrow
25g (1oz) butter
1 onion, peeled and finely chopped
450g (1lb) raw, lean minced beef
15g (½oz) plain flour
5ml (1 tsp) dried basil or oregano
1 egg, beaten
1 beef stock cube, crumbled
Salt and freshly ground black pepper to taste
15ml (1 tblsp) tomato puree

Wipe the marrow with a damp cloth. Cut both ends off the marrow and keep on one side. Scoop out the seeds with a spoon and discard. Melt the butter in a 1.75 litre (3 pint) mixing bowl for 1 minute on Full Power. Stir in the onion. Microwave on Full Power for 1 minute. Stir in all the remaining ingredients. Mix well. Secure one end of the marrow with wooden cocktail sticks. Stuff the marrow with the mince mixture. Secure the remaining end in place with wooden cocktail sticks. Place the marrow on a meat roasting rack and cover with cling film. Pierce. Microwave on Full Power for about 20 minutes, turning the marrow once halfway through cooking time. Allow to stand, covered with foil, for 5 minutes before serving. Cut into rings, and serve piping hot.

Brussels Sprouts with Chestnut and Bacon

PREPARATION TIME: 15 minutes
MICROWAVE TIME: 8 minutes
SERVES: 4 people

450g (1lb) fresh Brussels sprouts
15ml (1 tblsp) lemon juice
5ml (1 tsp) dried mixed herbs
30ml (2 tblsp) cold water
Salt and freshly ground black pepper to taste
75g (3oz) butter
225g (8oz) canned whole chestnuts, drained
3 rashers streaky bacon, de-rinded, cooked and chopped (see Garlic Mushrooms recipe)

Peel the sprouts and make a cross in the base of each one. Put the sprouts into a 1.2 litre (2 pint) casserole dish, or into a roasta bag. Add the lemon juice, herbs, water, and salt and pepper. Cover with a lid, or pierce the bag if used. Microwave on Full Power for 5 minutes. Stir or turn once, halfway through cooking time. Set aside for 5 minutes. Put the butter into a 300ml (½ pint) Pyrex jug and microwave on Power 4 or Simmer until melted (about 3 minutes). If using a roasta bag, tip the sprouts into serving dish. Add the chestnuts to the Brussels sprouts, stirring gently. Cover with a lid. Microwave on Full Power for 1 minute. Coat with melted butter, sprinkle with chopped bacon, and serve.

Brussels Sprouts with Chestnut and Bacon (top), Carrot and Parsnip Puree (centre) and Baked Stuffed Marrow (bottom).

Frozen Vegetable Chart

VEGETABLE AND WEIGHT	AMOUNT OF WATER	COOKING TIME	STANDING TIME
Asparagus 225g (8ozs)	30ml (2 tblsp)	7 minutes	5 minutes
Broccoli 225g (8ozs)	45ml (3 tblsp)	10 minutes	5 minutes
Brussels Sprouts 225g (8ozs)	30ml (2 tblsp)	4 minutes	3 minutes
Carrots 225g (8ozs)	30ml (2 tblsp)	6 minutes	3 minutes
Cauliflower Florets 225g (8ozs)	30ml (2 tblsp)	3 minutes	2 minutes
Courgettes 225g (8ozs)	Nil	4 minutes	2 minutes
Leeks 225g (8ozs)	30ml (2 tblsp)	6-7 minutes	2 minutes
Mixed Vegetables 225g (8ozs)	30ml (2 tblsp)	4 minutes	3 minutes
Mushrooms 225g (8ozs)	25g (1oz) butter and herbs	4 minutes	2 minutes
Baby Onions 225g (8ozs)	25g (1oz) butter	5 minutes	4 minutes
Peas 225g (8ozs)	Nil	4 minutes	2 minutes
Spinach 225g (8ozs)	Nil	5 minutes	3 minutes
Sweetcorn 225g (8ozs)	Nil	4 minutes	2 minutes

Carrot and Parsnip Puree

PREPARATION TIME: 15 minutes
MICROWAVE TIME: 13 minutes
SERVES: 4 people

225g (8oz) carrots, peeled
225g (8oz) parsnips, peeled
2.5ml (½ tsp) dried basil
45ml (3 tblsp) well-flavoured stock
30ml (2 tblsp) double cream
Salt and freshly ground black pepper
   to taste
Pinch grated nutmeg

Garnish
Carrot curls

Dice the peeled carrots and parsnips and place in a roasta bag in a 1.2 litre (2 pint) casserole. Add 30ml (2 tblsp) water and the basil. Snip the bag once at the base. Microwave on Full Power for 8 minutes, turning the bag over once halfway through cooking time. Set aside for 5 minutes. Empty the contents of the roasta bag into the goblet of a food processor or liquidizer. Add the stock and process until smooth. Add cream, salt and pepper, and nutmeg.

Process just to blend. Return to the casserole and cover with a lid. Microwave on Power 4, or Simmer, for 5 minutes. Garnish with carrot curls and serve.

Courgette Choice

PREPARATION TIME: 40-45 minutes
COOKING TIME: 10 minutes
SERVES: 4 people

450g (1lb) young courgettes, topped, tailed and washed
Salt and freshly ground black pepper
   to taste
450g (1lb) large firm tomatoes, skinned and sliced
2.5ml (½ tsp) dried tarragon
1 clove garlic, crushed
25g (1oz) butter

Arrange the sliced courgettes in a colander. Sprinkle generously with salt and leave to stand for 30 minutes. (This draws out the bitter juices.) Rinse well under cold running water. Drain. Layer the courgettes and tomatoes in a 1.2 litre (2 pint) casserole dish, starting and finishing with courgettes.

Season each layer with salt, pepper, tarragon and garlic. Dot the top with small knobs of butter. Cover tightly with a lid. Microwave on Full Power for 10 minutes. Allow to stand for 3 minutes before serving.

Cauliflower Cheese

PREPARATION TIME: 10 minutes
MICROWAVE TIME: 12 minutes
SERVES: 4 people

1 cauliflower, trimmed and divided into florets
15g (½oz) cornflour
300ml (½ pint) milk
5ml (1 tsp) made mustard
Salt and freshly ground black pepper
   to taste
75g (3oz) grated Cheddar cheese
25g (1oz) butter
½ red pepper, de-seeded and chopped

Arrange the florets of cauliflower in a roasta bag. Add 30ml (2 tblsp) water. Pierce the bag, and place in a 1.2 litre (2 pint) casserole. Microwave on Full Power for 7-8 minutes, turning the bag over once halfway through cooking time. Set aside, covered. Cream the cornflour with a little of the milk to a smooth paste. Stir in the mustard and salt and pepper to taste. Heat the remaining milk in a 1 litre (1¾ pint) jug for 2 minutes on Full Power. Pour the heated milk onto the cornflour mixture, stirring continuously. Return to the jug and microwave on Full Power for 2 minutes or until boiling. Beat in the cheese and butter, and any liquid from the cauliflower. Transfer cauliflower florets to a warmed serving dish. Pour the sauce over evenly. Sprinkle with the red pepper and serve immediately. The red pepper may be heated in a cup in the microwave for 1 minute on Full Power, if liked.

Ratatouille

PREPARATION TIME: 40 minutes
MICROWAVE TIME: 22-24 minutes
SERVES: 4 people

225g (½lb) courgettes
450g (1lb) aubergines
Salt and freshly ground black pepper
   to taste
50g (2oz) butter
1 medium onion, peeled and sliced
1 large clove garlic, crushed
A little oil
1 red pepper, de-seeded and sliced
425g (15oz) can tomatoes, chopped
2.5ml (½ tsp) dried oregano
50g (2oz) crumbled Danish Blue
   cheese

Wash the courgettes and aubergines. Cut off the ends and discard. Slice into ½ cm (¼ inch) slices and layer with a generous sprinkling of salt in a colander. Top with a plate and a weight and set aside to drain for 15 minutes. Rinse well under cold running water and drain. Put the butter in a 600ml (1 pint) measuring jug. Microwave on Full Power for 1-2 minutes until melted. Stir in the onion and garlic. Grease the sides and base of a 1.75-2.25 litre (3-4 pint) casserole or souffle dish with

Ratatouille (top), Courgette Choice (centre left) and Cauliflower Cheese (bottom).

oil. Layer the aubergines, courgettes and red pepper in the dish with the tomatoes, oregano, onion and garlic. Season each layer with salt and pepper. Cover with a lid. Microwave on Full Power for 20-22 minutes, removing the lid for the last 8 minutes. Turn the dish ¼ turn twice during the cooking time, if necessary. Top with the crumbled cheese and serve immediately.

Buttery Mashed Potato

PREPARATION TIME: 10 minutes
MICROWAVE TIME: 17 minutes
SERVES: 4-5 people

1kg (2lb) old potatoes, peeled
45ml (3 tblsp) milk
50g (2oz) butter
Salt and freshly ground black pepper to taste
50ml (2 tblsp) single cream
Chopped fresh parsley

Cut the potatoes into small, even sized pieces and put into a roasta bag with the milk and butter. Season. Secure the bag with an elastic band and stand in a 1.75 litre (3 pint) mixing bowl. Pierce the bag once at the base. Microwave on Full Power for 17 minutes, turning the bag over once halfway through the cooking time. Allow to stand for 5 minutes. Turn the potatoes and their liquid into the bowl and mash with a fork. Beat with a wooden spoon adding the cream. Turn into a serving dish. Fork up and sprinkle with the parsley. Serve.

Potatoes Gratinee

PREPARATION TIME: 20 minutes
MICROWAVE TIME: 26 minutes
SERVES: 4 people

750g (1½lb) old white potatoes, peeled and thinly sliced
300ml (½ pint) pouring white sauce
50g (2oz) grated cheese
45ml (3 tblsp) milk
Salt and freshly ground black pepper to taste
25g (1oz) butter
1 Recipe quantity of Crispy Topping (see recipe)

Soak the potato slices in cold water for a few minutes. Heat the sauce in a large jug for 1 minute on Full Power. Beat in the grated cheese, milk, and salt and pepper to taste. Grease a shallow dish with the butter. Arrange the drained potato slices, overlapping slightly, in the

Spinach Fiesta (top), Buttery Mashed Potato (far left) and Potatoes Gratinee (left).

base of the dish. Pour the sauce evenly over the top. Cover with cling film and pierce. Microwave on Power 7, or Roast, for 25 minutes. Stir once, gently, halfway through cooking time. Serve after 5 minutes standing time, sprinkled with the crispy topping.

Stuffed Baked Peppers

PREPARATION TIME: 10 minutes

MICROWAVE TIME: 14½-15½ minutes

SERVES: 4 people

4 large, even-sized peppers, about 225g (8oz) each
30ml (2 tblsp) water
350g (12oz) cooked chicken, pork or turkey
30ml (2 tblsp) drained, canned sweetcorn kernels
60ml (4 tblsp) soured cream
75g (3oz) chopped button mushrooms
Salt and freshly ground black pepper to taste

Cut the tops off the peppers and reserve. Scoop out the seeds and discard them. Stand the peppers upright in an oblong or round casserole dish. Add the water; cover and microwave on Full Power for 3½ minutes. Set aside. Combine all the remaining ingredients to make the filling and mix well. Drain the water from the peppers and divide the filling amongst them. Replace the tops. Cover with cling film and pierce. Microwave on Full Power for 11-12 minutes. Stand for 3 minutes before serving.

Garlic Mushrooms

PREPARATION TIME: 20 minutes

MICROWAVE TIME: 12½-14½

SERVES: 4 people

75g (3oz) butter
2 cloves garlic, crushed
350g (12oz) button mushrooms, stalks removed
4 rashers streaky bacon, de-rinded
100g (4oz) cream cheese
Salt and freshly ground black pepper to taste
15ml (1 tblsp) natural yogurt or soured cream
2.5ml (½ tsp) dried parsley

Garnish
Chopped fresh parsley

Place the butter and garlic into a small bowl and microwave on Power 4, or Simmer, for 3 minutes, or until melted. Using a pastry brush, brush the mushrooms all over, inside and out, with the melted butter. Arrange on a dinner plate, or baking sheet, in a circular fashion, leaving a space in the centre. Arrange the bacon on 2 sheets of absorbent kitchen paper, on a dinner plate, fat to outside. Cover with 1 piece absorbent kitchen paper. Microwave the bacon on Full Power for 2½-3 minutes. Set aside. Transfer the cream cheese to a 1.2 litre (2 pint) mixing bowl. Microwave, uncovered, on Defrost for 2 minutes. Stir in salt and pepper to taste, yogurt, dried parsley and chopped bacon. Soften the chopped onion in a cup for 45 seconds on Full Power. Stir into the cream cheese mixture. Fill the mushrooms with the cheese mixture. Microwave, uncovered on Roast, or Power 7, for 4-6 minutes. Serve immediately garnished with chopped parsley, on croutons of fried bread.

Spinach Fiesta

PREPARATION TIME: 20 minutes

MICROWAVE TIME: 22 minutes

SERVES: 4 people

225g (8oz) long grain rice
Salt and freshly ground black pepper to taste
3 frozen cod steaks
225g (8oz) frozen spinach
25g (1oz) butter
50ml (2 tblsp) milk
30ml (2 tblsp) canned tuna fish, drained
50g (2oz) Cheddar cheese, cubed
Chopped fresh parsley

Put the rice into a 1.75-2.25 litre (3-4 pint) mixing bowl. Pour on 600ml (1 pint) boiling water. Add 2.5ml (½ tsp) salt. Cover lightly with cling film and pierce once in the centre. Microwave on Full Power for 12 minutes. Set aside. Snip the fish packets open and microwave all 3 together, arranged on a dinner plate in a ring, for 6 minutes on Defrost. Turn each packet over, halfway through cooking. Set aside. Pierce the packet of spinach and place in a vegetable dish. Microwave on Full Power for 6 minutes. Set aside. Slip the cod steaks out of their packets and arrange on a pie plate in a ring.

Dot with butter. Season and spoon over the milk. Cover with cling film and pierce. Microwave on Full Power for 4 minutes. Drain the spinach. Chop and fork into the cooked rice. Add the tuna fish to the rice with the cheese. Drain the cooked cod and flake into the rice. Pile onto a warmed dish and serve, sprinkled with plenty of chopped parsley.

JACKET POTATOES WITH FILLINGS

Plain Jacket Potatoes

PREPARATION TIME: 15-20 minutes

MICROWAVE TIME: 15 minutes

SERVES: 4 people

4 x 200g (7oz) potatoes, scrubbed clean

Prick the potatoes with a fork and arrange in a ring on a dinner plate. Microwave uncovered, on Full Power, for 15 minutes. Wrap in a clean tea towel and set aside for 10-15 minutes. (The potatoes will continue to cook). Meanwhile prepare one of the fillings (all fillings serve 4 people).

Cottage Cheese with Prawns and Chives

Instead of pricking the potatoes, make a cross in the top of each one before baking.

225g (8oz) cottage cheese
15ml (1 tblsp) chopped chives
100g (4oz) peeled prawns
15ml (1 tblsp) soured cream
5ml (1 tsp) tomato puree
Sliced cucumber and whole prawns to garnish

Blend all the ingredients together, apart from the cucumber and prawns. Using a cloth, carefully push up each hot potato from the base, to form a water lily. Divide the filling between the potatoes. Garnish with the cucumber and whole prawns before serving.

Pilchards with Corn

30ml (2 tblsp) natural yogurt or mayonnaise
Salt and freshly ground black pepper to taste

350g (12oz) pilchards in tomato sauce
45ml (3 tblsp) drained canned sweetcorn kernels
4 spring onions, chopped

Cut the potatoes in half and carefully scoop out the flesh, leaving the skin intact. Put the potato flesh into a 1.75 litre (3 pint) mixing bowl. Mash well with a fork, adding the yogurt or mayonnaise and salt and pepper to taste. Open each pilchard and remove the backbone. Flake the pilchards into the potato; mix well, adding the sweetcorn and chopped spring onion. Pile the mixture back into the potato shells. Arrange in a serving dish. Cover with cling film. Microwave on Full Power for 4 minutes.

Baked Beans with Edam Cheese

425g (15.9oz) can baked beans in tomato sauce
225g (8oz) Edam cheese, cubed
Salt and freshly ground black pepper to taste

Garnish
Watercress

Empty the beans into a 900ml (1½ pint) casserole dish. Add the cheese and salt and pepper to taste. Cover with a lid and microwave on Power 7, or Roast, for 2½ minutes. Stir gently. Microwave on Power 7, or Roast, for 2½ minutes. Halve the potatoes after their standing time. Spoon the beans and cheese onto the potatoes. Garnish with watercress and serve.

Stuffed Baked Peppers (top), Jacket Potatoes with Fillings (centre) and Garlic Mushrooms (bottom).

Supper Dishes

Shish Kebabs

PREPARATION TIME: 10 minutes

MICROWAVE TIME: 8 minutes

SERVES: 3-4 people

350g (12oz) raw minced lamb
1 onion, finely chopped
10ml (2 tsp) lemon juice
5-10ml (1-2 tsp) mild curry powder
15ml (1 tblsp) soured cream
½ egg, beaten
25g (1oz) plain flour
30ml (2 tblsp) finely chopped fresh
   parsley
2.5ml (½ tsp) salt
15ml (1 tblsp) tomato sauce

Mix all the ingredients together.
Form the mixture into small balls.
Arrange the meatballs on a
microwave roasting rack in a ring.
Microwave, uncovered, on Power
7, or Roast, for 8 minutes. Serve
hot with yogurt sauce.

Yogurt Sauce

PREPARATION TIME: 5 minutes

SERVES: 4 people

150ml (5 fl oz) natural yogurt
5ml (1 tsp) granular mustard
10ml (2 tsp) tomato puree
5ml (1 tsp) concentrated mint sauce
5ml (1 tsp) lemon juice
5ml (1 tsp) caster sugar
30ml (2 tblsp) soured cream

Mix all the ingredients together
until well blended. Refrigerate until
required. Serve with Shish Kebabs.

Pasta Shells with Cheese and Bacon

PREPARATION TIME: 15 minutes

MICROWAVE TIME: 24 minutes

SERVES: 4 people

175g (6oz) dried pasta shapes
2.5ml (½ tsp) salt
15ml (1 tblsp) oil
225g (8oz) packet frozen mixed
   vegetables
5ml (1 tsp) cornflour
300ml (½ pint) milk

5ml (1 tsp) made mustard
Salt and freshly ground black pepper
   to taste
75g (3oz) grated Red Leicester cheese
2 bacon chops
1 Recipe Crispy Topping (see recipe)

Place the pasta in a 2.25-2.75 litre
(4-5 pint) mixing bowl. Add the
salt and the oil. Pour on 1.75 litres
(3 pints) boiling water. Cover
tightly with cling film and pierce
once in the centre. Microwave on
Full Power for 8 minutes. Set aside,
covered. Microwave the pierced
packet of vegetables in a suitable
dish, for 4 minutes on Full Power,
turning the packet over once
halfway through the cooking time.
Blend the cornflour with 15ml (1
tblsp) milk until smooth. Put the
remaining milk into a 1 litre (1¾
pint) jug and microwave on Full
Power for 3 minutes. Beat the
blended cornflour into the hot
milk together with the mustard and
salt and pepper to taste.
Microwave on Full Power for 2
minutes. Beat well adding the
cheese Microwave the bacon chops
on 2 sheets of absorbent kitchen
paper (with the fat facing
outwards). Microwave on Roast for
4 minutes. To assemble the dish:
drain the pasta and pile onto a
serving dish; drain the vegetables
and add to the pasta; chop the
bacon and mix into the pasta and
vegetables. Pour the cheese sauce
evenly over the top and top with
crispy crumbs. Microwave on
Power 5, or Roast, for 3 minutes.
Serve immediately.

Fish Fingers

PREPARATION TIME: 5 minutes

MICROWAVE TIME: 14 minutes

SERVES: 3-4 people

30ml (2 tblsp) cooking oil
8 frozen cod fish fingers

Preheat a large browning dish,
without a lid, for 7 minutes, on Full
Power. Put the oil into the heated
dish. Microwave on Full Power for
1 minute. Carefully press the fish
fingers into the oil. Microwave,
uncovered, on Full Power for 3

minutes. Turn each fish finger over
and microwave on Full Power for 3-
4 minutes. Drain on absorbent
kitchen paper and serve immediately (brown side uppermost).

Crispy Topping

PREPARATION TIME: 10 minutes

MICROWAVE TIME: 8 minutes

65g (2½oz) butter
100g (4oz) fresh brown breadcrumbs
50g (2oz) oatmeal

Put the butter into a 1.75 litre (3
pint) mixing bowl and microwave
on Full Power for 1½ minutes. Stir
in the breadcrumbs and oatmeal.
Microwave on Full Power for 2½
minutes. Stir with a fork.
Microwave on Full Power for 2
minutes. Stir. Microwave on Full
Power for 2 minutes. Allow to
stand for 5 minutes before using.
Alternatively, the topping may be
cooled and stored in an airtight
container. Serve as a crispy finish
for sweet and savoury dishes.

Kidney and Sausage Supper Dish

PREPARATION TIME: 20 minutes

MICROWAVE TIME: 18 minutes

SERVES: 4 people

450g (1lb) chipolata sausages
30ml (2 tblsp) oil
225g (8oz) lambs' kidneys, skinned,
   halved and cored
30ml (2 tblsp) tomato sauce
15ml (1 tblsp) Worcestershire sauce
Salt and freshly ground black pepper
   to taste
4 large, ripe tomatoes, skinned and
   chopped
225g (8oz) frozen peas
10ml (2 tsp) cornflour

Preheat the deep browning dish,
without the lid, for 4-7 minutes
according to size. Prick the sausages
and cut into 2.5cm (1 inch) pieces.
Add the oil and the pieces of
sausage to the preheated dish,
pressing the sausage against the
sides of the browning dish.

Microwave on Full Power for 2
minutes. Stir in the kidneys,
tomato sauce and Worcestershire
sauce. Cover with the lid and
microwave on Power 7, or on
Roast, for 5 minutes. Season with
salt and pepper and stir in the
tomatoes and peas. Mix the
cornflour to a smooth paste with
60ml (4 tblsp) water and stir in.
Microwave on Full Power for 2
minutes. Stir. Microwave on Full
Power for a further 2 minutes. Stir
and serve immediately.

Cowboy Supper

PREPARATION TIME: 15 minutes

MICROWAVE TIME: 13 minutes

SERVES: 4 people

425g (15.9oz) can baked beans
200g (7oz) can corned beef, chilled
Freshly ground black pepper to taste
½ beef stock cube, crumbled
50g (2oz) Cheddar cheese, cubed
1 French loaf

Empty the baked beans into a 1.75
litre (3 pint) casserole dish. Cover
with a lid. Microwave on Power 6
for 5 minutes. Gently stir in the
corned beef and season with
pepper. Add the stock cube. Cover
and microwave on Power 6 for 5
minutes. Add the cheese just
before serving.
To warm the bread, cut the bread
into pieces and arrange in a bread
basket, between absorbent paper
napkins. Microwave on Power 4, or
Simmer, for 3 minutes. Serve
immediately.

**Shish Kebabs with Yogurt
Sauce (top), Pasta Shells with
Cheese and Bacon (centre
right) and Kidney and Sausage
Supper Dish (bottom).**

Poached Eggs on Cheese on Toast

PREPARATION TIME: 10 minutes

MICROWAVE TIME: about 10 minutes

SERVES: 4 people

4 eggs
Salt and freshly ground black pepper to taste
Softened butter
4 slices toast
150g (5oz) grated cheese
Chopped chives

Put 15ml (1 tblsp) cold water into each of the 4 hollows of a microwave muffin pan or into 4 ramekin dishes. If using ramekins, arrange them in a ring on a dinner plate. Microwave on Full Power until the water boils. Carefully crack 1 egg into each hollow or dish. Prick each yolk once with a cocktail stick. Season with salt and pepper. Microwave on Simmer for about 4 minutes until the whites are just set. Leave aside. Butter the toast and top with the grated cheese. Microwave on Power 5, or Simmer, for about 4 minutes until melted. Slide the toasted cheese onto a serving dish and place an egg on top of each one. Sprinkle with chopped chives and serve immediately.

Cod and Prawn Supper Dish

PREPARATION TIME: 15 minutes

MICROWAVE TIME: 15½ minutes

SERVES: 4 people

4 x 75g (3oz) frozen cod steaks, thawed
50g (2oz) butter
Salt and freshly ground black pepper to taste
25g (1oz) flour
300ml (½ pint) milk
75g (3oz) grated Cheddar cheese
100g (4oz) peeled prawns
1 Recipe Crispy Topping (see recipe)

Garnish
Tomato wedges
Parsley

Arrange the fish steaks in a ring on a dinner plate. Divide half the butter into 4; put a small knob onto each fish steak. Season with salt and pepper and cover with cling film. Microwave on Full Power for 3½ minutes. Set aside. Microwave the remaining butter in a 1 litre (1¾ pint) jug for 1 minute on Full Power. Stir in the flour and then gradually stir in the milk; season to taste. Microwave on Full Power for 2 minutes. Beat well. Microwave on Full Power for a further 2 minutes. Beat in the cheese. Cut the fish into bite-size pieces and arrange in a suitable dish with the prawns. Pour the sauce evenly over the fish. Sprinkle with the crispy crumbs. Microwave on Power 4 for 7 minutes. Serve immediately, garnished with tomato and parsley.

Chicken with Ham

PREPARATION TIME: 15 minutes

MICROWAVE TIME: 13 minutes

SERVES: 4 people

350g (12oz) cooked chicken, roughly chopped
100g (4oz) cooked ham, chopped
60ml (4 tblsp) drained canned sweetcorn kernels with peppers
25g (1oz) butter
25g (1oz) flour
Salt and freshly ground black pepper to taste
300ml (½ pint) well flavoured chicken stock
75g (3oz) grated cheese
45ml (3 tblsp) single cream

Garnish
Sliced tomato and parsley

Arrange the chicken, ham and sweetcorn in a suitable dish. Melt the butter in a large jug for about 1 minute on Full Power. Stir in the flour and salt and pepper to taste. Stir in a little of the stock, blending it in well. Add the remaining stock. Microwave on Full Power for 2 minutes. Beat well with a balloon whisk. Microwave on Full Power for 2 minutes. Beat well. Beat in the cheese and the cream. Pour the sauce evenly over the meat. Microwave on Power 4, or Simmer, for about 8 minutes. Serve immediately, garnished with the tomato and parsley.

Sweet and Sour Pork

PREPARATION TIME: 25 minutes

MICROWAVE TIME: 29 minutes

SERVES: 4 people

15ml (1 tblsp) oil
½ red pepper, de-seeded and chopped
1 carrot, peeled and cut into strips
1 large onion, sliced
10cm (4 inch) cucumber, seeded and cut into strips
1 stem celery, chopped
450g (1lb) pork fillet, cubed
400g (14oz) can pineapple pieces in natural juice

**Fish Fingers (top right),
Poached Eggs on Cheese on
Toast (far left) and Chicken
with Ham (left).**

30ml (2 tblsp) soya sauce
10ml (2 tsp) tomato puree
15ml (1 tblsp) wine vinegar
Salt and freshly ground black pepper
    to taste
10ml (2 tsp) cornflour

Preheat the deep browning dish

without the lid for 4-7 minutes
according to size on Full Power. Put
the oil, pepper, carrot, onion,
cucumber and celery into the dish.
Stir well. Cover and Microwave on
Full Power for 4 minutes. Stir in all
remaining ingredients, apart from
the cornflour. Cover and

microwave on Full Power for 3
minutes and then on Power 4, or
Simmer, for 20 minutes. Cream the
cornflour with a little water and stir
into the pork mixture. Microwave
on Full Power for 2 minutes. Stir
and then serve immediately on a
bed of rice.

**Cowboy Supper (top) and
Sweet and Sour Pork (bottom).**

MICROWAVE COOKING
Fish Dishes

Plaice with Lemon

PREPARATION TIME: 12-15 minutes

MICROWAVE TIME: 9 minutes

SERVES: 4 people

4 plaice fillets (about 90g (3½oz) each), skinned
Salt and freshly ground black pepper to taste
Juice of ½ a lemon
30ml (2 tblsp) milk
100g (4oz) button mushrooms, sliced
25g (1oz) butter
120ml (4 fl oz) soured cream

Lay the plaice fillets out flat; season with salt and pepper and sprinkle with lemon juice. Roll up and secure with wooden cocktail sticks. Arrange the fillets close together in a dish and spoon over the milk; cover and microwave on Full Power for 5 minutes. Set aside. Put the mushrooms and butter into a small dish. Cover and microwave on Full Power for 2 minutes. Add the soured cream and stir in the juices from the fish. Microwave on Full Power for 2 minutes. Arrange the fish on a warmed serving dish. Pour over the sauce and serve immediately.

Curried Prawns with Chicken

PREPARATION TIME: 15 minutes

MICROWAVE TIME: about 22 minutes

SERVES: 4 people

50g (2oz) butter
1 medium onion, finely chopped
20ml (4 tsp) flour
20ml (4 tsp) mild curry powder
10ml (2 tsp) tomato puree
900ml (1½ pints) boiling chicken stock
15ml (1 tblsp) apple chutney
1 banana, thinly sliced
25g (1oz) raisins
Salt and freshly ground black pepper to taste
225g (8oz) peeled prawns
225g (8oz) cooked chicken, chopped
30ml (2 tblsp) lemon juice

Place the butter in a 2.25 litre (4 pint) casserole. Microwave on Full Power for 1-2 minutes. Stir in the onion. Microwave on Full Power for 1½ minutes. Stir in the flour and curry powder. Microwave on Full Power for 2 minutes. Stir in the tomato puree and gradually add the stock. Add the apple chutney, banana, raisins and salt and pepper to taste. Cover and microwave on Full Power for 12 minutes. Stir in the peeled prawns, chicken and lemon juice. Microwave on Full Power for 3-4 minutes.

Curried Prawns with Chicken (top left), Scampi Italienne (top right) and Plaice with Lemon (bottom).

Scampi Italienne

PREPARATION TIME: 10 minutes

MICROWAVE TIME: 10 minutes

SERVES: 4 people

½ red pepper, de-seeded and sliced
½ green pepper, de-seeded and sliced
50g (2oz) butter
1 small onion, finely chopped
1 clove garlic, crushed
150ml (¼ pint) dry white wine
15ml (1 tblsp) lemon juice
Salt and freshly ground black pepper to taste
450g (1lb) frozen shelled scampi, thawed

Garnish
Lemon butterflies
Savory

Put the red and green peppers, butter, onion and the garlic into a 1.75 litre (3 pint) casserole. Cover with the lid. Microwave on Full Power for 3 minutes. Stir in the white wine, lemon juice, salt and pepper to taste and the scampi. Cover and microwave on Full Power for 6-7 minutes, stirring once halfway through. Serve immediately, garnished with lemon butterflies and savory.

Special Fish Pie

PREPARATION TIME: 15 minutes

MICROWAVE TIME: 15 minutes

SERVES: 4 people

450g (1lb) young leeks, washed and cut into 4cm (1½ inch) lengths
4 large, firm tomatoes, skinned and sliced
10ml (2 tsp) mixed dried herbs
25g (1oz) butter
Salt and freshly ground black pepper to taste
350g (12oz) cod, skinned and filleted
30ml (2 tblsp) frozen sweetcorn kernels, thawed
50g (2oz) grated Cheddar cheese
15ml (1 tblsp) tomato sauce
450g (1lb) potatoes, peeled, cooked and mashed

Arrange the leeks and tomatoes in the base of a casserole dish; sprinkle with half the herbs. Dot the butter over the surface and season well with salt and pepper. Cover and microwave on Full Power for 5 minutes. Cut the fish into 2.5cm (1 inch) pieces. Arrange evenly over the vegetables and

season once again. Cover and microwave on Full Power for 7 minutes. Drain off excess liquid and add the sweetcorn. Add the cheese, tomato sauce and remaining herbs to the potato; beat well. Pile or pipe the potato on top of the fish and vegetables. Microwave, uncovered, on Full Power for about 3 minutes. Brown under a pre-heated grill, if desired, and serve immediately.

Mackerel with Apple Sauce

PREPARATION TIME: 30 minutes

MICROWAVE TIME: 15 minutes

SERVES: 4 people

4 fresh mackerel, heads and fins removed, and filleted (approx. 175g (6oz) per fish)
100g (4oz) fresh brown breadcrumbs
1 eating apple, peeled, cored and chopped
50g (2oz) shredded suet
5ml (1 tsp) lemon juice
10ml (2 tsp) finely chopped fresh parsley
1 onion, peeled and finely chopped
Salt and freshly ground black pepper to taste
1 egg, beaten
30ml (2 tblsp) apple juice

Sauce
750g (1½lb) cooking and eating apples (mixed), peeled, cored and sliced
10ml (2 tsp) lemon juice
10ml (2 tsp) caster sugar
15g (½oz) butter

Put the breadcrumbs, apple, suet, lemon juice, parsley and onion into a mixing bowl. Season to taste with salt and pepper. Mix with the beaten egg to bind. Divide the stuffing amongst the fish, pressing it well into each cavity. Make an incision with a sharp knife in the thickest side of each fish. Arrange the fish, nose to tail, in a shallow dish. Pour over the apple juice. Cover tightly with cling film and pierce. Microwave on Full Power for 8 minutes. Stand on one side while preparing the sauce. Put the apples into a 1.75 litre (3 pint) Pyrex mixing bowl with the lemon juice and sugar. Cover. Microwave on Full Power for 6-7 minutes. Allow to stand for 3 minutes. Beat together with the butter and the juices from the cooked fish. Serve immediately with the fish.

Trout with Almonds

PREPARATION TIME: 10 minutes

MICROWAVE TIME: about 19 minutes

SERVES: 4 people

4 rainbow trout, cleaned and gutted (approx 225g (8oz) per fish)
65g (2½oz) butter
1 clove garlic, crushed
Salt and freshly ground black pepper to taste
250ml (8 fl oz) double cream
50g (2oz) flaked almonds

Garnish
Fresh parsley

Use a very small amount of foil to mask the tail of each fish. Make 2 incisions in the thick side of each fish. Put 50g (2oz) of the butter into a suitable shallow dish and microwave on Full Power for 1½ minutes. Stir the garlic and salt and pepper into the butter. Arrange the fish, nose to tail, in the flavoured butter. Cover with cling film and pierce. Microwave on Full Power for 8 minutes. Turn each fish over once during cooking. Stand aside, covered. Put the almonds and the remaining butter into a soup bowl. Microwave on Full Power for 2 minutes. Stir. Microwave on Full Power for a further 2 minutes. Pour the cream over the fish, and microwave on Power 4 or, Simmer, for 5 minutes. Serve immediately sprinkled with the toasted nuts and garnished with parsley.

Devilled Herrings

PREPARATION TIME: 15-20 minutes

MICROWAVE TIME: 6-7 minutes

SERVES: 4 people

30ml (2 tblsp) dry mustard
15ml (1 tblsp) brown sugar
15ml (1 tblsp) malt vinegar
4 fresh herrings, about 225g (8oz) each
75ml (⅛ pint) white wine
1 medium onion, finely chopped
15ml (1 tblsp) finely chopped fresh parsley
Salt and freshly ground black pepper to taste
25g (1oz) butter

Blend together the mustard, sugar and vinegar. Cut the heads and the tails off the fish and remove the back-bones; flatten each fish.

Spread the mustard mixture inside the herrings and roll up. Secure with cocktail sticks. Arrange the fish in a suitable dish. Add the wine, parsley and salt and pepper to taste. Dot with butter. Cover tightly with cling film or a lid. Pierce if using cling film. Microwave on Full Power for 6-7 minutes. Stand for 3 minutes before serving.

Smoked Haddock with Scrambled Eggs

PREPARATION TIME: 5-10 minutes

MICROWAVE TIME: 11 minutes

SERVES: 3-4 people

450g (1lb) smoked haddock fillet
Salt and freshly ground black pepper to taste
150ml (¼ pint) milk
50g (2oz) butter
4 eggs
15ml (1 tblsp) finely chopped fresh parsley

Arrange the fish in a shallow container. Season with salt and pepper and add 30ml (2 tblsp) of the milk. Dot the fish with half the butter. Cover with cling film and pierce. Microwave on Full Power for 7 minutes. Set aside, covered. Make the scrambled egg: beat the eggs with the remaining milk in a 1.75 litre (3 pint) mixing bowl; season to taste and add the remaining butter. Microwave on Full Power for 2 minutes; beat well, using a balloon whisk. Microwave on Full Power for 2 minutes until light and fluffy. Carefully arrange the fish on a serving dish. Spoon the scrambled eggs either side of the fish. Sprinkle with the chopped parsley and serve immediately.

Special Fish Pie (top), Mackerel with Apple Sauce (centre) and Trout with Almonds (bottom).

Prawns Creole

PREPARATION TIME: 15 minutes
MICROWAVE TIME: 18 minutes
SERVES: 4 people

225g (8oz) long grain rice
600ml (1 pint) boiling chicken stock
2 medium size onions, chopped
½ red pepper, de-seeded and chopped
½ green pepper, de-seeded and
  chopped

225g (8oz) peeled prawns
425g (15oz) can pineapple segments
  in natural juice, drained
25g (1oz) seedless raisins
Salt and freshly ground black pepper
  to taste

Put the rice into a 1.75-2.25 litre (3-4 pint) mixing bowl. Pour on the boiling stock. Cover tightly with cling film and pierce once in the centre. Microwave on Full Power for 12 minutes. Set aside, covered with a clean tea towel. Put the onion and red and green pepper into a 1.2 litre (2 pint) mixing bowl. Cover with cling film and pierce. Microwave on Full Power for 3 minutes. Stir. Fork up the rice after 10 minutes standing time, and add the onions, peppers, prawns, pineapple, raisins and salt and pepper. Cover with cling film and pierce. Microwave on Full Power for 3 minutes to reheat. Serve immediately.

Smoked Haddock with
Scrambled Eggs (below left),
Prawns Creole (below) and
Devilled Herrings (below
right).

Meat Dishes

Sausagemeat Stuffing

PREPARATION TIME: 15 minutes
MICROWAVE TIME: 10 minutes
SERVES: 4 people

450g (1lb) pork sausagemeat
85g (3¼oz) packet parsley and
   thyme stuffing mix
15ml (1 tblsp) tomato sauce
5ml (1 tsp) made mustard
1 small onion, finely chopped
Salt and freshly ground black pepper
   to taste
150ml (¼ pint) boiling water

Put the sausagemeat into a 1.75 litre (3 pint) mixing bowl. Add all the remaining ingredients. Leave to stand for 3 minutes. Knead together until well mixed. Using dampened hands, form the sausagemeat mixture into 20 balls. Arrange on a large roasting rack, or in a ring on a large circular dish, on 2 sheets of absorbent kitchen paper. Microwave on Power 7, or Roast, for 10 minutes.

Savoury Mince with Dumplings

PREPARATION TIME: 20 minutes
MICROWAVE TIME: 23 minutes
SERVES: 4 people

2 rashers streaky bacon, de-rinded
   and chopped
1 medium onion, chopped
½ green pepper, de-seeded and
   chopped
750g (1½lb) raw minced beef or
   pork
1 beef stock cube, crumbled
2.5ml (½ tsp) mixed dried herbs
150ml (¼ pint) water
5ml (1 tsp) chive mustard
Salt and freshly ground black pepper
   to taste
425g (15.9oz) can butter beans,
   drained

Dumplings
100g (4oz) self-raising flour
50g (2oz) suet
2.5ml (½ tsp) dried tarragon

Put the bacon, onion and pepper into a soup bowl. Cover with cling film and pierce. Microwave on Full Power for 2 minutes. Put the mince into a 1.75 litre (3 pint) casserole dish. Microwave on Full Power for 4 minutes. Break down with a fork and stir in the onion mixture, stock cube, herbs, water and mustard. Season well with salt and pepper. Microwave on Power 6, or Roast, for 12 minutes. Stir in the butter beans. Set aside. To prepare the dumplings: mix together the flour, suet and tarragon. Bind with sufficient cold water to make an elastic dough. Divide into 6 dumplings and arrange on top of the mince. Cover with a lid and microwave on Power 7 for 4-5 minutes. Stand for 3 minutes before serving.

Mixed Meat Loaf

PREPARATION TIME: 30 minutes
MICROWAVE TIME: 27 minutes
SERVES: 6-8 people

1 clove garlic
175g (6oz) lean streaky bacon, de-
   rinded
450g (1lb) raw minced beef
225g (8oz) raw minced pork
175g (6oz) lambs' liver, finely
   chopped
175g (6oz) back bacon, de-rinded
   and finely chopped
50g (2oz) shredded suet
50g (2oz) fresh brown breadcrumbs
2.5ml (½ tsp) dried oregano
2.5ml (½ tsp) mixed dried herbs
Salt and freshly ground black pepper
   to taste
45ml (3 tblsp) sherry
1 egg, beaten

Glaze
30ml (2 tblsp) apricot jam or
   marmalade, sieved
5ml (1 tsp) French mustard
2.5ml (½ tsp) Bovril

Rub a 1.75 litre (3 pint) plastic bread baker with the clove of garlic. Lay the streaky bacon in the bread baker to line the base and the sides. In a large mixing bowl, mix the minced beef with the pork, liver, back bacon, suet, breadcrumbs and herbs. Season to taste. Beat together the sherry and the egg; add to the mixture and bind together. Transfer to the prepared bread baker. Smooth the top. Cover and microwave on Power 6, or Roast, for 27 minutes. Turn the dish ½ a turn twice during this time. Allow to stand for 10 minutes. Pour off the excess fat and carefully unmould the loaf. Mix all ingredients together for the glaze and brush over the top and sides of the meat loaf. Delicious hot or cold.

Cheesey Beef Cobbler

PREPARATION TIME: 30 minutes
MICROWAVE TIME: 20 minutes
SERVES: 4 people

450g (1lb) raw minced beef
1 onion, chopped
225g (8oz) can tomatoes, chopped
1 beef stock cube, crumbled
15ml (1 tblsp) bottled brown sauce
Celery salt and freshly ground black
   pepper to taste
30ml (2 tblsp) frozen peas

Scone Topping
225g (8oz) self-raising flour, sieved
   with 2.5ml (½ tsp) baking powder
50g (2oz) margarine or butter, chilled
50g (2oz) grated Cheddar cheese
2.5ml (½ tsp) mixed dried herbs
1 egg, mixed with 90ml (6 tblsp)
   milk
5ml (1 tsp) Bovril

Put the minced meat and onion into an 18cm (7 inch) souffle dish. Cover and microwave on Full Power for 4 minutes. Stir well with a fork. Stir in the tomatoes, stock cube, brown sauce and celery salt and pepper. Cover and microwave on Power 7, or Roast, for 10 minutes. Stir in the peas and set aside. Put the flour and baking powder into a 1.75 litre (3 pint) mixing bowl. Rub in the margarine or butter. Mix in the cheese and herbs. Add the beaten egg and milk and mix to a soft dough. Knead lightly. Roll the dough out to a thickness of 1cm (½ inch). Using a 5cm (2 inch) pastry cutter, cut the dough into scones. Arrange the scones on top of the mince. Cook, uncovered, on Full Power for 6 minutes. Serve immediately.

Note: to improve the colour of the scones mix the Bovril with a little water and use to brush the scones prior to cooking.

Lamb Curry

PREPARATION TIME: 20 minutes
MICROWAVE TIME: about
                    45 minutes
SERVES: 4 people

2 carrots, peeled and chopped
1 medium onion, chopped
25g (1oz) butter
25g (1oz) plain flour
15-20ml (3-4 tsp) mild curry powder
450g (1lb) lamb fillet, cubed
450ml (¾ pint) boiling chicken stock
15ml (1 tblsp) desiccated coconut
25g (1oz) sultanas
1 medium sized eating apple, peeled,
   cored and chopped
1 peach, peeled, stoned and roughly
   chopped
15ml (1 tblsp) tomato puree
30ml (2 tblsp) lemon juice
Salt and freshly ground black pepper
   to taste

Preheat a large browning dish, without the lid, for 3 minutes on Full Power. Put the carrots, onion and butter into the preheated dish. Microwave on Full Power for 2 minutes, covered. Stir in the flour, curry powder and meat. Microwave on Full Power for 4 minutes. Gradually add the stock, stirring all the time. Stir in the coconut, sultanas, apple, peach, tomato puree, lemon juice and seasoning to taste. Cover and

Lamb Curry (top left), Savoury Mince with Dumplings (top right) and Mixed Meat Loaf (bottom).

microwave on Full Power for 7 minutes. Stir. Microwave on Power 4, Simmer or Defrost, for 30-35 minutes. Stir twice during this time. Serve immediately.

Pasta with Pork and Liver

PREPARATION TIME: 15 minutes
MICROWAVE TIME: 25 minutes
SERVES: 4 people

30ml (2 tblsp) oil
1 medium onion, sliced
350g (12oz) raw minced pork
100g (4oz) chicken livers, minced
100g (4oz) mushrooms, chopped
225g (8oz) can tomatoes, chopped
45ml (3 tblsp) sherry
Salt and freshly ground black pepper to taste
1 beef stock cube, crumbled

175g (6oz) dried pasta shells
Chopped fresh parsley

Heat the browning dish, without the lid, for 4-6 minutes on Full Power, according to size. Put half the oil, the onion and minced meats into the preheated dish. Stir well. Microwave on Full Power for 4 minutes. Stir in all the remaining ingredients, apart from the pasta and the parsley. Cover with the lid and microwave on Full Power for 3 minutes. Stir. Microwave, covered, on Power 5, or Simmer, for 10 minutes. Allow to stand whilst preparing the pasta. To cook the pasta, place the remaining oil and the pasta into a 2.25-2.75 litre (4-5 pint) bowl. Add 1.75 litres (3 pints) water and 2.5ml (½ tsp) salt to the pasta. Cover and microwave on Full Power for 8 minutes. Allow to stand for 5 minutes. Drain the pasta and arrange on a serving dish. Spoon the meat sauce evenly over the pasta, and garnish with chopped parsley. Serve immediately.

Pasta with Pork and Liver (far left), Cheesey Beef Cobbler (below) and Sausagemeat Stuffing (below right).

Chicken Breasts in Garlic Cream Sauce

PREPARATION TIME: 10 minutes

MICROWAVE TIME: 17 minutes

SERVES: 4 people

50g (2oz) butter
1 clove garlic, crushed
1 medium onion, sliced
2 rashers bacon, de-rinded and chopped
50g (2oz) button mushrooms, sliced
2.5ml (½ tsp) dried basil
Salt and freshly ground black pepper to taste
4 chicken breasts, skinned and boned (about 150g (5oz) each)
300ml (½ pint) double cream

Garnish
Savory
Toasted flaked almonds

Melt the butter in a 1.75 litre (3 pint) casserole dish for 1-2 minutes on Full Power. Stir in the garlic, onion, bacon, mushrooms, basil and salt and pepper to taste. Cover and microwave on Full Power for 2 minutes. Arrange the chicken breasts on top of the vegetables. Cover and microwave on Power 7, or Roast, for 10 minutes. Season the cream and pour evenly over the top to coat. Microwave on Roast, or Power 7, for 3 minutes. Garnish with savory and almonds. Serve immediately.

Chicken Casserole

PREPARATION TIME: 15 minutes

MICROWAVE TIME: about 40 minutes

SERVES: 4 people

4 chicken portions, skinned (about 225g (8oz) each)
25g (1oz) butter
1 onion, finely chopped
2 stems celery, chopped
2 carrots, chopped
30ml (2 tblsp) drained canned sweetcorn kernels
10ml (2 tsp) cornflour
300ml (½ pint) chicken stock
Salt and paprika to taste

Put the butter into a 2.25 litre (4 pint) casserole dish. Microwave on Full Power for 1 minute. Stir in the onion, celery and carrots. Cover with a lid and microwave on Full Power for 3 minutes. Pour the stock into the casserole, and add salt to taste. Arrange the chicken pieces

on top of the vegetables, keeping the thickest part to the outside of the dish. Sprinkle each chicken piece with a little paprika. Microwave, covered, on Full Power for 4 minutes. Stir. Microwave on Power 4, Simmer or Defrost, for a further 30 minutes. Using a draining spoon, transfer the chicken to a warmed serving dish. Cover with a piece of foil and set aside. Cream the cornflour with a little water and stir into the casserole dish. Microwave on Full Power for 2-3 minutes, until boiling and thickened. Stir in the sweetcorn. Serve the chicken pieces with the vegetable sauce spooned over the top.

Sausage Suet Pudding

PREPARATION TIME: 30 minutes

MICROWAVE TIME: 21 minutes

SERVES: 4 people

Filling
225g (8oz) pork sausages, cut into 2.5cm (1 inch) pieces
225g (8oz) chicken livers, roughly chopped
25g (1oz) seasoned flour
15ml (1 tblsp) oil
1 medium onion, chopped
½ green pepper, de-seeded and chopped
300ml (½ pint) well flavoured boiling stock
Salt and freshly ground black pepper to taste

Suet Pastry
225g (8oz) self-raising flour
2.5ml (½ tsp) salt
5ml (1 tsp) baking powder
100g (4oz) finely grated (or shredded) suet
150ml (¼ pint) water

Toss the sausages and chicken livers in the seasoned flour. Put the oil into a 1.75 litre (3 pint) mixing bowl. Microwave on Full Power for 2 minutes. Stir in the onion and green pepper. Microwave on Full Power for 2 minutes. Stir the chicken livers and sausage into the onion. Cover and microwave on Power 8, or Roast, for 5 minutes. Carefully stir in the boiling stock and salt and pepper to taste. Microwave on Full Power for 2-3 minutes, until thickened. Stir and set aside while preparing the pastry. Sieve the flour, salt and baking powder into a bowl. Stir in the suet and mix to a soft dough with the water. Knead lightly. Roll out ⅔ of

the pastry and use to line a greased 900ml (1½ pint) boilable plastic pudding basin. Roll the remaining pastry into a circle. Fill the pastry-lined basin with the filling mixture. Dampen the pastry rim with cold water and top with the circle of pastry. Seal edges. Cut a small slit in the top to allow the steam to escape. Cover loosely with absorbent kitchen paper or cling film. Microwave on Power 7, or Roast, for 9 minutes. Stand for 5 minutes before serving.

Herby Roast Chicken

PREPARATION TIME: about 35 minutes

MICROWAVE TIME: about 36 minutes

SERVES: 6 people

75g (3oz) fresh brown breadcrumbs
50g (2oz) shredded suet
5ml (1 tsp) finely chopped fresh parsley
5ml (1 tsp) finely chopped fresh tarragon
1 eating apple, peeled, cored and chopped
5ml (1 tsp) lemon juice
Salt and freshly ground black pepper to taste
1 small onion, finely chopped
1 egg, beaten
1¾kg (4lb) chicken, giblets removed

Coating
50g (2oz) butter
10ml (2 tsp) chicken seasoning
5ml (1 tsp) paprika
2.5ml (½ tsp) mixed dried herbs

Garnish
Watercress

To make the stuffing, combine the breadcrumbs, suet, parsley, tarragon, apple, lemon juice and seasoning to taste. Put the onion into a small bowl and microwave on Full Power for 1 minute. Add the onion to the other ingredients. Bind together with the beaten egg.

**Chicken Casserole (top right),
Herby Roast Chicken (top left),
Chicken Breasts in Garlic
Cream Sauce (bottom right)
and Sausage Suet Pudding
(bottom left).**

Roasting Meats

TYPE OF MEAT	MICROWAVE POWER LEVEL	TIME PER 450g (1lb)	INTERNAL TEMPERATURE AFTER MICROWAVING	INTERNAL TEMPERATURE AFTER STANDING
Chops 1. Lamb	Power 7 or Roast Use pre-heated browning dish)	7-8 minutes	Turn the chops over once during cooking time.	
2. Pork	Power 7 or Roast (Use pre-heated browning dish)	9-10 minutes	Allow to stand for 5-10 minutes before serving.	
Beef (Boned & Rolled)	Power 7 or Roast	5-6 minutes *Rare* 7-8 minutes *Medium* 8-10 minutes *Well done*	57°C/130°F 65°C/150°F 70°C/160°F	62°C/140°F 70°C/160°F 78°C/170°F
Beef on the Bone	Power 7 or Roast	5 minutes *Rare* 6 minutes *Medium* 8 minutes *Well done*	57°C/130°F 65°C/150°F 70°C/160°F	62°C/140°F 70°C/160°F 78°C/170°F
Poultry (Unboned)	Full Power	7 minutes	85°C/185°F	94°C/190°F
Pork	Power 7 or Roast	10-11 minutes	82°C/180°F	85°C/185°F
Lamb	Power 7 or Roast	8-9 minutes	78°C/170°F	82°C/180°F

1. Have joints boned and rolled for best results.
2. Use a <u>microwave</u> meat thermostat to gauge when the meat should be removed from the microwave oven.
3. Any joint which is 1½kg (3lbs) or over will brown in the microwave oven, to increase the colouring, use a browning agent before cooking, or flash the meat under a pre-heated hot grill after standing time.
4. Turn the joint over once during the cooking time.
5. Use a microwave roasting rack, or an upturned saucer, placed in a suitable dish so as to allow the juices to drain.

Stuff the neck end of the bird with the stuffing. Truss. Weigh the stuffed bird and calculate the cooking time accordingly (7 minutes per 450g (1lb)). Use small amounts of foil to mask the wings and the stuffed area, to prevent overcooking. Arrange the chicken in a suitable roasting dish, on two upturned saucers, or on a microwave roasting rack. Melt the butter in the microwave for 1 minute on Full Power. Brush the butter all over the chicken. Combine the chicken seasoning, paprika and herbs together and sprinkle all over the chicken. Cover with a split roasta bag. Microwave on Full Power for the calculated time. Allow the chicken to stand, covered with a tent of foil, before serving. Garnish with watercress.

Devilled Pork Chops

PREPARATION TIME: 10 minutes
MICROWAVE TIME: 16 minutes
SERVES: 4 people

30ml (2 tblsp) oil
4 chump pork chops (about 175g (6oz) each)
100g (4oz) butter
15ml (1 tblsp) dry mustard
30ml (2 tblsp) fresh breadcrumbs
15ml (1 tblsp) soya sauce
10ml (2 tsp) Worcestershire sauce
15ml (1 tblsp) tomato chutney
Salt and paprika to taste

Preheat the browning dish (without the lid) for 4-7 minutes, according to size, on Full Power. Put the oil into the heated dish and microwave on Full Power for 1 minute. Put the 4 chops into the dish, pressing them down well. Microwave on Full Power for 2 minutes. Turn the chops over and microwave on Power 7, or Roast, for 10 minutes. Combine all the remaining ingredients in a mixing bowl. Spread over the partly cooked chops. Microwave on Power 7, or Roast, for a further 3 minutes.

Beef or Pork Burgers

PREPARATION TIME: 20 minutes
MICROWAVE TIME: 6-7 minutes
SERVES: 4 people

450g (1lb) raw minced beef or pork
1 small onion, finely chopped
50g (2oz) fresh breadcrumbs
1 stock cube, crumbled
2.5ml (½ tsp) dried parsley
Salt and freshly ground black pepper to taste
15ml (1 tblsp) tomato sauce
5ml (1 tsp) made mustard
1 egg, beaten
4 baps

Mix the mince, onion and breadcrumbs together. Add the stock cube and all the other ingredients, apart from the baps.

Mix well. Divide the mixture into 4 and form into burgers. Arrange on a microwave roasting rack, or other suitable dish, in a ring. Microwave on Full Power for 6-7 minutes, turning each burger over once halfway through cooking time. Split the baps and fill with the burgers.

Glazed Leg of Lamb

PREPARATION TIME: 25 minutes
MICROWAVE TIME: about 50 minutes
SERVES: 6 people

1¾kg (4lb) leg of lamb
2-3 cloves peeled garlic, cut into thin strips
Salt and freshly ground black pepper to taste
30ml (2 tblsp) tomato sauce
5ml (1 tsp) dry mustard
5ml (1 tsp) brown sugar
2.5ml (½ tsp) mixed dried herbs

Devilled Pork Chops (top right), Beef or Pork Burgers (centre left) and Glazed Leg of Lamb (bottom).

Make incisions all over the joint with a sharp knife; push a strip of garlic into each one. Season with salt and pepper. Combine the tomato sauce, mustard, brown sugar and herbs, and spread evenly over the joint. Arrange the joint on a roasting rack. Cover with a roasta bag. Microwave for 12 minutes on Full Power. Turn the joint over and microwave on Power 4, or Simmer, for 30-40 minutes or until the meat thermometer registers 70°C (160°F). Remove the joint. Cover with a tent of foil and allow to stand for 15 minutes before serving.

Rolled Roast Rib of Beef

| **PREPARATION TIME:** 18 minutes |
| **MICROWAVE TIME:** 30 minutes |
| **SERVES:** 6-8 people |

1¾kg (4lb) piece rib of beef, boned and rolled
Salt and freshly ground black pepper to taste
15ml (1 tblsp) tomato sauce
5ml (1 tsp) soft brown sugar

Stand the joint on the microwave roasting rack, in a suitable dish, keeping the fat side of the meat underneath. Season with salt and pepper. Microwave for 7 minutes, on Full Power. Turn the joint over and microwave on Roast, or Power 7, for 21 minutes. Remove from the microwave. Cover loosely with a tent of foil and allow to stand for 15 minutes. Spread the tomato sauce and brown sugar all over the fat. Microwave on Full Power for 2 minutes. (Check temperatures with a microwave thermometer. See chart).

Barbecue Lamb Chops

| **PREPARATION TIME:** 10 minutes, plus marinating time |
| **MICROWAVE TIME:** 16 minutes |
| **SERVES:** 6 people |

Marinade
30ml (2 tblsp) wine vinegar
60ml (4 tblsp) pure orange juice
15ml (1 tblsp) tomato sauce
5ml (1 tsp) soft brown sugar
5ml (1 tsp) French mustard
2.5ml (½ tsp) dried tarragon
5ml (1 tsp) mild curry powder
Salt and freshly ground black pepper to taste
5ml (1 tsp) oil
6 chump chops, each about 150g (5oz)

Rolled Roast Rib of Beef (top) and Barbecue Lamb Chops (left).

Blend all the ingredients together for the marinade, apart from the oil. Lay the chops in a large shallow dish and pour over the marinade. Cover and chill for at least two hours. Turn the chops over in the marinade, once or twice. Preheat a large browning dish for 7 minutes on Full Power. Put the oil and the drained chops into the dish, pressing the chops against the hot dish. Microwave, uncovered, on Full Power for 5 minutes. Turn the chops over. Microwave on Roast, or Power 7, for 3-4 minutes. Serve immediately.

Shepherd's Pie

| **PREPARATION TIME:** 30 minutes |
| **MICROWAVE TIME:** 38 minutes |
| **SERVES:** 4 people |

15ml (1 tblsp) cooking oil
2 courgettes, thinly sliced
1 small onion, finely chopped
450g (1lb) raw lean minced beef
15ml (1 tblsp) plain flour
Salt and freshly ground black pepper to taste
15ml (1 tblsp) tomato puree
60ml (4 tblsp) water
1 beef stock cube, crumbled
900g (2lb) potatoes
90ml (6 tblsp) milk
1 egg
15g (½oz) butter
30ml (2 tblsp) Red Leicester cheese, grated

Preheat a small browning dish on Full Power for 3½ minutes (if using a large browning dish preheat on Full Power for 5 minutes). Add the oil, courgettes and onion, and stir. Cover with a lid and microwave on Full Power for 2 minutes. Add the meat and microwave on Full Power for 3 minutes, stirring once. Add the flour, salt and pepper to taste, tomato puree, water and stock cube. Stir well and cover. Microwave on Power 7, or Roast, for 12 minutes, stirring after the first 4 minutes. Remove from the microwave oven and leave to stand. Meanwhile prepare the potatoes. Peel and dice the potatoes. Put them into a roasta bag with 60ml (4 tblsp) of the milk. Put the bag into a 1.75 litre (3 pint) bowl. Secure with a rubber band and pierce once at the base. Microwave on Full Power for 17 minutes (turn the bag over once during this time). Stand, covered, for 5 minutes. Drain the potatoes and mash them together with the egg, remaining milk and the butter. Pile the potato onto the meat mixture and sprinkle with the cheese. Microwave on Full Power for 3-4 minutes, until the cheese has melted and the pie is very hot. To speed this recipe up you can use reconstituted powdered potato.

Pork with Leeks and Grapes

PREPARATION TIME: 20 minutes

MICROWAVE TIME: 53 minutes

SERVES: 4-5 people

30ml (2 tblsp) oil
1 carrot, peeled and sliced
1 stick celery, chopped
225g (8oz) potato, peeled and diced
450g (1lb) young leeks, washed and sliced
750g (1½lb) boned shoulder of pork, cut into 2.5cm (1 inch) cubes
25g (1oz) plain flour
Salt and freshly ground black pepper to taste
½ pint well flavoured chicken stock
100g (4oz) seedless white grapes

Preheat the browning dish for 4 or 7 minutes, according to size. Add the oil, carrot, celery, potato and leeks to the heated dish. Cover with the lid. Microwave on Full Power for 4 minutes. Using a perforated spoon, transfer the vegetables to a dinner plate. Return the browning dish to the microwave, without the lid, for 1 minute on Full Power. Toss the meat in the flour and seasoning; stir into the dish, turning so that all sides come in contact with the hot skillet. Microwave, uncovered, for 3 minutes on Full Power. Stir in the drained vegetables, stock and extra seasoning to taste. Cover with the lid. Microwave, covered, on Power 5, or Simmer, for 40 minutes. Stir in the grapes and serve after a standing time of 5 minutes.

Turkey Fricassee

PREPARATION TIME: 20 minutes

MICROWAVE TIME: 12 minutes

SERVES: 4 people

25g (1oz) butter
25g (1oz) plain flour
300ml (½ pint) chicken or turkey stock
Salt and freshly ground black pepper to taste
100g (4oz) button mushrooms, sliced
½ red pepper, de-seeded and chopped

4 rashers streaky bacon, de-rinded and chopped
1 medium onion, chopped
350g (12oz) cooked turkey, chopped
100g (4oz) stuffed olives, halved
30ml (2 tblsp) single cream
1 egg yolk

To make the sauce: melt the butter in a 1 litre (1¾ pint) jug for 1 minute on Full Power. Stir in the flour to make a smooth paste. Gradually stir in the stock, mixing well. Season with salt and pepper. Microwave on Full Power for 2 minutes. Beat well with a balloon whisk. Microwave on Full Power for 2 minutes. Beat in the sliced mushrooms. Put the red pepper, bacon and onion into a 1.2 litre (2 pint) mixing bowl. Cover and microwave on Full Power for 2 minutes. Stir. Arrange the cooked turkey in a serving dish. Add the pepper mixture and most of the halved olives (reserve a few for decoration). Beat the cream and egg yolk into the sauce. Pour the sauce evenly over the vegetables and turkey. Cover with cling film and pierce. Microwave on Power 5 for 5 minutes. Allow to stand for 5 minutes before serving. Garnish with the remaining olives.

Stewed Steak with Garlic

PREPARATION TIME: 25 minutes

MICROWAVE TIME: about 1 hour 40 minutes

SERVES: 4 people

750g (1½lb) chuck steak, cubed
15ml (1 tblsp) seasoned flour
2 leeks, washed and sliced
1 medium onion, sliced
1 carrot, peeled and chopped
2 cloves garlic, crushed
30ml (2 tblsp) cooking oil
2 rashers streaky bacon, de-rinded and chopped
425g (15oz) can tomatoes, chopped
15ml (1 tblsp) tomato puree
Salt and freshly ground black pepper to taste
300ml (½ pint) well flavoured beef stock
2.5ml (½ tsp) dried parsley

Toss the meat in the seasoned flour. Put the leeks, onions, carrot and the garlic into a 1.2 litre (2 pint) dish. Cover and microwave on Full Power for 3 minutes. Stir and set aside. Preheat the large browning dish, without the lid, for

This page: Pork with Leeks and Grapes.

Facing page: Stewed Steak with Garlic (top), Shepherd's Pie (centre right) and Turkey Fricassee (bottom).

7 minutes on Full Power. Pour the oil into the dish and quickly stir in the bacon and the meat. Press the meat against the sides of the dish. Cover and microwave on Full Power for 4 minutes. Stir, and add all the remaining ingredients. Cover. Microwave on Full Power for 4 minutes, and then on Power 4, or Simmer, for 70 minutes. Stir once after the first 30 minutes. Stir, and allow to stand for 10 minutes before serving.

Sauces and Preserves

Basic Savoury White Sauce

PREPARATION TIME: 5 minutes
MICROWAVE TIME: 5 minutes
MAKES: 300ml (½ pint)

25g (1oz) butter
25g (1oz) plain flour
300ml (½ pint) milk or chicken stock
Salt and freshly ground black pepper
   to taste

Melt the butter in a 1 litre (1¾ pint) jug. Microwave on Full Power for 1 minute until very hot. Stir in the flour to form a roux. Gradually stir in all the milk or stock. Season to taste with salt and pepper. Microwave on Full Power for 2 minutes. Beat well with a balloon whisk. Microwave on Full Power for 2 minutes. Beat with a balloon whisk and serve.

Variations on Basic White Sauce
Cheese Sauce
Beat 50g (2oz) finely grated cheese and 5ml (1 tsp) made mustard into

Mushroom Sauce (above right), Basic Savoury White Sauce (far right) and Cheese Sauce (right).

the finished sauce. The heat of the sauce will melt the cheese.

Mushroom Sauce
Beat 50g (2oz) finely chopped mushrooms into the prepared

sauce. The heat of the sauce will cook the mushrooms.

Egg Sauce
Chop 1 hard-boiled egg (cooked conventionally). Beat into the prepared sauce.

Parsley Sauce
Beat 15ml (1 tblsp) chopped fresh parsley into the finished sauce.

Onion Sauce
Finely chop 1 medium sized peeled onion and put it into a bowl. Cover with cling film and pierce. Microwave on Full Power for 1-1½ minutes to soften. Beat the softened onion into the prepared sauce (the onion should be softened before the sauce is made).

Cranberry Sauce

PREPARATION TIME: 10 minutes
MICROWAVE TIME: 4 minutes
MAKES: about 400ml (⅔ pint)

1 orange
225g (8oz) frozen cranberries, defrosted
100g (4oz) granulated sugar

Finely grate the rind from the orange into a 1.2 litre (2 pint) mixing bowl. Squeeze the juice from the orange and make up to 150ml (¼ pint) with cold water. Put the cranberries, sugar, orange juice and water into the mixing bowl. Microwave on Full Power for 4 minutes. Stir once, halfway through cooking time. Stir and serve.

Custard Sauce

PREPARATION TIME: 5 minutes

MICROWAVE TIME: 4 minutes

MAKES: 600ml (1 pint)

30ml (2 tblsp) custard powder
50g (2oz) granulated sugar
600ml (1 pint) milk
30ml (2 tblsp) single cream

Put the custard powder and the sugar into a 1.2 litre (2 pint) mixing bowl. Mix to a smooth cream with a little of the milk. Put the remaining milk into a 1 litre (1¾ pint) jug and microwave on Full Power for 2 minutes. Pour the hot milk onto the blended custard powder, stirring well. Pour the custard back into the jug and microwave on Full Power for 2 minutes. Beat well with a balloon whisk. Allow to cool slightly before beating in the cream. Serve hot or cold.

Chocolate Sauce

PREPARATION TIME: 5 minutes

MICROWAVE TIME: 5 minutes

MAKES: about 300ml (½ pint)

25g (1oz) butter
15ml (1 tblsp) cocoa powder
300ml (½ pint) milk
15ml (1 tblsp) golden syrup

Melt the butter in a 1 litre (1¾ pint) jug for 1 minute on Full Power. Stir in the cocoa, mixing well. Gradually add the milk, stirring. Microwave on Full Power for 2 minutes. Beat well with a balloon whisk. Microwave on Full Power for 2 minutes. beat in the golden syrup. Serve immediately.

Beefy Tomato Sauce

PREPARATION TIME: 10 minutes

COOKING TIME: 20 minutes

MAKES: about 600ml (1 pint)

50g (2oz) butter
2 medium sized onions, finely
    chopped
50g (2oz) plain flour
750ml (1¼ pint) hot beef stock
30ml (2 tblsp) tomato puree
15ml (1 tblsp) vinegar
5ml (1 tsp) French mustard
5ml (1 tsp) soft brown sugar
5ml (1 tsp) Worcestershire sauce

15ml (1 tblsp) tomato sauce
Salt and freshly ground black pepper
    to taste

Melt the butter in a really large jug or mixing bowl for 1-2 minutes on Full Power. Stir in the onion and microwave, uncovered, for 3 minutes on Full Power. Stir in the flour, mixing well. Gradually add the stock, stirring continuously. Mix the puree with the vinegar and add to the sauce together with the French mustard, sugar, Worcestershire sauce, tomato sauce and salt and pepper to taste. Microwave on Full Power for 10 minutes. Beat well twice during this time. Turn on to Power 4, or Simmer, and microwave for a further 5 minutes. Beat well. Serve with meat balls, meat loaf, etc.

St Clement's Sauce

PREPARATION TIME: 10 minutes

MICROWAVE TIME: 3½ minutes

MAKES: about 200ml (⅓ pint)

45ml (3 tblsp) fine cut marmalade
Juice of 1 lemon
Juice of 1 orange
5ml (1 tsp) arrowroot

Put the marmalade and lemon and orange juices into a 1 litre (1¾ pint) jug. Microwave on Full Power for 1½ minutes. Stir well. Microwave on Full Power for 1 minute. Blend the arrowroot to a smooth paste with a little cold water. Stir into the jug. Microwave on Full Power for 30 seconds. Stir. Microwave on Full Power for a further 30 seconds. Stir and serve.

Plum Jam

PREPARATION TIME: 20 minutes

MICROWAVE TIME: 1 hour

MAKES: 1¼kg (2½lb)

Juice of 1 orange
900g (2lb) plums, halved and stoned
900g (2lb) granulated sugar

Put the juice and the plums into a large microwave container. Cover and microwave on Full Power for 10 minutes. Stir in the sugar to dissolve. Cover and microwave on Power 6 for about 40 minutes, or until setting point is reached. Test for setting. Pot and label in the usual way.

Strawberry Jam

PREPARATION TIME: 20 minutes,
    plus chilling
    overnight

COOKING TIME: 31 minutes

MAKES: about 1¼kg (2½lb)

900g (2lb) freshly picked
    strawberries, hulled
900g (2lb) granulated sugar

Place the hulled strawberries in a 2.75 litre (5 pint) microwave dish. Add the sugar and stir. Cover and leave overnight in the refrigerator. Stir well. Cover and microwave on Full Power for 7 minutes, until boiling point is reached. Microwave on Power 5, or Simmer, for 24 minutes, until setting point is reached. Test for setting. Pot and label in the usual way.

Green Tomato Chutney

PREPARATION TIME: 40 minutes

MICROWAVE TIME: 1¾-2 hours

MAKES: about 2¾kg (6lbs)

2 medium onions, finely chopped
350ml (12 fl oz) malt vinegar
250ml (8 fl oz) wine vinegar
1 small stem celery, chopped
2.5ml (½ tsp) mustard seed
1¾kg (4lb) green tomatoes, washed
    and chopped
2 large Bramley cooking apples,
    peeled, cored and chopped
175g (6oz) seedless raisins
1 clove garlic, crushed
4 peppercorns, 2 cloves and 2 chillies
    (tied in muslin)
450g (1lb) soft brown sugar
Salt and freshly ground black pepper
    to taste

Put the onions into a 750g (1½lb) pudding basin. Microwave on Full Power for 2 minutes. Put half the vinegar, the celery, mustard seed, tomatoes, apples, raisins, garlic and onions into a very large bowl.

Parsley Sauce (top), Cranberry Sauce (centre left), Onion Sauce (centre right) and Egg Sauce (bottom).

Crush the muslin bag with a rolling pin and add to the bowl. Stir. Cover and microwave on Full Power for 10 minutes. Stir in the sugar to dissolve. Add the remaining vinegar and season with salt and pepper to taste. Microwave on Full Power for 20-30 minutes. Remove the lid and stir well.

Microwave on Full Power, uncovered, for about 75 minutes until the mixture reduces and thickens. Stir twice during this time. Ladle into clean jam jars. Seal and label when cool. The chutney should be kept in a cool dark place for 2 months to mature, before using.

This page: Strawberry Jam (top), Plum Jam (centre right) and Green Tomato Chutney (bottom).

Facing page: Chocolate Sauce (top), St Clement's Sauce (centre left), Beefy Tomato Sauce (centre right) and Custard Sauce (bottom).

Sweets

Pear Upside Down Pudding

PREPARATION TIME: 25 minutes

MICROWAVE TIME: 9 minutes

SERVES: 6 people

Oil and caster sugar
45ml (3 tblsp) golden syrup
425g (15oz) can pear halves, drained
5 glace cherries, halved and rinsed
Recipe quantity Victoria Sandwich
mixture (see recipe)

Grease an 18cm (7 inch) souffle dish with oil and sprinkle the base and sides lightly with caster sugar. Spread the golden syrup over the bottom. Make an attractive pattern over the base with the pears and the glace cherries. Spoon the Victoria Sandwich mixture into the prepared dish. Smooth the top. Microwave on Full Power for 9 minutes. Allow to stand for 7 minutes in the dish before carefully turning out. Serve warm with custard or cream.

Apple and Blackcurrant Flan

PREPARATION TIME: 30 minutes

MICROWAVE TIME: 37 minutes

SERVES: 6 people

Base
150g (5oz) plain flour
150g (5oz) wholemeal flour
Pinch of salt
50g (2oz) margarine
50g (2oz) lard
1 egg and 30ml (2 tblsp) cold water,
beaten   together

Filling
450g (1lb) Bramley cooking apples,
   peeled, cored and sliced
225g (8oz) blackcurrants
50g (2oz) caster sugar
75g (3oz) ground almonds
25g (1oz) butter
2 egg yolks

Meringue
3 egg whites
175g (6oz) caster sugar
Glace cherries and angelica for
   decoration

To make the pastry, sieve the flours and salt into a mixing bowl. Rub in the margarine and lard until the mixture resembles fine breadcrumbs. Mix to a dough with the egg and cold water. Knead the dough lightly. Roll out and use to line a 25cm (10 inch) fluted flan dish. Press up pastry to come ½cm (¼ inch) above the rim of the dish.

Prick the sides and base with a fork. Refrigerate for 15 minutes. Using a single strip of foil, about 2.5cm (1 inch) wide, line the inside edge of the flan case. Place 2 sheets of absorbent kitchen paper in the base. Weigh down with a few baking beans. Microwave on Full Power for 6 minutes. Remove the foil, beans and absorbent paper.

This page: Mille Feuille (top), Apple Mousse (centre right) and Pear Upside Down Pudding (bottom).

Facing page: Chocolate Rice Krispie (top), Rhubarb Sunburst (centre right) and Creme Caramel (bottom).

Microwave on Full Power for 2-3 minutes. Set aside. Put the fruits into a 1.75 litre (3 pint) mixing bowl. Cover and microwave on Full Power for about 7-8 minutes, stirring once halfway through. Stir in sugar to dissolve and beat to a puree. Cool. Beat in the ground almonds, butter and egg yolk. Put the egg whites into a large, clean bowl and whisk until stiff and dry. Beat in the sugar, a little at a time, until a thick glossy meringue results. Spread the fruit mixture into the flan case. Pipe or spread the meringue mixture on top to cover completely. Put the flan into a pre-heated moderate oven, 180°C, 350°F, Gas Mark 4, for 15-20 minutes, until pale golden. Serve sprinkled with tiny pieces of cherry and angelica.

Mille Feuille

PREPARATION TIME: 15-20 minutes, plus cooling time

MICROWAVE TIME: 6 minutes

SERVES: 6 people

225g (8oz) puff pastry (you can use a small packet of frozen puff pastry)
225g (8oz) fresh strawberries
300ml (½ pint) double cream, whipped
25g (1oz) caster sugar
100g (4oz) icing sugar, sieved
Pink food colouring
25g (1oz) toasted flaked almonds

Roll the pastry out into a circle 20cm (8 inch) in diameter. Place on a large dinner plate and chill for 10 minutes. Microwave, uncovered, for 5-6 minutes, on Full Power. Turn the plate once halfway through the cooking time. Brown the top under a pre-heated hot grill for a few seconds, if required. Allow to cool completely. Hull strawberries and roughly chop them. Fold the strawberries into the cream with the caster sugar. Split the pastry horizontally into 3 layers and place the first layer on a serving dish. Spread thickly with strawberries and cream. Top with the second pastry layer and spread with more strawberries and cream. Add the final layer of pastry, browned side uppermost. Put the icing sugar into a basin. Add a few drops of pink food colouring and just enough boiling water to produce a smooth glacé icing. Ice the Mille Feuille using a teaspoon – see picture. Sprinkle with the cold, toasted almonds and serve immediately.

Creme Caramel

PREPARATION TIME: 15 minutes, plus chilling time

MICROWAVE TIME: 28 minutes

SERVES: 4 people

Caramel
175g (6oz) granulated sugar
120ml (4 fl oz) cold water

Custard
450ml (¾ pint) milk
4 eggs, lightly beaten
50g (2oz) caster sugar

To make the caramel, place the granulated sugar and water into a large Pyrex jug. Microwave on Full Power for 9-11 minutes, or until a golden caramel results. Swirl the caramel evenly around the inside of a suitable, lightly-greased 900ml (1½ pint) dish. Leave to set. Put the milk into a large, clean jug and microwave on Full Power for 2 minutes. Add the beaten eggs and caster sugar. Strain onto the set caramel. Cover with cling film and pierce. Stand the dish in a larger container, which will act as a water bath. Pour in sufficient boiling water to come halfway up the sides of the dish containing the creme caramel. Microwave on Power 5, or Simmer, for about 15 minutes or until the custard has set. Remove from the water bath. Carefully peel away the cling film and allow to cool. Chill until ready to serve. Turn out and serve very cold with whipped cream.

Apple Mousse

PREPARATION TIME: 20 minutes

MICROWAVE TIME: 7 minutes

SERVES: 6 people

750g (1½lb) Bramley cooking apples, peeled, cored and sliced
Juice of 1 lemon
3 cubes of lime jelly (from a packet jelly)
45ml (3 tblsp) caster sugar
200ml (⅓ pint) whipping cream
2 egg whites
1 red-skinned eating apple

Put the prepared cooking apples into a 1.75 litre (3 pint) casserole dish with half the lemon juice and the lime jelly. Cover with a lid and microwave on Full Power for about 7 minutes until the apples are pulpy (stir once during this time). Beat with a fork, beating in the sugar until melted. Set aside and allow to cool. Blend the cooled apple in a food processor or liquidizer until smooth. Add the half-whipped cream and process together for a few seconds. Whisk the egg whites in a clean bowl until they stand in soft peaks. Transfer the apple mixture to a large, clean bowl and fold in the beaten egg whites gently. Turn into a serving dish. Decorate with slices of eating apple, which have been brushed with the remaining lemon juice to prevent discolouration.

Rhubarb Sunburst

PREPARATION TIME: 10 minutes, plus chilling time

MICROWAVE TIME: 6 minutes

SERVES: 4 people

450g (1lb) fresh young rhubarb, cut into 2.5cm (1 inch) pieces
Finely grated rind and juice of 1 orange
15ml (1 tblsp) apricot jam
6 canned apricot halves, chopped

Place the rhubarb, orange rind and juice, and the jam into a 900ml (1½ pint) mixing bowl. Cover and microwave on Full Power for 6 minutes. Stir. Set aside to cool, and then chill. Stir in the chopped apricots. Serve with natural yogurt, ice cream or whipped double cream.

Chocolate Pudding with Cherries

PREPARATION TIME: 10 minutes

MICROWAVE TIME: 8½ minutes

SERVES: 4-6 people

75g (3oz) softened butter
75g (3oz) soft brown sugar
75g (3oz) self-raising flour
25g (1oz) cocoa powder
2 eggs
30ml (2 tblsp) milk
425g (15oz) can cherry pie filling

Put all ingredients, apart from the cherry pie filling, into a mixing bowl. Beat with a wooden spoon for 1 minute. Spoon into a lightly greased 900ml (1½ pint) plastic pudding basin. Microwave on Full Power for 3½-4 minutes, until well risen and springy to the touch. Set aside. Empty the cherry pie filling into a bowl and microwave on Full Power for 3 minutes, stirring after 1½ minutes. Turn the sponge pudding into a dinner plate. Spoon the hot cherry sauce over the top and serve immediately.

Chocolate Rice Krispie

PREPARATION TIME: 15 minutes, plus chilling time

COOKING TIME: 5 minutes

MAKES: 16-20 wedges

100g (4oz) margarine
50g (2oz) caster sugar
25g (1oz) cocoa powder
50g (2oz) golden syrup
100g (4oz) Rice Krispies

Lightly grease 2 x 20cm (8 inch) sandwich tins with a little of the margarine (these are not to be used in the microwave). Put the remaining margarine, cut into pieces, into a 1.75 litre (3 pint) mixing bowl with the caster sugar, cocoa powder and golden syrup. Microwave on Power 5 or Simmer for 4 minutes. Stir halfway through, and again at the end. Microwave on Full Power for a further 1 minute. Stir in the Rice Krispies, making sure that they are all coated with the chocolate mixture. Divide between the prepared tins and smooth level with a knife. Cool and then chill until set. Cut into finger wedges to serve. As an alternative, 50g (2oz) washed, seedless raisins may be stirred in with the Rice Krispies.

Apple Ginger Crisp

PREPARATION TIME: 15 minutes

MICROWAVE TIME: 9 minutes

SERVES: 4-6 people

450g (1lb) Bramley cooking apples peeled, cored and sliced
50g (2oz) demerara sugar
15ml (1 tblsp) orange juice
65g (2½oz) butter
225g (8oz) plain ginger biscuits, crushed
50g (2oz) flaked almonds

Place the apples, sugar and orange juice into a 1.5 litre (2½ pint) casserole dish. Cover and microwave on Full Power for 4-5 minutes. Stir and set aside. Put the butter into a 1.75 litre (3 pint) mixing bowl. Microwave on Power 7, or Roast, for about 2 minutes, until melted. Stir the biscuits and almonds into the melted butter. Mix well. Microwave on Full Power for 2 minutes. Stir well with a fork after 1 minute. Carefully spoon the biscuit crumble over the apples. Serve immediately with whipped cream or ice cream. This pudding can also be served cold.

Chocolate Pudding with Cherries (left), Apple Ginger Crisp (below left) and Apple and Blackcurrant Flan (bottom).

Tea Time Treats

Celebration Gateau

PREPARATION TIME: 40 minutes

MICROWAVE TIME: 14 minutes

MAKES: 1 gateau

Cake
Caster sugar and oil for preparing the dish
3 eggs
150g (5oz) self-raising flour
25g (1oz) cocoa powder
2.5ml (½ tsp) baking powder
175g (6oz) soft margarine
175g (6oz) caster sugar

Icing
225g (8oz) icing sugar, sieved
75g (3oz) butter
10ml (2 tsp) boiling water
5ml (1 tsp) liquid coffee essence
Few drops of vanilla essence

Decoration
1 packet sponge finger biscuits
175g (6oz) plain chocolate
1m 40cm (1½ yards) brown nylon ribbon, 2.5cm (1 inch) wide

Lightly grease a deep, 18cm (7 inch) diameter souffle dish with oil. Line the base with a circle of greaseproof paper and use a little caster sugar to dust the sides. Knock out any surplus. Put all the ingredients for the cake into a mixing bowl. Beat for 1 minute. Spoon into the prepared souffle dish and smooth the top. Microwave on Power 7, or Roast, for about 7 minutes, and then on Full Power for 2-3 minutes until the sponge has risen to the top of the souffle dish and is set. Allow to stand in the container for 10 minutes before turning out onto a clean tea towel which has been sprinkled with a little caster sugar. Cool completely.

To make the icing: gradually beat the sieved icing sugar into the butter, adding the boiling water. Take 15ml (1 tblsp) buttercream out of the bowl and beat the coffee essence into it. Beat the vanilla essence into the remaining butter cream. Cut the cake in half horizontally and sandwich together with some of the vanilla buttercream. Spread the vanilla buttercream around the sides and across the top of the cake. Pipe half

the cake with vanilla butter cream and the other half with the coffee buttercream. Arrange the prepared sponge fingers, like soldiers, around the edge of the cake – see picture. Tie brown ribbon around to finish the gateau.
To prepare the sponge fingers: measure 1 sponge finger against the cooked cake. Trim all the sponge fingers to the same size. Break the chocolate into a large mixing bowl and microwave on Power 4 for 3-4 minutes. Stir. Dip the rounded end of the sponge fingers into the melted chocolate to coat the top half of each one. Arrange on a tray and leave in a cool plac for 10-15 minutes to set.

Chocolate Icing

PREPARATION TIME: 5 minutes

MICROWAVE TIME: 2½ minutes

25g (1oz) soft margarine, chilled
22ml (1½ tblsp) cocoa powder, sieved
150g (5oz) icing sugar, sieved
30ml (2 tblsp) milk

Put the margarine and cocoa into a 1.2 litre (2 pint) bowl. Microwave on Power 5, or Simmer, for 2½ minutes, until the margarine has melted and is very hot. Stir once, halfway through. Beat in the icing sugar and the milk. Beat with a wooden spoon until thick and glossy. Use to coat the top and sides of the cake.

Collettes

PREPARATION TIME: 30 minutes

MICROWAVE TIME: 7½ minutes

MAKES: 12

175g (6oz) plain chocolate
50g (2oz) milk chocolate
60ml (tblspk double cream
15g (½oz) butter
10ml (2 tsp) brandy or coffee essence
36 paper sweet cases, separated into twelve groups of three cases

Break the plain chocolate into pieces and put into a 900ml (1½

pint) bowl. Microwave on Power 3, or Defrost, for 4-5 minutes. Stir. Using a small paint brush or teaspoon, coat the base and sides of each group of paper cases with the melted chocolate. Leave to set. Put the milk chocolate and the butter into a clean bowl. Microwave on Power 3, or Defrost, for 2-2½ minutes. Beat well for a few minutes. Beat in the brandy or coffee essence. Half whip the cream and fold into the milk chocolate mixture using a metal spoon. Chill until firm enough to pipe. Peel the paper cases away from the set chocolate and discard. Pipe rosettes of chocolate filling into the chocolate case. Serve immediately in new paper sweet cases.

Fruit and Almond Cake

PREPARATION TIME: 20 minutes

MICROWAVE TIME: 13-16 minutes

MAKES: 1 cake

Use the large Anchor Hocking ring mould, which should be lightly greased and coated with caster sugar.

175g (6oz) soft margarine
175g (6oz) soft brown sugar
2.5ml (½ tsp) liquid gravy browning
3 eggs, beaten
175g (6oz) self-raising flour
2-3 drops almond essence
25g (1oz) ground almonds
50g (2oz) seedless raisins
50g (2oz) glace cherries, washed and roughly chopped
30ml (2 tblsp) milk

Cream margarine and sugar until light and fluffy. Beat in the gravy browning and beaten eggs, a little at a time (add 15ml (1 tblsp) flour with each addition of egg to prevent curdling). Beat in the almond essence, ground almonds and milk. Fold in the remaining flour, and then the raisins and cherries. Place in the prepared ring mould and smooth the top. Microwave on Power 6, or Roast, for 12-14 minutes, and then on Full Power for 1-2 minutes until just set. Stand for 15 minutes, before turning out. When quite cold, the top may be sprinkled with a little sieved icing sugar.

Cheese and Paprika Scones

PREPARATION TIME: 20 minutes

MICROWAVE TIME: 5-6 minutes

MAKES: about 10

225g (8oz) self-raising flour
Pinch salt
Pinch paprika
50g (2oz) firm margarine
50g (2oz) Red Leicester cheese, grated
5ml (1 tsp) made mustard
1 egg
45ml (3 tblsp) milk
5ml (1 tsp) Bovril

Sieve the flour, salt and paprika into a 1.75 litre (3 pint) mixing bowl. Rub in the margarine and fork in the cheese. Beat the mustard and egg together and mix with the milk. Mix into the dry ingredients, using a round bladed knife, to form a soft dough. Knead on a lightly floured board. Roll out to a thickness of 1cm (½ inch). Cut into 6cm (2½ inch) rounds. Arrange the shaped scones in a ring on a non-metallic tray, leaving a gap in the centre. Mix 5ml (1 tsp) Bovril with a little boiling water and brush over the surface of the scones (do not cover). Microwave immediately on Power 7, or Roast, for 5-6 minutes. Transfer to a cooling rack and allow to stand for 2-3 minutes. Serve hot with butter, or cold if preferred. As an alternative to the Bovril glaze, the cooked scones may be flashed under a pre-heated hot grill to brown and crisp them.

Celebration Gateau (top), Collettes (centre left) and Fruit and Almond Cake (bottom).

Microwave Meringues (right),
Victoria Sandwich (below) and
Porridge (bottom right).

Porridge

PREPARATION TIME: 5 minutes

MICROWAVE TIME: 9 minutes

SERVES: 3 people

2 cups milk and water, mixed
2.5ml (½ tsp) salt
1 cup porridge oats
75g (3oz) demerara sugar
75g (3oz) butter

Put the milk, water and salt into a 1.75 litre (3 pint) mixing bowl. Stir in the porridge oats. Microwave on Full Power for 3 minutes. Stir. Microwave on Full Power for 3 minutes. Stir. Microwave on Full Power for 3 minutes. Turn into individual serving dishes. Sprinkle with the brown sugar and top with the butter. Serve immediately.

Microwave Meringues

PREPARATION TIME: 20 minutes

MICROWAVE TIME: about 8 minutes

MAKES: 10 sandwiched meringues

1 egg white
180ml (12 tblsp) icing sugar, sieved
Pink food colouring
175g (6oz) chocolate buttercream
Chocolate Vermicelli

Put the egg white into a 1.75 litre (3 pint) mixing bowl and beat until frothy. Gradually work in the icing sugar and mix to give a really stiff fondant. Divide the fondant into two portions. Knead a few drops pink food colouring into one portion of fondant. Roll both the fondants separately into small balls, each about the size of a marble. Arrange 4 balls of fondant in a ring on a large dinner plate. Microwave on Full Power for 1½ minutes. Allow to stand for 2 minutes before removing to a cooling tray. Repeat until all the mixture has

been cooked. Fill the cooled meringue halves with the chocolate buttercream. Sprinkle with a little vermicelli and serve in paper cake cases.

Victoria Sandwich

PREPARATION TIME: 15 minutes

MICROWAVE TIME: 7 minutes

MAKES: 1 cake

Oil
Caster sugar for dusting
3 eggs
175g (6oz) self-raising flour
175g (6oz) soft margarine
175g (6oz) caster sugar
2 drops liquid gravy browning
30ml (2 tblsp) milk
45ml (3 tblsp) strawberry jam

Lightly grease an 18cm (7 inch) souffle dish with oil; dust the sides with a little caster sugar. Place a circle of greaseproof paper in the base. Put the eggs, flour, margarine, caster sugar, gravy browning and milk into a mixing bowl. Beat for 1 minute. spoon into the prepared dish and smooth the top. Microwave on Full Power for about 7 minutes. Test by putting a wooden cocktail stick into the centre of the sponge after a 3 minute standing time. The cocktail stick should come out clean. Stand for 10 minutes. turn out into a wire cooling rack. When quite cold, split in half horizontally. Sandwich together with the jam. Serve with a little caster sugar sprinkled over the top.

Cream Slices

PREPARATION TIME: 15-20 minutes, plus cooling time

MICROWAVE TIME: 6-8 minutes

MAKES: about 6 slices

225g (8oz) puff pastry (small packet frozen puff pastry can be used)
Black cherry jam
45ml (3 tblsp) icing sugar, sieved
A few drops of pink food colouring

Roll the pastry into an oblong about 10cm (4 inch) wide and 30-35cm (12-14 inches) long. Cut in half, crossways. Dampen the surface of a suitable container. Lift one half of the pastry onto the prepared tray and microwave on Full Power for 3-4 minutes, until well puffed up (when the door is

Roast, for 6-7 minutes. The sponge should be well risen and just 'set'. Remove from the microwave oven and allow to stand for 5 minutes before turning out. Allow to become quite cold. To make the buttercream, mix the cocoa with 30ml (2 tblsp) boiling water to form a smooth paste. Beat with the butter and icing sugar until light and creamy. Split the cooled cake in half horizontally. Sandwich together with a little of the buttercream and arrange on a cake board. Use the remaining buttercream to completely coat the 'hedgehog'. Form a 'snout' for his nose. Fork all over. Cut most of the chocolate buttons in half and stud the hedgehog with these to represent the prickles. Use 1 whole chocolate button for his nose and 2 raisins for his eyes. Spread some green coconut around the base for grass.

Rich Fruit Cake

PREPARATION TIME: 30 minutes

MICROWAVE TIME: 40 minutes

MAKES: 1 cake

100g (4oz) soft margarine
100g (4oz) dark soft brown sugar
30ml (2 tblsp) black treacle
5ml (1 tsp) gravy browning
3 eggs
45ml (3 tblsp) milk
225g (8oz) self-raising flour, sieved
    with 5ml (1 tsp) mixed spice and a
    pinch of salt
500g (1lb 2oz) mixed dried fruit
    (sultanas, raisins, currants and
    peel)
25g (1oz) chopped blanched almonds
50g (2oz) glace cherries, washed and
    quartered
45ml (3 tblsp) sherry or brandy

Lightly grease a deep, 23cm (9 inch) diameter souffle dish. Line the base with a circle of ungreased greaseproof paper and dust the

opened, the pastry should hold its shape). Allow to stand for 2-3 minutes and then remove to a cooling tray. Repeat the process with the remaining half of the pastry. Allow to cool. Using a sharp knife, divide each layer into 3 slices. Sandwich each group of three layers together with the jam. Mix the icing sugar with a little boiling water to make a smooth, glossy icing. beat in a few drops pink food colouring. Quickly spread the icing over the top of each layered slice. Cut each one into 3 slices.

Mr Hedgehog Cake

PREPARATION TIME: 40 minutes

MICROWAVE TIME: 3½-7 minutes

MAKES: 1 cake

75g (3oz) softened margarine
75g (3oz) caster sugar
100g (4oz) self-raising flour
2 eggs
15ml (1 tblsp) milk
15ml (1 tblsp) cocoa powder
100g (4oz) butter
225g (8oz) icing sugar, sieved

1 packet chocolate buttons
2 raisins
Green coloured coconut for grass

To make the sponge, put the margarine, the caster sugar, flour, eggs and milk into a mixing bowl. Beat with a wooden spoon for 1 minute. Lightly grease the base and sides of a 900ml (1½ pint) Pyrex or plastic pudding basin. Fill with the sponge mixture and smooth the top. Microwave on Full Power for 3½ minutes, or on Power 6, or

This page: Mr Hedgehog Cake (top), Cream Slice (centre left) and Rich Fruit Cake (bottom).

Facing page: Pineapple Gateau (top right), Chocolate Pear Sponge (centre left) and Cheese and Paprika Scones (bottom).

sides with a little caster sugar (knocking out any surplus). Beat the margarine, sugar, treacle and gravy browning in a large mixing bowl until light and fluffy. Gradually beat in the eggs and the milk. Add 15ml (1 tblsp) flour with each addition of egg, to prevent it curdling. Fold in the remaining flour using a metal spoon. Fold in the fruits, nuts and glace cherries, together with the sherry or brandy. Spoon the mixture into the prepared container. Microwave on Power 4, Simmer or Defrost, for 40 minutes. Remove from the microwave oven and allow to stand in its dish for 20 minutes before turning out. When quite cold, the cake may be marzipanned and iced, or finished with glace fruits, and glazed. Allow the cake to mature for at least 1 month before using.

Date and Walnut Loaf Cake (below) and Crepes Suzette (bottom).

Crepes Suzette

PREPARATION TIME: 25 minutes

MICROWAVE TIME: about 24 minutes

SERVES: 4-6 people

Pancakes
120g (4oz) plain flour
Pinch salt
1 egg
150ml (¼ pint) milk
150ml (¼ pint) water
Cooking oil

Sauce
75g (3oz) butter
50g (2oz) caster sugar
Grated rind of 1 orange
Grated rind and juice of ½ a lemon
60ml (4 tblsp) brandy or Cointreau

Sieve the flour and salt into a bowl. Make a well in the centre. Add the egg and half of the milk. Beat well. Gradually beat in the remaining milk and the water. Beat in 5ml (1 tsp) oil. Allow to stand for 10 minutes. Fry the pancakes in the usual way, making 12 pancakes in all. Fold the 12 cooked pancakes in half and then in half again, to form triangles. Arrange in a shallow dish. To make the sauce, put the butter into a 1 litre (1¾ pint) jug and microwave on Defrost for 5 minutes, or until melted and hot. Stir in the sugar to dissolve. Add the fruit rinds, lemon juice, and the brandy or Cointreau. Microwave on Full Power for 2 minutes. Stir. Pour over the pancakes. Cover with cling film and microwave on Power 5, or Simmer, for 5 minutes. Turn each pancake over in the sauce before serving. Serve piping hot.

Pineapple Gateau

PREPARATION TIME: 30 minutes

MICROWAVE TIME: 7 minutes

MAKES: 1 gateau

Oil and caster sugar
1 recipe quantity Victoria Sandwich mixture (see recipe)
225g (8oz) can pineapple slices, drained
300ml (½ pint) whipping cream, whipped
100g (4oz) chopped blanched almonds, toasted
Angelica for decoration

Lightly grease an 18cm (7 inch) souffle dish or plastic pan with oil. Put a circle of greaseproof paper into the base of the dish; dust the base and sides with caster sugar (knock out any surplus). Spoon the

prepared Victoria Sandwich mixture into the dish, and smooth the surface. Microwave on Full Power for about 7 minutes. Allow to stand for 10 minutes before turning out onto a wire cooling rack. Once the cake is quite cold, remove the greaseproof paper. Split the cake in half horizontally. Chop 1 slice of pineapple and mix with 45ml (3 tblsp) of the whipped cream; use to sandwich the cake layers together. Spread some of the cream round the sides of the cake and roll it in nuts to coat evenly. Arrange on a serving dish. Spread the top with the remaining cream, piping it if liked. Decorate the top with pineapple and angelica – see picture.

Chocolate Pear Sponge

PREPARATION TIME: 15 minutes

MICROWAVE TIME: 6 minutes

MAKES: 1 sponge cake

120g (4oz) sugar
90g (3½oz) self-raising flour
15g (½oz) cocoa powder
2.5ml (½ tsp) baking powder
100g (4oz) soft margarine
15ml (1 tblsp) milk
5ml (1 tsp) mixed spice
100g (4oz) ripe pear, peeled, cored and chopped
Oil and caster sugar for preparing the souffle dish

Put all the ingredients, apart from the pear, into a 1.75 litre (3 pint) mixing bowl. Mix with a wooden spoon and then beat for 1 minute. Fold in the pear, using a metal spoon. Lightly grease an 18cm (7 inch) souffle dish; line the base with a circle of greaseproof paper and coat the sides with a little caster sugar. Turn the mixture into the prepared souffle dish and smooth the top. Microwave on Power 6, or Roast, for 4 minutes, and them on Full Power for 2 minutes. Allow to stand for 10 minutes before turning out onto a cooling rack. The cooling rack should be covered with a clean tea towel, sprinkled with a little caster sugar. When quite cold, ice the cake with chocolate icing.

Date and Walnut Loaf Cake

PREPARATION TIME: 15 minutes

COOKING TIME: 6 minutes

MAKES: 1 loaf

2 eggs
60ml (4 tblsp) milk
15ml (1 tblsp) golden syrup
5ml (1 tsp) gravy browning
100g (4oz) soft margarine
175g (6oz) self-raising flour
75g (3oz) soft brown sugar
75g (3oz) chopped stoned dates
1 small banana, sliced
50g (2oz) walnuts, chopped

Put the eggs, milk, syrup, gravy browning, margarine, flour and brown sugar into a large mixing bowl. Beat with a wooden spoon. Using a metal spoon, fold in the dates, banana and walnuts. Turn into a lightly greased 1.75 litre (3 pint) microwave bread baker. Microwave on Full Power for about 6 minutes, turning the dish a half turn, halfway through cooking time. Allow to stand in the bread baker for 10 minutes before turning out. Serve sprinkled with caster sugar

SOME INDIAN SPECIALITIES

Bread and Rice

Ubley Chawal
(BOILED RICE) 1

This method of cooking rice in a large quantity of water is very safe and ideal for all grades of rice, especially for starchy short and medium grades. Also for cooking large quantities as the fluffiness can be controlled. Use a few drops of lemon juice to whiten the rice.

COOKING TIME: 10-15 minutes

450g (1lb) Basmati rice
Pinch of salt
Few drops lemon juice

Wash rice in 4-5 changes of water until water is clear. Drain rice and put into a large pan. Fill pan with cold or tepid water 5-10cm (2-4 inches) above the rice level. Add pinch of salt and bring to boil gradually. When boiling, add drops of lemon juice, which bleaches the rice as well as cuts the starch formation. Boil for 7-10 minutes covered, or until the rice is almost cooked and has a hard core in the centre. Test by pressing a few grains of rice between thumb and fore-finger. Drain well and cover the top of the pan with a clean cloth or foil and put the lid on lightly. Replace on a very low heat. The moisture around the rice is enough to form steam and cook the core in 2-4 minutes. Serve with or without butter/ghee, with daal or curry.

Ubley Chawal
(BOILED RICE) 2

PREPARATION TIME: 5 minutes

COOKING TIME: 15 minutes

This method is good for long grain rice only, like Basmati, American, Deradun or Pahari rice. In cooking, the rice absorbs twice its dry measure of liquid. Bearing this in mind always measure rice with a cup or some such container and note. Then measure twice this amount of water.

450g (1lb) Basmati rice
Pinch of salt
Lemon juice

Wash rice in 4-5 changes of water until water is clear. Drain rice and put into a large pan. Fill the pan with measured quantity of water and let the rice soak for 10-15 minutes. The longer it stands the better the result. Add salt and lemon juice and gently bring to boil. Stir once or twice when boiling and cook covered until rice is almost cooked with a hard centre; about 7-10 minutes. Water should be totally absorbed. Do not stir rice during cooking. Keep on a low heat for a further 1-2 minutes to evaporate any remaining moisture and complete the cooking of the rice. Serve.

Sada Pulao (left), Meat Pulao (below, far left) and Ubley Chawal (below left).

Sada Pulao
(CUMIN FRIED RICE)

PREPARATION TIME: 5 minutes plus 15 minutes to soak the rice.

COOKING TIME: 15 minutes

450g (1lb) Basmati or American
 long grain rice
Water
75g (3oz) ghee or butter
5ml (1 tsp) cumin seed
1.25ml (¼ tsp) turmeric powder
5ml (1 tsp) salt

Measure rice with a cup and note. Wash rice in 4-5 changes of water. Drain well and add twice as much water as rice. Cover and set aside for 10-15 minutes. Heat ghee or butter and add cumin seed. Fry for a few seconds, do not allow to burn. Add strained rice, retaining water. Add turmeric and salt. Mix well and add strained water. Bring to the boil, cover and lower the temperature. Do not stir rice. Cook for 10-12 minutes until water is absorbed by the rice.
Serve with any curry.

Meat Pulao

PREPARATION TIME: 15 minutes

COOKING TIME: 1 hour

1 small onion, peeled and sliced
75g (3oz) ghee or butter
2.5cm (1 inch) stick cinnamon
6 green cardamoms
3 large cardamoms
6 cloves
1 bayleaf
5ml (1 tsp) whole black cumin seeds
5ml (1 tsp) ginger paste
5ml (1 tsp) garlic paste
225g (8oz) lean meat, cut into cubes
5ml (1 tsp) ground coriander
5ml (1 tsp) ground cumin
150ml (¼ pint) natural yogurt
5ml (1 tsp) salt
450g (1lb) Basmati rice

Fry onion until golden brown in ghee. Add cinnamon, cardamoms, cloves, bayleaf and cumin seed. Fry for 1 minute. Add ginger and garlic pastes and fry for ½ minute. Add meat and sprinkle with ground coriander and cumin. Stir and add yogurt and salt. Mix well, cover and cook for 10-12 minutes until yogurt is dry and oil separates. Add 300ml (½ pint) of water and cook until meat is tender, 20-25 minutes. Remove from heat. Strain meat from its liquid. Take a large saucepan and add washed rice. Add gravy from the meat by measuring with the same cup. Use twice as much gravy as rice. If short, make up with water. Add the meat and the spices. Check for salt and adjust. Bring to the boil and then lower the heat, give a stir and cover and cook on low heat without stirring for 10-15 minutes until water is totally absorbed by the rice. Serve with a curry.

Biryani

There are two methods of making biryani; one with uncooked meat and the other with cooked meat. Both styles give equally good results but have slightly different flavours.

Method 1

In this method meat is marinated and cooked with semi-cooked rice.

PREPARATION TIME: 15-20 minutes and at least 1 hour for meat to marinate.

COOKING TIME: 60-70 minutes

275g (10oz) meat cut into cubes (leg or shoulder of lamb)
150ml (¼ pint) natural yogurt
5ml (1 tsp) salt
5ml (1 tsp) ground coriander
5ml (1 tsp) ground cumin
5ml (1 tsp) chilli powder
2.5ml (½ tsp) turmeric powder
5ml (1 tsp) ginger paste
5ml (1 tsp) garlic paste
2 onions, peeled and sliced
Oil for frying
3-4 green chillis, chopped
2 sprigs fresh coriander leaves, chopped
450g (1lb) Basmati rice
2.5cm (1 inch) cinnamon stick
6 small cardamoms
6 cloves
2 bayleaves
5ml (1 tsp) black cumin seed
10ml (2 tsp) salt
50g (2oz) ghee, melted
5-10ml (1-2 tsp) saffron dissolved in 90ml (6 tblsp) milk

In a small bowl, mix meat, yogurt, salt, coriander, cumin, chilli and turmeric powder, ginger and garlic pastes. Cover and set aside to marinate for at least 1 hour. For best results marinate overnight.

For boiling rice
Fry onions until brown and crisp in plenty of oil. Drain on kitchen paper. Put the meat and marianade into a large saucepan with lid. Add half of the fried onions, half of the chopped chillis and coriander. Mix well. In a separate saucepan, wash rice in 3-4 changes of water, add lots of water together with the cinnamon, cardamom, cloves, bayleaves, black cumin and salt. Bring to the boil. Cook for 3-4 minutes until rice is half cooked. Drain well and put the steaming rice over the meat. Sprinkle with the remaining fried onions, chillis

and coriander leaves. Make 5-6 holes with the handle of a wooden spoon for steam to escape and pour saffron milk all over the rice. Sprinkle with lemon juice and melted ghee. Cover with the lid and place the pan on the stove to cook over a moderate heat. As soon as steam is visible, lower the temperature. Cook for 45-50 minutes rotating the pan, so that all areas receive even heat. The rice will cook with the steam formed by the milk and yogurt and moisture from the meat. Lower heat to minimum and cook for another 10 minutes. Serve biryani from one end of the saucepan, mixing meat with rice with the aid of a spoon. Serve with a mixed vegetable raita.

Method 2

This method is the layering method. It involves two stages:

Stage 1
Cooking the meat

Stage 2
Layering the meat with rice

1 onion, peeled and chopped
100g (4oz) ghee or
75-90ml (5-6 tblsp) oil
5ml (1 tsp) ginger paste
5ml (1 tsp) garlic paste
275g (10oz) meat (leg or shoulder of lamb), cubed
5ml (1 tsp) ground coriander
5ml (1 tsp) chilli powder
1.25ml (¼ tsp) turmeric powder
5ml (1 tsp) ground cumin
150ml (¼ pint) natural yogurt
5ml (1 tsp) salt
2.5ml (½ tsp) saffron
15ml (1 tblsp) milk
1 onion, peeled and thinly sliced
Oil for deep frying
450g (1lb) Basmati rice
2.5cm (1 inch) cinnamon stick
6 cloves
5ml (1 tsp) black cumin seed
1 bayleaf
6 small cardamoms
10ml (2 tsp) salt
2 sprigs fresh green coriander, chopped
2-3 green chillis, chopped
Juice of 1 lemon

Fry chopped onion in ghee or oil until light brown in a large pan. Add ginger and garlic pastes and fry for another ½ minute. Add meat and coriander, chilli, turmeric and cumin powder. Add yogurt and salt. Mix well and cook with lid on

for 10-15 minutes until dry. Add 350ml (12 fl oz) water. Cover and cook for 8-10 minutes on low heat until meat is tender and there is approx. 120ml (4 fl oz) gravy left.

For rice
Dissolve saffron in milk. Deep fry sliced onion in oil until crisp and brown and drain on kitchen paper. Wash rice in 4-5 changes of water. Add plenty of water and add cinnamon, cloves, black cumin, bayleaf and cardamom. Add salt and bring to boil. Cook until rice is nearly done. The rice should increase in size but have a hard centre. Drain well, leaving whole spices in the rice. Divide rice in two. Line the saucepan base with half the rice, and top with the cooked meat, saving the sauce. Sprinkle with half the fried onion, half the fresh coriander and chilli. Cover with the remaining rice. Sprinkle top with the remaining fried onion, chilli and coriander. Sprinkle with lemon juice and saffron milk. Pour the meat gravy all round. Make a few holes with the handle of the spoon for steam to rise. Cover and put on gentle heat for 4-5 minutes. Mix from one end before serving. Serve with mixed vegetable raita.

Tahiri

PREPARATION TIME: 10 minutes

COOKING TIME: 20 minutes

1 onion, peeled and sliced
75g (3oz) ghee or butter
2.5cm (1 inch) cinnamon stick
6 cloves
6 cardamoms
5ml (1 tsp) black cumin seed
5ml (1 tsp) whole black pepper
1-2 bayleaves
100-125g (4-5oz) shelled or frozen peas
450g (1lb) Basmati rice washed in 4-5 changes of water
460ml (16 fl oz) water
15-20ml (3-4 tsp) salt

Fry onion in ghee until light brown. Add cinnamon, cloves, cardamom, black cumin, pepper and bayleaf. Fry for ½ minute. Add peas and cook for 2 minutes. Add rice and 460ml (16 fl oz) water and salt. Bring to boil. Cover and lower heat to simmer. Cook for 10-12 minutes until rice is cooked and water is absorbed. Serve with vegetable or meat curry.

Vegetable Pulao

PREPARATION TIME: 15 minutes

COOKING TIME: 15 minutes

450g (1lb) Basmati or any long grain rice
75g (3oz) ghee or butter
1 onion, peeled and chopped
2.5cm (1 inch) cinnamon stick
1-2 bayleaves
6 small cardamoms
4 large cardamoms
6 cloves
3-4ml (3-4 tsp) salt
Water
225-275g (8-10oz) mixed vegetables, sliced
5ml (1 tsp) ground coriander
5ml (1 tsp) garam masala powder
1-4ml (1-4 tsp) turmeric powder
5ml (1 tsp) chilli powder
Salt to taste

Measure rice with a cup and note. Wash rice in 4-5 changes of water, drain well. Heat ghee and fry onion until light brown. Add cinnamon, bayleaf, cardamoms, and cloves. Fry for 1 minute. Add mixed vegetables and fry for 4-5 minutes. Add rice and sprinkle with coriander, garam masala, turmeric and chilli powder. Mix well. Add twice the measure of water. Add salt to taste. Bring to boil. Reduce heat, cover and gently cook for 12-15 minutes, without stirring, until water is completely absorbed. Serve by itself, with a raita or with a curry.

Recommended vegetables:- Can be used in any combination.

1-2 aubergines, cut in 1cm (½ inch) chunks
1-2 potatoes, diced
1-2oz shelled or frozen peas
1-2 carrots, peeled and diced
2oz sliced green beans
1-2oz corn kernels
2-3 cauliflower florets, cut into smaller pieces
1-2oz broad beans, frozen or shelled

Facing page: Vegetable Pulao (top), Khichri (left) and Shahi Pulao (bottom).

No leafy vegetables or pithy vegetables like marrow, courgettes, gourd etc. are advisable as they will make the pulao soggy. To colour the rice at random, do not use turmeric powder, but use food colouring, adding a few drops of any colour, at random, after the rice is semi-cooked and water is more-or-less absorbed.

Khichri
(KEDGEREE)

PREPARATION TIME: 6 minutes

COOKING TIME: 10-15 minutes

225g (8oz) Basmati rice
225g (8oz) red lentils
3-4ml (¾ tsp) salt, or to taste
2.5ml (½ tsp) turmeric
5ml (1 tsp) ground coriander
75g (3oz) butter
1 large onion, peeled and chopped
1-2 green chillis, chopped

Mix rice and lentils, measure with a cup and note. Wash in 4-5 changes of water. Drain and add twice the measure of water with the same cup. Add salt, turmeric and coriander. Bring to boil. Mix well by stirring gently. Lower the temperature, cover and cook over a gentle heat for 10-12 minutes until water is absorbed. In a frying pan, melt butter and fry onions golden brown. Add chopped chillis and pour over cooked khichri. Serve with poppadums and chutney.

Shahi Pulao
(NUT AND RAISIN PULAO)

PREPARATION TIME: 5-6 minutes.

COOKING TIME: 10-15 minutes.

450g (1lb) Basmati or long grain rice
75g (3oz) ghee or butter
2.5cm (1 inch) cinnamon stick
6 small cardamoms
2 large cardamoms
2 bayleaves
6 cloves
5ml (1 tsp) salt
Water
50-75g (2-3oz) raisins
50-75g (2-3oz) mixed nuts
    (almonds, cashew, pistachio)

Measure rice with a cup. Wash rice in 4-5 changes of water, drain. Heat ghee and fry cinnamon, cardamoms, bayleaves and cloves for half minute. Add washed rice,

salt and twice the quantity of water. Bring to boil gently. Stir once or twice. Reduce heat, add raisins and nuts, cover and cook for 10-12 minutes or until water is totally absorbed. Serve with meat or vegetable curry.

Jhinga Pulao
(PRAWN PULAO)

PREPARATION TIME: 6 minutes

COOKING TIME: 10-15 minutes

225g (8oz) long grain or Basmati rice
1 onion, peeled and chopped
75g (3oz) ghee or butter
2.5cm (1 inch) cinnamon stick
1 bayleaf
6 small cardamoms
6 cloves
5-10ml (1-2 tsp) ginger paste
5-10ml (1-2 tsp) garlic paste
225g (8oz) peeled and cooked prawns
15ml (1 tblsp) chopped fresh coriander
5ml (1 tsp) garam masala powder
1-2 green chillis
3-4ml (¾ tsp) salt

Measure rice and note. Wash in 3-4 changes of water. Drain and soak in twice the measure of water. Keep aside. Fry onion in ghee or butter until golden brown. Add cinnamon, bayleaf, cardamom and cloves, fry for 1 minute. Add ginger and garlic paste. Cook for ½-1 minute. Add prawns and sprinkle with coriander and garam masala. Add green chillis and salt. Stir in soaked rice and water. Mix well and bring to boil. Reduce heat, cover and cook until water is absorbed, about 10-15 minutes. Do not stir during cooking. Serve with curry. To colour pulao, add a few drops of red or orange food colour, 2-3 minutes before removing from heat. A pinch of saffron may be added along with the spices.

Pita

PREPARATION TIME: 10 minutes and 1 hour for dough to rest.

COOKING TIME: 30 minutes

10ml (2 tsp) dried yeast
5ml (1 tsp) sugar
Water
450g (1lb) refined or wholemeal flour
Pinch of salt
25g (1oz) butter or margarine

Mix yeast and sugar and add 30ml (2 tblsp) tepid water. Cover and let it rise. When it becomes frothy it is ready for use. Sift flour and salt, add butter and yeast mixture. Knead with water to make a pliable dough, cover and rest for 1 hour. Knead again and divide into 16 even-sized balls. Preheat oven to Gas Mark 5 (190°C-375°F). Roll each one out on lightly floured surface to a 15cm (6 inch) oblong or a circle. Bake in the oven on a tray for 7-10 minutes.

Saag Paratha

Paratha made with a leafy vegetable.

PREPARATION TIME: 10 minutes

COOKING TIME: 20 minutes

450g (1lb) wholemeal flour (atta)
Pinch of salt
75-100g (3-4oz) drained cooked spinach or
50g (2oz) boiled methi leaves
25g (1oz) butter
Vegetable ghee or butter ghee
Water

Sift flour and salt, add boiled spinach or methi and butter. Knead with water to make a soft, pliable dough. Knead well and rest for 5 minutes. Heat a non-stick frying pan or a Tawa. Make 16-18 even-sized balls. Roll each ball out onto a lightly floured surface into a 15-18cm (6-7 inch) circle. Place in Tawa. Cook for 1-3 minutes on low heat. Turn over and cook the other side. Apply vegetable ghee on both sides and shallow fry to light brown. Serve hot or cold.

Kulcha

Kulcha is yeast bread, deep fried.

PREPARATION TIME: 5-6 minutes and 5-6 hours for yeast to rise.

COOKING TIME: 3 minutes

5ml (1 tsp) dried yeast
5ml (1 tsp) sugar
Water
450g (1lb) rice flour
Pinch of salt
50g (2oz) ghee or butter
30ml (2 tblsp) natural yogurt
Oil

Take yeast and sugar and add 15ml (1 tblsp) tepid water. Cover and let it stand. When it becomes frothy it

is ready for use. Sift flour and salt. Add ghee or butter and yogurt. Knead with water to form a medium-hard dough. Make a well in the centre, add yeast mixture and knead. Let it rest for 5-6 hours in a warm place to rise. Knead again and make a soft, pliable dough. Make 20-25 even-sized balls. Heat oil and roll each ball into a 5-6cm (2-2½ inch) circle. Fry until lightly golden brown, about 2-3 minutes. Serve hot or cold with curry.

Stuffed Paratha

PREPARATION TIME: 10 minutes

COOKING TIME: 30 minutes

450g (1lb) wholemeal flour or chupati atta
Pinch of salt
25g (1oz) ghee or butter
Water
Ghee or oil for frying

Filling
A few florets of cauliflower, chopped
Pinch of salt
5ml (1 tsp) cumin seed
1.25ml (¼ tsp) chilli powder
5ml (1 tsp) ground coriander
Mix the above ingredients together.

Sift flour and salt. Add ghee or butter and knead with water to make a soft, pliable dough. Make 16-18 even-sized balls. Take a ball of dough, make a slight depression in the centre. Fill the centre with 5ml (1 tsp) of cauliflower mixture. Pull the surrounding dough from around the filling to gather at the top. Roll gently into a complete ball. On a lightly floured floor, roll each paratha into a 15-18cm (6-7 inch) round. On a preheated Tawa or frying pan, place the paratha. Let it cook for 2 minutes, until little brown specs appear. Flip over to the other side and cook for 2 minutes. Take a little ghee or oil and shallow fry parathas on both sides. Cook each side on low heat – until golden brown. Serve hot or cold with a curry.

Facing page: Biryani (top), Jhinga Pulao (centre left) and Tahiri (bottom right).

Nan

The actual taste of nan comes by baking the bread in a clay oven. Nan baked in gas or electric ovens does not have the same charcoal flavour.

PREPARATION TIME: 10-15 minutes and 2-3 hours for dough to rest.

COOKING TIME: 30-40 minutes

10ml (2 tsp) dried yeast
5ml (1 tsp) sugar
7.5ml (1½ tsp) bicarbonate of soda
Water
15ml (1 tblsp) sesame or onion seeds
450g (1lb) refined plain flour
Pinch of salt
25-35g (1-1½oz) butter, melted
60g (2½oz) natural yogurt

Mix yeast and sugar and add 15ml (1 tblsp) tepid water. When mixture becomes frothy it is ready for use. Sift flour and salt, add bicarbonate of soda. Make a well and add melted butter, yogurt and yeast mixture. Knead with sufficient water to give a smooth dough. Cover and rest to rise for 2-3 hours. Knead again and make 16-17 balls. Roll each ball into either an elongated flat bread – 15x25cm (6 x 10 ins) or a 15-18cm (6-7 inch) circle on a lightly floured surface. Coat with butter and sprinkle with a few onion or sesame seeds. Bake in oven, preheated to Gas Mark 6 (200°C or 400°F), for 5-6 minutes. When ready the bread will have brown spots on it. Serve hot.

Sheermaal

PREPARATION TIME: 10 minutes and time for yeast to rise.

COOKING TIME: 30-40 minutes

450g (1lb) self-raising flour
Pinch of salt
40ml (8 tsp) sugar
75g (3oz) butter or margarine
15ml (1 tblsp) dried yeast
1 cup tepid water
Milk
Sesame seed

Sift flour and salt, add 35ml (7 tsp) sugar. Add butter or margarine. Mix yeast with 1 cup water and add 5ml (1 tsp) sugar, mix and leave to rise. When frothy, add to flour. Knead with water to make a soft dough. Let it rest. When risen to twice its volume, knead again for 4-5 minutes. Divide into 10 equal portions. Roll each one out into a round or oblong shape of 5mm (¼ inch) thick. Brush with milk and sprinkle with sesame seeds. Preheat oven to Gas Mark 5 (190°C - 375°F) and bake for 5 minutes. Turn over and bake for a further 5 minutes until light brown and cooked.

Paratha

Parathas are shallow-fried breads.

PREPARATION TIME: 10 minutes

COOKING TIME: 25 minutes

450g (1lb) wholemeal flour (atta)
Pinch of salt
Water
Ghee for frying
Butter

Sift flour and salt. Add water and knead into a soft dough. Knead well and keep aside to rest for 5 minutes. Make 16-18 even-sized balls. Roll each ball out into a 5cm (2 inch) circle. Apply 1.25ml (¼ tsp) butter. Fold in half and apply a little butter and fold in half again to make a triangular shape. On a floured surface roll each into a 15cm (6 inch) triangle. Heat a frying pan or a Tawa. Place the paratha on it. Cook for 1-2 minutes. Flip over and cook for 2 minutes. Apply a little ghee on the surface and flip over and fry first side again. Repeat for second side. Both sides should be browned and pressed with a spatula to cook corners. Make the remaining parathas up as above and stack them. Serve hot or cold with curry.

Below: Saag Paratha (top left), Stuffed Paratha (top right) and Kulcha (bottom).

Facing page: Sheermal (top), Nan (centre) and Pita (bottom).

Roti/Chapati/Phulka

PREPARATION TIME: 6 minutes

COOKING TIME: 20 minutes

450g (1lb) plain wholemeal flour
(Atta)
Pinch of salt
130-175ml (4-6 fl oz) water

Sift flour and salt into a mixing bowl. Knead to a soft, pliable dough with water and leave to rest for 5 minutes. Make 16-20 even-sized balls and roll one ball out on lightly floured surface to a circle of 18cm (7ins). Heat a non-stick frying pan or Indian bread griddle known as 'Tawa'. Place the rolled circle on it. When little bubbles appear, turn over and cook for ½ minute. Place under preheated grill. The roti will swell, turn over to the other side. Make the rest in the same way and stack them. A little butter may be applied to keep the rotis soft on one side. Keep them well wrapped in a clean tea cloth or baking foil.

Alternative method:
The roti can be cooked for 1-1½ minutes on each side in the frying pan until little brown specs appear. Make them puff up by pressing with tea cloth to rotate the steam.

Puri

These are deep-fried, little, round breads.

PREPARATION TIME: 6 minutes

COOKING TIME: 10 minutes

450g (1lb) wholemeal flour or
chupati atta
Pinch of salt
50g (2oz) ghee or
45ml (3 tblsp) oil
Water
Oil for deep frying

Sift flour and salt and add ghee or oil. Knead with water to make a soft, pliable dough. Knead well and allow to stand for 5 minutes. Make 25-30 small balls. Roll each ball out into a small circle 5-6cm (2-2½ inches) in diameter. Heat oil, drop in a tiny bit of dough. When the dough surfaces immediately, the oil is ready. If not then wait for oil to heat to right temperature. Slide one puri into the oil. Press gently with a straining spoon. Turn over and the puri will swell. It may need a little pressing. Cook for 1-2 minutes until it is light brown. The side of the puri which goes in first, always has a thin crust, the other side will always have a thick side. When this thick side is light brown the puri is cooked. Fry all the puri and serve hot or cold with a curry or chutney, or both.

**Roti/Chapati/Phulka (left),
Paratha (top left) and Puri
(above).**

SOME INDIAN SPECIALITIES

Sherbets and Snacks

Lassi
(YOGURT SHERBET)

PREPARATION TIME: 5-7 minutes

300ml (½ pint) natural yogurt
50g (2oz) sugar
Pinch of salt
1 litre (1¾ pints) water
Pinch of saffron
10ml (2 tsp) lemon juice
Ice cubes

In a mixing bowl beat yogurt well, add sugar and salt, beat again and add water. Dissolve sugar by stirring well. Add saffron and lemon juice and serve with ice cubes.

Tandi Masala Chaaey
(SPICED ICED TEA)

PREPARATION TIME: 10 minutes.

600ml (1 pint) water
1 teabag or
10ml or 2 tsp orange peko tea leaves
Sugar to taste
4 cloves
2.5cm (1 inch) cinnamon stick
4 small cardamoms, seeds removed and ground
Crushed ice
Fresh lemon juice

Boil 150ml (¼ pint) of water. Put tea, sugar, cloves, cinnamon stick and crushed cardamom seeds in a teapot. Pour in boiling water and allow to stand for 2-4 minutes. Stir well, strain and mix with remaining cold water. Allow to cool. Mix and serve in tall glasses with crushed ice and lemon juice to taste.

This page: Lassi (left), Mint Barley (centre) and Tandi Masala Chaaey (right).

Facing page: Badam Ka Sherbet (left), Lemon Sherbet (centre) and Spiced Grape Sherbet (right).

(Normally served before the meal)

Green Mango Sherbet

PREPARATION TIME: 10-12 minutes

2 green, unripened mangoes
1 litre (1¾ pints) water
Pinch of salt
Sugar to taste
Crushed ice

Boil mangoes for 10 minutes. Remove from water and cool. Remove skin gently. Scrape all the pulp from around the stone and skin. Dissolve pulp in water. Add salt and sugar. Stir well to mix. Serve on a bed of ice.

Mint Barley

PREPARATION TIME: 15 minutes

600-750ml (1-1¼ pints) water
75g or 3oz broken barley
6-8 mint leaves, finely chopped
Pinch of salt
Sugar to taste
Fresh lemon juice

Boil 300ml (½ pint) water and add barley. Simmer for 5 minutes. Strain and discard barley. Add remaining water and finely chopped mint leaves. Add salt and sugar to taste. Chill and serve on ice with lemon juice.

Lemon Sherbet

PREPARATION TIME: 5 minutes

Sugar to taste
Pinch of salt
1.2 litres (2 pints) water
Juice of 2 lemons
5ml (1 tsp) grated lemon rind
Few mint leaves, bruised
Ice cubes

Dissolve sugar and salt in water. Add lemon juice and lemon rind. Add mint leaves and stir well. Serve in tall glasses with ice. 120ml (4 fl oz) of gin or vodka may be added.

Spiced Grape Sherbet

PREPARATION TIME: 10 minutes

225g (8oz) white seedless grapes
100g (4oz) black grapes, seeded
2 cloves
1 litre (1¾ pints) water
Pinch of salt
6 small cardamoms, seeds removed
   and crushed
Sugar to taste
10ml (2 tsp) lemon juice
Pinch of freshly ground pepper
Pinch of ground cinnamon
Crushed ice

Wash grapes and liquidise with cloves, strain through a sieve to collect juice. Add 1 cup/8 fl oz water to grapes and strain once again to collect the juice. Mix grape juice with remaining water and dissolve salt, crushed cardamom seeds and sugar. Add lemon juice, pepper and cinnamon. Mix well. Serve on crushed ice.

Passion Fruit Sherbet

PREPARATION TIME: 10 minutes

8-10 passion fruits
750ml (1¼ pints) water
Sugar
Pinch of salt
1-2 drops of red food colouring
   (optional)
Ice cubes

Cut passion fruits in half. Remove the pulp and blend with the water. Strain and dissolve sugar; add salt. Add red food colouring, if desired, this will make the sherbet pink. Serve with ice cubes.

Blackcurrant Sherbet

PREPARATION TIME: 10 minutes

100-175g or 4-6oz fresh or frozen
   blackcurrants
750ml (1¼ pints) water
50-60g or 2-3oz sugar
Pinch of salt
15ml (1 tblsp) lemon juice
Ice cubes

Mash blackcurrants in a bowl or blend them in a liquidiser. Add water and mix well, then strain. Dissolve sugar and salt and add lemon juice. Serve with ice cubes.

Badam Ka Sherbet
(ALMOND SHERBET)

PREPARATION TIME: 10 minutes

450ml (¾ pint) milk
150ml (¼ pint) water
60g (2½oz) sugar
15g (½oz) blanched almonds, soaked
   in water
15g (½oz) pistachio nuts, soaked
   and skins removed
Pinch of saffron
6 small cardamoms, seeds removed
   and crushed
3-4 drops rosewater
Ice cubes

Mix milk and water and dissolve sugar. Liquidise almonds and pistachio nuts with a little diluted milk. Dissolve saffron, add crushed seeds of cardamom and add rose essence. Serve with ice cubes or well chilled.

Dahi - Wada
(DAAL DUMPLINGS IN YOGURT)

PREPARATION TIME: 5 minutes
and 1 hour for soaking

COOKING TIME: 30 minutes

100g (4oz) urid daal, washed and
   soaked for 1 hour
50g (2oz) moong daal, washed and
   soaked for 1 hour
2.5ml (½ tsp) salt

2.5cm (1 inch) ginger root, peeled
   and finely chopped
1.25ml (¼ tsp) chilli powder or
2 green chillis, finely chopped
50g (2oz) mixed sultanas and raisins
Oil for deep frying

For Yogurt Sauce:
450-600ml (¾-1 pint) natural yogurt
1.25ml (¼ tsp) salt
2.5ml (½ tsp) cumin seed
Water to dip fried wada
2 sprigs coriander, chopped for
   garnish

Blend drained urid daal and moong daal with sufficient water in a liquidiser to make a very thick purée. Put liquidized urid and moong daal into mixing bowl, add salt, ginger, chillis and mixed fruits. Mix well. Heat oil for deep frying. Add small spoonfuls of the mixture to the hot oil to make small dumplings. To make more uniform wadas, you could wet your hands in water and form a little mixture into a flat, round shape before gently lowering the mixture into the oil. Fry both sides for 3-4 minutes or until golden brown. Drain on kitchen paper. Make all the wadas in this way. Mix yogurt and salt together. Soak fried wadas in water for 2-3 minutes. Gently squeeze out any excess water, arrange in a flat serving dish. Pour the yogurt evenly over them. In a hot frying pan, dry roast cumin and coriander seeds for 1-2 minutes. Place the roasted spices in folded

kitchen paper and, with a rolling pin, coarsely grind to a powder. Sprinkle ground spice mixture over the yogurt. Garnish with chopped, fresh green coriander. Alternatively, sprinkle with a pinch of paprika powder.

Pakoras or Bhajias
(DEEP FRIED CHICK PEA FLOUR FRITTERS)

PREPARATION TIME: 15 minutes

COOKING TIME: 10 minutes

100g (4oz) baisen flour (chick pea
   flour)
Pinch of salt
2.5ml (½ tsp) chilli powder
2.5ml (½ tsp) bicarbonate of soda
Water to make batter
Oil for deep frying

Vegetables and Fruits
1 small potato, peeled and sliced into
   ⅛ inch thick wafers
1 small aubergine, cut into thin slices
1 small onion, sliced
1 green pepper, seeded and sliced into
   rings
3-4 florets of cauliflower, separated
   into smaller pieces

Mix baisen flour, salt, chilli powder and soda and make a medium consistency batter with water. Mix well and allow to stand for 3-4 minutes. Heat oil for deep frying. Dip prepared vegetables one by one into the batter, coat well and fry them a few at a time for 4-5 minutes in hot oil until golden brown on both sides. Drain well. Serve hot or cold with chutney.

Other suggestions:
Pineapple rings, apples, tomatoes, spinach leaves, green chillis, bread slices cut in quarter, semi-ripe bananas, sweet potatoes, swede, parsnips, chicken and fish pieces.

This page: Blackcurrant Sherbet (centre) and Passion Fruit Sherbet (right).

Facing page: Pakoras (top), Ghoogni (centre left) and Dahi Wada (bottom).

Crispy Rolls or Curry Patties

PREPARATION TIME: 1 hour

COOKING TIME: 30 minutes

225-275g (8-10oz) plain flour
Salt
15ml (1 tblsp) cornflour
1.25ml (¼ tsp) bicarbonate of soda
25g (1oz) butter or margarine
Water
Paste

Take 2 tsp (10ml) flour and a little water to make a thick paste. Crispy rolls can be made with either a vegetable or meat filling. The rolls themselves are made in the same way for either filling. Sift flour, salt, cornflour and soda. Rub in butter. Make dough with water. Knead well and leave to stand for 10 minutes. Knead once again and divide into 4-6 portions. Roll each portion as thinly as possible on a lightly floured surface. Then cut 10cm (4 inch) squares. Heat frying pan and cook on both sides for ½ minute each. Make the rest similarly. Take a square wrapper and place a little filling slightly above one corner and fold corner over the filling. Bring the two side corners over as if to make the folds of an envelope. Secure with a little water and flour paste and press to seal. Roll over the folded edge to make a neat roll. Seal the flap with water and flour paste. Make all the rolls. Heat oil and fry a few at a time until golden brown. Drain on kitchen paper and serve hot with either chutney or tomato ketchup.

Vegetable Filling
1 onion
30ml (2 tblsp) oil
450g (1lb) potatoes, peeled and cubed
100g (4oz) shelled or frozen peas
Salt
5ml (1 tsp) ground black pepper
Oil for deep frying

Fry onion, in 30ml (2 tblsp) oil for 3-4 minutes. Add cubed boiled potatoes, peas and sprinkle with salt and pepper. Mix well and cook for 3-4 minutes. Cover and allow to cool.

Meat Filling
15ml (1 tblsp) oil
1 onion, peeled and sliced thinly
50g (2oz) grated cabbage
50g (2oz) grated carrots
50g (2oz) sliced green beans
50g (2oz) frozen peas
Salt

2.5ml (½ tsp) ground black pepper
50g (2oz) sprouted beans
225g (8oz) cooked meat (any kind) shredded
10-15ml (2-3 tsp) lemon juice

Heat oil and fry onions for 2 minutes. Add cabbage and carrots and fry for 3 minutes. Add green beans, peas and sprinkle with salt and black pepper. Cover and cook for 4-5 minutes. Add sprouted beans and stir fry for 2 minutes. Add shredded meat. Mix well, add lemon juice and stir the mixture. Cook for 2-3 minutes. Remove from heat, cool and use for filling.

Aloo-Bonda
(POTATO BALLS IN BATTER)

PREPARATION TIME: 20 minutes

COOKING TIME: 15 minutes

Batter
100g (4oz) baisen flour (chick pea flour)
Salt
Pinch of baking powder
1.25ml (¼ tsp) chilli powder
150ml (¼ pint) water
Oil for deep frying

Filling
450g (1lb) potatoes, boiled, peeled and cubed
1 onion, peeled and chopped
2 sprigs fresh green coriander, chopped
2.5cm (1 inch) ginger root, peeled and finely chopped
1-2 green chillis, chopped
15ml (1 tblsp) lemon juice or freshly ground black pepper to taste
Salt
10ml (2 tsp) dry mango powder

Sift flour and salt together with baking powder and chilli powder. Add water and mix well to make a smooth batter. If the batter is too thick add a little extra water; if thin add extra sifted baisen flour. Put aside to rest. In a large bowl, put cubed potatoes, chopped onions, coriander, ginger, chillis and lemon juice, mix well and sprinkle with pepper, salt and mango powder. Mix well and take a small lump to form a smooth ball, the size of a golf ball. Mould remaining mixture in the same way. Heat oil and dip potato bonda in baisen batter, coat well and slide them into the oil. Fry a few at a time until the bonda are golden brown. Drain on kitchen paper and serve hot with chutney. Aloo-bondas can be eaten cold, but they do not freeze well.

Dokhala

PREPARATION TIME: Overnight for soaking and 10-12 hours for fermenting.

COOKING TIME: 30-40 minutes

450g (1lb) channa daal (split chick pea), washed
1-2 green chillis
2.5cm (1 inch) ginger root, peeled and sliced
Salt to taste
Pinch of asafoetida
5ml (1 tsp) bicarbonate of soda
60ml (3½ fl oz) oil
6-8 curry leaves
2.5ml (½ tsp) mustard seed
45ml (3 tblsp) fresh grated coconut
2 sprigs coriander leaves, chopped

Soak channa daal overnight. Drain and grind with a little water, the green chillis and ginger to a coarse paste. Beat with a circular motion to incorporate air and leave to ferment for 10-12 hours (use a warm place like an airing cupboard and cover the pan). After it has fermented add salt, asafoetida, soda and half the oil. If too thick, add 30ml (2 tblsp) water. Beat again. Grease a flat 5-6cm (2-2½ inch) deep pie dish with oil. Spread the mixture on it about 2.5cm (1 inch) thick. Steam over a large saucepan for 15-20 minutes. Allow to cool slightly. Heat remaining oil, add curry leaves and mustard seeds and pour over dokhala evenly. Serve garnished with grated coconut and chopped coriander leaves, cut dokhala into 2.5cm (1 inch) square pieces. Dokhala can be frozen for future use.

Khari Sevian
(SAVOURY MINCE VERMICELLI)

PREPARATION TIME: 10 minutes

COOKING TIME: 20 minutes for mince and 10 minutes for sevian

1 onion, peeled and finely chopped
25g (1oz) ghee or
22ml (1½ tblsp) oil
2.5ml (½ tsp) ginger paste
1.25ml (¼ tsp) garlic paste
225g (8oz) lamb or beef mince

Salt
5ml (1 tsp) ground black pepper
50g (2oz) butter
225g (8oz) vermicelli, broken into
  smaller pieces
Juice of 1 lemon

Fry onion in ghee or oil for 3-4
minutes. Add ginger, garlic, mince
and salt. Fry for 6-7 minutes. Add
ground black pepper. Mix well.
Cover and cook until mince is dry.
Remove from heat and put aside.
In a non-stick pan, heat butter and
fry vermicelli for 1-2 minutes. Add
cooked mince and stir fry for 1
minute. Add 300ml (½ pint) water.
Cook until dry. Sprinkle with
lemon juice and serve hot.

**Khari Sevian (far left), Aloo
Bonda (below), Crispy Rolls
(centre) and Dokhala (bottom).**

Ghoogni
(GREEN PEA FRY OR SPICED GREEN PEAS)

PREPARATION TIME: 5 minutes
COOKING TIME: 10 minutes

1 onion, peeled and chopped
25g (1oz) ghee or
15ml (1 tblsp) oil
2 green chillis, cut in half
2.5cm (1 inch) ginger root, peeled and chopped
450g (1lb) shelled or frozen peas
1.25ml (¼ tsp) black ground pepper
2 sprigs fresh green coriander, chopped
1.25ml (¼ tsp) salt
Juice of 1 lemon

Fry onion in ghee or oil until tender (2-3 minutes), add green chillis and ginger. Fry for 1 minute and add green peas. Stir and cook for 5-6 minutes. Add black pepper, chopped coriander and salt. Cook for a further 2 minutes. Pour into a serving dish and sprinkle with lemon juice. Serve hot with tea.

Samosa
(DEEP FRIED STUFFED SAVOURY PASTRIES)

PREPARATION TIME: 30 minutes
COOKING TIME: 15 minutes

100-150g (4-5oz) plain flour
Pinch of salt
2.5ml (½ tsp) baking powder
25g (1oz) ghee or
22ml (1½ tblsp) oil
Water to mix

Flour paste
15ml (1 tblsp) flour mixed with little water to form thick paste
Oil for deep frying

Samosas may be made with either a vegetable or meat filling. The samosas are made in the same way for either filling. Sift flour and salt and add baking powder. Rub in ghee or oil and add the water, a little at a time, to form a dough. Knead well and set aside. When the filling has been made, knead dough again and make 16-20 even-sized balls. On lightly floured surface roll each ball into a thin circle 10-13cm (4-5 inch) round. Cut across the centre and apply the flour paste along the straight edge and bring the two corners together, overlapping slightly to make a cone. Secure by pressing the pasted edges together. Fill the cone with the filling, apply paste to the open mouth and seal the edge. Prepare the rest of the samosas in the same way. Heat oil. When it is moderately hot, fry samosas, a few at a time, until golden brown. Drain on kitchen paper and serve hot or cold with a sweet chutney or plain tomato ketchup.

For Vegetable Filling
15ml (1 tblsp) oil
1 onion, peeled and chopped
10ml (2 tsp) garam masala powder
2.5ml (½ tsp) salt
2.5ml (½ tsp) chilli powder
450g (1lb) potatoes, boiled, peeled, cubed and boiled for 4 to 5 minutes
50g (2oz) frozen or shelled peas
10ml (2 tsp) dry mango powder
Lemon juice

To make filling, heat oil and fry onion until just tender. Sprinkle with garam masala, salt and chilli powder. Fry for one minute and add drained potatoes and peas. Mix well and fry for 2-3 minutes until potatoes are tender. Sprinkle with mango powder or lemon juice. Allow to cool.

Meat Filling
1 onion, peeled and chopped
50g (2oz) ghee or
30ml (2 tblsp) oil
450g (1lb) mince (lamb or beef)
5ml (1 tsp) ginger paste
5ml (1 tsp) garlic paste
10ml (2 tsp) ground black pepper
2.5ml (½ tsp) salt

Fry onion until golden brown in ghee or oil. Add mince, ginger and garlic paste, black ground pepper and salt. Fry the mixture for 8-10 minutes until dry. Remove from pan and allow to cool. Samosas made with mince can be frozen either half fried or unfried. Fry straight from the freezer when required. They can also be thawed before frying without any damage or alteration to taste.

Tikia
(POTATO-MINCE PATTIES)

PREPARATION TIME: 20 minutes
COOKING TIME: 20-30 minutes

1 onion, peeled and chopped
25g (1oz) ghee or
15ml (1 tblsp) oil
225g (8oz) minced lamb or beef
100g (4oz) frozen or shelled peas
2 sprigs fresh green coriander leaves, chopped
2-3 small green chillis, chopped (optional)
5ml (1 tsp) ground black pepper
450g (1lb) boiled potatoes, peeled and mashed
5-10ml (1-2 tsp) salt
1-2 beaten eggs
Oil for frying

Fry onion in ghee or oil until just tender (2-3 minutes). Add mince, peas, coriander leaves, chillis and black pepper. Fry for 4-5 minutes. Cool and mix with mashed potatoes and salt. Make 20-25 small, flat burger shapes. Heat the oil in a frying pan and dip tikias in beaten egg to coat. Shallow fry in hot oil. Fry on each side for 2-3 minutes. Serve hot or cold with chutney.

Khageea
(SPICED SCRAMBLED EGG)

PREPARATION TIME: 6 minutes
COOKING TIME: 10 minutes

1 onion, peeled and chopped
30ml (2 tblsp) oil
2.5ml (½ tsp) chilli powder
1.25ml (¼ tsp) turmeric powder
1 green chilli, chopped
2 sprigs fresh coriander leaves, chopped
2 fresh tomatoes, chopped
Salt to taste
15ml (1 tblsp) water
4 well-beaten eggs

Fry onion in oil for 2 minutes. Add spices and green chilli and coriander leaves, stir fry for 1 minute. Add chopped, fresh tomatoes. Season with salt and sprinkle in the water. Add beaten eggs. Cover and cook on gentle heat for 6-7 minutes. Stir and mix egg over gentle heat. Khageea should look like spiced scrambled eggs. Serve with parathas for any meal, including a hearty breakfast.

Wada
(DAAL FRITTERS)

PREPARATION TIME: 2-3 hours
COOKING TIME: 20 minutes

100g (4oz) urid daal, washed and soaked for 2-3 hours
100g (4oz) yellow, dehusked moong daal, washed and soaked for 2-3 hours
Little water to grind
1 onion, peeled and finely chopped
5-10ml (1-2 tsp) salt
2-3 sprigs fresh coriander leaves, chopped
1 small green chilli finely chopped or
2.5ml (½ tsp) chilli powder
2.5cm (1 inch) ginger root, peeled and finely chopped
1.25ml (¼ tsp) bicarbonate of soda
Oil for deep frying

Grind drained urid and moong daal with a little water to a coarse, thick paste. Pour into a mixing bowl and add onion, salt, coriander leaves, chilli powder or green chillis, ginger and soda. Mix well and set aside for 4-5 minutes. Fry small spoonfuls of the mixture, a few at a time, for 3-4 minutes until golden brown. Drain and serve hot with chutney.

Omelette

PREPARATION TIME: 5 minutes
COOKING TIME: 5 minutes

2 eggs per person, white and yolk separated
1 small onion, finely chopped
1 fresh tomato, thinly sliced
1 green chilli, finely chopped
1 sprig coriander leaves, finely chopped
5ml (1 tsp) water
Salt to taste
15ml (1 tblsp) oil

Beat egg white until stiff. Add egg yolk and beat well. Mix in chopped onion, tomato, chilli, coriander and water. Grease a frying pan well with oil. Heat the pan and pour the egg mixture into it. Sprinkle with salt to taste. Cover and cook the omelette for 2-3 minutes until the sides leave the pan. With a flat

Facing page: Tikia (top left), Samosa (top right) and Wada (bottom).

spoon or spatula ease the base of the omelette and turn it over to cook the other side. Cover and cook for another 2-3 minutes. Serve hot with tomato ketchup or chutney, along with rotis or parathas.

Ganthia
(BAISEN STICKS)

PREPARATION TIME: 10 minutes

COOKING TIME: 10-15 minutes

225g (8oz) baisen flour (chick pea flour)
1.25-2.5ml (¼-½ tsp) salt
2.5ml (½ tsp) bicarbonate of soda
2.5ml (½ tsp) omum (ajwain)
20 whole peppercorns, crushed
Pinch of asafoetida
50ml (2½ fl oz) oil
Oil for frying
Water

Sift flour, salt, bicarbonate of soda and omum together. Add crushed peppercorns, asafoetida and 30ml (1½ fl oz) warm oil. Rub in well and knead with water to make a stiff dough. Take 5ml (1 tsp) oil, rub over dough and knead. Repeat 3-4 times until dough is quiet smooth. Pass lumps of dough, through sev mould or spaghetti machine, with a large hole setting. Fry baisen sticks in hot oil until golden brown and crisp over a low heat. Drain on kitchen paper and store in airtight containers. Serve with tea or drinks.

Egg Curry

PREPARATION TIME: 10 minutes

COOKING TIME: 20 minutes

1 large onion, peeled and chopped
25g (1oz) ghee or
15ml (1 tblsp) oil
2.5cm (1 inch) cinnamon stick
1 bayleaf
4 small cardamoms
6 cloves
5ml (1 tsp) garlic paste
5ml (1 tsp) ginger paste
5ml (1 tsp) ground coriander
5ml (1 tsp) ground cumin
1.25ml (¼ tsp) turmeric powder
5ml (1 tsp) garam masala powder
5ml (1 tsp) chilli powder
200-225g (7-8oz) canned tomatoes, crushed
Salt to taste
175ml (6 fl oz) water
4-6 eggs, hard boiled and shelled
2 sprigs fresh green coriander leaves, chopped
2 green chillis, chopped

Fry onion in oil for 2-3 minutes. Add cinnamon, bayleaf, cardamoms, cloves. Fry for 1 minute. Add ginger and garlic paste. Stir the mixture, add coriander, cumin, turmeric, garam masala and chilli powder. Add canned tomatoes and salt to taste. Cook the spices for 5 minutes. Add water, cover and bring to boil. Add eggs and cook for 10-12 minutes. Garnish with green chillis and fresh coriander leaves. The gravy can be increased or reduced as required. Serve with plain boiled rice.

Nimki and Papadi

PREPARATION TIME: 10 minutes

COOKING TIME: 15-20 minutes

225g (8oz) plain flour
1.25g (¼ tsp) salt
2.5ml (½ tsp) bicarbonate of soda
5ml (1 tsp) onion seed (kalongi)
2.5ml (½ tsp) omum
Pinch of asafoetida
50g (2oz) ghee or
45ml (3 tblsp) oil
Water
Oil for deep frying

Sift flour, salt, bicarbonate of soda, and add onion seed and omum. Add asafoetida and rub in ghee or oil. Knead with water to make a stiff dough. Knead for 3-4 minutes until smooth. Make 2 equal portions. Roll out each portion as thinly as possible, to about 3mm (⅛ inch) thickness. Then cut the first piece of dough diagonally into strips both ways to make small bite size diamond shapes and prick with fork. Roll out the other dough to a similar thickness and cut neat, round shapes with a clean, sharp jar lid or a biscuit cutter. Heat the oil and fry the shapes until golden brown and crisp. Drain on kitchen paper and allow to cool before storing them in jars or tins. These can be stored for up to 2 months. Serve with tea or drinks. The diamond shapes are called nimki and the round shapes are called papadi.

Ganthia (top) and Nimki and Papadi (bottom).

HEALTHY EATING

Introduction

For most of us, eating is one of life's great pleasures, with delectable flavours and aromas, and bright colours and textures, all stimulating our appetites. Unfortunately, these pleasurable aspects of food and eating often lead us to eat more than we need, and to crave for the wrong sorts of food. Wise decisions for healthy eating need to be made with some basic knowledge of nutrition.

What is Healthy Eating?

For optimum health we need a diet that regularly contains carbohydrates, proteins, fat, vitamins and minerals. Some foods are particularly rich in one nutrient, whereas others contain three or more. Each of the following nutrients is essential to the body.

Protein: for body growth and cell replacement.
Carbohydrate: for energy.
Fibre: aids digestion, and helps to prevent digestive-associated complaints.
Fat: concentrated source of energy; also provides vitamins A, D, E and K.
Vitamin A: for healthy eyes and strong bones and teeth.
Vitamin B: necessary for healthy skin, as well as the digestive and nervous system and blood formation.
Vitamin C: increases resistance to infection; aids healing of wounds.
Vitamin D: helps strengthen teeth and bones.
Calcium: strengthens teeth and bones; essential to the nervous system, muscles, heart and blood.

Iron: maintains haemoglobin in the blood.
Generally speaking, we all eat a diet which is too rich in fat (especially animal fat), too high in refined sugar, too high in salt, and too low in natural fibre.

General Guidelines for a Healthy Eating Pattern.

Eat white fish, chicken, turkey and veal as the main protein meats.
Eat low fat cheeses, such as curd and cottage cheese, rather than the high fat cheeses such as Cheddar.
Use skimmed milk in place of full fat milk, both for drinks and for cooking.
Use the minimum amount of margarine or butter for spreading on bread and toast, and use olive oil for cooking wherever possible.
If dishes need sweetening, use an unrefined sugar or honey – people who are also trying to lose weight can use an artificial sweetener instead (choose a good one).
Choose breads and cereals which are rich in fibre – wholemeal bread, brown rice, wholewheat pasta, etc.
Eat plenty of fresh fruits and vegetables, raw whenever possible.
Choose healthy cooking methods – poaching, baking, casseroling, etc. If frying is a necessary stage in a recipe, use the minimum amount of fat.

Recipes

All the recipes in this section have been put together in such a way that they not only offer a good balance of nutrients, but also follow the healthy eating guidelines listed above. They also taste delicious.

Facing page: Noodles with Kidney Beans and Pesto (top) and Cucumber with Yogurt, Dill and Burghul (bottom).

Soups and Starters

Houmus with Lime and Pine Kernels

PREPARATION TIME: 15 minutes, plus soaking and chilling time

COOKING TIME: 1 hour

SERVES: 4 people

100g (4oz) dried chick peas
Salt and freshly ground black pepper to taste
Juice of 2 limes
2 large cloves garlic, peeled and crushed
30ml (2 tblsp) natural yogurt
15ml (1 tblsp) tahina (sesame seed paste)
15ml (1 tblsp) pine kernels, lightly toasted and chopped

Garnish
Wedges of fresh lime

To Serve
Warm wholemeal pitta bread, or fingers of hot wholemeal toast

Soak the chick peas in cold water overnight. Drain the chick peas and put them into a pan with sufficient fresh cold water to cover; add 5ml (1 tsp) salt. Bring to the boil and simmer, covered, for 1 hour, until the chick peas are tender. Drain thoroughly and allow the chick peas to cool slightly. Put the chick peas into the liquidiser with the lime juice, garlic, yogurt, tahina, and salt and pepper to taste; blend until smooth. Cover and chill for 2-3 hours. Stir in the toasted pine kernels. Spoon into a bowl, or onto small serving plates, and garnish with wedges of lime. Serve with warm pitta bread, or fingers of hot toast.
Note: this houmus also makes a delicious dip to serve with sticks of raw vegetables.

Avocado and Smoked Salmon Mousse

PREPARATION TIME: 40 minutes, plus chilling time

SERVES: 4 people

1 large ripe avocado
Juice and grated rind of ½ lemon

150ml (¼ pint) natural yogurt
Salt and freshly ground black pepper to taste
2 drops Tabasco
60ml (4 tblsp) dry white wine
10ml (2 tsp) powdered gelatine
100g (4oz) smoked salmon trimmings, finely chopped
15ml (1 tblsp) chopped chives

Garnish
Lemon peel leaves
4 small curls smoked salmon

Peel, halve and stone the avocado. Chop the avocado flesh and put it into the liquidiser with the lemon juice and rind, yogurt, salt and pepper to taste, Tabasco and half

This page: Houmus with Lime and Pine Kernels (top right), Avocado and Smoked Salmon Mousse (top left), Leek and Cashew Nut Soup (bottom). Facing page: Spinach Ramekins (top), Courgette and Lemon Soup (centre left) and Chicken Liver and Tarragon Pate (bottom).

the white wine. Blend until smooth. Dissolve the gelatine in the remaining white wine and blend into the avocado mixture. Leave on one side until the mixture starts to thicken. Lightly grease 4 small decorative moulds. Mix the smoked salmon and chives into the thickened avocado mixture; spoon into the prepared moulds. Chill until set. Unmould the set mousses carefully onto small plates. Garnish with lemon peel leaves and small curls of smoked salmon.

Leek and Cashew Nut Soup

PREPARATION TIME:	15-20 minutes
COOKING TIME:	30-35 minutes
SERVES:	4 people

1 medium onion, thinly sliced.
30ml (2 tblsp) olive oil
1 clove garlic, peeled and crushed
6 medium size leeks, halved, washed and shredded
300ml (½ pint) skimmed milk
450ml (¾ pint) chicken stock
Salt and freshly ground black pepper to taste
75g (3oz) shelled cashew nuts, lightly toasted

Garnish
Matchstick strips of leek
A few lightly toasted cashew nuts, finely chopped (optional)

Fry the onion gently in the olive oil for 3 minutes. Add the garlic and shredded leeks and fry together for a further 3 minutes. Add the skimmed milk, chicken stock, and salt and pepper to taste. Bring to the boil and simmer gently for 20-25 minutes. Blend the soup in the liquidiser, together with the toasted cashew nuts, until smooth. Reheat the soup gently in a clean saucepan. Serve each portion garnished with a few strips of leek and a sprinkling of toasted cashews.

Spinach Ramekins

PREPARATION TIME:	25 minutes
COOKING TIME:	35 minutes
OVEN:	180°C, 350°F, Gas Mark 4
SERVES:	4 people

450g (1lb) fresh spinach, cooked and drained thoroughly
Salt and freshly ground black pepper to taste
Pinch ground nutmeg
2 eggs
2 egg yolks
60ml (4 tblsp) fresh wholemeal breadcrumbs
30ml (2 tblsp) natural yogurt
30ml (2 tblsp) grated Parmesan cheese
8-12 small spinach leaves

Garnish
Sprigs fresh dill
Small twists of lemon

Mix the cooked spinach with the salt and pepper to taste, nutmeg, whole eggs, egg yolks, breadcrumbs, yogurt and Parmesan cheese. Line 4 lightly greased cocotte dishes or ramekins with the spinach leaves, pressing them in well to fit the shape of the dishes. Spoon in the spinach and egg mixture carefully. Stand the dishes in a roasting tin an add sufficient hot water to come halfway up the sides. Bake in the oven for 35 minutes, until just set. The Spinach Ramekins can either be served hot or cold. Unmould each one carefully onto a small serving plate. Garnish with sprigs of fresh dill and twists of lemon, and serve with fingers of lightly buttered brown bread.
Note: the mixture can be baked in a small loaf tin, if preferred, and served cut into slices.

Spicy Rice Stuffed Mushrooms

PREPARATION TIME:	20 minutes
COOKING TIME:	20-25 minutes
OVEN:	190°C, 375°F, Gas Mark 5
SERVES:	4 people

12 medium size flat mushrooms
1 small onion, finely chopped
30ml (2 tblsp) olive oil
1 clove garlic, peeled and crushed
30ml (2 tblsp) chopped parsley
120ml (8 tblsp) cooked brown rice
1 egg, beaten
30ml (2 tblsp) grated Parmesan cheese
Salt and freshly ground black pepper to taste
Generous pinch ground cinnamon

Garnish
Small radicchio leaves
Sprigs fresh parsley

Remove the stalks from the mushrooms and chop the stalks finely. Peel the mushrooms and place them dark side uppermost in a lightly greased ovenproof dish. Fry the onion gently in half the olive oil for 2-3 minutes. Add the garlic and chopped mushroom stalks and fry for a further 3 minutes. Mix with the parsley, cooked brown rice, beaten egg, half the Parmesan cheese, salt and pepper to taste and the cinnamon. Spoon the savoury mixture on top of each mushroom and dribble over the remaining olive oil. Bake in the oven for 15-20 minutes. Serve piping hot, garnished with small radicchio leaves and parsley sprigs.

Celery and Hazelnut Soup

PREPARATION TIME:	15 minutes
COOKING TIME:	30-35 minutes
SERVES:	4 people

1 medium onion, thinly sliced
30ml (2 tblsp) olive oil
6-8 stems celery, finely chopped
1 bayleaf
Salt and freshly ground black pepper to taste
30ml (2 tblsp) ground hazelnuts
300ml (½ pint) skimmed milk
450ml (¾ pint) chicken stock

Garnish
Small celery leaves
A few flaked hazelnuts

Fry the onion gently in the olive oil for 3 minutes. Add the celery and fry for a further 3 minutes. Add the bayleaf, salt and pepper to taste, ground hazelnuts, skimmed milk and chicken stock. Bring to the boil and simmer gently for 20-25 minutes. Blend the soup in the liquidiser until smooth. Reheat the soup gently in a clean saucepan. Serve each portion garnished with a celery leaf and a sprinkling of flaked hazelnuts.

Courgette and Lemon Soup

PREPARATION TIME:	20 minutes, plus chilling time
COOKING TIME:	about 25 minutes
SERVES:	4 people

1 medium onion, thinly sliced
30ml (2 tblsp) olive oil
450g (1lb) courgettes, topped and tailed, and sliced
Finely grated rind of 1 lemon
450ml (¾ pint) chicken stock
Salt and freshly ground black pepper to taste
2 egg yolks
200ml (⅓ pint) natural yogurt

Garnish
Thin slices of courgette
Small sprigs of mint (optional)

Fry the onion gently in the olive oil for 3 minutes. Add the courgettes and fry for a further 2-3 minutes. Add the lemon rind, chicken stock and salt and pepper to taste. Bring to the boil and simmer, covered, for 20 minutes. Blend the soup in the liquidiser until smooth. If you are serving the soup hot, reheat the soup in a clean pan with the beaten egg yolks and yogurt – do not allow to re-boil. To serve the soup cold, cool the blended soup slightly and add the beaten egg yolks and yogurt. Chill thoroughly. Garnish each portion of soup with a thin slice of courgette and a sprig of mint.

Tomato and Orange Soup

PREPARATION TIME:	15 minutes
COOKING TIME:	about 25 minutes
SERVES:	4 people

1kg (2¼lbs) ripe tomatoes, skinned, seeded and chopped
15ml (1 tblsp) olive oil
1 clove garlic, peeled and crushed
Finely grated rind of ½ an orange
450ml (¾ pint) chicken stock
150ml (¼ pint) fresh orange juice
Salt and freshly ground black pepper to taste
5ml (1 tsp) honey

Garnish
Twists of orange peel
A little natural yogurt

Put the chopped tomatoes, olive oil, garlic and orange rind into a pan; cover the pan and 'sweat' gently over a moderate heat for 3-4 minutes. Add the chicken stock, orange juice, salt and pepper to taste, and the honey. Cover and simmer gently for 20 minutes. Blend the soup in the liquidiser until smooth. The prepared soup can either be served hot or chilled. Serve each portion garnished with a twist or two of orange peel and a swirl of natural yogurt.

Spicy Rice Stuffed Mushroom (right), Tomato and Orange Soup (below) and Celery and Hazelnut Soup (bottom).

Smoked Halibut with Yogurt and Lumpfish

PREPARATION TIME: 10-15 minutes

SERVES: 4 people

225g (8oz) smoked halibut, thinly sliced
60ml (4 tblsp) natural yogurt
30ml (2 tblsp) orange lumpfish roe
Salt and freshly ground black pepper to taste
Half a lemon

Garnish
Small sprigs fennel or dill

To Serve
Small triangles lightly buttered brown bread

Arrange the slices of smoked halibut on 4 small plates. Mix the yogurt with half the lumpfish and salt and pepper to taste. Add a squeeze of lemon juice. Squeeze the remaining lemon juice over the halibut. Spoon a little yogurt sauce into the centre of each portion; top with the remaining lumpfish roe. Garnish each portion with a few sprigs of fennel. Serve with triangles of buttered brown bread. Note: if you find smoked halibut difficult to buy, you can use smoked salmon instead.

Aubergine Puree with Crudites

PREPARATION TIME: 25-30 minutes

COOKING TIME: about 10 minutes

SERVES: 4 people

2 medium size aubergines
45ml (3 tblsp) olive oil
2 cloves garlic, peeled and crushed
Juice of 1 lemon
Salt and freshly ground black pepper to taste
10ml (2 tsp) chopped fresh mint

Garnish
Sprigs fresh mint

Grill the aubergines under a moderately hot grill until the skins blister and char – when squeezed with a cloth, the aubergines should feel soft in the centre. Rub the skins off the aubergines under a cold running tap. Squeeze the peeled aubergines in a piece of

clean muslin to remove as much of the bitter juices as possible. Put the aubergine flesh into a liquidiser and blend until smooth. Gradually blend in the olive oil, garlic, lemon juice and salt and pepper to taste. Stir in the chopped mint. Cover and chill briefly. Serve with vegetable crudites as dunks: sticks of carrot, cucumber, celery, pepper, small button mushrooms, strips of fennel, etc. Garnish with mint.

Chicken Liver and Tarragon Pate

PREPARATION TIME: 10-15 minutes

COOKING TIME: 7-8 minutes

SERVES: 4 people

1 small onion, finely chopped
15ml (1 tblsp) olive oil
1 clove garlic, peeled and crushed
15ml (1 tblsp) fresh tarragon, chopped
225g (8oz) chicken livers, roughly chopped
15ml (1 tblsp) brandy
30ml (2 tblsp) natural yogurt
Salt and freshly ground black pepper to taste

Garnish
Sprigs fresh tarragon or other herbs

To Serve
Hot wholemeal crusty bread, or toast

Fry the onion gently in the olive oil for 3 minutes. Add the garlic, tarragon and chicken livers and fry gently until sealed on the outside but still pink in the centre. Stir in the brandy and allow to bubble for 30 seconds. Put the chicken livers and their liquid into the liquidiser and blend until smooth. Mix in the yogurt and salt and pepper to taste. Spoon into one small terrine, or into several cocotte dishes, and chill. Garnish with fresh tarragon and serve with hot crusty bread or toast.
Note: if you are using small cocotte dishes, the surface of the pate can be smoothed level and a layer of aspic jelly spooned over the top prior to chilling.

Egg and Cheese Mousse with Watercress Sauce

PREPARATION TIME: 25-30 minutes, plus chilling time

COOKING TIME: 2-3 minutes

SERVES: 4 people

225g (8oz) curd cheese, or sieved cottage cheese
150ml (¼ pint) natural yogurt
150ml (¼ pint) chicken stock
10ml (2 tsp) powdered gelatine
Salt and freshly ground black pepper to taste
15ml (1 tblsp) chopped parsley
3 hard boiled eggs, shelled and finely chopped

Sauce
45ml (3 tblsp) chicken stock
1 bunch watercress
1 clove garlic, peeled and crushed
15ml (1 tblsp) pine kernels
60ml (4 tblsp) natural yogurt

Garnish
1 hard boiled egg yolk, sieved
Small sprigs watercress

Lightly grease 4 individual moulds or ramekin dishes. Beat the cheese with the yogurt and half the chicken stock until smooth. Dissolve the gelatine in the remaining chicken stock. Stir the gelatine into the cheese mixture, together with salt and pepper to taste, parsley, and the chopped hard boiled eggs. Spoon into the prepared moulds. Chill until set – about 3 hours. Meanwhile, make the sauce. Put the chicken stock, trimmed watercress and garlic into a small pan. Cover and simmer for 2-3 minutes. Cool slightly. Blend the watercress and its liquid in the liquidiser, together with the pine kernels, until smooth. Stir in the yogurt and chill. To serve, unmould each set mousse onto a small plate and spoon a pool of watercress sauce around each one. Garnish with a sprinkling of sieved egg yolk and a sprig of watercress.

This page: Aubergine Puree with Crudites (top) and Jellied Eggs en Cocotte (bottom).

Facing page: Egg and Cheese Mousse with Watercress Sauce (top) and Smoked Halibut with Yogurt and Lumpfish (bottom).

Stuffed Vine Leaves

PREPARATION TIME: 40 minutes

COOKING TIME: about 1 hour

SERVES: 6 people

100g (4oz) brown or wild rice
Salt and freshly ground black pepper
  to taste
450g (1lb) minced chicken
1 small onion, finely chopped
1 clove garlic, peeled and crushed
15ml (1 tblsp) chopped chives
15ml (1 tblsp) chopped fresh
  coriander
30ml (2 tblsp) chopped parsley
30ml (2 tblsp) chopped sultanas
15ml (1 tblsp) chopped pine kernels
Finely grated rind of ½ small orange
Juice of ½ lemon
225g (8oz) prepared vine leaves (see
  below)
600ml (1 pint) chicken stock and dry
  white wine, mixed

To Serve

Thinned natural yogurt
Mixed spice (optional)
Feathery sprigs of dill or fennel

Note: vine leaves are preserved in
brine, and this needs rinsing off
before they can be used. Put the
opened vine leaves into a large
bowl and cover with boiling water;
leave to stand until the vine leaves
can be easily separated. Rinse the
vine leaves in cold water and then
drain on absorbent paper, veined
sides uppermost.
Cook the rice in a pan of boiling
salted water for 8 minutes. Drain
thoroughly. Mix the par-cooked
rice with the minced chicken,
chopped onion, garlic, chives,
coriander, parsley, sultanas, pine
kernels, orange rind, lemon juice,
and salt and pepper to taste. Line
the base of a large, deep frying pan
with 4 large leaves. Divide the
prepared filling amongst the
remaining leaves, placing each
portion towards the base of the
leaf. Fold the stem of the leaf over
the filling and then fold in the
sides; roll up to form a sausage
shape. Place the prepared stuffed
vine leaves close together in the
pan; add salt and pepper to taste
and the mixed water and wine.
Cover the pan and simmer gently
for 50 minutes. Allow the stuffed
vine leaves to cool in their cooking
liquid. Chill the vine leaves for an
hour or two before serving. Serve
about 5 stuffed vine leaves per
person. Place a pool of yogurt onto
each serving plate and top with the
chilled vine leaves. Sprinkle with
mixed spice and garnish with dill.
Note: the vine leaves can be
marinated in a little oil and vinegar
dressing, if preferred, prior to
chilling.

My Gazpacho

PREPARATION TIME: 25 minutes,
plus chilling time

COOKING TIME: 2-3 minutes

SERVES: 4 people

300ml (½ pint) pure tomato juice
300ml (½ pint) chicken stock
½ small cucumber, seeded and
  chopped
450g (1lb) ripe tomatoes, skinned,
  seeded and chopped
6 spring onions, chopped
1 green pepper, seeded and chopped
1 red pepper, seeded and chopped
2 cloves garlic, peeled and crushed
2 anchovy fillets, chopped
15ml (1 tblsp) chopped fresh basil
15ml (1 tblsp) dry sherry
Salt and freshly ground black pepper
  to taste

Garnish

Thinly sliced cucumber
Small sprigs fresh basil

Put the tomato juice and chicken
stock into a pan with the chopped
cucumber, tomatoes, spring onions,
green and red peppers, garlic,
anchovies and basil. Bring to the
boil, covered, and then remove
immediately from the heat. Leave
to cool in the covered saucepan
(this allows all the flavours to
mingle). Once the vegetables and
their liquid are quite cool, blend in
the liquidiser until smooth,
together with the sherry and salt
and pepper to taste. Chill the soup
thoroughly for at least 4 hours. The
soup will be quite thick at this
stage, which is characteristic of a
'gazpacho'; however, it can be
thinned with a little extra chicken
stock if preferred. Ladle the soup
into bowls (usually glass ones),
adding a few ice cubes to each one.
Serve each portion garnished with
a few slices of cucumber and a sprig
of fresh basil.

Jellied Eggs en Cocotte

PREPARATION TIME: 30 minutes, plus chilling time

COOKING TIME: 2 minutes

SERVES: 4 people

4 tomatoes, skinned, seeded and chopped
1 clove garlic, peeled and finely chopped
15ml (1 tblsp) chopped parsley
Salt and freshly ground black pepper to taste
4 eggs
400ml (⅔ pint) beef consomme

Garnish
Finely chopped tomato, or small tomato 'roses'
Sprigs parsley

Mix the chopped tomatoes with the garlic, parsley, and salt and pepper to taste. Divide amongst 4 cocotte dishes. Lower the eggs into a pan of boiling water and cook for 2 minutes – the eggs should be just soft boiled. Cool the eggs under cold, running water. Carefully remove the shells and sit an egg in each cocotte dish. Spoon the consomme into each dish so that it covers the eggs – if the dishes are quite deep, you will need slightly more consomme than the quantity given above. Chill until set. Garnish each dish with a small tomato rose and a sprig of parsley. To make a tomato rose, peel a thin strip of outer flesh from a firm tomato using a small sharp knife or a potato peeler. Wind the tomato strip round and round, easing it out to form the shape of a rose head.

Stuffed Vine Leaves (far left) and My Gazpacho (left).

Fish and Seafood

Smoked Haddock and Egg Quiche

PREPARATION TIME: about 25 minutes

COOKING TIME: about 40 minutes

OVEN: 190°C, 375°F, Gas Mark 5

SERVES: 6 people

225g (8oz) wholemeal pastry
350g (12oz) smoked haddock fillet
Chicken stock
2 hard boiled eggs, chopped
15ml (1 tblsp) chopped chives
75g (3oz) grated cheese
300ml (½ pint) skimmed milk
3 eggs
Salt and freshly ground black pepper
    to taste

Garnish
2 hard boiled eggs
Finely chopped parsley

Roll out the pastry and use to line a 23cm (9 inch), deep fluted flan case; press up the edges well. Line with greaseproof paper and baking beans and bake 'blind' for 10 minutes. Meanwhile, poach the smoked haddock fillet gently in chicken stock for about 8 minutes, until just tender. Drain the fish and flake it, discarding any skin and bone. Put the flaked smoked haddock into the pastry case with the chopped hard boiled egg, chopped chives and grated cheese. Beat the skimmed milk with the eggs and salt and pepper to taste; pour into the pastry case. Bake for 30 minutes until the filling is just set. Meanwhile, prepare the garnish. Separate the hard boiled egg whites and yolks; chop the whites finely and sieve the yolks. The quiche can either be served hot or cold. Sprinkle the top with chopped egg white, sieved egg yolk and parsley.

Provençal Fish Stew

PREPARATION TIME: about 15 minutes

COOKING TIME: about 35 minutes

SERVES: 4 people

1 medium onion, finely chopped
2 cloves garlic, peeled and crushed
45ml (3 tblsp) olive oil
750g (1½lb) tomatoes, skinned, seeded and chopped
30ml (2 tblsp) tomato puree
600ml (1 pint) dry red wine
Salt and freshly ground black pepper
    to taste
1¼ litres (2 pints) mussels in their
    shells, scrubbed
8 large Mediterranean prawns
100g (4oz) peeled prawns
4 crab claws, partly shelled

To Serve
8 small slices stale French bread, or
    similar crusty bread
A little olive oil
1 large clove garlic
Bruised chopped parsley

Fry the onion gently in the olive oil for 3 minutes. Add the garlic and chopped tomatoes and fry gently for a further 3 minutes. Add the tomato puree and red wine and bring to the boil; simmer for 15 minutes. Add the mussels and

This page: Fish, Courgette and Lemon Kebabs (top), Smoked Haddock and Egg Quiche (bottom).

Facing page: Provencale Fish Stew (top) and Baked Sea Bass with Fennel and Vegetable Julienne (bottom).

simmer, covered, for 5 minutes. Add the whole Mediterranean prawns, peeled prawns and crab claws, and simmer for a further 5 minutes. Meanwhile, prepare the bread croutes. Brush the slices of French bread with a little olive oil and rub with the crushed clove of garlic. Grill until crisp and golden and then sprinkle with chopped parsley. Spoon the fish stew into a deep serving dish and top with the bread croutes. Serve immediately.

Chilled Fish Curry

PREPARATION TIME: 20 minutes, plus chilling time

COOKING TIME: about 6 minutes

SERVES: 4 people

225g (8oz) fresh salmon
350g (12oz) white fish fillet
Chicken stock
Salt and freshly ground black pepper to taste
150ml (¼ pint) mayonnaise
300ml (½ pint) natural yogurt
10ml (2 tsp) curry powder
Juice and grated rind of ½ lemon
100g (4oz) peeled prawns

Garnish
Sliced, peeled kiwi fruit
Sprigs fresh mint
Flaked coconut

Put the fresh salmon and white fish fillet into a shallow pan and add sufficient chicken stock to just cover. Add salt and pepper to taste; cover and simmer gently until the fish is just tender. Remove the fish carefully from the cooking liquid and allow to cool slightly. Mix the mayonnaise with the yogurt, curry powder, lemon juice and rind, and salt and pepper to taste. Thin the curry sauce down a little with a small amount of the fish cooking liquid. Flake the cooked salmon and white fish and stir lightly into the prepared curry sauce, together with the peeled prawns. Arrange the chilled fish curry on a serving dish and garnish with slices of kiwi fruit, sprigs of fresh mint and a scattering of flaked coconut.

Plaice Tartare

PREPARATION TIME: 25 minutes, plus chilling time

COOKING TIME: 6 minutes

SERVES: 4 people

450g (1lb) plaice or sole fillets
Skimmed milk
Salt and freshly ground black pepper to taste
60ml (4 tblsp) olive oil
Juice of ½ lemon
2.5ml (½ tsp) soft brown sugar
4 anchovy fillets, finely chopped
1 large clove garlic, peeled and crushed
30ml (2 tblsp) chopped parsley
2 hard boiled eggs

Garnish
Small wedges of lemon
Green olives
Capers

Put the fish fillets into a large, shallow pan with sufficient skimmed milk to just cover; add salt and pepper to taste. Cover the pan and poach the fish gently until just tender – about 6 minutes. Meanwhile, make the dressing. Mix the olive oil with the lemon juice, sugar, anchovy fillets, garlic, and salt and pepper to taste. Stir in the chopped parsley. Separate the egg yolks from the whites; chop the whites finely, and sieve the yolks. Add the chopped egg white to the dressing. Drain the cooked fish and flake it; mix lightly with the prepared dressing. Cover and chill for 1 hour. Spoon the prepared plaice tartare onto serving plates; sprinkle each portion with sieved egg yolk. Garnish with wedges of lemon, green olives and capers.

Baked Sea Bass with Fennel and Vegetable Julienne

PREPARATION TIME: 30 minutes

COOKING TIME: 35-40 minutes

OVEN: 190°C, 375°F, Gas Mark 5

SERVES: 4-6 people

1 sea bass, about 1.25kg (2½lb) in weight, scaled, gutted and cleaned
Salt and freshly ground black pepper to taste
15ml (1 tblsp) chopped fresh fennel
1 large clove garlic, peeled and finely chopped
Coarsely grated rind of ½ lemon
30ml (2 tblsp) olive oil
60ml (4 tblsp) dry white wine

Vegetable Julienne
2 large carrots, peeled and cut into thin strips
3 stems celery, cut into thin strips
100g (4oz) haricots vert

Garnish
Feathery sprigs of fennel or dill

Season the sea bass inside and out; put the chopped fennel, garlic and lemon rind into the cavity of the fish. Lay the fish on a rectangle of greased foil, sitting on a baking sheet; pinch up the edges of the foil. Brush the sea bass with olive oil and spoon over the dry white wine. Pinch the foil together over the fish to completely enclose it. Bake in the oven for 35-40 minutes (the foil can be folded back for the last 10 minutes cooking time, if liked). For the vegetable julienne, steam al the vegetables over gently simmering water for about 10 minutes – they should still be slightly crunchy. Arrange the cooked sea bass on a large, oval serving platter, and surround with small 'bundles' of the steamed vegetables. Garnish with sprigs of fennel.

Cod Steaks with Asparagus Sauce and Endive

PREPARATION TIME: 25 minutes

COOKING TIME: 25-30 minutes

OVEN: 190°C, 375°F, Gas Mark 5

SERVES: 4 people

4 even size cod steaks
30ml (2 tblsp) melted butter
Salt and freshly ground black pepper to taste
5ml (1 tsp) fennel seed
450g (1lb) asparagus
150ml (¼ pint) chicken stock
1 egg yolk
45ml (3 tblsp) natural yogurt

Garnish
Curly endive
Feathery pieces of fennel
Thin lemon slices or twists

Put the cod steaks into a lightly greased ovenproof dish. Brush with melted butter; season to taste with salt and pepper and sprinkle over the fennel seed. Cover with a piece of foil and bake for 25-30 minutes, until the fish is just tender. Meanwhile, make the sauce. Trim the asparagus so that you just have nice green tips (use the remaining stems for making soup, etc.). Tie the asparagus tips together and cook upright in a little boiling water until just tender. Drain carefully and reserve 4 tips for garnish. Put the rest of the cooked asparagus tips into the liquidiser with the chicken stock, egg yolk, yogurt and salt and pepper to taste; blend until smooth. Arrange the cooked cod cutlets on a serving dish, and spoon some of the asparagus sauce over the top. Garnish with small pieces of curly endive, feathery pieces of fennel, lemon slices and the reserved asparagus tips. Serve the remaining asparagus sauce separately.

Fish, Courgette and Lemon Kebabs

PREPARATION TIME: 30 minutes, plus chilling time

COOKING TIME: about 8 minutes

SERVES: 4 people

16 small, thin sole fillets, or 8 larger ones, cut in half lengthways
60ml (4 tblsp) olive oil
1 clove garlic, peeled and crushed
Juice of ½ lemon
Finely grated rind of ½ lemon
Salt and freshly ground black pepper to taste
3 drops Tabasco
3 medium size courgettes, cut into ½cm (¼ inch) slices
1 medium green pepper, halved, seeded and cut into 2.5cm (1 inch) pieces

Garnish
30ml (2 tblsp) coarsely chopped parsley

Roll up each sole fillet, Swiss-roll fashion, and secure with wooden cocktail sticks. Place them in a shallow dish. Mix the olive oil with the garlic, lemon juice, lemon rind, salt and pepper to taste and the Tabasco. Spoon evenly over the fish. Cover and chill for 2 hours. Remove the wooden cocktail sticks and carefully thread the rolled fish fillets onto kebab skewers together with the courgette slices and pieces of green pepper, alternating them for colour. Brush each threaded kebab with the lemon and oil marinade. Grill for about 8 minutes, under a moderately hot grill, carefully turning the kebabs once during cooking. Brush the kebabs during cooking with any remaining marinade. Place the kebas on a serving dish and sprinkle with chopped parsley.

Plaice and Mushroom Turnovers

PREPARATION TIME: 25 minutes, plus cooling time

COOKING TIME: about 35 minutes

OVEN: 200°C, 400°F, Gas Mark 6

SERVES: 4 people

4 large plaice fillets
Salt and freshly ground black pepper to taste
Skimmed milk
Finely grated rind of ½ lemon
100g (4oz) button mushrooms, thinly sliced
25g (1oz) butter
Juice of 1 lemon

Plaice Tartare (left) and Chilled Fish Curry (below).

cooked fillets carefully to a shallow serving dish and spoon over the prepared anchovy, caper and mint sauce. The sole fillets can either be served warm or chilled. Garnish with matchstick strips of orange peel and small sprigs of mint.

Taramasalata

PREPARATION TIME: about 20 minutes

SERVES: 4 people

3 slices wholemeal bread, crusts removed
75ml (5 tblsp) water
100g (4oz) smoked cod's roe, skinned
1 large clove garlic, peeled and crushed
Juice of 1 lemon
90ml (6 tblsp) olive oil
Salt and freshly ground black pepper to taste

To Serve
Wholemeal pitta bread
Olives (black or green)

Note: for special occasions, serve the taramasalata in a hollowed, cooked globe artichoke. Trim and cook the globe artichoke in the usual way. Drain thoroughly, upside-down, and brush lightly all over with oil and vinegar dressing. Pull out the centre leaves and remove the hairy choke. Brush inside with a little more dressing and fill with taramasalata – the outer leaves can then be pulled off and dipped into the taramasalata. Soak the bread in the water for 10 minutes; squeeze the bread lightly between the fingers. Put the bread into the liquidiser with the cod's roe, garlic, lemon juice and 15ml (1 tblsp) of the olive oil. Blend until smooth, and then gradually blend in the remaining olive oil. Season to taste with salt and pepper. Serve with warm pitta bread and olives, or as suggested above.

45ml (3 tblsp) hazelnut stuffing mix
350g (12oz) puff pastry (preferably the vegetable oil variety)
Beaten egg
Poppy seeds

Season each plaice fillet with salt and pepper to taste. Roll up each one Swiss-roll fashion and secure with a wooden cocktail stick. Place in a shallow pan and add sufficient skimmed milk to half cover; cover the pan and poach gently for 5 minutes. Drain the fish and allow to cool. Remove the wooden cocktail sticks. Put the lemon juice, mushrooms and butter into a small pan and cook gently for 5 minutes. Allow to cool and then stir in the hazelnut stuffing mix. Roll out the pastry quite thinly and cut 6 even sized circles, each about 15cm (6 inches) in diameter. Brush the pastry edges with beaten egg. Place a fish fillet in the centre of each

pastry circle and top with the mushroom and stuffing mixture; pull the pastry edges up and over the fish and pinch together to seal. Place on a lightly greased baking sheet and glaze with beaten egg. Bake in the oven for about 25 minutes, until well risen, puffed and golden. Serve piping hot.

Sole with Anchovy, Caper and Mint Sauce

PREPARATION TIME: 10-15 minutes

COOKING TIME: 10-12 minutes

SERVES: 4 people

30ml (2 tblsp) chopped fresh mint
60ml (4 tblsp) dry white wine
60ml (4 tblsp) olive oil
1 large clove garlic, peeled and finely chopped

Juice of 1 large orange
15ml (1 tblsp) capers
3 anchovy fillets, finely chopped
Salt and freshly ground black pepper to taste
8 good size sole fillets
Seasoned flour
25g (1oz) butter

Garnish
Matchstick strips orange peel
Small sprigs fresh mint

Mix half the chopped mint with the white wine, 45ml (3 tblsp) of the olive oil, the garlic, orange juice, capers, anchovy fillets and salt and pepper to taste. Dust the sole fillets very lightly in seasoned flour. Heat the remaining oil and the butter in a large, shallow pan with the remaining mint. Fry the sole fillets for 2-3 minutes on either side (you will find this easier if you fry the fillets in two batches). Remove the

This page: Plaice and Mushroom Turnovers (top) and Cod Steaks with Asparagus Sauce and Endive (bottom).

Facing page: Taramasalata (top) and Sole with Anchovy, Caper and Mint Sauce (bottom).

Meat Dishes

Stir Fried Calves' Liver with Peppers and Carrots

PREPARATION TIME:	15-20 minutes
COOKING TIME:	10-12 minutes
SERVES:	4 people

30ml (2 tblsp) olive oil
1 onion, thinly sliced
600g (1¼lb) calves' liver, cut into thin strips
Seasoned flour
60ml (4 tblsp) dry sherry
1 green pepper, seeded and cut into thin strips
3 large carrots, peeled and cut into thin strips
Salt and freshly ground black pepper to taste
1 clove garlic, peeled and cut into thin strips
100g (4oz) mung bean sprouts

Garnish
Sprigs fresh sage

Heat the olive oil in a large, shallow pan or wok; add the onion and stir fry for 3 minutes. Dust the strips of calves' liver in seasoned flour and add to the pan; stir fry until sealed on the outside but still pink in the centre. Add the sherry and bubble briskly; add 150ml (¼ pint) water or stock, green pepper, carrots, salt and pepper to taste and the garlic. Stir over a brisk heat for 3 minutes. Stir in the mung beans and heat through for 1 minute. Spoon into a serving dish and garnish with sprigs of fresh sage.

Chicken Moussaka

PREPARATION TIME:	about 30 minutes
COOKING TIME:	about 1 hour 5 minutes
OVEN:	190°C, 375°F, Gas Mark 5
SERVES:	6 people

60ml (4 tblsp) olive oil
1 medium onion, finely chopped
1 clove garlic, peeled and crushed
450g (1lb) minced raw chicken
30ml (2 tblsp) tomato puree
300ml (½ pint) chicken stock
30ml (2 tblsp) chopped parsley
Salt and freshly ground black pepper to taste
2 medium size aubergines, thinly sliced
150ml (¼ pint) natural yogurt
1 egg
50g (2oz) grated cheese
15ml (1 tblsp) grated Parmesan cheese

Heat half the olive oil in a pan; add the chopped onion and garlic and fry gently for 3 minutes. Add the minced chicken and fry until lightly browned. Add the tomato puree, chicken stock, parsley and salt and pepper to taste. Cover and simmer gently for 15 minutes. Lay the aubergine slices on lightly greased baking sheets and brush with the remaining olive oil; bake in the oven for 8 minutes. Arrange a layer of aubergine and then a layer of chicken in a lightly greased ovenproof dish; repeat the layers, finishing with a layer of aubergines. Beat the yogurt with the egg and grated cheese and spoon evenly over the top; sprinkle with the grated Parmesan. Bake in the oven for 35-40 minutes, until the top is bubbling and lightly golden. Serve piping hot.

Veal Casserole with Apricots and Prunes

PREPARATION TIME:	30 minutes
COOKING TIME:	about 1 hour 40 minutes
OVEN:	160°C, 325°F, Gas Mark 3
SERVES:	4 people

600g (1¼lb) boned leg of veal, cubed
Seasoned flour
45ml (3 tblsp) olive oil
1 large onion, thinly sliced
450g (1lb) fresh ripe apricots, skinned, halved and stoned
300ml (½ pint) chicken stock
300ml (½ pint) dry white wine
150ml (¼ pint) fresh orange juice
Salt and freshly ground black pepper to taste
75g (3oz) dried prunes, soaked overnight
75g (3oz) dried apricots, soaked overnight

Garnish
Matchstick strips of orange peel

Dust the cubed veal *lightly* in seasoned flour. Heat the oil in a pan; add the sliced onion and fry gently for 4 minutes. Meanwhile, put the halved and skinned fresh apricots into the liquidiser with the chicken stock and blend until smooth. Add the cubed veal to the onion and fry until evenly coloured on all sides. Gradually stir in the apricot puree, white wine and orange juice. Bring to the boil, stirring, and add salt and pepper to taste. Transfer to a casserole and add the drained prunes and apricots. Cover the casserole and cook in the oven for 1½ hours. Serve sprinkled with matchstick strips of orange peel.

Veal Paprika with Noodles

PREPARATION TIME:	10-15 minutes
COOKING TIME:	about 1 hour 15 minutes
SERVES:	4 people

1 medium onion, thinly sliced
30ml (2 tblsp) olive oil
600g (1¼lb) boned leg of veal, cubed
Seasoned flour
15ml (1 tblsp) paprika
15ml (1 tblsp) tomato puree
Bayleaf
450ml (¾ pint) chicken stock
150ml (¼ pint) skimmed milk
Salt and freshly ground black pepper to taste
100g (4oz) button mushrooms, sliced

To Serve
Cooked green noodles

Facing page: Veal Casserole with Apricots and Prunes (top) and Chicken Moussaka (bottom).

Fry the onion gently in the olive oil for 3 minutes. Dust the cubed veal *lightly* in seasoned flour and add to the onion; fry until the veal is evenly coloured on all sides. Add the paprika, tomato puree and bayleaf, and gradually stir in the stock and skimmed milk. Bring to the boil, stirring, and add salt and pepper to taste. Cover and simmer gently for 55 minutes. Add the sliced mushrooms and simmer for a further 10 minutes. Serve piping hot with cooked green noodles.

Rabbit in Mustard Sauce

PREPARATION TIME: 5 minutes

COOKING TIME: about 1 hour

SERVES: 4 people

4 rabbit joints
Seasoned flour
1 medium onion, thinly sliced
30ml (2 tblsp) olive oil
450ml (¾ pint) chicken stock
150ml (¼ pint) skimmed milk

15ml (1 tblsp) coarse grain mustard
30ml (2 tblsp) coarsely chopped parsley
Salt and freshly ground black pepper to taste

Garnish
Small puff pastry leaves

Dust the rabbit joints *lightly* in seasoned flour. Fry the sliced onion gently in the oil for 4 minutes; add the rabbit joints and fry until evenly coloured on all sides. Add

This page: Tarragon Chicken Pancakes (top) and Rabbit in Mustard Sauce (bottom).

Facing page: Stir Fried Calves' Liver with Peppers and Carrots (top) and Veal Paprika with Noodles (bottom).

the chicken stock, skimmed milk, mustard, parsley and salt and pepper to taste. Bring to the boil; cover and simmer gently for 40 minutes. Arrange on a serving dish or individual plates and garnish with pastry leaves.

Chicken with Blackcurrant Sauce and Mange Tout

PREPARATION TIME: 10-15 minutes

COOKING TIME: 12 minutes

SERVES: 4 people

4 chicken breasts, skinned and boned
Seasoned flour
Oil for shallow frying

Sauce
225g (8oz) fresh blackcurrants
Juice of 1 orange
150ml (¼ pint) red wine
Artificial sweetener to taste
Chicken stock

Garnish
Julienne strips orange peel
Cooked mange tout
4 lemon slices
Few whole fresh blackcurrants

Dust the chicken breasts lightly in seasoned flour; shallow fry gently in oil, for about 6 minutes on each side, until tender. Meanwhile, make the sauce. Put the blackcurrants into a pan with the orange juice, red wine, and sweetener to taste; cover and simmer gently until the blackcurrants are soft (this will only take a few minutes). Blend the sauce in the liquidiser until smooth. Reheat in a saucepan, adding sufficient stock to give a smooth coating consistency. Arrange the cooked chicken breasts on a serving dish. Spoon over the blackcurrant sauce and garnish with mange tout, strips of orange peel, and lemon slices topped with blackcurrants.

Chicken and Herb Loaf

PREPARATION TIME: 20-25 minutes

COOKING TIME: 50 minutes

OVEN: 190°C, 375°F, Gas Mark 5

SERVES: 6 people

450g (1lb) minced raw chicken
90ml (6 tblsp) wholemeal breadcrumbs
1 small onion, grated
1 clove garlic, peeled and crushed
30ml (2 tblsp) chopped parsley
15ml (1 tblsp) chopped fresh thyme
1 medium parsnip, peeled and grated
2 eggs, beaten
Salt and freshly ground black pepper to taste

Garnish
A little olive oil
15ml (1 tblsp) chopped parsley
Sprigs fresh rosemary

Mix the minced chicken with the breadcrumbs, onion, garlic, parsley, thyme, parsnip, beaten eggs and salt and pepper to taste. Spoon the mixture into a greased and lined loaf tin. Cover with a piece of greased foil. Bake in the oven for about 50 minutes, until cooked through – test with a skewer. For a brown top, remove the foil for the last 8-10 minutes. Brush the top of the loaf with the oil, while it is still hot, and sprinkle with the chopped parsley. Carefully take the loaf out of the tin, and serve either hot or cold, garnished with rosemary.

Chicken Andalusia

PREPARATION TIME: 15 minutes

COOKING TIME: 45 minutes

OVEN: 190°, 375°F, Gas Mark 5

SERVES: 4 people

4 small poussins
Salt and freshly ground black pepper to taste
Olive oil
4 small wedges of lime or lemon
4 bayleaves

Sauce
1 small onion, thinly sliced
30ml (2 tblsp) olive oil
1 clove garlic, peeled and crushed
450g (1lb) tomatoes, skinned, seeded and chopped
150ml (¼ pint) red wine
150ml (¼ pint) chicken stock
15ml (1 tblsp) tomato puree
2 green chillies, thinly sliced
1 small red pepper, seeded and cut into thin strips
1 small green pepper, seeded and cut into thin strips
30ml (2 tblsp) chopped blanched almonds
15ml (1 tblsp) pine kernels
12 small black olives
15ml (1 tblsp) raisins

Season the poussins inside and out with salt and pepper. Rub olive oil into the skin and push a wedge of lemon or lime and a bayleaf into the centre of each one. Roast the poussins in the oven for 45 minutes, until just tender (if they start to get too brown, cover them with foil during cooking). Meanwhile, make the sauce. Fry the sliced onion gently in the oil for 3 minutes; add the remaining sauce ingredients and simmer for 10 minutes. Arrange the poussins on a serving dish and spoon over the hot sauce.

Chicken Escalopes

PREPARATION TIME: 20 minutes, plus chilling time

COOKING TIME: 10 minutes

SERVES: 4 people

4 chicken escalopes
Beaten egg
Seasoned flour
60ml (4 tblsp) wholemeal breadcrumbs
15ml (1 tblsp) chopped fresh sage
25g (1oz) butter
15ml (1 tblsp) olive oil

Sauce
75ml (⅛ pint) low calorie mayonnaise
150ml (¼ pint) natural yogurt
5ml (1 tsp) grated fresh horseradish
30ml (2 tblsp) chopped walnuts

Garnish
175g (6oz) French beans, lightly cooked
4 thin slices lemon
15ml (1 tblsp) chopped walnuts

Dust the escalopes lightly in seasoned flour; dip into beaten egg and then coat with a mixture of breadcrumbs and sage. Chill for 30 minutes. Heat the butter and oil in a large, shallow pan; add the prepared escalopes and fry gently for 5 minutes on each side until lightly golden and tender. Keep warm. For the sauce: mix all the ingredients together. Arrange the cooked escalopes on a serving dish and garnish with the cooked beans and lemon slices topped with chopped walnuts. Spoon the sauce over the chicken.

Tarragon Chicken Pancakes

PREPARATION TIME: about 10 minutes

COOKING TIME: 5-10 minutes

SERVES: 4 people

8 small wholemeal pancakes (using wholemeal flour and skimmed milk in the batter)
A little melted butter
22g (¾oz) butter

Chicken with Blackcurrant
Sauce and Mange Tout (left)
and Chicken Escalopes (below).

22g (¾oz) plain flour
300ml (½ pint) skimmed milk
Salt and freshly ground black pepper
  to taste
225g (½lb) cooked chicken, chopped
1 avocado pear (not over-ripe),
  peeled, halved, stoned and
  chopped
15ml (1 tblsp) chopped fresh tarragon

Brush the cooked pancakes lightly with melted butter and keep them warm in a parcel of foil in a moderately hot oven. Melt the butter and stir in the flour; cook, stirring, for 1 minute. Gradually stir in the skimmed milk; bring to the boil until the sauce has thickened. Add salt and pepper to taste and stir in the chopped chicken, avocado and tarragon. Fold each pancake in half, and then in half again, to form a triangle. Fill each folded pancake with the chicken

and avocado mixture and serve piping hot. Garnish with sprigs of fresh tarragon, if liked.

Chicken Breasts with Plum and Cinnamon Sauce

PREPARATION TIME: 15 minutes
COOKING TIME: about 20 minutes
SERVES: 4 people

4 chicken breasts, skinned and boned
Seasoned flour
Olive oil for frying

Sauce
1 small onion, finely chopped
15g (½oz) butter

350g (12oz) ripe red plums, halved
  and stoned
Pinch ground cinnamon
Salt and freshly ground black pepper
  to taste
Artificial sweetener to taste
150ml (¼ pint) red wine

Garnish
Whole poached plums
Chopped fresh thyme
Small sprigs fresh thyme

Dust the chicken breasts lightly in seasoned flour. Shallow fry the chicken breasts in olive oil for about 6 minutes on each side, until tender. Meanwhile, prepare the sauce. Fry the chopped onion gently in the butter for 3 minutes; add the remaining sauce ingredients and simmer until the plums are soft and 'mushy'. The sauce can either be left as it is, or it

can be blended in the liquidiser or sieved. Reheat the sauce if necessary, thinning it to the desired consistency. Arrange the chicken breasts on a serving dish and spoon over the hot plum sauce. Garnish with a few whole poached plums, a sprinkling of thyme, and a few small sprigs of fresh thyme.

This page: Turkey, Chestnut and Sage en Croute.

Facing page: Turkey Meatballs with Sweet and Sour Sauce (top) and Sweetbreads and Courgette Tarts (bottom).

Turkey, Cauliflower and Almond au Gratin

PREPARATION TIME: 20-25 minutes

COOKING TIME: about 16 minutes

SERVES: 4 people

1 medium size cauliflower
Juice of ½ lemon
Salt and freshly ground black pepper to taste
22g (¾oz) butter
22g (¾oz) flour
300ml (½ pint) skimmed milk
175g (6oz) cooked turkey, cut into thin strips
100g (4oz) grated cheese
30ml (2 tblsp) flaked almonds

Divide the cauliflower into good size florets; cook in boiling salted water to which you have added the lemon juice and salt to taste, until just tender. Meanwhile, make the sauce. Melt the butter in a pan; stir in the flour and cook for 1 minute. Gradually stir in the skimmed milk and bring to the boil; add salt and pepper to taste and stir until thickened. Add the strips of turkey and half the grated cheese to the sauce. Arrange the florets of cooked cauliflower in a greased heatproof dish and spoon over the prepared sauce; sprinkle with the almonds and remaining cheese and brown under a hot grill.

Turkey Meatballs with Sweet and Sour Sauce

PREPARATION TIME: 20-25 minutes, plus chilling time

COOKING TIME: about 35 minutes

SERVES: 4 people

1 small onion, finely chopped
30ml (2 tblsp) olive oil
450g (1lb) minced raw turkey
1 clove garlic, peeled and crushed
30ml (2 tblsp) chopped parsley
30ml (2 tblsp) finely chopped almonds
Salt and freshly ground black pepper to taste
1.25ml (¼ tsp) mixed spice
15ml (1 tblsp) chopped raisins
30ml (2 tblsp) wholemeal breadcrumbs
1 egg, beaten

Sauce
1 small onion, thinly sliced
300ml (½ pint) pure tomato juice
30ml (2 tblsp) tomato puree
Juice of ½ lemon
15ml (1 tblsp) honey

1 green chilli, thinly sliced
2 slices fresh pineapple, finely chopped
1 medium red pepper, seeded and cut into thin strips
2 carrots, peeled and coarsely grated

For the meatballs: fry the onion gently in the olive oil for 4 minutes. Mix with the minced turkey, garlic, parsley, almonds, salt and pepper to taste, mixed spice, raisins, breadcrumbs and beaten egg. Form into small balls, about the size of a table tennis ball. Chill for 30 minutes. For the sauce: put all the ingredients into a shallow pan; bring to the boil and simmer gently for 10 minutes. Add the shaped meatballs and turn them in the sauce. Cover and simmer gently for a further 20 minutes, until the meatballs are tender – if the sauce evaporates too quickly, add a little stock or water. Serve piping hot with cooked brown rice or wholewheat pasta.
Note: the shaped meatballs can be lightly fried in a little oil, before being added to the sauce, if liked.

Chicken Breasts with Plum and Tarragon Sauce (far right) and Calves' Liver Mousse with Cherry and Marsala (below).

Turkey, Chestnut and Sage en Croute

PREPARATION TIME: 35 minutes, plus chilling time

COOKING TIME: about 55 minutes

OVEN: 200°C, 400°F, Gas Mark 6, and then 180°C, 350°F, Gas Mark 4

SERVES: 6-8 people

450g (1lb) minced raw turkey
1 small onion, finely chopped
45ml (3 tblsp) chestnut puree (unsweetened)
15ml (1 tblsp) chopped fresh sage
1 clove garlic, peeled and crushed
Salt and freshly ground black pepper to taste
45ml (3 tblsp) fresh brown breadcrumbs
1 egg, beaten
450g (1lb) puff pastry (preferably vegetable oil based)
Beaten egg to glaze

Mix the minced turkey with the onion, chestnut puree, sage, garlic, salt and pepper to taste, and brown breadcrumbs. Bind with the beaten egg. Form into a fat, cylindrical sausage, and chill while you prepare the pastry coating. Divide the pastry into two portions, one slightly larger than the other; roll out thinly on a floured surface into two rectangles, one slightly larger than the other. Trim neatly, reserving the trimmings. Place the smaller rectangle of pastry into a dampened baking sheet; brush the edges with beaten egg. Place the turkey 'sausage' in the centre. Lay the larger rectangle of pastry over the top, and pinch the joining pastry edges together to seal (the pastry should fit snugly around the filling). Trim off excess pastry. Glaze the pastry all over with beaten egg and decorate with shapes cut from the pastry trimmings; glaze the pastry decorations. Bake in the oven at the higher temperature for 20 minutes; reduce to the lower temperature and bake for a further 35 minutes, covered with a piece of foil. Serve hot or cold, cut into slices.

Calves' Liver Mousse with Cherry and Marsala

PREPARATION TIME: 25 minutes, plus chilling time

COOKING TIME: 10-12 minutes

SERVES: 6 people

450g (1lb) calves' liver
30ml (2 tblsp) marsala
300ml (½ pint) chicken stock
1 clove garlic, peeled and crushed
Salt and freshly ground black pepper to taste
300ml (½ pint) natural yogurt
20ml (4 tsp) powdered gelatine
60ml (4 tblsp) water
4 spring onions, chopped

Sauce
225g (8oz) fresh cherries, de-stalked and pitted
150ml (¼ pint) red wine
45ml (3 tblsp) marsala
Artificial sweetener to taste
5ml (1 tsp) cornflour
Juice of 1 orange

Garnish
Mint leaves
Few fresh cherries

Grease a 900ml (1½ pint) mould. Cook the calves' liver in the chicken stock and marsala until just tender – this will only take a few minutes. Put the liver and its liquid into the liquidiser and blend, until smooth, with the garlic and salt and pepper to taste. Stir in the yogurt. Dissolve the gelatine in the water and add to the liver mixture together with the chopped spring onions. Spoon into the mould and chill until set. For the sauce: put the cherries into a pan with the red wine, marsala and sweetener to taste; cover and cook until the cherries are just soft. Blend the cornflour with the orange juice and add to the cherry sauce; stir over the heat until thickened. Unmould the chilled mousse onto a serving dish and garnish with mint leaves and a few fresh cherries. Serve with the *warm* cherry sauce.

Sweetbread and Courgette Tarts

PREPARATION TIME: 40 minutes, plus chilling time

COOKING TIME: about 35 minutes

OVEN: 190°C, 375°F, Gas Mark 5

SERVES: 4 people

350g (12oz) shortcrust pastry
225g (8oz) calves' sweetbreads, soaked for 3 hours
Beaten egg
25g (1oz) butter
Finely grated rind of 1 lemon
1 clove garlic, peeled and crushed
4 courgettes, finely shredded
Salt and freshly ground black pepper to taste
Juice of ½ lemon

Divide the pastry into 4 equal portions; roll each one out to a circle and use to line an individual tartlet tin, about 10cm (4 inches) in diameter. Press up the pastry edges well. Line with greaseproof paper and baking beans, and chill for 30 minutes. Rinse the sweetbreads under cold water. Drain the sweetbreads, put them into a pan and add sufficient cold water to cover; bring to the boil slowly, covered, and simmer for 8 minutes. Drain and rinse; remove any muscly parts and skin, and chop into pieces. Bake the pastry cases for 10 minutes. Remove the paper and beans and brush the rim of each pastry case with beaten egg. Return to the oven for a further 8 minutes. Melt the butter with the lemon rind. Add the garlic and chopped sweetbreads and fry for 4 minutes. Add the shredded courgettes and salt and pepper to taste and fry together for a further 3 minutes. Spoon the hot filling into the pastry cases, squeeze over the lemon juice and serve immediately.

Chicken and Herb Loaf (top right), Chicken Andalusia (centre left) and Turkey, Cauliflower and Almond au Gratin (bottom).

HEALTHY EATING

Vegetables and Salads

Stir Fried Peas with Lentil Sprouts and Leeks

PREPARATION TIME: 10 minutes

COOKING TIME: about 10 minutes

SERVES: 4 people

1 medium onion, thinly sliced
2 cloves garlic, peeled and cut into thin slivers
60ml (4 tblsp) olive oil
225g (8oz) mange tout peas, topped and tailed
2 large leeks, split, washed, and cut into thin strips
100g (4oz) lentil sprouts
Salt and freshly ground black pepper to taste
15ml (1 tblsp) chopped coriander

Stir fry the onion and garlic in the olive oil for 3 minutes, either in a wok or in a large, deep frying pan. Add the mange tout and leeks and stir fry for a further 4-5 minutes. Add the lentil sprouts, salt and pepper to taste and the coriander, and stir fry for a further 3 minutes. Serve piping hot with a really good soya sauce, or a peanut sauce. For a quick peanut sauce: put 75g (3oz) shelled peanuts into the liquidiser with 1 clove garlic, peeled, 1 small onion, chopped and 200ml (⅓ pint) chicken stock; blend until smooth.

Rice and Tuna Stuffed Aubergines

PREPARATION TIME: 40 minutes

COOKING TIME: about 50 minutes

OVEN: 190°C, 375°F, Gas Mark 5

SERVES: 4 people

4 small aubergines
45ml (3 tblsp) olive oil
Salt and freshly ground black pepper to taste
1 small onion, finely chopped
1 clove garlic, peeled and crushed
90ml (6 tblsp) cooked brown or wild rice
200g (7oz) can tuna, drained and coarsely flaked
15ml (1 tblsp) mayonnaise

5ml (1 tsp) curry powder
4 tomatoes, skinned, seeded and chopped
15ml (1 tblsp) coarsely chopped parsley

Cut the aubergines in half langthways. Score the cut surfaces lightly with a sharp knife, at regular intervals. Brush lightly with oil and sprinkle with salt. Place on a greased baking sheet and bake in the oven for 15 minutes. Carefully scoop the centre flesh from each half aubergine, making sure that you do not break the skin. Fry the chopped onion gently in 30ml (2 tblsp) of the olive oil for 3 minutes. Add the garlic, scooped aubergine flesh, and salt and pepper to taste; fry gently for a further 2 minutes. Add the flaked tuna, mayonnaise,

This page: Okra in Light Curry Sauce (top) and Stir Fried Peas with Lentil Sprouts and Leeks (bottom).

Facing page: Courgette, Caper and Anchovy Salad (top) and Rice and Tuna Stuffed Aubergines (bottom).

curry powder, chopped tomato and parsley, and mix together. Fill the aubergine 'shells' with the savoury rice mixture and place in a lightly greased ovenproof dish. Sprinkle with the remaining olive oil. Bake in the oven for about 25 minutes. Serve piping hot.

Courgette, Caper and Anchovy Salad

PREPARATION TIME: 15-20 minutes

SERVES: 4 people

450g (1lb) courgettes
1 small onion, thinly sliced
15ml (1 tblsp) capers
4-6 anchovy fillets, chopped
15ml (1 tblsp) anchovy oil (drained from the can of anchovy fillets)
30ml (2 tblsp) olive oil
30ml (2 tblsp) tarragon vinegar
Juice of ½ lemon
Salt and freshly ground black pepper to taste

Garnish
2 medium size heads of chicory (optional)
2 whole anchovy fillets

The secret of this salad is to slice the raw courgettes really thinly – you can do this with a sharp knife, but it is much easier if you use the slicing blade on a food processor or a mandolin. Top and tail the courgettes, and slice them very thinly. Mix the sliced courgettes with the onion, capers and chopped anchovy fillets. Mix the anchovy oil, olive oil, tarragon vinegar and lemon juice together; add salt and pepper to taste. Stir the dressing into the prepared salad ingredients. Separate the leaves from each head of chicory and use to line a salad bowl. Spoon the prepared salad into the centre and garnish with anchovy fillets.

Okra in Light Curry Sauce

PREPARATION TIME: 10 minutes

COOKING TIME: 30-35 minutes

SERVES: 4 people

1 medium onion, roughly chopped
Small piece fresh root ginger, chopped
1 large clove garlic, peeled
50g (2oz) shelled peanuts
15ml (1 tblsp) fresh coriander sprigs
15ml (1 tblsp) chopped parsley
5ml (1 tsp) ground turmeric
2.5ml (½ tsp) ground cumin
30ml (2 tblsp) olive oil
1 small onion, thinly sliced
300ml (½ pint) chicken stock
Salt and freshly ground black pepper to taste
450g (1lb) okra

Garnish
Flaked coconut (optional)
Sprigs fresh coriander

To Serve
Natural yogurt
Wedges of lime

Put the chopped onion, root ginger, garlic, peanuts, coriander, parsley, turmeric and cumin into the liquidiser; blend until smooth. Heat the olive oil in a large, shallow pan; add the sliced onion and fry gently for 3 minutes. Add the liquidised spice mixture and cook for 1 minute. Add the stock and salt and pepper to taste; bring to the boil and simmer for 5 minutes. Add the okra and cover the pan; simmer gently for 20-25 minutes, until the okra is just tender. Spoon into a serving dish and sprinkle with the flaked coconut. Garnish with fresh coriander. Serve accompanied by a bowl of well-chilled yogurt and lemon wedges for squeezing.

Radicchio and Sweetbread Salad

PREPARATION TIME: 40 minutes, plus standing time

COOKING TIME: 18-20 minutes

SERVES: 4

4 calf's sweetbreads
90ml (6 tblsp) olive oil
1 clove garlic, peeled and crushed
Salt and freshly ground black pepper to taste
2 medium size heads radicchio
4 large cooked asparagus tips
100g (4oz) firm white button mushrooms, thinly sliced
30ml (2 tblsp) white wine vinegar
15ml (1 tblsp) chopped fresh sage (optional)

Garnish
Sprig fresh basil

Soak the sweetbreads in cold water for 3 hours; change the water once or twice during this time. Rinse them under cold water. Drain the sweetbreads; put them into a pan and add sufficient cold water to cover. Bring to the boil slowly; cover and simmer for 8-10 minutes. Drain and rinse under cold water once again. Remove any muscle or fatty parts. Put the prepared sweetbreads between two plates and weight down; leave to stand in a cool place for 1 hour. Slice the pressed sweetbreads evenly. Heat half the olive oil in a large, shallow pan. Add the sweetbread slices, garlic and salt and pepper to taste and fry gently for 5 minutes; flip the sweetbread slices over and fry for a further 3-4 minutes. Meanwhile, prepare the salad ingredients. Cut the heads of radicchio into quarters and arrange on a large, flat plate. Arrange the asparagus tips and mushroom slices between the wedges of radicchio. Mix the wine vinegar with the remaining olive oil, salt and pepper to taste and the chopped sage. Spoon the dressing evenly over the salad and top with the fried sweetbread slices and their juices. Garnish with basil. Serve immediately.

Turkey Caesar Salad

PREPARATION TIME: 20 minutes

COOKING TIME: 4-5 minutes

SERVES: 4-6 people

1 Cos lettuce
Few young spinach leaves
Juice of 1 lemon
5ml (1 tsp) French mustard
90ml (6 tblsp) olive oil
2 cloves garlic, peeled and crushed
10ml (2 tsp) Worcestershire sauce
3 drops Tabasco
4 anchovy fillets, chopped
Salt and freshly ground black pepper to taste
1 egg
2 slices wholemeal bread, cut into small cubes
175g (6oz) cooked turkey, cut into thin strips

Tear the lettuce into pieces and put into a salad bowl with the young spinach leaves. Mix the lemon juice with the French mustard, 45ml (3 tblsp) of the olive oil, half the garlic, the Worcestershire sauce, Tabasco, anchovy fillets and salt and pepper to taste. Put the egg into a pan of boiling water and cook for *just 45 seconds* – the white and yolk must still be very runny. Carefully crack the egg and scoop all the centre egg into the dressing; beat well. Heat the remaining olive oil with the rest of the garlic in a large shallow pan; add the small cubes of wholemeal bread and fry until crisp and golden. Add the croutons, turkey strips and prepared dressing to the salad greens and toss well together. Serve immediately.

Brown Rice, Pineapple, Peanut and Red Pepper Salad

PREPARATION TIME: 15 minutes, plus cooling time

COOKING TIME: 10-15 minutes

SERVES: 4 people

100g (4oz) brown or wild rice
Salt and freshly ground black pepper to taste
Juice of 1 orange
60ml (4 tblsp) olive oil
5ml (1 tsp) clear honey
2 slices fresh pineapple, peeled and chopped
30ml (2 tblsp) shelled peanuts
1 large red pepper, seeded and cut into thin strips
Peeled segments of 2 large oranges

Cook the rice in boiling salted water until just tender. Meanwhile, prepare the orange dressing. Mix the orange juice, olive oil and

Radicchio and Sweetbread Salad (right) and Turkey Caesar Salad (below).

honey together, and season to taste with salt and pepper. Drain the cooked rice thoroughly, and stir in the prepared dressing while the rice is still warm. Allow to cool. Mix in the pineapple, peanuts, and red pepper. Spoon into a shallow salad bowl and garnish with the orange segments.

Fisherman's Wholewheat Pasta Salad

PREPARATION TIME: 20 minutes, plus cooling time

COOKING TIME: about 10 minutes

SERVES: 4 people

175g (8oz) wholewheat pasta shapes (shells, wheels, etc.)
Salt and freshly ground black pepper to taste
60ml (4 tblsp) olive oil
30ml (2 tblsp) dry white wine
15ml (1 tblsp) chopped parsley
3 spring onions, chopped
100g (4oz) shelled cooked mussels
75g (3oz) peeled prawns
100g (4oz) flaked crabmeat
12 black olives

Garnish
Large peeled prawns

Cook the wholewheat pasta in a large pan of boiling salted water until just tender – about 10 minutes. Meanwhile, prepare the dressing. Mix the olive oil with the white wine, parsley, and salt and pepper to taste. Drain the cooked pasta thoroughly and stir in the prepared dressing. Allow to cool. Mix in the chopped spring onion, and then carefully stir in the shellfish; add the black olives. Spoon into one large salad bowl, or four individual ones.

Potato and Hazelnut Nests

PREPARATION TIME: 30 minutes, plus chilling time

COOKING TIME: 35 minutes

OVEN: 190°C, 375°F, Gas Mark 5

SERVES: 6 people

750g (1½lb) potatoes, peeled
Salt and freshly ground black pepper to taste

22g (¾oz) butter
2 egg yolks
15ml (1 tblsp) natural yogurt
30ml (2 tblsp) finely chopped hazelnuts
225g (8oz) low fat cream cheese
15ml (1 tblsp) chopped chives (optional)

Garnish
A few flaked or coarsely chopped hazelnuts
Parsley

Cook the potatoes in boiling salted water until just tender. Drain them thoroughly. Mash the potatoes. Return the mashed potato to a clean saucepan and stir over a gentle heat to 'dry' them out. Remove from the heat and beat in the butter, egg yolks, salt and pepper to taste, yogurt and chopped hazelnuts. Using a large piping bag fitted with a wide star nozzle, pipe the potato mixture into 6 nest shapes on a lightly greased baking sheet. Chill for 30

This page: Potato, Lentil and Cheese Pie (top), Potato and Hazelnut Nests (centre) and Parsnip, Orange and Ginger Puree (bottom).

Facing page: Fisherman's Wholewheat Pasta Salad (top) and Brown Rice, Pineapple, Peanut and Red Pepper Salad (bottom).

minutes. Bake in the oven until pale golden – about 15 minutes (the potato nests can be glazed with beaten egg before baking, if liked). Beat the cream cheese until soft and add the chopped chives and salt and pepper to taste. As soon as the potato and hazelnut nests come out of the oven, put a spoonful of the flavoured cream cheese in the centre of each one and sprinkle with the flaked hazelnuts. Garnish with parsley. Serve immediately. They make a delicious accompanying vegetable to fish.

Mushrooms Monegasque

PREPARATION TIME: 10 minutes, plus chilling time

COOKING TIME: about 13 minutes

SERVES: 4 people

450g (1lb) tomatoes, skinned, seeded and chopped
150ml (¼ pint) red wine
30ml (2 tblsp) tomato puree
Pinch ground ginger
Salt and freshly ground black pepper to taste
1 clove garlic, peeled and finely chopped
2 spring onions, finely chopped
30ml (2 tblsp) raisins
225g (8oz) small button mushrooms

To Serve
Crusty wholemeal bread or rolls

Put the chopped tomatoes, red wine, tomato puree, ground ginger, salt and pepper to taste, and the garlic into a shallow pan. Simmer for 6-8 minutes. Add the spring onions, raisins and button mushrooms; cover the pan and simmer for 5 minutes. Allow to cool and then chill very thoroughly. Serve in small, shallow dishes, accompanied by crusty wholemeal bread.

Fennel au Gratin

PREPARATION TIME: 15 minutes

COOKING TIME: 25-30 minutes

OVEN: 190°C, 375°F, Gas Mark 5

SERVES: 4 people

4 medium size heads of fennel
Juice of 1 lemon
Salt and freshly ground black pepper to taste
25g (1oz) butter
22g (¾oz) flour
150ml (¼ pint) skimmed milk
150ml (¼ pint) dry white wine
60ml (4 tblsp) natural yogurt
2.5ml (½ tsp) chive mustard
75g (3oz) grated Gruyere cheese

Garnish
15ml (1 tblsp) chopped chives

Trim both ends of the fennel – reserve any feathery tops for garnish. Peel off any discoloured patches from the fennel. Cut each head in half lengthways. Put the fennel into a pan of boiling water to which you have added the lemon juice and 5ml (1 tsp) salt; simmer steadily for 5 minutes. Drain the par-cooked fennel thoroughly. Melt the butter in a pan and stir in the flour; gradually stir in the milk and white wine. Bring to the boil and stir until lightly thickened. Beat in the yogurt, chive mustard, half the grated cheese, and salt and pepper to taste. Arrange the fennel in a lightly greased ovenproof dish and spoon the sauce evenly over the top; sprinkle with the remaining grated cheese. Bake in the oven for 25-30 minutes, until the sauce is golden. Garnish with the chopped chives and any reserved pieces of feathery fennel.

Potato, Lentil and Cheese Pie

PREPARATION TIME: 25 minutes

COOKING TIME: 1 hour 15 minutes

OVEN: 190°C, 375°F, Gas Mark 5

SERVES: 4 people

225g (8oz) lentils, soaked overnight
600ml (1 pint) chicken stock
1 small onion, finely chopped
25g (1oz) butter
25g (1oz) flour
60ml (4 tblsp) natural yogurt
1 egg, beaten
Salt and freshly ground black pepper to taste
450g (1lb) medium size potatoes, peeled, par-boiled, and thinly sliced
75g (3oz) grated cheese

Garnish
A little crumbled fresh rosemary

Cook the drained, soaked lentils in three quarters of the stock, with the chopped onion, until tender – about 30 minutes. Drain thoroughly. Melt the butter in a pan and stir in the flour; add the remaining 150ml (¼ pint) stock, and stir over the heat until thickened. Season to taste with salt and pepper and stir in half the yogurt. Stir the prepared sauce into the cooked lentils. Put the lentil mixture into a lightly greased ovenproof dish. Beat the remaining yogurt with the egg and salt and pepper to taste. Arrange the potato slices, overlapping, on top of the lentil mixture; brush all the potato slices with the egg and yogurt mixture, and sprinkle with the grated cheese. Bake in the oven for 40-45 minutes, until a rich golden brown. Sprinkle with the rosemary and serve piping hot.

Mushrooms Monegasque (top) and Fennel au Gratin (right).

Broccoli and Almond Risotto

PREPARATION TIME: 5 minutes

COOKING TIME: about 35 minutes

SERVES: 4 people

1 medium onion, finely chopped
30ml (2 tblsp) olive oil
175g (6oz) brown or wild rice
750ml (1¼ pint) chicken stock
Salt and freshly ground black pepper to taste
30ml (2 tblsp) chopped, toasted almonds
450g (1lb) broccoli, divided into small florets
50g (2oz) grated Parmesan cheese

Garnish
Lightly toasted flaked almonds

Fry the onion gently in the olive oil for 3 minutes. Add the rice and stir over the heat for 1 minute, until the rice is evenly coated with oil. Gradually stir in the chicken stock. Bring to the boil and add salt and pepper to taste and the chopped almonds; cover and simmer for 20 minutes. Add the florets of broccoli; cover and simmer for a further 8 minutes, until all the stock has been absorbed. Stir in the Parmesan cheese and spoon into a serving dish; sprinkle with the toasted almonds and serve piping hot.

Parsnip, Orange and Ginger Puree

PREPARATION TIME: 15-20 minutes

COOKING TIME: about 25 minutes

SERVES: 4 people

750g (1½lb) parsnips, peeled and roughly chopped
2 thin strips orange peel
Salt and freshly ground black pepper to taste
25g (1oz) butter
2 egg yolks
Generous pinch ground ginger
Finely grated rind of ½ orange
15ml (1 tblsp) chopped preserved stem ginger

Garnish
Finely chopped parsley
Peeled segments of orange

Put the parsnips into a pan with the strips of orange peel, salt and pepper to taste, and sufficient water to just cover. Bring to the boil and simmer, covered, until the parsnips are just tender. Drain very thoroughly, removing the strips of orange peel. Mash the cooked parsnips and return to a clean pan; stir over a gentle heat to 'dry' the parsnip puree. Beat in the butter, egg yolks, grated orange rind, salt and pepper to taste and the chopped stem ginger. Heat through and spoon into a serving dish. Garnish with chopped parsley and orange segments, and serve the puree piping hot.

Pasta, Rice and Pulses

Pasta Shells with Agliata Sauce

PREPARATION TIME: 10 minutes

COOKING TIME: about 8 minutes

SERVES: 4 people

275g (10oz) wholemeal or plain pasta shells
Salt and freshly ground black pepper to taste

Sauce
90ml (6 tblsp) olive oil
45ml (3 tblsp) coarsely chopped parsley
2 cloves garlic, peeled
15ml (1 tblsp) pine kernels
15ml (1 tblsp) blanched almonds

Cook the pasta shells in a large pan of boiling salted water until just tender. Meanwhile, make the sauce. Put all the ingredients into a liquidiser and blend until smooth; add salt and pepper to taste. Drain the hot, cooked pasta shells and toss together with the prepared sauce. Serve immediately.

Chick Pea, Mint and Orange Salad

PREPARATION TIME: 15-25 minutes

SERVES: 4 people

175g (6oz) dried chick peas, soaked overnight and cooked
30ml (2 tblsp) chopped fresh mint
1 clove garlic, peeled and crushed
Salt and freshly ground black pepper to taste
Juice of 1 orange
Rind of 1 orange, cut into matchstick strips
45ml (3 tblsp) olive oil
Segments from 2 large oranges

Garnish
Fresh mint leaves

Mix the chick peas with half the chopped mint, garlic, and salt and pepper to taste. Mix the orange juice, strips of orange rind and olive oil together; stir into the chick

peas. Lightly mix in the orange segments and garnish with the remaining chopped mint.

Noodle and Ratatouille Bake

PREPARATION TIME: 25-30 minutes

COOKING TIME: 35-40 minutes

OVEN: 190°C, 375°F, Gas Mark 5

SERVES: 4 people

1 medium onion, thinly sliced
30ml (2 tblsp) olive oil
2 cloves garlic, peeled and finely chopped
1 large green pepper, seeded and cut into cubes
1 large red pepper, seeded and cut into cubes

This page: Chick Pea, Mint and Orange Salad (top) and Spinach and Feta Cheese Lasagne (bottom).

Facing page: Pasta Shells with Agliata Sauce (top) and Noodle and Ratatouille Bake (bottom).

1 medium aubergine, cubed
6 tomatoes, skinned, seeded and
    chopped
15ml (1 tblsp) tomato puree
45ml (3 tblsp) red wine
Salt and freshly ground black pepper
    to taste
100g (4oz) green noodles, cooked
75g (3oz) grated cheese

Fry the onion gently in the olive oil
for 4 minutes; add the garlic, red
and green peppers, aubergine and
chopped tomatoes and cook
covered for 5 minutes. Add the
tomato puree, wine and salt and
pepper to taste; simmer gently for
10-15 minutes, until the vegetables
are almost soft. Remove from the
heat and stir in the cooked
noodles. Spoon into a shallow
flameproof dish and sprinkle with
the grated cheese. Bake in the oven
for 15 minutes (alternatively, the
dish can be flashed under a
preheated grill).

Spaghetti with Sweetbread Carbonara

PREPARATION TIME: 10-15
                              minutes

COOKING TIME: 10 minutes

SERVES: 4 people

1 onion, chopped
45ml (3 tblsp) olive oil
350g (12oz) wholemeal spaghetti
Salt and freshly ground black pepper
    to taste
225g (8oz) calves' sweetbreads,
    blanched, skinned and chopped
90ml (6 tblsp) dry white wine
4 eggs
50g (2oz) grated Parmesan cheese
30ml (2 tblsp) chopped fresh basil
1 clove garlic, peeled and crushed

Fry the onion gently in the olive oil
for 5 minutes. Meanwhile, cook
the spaghetti in a large pan of
boiling salted water for about 10
minutes, until just tender. Add the
chopped sweetbreads to the onion
and fry gently for 4 minutes. Add
the white wine and cook briskly
until it has almost evaporated. Beat
the eggs with the Parmesan cheese,
basil, garlic, and salt and pepper to
taste. Drain the hot, cooked
spaghetti thoroughly; immediately
stir in the beaten egg mixture and
the sweetbreads, so that the heat
from the spaghetti cooks the egg.
Garnish with basil and serve
immediately.

Wild Rice and Egg Scramble

PREPARATION TIME: 10 minutes

COOKING TIME: 7-8 minutes

SERVES: 4 people

175g (6oz) wild or brown rice,
    cooked
15g (½oz) butter
1 small onion, thinly sliced
30ml (2 tblsp) olive oil
3 eggs
2.5ml (½ tsp) mixed herbs
Salt and freshly ground black pepper
    to taste

Garnish
Chopped parsley

Heat the cooked rice through
gently with the butter. Fry the
onion gently in the olive oil for 3-4
minutes. Beat the eggs with the
herbs, salt and pepper to taste, and
15ml (1 tblsp) water. Add the
beaten egg mixture to the onion
and scramble lightly. Combine the
hot rice and the scrambled egg and
onion and serve immediately.

Pasta Shapes with Green Mayonnaise and Crab

PREPARATION TIME: 25 minutes

COOKING TIME: 8-10 minutes

SERVES: 4 people

Green Mayonnaise
60ml (4 tblsp) mayonnaise
150ml (¼ pint) natural yogurt
45ml (3 tblsp) cooked spinach
1 clove garlic, peeled
Salt and freshly ground black pepper
    to taste
350g (12oz) pasta shapes – shells,
    wheels, twists, etc
Juice of 1 lemon
30ml (2 tblsp) olive oil
175g (6oz) flaked crabmeat, or crab
    flavoured sticks, shredded

Garnish
Parsley sprigs

For the green mayonnaise: put all
the ingredients into the liquidiser
and blend until smooth. Cook the
pasta shapes in boiling salted water

until tender. Drain thoroughly and
toss in the lemon juice and olive
oil, adding salt and pepper to taste.
Mix in the flaked crabmeat. Spoon
into a serving dish and serve warm,
garnished with parsley.

Spinach and Feta Cheese Lasagne

PREPARATION TIME: 20-25
                              minutes

COOKING TIME: about 35
                          minutes

OVEN: 190°, 375°F, Gas Mark 5

SERVES: 6 people

450g (1lb) cooked and drained
    spinach (or thawed frozen spinach)
Generous pinch grated nutmeg
Salt and freshly ground black pepper
    to taste
30ml (2 tblsp) natural yogurt
1 clove garlic, peeled and crushed
1 egg yolk
175g (6oz) Feta cheese, crumbled
225g (8oz) green or wholewheat
    lasagne (the non pre-cook variety)

Sauce
150ml (¼ pint) natural yogurt
1 egg, beaten
30ml (2 tblsp) grated Parmesan
    cheese
3 firm tomatoes, sliced

Mix the cooked spinach with
nutmeg and salt and pepper to
taste; stir in the yogurt, garlic, egg
yolk and crumbled Feta cheese.
Layer the lasagne and spinach
mixture in a lightly greased
ovenproof dish, starting with
spinach and finishing with lasagne.
For the sauce: mix the yogurt with
the beaten egg and half the grated
Parmesan cheese; spoon over the
lasagne. Top with the sliced tomato
and the remaining Parmesan
cheese. Bake in the oven for about
35 minutes, until golden. Serve
piping hot.

**This page: Wild Rice and Egg
Scramble (top) and Pasta Shapes
with Green Mayonnaise and
Crab (bottom).**

**Facing page: Chicken Liver
Risotto with Red Beans (top)
and Spaghetti with Sweetbread
Carbonara (bottom).**

Rice and Vegetable Loaf with Yogurt and Mint Sauce

PREPARATION TIME: 25-30 minutes	
COOKING TIME: 53 minutes	
OVEN: 190°C, 375°F, Gas Mark 5	
SERVES: 6-8	

1 small onion, finely chopped
30ml (2 tblsp) olive oil
1 clove garlic, peeled and crushed
225g (8oz) wild rice, cooked and drained (not rinsed)
3 courgettes, finely shredded
2 medium size carrots, finely shredded
30ml (2 tblsp) chopped parsley
Salt and freshly ground black pepper to taste
5ml (1 tsp) chopped fresh thyme
2-3 eggs, beaten
75g (3oz) grated cheese

Garnish
Fresh mint

Fry the onion gently in the olive oil for 3 minutes. Mix together with all the remaining ingredients, adding sufficient beaten egg to give a stiff yet moist consistency. Spoon the mixture into a deep, greased and lined loaf tin, smoothing the surface level. Cover with a piece of lightly greased foil. Bake in the oven for 50 minutes. Allow to cool slightly in the tin before turning out. Serve the rice and vegetable loaf cut into slices, and accompanied by the yogurt and mint sauce. Garnish with mint. For the sauce: mix 150ml (¼ pint) natural yogurt with salt and freshly ground black pepper to taste and 15ml (1 tblsp) chopped mint.

225g (8oz) black eye beans, soaked
  overnight
Salt and freshly ground black pepper
  to taste
1 small onion, thinly sliced
1 green pepper, seeded and finely
  chopped
Juice of ½ lemon
30ml (2 tblsp) cashew nuts, whole or
  roughly chopped

Dressing
150ml (¼ pint) natural yogurt
10ml (2 tsp) curry powder
30ml (2 tblsp) fresh pineapple juice
1 clove garlic, crushed

Garnish
Curry powder

Simmer the beans in salted water until tender. Drain. Mix the black eye beans with the onion and green pepper. Stir in the lemon juice, salt and pepper to taste and the cashew nuts. For the dressing: mix all the ingredients together, adding salt and pepper to taste. Spoon the bean salad into a bowl, and spoon the prepared dressing over the top. Sprinkle with curry powder.

Chicken Liver Risotto with Red Beans

PREPARATION TIME: 15 minutes
COOKING TIME: about 28 minutes
SERVES: 4 people

1 medium onion, finely chopped
30ml (2 tblsp) olive oil
1 clove garlic, peeled and crushed
175g (6oz) brown or wild rice
750ml (1¼ pints) chicken stock
Salt and freshly ground black pepper
  to taste
225g (8oz) chicken livers, chopped
25g (1oz) butter
175g (6oz) cooked red kidney beans
15ml (1 tblsp) chopped parsley

Fry the onion gently in the olive oil for 3 minutes. Add the garlic and the rice and stir over the heat for 1 minute, until the rice is evenly coated with oil. Gradually stir in the chicken stock. Bring to the boil and add salt and pepper to taste; cover and simmer for 20 minutes. Meanwhile, fry the chopped chicken livers in the butter for about 4 minutes, until sealed on the outside but still pink in the centre. Drain the chicken livers with a slotted spoon and stir into the cooked rice, together with the red kidney beans and chopped parsley. Heat through. Serve hot with grated Parmesan cheese, if liked.

Cucumber with Yogurt, Dill and Burghul

PREPARATION TIME: 25 minutes
SERVES: 4 people

90ml (6 tblsp) burghul
1 clove garlic, peeled and crushed
Juice of 1 lemon
60ml (4 tblsp) olive oil
15ml (1 tblsp) fresh dill
Salt and freshly ground black pepper
  to taste
½ a large cucumber, halved, seeded
  and chopped
30ml (2 tblsp) natural yogurt

Garnish
Coarsely grated lemon rind
Sprigs of fresh dill

Soak the burghul in sufficient warm water to cover, for 10 minutes. Squeeze the drained burghul in a clean cloth to remove excess moisture. Mix the prepared burghul with the garlic, lemon juice, oil, dill and salt and pepper to taste. Stir in the cucumber and the yogurt. Spoon into a serving dish and garnish with lemon rind and dill.
Note: instead of mixing the yogurt into the burghul, make a well in the centre of the prepared burghul and spoon the yogurt into the centre.

Noodles with Fresh Tomato Sauce

PREPARATION TIME: 10-15 minutes
COOKING TIME: 6-8 minutes
SERVES: 4 people

450g (1lb) tomatoes, skinned and
  roughly chopped
1 small onion, peeled and chopped
1 clove garlic, peeled and chopped
15ml (1 tblsp) chopped parsley
15ml (1 tblsp) chopped basil
200ml (⅓ pint) olive oil
Salt and freshly ground black pepper
  to taste
350g (12oz) noodles (green, yellow, or
  wholemeal)

Garnish
Sprigs fresh basil

Put the tomatoes, onion, garlic, herbs, olive oil, and salt and pepper to taste into the liquidiser and blend until smooth. Cook the noodles in boiling salted water until just tender. Drain thoroughly. Toss the cooked noodles in the prepared tomato sauce. Garnish with sprigs of fresh basil and serve immediately.

Black Eye Beans with Curry Dressing (far left) and Noodles with Fresh Tomato Sauce (above left).

Noodles with Kidney Beans and Pesto

PREPARATION TIME: 5 minutes
COOKING TIME: about 10 minutes
SERVES: 4 people

225g (8oz) wholemeal or plain
  noodles
Salt and freshly ground black pepper
  to taste
1 small onion, finely chopped
30ml (2 tblsp) olive oil
1 clove garlic, peeled and crushed
10ml (2 tsp) Pesto sauce (see recipe)
225g (8oz) cooked red kidney beans

Garnish
Sprigs fresh basil

Cook the noodles in a large pan of boiling salted water until just tender. Meanwhile, fry the onion gently in the olive oil for 3 minutes; mix in the garlic and Pesto sauce. Drain the cooked noodles thoroughly; add to the onion and pesto mixture, together with the red kidney beans. Stir over a gentle heat for 1-2 minutes and serve piping hot, garnished with basil.

Black Eye Beans with Curry Dressing

PREPARATION TIME: 10-15 minutes
COOKING TIME: 35-40 minutes
SERVES: 4 people

Skillet Rice Cake

PREPARATION TIME: 25 minutes

COOKING TIME: about 15 minutes

SERVES: 4 people

1 medium onion, thinly sliced or chopped
1 clove garlic, peeled and chopped
30ml (2 tblsp) olive oil
15ml (1 tblsp) chopped fresh thyme
1 red pepper, seeded and thinly sliced
1 green pepper, seeded and thinly sliced
4 eggs
Salt and freshly ground black pepper to taste
90ml (6 tblsp) cooked brown or wild rice
45ml (3 tblsp) natural yogurt
75g (3oz) grated cheese

Garnish
Chopped fresh thyme

Fry the chopped onion and garlic gently in the olive oil in a frying pan for 3 minutes. Add the thyme and sliced peppers and fry gently for a further 4-5 minutes. Beat the eggs with salt and pepper to taste. Add the cooked rice to the fried vegetables and then add the beaten egg; cook over a moderate heat, stirring from time to time, until the egg starts to set underneath. Spoon the yogurt over the top of the part-set egg and sprinkle with the cheese. Place under a moderately hot grill until puffed and golden. Serve immediately, straight from the pan.

Italian Pasta Pie

PREPARATION TIME: 35 minutes

COOKING TIME: 1 hour 5 minutes

OVEN: 190°C, 375°F, Gas Mark 5

SERVES: 6-8 people

600g (1¼lbs) puff pastry
450g (1lb) fresh spinach, cooked and drained thoroughly
175g (6oz) curd cheese
1 clove garlic, peeled and crushed
Salt and freshly ground black pepper to taste
Generous pinch ground nutmeg
100g (4oz) pasta shapes, cooked until just tender
75g (3oz) shelled mussels
15ml (1 tblsp) chopped fresh basil
1 egg, beaten

Sauce

1 medium onion, finely chopped
1 clove garlic, peeled and finely
 chopped
30ml (2 tblsp) olive oil
200ml (⅓ pint) red wine
30ml (2 tblsp) tomato puree
15ml (1 tblsp) chopped fresh thyme
Salt and freshly ground black pepper
 to taste
225g (8oz) finely chopped cooked
 chicken
6 tomatoes, skinned, seeded and
 chopped
5ml (1 tsp) Pesto sauce (see recipe)
15ml (1 tblsp) chopped cashew nuts
15ml (1 tblsp) chopped walnuts
350g (12oz) spaghetti, plain or
 wholemeal

Garnish
Chopped walnuts

Fry the onion and garlic in the olive oil for 3 minutes. Add the red wine, tomato puree, thyme and salt and pepper to taste. Bring to the boil and simmer for 10 minutes. Add the chopped chicken, chopped tomatoes, Pesto sauce, cashew nuts and walnuts; simmer the sauce for a further few minutes. Meanwhile, cook the spaghetti in boiling salted water for 8-10 minutes, until just tender. Drain the spaghetti thoroughly. If the sauce is too thick for your liking, thin it down with a little hot stock or water. Pile the cooked spaghetti into a serving dish and spoon the hot sauce over the top. Sprinkle with extra chopped walnuts and serve immediately.

To Glaze Pastry
Beaten egg
Grated Parmesan cheese

Roll out ⅔ of the puff pastry quite thinly and use to line the sides and base of a loose-bottomed 18cm (7 inch) round cake tin; press the pastry carefully into the shape of the tin, avoiding any cracks or splits. Roll out the remaining pastry to a circle large enough to cover the top of the cake tin generously. Mix the spinach with the curd cheese, garlic, salt, pepper and nutmeg to taste, cooked pasta,

mussels and the beaten egg; spoon the filling into the pastry lined tin. Brush the rim of the pastry with beaten egg; lay the rolled out portion of pastry over the filling and press the adjoining pastry edges together to seal. Trim off the excess pastry, and pinch the edges decoratively. Cut decorative shapes from the pastry trimmings and fix on top of the pie; glaze with beaten egg and sprinkle with grated Parmesan cheese. Bake in the oven for 45 minutes; cover with a piece of foil and cook for a further 20 minutes. Unmould carefully from

the tin and serve the pie hot, cut into wedges.
Note: the top of the pie can be sprinkled with a few pine kernels prior to baking, if liked.

Spaghetti with Chicken Bolognese and Nuts

PREPARATION TIME:	15-20 minutes
COOKING TIME:	15 minutes
SERVES:	4 people

Facing page: Italian Pasta Pie (top) and Spaghetti with Chicken Bolognese and Nuts (bottom).

This page: Rice and Vegetable Loaf with Yogurt and Mint Sauce (top) and Skillet Rice Cake (bottom).

Desserts and Cakes

Ricotta Pancakes with Honey and Raisin Sauce

PREPARATION TIME: 10 minutes

COOKING TIME: 2-3 minutes

SERVES: 4 people

Sauce
60ml (4 tblsp) clear honey
Juice ½ lemon
15ml (1 tblsp) raisins
15ml (1 tblsp) pine kernels

Filling
225g (8oz) curd cheese, or Ricotta
Grated rind of ½ lemon
30ml (2 tblsp) raisins
15ml (1 tblsp) chopped pine kernels

8 small, hot pancakes

To Decorate
Twists of lemon

For the sauce: put all the ingredients into a small pan and warm through gently. For the filling: beat the cheese and the lemon rind until soft; mix in the raisins and pine kernels. Divide the filling amongst the hot pancakes and either roll them up, or fold them into triangles. Arrange the pancakes on warm plates, spoon the sauce over the top and decorate with twists of lemon. Serve immediately.

Almond Stuffed Figs

PREPARATION TIME: 25 minutes

SERVES: 4 people

4 large ripe figs
60ml (4 tblsp) ground almonds
30ml (2 tblsp) orange juice
30ml (2 tblsp) finely chopped dried apricots

Sauce
60ml (4 tblsp) natural yogurt
Finely grated rind of ½ orange

Garnish
Wedges of ripe fig
Wedges of lime
Ground cinnamon

Make a cross cut in each fig, without cutting right down and through the base. Ease the four sections of each fig out, rather like a flower head. Mix the ground allmonds with the orange juice and chopped dried apricots; press into the centre of each fig. For the sauce: mix the yogurt with the orange rind, and thin down with *a little* water. Spoon a pool of orange flavoured yogurt onto each of 4 small plates; sit a stuffed fig in the centre of each one. Decorate with wedges of fig and lime and a sprinkling of ground cinnamon.

Honey and Apple Tart

PREPARATION TIME: about 45 minutes

COOKING TIME: 35-40 minutes

OVEN: 190°C, 375°F, Gas Mark 5

SERVES: 6 people

75g (33oz) wholemeal flour
75g (3oz) plain white flour
75g (3oz) butter
1 egg yolk
45ml (3 tblsp) cold water

Filling
300ml (½ pint) unsweetened apple puree
15ml (1 tblsp) honey
2 egg yolks
30ml (2 tblsp) ground almonds
3 large eating apples, quartered, cored and thinly sliced
A little pale soft brown sugar

Glaze
45ml (3 tblsp) clear honey, warmed

For the pastry: put the flours into a bowl; add the butter in small pieces and rub in. Beat the egg yolk with 30ml (2 tblsp) of the water and add to the dry ingredients; mix to a soft yet firm dough, adding a little extra water as necessary (wholemeal flour varies from batch to batch as to how much liquid it will absorb). Roll out the dough on a floured surface and use to line a 23cm (9 inch) loose-bottomed, fluted flan tin; pinch up the edges well. Prick the base. For the filling: mix the apple puree with the brandy, egg yolks, honey and ground almonds. Spread over the base of the pastry case. Arrange the apple slices in overlapping, concentric circles on top of the apple and almond filing. Dust lightly with soft brown sugar. Bake in the oven for 35-40 minutes (if the apples start to brown too much, cover the filling with a circle of foil). As soon as the flan comes out of the oven, brush the apple top with warmed honey. This flan can be served cold, but it is best served warm.

Prune, Apricot and Nut Torten

PREPARATION TIME: 30 minutes. plus 'plumping' time

COOKING TIME: 25 minutes

OVEN: 190°C, 375°F, Gas Mark 5

SERVES: 6-8 people

100g (4oz) dried apricots
100g (4oz) dried prunes
300ml (½ pint) red wine, or dry cider

Nut Shortcake
100g (4oz) butter
50g (2oz) soft brown sugar
100g (4oz) wholemeal flour
50g (2oz) ground hazelnuts
45ml (3 tblsp) finely chopped walnuts

Glaze
30ml (2 tblsp) clear honey, warmed

To Decorate
15ml (1 tblsp) pine kernels
15ml (1 tblsp) hazelnuts

Put the apricots and prunes into a bowl. Warm the wine or cider and pour it over the dried fruits; leave them to 'plump' for 4 hours. For the shortcake: work the butter, brown sugar, flour and ground hazelnuts together. Knead lightly to a smooth dough, working in the chopped walnuts. Press evenly over the base of a 23cm (9 inch) fluted, loose-bottomed flan tin. Bake in the oven for 15 minutes. Drain the plumped prunes and apricots thoroughly on absorbent paper. Remove the shortcake from the oven and arrange the plumped fruits on top. Cover with a piece of foil and return to the oven for a further 10 minutes. Remove the shortcake carefully from its tin. Glaze the fruits on top with the warmed honey and sprinkle with the nuts. This is absolutely delicious served warm from the oven, but is equally good served cold.

Ricotta Pancakes with Honey and Raisin Sauce (right) and Almond Stuffed Figs (below).

Passion Fruit Ice Cream

PREPARATION TIME: 20 minutes, plus freezing time

SERVES: 4 people

6 passion fruit
300ml (½ pint) thick natural yogurt
2 egg yolks
10ml (2 tsp) honey

To Decorate
1-2 passion fruit, halved and scooped

For the ice cream: halve the passion fruit and scoop all the centre pulp into a bowl. Add the yogurt, egg yolks and honey, and mix well together. Pour into a shallow container and freeze until firm. Scoop the ice cream into stemmed glasses and trickle a little passion fruit pulp over each portion. Serve immediately.
Note: this ice cream goes *very* hard, and needs to be removed from the freezer several minutes before scooping.

Strawberry and Melon Salad

PREPARATION TIME: 25 minutes

SERVES: 4 people

225g (8oz) large strawberries, hulled
1 small Charentais or Ogen melon
Juice of 1 orange
15ml (1 tblsp) brandy

To Decorate
Small sprigs fresh mint

Slice the strawberries quite thinly. Halve and de-seed the melon and then scoop it into small balls (there is a special cutter for doing this, but you can do it with a coffee spoon). Arrange the strawberry slices and melon balls on individual glass plates. Mix the orange juice with the brandy and dribble over the fruit. Decorate with mint.

This page: Prune, Apricot and Nut Torten (top) and Honey and Apple Tart (bottom).

Facing page: Passion Fruit Ice Cream (top) and Strawberry and Melon Salad (bottom).

Jellied Grape Shortcake

PREPARATION TIME: 45 minutes, plus cooling and chilling

COOKING TIME: about 20 minutes

OVEN: 190°C, 375°F, Gas Mark 5

SERVES: 6 people

50g (2oz) butter
25g (1oz) soft brown sugar
50g (2oz) wholemeal flour
25g (1oz) ground almonds

Jelly Topping
225g (8oz) green grapes, halved and de-pipped
600ml (1 pint) water
Thinly pared rind of 2 lemons
15ml (1 tblsp) honey
15g (½oz) powdered gelatine
30ml (2 tblsp) water
Yellow food colouring

Work the butter, brown sugar, flour and ground almonds together. Knead lightly to a smooth dough. Press evenly over the base of a 20cm (8 inch) loose-bottomed cake tin. Bake in the oven for 12-15 minutes, until the shortcake is pale golden. Remove from the oven and allow to cool completely. Lightly grease the sides of the cake tin above the baked shortcake. Arrange the halved grapes on top of the shortcake. Put the water and lemon rind into a pan; bring to the boil and allow to bubble briskly for 5 minutes. Remove the pan from the heat and allow the liquid to cool. Strain the lemon liquid and measure off 450ml (¾ pint). Stir in the honey. Dissolve the gelatine in the 30ml (2 tblsp) water and add to the lemon liquid (it can be tinted with a few drops of yellow food colouring at this stage, if liked). Leave in a cool place until it starts to set; pour the setting jelly over the grapes, making sure that the top surface is level. Chill for 2-3 hours until set. Serve cut into wedges.

Hazelnut and Apple Meringue Torten

PREPARATION TIME: 25-30 minutes

COOKING TIME: 45 minutes

OVEN: 190°C, 375°F, Gas Mark 5, then 160°C, 325°F, Gas Mark 3

SERVES: 6-8 people

100g (4oz) butter
50g (2oz) soft brown sugar
100g (4oz) wholemeal flour
50g (2oz) ground hazelnuts
30ml (2 tblsp) chopped hazelnuts
2 egg whites
75g (3oz) golden granulated sugar
300ml (½ pint) thick unsweetened apple puree

Work the butter, brown sugar, wholemeal flour and ground hazelnuts to a soft, smooth dough. Knead lightly and work in the chopped hazelnuts. Press evenly over the base of a 23cm (9 inch) fluted, loose-bottomed flan tin. Bake in the oven for 10 minutes. Meanwhile, whisk the egg whites until stiff but not 'dry'; gradually whisk in the golden granulated sugar. Remove the shortcake from the oven and pipe or swirl the meringue in a border around the edge. Return to the oven, lower the heat, and bake for a further 35 minutes, until golden. Fill immediately with the apple puree and serve while still warm.

Jellied Grape Shortcake (far right) and Chestnut Parfait (right).

Chestnut Parfait

PREPARATION TIME: 15 minutes

SERVES: 4 people

225g (8oz) unsweetened chestnut
  puree
15ml (1 tblsp) honey
15ml (1 tblsp) brandy
60ml (4 tblsp) thick natural yogurt
Generous pinch ground cinnamon

To Decorate
Small cinnamon sticks

Beat the chestnut puree with the
honey and brandy; blend in the
yogurt and cinnamon. Spoon into
glass custard cups or stemmed
glasses. Spike each one with a
cinnamon stick.
Note: this is very rich, and you may
prefer to make the above quantities
serve 6 small portions.

Iced Kiwi Fruit and Yogurt Pudding

PREPARATION TIME: 15 minutes,
plus chilling time

SERVES: 4 people

300ml (½ pint) thick natural yogurt
Artificial sweetener to taste, or a little
  honey
4 kiwi fruit, peeled and chopped
2 kiwi fruit, peeled and thinly sliced

Mix the yogurt with sweetener or
honey to taste, and stir in the
chopped kiwi fruit. Place slices of
kiwi fruit so that they stand upright
against the sides of 4 stemmed
glasses; spoon the yogurt and kiwi
fruit mixture into the centre. Chill
briefly, for about 20-30 minutes,
before serving.

Glazed Cherry Rice Pudding

PREPARATION TIME: 20 minutes, plus cooling and chilling time

COOKING TIME: 45 minutes to 1 hour

SERVES: 4-6 people

60g (2oz) brown rice
25g (1oz) soft brown sugar
600ml (1 pint) skimmed milk
2.5ml (½ tsp) vanilla essence
Generous pinch ground nutmeg
30ml (2 tblsp) thick natural yogurt

225g (8oz) fresh cherries, de-stalked and pitted
150ml (¼ pint) pure red grape juice
150ml (¼ pint) water
10ml (2 tsp) powdered gelatine

Put the rice, sugar, skimmed milk, vanilla essence and nutmeg into a solid based pan; bring to the boil and simmer gently for ¾-1 hour, until the rice mixture is thick and creamy. Allow to cool and then beat in the yogurt. Spoon into a glass bowl and arrange the cherries on the top. Mix the grape juice with half the water; dissolve the gelatine in the remaining water and then add to the grape juice. Leave in a cool place until syrupy. Spoon the red glaze evenly over the cherries. Chill until set.

This page: Banana, Almond and Orange Truffles (top) and Hazelnut and Apple Meringue Torten (bottom).

Facing page: Iced Kiwi Fruit and Yogurt Pudding (top) and Glazed Cherry Rice Pudding (bottom).

Mango and Orange Mousse

PREPARATION TIME: 35-40 minutes, plus chilling time

SERVES: 4-6 people

450ml (¾ pint) fresh mango pulp
Finely grated rind of ½ orange
Artificial sweetener to taste
15g (½oz) powdered gelatine
30ml (2 tblsp) orange juice
30ml (2 tblsp) natural yogurt
2 egg whites

To Decorate

Twisted strips orange peel

Mix the mango pulp with the orange rind and artificial sweetener to taste. Dissolve the gelatine in the orange juice. Add to the mango pulp, together with the yogurt. Leave until the mixture is on the point of setting. Whisk the egg whites until stiff but not 'dry', and fold lightly but thoroughly into the thickened mango mixture. Spoon into stemmed glasses and chill until set. Decorate with twisted strips of orange peel.

No Sugar Fresh Mincemeat Tarts (top right), Lemon Yogurt Cake (above) and Muesli Biscuits (far right).

Banana, Almond and Orange Truffles

PREPARATION TIME: 25 minutes
MAKES: 10

2 bananas, peeled
Juice of ½ orange
Finely grated rind of 1 orange
100g (4oz) ground almonds
30ml (2 tblsp) finely chopped
    blanched almonds
15ml (1 tblsp) dark, soft brown sugar
Plain chocolate vermicelli

Mash the bananas with the orange juice and rind; mix in the ground almonds, chopped almonds and brown sugar. Chill the mixture until it is firm enough to shape. Roll into small balls, about the size of a ping pong ball. Roll each one in chocolate vermicelli so as to give an even coating. Chill once again.

No Sugar Fresh Mincemeat Tarts

PREPARATION TIME: 30 minutes
COOKING TIME: 20-25 minutes
OVEN: 190°C, 375°F, Gas Mark 5
MAKES: 4

1 eating apple, cored and finely
    chopped
30ml (2 tblsp) raisins
30ml (2 tblsp) currants
15ml (1 tblsp) chopped pitted dates
15ml (1 tblsp) chopped nuts (any
    variety)
30ml (2 tblsp) clear honey

Pastry
100g (4oz) wholemeal flour
100g (4oz) plain white flour
100g (4oz) butter
1 egg yolk
45ml (3 tblsp) water

Glaze
Beaten egg white
Caster sugar

Mix the chopped apple with the raisins, currants, chopped dates, nuts and honey. Keep covered while you make the pastry. Put the flours into a mixing bowl and rub in the butter. Mix the egg yolk with 30ml (2 tblsp) cold water; add to the sieved flours and mix to a soft, smooth dough, adding a little extra water if necessary. Roll out the dough quite thinly and use to line 4 individual tartlet tins (preferably with loose bottoms). Press up the edges well, trimming off excess pastry. Roll out the pastry trimmings and cut into thin strips. Fill the pastry cases with the fresh mincemeat, and lay a lattice of pastry strips over the top of each one. Press the strips to the side of the pastry case to seal. Glaze the strips and edges of the tarts with beaten egg white and sprinkle lightly with sugar. Bake in the oven for 20-25 minutes, until golden. Serve warm or cold.
Note: these are not little tarts, like jam tarts, and the pastry cases need to be about 10cm (4 inches) in diameter.

Lemon Yogurt Cake

PREPARATION TIME: 45 minutes
COOKING TIME: about 25
    minutes
OVEN: 190°C, 375°F, Gas Mark 5
SERVES: 8-10 people

6 eggs
175g (6oz) soft brown sugar
175g (6oz) plain flour
Pinch mixed spice
Finely grated rind of 2 lemons
60ml (4 tblsp) water
30ml (2 tblsp) clear honey

Filling
225g (8oz) curd cheese
30ml (2 tblsp) clear honey
Finely grated rind and juice of ½
    lemon
Few drops vanilla essence
30ml (2 tblsp) natural yogurt

Langues de chat biscuits
200ml (⅓ pint) thick natural yogurt
Matchstick strips lemon peel

Grease 3 large sandwich tins, each 23cm (9 inches) in diameter; dust each one lightly with flour. Whisk the eggs and brown sugar together until thick, light and creamy (when the whisk is lifted free from the mixture it should leave a trail on the surface). Sieve the flour and spice and fold lightly but thoroughly into the whisked mixture. Divide the mixture amongst the prepared tins, tilting them so that the mixture spreads evenly. Bake the sponge layers for 25 minutes. Allow them to shrink slightly from their tins before turning the baked sponges onto cooling racks. Put the lemon rind and water into a small pan; boil briskly until reduced by one half. Add the honey to the remaining lemon liquid and heat through together. Trickle the honey and lemon syrup over each sponge layer. For the filling: soften the curd cheese and beat with the honey, lemon rind and juice, vanilla essence and yogurt until smooth. Sandwich the three sponge layers together with the cheese filling, saving a few spoonfuls for fixing the biscuits to the sides of the cake. Fix langues de chat biscuits all around the sides of the assembled cake; attach each one with a little of the cheese filling. Spread the top of the cake with thick yogurt and decorate with matchstick strips of lemon peel.

Lemon and Ginger Cheesecake

PREPARATION TIME: 45 minutes,
plus chilling time
SERVES: 6-8 people

40g (1½oz) butter, melted
25g (1oz) soft brown sugar
75g (3oz) oatmeal biscuits, crushed

Filling
175g (6oz) curd cheese
2 eggs, separated
Finely grated rind of 1 lemon
50g (2oz) light, soft brown sugar
150ml (¼ pint) natural yogurt
15g (½oz) powdered gelatine
45ml (3 tblsp) water
Juice of ½ lemon
3 pieces preserved stem ginger, rinsed
    in warm water and chopped

To Decorate
60ml (4 tblsp) thick natural yogurt
Fine matchstick strips lemon peel,
    or twists of lemon

Lightly grease an 18cm (7 inch) loose-bottomed cake tin. For the base: mix the melted butter, soft brown sugar and crushed biscuits together; press evenly over the base of the tin. Chill while you make the filling. For the filling: beat the curd cheese with the egg yolks, lemon rind, soft brown sugar and yogurt. Dissolve the gelatine in the water and add to the cheese mixture, together with the lemon juice; leave on one side until the mixture is on the point of setting. Whisk the egg whites until stiff but not 'dry', and fold lightly but thoroughly into the cheese mixture, together with the chopped ginger. Spoon the mixture into the prepared cake tin, smoothing the surface level. Chill for 3-4 hours, until the filling has set. Unmould the cheesecake carefully. Swirl natural yogurt over the top of the cheesecake and decorate with strips of lemon peel or lemon twists.

Muesli Biscuits

PREPARATION TIME: 20 minutes
COOKING TIME: 15 minutes
OVEN: 190°C, 375°F, Gas Mark 5
MAKES: about 20

100g (4oz) softened butter
100g (4oz) soft brown sugar
1 egg, beaten
100g (4oz) wholemeal flour
50g (2oz) muesli
30ml (2 tblsp) flaked almonds

Beat the margarine and sugar together until light and fluffy. Beat in the egg, adding a little flour if the mixture shows signs of curdling. Work in the remaining flour, muesli and flaked almonds. Shape the mixture into small balls, using floured hands. Place on greased baking sheets, allowing room for spreading. Flatten the balls of biscuit dough slightly. Bake in the oven for 15 minutes until crisp and golden. Allow to cool slightly before removing the baked biscuits to a cooling rack.

Date and Pistachio Shortbreads

PREPARATION TIME: 20 minutes
COOKING TIME: 12-15 minutes
OVEN: 190°C, 375°F, Gas Mark 5
MAKES: about 12

100g (4oz) butter
50g (2oz) soft brown sugar
100g (4oz) wholemeal flour
50g (2oz) ground almonds
75g (3oz) stoned dates, chopped
30ml (2 tblsp) chopped shelled
    pistachios

To Decorate
Chopped shelled pistachios

Work the butter, brown sugar, wholemeal flour and ground almonds to a soft, smooth dough. Knead lightly, working in the chopped dates and pistachios. Press the mixture into small boat-shaped moulds. Press a few chopped pistachios into the top of each uncooked shortbread. Bake in the oven for 12-15 minutes.

Apricot and Walnut Teabread

PREPARATION TIME: 20 minutes

COOKING TIME: 1 hour 3 minutes

OVEN: 160°C, 325°F, Gas Mark 3

MAKES: 1 loaf

175g (6oz) softened butter
175g (6oz) light soft brown sugar
3 eggs, beaten
225g (8oz) wholemeal flour
7.5ml (1½ tsp) baking powder
30ml (2 tblsp) milk
100g (4oz) dried apricots, chopped
50g (2oz) chopped walnuts

To Decorate
30ml (2 tblsp) clear honey, warmed
Extra chopped dried apricots

Lightly grease a 1kg (2lb) loaf tin, and line the base with a piece of greased greaseproof paper. Cream the butter and sugar until light and fluffy. Gradually beat in the eggs, adding a little flour if the mixture shows signs of curdling. Mix in the flour and baking powder, together with the milk, and finally stir in the chopped apricots and nuts. Put the mixture into the prepared loaf tin, smoothing the top level. Bake in the oven for 1 hour 30 minutes. If the top of the loaf starts to darken too much, cover it with a piece of foil. As soon as the loaf comes out of the oven, brush the top with the warmed honey and sprinkle with the chopped apricots. Leave to cool in the tin for a few minutes before turning out.

Golden Pistachio Meringues

PREPARATION TIME: 15-20 minutes

COOKING TIME: 1 hour

OVEN: 110°C, 225°F, Gas Mark ¼

MAKES: about 6

2 egg whites
100g (4oz) golden granulated sugar

Filling
100g (4oz) curd cheese
15ml (1 tblsp) clear honey
30ml (2 tblsp) chopped shelled pistachios

To Decorate
Chopped shelled pistachios

Whisk the egg whites until stiff but not dry and then gradually whisk in the golden granulated sugar. Pipe into 6 nest shapes on lightly greased and floured baking sheets. Bake in the oven for 1 hour. The meringues should be fairly crisp but they should not 'colour'. Allow to cool. For the filling: cream the cheese until soft; beat in the honey and chopped pistachios. Fill the meringue nests with the cheese filling. Sprinkle each one with extra pistachios.

Cinnamon and Peanut Cookies

PREPARATION TIME: 15-20 minutes

COOKING TIME: 20 minutes

OVEN: 180°C, 350°F, Gas Mark 4

MAKES: about 20

100g (4oz) softened butter
100g (4oz) soft brown sugar
1 egg, beaten
60ml (4 tblsp) clear honey
250g (9oz) wholemeal flour
2.5ml (½ tsp) ground cinnamon
5ml (1 tsp) baking powder
Pinch salt
75g (3oz) shelled peanuts

Cream the butter and sugar until well mixed (do not over-beat). Mix in the beaten egg and honey and then mix in the flour, cinnamon, baking powder and salt. Put heaped teaspoons of the mixture onto greased baking sheets, allowing room for spreading; flatten each one slightly with the rounded side of a dampened spoon. Stud the tops with peanuts. Bake in the oven for 20 minutes.
Note: for really golden topped biscuits bake them as above for just 15 minutes; brush each one with beaten egg and return to the oven for a further 5 minutes.

This page: (left picture) Cinnamon and Peanut Cookies (top) and Golden Pistachio Meringues (bottom). (Right picture) Mango and Orange Mousse (top) and Lemon and Ginger Cheesecake (bottom).

Facing page: Apricot and Walnut Teabread (top) and Date and Pistachio Shortbreads (bottom).

Drinks, Sauces and Dressings

Tropical Fruit Flummery

PREPARATION TIME: 10 minutes

SERVES: 4 people

3 kiwi fruit, peeled and chopped
2 ripe nectarines, halved, stoned and
    chopped
2 slices fresh pineapple, peeled and
    chopped
Juice of 1 fresh lime
300ml (½ pint) unsweetened
    pineapple juice

To Decorate
Slices of peeled kiwi fruit, or lime

Put the kiwi fruit, nectarines,
pineapple, lime juice and pineapple
juice into the liquidiser and blend
until smooth. Pour into tall glasses
and top up with iced water (either
mineral or tap water). Decorate the
rim of each glass with a slice of kiwi
fruit or lime.

Mulled Apple and Honey

PREPARATION TIME: 5 minutes

COOKING TIME: 4 minutes

SERVES: 4 people

450ml (¾ pint) unsweetened apple
    juice
150ml (¼ pint) water
10ml (2 tsp) honey
2 cinnamon sticks, split in half
6 cloves
3 strips lemon peel

To Serve
4 cinnamon sticks

Put the apple juice into a pan with
the water, honey, broken cinnamon
sticks, cloves and lemon peel;
simmer very gently for 4 minutes.
Remove the broken cinnamon
sticks and pour liquid into heatproof glasses. Spike each drink with
a whole cinnamon stick and serve.

Spicy Fresh Mango Juice

PREPARATION TIME: 15 minutes

SERVES: 4 people

300ml (½ pint) fresh mango pulp
Juice of 1 lemon
15ml (1 tblsp) clear honey
Generous pinch ground ginger
Generous pinch nutmeg
150ml (¼ pint) unsweetened orange
    juice
150ml (¼ pint) water
1 small piece fresh root ginger

To Decorate
4 rings of orange

Put the mango pulp, lemon juice,
honey, ground ginger, nutmeg,
orange juice and water into the
liquidiser and blend until smooth.
Pour into 4 glasses, adding two or
three ice cubes to each one. Put the
piece of root ginger into a garlic
crusher and squeeze a few drops
into each glass. Slide a ring of
orange over the rim of each glass
and serve.

**This page: Tropical Fruit
Flummery (top) and Grapefruit
Shrub (bottom).**

**Facing page: Spicy Fresh Mango
Juice (right) and Mulled Apple
and Honey (left).**

Almond and Tarragon French Dressing

PREPARATION TIME: 5 minutes

MAKES: about 300ml (½ pint)

200ml (⅓ pint) good green olive oil
60ml (4 tblsp) tarragon vinegar
15ml (1 tblsp) chopped fresh tarragon
1 clove garlic, peeled and crushed
Salt and freshly ground black pepper
   to taste
30ml (2 tblsp) finely chopped
   blanched almonds

Mix all the ingredients together. Keep in a screw topped bottle or jar, in a cool place (not in the refrigerator).

Pesto Sauce

PREPARATION TIME: 5 minutes

MAKES: about 200ml (½ pint)

1 large bunch fresh basil
4 cloves garlic, peeled
45ml (3 tblsp) pine kernels
150ml (¼ pint) good green olive oil
15ml (1 tblsp) lemon juice
Salt and freshly ground black pepper
   to taste

Put all the ingredients into the liquidiser and blend until fairly smooth; the sauce should still have a little texture to it. Keep in a screw top jar in the refrigerator, for no more than a week. Serve with cooked pasta, with cold meats such as Italian ham, and with cooked game and poultry.

Fresh Tomato and Basil Sauce

PREPARATION TIME: 10-15
                  minutes

MAKES: 450ml (¾ pint)

1 small onion, finely chopped
450g (1lb) tomatoes, skinned, seeded
   and chopped
30ml (2 tblsp) tomato puree
5ml (1 tsp) honey
5ml (1 tsp) finely grated orange rind
2 cloves garlic, peeled
Salt and freshly ground black pepper
   to taste
150ml (¼ pint) red wine
150ml (¼ pint) chicken stock
30ml (2 tblsp) coarsely chopped fresh
   basil

Put all the sauce ingredients into the liquidiser and blend until smooth. If the sauce is too thick for your liking, thin it down a little with extra chicken stock. Can be kept in the refrigerator for up to 3 days. Serve with cooked pasta, with cooked fish, or as the base for a cold soup.

Low Fat Yogurt 'Mayonnaise'

PREPARATION TIME: 5-10
                  minutes

MAKES: about 300ml (½ pint)

2 egg yolks
15ml (1 tblsp) white wine vinegar
5ml (1 tsp) chive mustard
1 clove garlic, peeled and crushed
Salt and freshly ground black pepper
   to taste
300ml (½ pint) thick natural yogurt

Beat the egg yolks with the vinegar; beat in the remaining ingredients. This is thinner than a standard oil-based mayonnaise, but equally delicious. Serve with salads, cooked fish, over cooked vegetables, etc. Will keep in the refrigerator for up to 4 days.

Grapefruit Shrub

PREPARATION TIME: 10-15
                  minutes

SERVES: 4 people

Peeled segments from 2 grapefruit
300ml (½ pint) unsweetened
   grapefruit juice
150ml (¼ pint) water
30ml (2 tblsp) clear honey
2 egg whites

To Decorate
Small sprigs fresh mint or grated
   lemon rind

Put the grapefruit segments, grapefruit juice, water and honey into the liquidiser and blend until smooth. Add the egg whites and blend once again until frothy. Pour into glasses, making sure that a good portion of the white 'froth' goes into each one. Decorate with mint or lemon rind.

This page: Almond and Tarragon French Dressing (top) and Low Fat Yogurt 'Mayonnaise' (bottom).

Facing page: Pesto Sauce (top) and Fresh Tomato and Basil Sauce (bottom).

CHINESE CUISINE

Introduction to Chinese Cooking

As in any other style of cooking, Chinese food is a symbol of life and good health, forming a central part of family and social activity for many people. Through cooking, one demonstrates personal inventiveness and creativity, as well as one's cultural background, so cooking can always be seen as a pleasurable activity.

In Chinese cooking, the preparation is of great importance. Many dishes require very fine chopping and shredding of the various ingredients, and they are combined in a very orderly manner. Those ingredients which are not easily available in the Western world can be substituted by others in the recipes. It is not necessary to use only Chinese utensils as these dishes can easily be prepared using basic kitchen equipment.

The main cooking technique used to produce good Chinese food is stir-frying. A wok is ideal, but a deep, non-stick skillet will serve the purpose just as well. Stir-frying requires good temperature control and this is easily learnt through practice. The wok or pan should be heated, then the temperature reduced before adding oil. If the utensil is too hot the oil will burn, giving a charred, oily taste to the food, which may burn, too! The heat should be progressively raised for the addition of other ingredients. The whole process may take between five and seven minutes. Remember, never overcook, as this will not only destroy the crispness of the food, but also its flavor and goodness.

Chinese food incorporates six basic flavors, just like Indian food. They are: sweet, sour, salty, spicy, pungent and hot. Their employment and respective proportions must be well balanced. Flavoring is always supplemented by ready-prepared sauces, the most essential of which is soy sauce. Others commonly used are oyster and plum sauces.

Finally, garnishing should not be neglected, as presentation is every bit as important as preparation. After all, what appeals to the eye also appeals to the mind and thence to heart and stomach. A slice of cleverly carved carrot, a thin sliver of tomato and carefully arranged parsley or coriander, can add that all-important dash of color.

Cooking is always a pleasure, especially Chinese cooking. It is a challenge and a way to explore one's creative talents. In any case, who does not want their efforts to be rewarded by the pleasure of an exquisite meal?

CHINESE CUISINE

Snacks

Four Happiness Dumplings

PREPARATION TIME: 30-45 minutes for pastry; 20-30 minutes for filling

COOKING TIME: 20 minutes

Pastry
225g (8oz) plain flour
Pinch of salt
200ml (⅓ pint) boiling water

Put the flour and salt into a bowl. Add the boiling water and mix quickly to make a dough. Cover and allow to stand for 20-30 minutes. Knead the dough for 2-3 minutes, sprinkling the work surface with a little cornflour if needed. Divide the dough into 30-35 equal portions and roll each one to a circle 6cm (2½") in diameter.

Filling
175g (6oz) boned loin of pork, finely chopped or minced
2 black mushrooms, soaked and diced
50g (2oz) mixed vegetables, peeled and finely chopped (peas, carrots, celery, etc.)
2.5ml (½ tsp) brown sugar or maltose
10ml (2 tsp) light soya sauce
1.25ml (¼ tsp) freshly ground black pepper
1 egg
5-6 chives, finely chopped
Salt to taste
15ml (1 tblsp) oil
7.5ml (1½ tsp) cornflour
30ml (2 tblsp) flour mixed with a little cold water to a smooth paste

Mix the pork with the mushrooms, mixed vegetables, sugar, soya sauce, black pepper, egg, chives and salt to taste. Add the oil and cornflour and mix well with a fork. Divide filling into 30 to 35 equal portions. Fill each dumpling wrapper with a portion of filling and shape into crescent shape dumplings. Steam them in an ordinary steamer or a Chinese bamboo steamer for about 20 minutes. Serve with a dip and chilli sauce. To make the crescent shape, place a wrapper on a flat surface, put a little filling in the centre, spread the edges with a little flour and water paste and pinch the edges of the wrapper together to seal. Pull one corner of the filled wonton around and over the other corner. Press to seal.

Steamed Shrimp Pancakes

PREPARATION TIME: 1 hour
COOKING TIME: 10-15 minutes

175g (6oz) plain flour or high gluten flour
50g (2oz) cornflour
1.25ml (¼ tsp) salt
15ml (1 tblsp) oil
45ml (3 tblsp) beaten egg
30ml (2 tblsp) water
30ml (2 tblsp) flour mixed with cold water to a smooth paste

Filling
150g (6oz) shrimps, boiled and finely chopped
2 spring onions, bulb only, finely chopped
1.25ml (¼ tsp) salt or to taste
5ml (1 tsp) cornflour to bind

Sieve the flour, cornflour and salt into a bowl. Add the oil, beaten egg and water and mix to make a stiff dough. Leave for 30 minutes to rest. Knead well for 5-6 minutes and roll into 25-30 15cm (6") circles on greaseproof paper. Place the filling in the centre and flatten. Spread flour and water paste around the edge of each pancake and fold up from one end to make a roll. Arrange the pancakes in a greased ordinary or Chinese bamboo steamer and cook over boiling water for 10-15 minutes. Serve piping hot with chilli or soya sauce dip.

Filling
To make the filling mix all the ingredients except the cornflour together, and then bind with the cornflour.

Alternative
To make rice pancakes, soak 100g (4oz) rice for 10 minutes. Grind with water to make a very fine paste of batter consistency. Add 15ml (1 tblsp) oil and mix well. Line a steamer with fine muslin and spoon in a little batter; spread it out into a thin pancake. Steam for 5 minutes. Place a little filling on the pancake and roll up. Steam for 10 minutes and serve piping hot with a dip.

Steamed Open Dumplings

PREPARATION TIME: 1 hour
COOKING TIME: 10-15 minutes

Filling
100g (4oz) peeled prawns, finely chopped
175g (6oz) pork or beef, minced
2 black mushrooms, soaked and finely chopped
Salt to taste
2.5ml (½ tsp) brown sugar

Seasoning
2.5ml (½ tsp) monosodium glutamate (optional)
15ml (1 tblsp) cornflour
5ml (1 tsp) dark soya sauce
5ml (1 tsp) light soya sauce
1.25ml (¼ tsp) freshly ground black pepper
15ml (1 tblsp) sesame oil
24 wonton wrappers

Mix the minced pork, prawns, mushrooms, salt and sugar together. Add the seasoning ingredients and mix well. Allow to stand for 30 minutes. Take each wonton wrapper and spoon a little filling in the centre. Fold up the edges around the filling but do not completely enclose it. (An open ended dumpling is produced with the sides of the wrapper gathered around the filling.) Flatten the base by pressing it slightly so that it will stand upright in a steamer. Grease an ordinary steamer or a bamboo steamer and arrange the dumplings in it. Steam for 15-20 minutes. Serve hot with a dip.

Wontons with Pork and Shrimp Filling

PREPARATION TIME: 30 minutes

COOKING TIME: 10-15 minutes

175g (6oz) lean pork, minced
Oil
175g (6oz) peeled shrimps, finely chopped
3 spring onions, finely chopped
2.5ml (½ tsp) ground white pepper
15ml (1 tblsp) soya sauce
7.5ml (1½ tsp) rice wine or dry sherry
2.5ml (½ tsp) salt, or to taste
7.5ml (1½ tsp) cornflour blended with 30ml (2 tblsp) water
40-50 wonton wrappers
30ml (2 tblsp) plain flour, mixed with a little cold water to a smooth paste

Fry pork in 30ml (2 tblsp) oil until it loses its pink colour. Add shrimps and onions and fry for 3-4 minutes. Add pepper, soya sauce and wine. Season with salt and stir fry for 1-2 minutes. Add the blended cornflour and stir over a moderate heat until thickened. Allow to cool before filling the wontons. Divide filling into 40-50 equal portions. Take a wonton wrapper, moisten the edges with the flour and water paste. Place a portion of filling in the centre of the wonton and gather up the edges to make a neat round, or shape in such a way as to make a triangle or any other shape that you prefer. Once you have shaped all the wontons, deep-fry them in hot oil until crisp and golden. You will need to fry them in 3 or more batches. Drain well on absorbent paper before serving.

Fried Meat Dumplings

PREPARATION TIME: 10 minutes
COOKING TIME: about 15 minutes

30ml (2 tblsp) cooking oil
225g (8oz) lean, minced beef or lamb
2 spring onions, chopped
30ml (2 tblsp) light soya sauce
2.5ml (½ tsp) salt
22.5ml (1½ tblsp) rice wine or dry sherry
10ml (2 tsp) cornflour mixed with 30ml (2 tblsp) water

Dumpling wrappers (see recipe)
30ml (2 tblsp) plain flour mixed to a
paste with cold water
Oil for deep frying

Heat the 30ml (2 tblsp) oil in a pan and fry the minced meat and onion for 2-3 minutes. Add the soya sauce, salt and wine. Cook gently for 2 minutes and then stir in the cornflour and water mixture. Stir over the heat until the mixture thickens. Put the meat mixture into a dish and leave to cool. Divide into equal portions – about 48. Take a round dumpling wrapper and place a portion of filling in the centre. Moisten the edges of the wrapper with a little flour and water paste, gather the edges up and over the filling and pinch together to seal. Shape neatly. Continue to make the remaining dumplings in the same way. Deep-fry the dumplings in moderately hot oil, cooking a few dumplings at a time, until they are golden brown. Drain thoroughly on absorbent paper. Serve with chilli sauce dip.

Dumpling Wrappers
(Chiao Tze P'i)

PREPARATION TIME: 50-60 minutes

275g (10oz) plain flour
200ml (⅓ pint) cold water

Makes 40-50 wrappers

Sieve the flour into a bowl and add the cold water, a little at a time, and mix to a firm dough. Knead the dough on a flat surface for 4-5 minutes. Cover with a damp cloth or wrap in cling film. Leave to stand at room temperature for 30-40 minutes. Roll out on a well-floured surface as thinly as possible, until almost transparent. Cut into round or square pieces to suit your requirements. Use within a few hours of making otherwise they will dry out.

Wonton Wrappers

PREPARATION TIME: 5-6 hours (including standing time)

120g (4¼oz) high gluten flour
30ml (2 tblsp) beaten egg
30ml (2 tblsp) cold water
Cornflour
Makes 40-50 wrappers

Sieve flour and gradually add the beaten egg and water mixed together. Mix to a stiff dough. Knead firmly for 5-6 minutes and wrap in cling film. Leave to stand at room temperature for 4-5 hours. Roll out into a very large square on a work surface dusted with cornflour. The pastry should be almost transparent. Cut into 40-50 7.5cm (3″) round or square wrappers. Dust each wrapper with cornflour before stacking. Store the wrappers, wrapped securely in cling film, in the refrigerator, for up to 24 hours. If they are allowed to dry out they will split during cooking.

Spring Roll Wrappers

PREPARATION TIME: 20 minutes, plus chilling time

100g (4oz) strong plain flour
1 egg, beaten
A little cold water

Makes 12 wrappers

Sieve the flour into a bowl. Make a well in the centre and add the beaten egg and a little cold water. Mix to a soft yet firm dough, adding a little extra water if necessary. Knead the dough until it is really pliable. (This helps to make the gluten work.) Chill, covered, for 4 hours or overnight. Allow to come back to room temperature. Roll out the dough on a well-floured surface to about 5mm (¼″) thick. Cut into 12 equal pieces, and then roll each piece to a square about 15x15cm (6x6″) – each square should be very thin.

Spring Rolls

PREPARATION TIME: 20-30 minutes

COOKING TIME: about 20 minutes

225g (8oz) lean, raw pork or beef, finely shredded
100g (4oz) prawns or shrimps (either uncooked or boiled), shelled
4 spring onions, finely chopped
Cooking oil
10ml (2 tsp) fresh root ginger, peeled and shredded
100g (4oz) white cabbage, shredded
75g (3oz) bean sprouts
15ml (1 tblsp) soya sauce
Salt to taste
12 spring roll wrappers, each 15cm (6″) square (see recipe)
30ml (2 tblsp) plain flour, mixed with a little cold water to a smooth paste

Fry the shredded pork, prawns or shrimps and the spring onions in 15ml (1 tblsp) of cooking oil for 2-3 minutes. Add the ginger, cabbage and bean sprouts, and stir fry for 2-3 minutes. Add soya sauce, and season with a little salt if desired. Remove from the heat and allow to cool. Lay out the spring roll wrappers on a clean working surface, with one point of each wrapper facing you. Divide the filling mixture into 12 equal portions and place one portion of filling just above the front point of each wrapper. Fold in the opposite side points, so that they overlap slightly like an envelope – secure the side points with a little flour and water paste. Starting with the point facing you, roll each wrapper up around the filling, securing the remaining point with a little flour and water paste. Repeat in exactly the same way with the remaining spring roll wrappers. They will keep a better shape if you chill them for 1 hour before cooking. Deep fry over a medium heat until golden brown and crisp. Drain thoroughly on absorbent paper and serve hot with a selection of dips or chilli sauce. The spring rolls can be frozen, uncooked.

This page: **Fried Meat Dumplings (top right), Spring Rolls (centre left) and Wontons with Pork and Shrimp Filling (bottom).** Facing page: **Spiced Beef (top), Steamed Beef Szechuan Style (bottom left) and Beef with Green Pepper and Chilli (bottom right).**

CHINESE CUISINE
Meat Dishes

Spiced Beef

PREPARATION TIME: 30 minutes

COOKING TIME: 5-6 minutes

Marinade
5ml (1 tsp) sugar
2-3 star anise, ground
2.5ml (½ tsp) ground fennel
15ml (1 tblsp) dark soya sauce
1.25ml (¼ tsp) monosodium
glutamate (optional)

450g (1lb) fillet of beef, cut into
2.5cm (1") strips
2.5cm (1") fresh root ginger, peeled
and crushed
2.5ml (½ tsp) salt
30ml (2 tblsp) oil
4 spring onions, sliced
2.5ml (½ tsp) freshly ground black
pepper
15ml (1 tblsp) light soya sauce

Mix the marinade ingredients
together. Add the beef strips,
ginger and salt, and marinate for 20
minutes. Heat the oil in wok and
stir fry the onions for 1 minute.
Add beef, ground pepper and soya
sauce and stir fry for 4-5 minutes.
Serve with a dip.

Steamed Beef Szechuan Style

PREPARATION TIME: 40 minutes

COOKING TIME: 15 minutes

3 slices fresh root ginger, minced
5ml (1 tsp) salt
5ml (1 tsp) sugar
Freshly ground black pepper
15ml (1 tblsp) oil
30ml (2 tblsp) rice wine or dry sherry
22.5ml (1½ tblsp) chilli bean paste
30ml (2 tblsp) dark soya sauce
3-4 spring onions, finely chopped
450g (1lb) fillet of beef, cut into 5cm
(2") long strips
100g (4oz) ground rice
1 large lotus leaf or several cabbage
leaves

For the marinade, mix the ginger,
salt, sugar, pepper, oil, wine, bean
paste, soya sauce and half of the
spring onions. Add beef strips and
mix well. Leave to marinate for 15-

20 minutes. Heat the wok and dry-
roast the ground rice for 2-4
minutes till rice changes colour
from white to light brown. Roll the
marinated beef in the roasted
ground rice to give a thin, even
coating. Line the bamboo steamer
with a well-oiled lotus leaf or a few
old and tough cabbage leaves.
Arrange the coated beef strips in a
neat pile on top. Steam fairly

quickly for 10-15 minutes over
boiling water. Garnish with the
remaining chopped spring onions
before serving. Serve hot with chilli
sauce.

Beef with Green Pepper and Chilli

PREPARATION TIME: 30 minutes

COOKING TIME: 10-12 minutes

450g (1lb) fillet of beef, cut into
2.5cm (1") strips

Seasoning
30ml (2 tblsp) dark soya sauce
5ml (1 tsp) sesame oil
Pinch bicarbonate of soda
1.25ml (¼ tsp) ground black pepper
2.5ml (½ tsp) salt

Oil for cooking
2 green peppers, seeded and thinly
  sliced
1 onion, peeled and sliced
2 spring onions, chopped
2.5cm (1") fresh root ginger, peeled
  and sliced
2 garlic cloves, peeled and chopped
3 green chillis, sliced

Sauce
30ml (2 tblsp) chicken stock
2.5ml (½ tsp) monosodium
  glutamate (optional)
5ml (1 tsp) dark soya sauce
Salt to taste
Few drops sesame oil

Marinate beef with the seasoning
ingredients for 15 minutes. Heat
30ml (2 tblsp) oil and stir fry green
peppers and onions for 2 minutes.
Remove to a plate. Reheat wok,
add 30-45ml (2-3 tblsp) oil and fry
ginger, garlic and green chillis for 1
minute. Add beef and stir fry for 4-
5 minutes. Add sauce ingredients,
mixed together, and the fried
peppers and onions. Stir fry for a
further 2 minutes and serve.

Diced Pork with Sweet Corn

PREPARATION TIME: 25 minutes

COOKING TIME: 15-20 minutes

Marinade
Pinch salt
10ml (2 tsp) dark soya sauce
1.25ml (¼ tsp) sugar
5ml (1 tsp) rice wine
15ml (1 tblsp) water

175g (6oz) pork loin, diced
Oil for deep frying
2 slices fresh root ginger, peeled and
  diced
1 clove garlic, peeled and chopped
250ml (8 fl oz) chicken stock

Seasoning
1.25ml (¼ tsp) salt
1.25ml (¼ tsp) freshly ground black
  pepper
1.25ml (¼ tsp) sugar
5ml (1 tsp) rice wine or dry sherry
Few drops sesame oil

5ml (1 tsp) cornflour mixed with
  15ml (1 tblsp) water

250ml (8 fl oz) creamed sweet corn
1 egg, well beaten
4 spring onions, chopped

Mix the marinade ingredients
together. Add the pork and leave
to marinate for 15 minutes. Drain
the pork and discard the liquid.
Heat the wok and pour in the oil
for deep frying. Fry the pork until
light brown. Remove the pork and
drain. Reserve the oil for future
use. Heat 15ml (1 tblsp) oil in the
wok, add the ginger and pork. Stir
fry for 3 minutes. Add the stock
and simmer for 3 minutes. Add the
seasoning ingredients and simmer
for 2-3 minutes. Add the blended
cornflour and water and simmer
until the sauce thickens. Add the
sweet corn and beaten egg and
cook for 2-3 minutes. Serve
sprinkled with chopped onions.
Serve this dish with plain boiled
rice or noodles.

Pork Stuffed Mushrooms

PREPARATION TIME: 15-20
  minutes

COOKING TIME: 12 minutes

Filling
1 egg
10ml (2 tsp) cornflour
10ml (2 tsp) rice wine or dry sherry
1.25ml (¼ tsp) minced fresh root
  ginger
6 water chestnuts, finely chopped
50g (2oz) peeled shrimps, chopped
175g (6oz) lean pork, minced
1.25ml (¼ tsp) salt
1.25ml (¼ tsp) freshly ground black
  pepper
2.5ml (½ tsp) sugar
10ml (2 tsp) chilli sauce

16 large, open mushrooms
600ml (1 pint) chicken stock
Oil

Mix all the filling ingredients
together. Remove the mushroom
stalks. Divide the filling into 16
portions. Bring the chicken stock
to the boil. Add the mushrooms
and leave to stand off the heat for 5
minutes, covered. Drain the
mushrooms and discard the stock.
Top each mushroom with a portion
of filling. Put the stuffed
mushrooms into a well-oiled
steamer. Steam for 10-12 minutes
over boiling water. Serve as a snack,
as a starter or as a side dish.
Alternatively, serve with a simple
sauce made from thickened
chicken broth. Pour the sauce over
the steamed mushrooms.

Sliced Pork in Wine Sauce

PREPARATION TIME: 30 minutes
COOKING TIME: about 16 minutes

Seasoning
15ml (1 tblsp) red vinegar
15ml (1 tblsp) light soya sauce
15ml (1 tblsp) rice wine or dry sherry
10ml (2 tsp) soya paste
5ml (1 tsp) freshly ground black pepper
5ml (1 tsp) salt
5ml (1 tsp) Shao Hsing wine

450g (1lb) pork fillet, cut into 5cm (2") long thin slices
15ml (1 tblsp) cornflour
60ml (4 tblsp) oil

2.5cm (½") fresh root ginger, finely chopped
3 spring onions (or scallions), chopped
1 green pepper, seeded and diced

Sauce
10ml (2 tsp) cornflour
60ml (4 tblsp) dry white wine
120ml (4 fl oz) chicken stock
10ml (2 tsp) dark soya sauce
5ml (1 tsp) sugar
2.5ml (½ tsp) salt

Mix the seasoning ingredients together. Add the pork slices and leave to marinate for 10-15 minutes. Drain the pork and roll in the cornflour. Leave on one side. Discard the marinade. Heat half the oil in the wok until smoking. Add the pork, reduce the heat, and

Diced Pork with Sweet Corn (far left), Sliced Pork in Wine Sauce (top left) and Pork Stuffed Mushrooms (left).

**Steamed Pork with Salted Cabbage (top), Pork with
Green Pepper (centre right) and Pork Chop Suey (bottom).**

golden brown and tender. Remove
and drain on kitchen paper. Fry all
the meat balls and serve with
chopped spring onions and green
pepper rings sprinkled on top.
Serve as a snack, as a starter or as a
side dish.

Pork Chop Suey

PREPARATION TIME: 35 minutes
COOKING TIME: 10 minutes

Marinade
15ml (1 tblsp) water
2.5ml (½ tsp) bicarbonate of soda
10ml (2 tsp) dark soya sauce

*225g (½ lb) pork fillet, sliced into
   5cm (2″) pieces*
*45ml (3 tblsp) cooked oil or cooking
   oil*
1 onion, peeled and cut into pieces
1 clove of garlic, peeled and sliced
25g (1oz) bamboo shoots, sliced
175g (6oz) bean sprouts

Seasoning
Pinch salt
Pinch freshly ground black pepper
*Pinch monosodium glutamate
   (optional)*
45ml (3 tblsp) light soya sauce
5ml (1 tsp) sugar
5ml (1 tsp) cornflour

Sauce
5ml (1 tsp) cornflour
15ml (1 tblsp) water

Mix the marinade ingredients
together. Add the pork and leave
for 15 minutes to marinate. Drain
the pork and discard the marinade.
Heat the oil in the wok and stir fry
pork for 2-3 minutes. Remove the
pork. Add the onions, garlic and
bamboo shoots to the wok and stir
fry for 1-2 minutes. Add the
bean sprouts and stir fry for 2
minutes. Remove onto a dish and
add the mixed seasoning
ingredients. Leave for 10 minutes.
Return the pork and the vegetables
to the wok. Add the blended sauce
ingredients. Bring to the boil gently,
stirring until the sauce thickens.
Serve immediately.

stir fry for 4-6 minutes until lightly
browned. Remove the pork and
keep on one side. Discard any oil
left in the wok. Add the remaining
oil to the wok and stir fry the
onions, ginger and green pepper for
3-5 minutes. Return the fried pork
to the wok and cook for a further
2-3 minutes with the vegetables.
Remove onto a serving dish. Mix
the cornflour from the sauce
ingredients with 30ml (2 tblsp)
water. Add the remaining sauce
ingredients to the wok and bring to
the boil. Add the blended
cornflour. Stir and simmer until the
sauce thickens, simmer for 1-2
minutes. Pour over the pork and
serve.

Deep Fried Pork Meat Balls

PREPARATION TIME: 25 minutes
COOKING TIME: about 12
                     minutes

*450g (1lb) lean pork, coarsely
   minced*
1 small onion, finely chopped
1 green chilli, chopped
*Salt and freshly ground black pepper
   to taste*
*2.5cm (½″) fresh root ginger, peeled
   and finely chopped*
1 egg, beaten
15ml (1 tblsp) cornflour
10ml (2 tsp) dark soya sauce

*2 sprigs Chinese parsley, finely
   chopped*
5ml (1 tsp) cooked oil
Oil for deep frying
*2 spring onions, chopped (for
   garnishing)*
*1 green pepper, seeded and cut into
   rings (for garnishing) (optional)*

Mix the minced pork with the
chopped onion, chilli, salt and
pepper to taste, chopped ginger,
beaten egg, cornflour, soya sauce,
parsley and cooked oil. Leave to
stand for 10 minutes. Mould into
16 even-sized balls. Heat the oil in
the wok for deep frying and slide a
few pork balls into the oil. Fry over
a gentle heat for 5-6 minutes until

**Facing page: Fried Pork with
Vegetables (top left), Bean
Sprouts with Chopped Pork
(centre right) and Deep Fried
Pork Meat Balls (bottom).**

Braised Hong Kong Beef

PREPARATION TIME: 30 minutes

COOKING TIME: about 15-17 minutes

30ml (2 tblsp) oil
450g (1lb) fillet of beef, sliced into matchstick-size strips
1 onion, peeled and sliced
2.5cm (1") fresh root ginger, peeled and cut into thin strips
3-4 fresh tomatoes, cut into thin wedges
225g (½lb) carrots, scraped and cut into 5cm (2") sticks
10ml (2 tsp) brown sugar
2.5ml (½ tsp) five spice powder
30ml (2 tblsp) light soya sauce
15ml (1 tblsp) rice wine or dry sherry
30ml (2 tblsp) water
Salt to taste

Heat the oil in a wok and fry the beef for 3-4 minutes. Add the onion, ginger, tomatoes and carrots. Stir fry for 2-3 minutes. Add the sugar, five spice powder, soya sauce, wine and water. Season with salt to taste and cook gently for 8-10 minutes. Serve as a side dish.

Pork with Green Pepper

PREPARATION TIME: 20 minutes

COOKING TIME: 1 hour 15 minutes

450g (1lb) pork fillet, cut into 5cm (2") strips

Seasoning
1.25ml (¼ tsp) sugar
1.25ml (¼ tsp) monosodium glutamate (optional)
5ml (1 tsp) light soya sauce
10ml (2 tsp) sweet bean paste
10ml (2 tsp) Shao Hsing wine or dry sherry
60ml (4 tblsp) chicken stock

Oil for deep frying
2 cloves garlic, peeled and cut into thin strips
1 green pepper, seeded and sliced into strips
1 green chilli, sliced into strips
1 red chilli, cut in half then sliced into strips

Sauce
5ml (1 tsp) cornflour
15ml (1 tblsp) water

Boil the pork in water for ¾ hour until cooked. Drain the pork and discard the water. Mix the seasoning ingredients together and stir in the pork. Leave to stand for 10 minutes. Heat the wok and add the oil for deep frying. When oil is very hot fry the drained pork for a few minutes until golden brown. Remove and drain the pork and keep the oil for future use. Reheat the wok and add 5ml (1 tsp) oil and stir fry the garlic for 1 minute. Add the pepper and chillis and stir fry for 1 minute. Add the remaining seasoning mixture and the pork. Stir fry over a gentle heat for 1-2 minutes and then add the blended sauce ingredients. Cook until the sauce thickens. Remove from the heat and serve immediately. Serve with mixed fried rice or rice noodles.

Steamed Pork with Salted Cabbage

PREPARATION TIME: 25 minutes

COOKING TIME: 2 hours

450g (1lb) fillet pork cut into 1cm (½") thick slices
Salt
175g (6oz) cabbage, shredded (Chinese white or plain green cabbage)

Seasoning
15ml (1 tblsp) sugar
30ml (2 tblsp) cooked oil
5ml (1 tsp) monosodium glutamate (optional)
60ml (4 tblsp) stock or water
Salt and freshly ground black pepper

15ml (1 tblsp) dark soya sauce
Oil for deep frying

Sauce
5ml (1 tsp) cornflour
15ml (1 tblsp) water

Boil the pork in 450ml (¾ pint) water for ¾ hour until tender. Drain the pork and discard the water. Boil 450ml (¾ pint) fresh water with 5ml (1 tsp) salt and add the cabbage. Cook for 2 minutes. Drain, rinse in cold water and then drain again. Season the cabbage with 5ml (1 tsp) of the sugar and 15ml (1 tblsp) of the cooked oil. Mix well and keep on one side. Place the pork in a dish and mix with the dark soya sauce. Leave for 10 minutes. Drain. Mix all the seasoning ingredients together. Heat the oil for deep frying and fry the pork until it turns lightly golden. Drain and add to the seasoning mixture. Keep the oil for future use. Place the pork and the seasoning mixture into a deep dish and put the boiled cabbage on top. Cover and steam over boiling water for 1 hour. Drain off any excess liquid and retain. Heat the wok and add the cabbage liquid. Add the blended sauce thickening of cornflour and water. Stir over the heat until the sauce thickens. Pour over the cabbage and pork and serve.

Bean Sprouts with Chopped Pork

PREPARATION TIME: 15 minutes

COOKING TIME: 10 minutes

225g (½ lb) lean pork, chopped finely or coarsely minced

Marinade
2.5ml (½ tsp) salt
15ml (1 tblsp) light soya sauce
1 egg white, beaten
5ml (1 tsp) cornflour

450g (1lb) bean sprouts
Oil for cooking

Seasoning
2.5ml (½ tsp) salt
2.5ml (½ tsp) sugar
2.5ml (½ tsp) monosodium glutamate (optional)
10ml (2 tsp) soya sauce
5ml (1 tsp) rice wine or dry sherry
15ml (1 tblsp) oyster sauce

2.5cm (½") fresh root ginger, peeled and thinly sliced
2-3 spring onions, chopped
120ml (4 fl oz) chicken stock

Sauce
2.5ml (½ tsp) cornflour or arrowroot
15ml (1 tblsp) water or stock
Few drops of sesame oil

Mix the pork with the marinade ingredients and keep on one side for 10 minutes. Trim the bean sprouts and chop them coarsely. Heat the wok and 30ml (2 tblsp) oil. Stir fry the bean sprouts for 1 minute to evaporate excess water and moisture. Remove the bean sprouts and keep on a plate. Mix the seasoning ingredients together. Heat 45ml (3 tblsp) oil in the wok until it smokes. Stir fry the pork for 2 minutes and then add the ginger, onions and bean sprouts. Stir fry for 2-3 minutes. Add the seasoning ingredients and stir fry for 1 minute. Add the chicken stock and the blended sauce ingredients. Cook until the sauce thickens. Serve immediately.

Spiced Liver (top), Sliced Beef in Oyster Sauce (centre right) and Braised Hong Kong Beef (right).

Oil for frying
1 small onion, peeled and thickly
    sliced
3 spring onions, chopped lengthways
2 leeks, white part only, cut into 4cm
    (1½″) slices
5ml (1 tsp) sesame oil

Mix the marinade ingredients with the beef strips. Leave to marinate for 20 minutes. Mix all the seasoning ingredients together in a small bowl. Heat 30ml (2 tblsp) oil in a wok and when it is smoking, add the beef. Reduce the heat and stir fry for 4-5 minutes. Remove the meat and keep the oil for future use. Heat the wok, add 30ml (2 tblsp) fresh oil and stir fry the onion and leeks for 2 minutes. Add seasoning mixture and beef and stir fry for 1-2 minutes. Sprinkle sesame oil over the top and mix well. Serve immediately. Use as a main dish or a side dish.

Shredded Beef with Vegetables

PREPARATION TIME: 15 minutes

COOKING TIME: 10 minutes

225g (8oz) lean beef, cut into thin
    strips
Pinch salt
60ml (4 tblsp) oil
2 red and green chillis, cut in half
    then sliced into strips
5ml (1 tsp) black vinegar
1 stem of celery, cut into 5cm (2″)
    thin strips
2 carrots, cut into 5cm (2″) thin strips
1 leek, white part only, sliced into
    5cm (2″) thin strips
2 cloves of garlic, peeled and finely
    chopped

Seasoning
5ml (1 tsp) light soya sauce
5ml (1 tsp) dark soya sauce
10ml (2 tsp) Shao Hsing wine
5ml (1 tsp) sugar
Pinch monosodium glutamate
    (optional)
2.5ml (½ tsp) freshly ground black
    pepper

This page: Stir Fried Beef with Spring Onions (top), Shredded Beef with Vegetables (centre left) and Sesame Beef with Dates (bottom). Facing page: Beef with Green Beans (top), Beef Steak with Ginger (centre right) and Sweet and Sour Beef (bottom).

Spiced Liver

PREPARATION TIME: 10 minutes

COOKING TIME: 20 minutes

450g (1lb) lamb's liver, cut into
    2.5cm (1″) cubes
120ml (8 tblsp) soya sauce
3-4 spring onions, chopped
30ml (2 tblsp) rice wine or dry sherry
10ml (2 tsp) sugar
2.5cm (1″) fresh root ginger, peeled
    and finely chopped
2.5ml (½ tsp) freshly ground black
    pepper
Pinch anise powder

Boil the liver in sufficient water to just cover, for 3-4 minutes. Drain well. Add soya sauce, spring onions, wine, sugar, ginger, pepper and anise powder. Simmer gently for 10-15 minutes, covered, until the liver is tender. Serve as a side dish.

Stir Fried Beef with Spring Onions

PREPARATION TIME: 30 minutes

COOKING TIME: 10 minutes

Marinade
15ml (1 tblsp) cornflour or arrowroot
1 egg white
15ml (1 tblsp) oil
5ml (1 tsp) bicarbonate of soda
450g (1lb) beef fillet, cut into 2.5cm
    (1″) strips

Seasoning
5ml (1 tsp) Shao Hsing wine
15ml (1 tblsp) light soya sauce
5ml (1 tsp) dark soya sauce
2.5ml (½ tsp) salt
2.5ml (½ tsp) freshly ground black
    pepper
5ml (1 tsp) monosodium glutamate
    (optional)

Put the beef into a bowl and sprinkle with salt; rub salt into meat. Heat 5ml (1 tsp) oil in a wok until it begins to smoke. Reduce heat and add beef and chillis and stir fry for 4-5 minutes. Add remaining oil, and stir fry beef until it turns crispy. Add vinegar and mix until it evaporates then add celery, carrots, leeks and garlic. Stir fry for 2 minutes. Mix the seasoning ingredients and pour over the beef and cook for 2 minutes. Serve immediately.

Steamed Lamb with Mushroom Sauce

PREPARATION TIME: 20-25 minutes

COOKING TIME: 2 hours 10 minutes

1kg (2¼lb) boned leg of lamb, cut into 2.5cm (1") cubes
2 onions, thinly sliced
Salt and freshly ground black pepper
10ml (2 tsp) oil
2 cloves of garlic, peeled and sliced
5ml (1 tsp) cornflour
Pinch monosodium glutamate (optional)
75ml (5 tblsp) light soya sauce
45ml (3 tblsp) rice wine or dry sherry
5ml (1 tsp) crushed black pepper
2.5cm (1") fresh root ginger, peeled and thinly sliced
Few drops sesame oil

Put the lamb into a saucepan and add sufficient water to cover. Boil for 5 minutes. Drain the lamb and retain the water. Arrange the lamb cubes in a deep dish and sprinkle the onions on top. Season with pepper and salt. Heat the oil in a wok and fry the garlic until brown. Remove the garlic and discard. Mix together the cornflour, monosodium glutamate, soya sauce, wine, crushed pepper, ginger and 60ml (4 tblsp) reserved water. Stir the cornflour mixture into the oil in the wok and cook for 1-2 minutes. Pour over the lamb. Cover the lamb with overlapping foil and tie around the rim. Put the dish in a steamer and steam over boiling water for 2 hours. Serve with the sesame oil sprinkled over the lamb.

Lamb with Tomatoes

PREPARATION TIME: 20 minutes

COOKING TIME: about 10 minutes

10ml (2 tsp) cornflour
2.5ml (½ tsp) salt
15ml (1 tblsp) light soya sauce
60ml (4 tblsp) water
45ml (3 tblsp) oil
1cm (½") fresh root ginger, sliced
225g (½lb) lamb fillet, cut across the grain in thin strips of 1x5cm (½x2")
2 spring onions, chopped
1 onion, peeled and cut into 2.5cm (1") pieces
1 green pepper, seeded and cut into strips
5ml (1 tsp) curry powder
3-4 small, firm tomatoes, cut into 1cm (½") pieces

Mix the cornflour, salt, soya sauce, water and 5ml (1 tsp) of the oil together. Keep on one side. Heat the remaining oil in a wok and fry the ginger and lamb for 2-3 minutes. Add the onions, green pepper and curry powder and stir fry for 3-4 minutes. Stir in the cornflour mixture and cook for 1 minute. Add the tomatoes and cook until the sauce thickens. Serve as a side dish.

Mongolian Lamb with Onions

PREPARATION TIME: 20 minutes

COOKING TIME: 8-10 minutes

450g (1lb) lean, boned lamb, cut into 5x50mm (¼x2") strips
1 egg white
2 cloves of garlic, sliced
2.5ml (½ tsp) five spice powder
1cm (½") fresh root ginger, peeled and thinly sliced
15ml (1 tblsp) cornflour
15ml (1 tblsp) light soya sauce
45ml (3 tblsp) rice wine or dry sherry
30ml (2 tblsp) water
45ml (3 tblsp) cooked oil
6 spring onions, chopped

Mix the lamb with the egg white, garlic, five spice powder, ginger root and 5ml (1 tsp) cornflour and 5ml (1 tsp) soya sauce. Keep on one side. Mix the remaining cornflour,

Lamb with Tomatoes (below left), Steamed Lamb with Mushroom Sauce (right) and Mongolian Lamb with Onions (below right).

soya sauce, wine and water together. Heat the wok and add the oil. When it begins to smoke, add the beef mixture. Reduce the heat and stir fry for 3-4 minutes until the meat browns slightly. Remove and keep on one side. Add the onions and the cornflour, soya sauce and wine mixture to the wok. Stir until it thickens. Return the meat to the wok and simmer gently for 3-4 minutes, or until the meat is tender. Serve as a main dish.

Sweet and Sour Beef

PREPARATION TIME: 15 minutes

COOKING TIME: 15 minutes

Batter
100g (4oz) plain flour
7.5ml (1½ tsp) baking powder
60ml (4 tblsp) cornflour
15ml (1 tblsp) oil
45ml (3 tblsp) oil
225g (8oz) fillet of beef, cut into 2.5cm (1") cubes

1 onion, peeled and cut into wedges
2.5cm (1") fresh root ginger, peeled and thinly sliced
1 clove garlic, peeled and thinly sliced
1 green pepper, seeded and chopped

Sweet and Sour Sauce
60ml (4 tblsp) sugar
1.25ml (¼ tsp) salt
60ml (4 tblsp) red or malt vinegar
5ml (1 tsp) fresh root ginger, peeled and minced
90ml (6 tblsp) water

15ml (1 tblsp) cornflour or arrowroot
10ml (2 tsp) cooked oil
Few drops food colouring
Oil for deep frying

For the batter: sieve the flour, baking powder and cornflour. Beat in the oil and add sufficient water to make a thick, smooth batter. Heat the 45ml (3 tblsp) oil in a wok and stir fry the beef for 2 minutes. Remove the beef. Fry the onion, ginger, garlic and green pepper for 2-3 minutes in the same oil. Remove the wok from the heat. Mix the sauce ingredients together and add to the wok. Return the wok to the heat and bring to the boil gently. Lower the heat and simmer gently for 2-3 minutes until thick and clear. Meanwhile, dip the beef cubes into the batter and deep fry in hot oil until golden brown and crisp. Drain on absorbent paper. Arrange in a deep dish and pour the hot sauce over the beef. Serve with a chow mein dish or fried rice. Thinly sliced carrots, cucumber and courgette may also be added along with the onion, ginger and green pepper.

Barbecued Pork
(Kan Hsiang Ch'a Shao or Char Siu)

PREPARATION TIME: 3 hours

COOKING TIME: 1 hour to 1 hour 30 minutes

2kg (4½lb) loin of pork

Seasoning
15ml (1 tblsp) ginger juice
Few drops red food colouring
75ml (5 tblsp) sugar
200ml (⅓ pint) light soya sauce
5ml (1 tsp) salt
15ml (1 tblsp) Mue Kwe Lo wine (or a mixture of 10ml (2 tsp) dry sherry and 5ml (1 tsp) apricot brandy)

225g (½lb) honey, melted

Remove the bones from the loin of pork. Cut pork into 4cm (1½") wide strips. With the aid of a fork scrape the surface of the pork lightly to form grooves in which the seasoning can lodge. Mix the seasoning ingredients together and rub well into the pork strips. Leave to marinate for at least 1½ hours. Thread the pork strips onto a long metal skewer and hang to dry for 1 hour. Put the pork onto a wire rack in a roasting tin. Brush with melted honey and roast in the oven 180°C, 350°F, Gas Mark 4, for 1-1½ hours, basting with honey frequently. When cooked, brush the pork with any remaining honey and leave to 'dry' slightly. Serve hot or cold, sliced thinly on a serving plate.

Pork Spare Ribs

PREPARATION TIME: 25 minutes

COOKING TIME: 40-45 minutes

16-20 spare ribs
5ml (1 tsp) salt
Oil
5ml (1 tsp) ginger paste
5ml (1 tsp) garlic paste

Pork Meat Balls in Sauce (left), Pork Spare Ribs (above) and Barbecued Pork (right).

5ml (1 tsp) onion paste
Pinch monosodium glutamate
  (optional)
5ml (1 tsp) light soya sauce
5ml (1 tsp) cornflour
1 egg
2.5ml (½ tsp) Shao Hsing wine
2.5ml (½ tsp) chilli oil

Sauce
45ml (3 tblsp) sugar
45ml (3 tblsp) black vinegar
15ml (1 tblsp) tomato ketchup
  (optional)
5ml (1 tsp) cornflour
5ml (1 tsp) water
15ml (1 tblsp) dark soya sauce
2.5ml (½ tsp) salt
2.5ml (½ tsp) freshly ground black
  pepper

Trim excess fat from spare ribs and rub with salt. Add 60ml (4 tblsp) oil to the wok and fry the ginger, garlic and onion for 1-2 minutes. Add the spare ribs and stir fry for 6 minutes. Remove to a dish and add the monosodium glutamate, light soya sauce, cornflour, egg, wine and chilli oil. Marinate for 10 minutes. Prepare the sauce by mixing all the ingredients together in the wok and bringing them gently to the boil. Simmer for 2-3 minutes and add the spare ribs along with their marinade. Stir fry until the liquid is

reduced to half its original quantity. Put all the ingredients onto a baking tray and spread out evenly. Bake at 190°C, 375°F, Gas Mark 5, for 25 minutes. Baste occasionally with the liquid from the tray and oil. The spare ribs should have browned well and be well coated with seasoning. Serve hot or cold.

Pork Meat Balls in Sauce
(Sha Kwo Shih-tzu-Tou)

PREPARATION TIME: 25 minutes

COOKING TIME: 45 minutes

Seasoning
Pinch monosodium glutamate
  (optional)
15ml (1 tblsp) Shao Hsing wine
2cm (1") fresh root ginger, peeled and
  ground
2 spring onions, white part only,
  minced
2.5ml (½ tsp) salt
10ml (2 tsp) cornflour
450g (1lb) lean pork, minced
25g (1oz) bamboo shoots, chopped
50g (2oz) dried Chinese mushrooms,
  soaked, drained and sliced
1 egg, beaten
Cornflour to roll the meat balls in

175g (6oz) Chinese white cabbage,
  cut into 7.5cm (3") pieces or 225g
  (8oz) ordinary green leafy cabbage,
  cut into 7.5cm (3") pieces
15ml (1 tblsp) cooked oil
Oil for deep frying
15ml (1 tblsp) cornflour
45ml (3 tblsp) water
1 small onion, peeled and finely
  chopped
2.5cm (1") fresh root ginger, peeled
  and finely chopped
300ml (½ pint) chicken stock

Sauce
Salt to taste
2.5ml (½ tsp) monosodium
  glutamate (optional)
15ml (1 tblsp) light soya sauce
5ml (1 tsp) dark soya sauce
15ml (1 tblsp) cooked oil

Mix seasoning ingredients together. Add the pork, bamboo shoots, mushrooms and egg and mix well. Shape into 15-16 even-sized balls and roll them in cornflour. Keep aside on a dish. Blanch cabbage for 1 minute in boiling water and the cooked oil. Drain the cabbage and discard the water. Heat the wok and add the oil for deep frying. When quite hot deep-fry the meat balls, a few at a time, for 4-5 minutes. Remove and drain. Keep warm in a large casserole dish.

Keep oil for future use. Mix the 15ml (1 tblsp) cornflour with the 45ml (3 tblsp) water and keep aside. Reheat the wok and add 5ml (1 tsp) deep frying oil. Stir fry the onion and ginger for 2 minutes. Add the chicken stock and stir in the blended sauce ingredients. Bring to the boil and add the meat balls. Simmer gently for 30 minutes. Add the cabbage, sesame oil and the blended cornflour mixture. Stir over the heat until the sauce thickens.

Sesame Beef with Dates

PREPARATION TIME: 20 minutes, plus 30 minutes to marinate

COOKING TIME: 12-15 minutes

Seasoning A
2.5ml (½ tsp) bicarbonate of soda
15ml (1 tblsp) light soya sauce
15ml (1 tblsp) oil
7.5ml (1½ tsp) cornflour
450g (1lb) beef fillet, thinly sliced
    into 5cm (2") pieces
20 dried dates (red or dark), soaked
    and stoned

Seasoning B
5ml (1 tsp) monosodium glutamate
    (optional)
7.5ml (1½ tsp) sugar
10ml (2 tsp) bean paste
200ml (⅓ pint) beef stock, or made
    with stock cube
Salt to taste
60ml (4 tblsp) cooked oil or plain oil
2.5cm (1") fresh root ginger, peeled
    and thinly sliced
2 spring onions, sliced

Sauce
15ml (1 tblsp) cornflour
30ml (2 tblsp) water or stock
30ml (2 tblsp) sesame seeds

Mix the ingredients for seasoning A. Mix with the beef and marinate for 30 minutes. Drain meat and discard marinade. Drain soaked dates; slice most of them into 4 long pieces, leaving a few whole. Mix the dates with seasoning B. Heat oil in a wok and stir fry beef for 4-5 minutes. Add ginger, spring onions, dates and the seasoning B and gently bring to the boil. Add the blended sauce ingredients. Cover and simmer for 3-4 minutes over a gentle heat until the sauce thickens and becomes clear. Remove from the heat, place on a serving dish and keep warm. Heat a wok or frying pan and add the sesame seeds. Dry roast for 2

minutes until they begin to crackle and turn golden brown. Sprinkle over the beef and serve immediately.

Shredded Pork with Preserved Vegetables

PREPARATION TIME: 30 minutes

COOKING TIME: 6-8 minutes

Pinch monosodium glutamate
    (optional)
10ml (2 tsp) cornflour
Salt and freshly ground black pepper
    to taste
225g (½ lb) lean pork, shredded
Oil
2.5cm (1") fresh root ginger, peeled
    and shredded
50g (2oz) shelled green peas
2.5ml (½ tsp) sugar
10ml (2 tsp) Shao Hsing wine or dry
    sherry
225g (8oz) Shanghai preserved
    vegetables (mixed), in brine
5ml (1 tsp) sesame oil

Mix the monosodium glutamate, cornflour and a pinch of salt. Add the pork and let it stand for 15 minutes. Heat the oil in a wok and deep fry the pork for 3 minutes. Remove the pork and drain. Reserve oil for future use. Reheat wok and add 10ml (2 tsp) deep fried oil. Stir fry the ginger and green peas for 1 minute. Add the pork and sprinkle with the sugar, wine and salt and pepper to taste. Stir fry for another minute and add the well-drained, preserved vegetables. Allow to heat through and then stir gently. Sprinkle on the sesame oil and serve. Serve as a side dish or on a bed of plain fried noodles.

Beef Steak with Ginger

PREPARATION TIME: 20-25 minutes

COOKING TIME: 10-12 minutes

Seasoning
2.5ml (½ tsp) bicarbonate of soda
45ml (3 tblsp) light soya sauce
30ml (2 tblsp) rice wine or dry sherry
2.5ml (½ tsp) salt
2.5ml (½ tsp) ground black pepper
1.25cm (½ tsp) fresh root ginger,
    peeled and minced
225g (½lb) beef fillet, sliced into
    2.5cm (1") pieces

Sauce
5ml (1 tsp) sugar
1.25ml (¼ tsp) monosodium
    glutamate (optional)
15ml (1 tblsp) dark soya sauce
45ml (3 tblsp) stock
Few drops sesame oil
5ml (1 tsp) Shao Hsing wine
60ml (4 tblsp) oil
2.5cm (1") fresh root ginger, peeled
    and thinly sliced
4 spring onions, chopped
50g (2oz) bamboo shoots, thinly
    sliced
2 green chillis, sliced

Mix the seasoning ingredients with the minced ginger. Add the beef and marinate for 20 minutes. Drain the beef and discard the marinade. Mix the sauce ingredients together. Heat 45ml (3 tblsp) oil in the wok and fry the sliced ginger and onions for 2 minutes. Add the bamboo shoots and chillis and stir fry for 1-2 minutes. Remove to a plate. Add the remaining oil to the wok and fry the beef for 2-3 minutes. Add fried vegetables and stir fry for 2 minutes. Add well-stirred sauce ingredients and simmer gently until the mixture thickens. Simmer for another 1-2 minutes. Remove from heat and serve.

Beef with Green Beans

PREPARATION TIME: 30 minutes

COOKING TIME: 12 minutes

Seasoning
2.5ml (½ tsp) bicarbonate of soda
5ml (1 tsp) cornflour
15ml (1 tblsp) light soya sauce
30ml (2 tblsp) water
5ml (1 tsp) cooked oil
450g (1lb) lean beef, thinly sliced
    into 2.5cm (1") pieces

Sauce
1.25ml (¼ tsp) salt
5ml (1 tsp) monosodium glutamate
    (optional)
5ml (1 tsp) light soya sauce
5ml (1 tsp) dark soya sauce
5ml (1 tsp) Shao Hsing wine
    (optional)
120ml (4 fl oz) stock
10ml (2 tsp) cornflour
45ml (3 tblsp) oil
2 cloves of garlic, peeled and sliced
1 onion, peeled and cut into wedges
2.5cm (1") fresh ginger root, peeled
    and sliced thinly
175g (6oz) Chinese long beans, cut
    into 7.5cm (3") pieces, or whole
    tender green beans
Salt and freshly ground black pepper
    to taste

Mix seasoning ingredients together. Add the beef and marinate for 20 minutes. Drain the meat and discard the marinade. Mix the sauce ingredients together. Heat 30ml (2 tblsp) oil in the wok until it smokes. Reduce the heat add the garlic and the beef, and stir fry for 3-4 minutes. Remove the meat and keep on one side. Add the remaining oil to the wok and add the onion, ginger and long beans and stir fry for 2-3 minutes. Add fried beef. Cover and fry for a further 1 minute. Stir in the sauce ingredients and bring to the boil. Simmer gently for 2-3 minutes. Season with salt and pepper. Remove from heat and serve.

Sweet and Sour Pork

PREPARATION TIME: 20 minutes, plus 20 minutes to marinate

COOKING TIME: 15-20 minutes

Batter
45ml (3 tblsp) flour
15ml (1 tblsp) cornflour
7.5ml (1½ tsp) bicarbonate of soda
30ml (2 tblsp) oil

350g (12oz) lean pork, cut into
    2.5cm (1") cubes

Seasoning
5ml (1 tsp) sugar
5ml (1 tsp) salt
30ml (2 tblsp) light soya sauce
5ml (1 tsp) dark soya sauce
15ml (1 tblsp) cooked oil
15ml (1 tblsp) water

Cornflour
Oil for deep frying
2 cloves garlic, cut into thin strips
1 large onion, peeled and cut into
    1cm (½") pieces
1 carrot, sliced into 3x25x50mm
    (⅛x1x2") thin pieces
Pinch salt

Sweet and Sour Sauce
45ml (3 tblsp) sugar
15ml (1 tblsp) tomato purée
250ml (8 fl oz) chicken stock or water
60ml (4 tblsp) red or white vinegar
5ml (1 tsp) light soya sauce
Few slices fresh root ginger, peeled
15ml (1 tblsp) cornflour or arrowroot
Few drops of red food colouring
10ml (2 tsp) cooked oil

Mix the batter ingredients together, adding sufficient water to make a thick coating batter. Wash and drain the pork. Mix with the seasoning ingredients and marinate

Seasoning

7.5ml (1½ tsp) light soya sauce
Few drops sesame oil
Salt and freshly ground black pepper
   to taste
15ml (1 tblsp) oil
15ml (1 tblsp) water
15ml (1 tblsp) cornflour
Pinch monosodium glutamate
   (optional)

225g (½ lb) pork fillet, cut into cubes
1 carrot, thinly sliced
1 onion, peeled and cut into pieces
3 spring onions, chopped
2.5cm (1″) fresh root ginger, peeled
   and thinly sliced

Sauce

90ml (6 tblsp) stock
5ml (1 tsp) cornflour

Cook the walnuts in boiling water
for 3-4 minutes. Drain the nuts
thoroughly. Deep fry the walnuts
until lightly browned. Remove and
drain. Use oil for cooking. Mix the
seasoning ingredients together and
add the pork. Leave to marinate for
15 minutes. Discard marinade.
Heat 30ml (2 tblsp) oil in the wok
and stir-fry the carrots for 2
minutes. Add the onions and root
ginger and stir fry for 1 minute.
Add 10ml (2 tsp) of the sauce
stock and remove to a plate. Add
the drained pork cubes and 15ml
(1 tblsp) oil to the wok and stir fry
for 4-5 minutes. Mix the remaining
stock and the cornflour together
for the sauce. Return the walnuts
and carrots to the wok, together
with the blended sauce ingredients.
Mix well and simmer until the
sauce thickens. Remove and serve
immediately. Serve with rice
noodles or fried rice.

for 15-20 minutes. Drain the pork
and discard the marinade. Roll the
pork cubes in cornflour. Heat the
oil for deep frying. Dip the pork
cubes in batter and fry in the hot
oil until golden brown. Fry a few at
a time until all the pork has been
fried. Drain well and keep warm in
a low oven. Heat wok and add
10ml (2 tsp) deep fried oil. Stir fry
the garlic, onions and carrots for 3-
4 minutes. Season with salt and fry
for a further minute. Mix the sweet
and sour sauce ingredients together
and add to the wok. Stir the
mixture until it thickens. Pour over
the fried pork cubes and serve
immediately. Note: sliced green
peppers can also be added along
with the carrots and onions.

Diced Pork with Walnuts

| **PREPARATION TIME:** 30 minutes |
| **COOKING TIME:** 16-18 minutes |

100g (4oz) shelled walnuts
Oil for deep frying

**Sweet and Sour Pork (top right),
Diced Pork with Walnuts
(centre) and Shredded Pork with
Preserved Vegetables (bottom
left).**

CHINESE CUISINE
Poultry Dishes

Roast Crispy Duck

PREPARATION TIME: 15-20 minutes plus 6-8 hours to dry

COOKING TIME: 1 hour 30 minutes

2kg (4½lb) duck or goose, prepared for cooking
250ml (8 fl oz) water
6 large scallions or 12 spring onions, cut into 5cm (2 inch) lengths
60ml (4 tblsp) maltose or golden syrup
2.5ml (½ tsp) red food colouring
30ml (2 tblsp) tomato purée

Wash the duck and pat it dry on a clean cloth. Ease the fingers between the skin and flesh of the duck, starting at the neck end and working the length of the bird. Put a stick or large skewer through the neck and the cavity of the duck to wedge it securely. This will make the duck easier to handle. Hold the duck over the sink and pour boiling water all over it. Pat the duck dry. Melt half the maltose and dissolve in the water. Stand the duck on a rack over a deep tray. Slowly pour the maltose liquid over the duck. Pour the maltose liquid over the duck 3 or 4 times. Leave the duck in a cool place for 6-8 hours, or overnight, until the skin is dry. Remove the stick. Stand the duck on a rack in a roasting tin. Preheat the oven to 200°C, 400°F, Gas Mark 6 and cook for 30 minutes. Turn over and cook the underside for a further 30 minutes. Melt the remaining maltose with the tomato purée and add the food colouring. Spread over the duck and cook for a further 30 minutes. (The duck should have a crisp, red skin.) Remove the duck skin in squares. Slice the duck flesh and serve with the skin on the top. Serve the following dip as an accompaniment.

Duck Dip

100g (4oz) sugar
60ml (4 tblsp) sweet bean paste
30ml (2 tblsp) sesame oil
120ml (4 fl oz) water

Heat the wok and add the mixed ingredients. Cook for 3-4 minutes until the sugar has dissolved and the dip is smooth. Serve in individual cups.

Sliced Duck with Bamboo Shoots

PREPARATION TIME: 30 minutes

COOKING TIME: 10 minutes

1kg (2¼lb) small duck
5ml (1 tsp) monosodium glutamate (optional)
12.5ml (2½ tsp) cornflour
30ml (2 tblsp) water
100g (4oz) broccoli, chopped
45ml (3 tblsp) oil
2-3 spring onions, chopped
2.5cm (1 inch) fresh root ginger, peeled and thinly sliced
1 clove garlic, peeled and finely chopped
100g (4oz) bamboo shoots, sliced
2.5ml (½ tsp) sugar
Salt and freshly ground black pepper to taste
60ml (4 tblsp) chicken stock
10ml (2 tsp) rice wine or sweet sherry
Few drops sesame oil

Cut the duck flesh into bite-size pieces, removing all the bones. Mix the MSG, 7.5ml (1½ tsp) cornflour and 15ml (1 tblsp) water together. Stir into the duck. Marinate for 20 minutes. Cook the broccoli in boiling water for 1 minute. Drain thoroughly. Heat the wok and add the oil. Stir fry the onions, ginger, garlic and bamboo shoots for 1-2 minutes. Add the duck pieces and stir fry for 2-3 minutes. Add the sugar, salt and pepper to taste, stock, rice wine and sesame oil. Stir fry for 3 minutes. Add the remaining cornflour and water blended together. Stir over the heat until the sauce thickens. Serve immediately, as a side dish.

Duck with Ginger and Pineapple

PREPARATION TIME: 20 minutes

COOKING TIME: 2 hours to 2 hours 45 minutes

1.25cm (½ inch) fresh root ginger, peeled and crushed
2kg (4½lb) duck
Salt and freshly ground black pepper to taste
45ml (3 tblsp) oil
10cm (4 inches) fresh root ginger, peeled and thinly sliced
50g (2oz) bean sprouts
3 spring onions, chopped
2 carrots, peeled, sliced and blanched in boiling water for 2 minutes
10ml (2 tsp) brown sugar
15ml (1 tblsp) wine vinegar
5ml (1 tsp) white vinegar
225g (8oz) can pineapple chunks in syrup
15ml (1 tblsp) cornflour mixed with 30ml (2 tblsp) water

Mix together the crushed ginger, half of the soya sauce and salt and pepper to taste. Wash the duck and pat it dry. Rub the outside of the duck with salt and put on a wire rack in a roasting tin. Roast at 180°C, 350°F, Gas Mark 4, for 30 minutes. Brush the ginger and soya sauce mixture over the duck. Baste frequently with the sauces from the pan and roast for 2 hours, turning the bird occasionally to brown all sides. Remove and slice the duck in small pieces. Heat the oil in a wok and stir fry the sliced ginger, bean sprouts, onions and carrots for 1-2 minutes. Add the duck slices and cook for 1 minute. Then add the brown sugar, vinegar and pineapple chunks in their syrup. Bring to the boil and cook for 2-3 minutes. Add the blended cornflour and cook until the sauce thickens. Serve as a main dish along with noodles or rice.

This page: Stewed Chicken and Pineapple (top right), Fried Shredded Chicken on Cabbage (centre left) and Chicken and Cashew Nuts (bottom right).

Facing page: Sliced Duck with Bamboo Shoots (top), Duck with Ginger and Pineapple (bottom left) and Roast Crispy Duck (bottom right).

Chicken Green Chilli

PREPARATION TIME: 10 minutes, plus 10 minutes to marinate

COOKING TIME: 10 minutes

Sauce
5ml (1 tsp) light soya sauce
5ml (1 tsp) dark soya sauce
Salt to taste
10ml (2 tsp) cornflour
5ml (1 tsp) sesame oil
5ml (1 tsp) malt vinegar
250ml (8 fl oz) chicken stock

Seasoning
Salt to taste
Freshly ground black pepper to taste
Pinch monosodium glutamate (optional)
30ml (2 tblsp) dark soya sauce
15ml (1 tblsp) light soya sauce
5ml (1 tsp) cornflour
10ml (2 tsp) rice wine or dry sherry

450g (1lb) boned chicken, cut into bite-size pieces
45ml (3 tblsp) oil
3 spring onions, chopped
2.5cm (1") fresh root ginger, peeled and sliced
2 cloves of garlic, peeled and sliced
1 green pepper, seeded and chopped
2-3 green chillis, sliced lengthways

Mix the sauce ingredients together. Mix the seasoning ingredients together and add the chicken. Marinate for 10 minutes. Drain the chicken and discard the liquid. Heat 15ml (1 tblsp) oil and stir fry the onions, ginger and garlic for 2 minutes. Remove to a dish. Add the remaining oil and stir fry the chicken for 3 minutes. Add the blended green peppers and chillis and stir fry for 2 minutes. Add the onion mixture and the well-blended sauce ingredients and cook for 3-4 minutes until the sauce thickens. Serve immediately.

Chicken and Mushrooms

PREPARATION TIME: 15 minutes, plus 10 minutes to marinate

COOKING TIME: 10-12 minutes

Seasoning
2.5ml (1/2 tsp) salt
30ml (2 tblsp) light soya sauce
10ml (2 tsp) cornflour
5ml (1 tsp) rice wine or dry sherry
Pinch monosodium glutamate (optional)

225g (1/2lb) chicken breast, cut into bite-size pieces

Sauce
Salt to taste
Freshly ground black pepper to taste
15ml (1 tblsp) light soya sauce
250ml (8 fl oz) chicken stock
10ml (2 tsp) cornflour or arrowroot
5ml (1 tsp) oyster sauce
30ml (2 tblsp) oil

1 onion, peeled and chopped
1 clove of garlic, sliced
1cm (1/2") fresh root ginger, peeled and thinly sliced
3 dried black mushrooms, soaked and sliced
50g (2oz) open mushrooms, sliced
50g (2oz) button mushrooms, sliced

Mix the seasoning ingredients together. Marinate the chicken in the seasoning mixture for 10 minutes. Mix the sauce ingredients together. Heat the oil in a wok and fry the onion, garlic and ginger for 2-3 minutes. Remove and keep on one side. Fry the drained chicken in the remaining oil for 4 minutes. Add the mushrooms and stir fry for 1 minute. Add a little extra oil if necessary. Return the fried onion mixture to the wok and stir fry until well mixed. Pour the blended sauce ingredients into the wok and cook gently until the sauce thickens. Serve piping hot.

Chicken Fry with Sauce (below right), Chicken Green Chilli (below centre) and Chicken and Mushrooms (far right).

Chicken Fry with Sauce

PREPARATION TIME: 20 minutes
COOKING TIME: about 24 minutes

15ml (1 tblsp) cooked oil
5ml (1 tsp) sesame oil
25g (1oz) sesame seeds

Sauce

2 cloves of garlic, minced
2 spring onions, finely chopped or minced
5ml (1 tsp) Chinese black vinegar or brown malt vinegar
45ml (3 tblsp) dark soya sauce
5ml (1 tsp) light soya sauce
2.5ml (½ tsp) monosodium glutamate (optional)
2.5ml (½ tsp) salt
7.5ml (1½ tsp) sugar
8 chicken thighs, or 450g (1lb) chicken, cut into small joints

Heat the wok and add the oils. Stir fry the sesame seeds till they change colour to golden brown. Remove onto a dish. Mix sauce ingredients together and add the sesame seeds. Wipe the wok and add the chicken. Add sufficient water to cover, and cook for 20 minutes until the chicken is tender. De-bone the chicken and quickly cut into bite-size pieces. Arrange the chicken on a plate and spoon the sauce over the top. Serve immediately.

Stewed Chicken and Pineapple

PREPARATION TIME: 30 minutes
COOKING TIME: 15 minutes

Seasoning

30ml (2 tblsp) light soya sauce
15ml (1 tblsp) oil
15ml (1 tblsp) cornflour
5ml (1 tsp) salt
2.5ml (½ tsp) sesame oil
30ml (2 tblsp) water
750g (1½lb) boned chicken breast, cut into cubes

Sauce

7.5ml (1½ tsp) cornflour
250ml (8 fl oz) water or chicken stock
10ml (2 tsp) dark soya sauce
Salt to taste
30ml (2 tblsp) oil
1 onion, peeled and cut into chunks
2 spring onions, finely chopped
2.5cm (1") fresh root ginger, peeled and thinly sliced
4-5 pineapple rings, cut into chunks

Mix the seasoning ingredients together. Add the cubed chicken and marinate for 10-12 minutes. Mix the sauce ingredients together in a bowl. Heat the oil in a wok and fry the onions for 2 minutes until just tender. Add the drained chicken and fry for 3-4 minutes. Add the root ginger and fry for 1 minute. Add any remaining marinade and the sauce ingredients and bring to the boil. Cook, stirring, until the sauce thickens then add the pineapple chunks. Heat through. Remove from the heat and serve with fried rice.

Chicken Chop Suey

PREPARATION TIME: 30 minutes

COOKING TIME: 15 minutes

30ml (2 tblsp) light soya sauce
5ml (1 tsp) brown sugar
Salt to taste
450g (1lb) boned chicken, cut into 2.5cm (1″) pieces
30ml (2 tblsp) cooking oil
1 onion, cut into chunks
225g (8oz) bean sprouts
10ml (2 tsp) sesame oil
1.25g (¼ tsp) monosodium glutamate (optional)
15ml (1 tblsp) cornflour
250ml (8 fl oz) chicken stock

Mix the soya sauce with the sugar and salt and add the chicken pieces. Allow to marinate for 5 minutes. Drain the chicken and reserve the marinade. Heat the wok and add the oil. Fry the chicken for 2-3 minutes. Remove the chicken. Fry the onions for 2-3 minutes and add the beansprouts. Stir fry for 4-5 minutes. Return the chicken to the pan and add the sesame oil. Dissolve the monosodium glutamate and the cornflour in the stock and pour over the chicken mixture. Cook for 2-3 minutes, stirring, until the sauce thickens. Serve as a side dish.

Deep Fried Crispy Chicken

PREPARATION TIME: 3 hours

COOKING TIME: 13-14 minutes

1.5kg (3-3½lb) chicken, prepared for cooking

Seasoning
5ml (1 tsp) salt
2.5ml (½ tsp) five spice powder
40g (1½oz) maltose
30ml (2 tblsp) malt vinegar
150ml (¼ pint) white vinegar
Oil for deep frying

Wash the chicken and hang it up by a hook to drain and dry. The skin will dry quickly. Pour boiling water over the chicken 4-5 times, to partially cook the skin. This will make the skin crisp during frying. Rub salt and five spice powder well inside the chicken cavity. Dissolve the maltose and vinegars in a pan over a gentle heat. Pour over the chicken. Repeat several times, catching the maltose solution in a drip tray. Leave the chicken to hang and dry for 1½-2 hours, until the skin is smooth and shiny. Heat the oil for deep frying. Deep fry the chicken for 10 minutes. Ladle hot oil carefully over the chicken continually, until the chicken is deep brown in colour. (The skin puffs out slightly.) Cook for a further 3-4 minutes and remove from the oil. Drain on absorbent paper. Cut into small pieces and serve with a dip.

Chicken and Cashew Nuts

PREPARATION TIME: 15 minutes

COOKING TIME: 15 minutes

350g (12oz) chicken breast, sliced into 2.5cm (1″) pieces
15ml (1 tblsp) cornflour

Seasoning
5ml (1 tsp) salt
5ml (1 tsp) sesame oil
15ml (1 tblsp) light soya sauce
2.5ml (½ tsp) sugar
Oil for deep frying
100g (4oz) cashew nuts
2 spring onions, chopped
1 small onion, peeled and cubed
2.5cm (1″) fresh root ginger, peeled and sliced
2 cloves of garlic, sliced
75g (3oz) snow peas (mange tout)
50g (2oz) bamboo shoots, thinly sliced

Sauce
10ml (2 tsp) cornflour
15ml (1 tblsp) Hoi Sin sauce
250ml (just over ⅓ pint) chicken stock
Pinch monosodium glutamate (optional)

Roll the chicken pieces in cornflour. Discard the remaining cornflour. Mix the seasoning ingredients together and pour over chicken. Leave to stand for 10 minutes. Heat oil for deep frying and fry cashew nuts until golden brown. Remove the nuts and drain on kitchen paper. Heat 30ml (2 tblsp) oil in a wok and stir fry the onions, ginger and garlic for 2-3 minutes. Add snow peas and bamboo shoots and stir fry for 3 minutes. Remove the fried ingredients. Add 15ml (1 tblsp) oil to the wok and fry the chicken for 3-4 minutes. Remove the chicken. Clean the wok and add a further 10ml (2 tblsp) oil and return chicken, cashew nuts and fried onions etc. to the wok. Prepare the sauce by mixing the cornflour, Hoi Sin sauce, chicken stock and monosodium glutamate together. Pour over the chicken. Mix well and cook until the sauce thickens and becomes transparent. Serve hot with a chow mein dish. Alternatively, a few chunks of pineapple will add extra zest to the dish.

Fried Shredded Chicken on Cabbage

PREPARATION TIME: 20 minutes

COOKING TIME: 12 minutes

450g (1lb) Chinese white cabbage, cut into 2.5cm (1″) pieces
Pinch bicarbonate of soda

Seasoning
15ml (1 tblsp) light soya sauce
15ml (1 tblsp) cornflour
1.25ml (¼ tsp) sesame oil
1.25ml (¼ tsp) freshly ground black pepper
2.5ml (½ tsp) sugar
2.5ml (½ tsp) salt
15ml (1 tblsp) water
15ml (1 tblsp) oil
Pinch monosodium glutamate (optional)
30ml (2 tblsp) oil
1 onion, peeled and roughly chopped
2.5cm (1″) fresh root ginger, peeled and thinly sliced
450g (1lb) boned chicken breasts, shredded
4-6 mushrooms, sliced

Sauce
45ml (3 tblsp) chicken stock
1.25ml (¼ tsp) sesame oil
5ml (1 tsp) light soya sauce
5ml (1 tsp) cornflour
5ml (1 tsp) monosodium glutamate (optional)

Wash cabbage and blanch in boiling water with a pinch of bicarbonate of soda for 2 minutes. Drain well. Mix the seasoning ingredients together. Heat the wok and add the oil. Fry the onions, ginger and chicken for 2-3 minutes. Add the mushrooms and fry for further 2 minutes. Add the stock and cook for 4-5 minutes. Mix the

sauce ingredients together and pour over the chicken. Cook for 2 minutes. Serve immediately.

Steamed Chicken

PREPARATION TIME: 20-30 minutes

COOKING TIME: 15-20 minutes

750g (1½lb) boned chicken

Seasoning
15ml (1 tblsp) light soya sauce
5ml (1 tsp) brown sugar
5ml (1 tsp) salt
15ml (1 tblsp) cornflour
30ml (2 tblsp) oil or cooked oil
2.5ml (½ tsp) monosodium glutamate (optional)
100g (4oz) dried mushrooms, soaked in boiling water for 5 minutes and sliced, or ordinary mushrooms
1cm (½″) fresh root ginger, peeled and sliced
4 spring onions, finely chopped
30ml (2 tblsp) stock or water, if needed

Cut the chicken into 2.5cm (1″) pieces. Mix the seasoning ingredients together and mix with the chicken. Leave to marinate for 15 minutes. Place a plate in a steamer and put the chicken, mushrooms, ginger, half the onion and the stock on top. Steam over boiling water for 15-20 minutes. Serve with the remaining onions sprinkled over the chicken. The steaming can also be done on a greased lotus leaf or a banana leaf. The flavour is quite stunning.

Tangerine Peel Chicken

PREPARATION TIME: 30 minutes

COOKING TIME: 12-15 minutes

450g (1lb) boned chicken breast, cut into 2.5cm (1″) pieces

Facing page: Chicken Chop Suey (top left), Steamed Chicken (centre right) and Deep Fried Crispy Chicken (bottom left).

Seasoning
2.5ml (½ tsp) salt
7.5ml (1½ tsp) sugar
2.5ml (½ tsp) monosodium glutamate (optional)
5ml (1 tsp) dark soya sauce
10ml (2 tsp) light soya sauce
5ml (1 tsp) rice wine or dry sherry
10ml (2 tsp) malt vinegar
5ml (1 tsp) sesame oil
10ml (2 tsp) cornflour

Oil for deep frying
1-2 red or green chillis, chopped
1.25cm (½") fresh root ginger, peeled and finely chopped
5cm (2") dried tangerine peel, coarsely ground or crumbled
2 spring onions, finely chopped
Sauce
2.5ml (½ tsp) cornflour
15-30ml (1-2 tblsp) water or stock

Mix the chicken pieces with the seasoning ingredients and stir well. Leave to marinate for 10-15 minutes. Remove the chicken pieces and reserve the marinade. Heat wok and add the oil for deep frying. Once it starts to smoke add the chicken pieces and fry for 4-5 minutes until golden. Drain chicken on kitchen paper. Tip off the oil, leaving 15ml (1 tblsp) oil in the wok, and stir fry the chillis, ginger, tangerine peel and onions for 2-3 minutes. When they begin to colour add the chicken and stir fry for 1 minute. Mix the reserved marinade with the sauce ingredients and pour over the chicken. Stir and cook for 2-3 minutes until the sauce thickens and the chicken is tender. Serve immediately.

Roast Spiced Duck

PREPARATION TIME: 3-4 hours to dry, and 1 hour to glaze
COOKING TIME: 1 hour

2kg (4½lb) duck or small goose
5ml (1 tsp) five spice powder
7.5ml (1½ tsp) salt
60ml (4 tblsp) maltose or golden syrup
5ml (1 tsp) white vinegar
10ml (2 tsp) malt or red vinegar
Oil

Wash and dry the duck. Rub in the five spice powder and salt. Close the cavities of the duck by securing both ends with small skewers. Mix the maltose and vinegar together with a little water and bring to the boil. Spoon this liquid over the duck several times, collecting the liquid in a tray. Hang the duck by its neck for 3-4 hours to dry.

Preheat the oven to 230°C, 450°F, Gas Mark 8. Place the duck in a roasting tin. Rub oil into the skin. Roast in the oven for 1 hour, basting with any remaining maltose and vinegar liquid. If the duck is not quite tender, cook for a little longer. Slice the duck onto a warmed serving dish and serve immediately.

Roast Peking Duck

PREPARATION TIME: 15 minutes plus 2-3 hours to dry out the skin
COOKING TIME: 1 hour 20 minutes

2kg (4½lb) duck or small goose
1 litre (1¾ pints) boiling water
30ml (2 tblsp) maltose or golden syrup
250ml (8 fl oz) water
2-3 seedless oranges, peeled and cut into rings
30ml (2 tblsp) oil
Salt and freshly ground black pepper

Sauce
10ml (2 tsp) cornflour
60ml (4 tblsp) water or stock
Pinch monosodium glutamate (optional)
10ml (2 tsp) light soya sauce
5ml (1 tsp) rice wine or dry sherry

To Garnish
4 spring onions, cut into 5cm (2 inch) lengths

Wash and dry the duck. Put a stick or skewer through the neck and the cavity of the duck so that it is easier to handle. Hold the bird over the sink and pour the boiling water over it. Hang the duck up to dry. Melt the maltose and water together and spoon over the duck several times, catching the liquid on a drip tray each time. Leave the duck to dry for 2-3 hours in a cool place. Save any liquid that drops off. Preheat the oven to 200°C, 400°F, Gas Mark 6. Place the duck, breast side down, in a roasting tin and roast for 30 minutes. Lift out the duck. Put the orange rings into the tin and sit the duck on top, breast side uppermost. Baste with the oil and season with salt and pepper. Roast for a further 45-50 minutes until tender. Cut off the duck joints and slice the breast meat. Arrange with the orange slices on a serving dish and keep warm.

To Make the Sauce
Mix the sauce ingredients together and add any reserved maltose liquid. Bring to the boil gently, stirring, until the sauce thickens. Pour over the cooked duck and sprinkle with the onions. This is served either as a main dish or as a side dish.

Steamed Duck in Wine Sauce

PREPARATION TIME: 20 minutes
COOKING TIME: 3 hours 30 minutes

2kg (4½lb) duck
150ml (¼ pint) Kao Liang wine or mild red wine
2.5ml (½ tsp) monosodium glutamate (optional)

Roast Spiced Duck (top), Roast Peking Duck (above) and Steamed Duck in Wine Sauce (right).

2.5cm (1 inch) fresh root ginger,
   peeled and thinly sliced
3 spring onions, chopped
5ml (1 tsp) salt
5ml (1 tsp) sugar
5ml (1 tsp) cornflour

Place the duck in a large pot. Add
water to cover and boil for 5-7
minutes. Remove the duck and
drain well. Mix all the remaining
ingredients together apart from the
cornflour. Place the duck in a deep
dish and stand over a steamer. Pour
the wine mixture over the duck.
Cover and steam for 2-3 hours
until the duck is quite tender.
Remove the duck and strain the

cooking liquid. Place the duck on a
serving dish, either whole or cut
into slices. Blend the cooking liquid
with the cornflour. Bring to the boil
and stir until thickened. Pour over
the duck. Serve immediately.

Chicken Chow Mein

PREPARATION TIME: 30 minutes

COOKING TIME: 20 minutes

450g (1lb) egg noodles or spaghetti,
   broken into small pieces
1 onion, peeled and thinly sliced
50g (2oz) mushrooms, sliced
3 spring onions, chopped
2 cloves of garlic, peeled and chopped
Salt to taste
Pinch monosodium glutamate
60ml (4 tblsp) oil
175g (6oz) chicken meat, finely
   shredded
30ml (2 tblsp) light soya sauce
5ml (1 tsp) sugar
15ml (1 tblsp) rice wine or dry sherry
90ml (6 tblsp) chicken stock

Cook the noodles in boiling, salted
water for 4-5 minutes until tender.
Drain and rinse under cold water.
Drain once again and add 30ml (2
tblsp) oil; mix well to prevent the
noodles from sticking together.
Heat 30ml (2 tblsp) oil in a wok
and fry the onions and garlic for 2
minutes. Add chicken and stir fry
for 3-4 minutes. Add mushrooms.
Sprinkle over the wine, sugar, soya
sauce, monosodium glutamate and

salt to taste. Cook until the
mixture is fairly dry. Add noodles
and stir well to mix. Sprinkle over
the stock and cook once again until
dry. Serve with chilli sauce and
dark soya sauce. 50g (2oz) sliced
green beans, 50g (2oz) peas or 50g
(2oz) shredded carrot may also be
added, along with the chicken
pieces.

Peking Duck with Pancakes

PREPARATION TIME: for duck 2-3
hours; for pancakes 6 minutes

COOKING TIME: for duck 1 hour
20 minutes; for pancakes 15
minutes

2kg (4½lb) Peking duck, roasted
16-20 spring onions, sliced into
   7.5cm (3 inch) pieces

Pancakes (Po Ping)
450g (1lb) flour
Pinch salt
15ml (1 tblsp) corn oil
5ml (1 tsp) sesame oil
Tepid water for kneading
Flour for rolling

To Make Pancakes
Sift the flour and salt into a mixing
bowl. Make a well in the centre and
add the corn oil and water, a little
at a time, and work in the flour.
Make a pliable dough. Remove
from the bowl and knead well for
2-3 minutes. Cover with a damp,

clean cloth and allow to rest for 10 minutes. Knead again for 1 minute and divide the dough into 16-20 even-sized balls. Roll each ball in flour and roll out into a 10-15cm (4-6 inch) circle. Place a frying pan on the heat and when moderately hot place the rolled circle of dough on it; cook for ½-1 minute. Little bubbles will appear; flip over and allow to cook for 1-1½ minutes. Pick the pancake up and check whether little brown specks have appeared on the undersides; if not, then cook for a few seconds more. Use a clean tea towel to press the pancakes gently, this will circulate the steam and cook the pancakes. Prepare the rest of the pancakes in the same way and keep them stacked, wrapped in foil to keep them warm.

To Make Dip

60ml (4 tblsp) sugar
60ml (4 tblsp) bean paste (sweet)
15ml (1 tblsp) sesame oil
15ml (1 tblsp) corn oil or peanut oil
120ml (4 fl oz) water

Other Dips, Ready Prepared

60ml (4 tblsp) Hoi Sin sauce
60ml (4 tblsp) Chinese barbecue
sauce

Mix sugar, bean paste and water together. Warm the wok, add the oil and then the sugar mixture. Bring to boil and, when the sugar has melted, remove and put in a bowl. Place the duck on a cutting board and cut thin slices from the breast area and thighs. Place a pancake on an individual plate, cover with a slice of duck and a few strips of onion, spread on a dip of your choice, roll up like a pancake and eat. To make very crisp duck, cut duck into large joints and deep fry them till crispy.

Sweet and Sour Chicken

PREPARATION TIME: 30 minutes
COOKING TIME: 20 minutes

2.5ml (½ tsp) salt
10ml (2 tsp) cornflour or arrowroot
1 chicken breast, cut into 1cm (½")
cubes
1 onion, peeled and roughly chopped
into 1cm (½") chunks
25g (1oz) bamboo shoots, sliced
1 green pepper, seeded and thinly
sliced

2.5cm (1") fresh root ginger, peeled
and thinly sliced
2 carrots, scraped and thinly sliced
into 2.5cm (1") long pieces
1 garlic clove, peeled and chopped
30ml (2 tblsp) oil

Batter

100g (4oz) plain flour
25g (1oz) cornflour
1 small egg
Oil for deep frying

Sauce

15ml (1 tblsp) soft brown sugar
15ml (1 tblsp) red wine vinegar or
white vinegar
15ml (1 tblsp) soya sauce
15ml (1 tblsp) tomato purée
450ml (¾ pint) chicken stock
Pinch monosodium glutamate
(optional)
10ml (2 tsp) cornflour or arrowroot

Mix salt and cornflour and roll chicken pieces in it. Make the batter by mixing the sieved flour and cornflour with the egg and sufficient water to make a thick batter. Beat well. Heat oil for deep frying. Dip the chicken pieces into the batter and deep-fry until golden brown and crisp. Drain on absorbent paper and keep warm.

Heat the 30ml (2 tblsp) oil in a wok and stir fry the onions, ginger and garlic for 2-3 minutes. Add the carrots and fry for 2 minutes. Add the green peppers and fry for 2 minutes. Add bamboo shoots, season with salt and stir well. Mix all the sauce ingredients together. Pour over the cooked vegetables. Cook for 2-3 minutes, until the sauce thickens. The sauce should become transparent. Arrange fried chicken pieces on a serving dish and pour the sweet and sour sauce over them. Serve as a side dish.

This page: Peking Duck with Pancakes.

Facing page: Tangerine Peel Chicken (top), Sweet and Sour Chicken (centre left) and Chicken Chow Mein (bottom).

Fish and Seafood

Prawns with Broccoli

PREPARATION TIME: 10 minutes

COOKING TIME: 8-10 minutes

450g (1lb) peeled prawns
Oil for deep frying

Sauce
120ml (4 fl oz) chicken stock
10ml (2 tsp) cornflour
Freshly ground black pepper and salt
 to taste
Pinch monosodium glutamate
 (optional)
5ml (1 tsp) sugar

Seasoning
30ml (2 tblsp) cooked oil, or oil from
 deep frying the prawns
Pinch salt
2.5ml (½ tsp) sugar
Pinch monosodium glutamate
 (optional)
10ml (2 tsp) cornflour

250g (8oz) Chinese broccoli, or
 English broccoli, cut into 8cm (3″)
 pieces
1 carrot, peeled and sliced
2 cloves garlic, peeled and chopped
1cm (½″) fresh root ginger, peeled
 and chopped

Deep fry the prawns in hot oil for
1-2 minutes. Drain the prawns and
keep on one side. Keep the oil. Mix
the sauce ingredients together. Mix
the seasoning ingredients together
in a separate bowl. Cook the
broccoli in boiling water for 1
minute. Drain and add cold water
to cover. Drain once again and mix
the broccoli with the seasoning
ingredients. Heat the wok and add
30ml (2 tblsp) cooked oil. Add the
carrot, garlic and ginger and stir fry
for 1 minute. Add the broccoli and
stir fry for 1 minute more. Add the
prawns and stir fry for ½ minute
then add the blended sauce
ingredients. Cook gently until the
sauce thickens. Serve immediately.

Shrimps with Beancurd

PREPARATION TIME: 10 minutes

COOKING TIME: 8 minutes

450g (1lb) peeled shrimps

Seasoning
5ml (1 tsp) light soya sauce
Pinch salt
5ml (1 tsp) sugar
5ml (1 tsp) cornflour

2.5cm (1″) fresh root ginger, peeled
 and finely chopped
30ml (2 tblsp) oil
1 clove of garlic, peeled and chopped
1 red chilli, chopped
2-3 beancurd cakes, cubed
60ml (4 tblsp) chicken stock

5ml (1 tsp) cornflour
30ml (2 tblsp) water

Mix the shrimps with the
seasoning ingredients and half of
the ginger. Heat the oil and stir fry
the ginger and shrimps for 2
minutes. Add the garlic and fry for
1 minute. Add the chilli, cubed
beancurd and stock. Simmer for 2-
3 minutes. Mix the cornflour with
the water and remaining crushed
ginger and pour over the shrimp
mixture. Simmer gently until the
sauce thickens. Serve immediately.

Prawns in Hot Sauce

PREPARATION TIME: 10 minutes

COOKING TIME: 6 minutes

350g (12oz) cooked unshelled
 prawns

Seasoning
5ml (1 tsp) malt vinegar
5ml (1 tsp) Shao Hsing wine
Pinch salt

Sauce
5ml (1 tsp) cornflour mixed with
 15ml (1 tblsp) water
10ml (2 tsp) tomato purée
Salt and freshly ground black pepper
 to taste
10ml (2 tsp) sugar

2.5ml (½ tsp) monosodium
 glutamate (optional)
5ml (1 tsp) hot chilli sauce
180ml (6 fl oz) chicken stock
30ml (2 tblsp) cooked oil

Wash prawns and drain well. Mix
the seasoning ingredients together.
Mix the sauce ingredients together
in a separate bowl. Heat the oil in a
wok and deep fry the prawns for 1
minute. Remove the prawns and
drain. Keep the oil. Reheat the wok
and add 10ml (2 tsp) oil and stir fry
the onion, celery and garlic for 1
minute. Add prawns and the
blended sauce ingredients. Bring to
the boil and simmer gently for 3-4
minutes. Stir in the seasoning
mixture.

Fish in Wine Sauce

PREPARATION TIME: 20 minutes

COOKING TIME: 15 minutes

Marinade
1.25ml (¼ tsp) salt
1 egg white
10ml (2 tsp) cornflour
5ml (1 tsp) wine vinegar

275-350g (10-12oz) mullet or carp
 fillet, cut into 5cm (2 inch) slices
Oil for deep frying
250ml (8 fl oz) chicken stock

**Prawns in Hot Sauce (top right), Shrimps with Bean
Curd (centre right) and Prawns with Broccoli
(bottom right).**

Seasoning

Pinch monosodium glutamate
  (optional)
Pinch salt
Pinch freshly ground black pepper
5ml (1 tsp) sugar
10ml (2 tsp) cornflour
15ml (1 tblsp) water
1 cloud ear fungus, soaked and
  boiled for 2 minutes, and then
  chopped
2 dried Chinese mushrooms, soaked
  and sliced

Mix the marinade ingredients together. Marinate the fish in the marinade for 10 minutes. Heat a generous quantity of oil in the wok and deep fry the fish pieces, a few at a time, until the flesh is white. Remove and drain the fish. Keep the oil for future use. Clean the wok. Add the chicken stock to the wok and bring to the boil. Simmer gently and stir in the seasoning ingredients. Simmer for a few seconds and then add the cornflour blended with the water. Add the fish and simmer until the sauce thickens. Add the fungus and mushrooms. Simmer for 1 minute. Serve immediately.

Fish with Chicken and Vegetables

PREPARATION TIME: 25 minutes
COOKING TIME: 15 minutes

450g (1lb) pomfret, plaice or lemon
  sole fillets, cut into 5cm (2 inch)
  pieces
225g (8oz) boned chicken, cut into
  5cm (2 inch) slices
6 dried Chinese mushrooms, soaked
  and sliced
50g (2oz) button mushrooms, sliced
50g (2oz) bamboo shoots, sliced
50g (2oz) mustard green, kale, or
  broccoli or 4 asparagus tips
100g (4oz) mixed vegetables (peas,
  carrots, bean sprouts, etc)
1 small onion, peeled and sliced
5ml (1 tsp) salt
Cooked oil

Marinade

1.25ml (¼ tsp) salt
5ml (1 tsp) white pepper
2.5ml (½ tsp) monosodium
  glutamate (optional)
10ml (2 tsp) cornflour
15ml (1 tblsp) cooked oil
1.25ml (¼ tsp) sesame oil

Sauce

250ml (8 fl oz) chicken stock
Salt to taste
Freshly ground black pepper to taste
2.5ml (½ tsp) monosodium
  glutamate (optional)
10ml (2 tsp) cooked oil
5ml (1 tsp) lemon juice

Wash the fish and drain. Mix the
marinade ingredients together and
marinate fish for 10-15 minutes.
Blanch the mustard green, kale or
broccoli in boiling, salted water for
1 minute. Drain and keep on one
side. Heat the wok with 15ml (1
tblsp) cooked oil and stir fry the
mixed vegetables and the onions
for 2 minutes. Add the mustard
green and stir fry for 1 minute.
Drain and remove onto a plate.
Brush a deep plate with cooked oil
and arrange the drained fish,
mushrooms, chicken and bamboo
shoots in alternate rows. Place the
dish over a steamer. Cover and
steam over boiling water for 7
minutes until cooked. Remove the
steamer from heat and keep on one
side. Heat the wok and add the
sauce ingredients and fish
marinade. Bring to the boil and
simmer for 1 minute, until
thickened. Put the steamed fish,
mushrooms etc. onto a serving
plate and pour the hot sauce over
the top. Serve immediately.

Fish with Vegetables and Bean Curd

PREPARATION TIME: 20 minutes
COOKING TIME: 15 minutes

4 squares bean curd, cut into 2.5cm
  (1 inch) squares

Sauce B

15ml (1 tblsp) Shao Hsing wine
15ml (1 tblsp) dark soya sauce
15ml (1 tblsp) light soya sauce
10ml (2 tsp) sugar
Pinch salt
Pinch white pepper
900ml (1½ pints) chicken stock
225g (8oz) cod fillet, cut into 5cm (2
  inch) slices

Seasoning for Fish A

2.5ml (½ tsp) salt
2.5ml (½ tsp) Shao Hsing wine
22.5ml (1½ tblsp) cornflour
45ml (3 tblsp) oil

Seasoning for Cabbage C

2.5ml (½ tsp) sugar
Pinch salt
5ml (1 tsp) cornflour
2.5cm (1 inch) fresh root ginger,
  peeled and shredded
2 spring onions, chopped

22.5ml (1½ tblsp) cornflour mixed
  with 30ml (2 tblsp) water
25g (1oz) bean sprouts
Few slices of pepper, diced
1 small carrot, chopped
25g (1oz) shelled or frozen peas

Soak the bean curd in cold water
for 2 minutes. Drain well. Mix the
sauce B ingredients and keep on
one side. Wash the fish and drain
well. Mix seasoning A ingredients
and marinate fish for 10-12
minutes. Heat the wok and add
half the oil. When very hot, add
the cabbage and seasoning C
ingredients and stir fry for about 2
minutes. Drain the cabbage well.
Discard any liquid. Heat wok and
add the remaining oil. Add the
ginger and onions and stir fry for 1
minute. Add sauce B ingredients
and bring to the boil. Add fish and
boil for 1 minute. Add the
beancurd and simmer over a low
heat for 5-6 minutes. (The
bean curd should become spongy
to the touch.) Add the blended
cornflour and water. Stir and
simmer until the sauce thickens.
Add the cabbage and simmer for a
further 2 minutes. Serve
immediately.

Boiled Prawns

PREPARATION TIME: 5 minutes,
plus 10 minutes for the sauce
COOKING TIME: 10-15 minutes

Sauce

30ml (2 tblsp) dark soya sauce
45ml (3 tblsp) light soya sauce
1cm (½") fresh root ginger, peeled
  and shredded
2 spring onions, finely chopped
1 red chilli, seeded and shredded
60ml (4 tblsp) cooked oil
10ml (2 tsp) tomato purée

1kg (2 lb) medium or large
  uncooked prawns in their shells
Salt

Mix the sauce ingredients together.
Wash the prawns and drain. Place
the prawns into a wire basket and
lower into a large pan of boiling,
salted water. Boil for 10-12
minutes. Drain. Serve the drained
hot prawns with small bowls of
sauce for dipping.

Cantonese Prawns

PREPARATION TIME: 10 minutes
COOKING TIME: 15 minutes

45ml (3 tblsp) oil
2 cloves garlic, finely crushed
450g (1lb) peeled prawns
5cm (2") root ginger, peeled and
  finely chopped
100g (4oz) uncooked pork or bacon,
  finely chopped

Sauce

15ml (1 tblsp) rice wine or dry sherry
15ml (1 tblsp) light soya sauce
5ml (1 tsp) sugar
250ml (8 fl oz) stock or water
15ml (1 tblsp) cornflour mixed with
  30ml (2 tblsp) stock or water

2-3 spring onions, chopped
2 eggs, lightly beaten

Heat 15ml (1 tblsp) oil in a wok.
Add the garlic and fry for 1 minute.
Add the prawns and stir fry for 4-5
minutes. Remove to a dish. Keep
warm. Add the remaining oil to the
wok and fry the ginger and pork for
3-4 minutes until it loses its
colour. Add the mixed sauce
ingredients to the wok and cook
for 1 minute. Add the onions and
cook for 1 minute. Add the beaten
eggs and cook for 1-2 minutes,
without stirring, until it sets. Spoon
the egg mixture over the prawns.

Alternatively, add the prawns along with the beaten eggs. Allow the eggs to set and then mix gently. Serve at once.

Prawns and Ginger

PREPARATION TIME: 10 minutes

COOKING TIME: 10 minutes

30ml (2 tblsp) oil
675g (1½ lb) peeled prawns
2.5cm (1") fresh root ginger, peeled and finely chopped
2 cloves garlic, peeled and finely chopped
2-3 spring onions, chopped lengthways into 2.5cm (1") pieces
1 leek, white part only, cut into strips.
100g (4oz) shelled peas
175g (6oz) bean sprouts

Seasoning
30ml (2 tblsp) dark soya sauce
5ml (1 tsp) sugar
Pinch monosodium glutamate (optional)
Pinch of salt

Heat the oil in a wok and stir fry the prawns for 2-3 minutes. Remove the prawns to a dish. Reheat the oil and add the ginger and garlic and fry for 1 minute. Add the onions and stir fry for 1 minute. Add the leek, peas and bean sprouts. Stir fry for 2-3 minutes. Sprinkle over the seasoning ingredients and return the prawns to the wok. Cover and cook for 2 minutes. Serve immediately.

Shrimp and Cauliflower

PREPARATION TIME: 15 minutes

COOKING TIME: 14-15 minutes

45ml (3 tblsp) oil
1 clove of garlic, peeled and finely chopped
450g (1lb) shrimps, peeled
275g (10oz) cauliflower florets, cut into smaller pieces
250ml (8 fl oz) water or stock
Salt to taste
175g (6oz) shelled peas

Facing page: Fish with Vegetables and Bean Curd (top), Fish in Wine Sauce (centre right), Fish with Chicken and Vegetables (bottom). This page: Prawns and Ginger (top), Boiled Prawns (centre) and Cantonese Prawns (bottom right).

Sauce
10ml (2 tsp) cornflour
30ml (2 tblsp) stock or water
Freshly ground black pepper to taste

Heat the oil in a wok and fry the garlic for 2 minutes. Add the shrimps and cook for 3 minutes. Remove the shrimps. Add cauliflower and fry for 2-3 minutes, stirring constantly. Add stock, cover and simmer for five minutes. Add salt to taste and the peas and cook for a further 2-3 minutes. Return the shrimps to the wok and stir well. Add the blended sauce ingredients and gently simmer until it thickens. Serve immediately.

Snow Peas with Shrimps

PREPARATION TIME: 10 minutes

COOKING TIME: 6-8 minutes

5ml (1 tsp) cornflour
5ml (1 tsp) sugar
5ml (1 tsp) dark soya sauce
15ml (1 tblsp) water
45ml (3 tblsp) oil
450g (1lb) peeled shrimps
180ml (6 fl oz) chicken stock
2.5ml (½ tsp) salt
100g (4oz) snow peas (mange tout)
75g (3oz) water chestnuts, sliced
1 small onion, peeled and cut into small pieces
1 stem celery, cut into 5mm (¼") pieces
Pinch monosodium glutamate (optional)

Mix together the cornflour, sugar, soya sauce and water. Heat the oil in a wok. Add the shrimps and stir fry for 2 minutes. Add the stock, salt, snow peas, water chestnuts, onions and celery. Cover and cook for 2 minutes. Stir in the monosodium glutamate. Stir in the cornflour mixture and simmer gently until the sauce thickens. Serve as a side dish.

Prawns with Cashew Nuts

PREPARATION TIME: 10 minutes

COOKING TIME: 7-8 minutes

45ml (3 tblsp) oil
50-75g (2-3oz) cashew nuts
10ml (2 tsp) cornflour
250ml (8 fl oz) chicken stock or water

1 onion, peeled and cut into small pieces
25g (1oz) sliced green beans
50g (2oz) Chinese cabbage or white cabbage, shredded
50g (2oz) bamboo shoots, sliced
450g (1lb) peeled prawns
Salt and freshly ground black pepper to taste
4 rings pineapple, cut into chunks
Pinch monosodium glutamate (optional)

Heat 15ml (1 tblsp) oil in a wok and stir fry the cashew nuts until light brown. Remove the nuts and keep on one side. Mix the cornflour with 30ml (2 tblsp) water or stock and keep on one side. Reheat the wok with the remaining oil and fry the onion for 1 minute. Add the beans, cabbage and bamboo shoots and stir fry for 2-3 minutes. Add the cashew nuts and prawns and then add the remaining stock, salt and pepper, and the pineapple. Simmer for 1 minute and then add the MSG and cornflour mixture and cook until the sauce thickens. Serve immediately.

Shrimp and Cauliflower (top right), Prawns with Cashew Nuts (centre left) and Snow Peas with Shrimps (bottom).

CHINESE CUISINE
Vegetables

Braised Cauliflower with Chilli

PREPARATION TIME: 5 minutes
COOKING TIME: 10 minutes

60ml (4 tblsp) oil
2.5cm (1 inch) fresh root ginger, peeled and thinly sliced
1 small cauliflower, cut into 2.5cm (1 inch) florets
2-3 green or red chillis, sliced into quarters and seeded
3 spring onions
Salt to taste
5ml (1 tsp) sugar
300ml (½ pint) chicken stock
5ml (1 tsp) cornflour or arrowroot
15ml (1 tblsp) water

Heat the wok and add the oil. Stir fry the ginger for 1 minute. Reduce the heat and add the cauliflower and chillis. Stir fry for 3-4 minutes. Add the spring onions, season with salt and sprinkle with sugar. Mix for 1 minute and then add the stock. Cover and cook for 2 minutes. Add the blended cornflour and water and stir over the heat until the sauce has thickened.

Fried Bean Curd with Mushrooms

PREPARATION TIME: 15 minutes
COOKING TIME: 12-15 minutes

225g (8oz) mushrooms (button or open) sliced

Seasoning
15ml (1 tblsp) rice wine or dry sherry
10ml (2 tsp) sugar
4 dried Chinese mushrooms, soaked and sliced
Pinch bicarbonate of soda
225g (8oz) mustard green or spinach, cut into 7.5cm (3 inch) pieces
4 squares bean curd (tau fu), cubed
Oil
2.5cm (1 inch) fresh root ginger, peeled and shredded
2 spring onions, chopped
50g (2oz) cooked ham, shredded

Sauce
15ml (1 tblsp) oyster sauce
5ml (1 tsp) dark soya sauce

15ml (1 tblsp) cornflour
60ml (4 tblsp) stock or water
Freshly ground black pepper

Blanch the fresh mushrooms in water for 1 minute. Drain the mushrooms and discard the water. Mix the seasoning ingredients together and marinate the mushrooms for 5-6 minutes. Discard marinade. Bring 1.2 litres (2 pints) of water to the boil and add the bicarbonate of soda and salt. Blanch the greens for 2 minutes. Drain the greens. Discard water. Sprinkle 2.5ml (½ tsp) salt over the bean curd. Deep fry in hot oil until golden brown. Drain and remove. Heat 30ml (2 tblsp) oil in the wok and stir fry the ginger, onions and ham for 2-3 minutes. Return the mushrooms to the wok and mix with the ginger and onions. Add the blended sauce ingredients and bring to boil. Add the bean curd and simmer until the sauce thickens. Arrange the greens on a dish and pour the sauce over them. Sprinkle with freshly ground black pepper.

Fried Vegetables with Ginger

PREPARATION TIME: 10 minutes
COOKING TIME: 13-15 minutes

1kg (2¼ lb) mixed Chinese green vegetables (cabbage, spinach, kale, broccoli, Chinese leaf etc.)
50g (2oz) snow peas (mange tout)
5ml (1 tsp) bicarbonate of soda
10ml (2 tsp) sugar
5ml (1 tsp) salt
15ml (1 tblsp) cooked oil
45ml (3 tblsp) oil
2.5cm (1 inch) fresh root ginger, peeled and shredded
1 green pepper, seeded and diced
1 green or red chilli, sliced into strips

Sauce
10ml (2 tsp) dark soya sauce
5ml (1 tsp) sugar
250ml (8 fl oz) chicken stock
10ml (2 tsp) cornflour
5ml (1 tsp) five spice powder

To Serve
2.5ml (½ tsp) sesame oil
Freshly ground black pepper to taste

Cut greens into 7.5cm (3 inch) pieces. Bring a large pan of water to the boil and add the seasoning ingredients. Add the snow peas and greens and cook for 4-5 minutes. Drain green vegetables and discard water. Add 15ml (1 tblsp) oil to the vegetables and keep covered. Heat the remaining oil in the wok and stir fry the ginger for 1 minute. Add the green pepper and chillis and stir fry for 1-2 minutes. Add the blended sauce ingredients and stir well. Simmer gently for 3-4 minutes. Add the green vegetables and cook for 1 minute. Serve immediately, sprinkled with sesame oil and pepper.

Bamboo Shoots with Green Vegetables

PREPARATION TIME: 10 minutes
COOKING TIME: 10-12 minutes

Oil for cooking
225g (8oz) spinach, or chopped broccoli

Seasoning
120ml (4 fl oz) chicken stock or water
1.25ml (¼ tsp) monosodium glutamate (optional)
1.25ml (¼ tsp) salt
1.25ml (¼ tsp) sugar
100g (4oz) bamboo shoots, sliced

Sauce
5ml (1 tsp) light soya sauce
Pinch monosodium glutamate
5ml (1 tsp) cornflour
10ml (2 tsp) water
15ml (1 tblsp) cooked oil

Heat 30ml (2 tblsp) oil in the wok. Fry the spinach for 2 minutes and add the mixed seasoning ingredients. Simmer for 1 minute and remove from the wok onto a

Fried Vegetables with Ginger (top right), Mustard Green with Crab Sauce (centre left) and Fried Bean Curd with Mushrooms (bottom).

dish. Heat the wok and add 15ml (1 tblsp) oil. Add the bamboo shoots and fry for 1-2 minutes. Return the spinach mixture to the wok. Cook for 3 minutes. Mix together the ingredients for thickening the sauce. Add to the wok and cook for 1-2 minutes. Serve with roast Peking duck, or as a side dish.

Braised Aubergine and Chicken with Chilli

PREPARATION TIME: 10 minutes

COOKING TIME: about 15 minutes

90ml (3 fl oz) oil
2 cloves of garlic, peeled and sliced
450g (1lb) aubergine, cut into 5x6cm (2x2½ inch) pieces
15ml (1 tblsp) soya bean paste (or canned red kidney beans, made into paste)
2.5ml (½ tsp) ground dry chilli or chilli powder
Salt
450ml (¾ pint) chicken stock
2.5cm (1 inch) fresh root ginger,

peeled and sliced
2-3 spring onions, chopped
225-275g (8-10oz) chicken, shredded (cooked or uncooked)

Seasoning
30ml (2 tblsp) light soya sauce
2.5ml (½ tsp) sugar
15ml (1 tblsp) cornflour or arrowroot
30ml (2 tblsp) stock or water, if needed

Heat 60ml (4 tblsp) oil in the wok and stir fry the garlic for 2 minutes. Add the aubergine, which will soak up all the oil. Stir fry for 3-4 minutes, stirring constantly to avoid burning. Add the bean paste, chilli powder and salt to taste, and mix well. Add the chicken stock. Cover and cook for 4-6 minutes, simmering gently. Remove the aubergine and arrange on a dish. Save the sauce. Clean the wok and heat the remaining oil. Stir fry the ginger for 1 minute. Add the onions and chicken and stir fry for 2 minutes. Add the blended seasoning ingredients and the reserved aubergine sauce and simmer gently until it thickens. Pour over the aubergine and serve immediately.

Szechuan Aubergine

PREPARATION TIME: 15 minutes

COOKING TIME: 18-20 minutes

Oil
1 large European aubergine or
450g (1lb) oriental aubergines, cut into 5cm (2 inch) long and 1cm (½ inch) thick strips
3 cloves garlic, peeled and finely sliced
2.5cm (1 inch) fresh root ginger, peeled and shredded
1 onion, peeled and finely chopped
2 spring onions, chopped
100g (4oz) cooked and shredded chicken
1 red or green chilli, cut into strips

Seasoning
120ml (4 fl oz) chicken stock
5ml (1 tsp) sugar
5ml (1 tsp) red vinegar or wine vinegar
2.5ml (½ tsp) salt
2.5ml (½ tsp) freshly ground black pepper

Sauce
5ml (1 tsp) cornflour
15ml (1 tblsp) water
5ml (1 tsp) sesame oil

Heat the wok and add 45ml (3 tblsp) oil. Add the aubergine and stir fry for 4-5 minutes. The aubergines absorb a lot of oil; keep stirring or else they will burn. Remove from wok and keep on one side. Heat the wok and add 30ml (2 tblsp) oil. Add the garlic and ginger and fry for 1 minute. Add the onions and fry for 2 minutes. Add the chicken and chilli. Cook for 1 minute. Return the aubergines to the wok. Add the blended seasoning ingredients and simmer for 6-7 minutes. Stir in the blended sauce ingredients and simmer until the sauce thickens. Serve with extra sesame oil if desired. This dish goes well with Yung Chow fried rice or rice supreme.

Lettuce and Bean Sprouts with Soya Sauce

PREPARATION TIME: 15 minutes

COOKING TIME: 5 minutes

100g (4oz) bean sprouts (moong or soya)
225g (8oz) sweet lettuce
15ml (1 tblsp) oil
2.5cm (1 inch) fresh root ginger, peeled and shredded
1 green or red chilli, seeded and split in half
Salt and freshly ground black pepper

Sauce
30ml (2 tblsp) light soya sauce
5ml (1 tsp) dark soya sauce
10ml (2 tsp) medium white wine or rice wine
2.5ml (½ tsp) sugar
Salt and freshly ground black pepper to taste
2.5ml (½ tsp) sesame oil

Trim the bean sprouts by pinching off the grey and brown ends, as they impart a bitter taste to the dish. Pick off bean seed skin if using soya beans. Cut soya bean sprouts in 2-3 pieces. Rinse in cold water and drain. Wash and drain lettuce before shredding into 5cm (2 inch) pieces. Heat the oil in the wok and stir fry the ginger and chilli for 1 minute. Add the lettuce and toss

for 1 minute. Drain and remove on to a plate. Place the bean sprouts in a colander and pour boiling water over them. Drain thoroughly and add to the lettuce. Sprinkle with salt and pepper and keep covered. Mix the sauce ingredients together in the wok. Stir over the heat until blended. Pour this sauce over the vegetables and serve immediately.

Sweet and Sour Cabbage

PREPARATION TIME: 10 minutes

COOKING TIME: 10 minutes

450g (1lb) white cabbage, shredded
2.5ml (½ tsp) bicarbonate of soda
5ml (1 tsp) salt
10ml (2 tsp) sugar
15ml (1 tblsp) oil

Sauce
30ml (2 tblsp) sugar
30ml (2 tblsp) wine vinegar
250ml (8 fl oz) chicken stock or water
Pinch salt

15ml (1 tblsp) cornflour or arrowroot
Few drops red food colouring
5ml (1 tsp) tomato purée

Boil the cabbage in a large pan of water with the bicarbonate of soda, salt and sugar for 2-3 minutes. Drain the cabbage and discard the boiling water. Keep the cabbage in cold water for 5 minutes. Drain and keep on one side. Heat the wok and add the oil. Fry the cabbage until it is heated through. Remove on to a serving dish. Add the well-stirred sauce ingredients to the wok and gently bring to the boil, stirring. Stir over the heat until the sauce thickens. Pour over the cabbage and serve immediately.

Facing page: Bamboo Shoots with Green Vegetables (top right), Sweet and Sour Cabbage (centre left), Szechuan Aubergine (bottom).

This page: Lettuce and Bean Sprouts with Soya Sauce (left), Braised Aubergine and Chicken with Chilli (centre) and Braised Cauliflower with Chilli (right).

Egg Dishes and Curry

Lamb Curry

PREPARATION TIME: 15 minutes

COOKING TIME: 50 minutes

30ml (2 tblsp) oil
1 onion, peeled and chopped
2.5cm (1 inch) fresh root ginger,
    peeled and chopped
2 cloves of garlic, chopped
450g (1lb) lean, boned lamb, cut into
    cubes
1-2 carrots, scraped and sliced
5ml (1 tsp) five spice mixture
Salt to taste
2 chillis, chopped
15ml (1 tblsp) tomato purée
10ml (2 tblsp) cornflour
1 green pepper, seeded and chopped

Heat the oil and fry the onion for 2
minutes. Add the ginger and garlic
and fry for 1 minute. Add the lamb
and carrots and stir fry for 3-4
minutes. Sprinkle over the five
spice powder and add the salt,
chillis and tomato purée. Stir in
300ml (½ pint) water. Cover and
simmer for 30-35 minutes. Mix
30ml (2 tblsp) water with the
cornflour and add to the curry.
Add the green pepper and simmer
for 5 minutes. Serve with rice.

Prawn Curry

PREPARATION TIME: 10 minutes

COOKING TIME: 8 minutes

30ml (2 tblsp) oil
1 onion, peeled and chopped
1 carrot, cut into strips
75g (3oz) snow peas (mange tout)
2.5cm (1 inch) fresh root ginger,
    peeled and chopped
2 cloves garlic, chopped
450g (1lb) prawns, peeled
7.5ml (1½ tsp) curry powder
Salt to taste
2 green chillis, sliced
10ml (2 tblsp) cornflour

Heat the oil and fry the onions for
2 minutes. Add the carrot and
snow peas and fry for 2 minutes.
Add the ginger, garlic and prawns
and stir fry for 1-2 minutes.
Sprinkle over the curry powder
and add the salt, green chillis and
300ml (½ pint) water. Mix the
cornflour with 15ml (1 tblsp) water
and add to the curry. Cook gently
until the curry thickens. Serve with
rice.

Chicken Curry

PREPARATION TIME: 15 minutes

COOKING TIME: 40 minutes

30ml (2 tblsp) oil
1 onion, peeled and chopped
2 cloves of garlic, peeled and chopped
2.5cm (1 inch) fresh root ginger,
    peeled and finely chopped
1.5kg (3lb) chicken, boned and cut
    into small pieces
10ml (2 tsp) curry powder
5ml (1 tsp) chilli powder
2.5ml (½ tsp) salt
100g (4oz) mixed frozen vegetables
1 green pepper, seeded and chopped
10ml (2 tsp) cornflour

Heat the oil and fry the onions for
2 minutes. Add the garlic, ginger
and chicken and fry gently for 5
minutes. Add the curry powder,
chilli powder, salt and 450ml (¾
pint) of water. Cover and cook
gently until the chicken is tender.
Add the mixed vegetables and
green pepper and cook for 3-4
minutes. Add the cornflour,
dissolved in 30ml (2 tblsp) water,
and simmer until the sauce
thickens. Serve with plain boiled
rice.

Shrimp Fu Yung

PREPARATION TIME: 10 minutes

COOKING TIME: 4 minutes for
filling; 3-4 minutes for each
pancake

Oil
1-2 cloves of garlic, chopped
100g (4oz) shrimps, peeled
100g (4oz) green beans, sliced
1 carrot, shredded
6 eggs
Salt and freshly ground black pepper
    to taste
250ml (8 fl oz) chicken stock
1.25ml (¼ tsp) salt
10ml (2 tsp) soya sauce
5ml (1 tsp) sugar
5ml (1 tsp) vinegar
5ml (1 tsp) cornflour

Heat 30ml (2 tblsp) oil in a wok.
Add the garlic and stir fry for 1
minute. Add the shrimps and stir
fry for 1 minute. Add the beans
and carrots and stir fry for 2
minutes. Remove and keep on one
side. Beat the eggs with salt and
pepper to taste, and add the cooled

shrimp mixture. Clean the wok
and heat 5ml (1 tsp) oil. Pour in
60ml (4 tblsp) of the egg mixture
and cook like a pancake. When the
egg is set, turn the pancake over
and cook on the other side until
lightly golden. Place on a warm
platter and keep warm.

To Make the Sauce
Beat the stock with the other sauce
ingredients and stir over a gentle
heat until the sauce thickens. Serve
the pancakes with this sauce.
Makes 6-8 servings.

Egg Fu Yung

PREPARATION TIME: 5 minutes

COOKING TIME: 8-10 minutes

6 eggs
22.5ml (1½ tblsp) soya sauce
3-4 spring onions, chopped
Salt and freshly ground black pepper
    to taste
45ml (3 tblsp) oil
100g (4oz) bean sprouts

Beat the eggs and soya sauce
together and add the spring onions
and salt and pepper to taste. Heat
the oil in a frying pan or wok and
stir fry the bean sprouts for 2-3
minutes. Pour in the beaten egg
mixture. Leave over a moderate
heat to set and then put under the
grill to set and brown the top. Cut
into wedges and serve immediately.
Alternatively, stir the mixture
while it is cooking so that it turns
out like scrambled egg.

Prawns in Egg Custard

PREPARATION TIME: 5 minutes

COOKING TIME: 20 minutes

8 eggs
Salt and freshly ground black pepper
    to taste
Pinch monosodium glutamate
    (optional)
5ml (1 tsp) Shao Hsing wine
300ml (½ pint) chicken stock
300ml (½ pint) water
450g (1lb) prawns, peeled
10ml (2 tsp) cooked oil

Beat the eggs in a bowl, add the
seasoning, MSG and wine. Bring
the stock and water to the boil and

add to the eggs. Add prawns and
set the bowl over a steamer. Cover
and steam over simmering water
for about 15-20 minutes, until the
custard has set. Serve with the
cooked oil spooned over the top.

Stir Fried Eggs with Shredded Meats and Vegetables

PREPARATION TIME: 15-20
    minutes

COOKING TIME: 15 minutes

50g (2oz) cooked chicken, shredded
75g (3oz) cooked pork or beef,
    shredded
Salt to taste
1.25ml (¼ tsp) soya sauce
60ml (4 tblsp) oil
4 eggs, beaten
2 spring onions, chopped
50g (2oz) dried mushrooms, soaked
    and sliced
50g (2oz) button mushrooms, sliced
2 cloud ear fungus, boiled in water
    for 3 minutes and thinly sliced
175g (6oz) Chinese white cabbage,
    broccoli or green leafy cabbage,
    shredded
1-2 green or red chillis, chopped
2 sprigs Chinese parsley, chopped
Pinch monosodium glutamate
    (optional)

Put the chicken and pork into a
bowl with 1.25ml (¼ tsp) salt and
the soya sauce. Leave for 10
minutes. Heat the wok and add
30ml (2 tblsp) oil. Add the beaten
eggs and stir fry for 2-3 minutes
until they resemble scrambled egg.
Keep on one side. Reheat the wok
and add the remaining oil. Fry the
onions and meats for 2 minutes.
Remove from the wok and keep on
one side. Stir fry the cabbage and
chillis in the wok for 1-2 minutes.
Cover and gently cook in its own
juice until tender – approx 3-4
minutes. Return the meats,
mushrooms and egg to the cabbage
and add the parsley and MSG. Stir
fry for 1-2 minutes. Serve with
extra soya sauce and Shao Hsing
wine sprinkled over it, if desired.

Lamb Curry (right), Prawn Curry (below) and Chicken Curry (bottom).

Marbled Eggs

PREPARATION TIME: 10 minutes

COOKING TIME: 1 hour 10 minutes to 1 hour 15 minutes

These are eaten cold, dipped in a sauce, as a starter or a snack. Allow 1 egg per person.

6-8 eggs
45ml (3 tblsp) tea leaves
2.5cm (1 inch) cinnamon stick
2-3 star anise
30ml (2 tblsp) dark soya sauce
30ml (2 tblsp) light soya sauce

Boil the eggs for 8-10 minutes until hard boiled. Drain and cool quickly by placing in iced water. Tap each egg shell with the back of a spoon until cracks appear all over. Bring enough water to the boil to cover the eggs. Add tea leaves, cinnamon, star anise, soya sauces and stir. Add the eggs and simmer gently for at least 1 hour. Allow to cool and then shell before serving.

Egg Pancakes with Filling

PREPARATION TIME: 10 minutes

COOKING TIME: 6-7 minutes for each pancake

6 eggs
Salt and freshly ground black pepper to taste
100g (4oz) lean pork, finely chopped or ground
50g (2oz) button mushrooms, chopped
5ml (1 tsp) rice wine or dry sherry
5ml (1 tsp) light soya sauce
2.5ml (½ tsp) sugar
2.5ml (½ tsp) fresh root ginger, minced
Oil

Beat the eggs and season with salt and pepper. Mix the pork with the mushrooms, wine, soya sauce, sugar and ginger. Add salt and pepper to taste and mix well. Heat the wok and add 5ml (1 tsp) oil. Spoon in 30ml (2 tblsp) of the beaten egg and spread into a 7½cm (3 inch) circle. Place 10ml (2 tsp) filling into the centre of the egg. When the underside of the egg sets but the top is still moist, fold the egg circle over to make a crescent shape; press gently to seal the edges. Cook for 4 minutes on a low heat to cook the filling. Make the remaining pancakes in the same way. Serve with a chilli sauce or dip, or with stir fried vegetables as a main dish.

Noodles with Pork Fu Yung

PREPARATION TIME: 20 minutes

COOKING TIME: about 20 minutes

2.5ml (½ tsp) bicarbonate of soda
15ml (1 tblsp) water
225g (8oz) pork, thinly sliced
225g (8oz) cake noodles
10ml (2 tsp) cornflour
Few drops sesame oil
Salt and freshly ground black pepper to taste
2.5ml (½ tsp) sugar
Oil
2 cloves of garlic, finely chopped
2.5cm (1 inch) fresh root ginger, peeled and sliced
2-3 spring onions, chopped
6 eggs, well beaten

Mix the bicarbonate of soda and the water together. Mix in the pork and marinate for 10-12 minutes. Drain. Cook the noodles in boiling, salted water for 3-4 minutes. Drain, rinse in cold water and drain once again. Toss in 15ml (1 tblsp) oil. Heat 30ml (2 tblsp) oil in the wok and brown the garlic. Add 5ml (1 tsp) salt and the noodles and stir fry for 3-4 minutes, until they turn light brown. Remove and keep on one side. Heat sufficient oil for deep frying in the wok and deep fry the pork for 3-4 minutes, drain and remove. Tip off the oil. Heat 15ml (1 tblsp) oil in the wok. Add the ginger and onions and stir fry for 1-2 minutes. Add the pork and then pour in the beaten eggs, mixing well. Add the cornflour, sesame oil and sugar and cook until the mixture thickens. Pour over the noodles and serve immediately.

This page: **Marbled Eggs (top), Noodles with Pork Fu Yung (centre right) and Stir Fried Eggs with Shredded Meats and Vegetables (bottom left).**

Facing page: **Prawns in Egg Custard (top left), Egg Pancakes with Filling (top right), Shrimp Fu Yung (centre left) and Egg Fu Yung (bottom right).**

CHINESE CUISINE

Rice and Noodles

Rice with Minced Beef

PREPARATION TIME: 10 minutes
COOKING TIME: 25 minutes

30ml (2 tblsp) cooking oil
225g (8oz) minced beef
3 spring onions, chopped
1.25cm (½ inch) fresh root ginger,
　peeled and sliced
2 cloves garlic, peeled and sliced
15ml (1 tblsp) soya sauce
1 green pepper, seeded and chopped
450g (1lb) rice, thoroughly washed
2.5ml (½ tsp) salt
5ml (1 tsp) freshly ground black
　pepper, or to taste

Heat the oil and fry the mince,
onions, ginger and garlic for 5
minutes. Add the soya sauce and
green pepper and fry for 5-6
minutes. Cook the rice with 2.5cm
(1 inch) water above the rice level
with the salt for 5-6 minutes or
until the rice is semi-cooked and
the water is almost absorbed.
Spread the mince evenly over the
rice. Cover and cook for 6-8
minutes over a very gentle heat.
Remove and serve well mixed.
Season with salt and pepper to
taste.

Assorted Meat Congee

PREPARATION TIME: 20 minutes
COOKING TIME: 1 hour
　　　　　　　　45 minutes

450g (1lb) rice
Scant 2½ litres (4 pints) chicken
　stock
100g (4oz) tripe, well washed and
　chopped (optional)
100g (4oz) pig's or lamb's liver, sliced
100g (4oz) cooked beef, ham, lamb,
　chicken or pork, chopped
100g (4oz) white fish fillets, thinly
　sliced
5ml (1 tsp) sesame oil
3 spring onions, chopped
7.5ml (1½ tsp) salt, or to taste
7.5ml (1½ tsp) freshly ground black
　pepper
1.25cm (½ inch) fresh root ginger,
　peeled and sliced

Wash the rice well and put it into a
large saucepan. Add the chicken

stock and the tripe (if used). Cook
gently for 1-1½ hours or until the
tripe is well cooked and the rice has
become a soft pulp. In a separate
saucepan, boil the sliced liver for 5
minutes in water. Drain and add to
the rice. Add the cooked meat,
fish, sesame oil, half the onions, salt
and pepper and the slices of ginger.
Cook for further 10-15 minutes
covered. Pour into large bowls and
serve topped with the remaining
chopped onions.

Rice Supreme

PREPARATION TIME: 10 minutes
COOKING TIME: 15 minutes

45ml (3 tblsp) cooking oil
15ml (1 tblsp) light soya sauce
2 eggs, beaten
1 small onion, peeled and finely
　sliced
50g (2oz) shrimps, peeled
50g (2oz) prawns, peeled

50g (2oz) white fish, cubed
2 spring onions, finely chopped
50g (2oz) green pepper, seeded and
　cut into strips
450g (1lb) rice, cooked and cooled
Salt to taste
5ml (1 tsp) freshly ground black
　pepper
45ml (3 tblsp) tomato ketchup
50g (2oz) frozen peas

Heat 15ml (1 tblsp) oil in the wok
and pour in the beaten eggs. Cook
to make a thin omelette. Cut into
thin strips. Heat 15ml (1 tblsp) oil
in the wok and stir fry the onion
for 2 minutes. Add the shrimps,
prawns and fish and stir fry for 3-4
minutes. Remove the fish mixture
to a plate. Heat the remaining oil in
the wok. Add half the spring
onions and the green pepper and
stir fry for 2 minutes. Add the rice
and season with salt and pepper.
Add the tomato ketchup, peas,
fried fish, prawns and shrimps. Add
the soya sauce and stir fry for 3
minutes. Serve with the egg strips
arranged on top of the rice.

Vegetable Rice

PREPARATION TIME: 10 minutes
COOKING TIME: 5-8 minutes

450g (1lb) rice, cooked
175g (6oz) Chinese cabbage or
　Chinese leaves, shredded
100g (4oz) sliced green beans
100g (4oz) frozen peas
3 spring onions, chopped
15ml (1 tblsp) light soya sauce
Salt to taste

Rinse the cooked rice in cold water
and drain. Put the moist rice into a
pan. Arrange the Chinese cabbage,
sliced beans, peas and onions on
top. Cover and cook over a gentle
heat for 4-6 minutes. Sprinkle with
soya sauce and add salt to taste.
Stir the vegetables evenly into the
rice and raise the heat for a few
seconds. Serve immediately.

Plain Fried Rice

PREPARATION TIME: 5 minutes,
plus cooling time
COOKING TIME: 10-11 minutes

450g (1lb) Patna or long grain rice
1.25ml (¼ tsp) monosodium
　glutamate
30ml (2 tblsp) oil
Salt

Wash the rice in 4-5 changes of
cold water. Drain the rice and put
into a large pan or wok. Add
sufficient cold water to come
2.5cm (1 inch) above the level of
the rice. Bring to the boil. Stir once
and reduce the heat to simmer.
Cover and cook gently for 5-7
minutes until the water has been

This page: **Vegetable Rice (top),
Assorted Meat Congee (centre
right) and Rice Supreme
(bottom).**

Facing page: **Yang Chow Fried
Rice (top), Plain Fried Rice
(centre left) and Rice with
Minced Beef (bottom).**

totally absorbed and the rice is separate and fluffy, with the necessary amount of stickiness to be handled by chopsticks. (If necessary cook for a little longer.) Spread the rice out on a tray and cool. Sprinkle with the monosodium glutamate. Heat the oil in a wok or large frying pan and add the rice. Stir fry for 1-2 minutes. Add salt to taste and stir fry for a further 1-2 minutes.

Yang Chow Fried Rice

PREPARATION TIME: 10 minutes

COOKING TIME: 6-8 minutes

45ml (3 tblsp) cooking oil
1 egg, beaten
100g (4oz) cooked meat, chopped (pork, lamb, beef)
100g (4oz) cooked prawns or shrimps, shelled and chopped
50g (2oz) shelled green peas
2 spring onions, chopped
450g (1lb) dry, cooked rice
Salt to taste
5ml (1 tsp) monosodium glutamate (optional)

Heat 15ml (1 tblsp) oil in a wok. Fry the beaten egg until set, and break into small lumps. Remove the egg. Add the remaining oil and fry the meat, shrimps, peas and onions for 1-2 minutes. Add the cooked rice and sprinkle with salt and monosodium glutamate. Fry for 3 minutes. Mix in the cooked egg and serve immediately.

Sizzling Rice or Singing Rice

PREPARATION TIME: 50 minutes

COOKING TIME: 2 hours, plus time for deep frying sizzling rice

100g (4oz) short grained rice

When rice is cooked, the crust that forms on the bottom of the pot can be dried and then deep fried. When it is immersed in gravy or soup it makes a sizzling noise, hence the name. Once made or collected, the rice crusts can be kept for months.

To Make a Rice Crust
Wash rice in 4-5 changes of water until the water runs clear. Drain the rice and put it into a pan with 300ml (½ pint) of water; bring to the boil. Reduce heat to low and cook for 20 minutes, simmering gently. Turn off the heat and let the rice stand covered for 25-30 minutes. Take a non-stick frying pan and transfer the rice to it. Spread evenly to a thickness of 1cm (½ inch). Cook on a very gentle heat for 40-50 minutes. Turn over and cook gently for another hour. The rice should be very dry. Break into 5cm (2 inch) squares and store in a glass jar with a lid.

To Cook Sizzling Rice
Pour oil into a pan to a depth of 5cm (2 inches) and bring to a moderately high temperature (190°C or 375°F). Add the rice squares and fry until golden brown. Remove and drain on kitchen paper. Serve with soup or any stir fried dish.

Shrimp Egg Rice

PREPARATION TIME: 20 minutes

COOKING TIME: 17-18 minutes

450g (1lb) long or medium grained rice
2 eggs
2.5ml (½ tsp) salt
60ml (4 tblsp) oil
2 spring onions, chopped
1 large onion, peeled and chopped
2 cloves garlic, peeled and chopped
100g (4oz) peeled shrimps
50g (2oz) shelled peas
30ml (2 tblsp) dark soya sauce

To Cook the Rice
Wash rice in 4-5 changes of water. Add cold water to 2.5cm (1 inch) above the rice level and bring to the boil. Stir once and reduce the heat to simmer. Cover the pan and gently cook the rice for 5-7 minutes until the rice is dry and the liquid has been totally absorbed. Remove from the heat, add cold water to cover and drain thoroughly. Spread the rice on a serving tray and separate the grains with a fork.
Beat the eggs in a bowl and season with a pinch of salt. Heat the wok and add 15ml (1 tblsp) oil. Add the onions and stir fry for 2 minutes. Add the beaten eggs. Allow to set slightly and then stir the mixture until it scrambles. Remove onto a plate. Heat the wok and add 15ml (1 tblsp) oil. Fry the garlic for 1 minute then add the shrimps and cook for 2 minutes. Add the peas, and stir fry for 1 minute. Remove

onto a plate. Heat the wok and add the remaining oil, a little salt to taste and the cooked rice. Stir fry to heat the rice through. Stir in the soya sauce, shrimp mixture and the cooked eggs, gently stirring the mixture to blend. Serve immediately.

Shrimp Egg Rice (below), Sizzling Rice or Singing Rice (bottom left) and Plain Rice (bottom right).

Plain Rice

PREPARATION TIME:	5 minutes
COOKING TIME:	5-7 minutes

450g (1lb) rice
Pinch salt
10ml (2 tsp) oil

To make a bowl of plain rice, take any grade of long or medium grained rice. Wash the rice in 4-5 changes of water and then add enough cold water to come 2.5cm (1 inch) above the rice level. Add the salt and oil and bring to the boil. Stir once. Cover and simmer gently for 5-7 minutes until the water has been totally absorbed. Remove from the heat and serve. Plain boiled rice should be fluffy, yet have enough moisture around the rice so that the grains can be picked up easily by chopsticks.

Noodles in Soup

PREPARATION TIME:	10 minutes
COOKING TIME:	6-8 minutes

450g (1lb) small rounds of noodle cakes.
Salt
1.3 litres (2¼ pints) chicken or beef broth, or thick stock
100g (4oz) cooked shredded chicken
2 eggs, hard boiled and sliced
100g (4oz) Chinese napa cabbage, finely shredded (or iceberg lettuce)
2 spring onions, thinly sliced

2 sticks celery, chopped
50g (2oz) leek, chopped
2 spring onions, shredded
60ml (4 tblsp) stock
30ml (2 tblsp) soya sauce

Soak the rice noodles in warm water for 10-15 minutes. Drain thoroughly. Heat half the oil in a wok. Add the chicken, shrimps, bamboo shoots, celery, leeks and spring onions and stir fry for 2-3 minutes. Add the stock and salt and pepper to taste. Simmer for 2 minutes and then drain the chicken and vegetables. Heat the remaining oil, add the rice noodles and stir over the heat for 1 minute. Add the soya sauce and stir into the chicken and vegetable mixture. Cook together for 2-3 minutes. Serve immediately. Boiled prawns may also be added along with the chicken.

Meat and Prawn Chow Mein

PREPARATION TIME: 20 minutes

COOKING TIME: 12-15 minutes

450g (1lb) dried Chinese noodles or broken spaghetti
Salt to taste
60ml (4 tblsp) oil
2-3 spring onions, chopped
100g (4oz) cooked ham, shredded
100g (4oz) peeled prawns
100g (4oz) shredded carrots
100g (4oz) green beans, sliced
5ml (1 tsp) sugar
15ml (1 tblsp) rice wine or dry sherry
100g (4oz) cooked chicken, shredded
100g (4oz) bean sprouts
37ml (2½ tblsp) soya sauce

Cook the noodles in boiling, salted water for 4-5 minutes. Rinse under cold water and drain thoroughly. Toss in 15ml (1tblsp) oil. Heat the remaining oil in a wok. Add the onions, ham, prawns, carrots and green beans and stir fry for 2-3 minutes. Add the salt, sugar, wine, chicken and bean sprouts. Cook for 2 minutes. Add the cooked noodles and soya sauce. Cook for 1-2 minutes. Serve immediately.

Cook the noodles in boiling, salted water for 5 minutes. Drain thoroughly. Heat the broth or stock and add salt to taste. Serve the cooked noodles in bowls, and pour over the hot broth. Garnish with chicken, sliced eggs, cabbage and spring onions.

Stir Fried Shanghai Noodles

PREPARATION TIME: 10 minutes

COOKING TIME: 5-6 minutes

100g (4oz) white cabbage, shredded
2.5ml (½ tsp) sesame oil
45ml (3 tblsp) cooked oil
100g (4oz) cooked chicken or pork, shredded
450g (1lb) thick Shanghai noodles, cooked until just tender
30ml (2 tblsp) soya sauce
2.5ml (½ tsp) monosodium glutamate (optional)
Freshly ground black pepper to taste

Cook the cabbage in boiling water for 1 minute. Drain thoroughly. Heat the oils in a wok. Add the meat and stir fry for 2-3 minutes. Add the cooked noodles, soya sauce, monosodium glutamate and salt and pepper to taste. Add the cabbage, heat through and serve immediately.

Deep Fried Noodles
Boil noodles for 5 minutes. Drain thoroughly on absorbent paper. Deep fry in hot oil until crisp and golden.

Fried Rice Noodles

PREPARATION TIME: 25 minutes

COOKING TIME: 10 minutes

450g (1lb) rice noodles
45ml (3 tblsp) oil
100g (4oz) cooked chicken, shredded
50g (2oz) peeled shrimps
50g (2oz) bamboo shoots, sliced

This page: Deep Fried Noodles (top), Stir Fried Shanghai Noodles (centre), Fried Rice Noodles (bottom). Facing page: Meat and Prawn Chow Mein (top), Noodles in Soup (centre), Rice Noodles Singapore Style (bottom).

Rice Noodles Singapore Style

PREPARATION TIME: 15 minutes, plus soaking time for noodles

COOKING TIME: about 15 minutes

225g (8oz) rice noodles
Oil
2 eggs, beaten
1.25cm (½ inch) fresh root ginger, peeled and shredded
100g (4oz) bean sprouts
100g (4oz) cooked ham, pork or chicken, shredded
50g (2oz) chives, finely chopped
2 cloves garlic, finely chopped
Salt to taste
15ml (1 tblsp) chicken stock
30ml (2 tblsp) soya sauce
3 spring onions, chopped

Soak the rice noodles in warm water for 10 minutes and then drain well. Heat 15ml (1 tblsp) oil in a frying pan or wok and fry the beaten eggs to make a thin pancake. Slide onto a plate and cut into thin strips. Heat the wok or frying pan and add 15ml (1 tblsp) oil. Fry the ginger and bean sprouts for 2 minutes. Slide onto a plate. Heat the wok or frying pan with a further 15ml (1 tblsp) oil and fry the pork or chicken and the chives for 1-2 minutes. Slide onto a plate. Heat 30ml (2 tblsp) oil in the wok or frying pan and brown the garlic. Add the rice noodles and stir fry for 2-3 minutes. Add salt to taste, chicken stock, bean sprouts and pork or chicken. Mix well, sprinkle with soya sauce and stir over the heat for 1 minute. Top with the strips of egg pancake and spring onions and serve immediately.

Noodles with Beef and Almonds

PREPARATION TIME: 15 minutes

COOKING TIME: 10 minutes

45ml (3 tblsp) oil
1 onion, chopped
4 cloves of garlic, chopped
2.5cm (1 inch) fresh root ginger, peeled and sliced
225g (8oz) beef, thinly sliced
50g (2oz) carrots, diced
50g (2oz) sliced green beans
50g (2oz) water chestnuts, sliced
50g (2oz) mushrooms, sliced
2 green chillis, sliced in half
Salt

5ml (1 tsp) sugar
5ml (1 tsp) monosodium glutamate (optional)
250ml (8 fl oz) chicken stock
100g (4oz) blanched almonds
450g (1lb) noodles, cooked until just tender

Heat 30ml (2 tblsp) oil in a wok. Fry the onion, garlic, ginger and beef for 3 minutes. Add the carrots and green beans and fry for 2 minutes. Add the water chestnuts, mushrooms and green chillis and fry for 1 minute. Add salt, sugar, MSG and stock. Simmer for 1 minute. Remove to a dish and keep warm. Clean the wok and add the remaining oil. Fry the almonds and noodles for 1-2 minutes. Mix with the cooked vegetables and season with soya sauce. Serve immediately.

Egg Noodles with Meat Sauce

PREPARATION TIME: 15 minutes

COOKING TIME: 20-22 minutes

45ml (3 tblsp) oil
3 cloves garlic, chopped
2.5cm (1 inch) fresh root ginger, peeled and shredded
1 onion, chopped
1 green pepper, seeded and sliced
450g (1lb) beef mince
2.5ml (½ tsp) salt
10ml (2 tsp) tomato purée
15ml (1 tblsp) soya sauce
2.5ml (½ tsp) freshly ground black pepper
120ml (4 fl oz) chicken stock
5ml (1 tsp) cornflour
450g (1lb) egg noodles
2 spring onions, chopped

Heat 30ml (2 tblsp) oil in a wok. Fry the garlic and ginger for 1-2 minutes. Add the onion and fry for 2-3 minutes. Add the green pepper and the beef mince and fry for 1 minute. Add half the salt, tomato purée, soya sauce and ground pepper. Fry for a further 3 minutes. Blend the stock and cornflour and add to the wok. Cook until thickened and the meat is tender. Meanwhile, cook noodles in boiling, salted water for 3-4 minutes, and drain. Rinse in cold

water and drain once again. Heat the remaining oil in a pan. Add the noodles and toss over the heat until heated through. Arrange on a plate and top with the meat sauce. Garnish with chopped spring onions.

Fried Noodles with Shredded Chicken

PREPARATION TIME: 15 minutes

COOKING TIME: about 10 minutes

Oil
225g (8oz) cooked chicken, shredded
1 clove of garlic, chopped
2-3 spring onions, chopped
100g (4oz) whole green beans (or long Chinese beans, cut into 7.5cm (3 inch) pieces)
450g (1lb) noodles, cooked until just tender
15ml (1 tblsp) cornflour
250ml (8 fl oz) chicken stock
15ml (1 tblsp) soya sauce
15ml (1 tblsp) oyster sauce
5ml (1 tsp) wine
5ml (1 tsp) sugar
1.25ml (¼ tsp) salt

Heat 30ml (2 tblsp) oil in a wok and cook the chicken for 2 minutes. Remove the chicken. Add the garlic, spring onions and beans and fry for 2 minutes. Remove the vegetables. Heat 30ml (2 tblsp) oil in the wok and toss the pre-boiled noodles over the heat for 2 minutes. Arrange on a plate and keep warm. Return the fried chicken, onion and green beans to the wok and stir fry for 1 minute. Dissolve the cornflour in the chicken stock and add to the wok. Add the soya sauce, oyster sauce, wine, sugar and salt and pepper to taste. Simmer until the sauce is thick. Pour over the bed of noodles and serve immediately.

This page: Noodles with Beef and Almonds (top), Egg Noodles with Meat Sauce (centre) and Fried Noodles with Shredded Chicken (bottom).

Facing page: Chinese Bean Buns (top), Red Bean Filled Dim Sums (centre right) and Candied Apples (bottom).

CHINESE CUISINE
Sweets

a chopstick on each circle of dough to mark it in half, and then in half again. Cut along the marks to within ⅓ of the centre. Place one portion of filling in the centre of the dough circle and fold the cut ends in to meet in the centre, to form a rosette. Secure by pinching ends of dough together. Place a piece of greased foil over the pinched ends and place the buns on a greased baking tray. Brush with a little milk. Bake at 190°C, 375°F, Gas Mark 5 for 20-25 minutes.

Red Bean Filled Dim Sums

PREPARATION TIME: 45-50 minutes

COOKING TIME: 10-12 minutes

50g (2oz) sugar
300ml (½ pint) warm water
15ml (1 tblsp) dried yeast
450g (1lb) plain flour
30ml (2 tblsp) melted lard
1 egg white, beaten

Filling
275g (10oz) sweet bean paste, ready made
Red food colouring

Dissolve the sugar in the warm water and add the yeast. Stir until dissolved. Leave in a warm place until frothy. Sift the flour into a mixing bowl and add the melted lard and the yeast mixture. Mix together. Turn the mixture onto a floured surface and knead to a smooth and elastic dough. Roll into a long sausage and divide into 24 equal portions. Roll each portion into a 5cm (2 inch) flat circle. Brush edges of dough with beaten egg white. Place 15ml (1 tblsp) of filling into the centre of each circle and pull the dough around it to enclose the filling. Pleat the open edges in a circular fashion, so that a small opening is left in the middle of the pleating. Place a small piece of greased foil over the pleats on each dim sum. Leave for 10-12 minutes until the dough becomes springy to the touch. Put a dab of red food

Chinese Bean Buns

PREPARATION TIME: about 2 hours, including proving time

COOKING TIME: about 30 minutes

60ml (2 fl oz) milk
50g (2 oz) sugar
2.5ml (½ tsp) salt
25g (1oz) lard
60ml (2 fl oz) warm water
10ml (2 tsp) dried yeast
1 egg, beaten
275g (10oz) plain flour

Bring the milk almost to the boil. Stir in the sugar, salt and lard. Cool slightly. Put the warm water and yeast into a bowl and stir to mix. Add the lukewarm milk mixture. Add the beaten egg and 225g (8oz) of the flour and beat until smooth. Add the remaining flour and mix to a dough. Turn dough out onto a well-floured board and knead until smooth and elastic. Place in a greased bowl. Brush the dough with oil and cover. Leave to rise in a warm place until doubled in size (about 1 hour).

Filling
100g (4oz) sweet bean paste
25g (1oz) sugar
25g (1oz) chopped walnuts
15ml (1 tblsp) lard

Heat the filling ingredients together in a wok for 5-6 minutes until smooth and shiny. Remove and cool. Divide the filling into 12-14 portions. Knead the risen dough again for 2 minutes and then divide the dough into 12-14 portions. Flatten into thick, circular shapes 10cm (4 inches) in diameter. Place colouring on each dim sum. Arrange the dim sums in a bamboo steaming basket and steam over boiling water for 10-12 minutes. The dim sums are ready when they are dry and smooth. Alternatively they can be baked at 180°C, 350°F, Gas Mark 4, for about 20 minutes.

Agar-Agar Pudding

PREPARATION TIME: 5 minutes

COOKING TIME: 4-5 minutes

600ml (1 pint) milk
100g (4oz) sugar
25g (1oz) ground almonds
50g (2oz) agar-agar (also called Chinese grass)
25g (1oz) blanched and chopped almonds

Mix the milk, sugar and ground almonds together in a pan and stir over the heat for 4 minutes. Add the agar-agar and stir until dissolved. Stir in the chopped almonds. Pour into a shallow dish 2.5cm (1 inch) deep. Cool and keep in refrigerator until set. Serve chilled, cut into diamond or square shapes.

Almond Cookies
Makes 60 cookies

PREPARATION TIME: 20 minutes

COOKING TIME: 12-15 minutes

225g (8oz) lard
100g (4oz) caster sugar
50g (2oz) brown sugar
1 egg, beaten
Few drops almond essence
275g (10oz) plain flour
Pinch salt
7.5ml (1½ tsp) baking powder
75g (3oz) blanched almonds
1 egg yolk
30ml (2 tblsp) water

Cream the lard with the caster sugar and the brown sugar until light and fluffy. Add the egg and almond essence and beat until smooth. Sift the flour, salt and baking powder. Mix the dry ingredients into the creamed mixture. Shape into small balls on a lightly floured surface. Flatten slightly and press an almond into the centre of each one. Place onto a greased baking sheet. Mix the egg yolk with the water. Brush the cookies with the egg glaze. Bake at 180°C, 350°F, Gas Mark 4, for 12-15 minutes.

Sweet Almond Pudding

PREPARATION TIME: 4-5 minutes

COOKING TIME: 6 minutes

175g (6oz) blanched almonds
450ml (¾ pint) water
175g (6oz) sugar
45ml (3 tblsp) rice powder, or ground rice
150ml (¼ pint) milk

Blend the blanched almonds and water in the liquidiser. Put into a pan and bring to the boil. Add the sugar and stir over the heat until the sugar has dissolved. Add the rice slowly to the milk and stir gradually into the simmering sugar and almond mixture. Cook gently until the mixture thickens. Remove from the heat and pour into a serving dish. Serve hot or cold.

Sweet Dumplings

PREPARATION TIME: 10 minutes

COOKING TIME: 15-20 minutes

Oil
75g (3oz) sugar
100g (4oz) plain red bean paste
50g (2oz) desiccated coconut
4 egg whites
15ml (1 tblsp) plain flour
45ml (3 tblsp) cornflour
Icing sugar

Heat 15ml (1 tblsp) oil in a wok and add the sugar, bean paste and coconut. Stir fry for 4-5 minutes until the sugar melts and the paste is smooth and shiny. Fry for a few minutes more and then allow to cool on a dish. Whisk the egg whites until stiff and mix with the plain flour and cornflour to a smooth batter. Beat well. Clean the wok and heat sufficient oil for deep frying. Make 10-12 even-sized balls from the bean paste mixture. Dip each ball into the batter and then

deep fry for 3-4 minutes until golden and crisp. Fry a few at a time and drain on kitchen paper. Dust with icing sugar before serving.

Stuffed Lychees

PREPARATION TIME: 20 minutes

450g (1lb) canned lychees, stones removed
225g (8oz) canned pineapple rings
Few drops vanilla essence or almond essence

Drain the lychees into a bowl, reserving the juice. Drain the pineapple rings and reserve the liquid. Slice each pineapple ring into 2.5cm (½ inch) long strips. Press one or two strips of pineapple into each lychee. Arrange the pineapple-filled lychees in a deep serving dish. Mix the pineapple and lychee liquid with a few drops of essence. Spoon over the stuffed fruits. Serve well chilled. Alternatively, stuff the lychees with maraschino cherries, mango, canned pears, oranges etc.

Facing page: Sweet Dumplings (top), Almond Cookies (centre left) and Date Cake (bottom right).

Chocolate Roulade (above),
Devil's Food Cake (right) and
Family Chocolate Cake (far
right).

COOKING WITH CHOCOLATE

Introduction

Rich, dark and luxuriously smooth and enticing, chocolate remains one of the most popular ingredients for both everyday and exotic desserts, cakes and confectionery. These mouth-watering recipes have been specially selected for their variety as well as their relative ease of preparation: recipes which are bound to delight all those with a passion for chocolate cuisine.

Hints For Cooking With Chocolate
The amount of cocoa butter added to chocolate determines how the chocolate can be used.

Cooking Chocolate
This is not to be confused with cake covering. Cooking chocolate has some cocoa butter replaced with palm kernel oil or coconut oil. Flavourings are used to make the chocolate less expensive and easy to use; it can be used for any chocolate cooking or decoration.

Milk Chocolate
This is rarely used in cooking as it does not give a strong enough flavour, but it can be used for making Easter Eggs and in other recipes that require a delicate flavour.

Couverture
This is a chocolate containing a high proportion of cocoa butter, which gives it a smooth, glossy appearance. Couverture chocolate requires repeated heating and cooling, or tempering; a professional method of working with chocolate.

White Chocolate
This variety has a relatively high sugar content. It is used in some recipes in this book but great care should be taken when using this as it is difficult to melt and has a tendency to go grainy if overheated.

Plain Chocolate
This chocolate has a rich, dark flavour and is used in most recipes where chocolate is called for. Plain eating chocolate can always be used but there are also some varieties of plain chocolate available which are specially recommended for cooking.

Bitter Chocolate
This is not easy to buy but it can be made as required. To make plain chocolate bitter add 5ml (1 tsp) instant coffee powder or granules (or 5ml (1 tsp) cocoa powder) for every 50g (2oz) of chocolate.

Chipped and Grated Chocolate
Chocolate can be chipped and grated either manually or in a food

processor. When grating chocolate, refrigerate for 30 minutes, then hold the chocolate with kitchen paper to prevent it from melting.

Cocoa Powder and Drinking Chocolate
Often used in baking but make sure the lumps are removed. It is best used blended with hot (not boiling) water, so that it forms a smooth paste. Add the paste to the recipe as required.

Melting Chocolate
This should be done carefully as it is particularly important. Break the chocolate into pieces and put in a bowl over a pan of simmering water, or into the top of a double boiler if you have one. When using an electric cooker turn off the heat once the water has boiled. Make sure the bowl fits well into the saucepan so that no steam or water goes into the chocolate. Note: if the chocolate goes solid add a little vegetable oil and beat well.

Microwave Melting
This is a clean and easy way to work with chocolate. Break the chocolate into pieces and put into a suitable bowl. Cover with cling film and melt following the manufacturers instructions. The timing will depend on the quantity of chocolate and the size of the bowl.

Decorating with Chocolate

Chocolate for Dipping
This chocolate has a high proportion of vegetable fat and is less expensive than couverture. Melt the chocolate, which you may find easier to use if you add 15ml (1 tblsp) of vegetable oil to every 175g (6oz) of chocolate.

Chocolate Leaves
These are made by using rose leaves, although any leaves with good strong veins can be used. *Make sure that the leaves you select are not poisonous.* Wash and dry the leaves thoroughly, melt the chocolate and, using a small paintbrush, brush the underside of the leaves with the chocolate. Alternatively you can dip the undersides of the leaves in the chocolate, then place them on non-stick silicone paper or greaseproof paper, chocolate side up. When the chocolate is hard peel off the leaves.

Chocolate Curls
Make sure the chocolate is neither too warm, as it will be too soft to hold a cult, nor too cold, since it will become brittle and may crumble. Using a small knife or even a vegetable peeler make curls by gently shaving the chocolate with the blade.

Craque
To produce these glamorous, long curls, melt the chocolate and spread it with a palette knife onto an ungreased, laminated or marble surface. The chocolate should be 0.5cm (¼ inch) thick. Leave it to set, then scrape it up in curls by holding a knife at an angle of 45° and pushing it away from you.

Shapes
To make shapes, melt and pour the chocolate onto an ungreased, laminated or marble surface then, when set, cut into shapes with a sharp knife.

Cakes and Gateaux

Chocolate Fudge Cake

PREPARATION TIME: 15 minutes

COOKING TIME: 45-50 minutes

OVEN TEMPERATURE: 160°C, 325°F, Gas Mark 3

MAKES: 1 cake, 23cm (9 inches) in diameter

200g (7oz) plain flour
5ml (1 tsp) bicarbonate of soda
5ml (1 tsp) baking powder
30ml (2 tblsp) cocoa powder
150g (5oz) brown sugar
30ml (2 tblsp) golden syrup
2 eggs
150ml (¼ pint) oil
300ml (½ pint) milk

Chocolate Icing
175g (6oz) plain chocolate, grated
30ml (2 tblsp) single cream

To Decorate
Chocolate shavings

Grease and line a 23cm (9 inch) cake tin. Sieve the dry ingredients together in a bowl and add the sugar. Make a well in the centre and add the syrup, eggs, oil and the milk. Beat them all together until smooth. Pour the cake mixture into the cake tin. Bake in the oven for 45 minutes. When cooked, leave the cake in the tin for a few minutes before turning it out onto a wire rack. To make the icing: heat the chocolate and cream in a small, heavy saucepan until melted. Cool the mixture slightly and pour over the cake; drag the surface with a fork when it is nearly dry, and decorate with the chocolate shavings.

Chocolate Spice Cake

PREPARATION TIME: 30 minutes

COOKING TIME: 40-50 minutes

OVEN TEMPERATURE: 180°C, 350°F, Gas Mark 4

MAKES: 1 cake, 20cm (8 inches) in diameter

5 eggs, separated
175g (6oz) caster sugar
75g (3oz) plain chocolate, melted
75g (3oz) plain flour
2.5ml (½ tsp) ground nutmeg

2.5ml (½ tsp) ground cinnamon
2.5ml (½ tsp) ground cloves

Cinnamon Topping
Ground cinnamon
Icing sugar

Butter and line a 20cm (8 inch) spring form cake tin with greaseproof paper (use a tin that has a central funnel). Brush the paper with melted butter and dust with flour. Put the egg yolks and sugar into a mixing bowl and beat

them well until the mixture will fall from the whisk in a thick ribbon. Stir in the melted chocolate. Sieve together the flour, nutmeg, cinnamon and cloves, and fold into the cake mixture. Whisk the egg whites until stiff but not dry. Gently fold in the beaten egg whites, a little at a time. Pour the mixture into the tin. Bake in a pre-heated oven for 40-50 minutes, or until a skewer inserted into the middle comes out clean. Remove the cake from the oven and let it

This page: Chocolate Fudge Cake (top) and Chocolate Almond Cake (bottom).

Facing page: Chocolate Spice Cake (top) and Chocolate Potato Cake (bottom).

Chocolate Roulade (above) and
Chocolate Orange Cake (right).

cool in the tin on a wire rack, for 10 minutes. Turn the cake out to cool completely. Dust the top of the cake with a little ground cinnamon and/or icing sugar.

Chocolate Roulade

PREPARATION TIME: 35 minutes

COOKING TIME: 15-20 minutes

OVEN TEMPERATURE: 180°C 350°F, Gas Mark 4

MAKES: 1 roulade, 23cm (9 inch) long

15ml (1 tblsp) instant coffee
15ml (1 tblsp) hot water
100g (4oz) plain chocolate, chopped or grated

4 eggs, separated
100g (4oz) caster sugar

To Decorate
300ml (½ pint) double cream
Icing sugar

Grease and line a 33x23cm (13x9 inch) Swiss roll tin. Mix the coffee with the hot water and add the chocolate; stand in a bowl over a saucepan of hot water, and stir until the chocolate has melted. Allow the mixture to cool. Whisk together the egg yolks and sugar until thick, then fold into the chocolate mixture. Whisk the egg whites until stiff but not dry, and fold lightly into the mixture. Pour the mixture into the prepared tin. Bake in the oven for 15-20 minutes. Immediately after taking the cake

out of the oven, cover the cake in its tin with a damp tea towel, and leave it to stand overnight. To decorate: carefully turn the cake out onto a sheet of greaseproof paper which has been sprinkled with caster sugar; remove the lining paper. Whip the cream until it holds its shape and spread over the cake (reserve a little for piping). Roll up the cake, like a Swiss roll, and dust it with icing sugar. Pipe the remaining cream down the centre or around the roulade.

Chocolate Orange Cake

PREPARATION TIME: 30 minutes

COOKING TIME: 40 minutes

OVEN TEMPERATURE: 180°C, 350°F, Gas Mark 4

MAKES: 1 cake, 20cm (8 inches) in diameter

225g (8oz) plain flour
75g (3oz) cocoa powder

225g (8oz) butter
275g (10oz) caster sugar
2 eggs, beaten
250ml (8 fl oz) buttermilk

Icing
225g (8oz) butter
Grated rind of 1 orange
225g (8oz) icing sugar, sieved
Juice of ½ an orange

To Decorate
Fresh orange segments or slices

Grease and line two 20cm (8 inch) sandwich tins. Sieve together the cocoa and the flour. Cream the butter and sugar together until light and fluffy; gradually add the beaten eggs. Stir the buttermilk into the mixture, and then fold in the cocoa and flour. Turn the mixture into the prepared tins. Bake for 40 minutes. Remove the cakes from the oven; turn out of the tins and allow to cool on a wire rack. When the cakes are cold, split each cake into two layers. To make the icing: cream the butter with the orange rind until soft; beat in the icing sugar, alternately with the orange juice. Sandwich the cakes together with some of the butter icing and spread the remaining icing on the top and the sides of the cake. "Rough" with a fork and decorate with the orange slices or segments.

283

Austrian Sachertorte

PREPARATION TIME: 40 minutes, plus cooling time

COOKING TIME: 1 hour 15 minutes

OVEN TEMPERATURE: 180°C, 350°F, Gas Mark 4

MAKES: 1 cake, 20cm (8 inches) in diameter

Torte
150g (5oz) plain dark chocolate, grated
15ml (1 tblsp) warm water
150g (5oz) butter
150g (5oz) icing sugar
5 eggs, separated
150g (5oz) self-raising flour
25g (1oz) cornflour
15ml (1 tblsp) rum, or strong black coffee
75ml (5 tblsp) sieved apricot jam

Icing
120ml (4 fl oz) double cream
10ml (2 tsp) brandy
100g (4oz) plain dark chocolate, grated
50g (2oz) milk chocolate, grated
Icing sugar to dust

Grease and flour a 20cm (8 inch) round cake tin. Melt the chocolate in a basin with the warm water. Cream the butter and icing sugar together until light and fluffy. Beat in the chocolate gradually. Beat in the egg yolks one at a time. Sieve together the flour and the cornflour and fold it into the chocolate mixture. Whisk the egg whites until stiff but not dry. Beat a third of the egg whites into the mixture then fold in the remainder. Spoon the mixture into the prepared cake tin. Bake for 50 minutes to 1 hour, until firm to the touch. Turn out and cool on a wire rack. Split the cake in half horizontally, sprinkle with rum or coffee, and sandwich together with 30ml (2 tblsp) apricot jam. Place

Chocolate and Almond Cake

PREPARATION TIME: 45 minutes

COOKING TIME: 40-45 minutes

OVEN TEMPERATURE: 160°C, 325°F, Gas Mark 3

MAKES: 1 cake, 20cm (8 inches) in diameter

175g (6oz) butter or margarine
175g (6oz) caster sugar
100g (4oz) plain chocolate, melted
50g (2oz) ground almonds
4 eggs, separated
50g (2oz) self-raising flour
25g (1oz) cornflour

Icing
30ml (2 tblsp) cocoa powder
30ml (2 tblsp) hot water
75g (3oz) butter or margarine
225g (8oz) icing sugar

To Decorate
50g (2oz) chopped toasted almonds
16 whole almonds, half dipped in melted chocolate

Grease and line two 20cm (8 inch) sandwich tins. Cream the butter and sugar together until light and fluffy. Beat together the melted chocolate, ground almonds, and egg yolks, and add to the butter and sugar mixture. Fold the flour and cornflour into the mixture.

Whisk the egg whites until stiff but not dry; fold into the cake mixture. Divide the mixture between the two tins. Bake in the oven for 40-45 minutes. Turn out and cool on a wire rack. To make the icing: blend the cocoa powder with the hot water. Beat together the butter and icing sugar until well mixed. Mix in the cocoa mixture. Use two-thirds of the icing to sandwich the cakes together, and cover the sides. Put the toasted nuts on a sheet of greaseproof paper and roll the sides of the sandwiched cakes over the nuts. Smooth the remaining icing over the top of the cake. Decorate with the whole almonds, half dipped in melted chocolate.

This page: Humpty Dumpty (top) and Moon Cake (bottom).

Facing page: Loganberry Torte (top) and Austrian Sachertorte (bottom).

the cake on a wire rack. Brush all over with the remaining jam. To make the icing: place the cream in a saucepan with the brandy and bring just to the boil. Add the grated plain dark chocolate and stir until thick and smooth. Pour the chocolate mixture evenly over the cake and leave it to set. Melt the milk chocolate and place in a greaseproof piping bag fitted with a plain "writing" nozzle. Pipe "Sachertorte" across the top. Dust with icing sugar if liked.

Chocolate Raspberry Torte

PREPARATION TIME: 45 minutes

COOKING TIME: 35-40 minutes

OVEN TEMPERATURE: 160°C, 325°F, Gas Mark 3

MAKES: 1 cake, 30cm (12 inches) in diameter

1 recipe Family Chocolate Cake mixture (see recipe)
65ml (2½ fl oz) rum or Framboise
75g (3oz) raspberry jam
450g (1lb) fresh raspberries
Bittersweet Butter Cream (see recipe)
20 chocolate leaves (see recipe)

Chocolate Icing
10ml (2 tsp) oil
25g (1oz) butter
175g (6oz) plain dark chocolate, grated
15ml (1 tblsp) Framboise or rum

Grease and flour a 30cm (12 inch) deep pizza pan. Fill with the cake mixture. Bake until it springs up when pressed on top. Leave to cool in the tin for 5 minutes. Remove from the tin and let the cake cool on a wire rack for at least 2 hours. Slice the cake into two layers, horizontally, using a long knife. Sprinkle the cut surfaces with either the Framboise or rum. Spread one layer of the cake with raspberry jam and then with bittersweet butter cream; sandwich the cake back together again. Turn the cake upside down and chill. To make the icing, put the oil and butter into a saucepan and stir constantly over a medium heat. Let the mixture simmer for a minute.

Remove from the heat and add the chocolate and the Framboise or rum. Whisk until the chocolate has melted and the icing is smooth. Let the icing cool and spread the icing over the top and sides of the cake. Put the raspberries on the top of the cake, in the middle, and put the chocolate leaves round the circle of raspberries. Refrigerate the cake for 1 hour. Note: this cake is best consumed on the day it is made.

Loganberry Torte

PREPARATION TIME: 25 minutes

COOKING TIME: 45 minutes

OVEN TEMPERATURE: 180°C, 350°F, Gas Mark 4

MAKES: 1 cake, 20cm (8 inches) in diameter

4 eggs, separated
100g (4oz) caster sugar
25g (1oz) cocoa powder
50g (2oz) fresh white breadcrumbs
100g (4oz) ground almonds

Filling
60ml (4 tblsp) loganberry jam
150ml (¼ pint) double cream, whipped

To Decorate
Fresh loganberries (or raspberries)
Cocoa powder to dust

Grease and line a 20cm (8 inch) round cake tin. Beat the egg yolks and sugar until thick and fluffy. Sieve the cocoa powder into the breadcrumbs. Fold into the egg yolks. Whisk the egg whites in a large, dry bowl until they are fluffy and stiff. Fold half the egg whites into the cake mixture taking care not to deflate the meringue; fold in the almonds followed by the remaining egg whites. Put the mixture into the prepared cake tin. Bake in the oven for 45 minutes. Cool in the tin for a few minutes, and then turn onto a wire rack to cool. Split the cake in half horizontally. Spread one layer of the cake with the jam, and then with half the whipped cream. Pipe the remaining cream on the top of the cake and garnish with loganberries, or raspberries. Dust the cake with cocoa powder.

Devil's Food Cake

PREPARATION TIME: 35 minutes

COOKING TIME: 1 hour 45 minutes-2 hours

OVEN TEMPERATURE: 150°C, 300°F, Gas Mark 2

MAKES: 1 cake, 20cm (8 inches) in diameter

175g (6oz) butter or margarine
175g (6oz) soft brown sugar
2 eggs, beaten
175g (6oz) golden syrup
50g (2oz) ground almonds
175g (6oz) plain flour
50g (2oz) cocoa powder
150ml (¼ pint) milk
1.25ml (¼ tsp) bicarbonate of soda

American Frosting
1 egg white
175g (6oz) icing sugar
15ml (1 tblsp) golden syrup
45ml (3 tblsp) water
Pinch of salt
5ml (1 tsp) lemon juice

To Decorate
Chocolate curls

Grease and line a 20cm (8 inch) cake tin with greaseproof paper. Cream the butter and sugar together until light and fluffy. Add the eggs gradually, beating well after each addition. Sieve together all the dry ingredients. Add the golden syrup and the milk to the creamed mixture. Fold in the dry ingredients and beat well with a wooden spoon. Pour the mixture into the prepared cake tin. Bake until a skewer inserted in the centre comes out clean. Turn out and cool on a wire rack. To make the frosting: place all the frosting ingredients into a basin over a saucepan of hot water; whisk until the icing stands in peaks. Remove from the heat and continue whisking until the mixture has cooled. Spread over the cake using a palette knife. (The frosting must be used as soon as it is made.) Decorate with the chocolate curls.

Truffle Torte (top) and Chocolate Raspberry Torte (right).

Humpty Dumpty

PREPARATION TIME: 50 minutes

COOKING TIME: 40-50 minutes

OVEN TEMPERATURE: 160°C, 325°F, Gas Mark 3

MAKES: 1 cake

225g (8oz) butter or margarine
225g (8oz) caster sugar
4 eggs, lightly beaten
175g (6oz) self-raising flour
5ml (1 tsp) baking powder
30ml (2 tblsp) cocoa powder
350g (12oz) Butter Icing (see recipe)
Smarties
Liquorice strips
225g (8oz) marzipan

Grease a 600ml (1 pint) pudding basin, and grease and line an 18cm (7 inch) square shallow tin. Cream the butter and sugar together until light and fluffy. Beat in the eggs and then sieve the flour and baking powder into the mixture. Mix the cocoa powder with a little water to make a paste. Mix this into the cake mixture. Put two-thirds of the cake mixture into the pudding basin and the rest into the tin. Bake the pudding cake for 40-50 minutes, and the square cake for 30 minutes. Cool on a wire rack. To ice the cake: cut the square cake in half and then cut each half into 4 rectangles. Using the rectangles of cake as bricks, make a wall 2 bricks high and 4 across, sandwiching them together with butter icing. Spread some of the remaining icing on the top of the wall. Cover the pudding basin cake completely with butter icing and put Humpty's eyes and nose on, using smarties.

Use the liquorice to make a mouth. Roll out the marzipan and shape legs and arms. Fix in position with cocktail sticks. You can even make a little hat, by making a marzipan cup and pulling out a brim.

Chocolate Potato Cake

PREPARATION TIME: 55 minutes, plus cooling time

COOKING TIME: 30 minutes

OVEN TEMPERATURE: 190°C, 375°F, Gas Mark 5

MAKES: 1 two layer cake, 18cm (7 inches) in diameter

100g (4oz) hot mashed potato
30ml (2 tblsp) double cream
200g (7oz) sugar
50g (2oz) plain chocolate, melted
65g (2½oz) unsalted butter, softened
15-20ml (3-4 tsp) bicarbonate of
*   soda*
30ml (2 tblsp) water
3 eggs, separated
100g (4oz) plain flour
5ml (1 tsp) baking powder
2.5ml (½ tsp) rum
50ml (2 fl oz) milk
1.25 (¼ tsp) salt

Cocoa and Rum Icing
40g (1½oz) unsalted butter
225g (8oz) icing sugar
30ml (2 tblsp) cocoa powder
1.25ml (¼ tsp) salt
10ml (2 tsp) rum
22ml (1½ tblsp) strong black coffee

Butter and line two 18cm (7 inch) round sandwich tins with grease-proof paper. Brush the paper with a little melted butter and dust with flour. Mix the mashed potato and cream together in a bowl over a saucepan of hot water. Beat the softened butter and sugar together until soft and creamy. Add the potato and cream mixture to the butter and sugar and stir in the melted chocolate. Dissolve the bicarbonate of soda in the water and add to the mixture. Beat the egg yolks into the mixture one at a time. Sieve together the flour, baking powder and salt. Fold the flour into the mixture, adding the milk and rum alternately. Whisk the egg whites until stiff but not dry. Gently fold in a third of the egg whites, and then fold in the remainder. Divide the mixture between the tins. Bake in a pre-heated oven for 30 minutes, or until a skewer inserted into the centre comes out clean. Leave the

cakes in the tins for 5 minutes before turning them out onto a wire rack to cool. For the icing: beat the butter until soft and creamy. Sieve together the icing sugar, cocoa powder and salt; beat into the butter. Stir in the rum and coffee. Spread a layer of icing on top of one cake and sandwich the cakes together; ice the top and sides of the cake with the remaining icing.

Black Forest Gateau

PREPARATION TIME: 35 minutes

COOKING TIME: 55 minutes

OVEN TEMPERATURE: 160°C, 325°F, Gas Mark 3

MAKES: 1 cake, 18cm (7 inches) in diameter

100g (4oz) plain chocolate, grated
100g (4oz) self-raising flour
25g (1oz) cornflour
Generous pinch salt
150g (5oz) butter, softened
100g (4oz) caster sugar
4 eggs, separated
300ml (½ pint) double cream,
*   whipped*
45ml (3 tblsp) black cherry jam

To Decorate
100g (4oz) plain chocolate, grated

Grease and line an 18cm (7 inch) round cake tin. Melt the chocolate in a basin over hot water. Sieve the flours and salt together. Cream the butter and sugar together until light and fluffy. Add the melted chocolate and egg yolks and beat well. Beat the egg whites until they are stiff and form peaks. Fold the

This page: Chocolate Mushroom Cake (top) and Chocolate Valentine Basket (bottom).

Facing page: Black Forest Gateau (top) and Devil's Food Cake (bottom).

egg whites lightly but thoroughly into the cake mixture. Spoon the mixture into the prepared cake tin. Bake in the oven for 55 minutes. Cool the cake in the tin and then turn it out onto a wire rack. Split

the cake into two, horizontally. Spread one half with the jam and then with a third of the cream; sandwich together with the remaining cake layer. Spread one half of the remaining cream over the top of the cake. Fit a large star nozzle to a piping bag and fill with the remaining cream. Pipe 8 rosettes on the top of the cake. Sprinkle the grated chocolate on the top of the cake. (You can top each rosette of cream with a black cherry, if liked.)

Chocolate Lemon Cake

PREPARATION TIME:	30 minutes
COOKING TIME:	40-45 minutes
OVEN TEMPERATURE:	180°C, 350°F, Gas Mark 4
MAKES:	1 1kg (2lb) cake

175g (6oz) butter or margarine
175g (6oz) soft brown sugar
3 eggs
Grated rind of 1 lemon
225g (8oz) self-raising flour
100g (4oz) plain chocolate, melted

Icing
175g (6oz) butter
450g (1lb) icing sugar, sieved
30ml (2 tblsp) lemon juice

To Decorate
Crystallised orange and lemon slices

Grease and line a 1kg (2lb) rectangular tin or loaf tin. Cream the butter and sugar together until light and fluffy. Beat in the eggs, one at a time, adding a little sieved flour with each egg. Beat in the lemon rind and remaining flour, and then the chocolate. Pour into the prepared tin. Bake in the oven for 40-45 minutes. Turn onto a wire rack to cool. To make the icing: put all the ingredients into a mixing bowl and beat together with a wooden spoon until well mixed. Cut the cake in half and use half the butter cream to sandwich the cake together. Spread the remaining icing on the top of the cake and decorate with crystallised orange and lemon slices.

Chocolate Valentine Basket

PREPARATION TIME:	25 minutes
COOKING TIME:	40-45 minutes
OVEN TEMPERATURE:	160°C, 325°F, Gas Mark 3
MAKES:	1 heart-shaped cake

1 recipe Family Chocolate Cake mixture (see recipe)

Icing
150g (5oz) butter
350g (12oz) icing sugar
15ml (1 tblsp) milk
30ml (2 tblsp) hot water
15ml (1 tblsp) cocoa powder
Sweets for filling

Bake the Family Chocolate Cake mixture in two 20cm (8 inch) heart-shaped sandwich tins, for 40-45 minutes. Leave to cool on a wire rack. Cream the butter and the icing sugar together with the milk. Mix the hot water and cocoa powder into a paste. Add this to the butter mixture and cream well. Fit two piping bags with nozzles; one a ribbon nozzle, and the other a plain writing nozzle. Fill the bags with the butter cream. Hold the ribbon nozzle sideways and pipe three evenly-spaced lines, one above the other, on one of the cakes. The three lines should all be the same length. Pipe a vertical line, using the writing tube, along the edge of the basket weaving. Continue this process until the cake is covered. Cover the outermost edge and the sides of the remaining cake in the same way. This will now be the base, and the completely covered cake the lid. Arrange the lid at an angle on top of the lower cake and fill the inside with sweets.

Moon Cake

PREPARATION TIME:	20 minutes
COOKING TIME:	35 minutes
OVEN TEMPERATURE:	180°C, 350°F, Gas Mark 4
MAKES:	1 cake, 23cm (9 inches) in diameter

This cake is fun to make and to eat. The mixture bubbles during baking and leaves a cake with a rocky, moon-like surface.

200g (7oz) self-raising flour
100g (4oz) granulated sugar
100g (4oz) brown sugar
5ml (1 tsp) salt
60ml (4 tblsp) cocoa powder
75ml (5 tblsp) melted butter
5ml (1 tsp) vanilla essence
5ml (1 tsp) baking powder
15ml (1 tblsp) white wine vinegar
150ml (¼ pint) milk
100g (4oz) marshmallows
Icing sugar

Put the flour, sugar, salt and cocoa directly into a 23cm (9 inch) cake tin and stir well until you have a light brown moon sand texture. Make a big crater in the middle of the sand so you can see the base of the tin, then a medium sized crater somewhere else in the sand, and a smaller crater on the other side (make sure that they are well apart). Spoon the baking powder into the medium sized crater. Spoon the melted butter into the large crater and the vanilla into the smallest crater. Now pour the vinegar into the medium sized crater and it will bubble and foam, and become "volcanic". When this stops, pour the milk over the moon sand and stir well. The sand will now look like mud. Scatter the marshmallows over the surface. Bake for 35 minutes. (Test with a cocktail stick or skewer to see that the cake is done.) Dust with icing sugar and serve from the tin.

Chocolate Mushroom Cake

PREPARATION TIME:	1 hour
COOKING TIME:	3 hours
OVEN TEMPERATURE:	110°C, 225°F, Gas Mark ¼
MAKES:	1 cake, 23cm (9 inches) in diameter

1 recipe Family Chocolate Cake mixture (see recipe)
Icing recipe for Family Chocolate Cake
50g (2oz) white chocolate, melted
3 chocolate flakes
Icing sugar

Meringue Mushrooms
2 egg whites
100g (4oz) caster sugar
Oil for greasing
Cocoa powder
75g (3oz) plain chocolate, melted

Make the Family Chocolate Cake as instructed. Bake as directed and coat with icing. Fill a piping bag fitted with a small writing nozzle with the melted white chocolate. Pipe a spiral of melted white chocolate on top of the cake, working from the middle outwards. Cut the chocolate flakes in half, dust them with icing sugar, and stick them around the sides of the cake to represent bark. To make the meringues: beat the egg whites in a bowl until they are stiff but not dry. Add the sugar slowly, beating well after each addition. Lightly oil a baking tray and cover with greaseproof paper. Fit a piping bag with a 1-2cm (½-¾ inch) plain nozzle. Fill the bag with the meringue mixture. Pipe 12 mushroom stems on half the baking sheet. Lift the bag vertically until the stems are 4-5cm (1½-2 inches) high. Cut the meringue away from the nozzle. Then pipe 12 even rounds of meringue 4-5cm (1½-2 inches) in diameter and 2cm (3-4 inches) thick. (These make the mushroom tops; make sure that they are flat.) Sieve the cocoa powder over the meringues and then bake in a pre-heated oven until they are dried out (about 3 hours). Leave to cool. When the meringues are cool, spread melted chocolate on the underside of each mushroom top and fix the stem onto the chocolate. Leave to cool until the chocolate has set. Remove the mushrooms and stick a few of them on the cake, using a little more melted chocolate. Lay the others around the cake, to be eaten separately.

Chocolate Brandy Snap Gateau

PREPARATION TIME:	40 minutes
COOKING TIME:	25-30 minutes
OVEN TEMPERATURE:	180°C, 350°F, Gas Mark 4
MAKES:	1 gateau, 20 cm (8 inches) in diameter

3 eggs
75g (3oz) caster sugar
15g (½oz) cocoa powder
2.5ml (½ tsp) baking powder
65g (2½oz) plain flour

Filling and Decoration
300ml (½ pint) double cream
100g (3.5oz) packet brandy snaps
25g (1oz) plain chocolate, melted

Grease and line two 20cm (8 inch) sandwich tins. Place the eggs and sugar in a basin and whisk over a saucepan of hot water until thick and pale. Remove from the heat and whisk until cool. Sieve together the cocoa powder, baking powder and flour, and gently fold into the mixture. Divide the mixture between the two prepared tins. Bake for 25-30 minutes. Turn out carefully onto a wire rack and cool. Whip the cream until thick and use a little to sandwich the cakes together. Spread a little cream around the sides and secure the brandy snaps round the edge of the cake. Spread the remaining cream on the top of the cake. Put the melted chocolate into a greaseproof piping bag with a small hole, and drizzle over the cream; swirl it with a skewer.

Chocolate Brandy Snap Gateau (right) and Chocolate Lemon Cake (below).

Truffle Torte

PREPARATION TIME: 1 hour

COOKING TIME: 1 hour 15 minutes

OVEN TEMPERATURE: 180°C, 350°F, Gas Mark 4

MAKES: 1 cake, 18cm (7 inches) in diameter

100g (4oz) unsalted butter, softened
100g (4oz) caster sugar
3 eggs, separated
100g (4oz) plain chocolate, melted
25g (1oz) plain flour
150g (5oz) finely ground hazelnuts

Chocolate Icing
150ml (¼ pint) double cream
150g (5oz) plain chocolate, broken into pieces

Butter and line an 18cm (7 inch) springform cake tin with greaseproof paper. Brush the paper with a little melted butter and dust with flour. Beat the butter until soft and creamy. Add the sugar and continue to beat until light and fluffy. Add the egg yolks, one at a time, and beat well. Stir in the melted chocolate. Sieve together the flour and the ground hazelnuts and fold them into the cake mixture. Beat the egg whites until stiff but not dry. Gently fold in the beaten egg whites. Pour the mixture into the prepared tin. Bake in the pre-heated oven for about 1 hour. (When cooked the cake should be springy to the touch.) Remove from the oven and leave the cake in its tin for 5 minutes. Turn onto a wire rack and cool completely. To make the chocolate icing: put the cream into a saucepan and bring to the boil. Add the chocolate, stirring until the chocolate has melted, and the mixture is thick and smooth. Pour the icing evenly over the cake before it has a chance to set. Decorate with piped chocolate wirls (see Cookies and Confections recipe).

Family Chocolate Cake

PREPARATION TIME: 25 minutes

COOKING TIME: 45-50 minutes

OVEN TEMPERATURE: 160°C, 325°F Gas Mark 3

MAKES: 1 cake, 23cm (9 inches) in diameter

200g (7oz) plain flour
5ml (1 tsp) bicarbonate of soda

5ml (1 tsp) baking powder
30ml (2 tblsp) cocoa powder
150g (5oz) soft brown sugar
30ml (2 tblsp) golden syrup
2 eggs
150ml (¼ pint) oil
150ml (¼ pint) milk

Icing
175g (6oz) plain chocolate, chopped or grated
30ml (2 tblsp) single cream

To Decorate
Walnut halves

Grease and line a 23cm (9 inch) cake tin. Sieve all the dry ingredients together in a large bowl. Put the sugar, syrup, eggs, oil and milk into a well in the centre of the dry ingredients. Beat thoroughly until the mixture is smooth. Pour the mixture into the prepared cake tin. Bake for 45-50 minutes until a skewer inserted in the centre of the cake comes out clean. Leave the baked cake in its tin for a few minutes and turn onto a wire rack to cool. To make the icing: place the chocolate and cream into a small, heavy-based pan and heat gently until melted. Cool slightly and pour evenly over the cake. Decorate with walnuts.

Chocolate Cup Cakes

PREPARATION TIME: 20 minutes

COOKING TIME: 15 minutes

OVEN TEMPERATURE: 180°C, 350°F, Gas Mark 4

MAKES: 18

100g (4oz) soft margarine
100g (4oz) caster sugar
2 eggs
75g (3oz) self-raising flour
25g (1oz) cocoa powder

Fudge Icing
15ml (1 tblsp) golden syrup
450g (1lb) granulated sugar
50g (2oz) unsalted butter
50g (2oz) cocoa powder

Line 2 bun trays with 18 paper cake cases. Put all the cake ingredients into a bowl and beat together with a wooden spoon, until smooth and glossy. Put one small spoonful of the mixture into each of the cake cases. Bake in the centre of the oven for 15 minutes or until they are firm to touch. To make the icing: put the syrup into a saucepan with 250ml (8 fl oz) cold water, the sugar, butter and cocoa powder; stir over a low heat until the sugar dissolves. Boil the mixture until a

little will form a soft ball when dropped into cold water. (Do not stir the mixture, just cut it with a wooden spoon occasionally.) Remove the mixture from the heat and allow it to cool for 10 minutes. Beat it with a wooden spoon until the mixture begins to thicken to a coating consistency. Pour the mixture over the cup cakes and allow it to set. (If the icing sets before it has covered all the cakes, melt it gently.)

Spider's Web

PREPARATION TIME: 50 minutes

COOKING TIME: 35 minutes

OVEN TEMPERATURE: 190°C, 375°F, Gas Mark 5

MAKES: 1 cake, 19cm (7½ inches) in diameter

150g (5oz) self-raising flour
50g (2oz) cocoa powder
2.5ml (½ tsp) bicarbonate of soda
100g (4oz) soft margarine
225g (8oz) dark soft brown sugar
2 eggs
10ml (2 tsp) peppermint essence
25g (1oz) ground almonds
150ml (¼ pint) soured cream

To Decorate
100g (4oz) dark plain chocolate, grated
175g (6oz) icing sugar
1 plain chocolate drop
Green food colouring
Peppermint essence
225g (8oz) Butter Icing (see recipe)
1 liquorice shoe-lace
1 chocolate-covered marshmallow
1 packet white chocolate buttons

Grease and line two 19cm (7½ inch) cake tins. Sieve the flour, cocoa powder and bicarbonate of soda into a bowl and then add all the other ingredients. Mix well

This page: Chocolate Cup Cakes (top) and Family Chocolate Cake – shown with candy covered chocolate sweets – (bottom).

Facing page: Nouvelle – Truffle Cake (top) and Sherry Cream Pie (bottom).

until they are blended. Divide the mixture between the two tins. Slightly hollow out the centres so that the tops will be flat when baked. Bake in the oven for 35 minutes, until a knife inserted through the centre comes out clean. Cool the cakes slightly in their tins and then turn onto a wire rack. Melt half the chocolate in a bowl over a pan of simmering water. Mix the sieved icing sugar with a few drops of water to give a coating consistency. Put the melted chocolate into a piping bag fitted with a small, plain nozzle. Cover the top of one of the cakes with the white icing. Immediately pipe a spiral of chocolate onto the white iced cake, working outwards from the centre. To make the web, mark out 12 lines by drawing a skewer across the icing, from the centre outwards. Put the plain chocolate drop in the centre and leave to set. Add a little green colouring and peppermint essence to the butter icing. Spread some of the green peppermint butter icing over the un-iced cake and place the iced cake on top. Spread some of the remaining green icing around the sides of the cake. Sprinkle the remaining grated chocolate around the sides of the cake. To make the spider: cut the liquorice into 8 equal lengths. Stick each length into the side of the chocolate marshmallow and trim the two front legs, making them a little shorter than the others. Using a little icing, stick two white buttons on the front of the marshmallow for eyes. Put small liquorice trimmings onto the white chocolate drops, fixing them in place with a little more icing. Place the spider on the cake.

Birthday Salute
Tanks

PREPARATION TIME: 45 minutes	
COOKING TIME: 25 minutes	
OVEN TEMPERATURE: 190°C, 375°F Gas Mark 5	

1 recipe Family Chocolate Cake mixture (see recipe)
350g (12oz) Chocolate Butter Icing (see recipe)
1 packet chocolate buttons
6 chocolate flakes

Grease and line an 18cm (7 inch) square cake tin. Fill the tin with the family chocolate cake mixture and spread evenly in the tin. Bake as instructed, then leave to cool on a wire rack. Cut the cake in half. Cut off a piece from each half, measuring 9x5cm (3½x2 inches).

Spider's Web (above) and Birthday Salute (right).

Cover the larger cake pieces with butter icing. Put the smaller pieces of cake on top of the larger pieces of cake, slightly towards the back. Stick 5 chocolate buttons along both of the longer sides of each lower cake. Then put one button on top for the hatch lid. Reserve two chocolate flakes, then cut the rest into short lengths. Lay the short lengths as tracks around the outer edges of the cakes. Push the whole flakes into the front of the smaller cakes to make the gun barrels.

Cannon

PREPARATION TIME: 10 minutes	
COOKING TIME: 12 minutes	
OVEN TEMPERATURE: 200°C, 400°F, Gas Mark 6	

3 eggs
75g (3oz) caster sugar
Vanilla essence
75g (3oz) plain flour
25g (1oz) cocoa powder
22ml (1½ tblsp) warm water
1 recipe Chocolate Butter Icing

To Decorate
Icing sugar
4 large chocolate flakes
Chocolate balls

Grease and line a 23cm (9 inch) Swiss roll tin. Whisk the eggs, sugar, and a few drops of vanilla essence in a bowl over a pan of hot water until pale and thick. (Use an electric whisk if possible.) Sieve together the flour and cocoa powder, and then fold into the egg mixture with the water. Turn the mixture into the prepared tin and spread evenly. Bake for 12 minutes until the cake has risen. Sprinkle some caster sugar onto a sheet of greaseproof paper and turn the cake out onto the paper. Peel off the lining paper which may be stuck to the cake, and trim off any crisp edges that may be around the cake. Lay a piece of greaseproof paper over the top of the cake and roll up the cake with the greaseproof paper inside. Leave to cool on a wire rack. Unroll the cake and remove the paper. Spread with some of the butter icing and re-roll.

Dust the cake with icing sugar. To decorate: fit a star nozzle onto a piping bag and fill with some of the butter cream. Cut the Swiss roll into 12 pieces, then cut 4 of the slices in half. Place two halves side by side, standing them on their flat edges. With a dab of butter cream, attach two whole slices on each of the sides. Pipe stripes of butter icing down the middle of each cannon and lay the flake on it, angled up at one end. Next to the cannon place a pile of chocolate balls, to represent cannon balls.

Chocolate Nut Gateau

PREPARATION TIME: 30 minutes, plus chilling

MAKES: 1 gateau, 18cm (7 inches) in diameter

25g (1oz) butter
15ml (1 tblsp) golden syrup
40g (1½oz) Rice Krispies

Filling
40g (1½oz) cornflour
15ml (1 tblsp) cocoa powder
450ml (¾ pint) milk
150ml (¼ pint) chocolate flavoured yogurt
15ml (1 tblsp) hazelnuts, skinned and roughly chopped

Topping
150ml (¼ pint) hazelnut-flavoured yogurt
75ml (5 tblsp) double cream, whipped

To Decorate
Grated chocolate
8 whole hazelnuts

Melt the butter and syrup in a saucepan. Add the Rice Krispies and mix well until they are coated with the butter syrup. Press the mixture into the base of an 18cm (7 inch) fluted flan ring, placed on a serving plate. Leave to cool. For the filling: mix the cornflour and cocoa powder with a little of the milk. Heat the remaining milk until boiling and pour onto the cornflour mixture, stirring constantly. Return the mixture to the pan and return to the heat; simmer for a few minutes, until thickened. Remove the saucepan from the heat and stir in the chocolate yogurt and chopped hazelnuts. Pour the mixture over the crisp base. For the topping: mix the nut yogurt with the whipped cream and spread it over the

chocolate mixture. Put the flan in the refrigerator and chill until set. Carefully remove the flan ring and decorate with grated chocolate and whole hazelnuts. Serve with chocolate sauce if desired.

Chocolate Pistachio Loaf

PREPARATION TIME: 20 minutes

COOKING TIME: 1 hours 15 minutes-1 hour 30 minutes

OVEN TEMPERATURE: 180°C, 350°F, Gas Mark 4

MAKES: One 450g (1lb) loaf

100g (4oz) self-raising flour
100g (4oz) butter or margarine, softened
50g (2oz) caster sugar
50g (2oz) plain chocolate, chopped
50g (2oz) pistachio nuts, chopped
25g (1oz) ground almonds
2 eggs
30ml (2 tblsp) milk

Icing
175g (6oz) plain chocolate, chopped or grated
A knob of butter

To Decorate
A few pistachio nuts, chopped

Grease and line a 450g (1lb) loaf tin. Put all the cake ingredients into

a mixing bowl and beat until they are well mixed. Pour the mixture into the prepared tin. Bake in a pre-heated oven for 1 hour 15 minutes, or until cooked. Turn the cake out of the tin and leave to cool on a wire rack. For the icing: melt the chocolate in a basin over a pan of hot water; beat the knob of butter (the size of a walnut) into the chocolate and pour evenly over the cake. Sprinkle with chopped pistachio nuts.

Chocolate Knitting

PREPARATION TIME: 45 minutes

COOKING TIME: 40-45 minutes

OVEN TEMPERATURE: 160°C, 325°F, Gas Mark 3

MAKES: 1 cake, 23cm (9 inches) square

1 recipe Family Chocolate Cake mixture (see recipe)
Butter Icing (see recipe)
10ml (2 tsp) cocoa powder
1 packet of sugar strand cake decorations
2 large wooden knitting needles
10 chocolate flakes
25cm (10 inch) square cake board

Bake the family chocolate cake mixture in a 23cm (9 inch) square cake tin, as directed. Cut the cake in half and sandwich the two

halves together using some of the butter icing. Put on the cake board. Mix the cocoa powder with 10ml (2 tsp) boiling water and add this to the remaining butter icing. Mix until smooth. Then add an extra 15ml (1 tblsp) icing sugar to the icing so it will pipe better. Spread some of this icing over the top of the cake. With a warmed knife, cut 4 flakes in half and arrange them along the edge of the cake. Cut 4 flakes into quarters and place them with two pieces alternately, vertically and horizontally. Then cut two flakes into eight and repeat this process. Put the knitting needles into the cake; one goes on top, and the other goes through the centre filling, so that the handles cross. Use the remaining icing to fill a piping bag fitted with a star nozzle. Pipe sticks of icing over the top needle. Sprinkle the sugar strands over the top of the cake in a flaked pattern.

Dart Board

PREPARATION TIME: 45 minutes

COOKING TIME: 35 minutes

OVEN TEMPERATURE: 160°C, 325°F, Gas Mark 3

MAKES: 1 cake, 25cm (10 inches) in diameter

225g (8oz) butter
175g (6oz) soft light brown sugar
4 eggs
175g (6oz) golden syrup
25g (1oz) cocoa powder
225g (8oz) self-raising flour
5ml (1 tsp) mixed ground spice
2.5ml (½ tsp) ground ginger

To Decorate
30cm (12 inch) cake board
45ml (3 tblsp) apricot jam
350g (12oz) Butter Icing (see recipe)
Generous pinch ground ginger
Grated chocolate
1 liquorice wheel
Small darts

Grease and line two 25cm (10 inch) round cake tins. Cream the butter and sugar together; beat in the eggs slowly, followed by the golden syrup. Mix the cocoa powder with a few drops of water and make into a paste. Fold the flour into the cake mixture and then divide the mixture into two. Add the cocoa paste to one portion; sieve the mixed spice and ground ginger into the other portion, and add a little milk if necessary. Spread the two mixtures into their separate tins and hollow out the centres so the cakes will have a flat top when cooked. Bake in a pre-heated oven for 35 minutes. Leave to cool upside down on a wire rack, removing the paper. Put an 18cm (7 inch) round plate on each cake and, using it as a guide, cut out a circle from the middle of each cake. Remove the circles and cut them into 20 even wedges. Put the ginger outer circle on the cake board and put the wedge slices – alternating between chocolate and ginger – in a circular pattern in the centre. Spread the top of the cake with jam and lay the chocolate ring on top of the ginger ring. Then repeat the process with the remaining wedges, reversing the colours to get a chequered effect. Beat the butter icing with the ginger and spread some of it around the sides of the cake. Cover the sides of the cake with grated chocolate. Fill a piping bag fitted with a plain writing nozzle with butter icing. Pipe the numbers on the cake in the correct order. Fit a star nozzle to the piping bag, refill with the remaining butter icing, and pipe shells for the scoring circles. Pipe a line around the top and bottom of the outer edges and stick the liquorice wheel in the centre for the bullseye. Put on the darts for decoration.

Facing page: Chocolate Knitting (top) and Dart Board (bottom).

This page: Chocolate Pistachio Loaf (top) and Chocolate Nut Gateau (bottom).

COOKING WITH CHOCOLATE

Desserts and Pastries

Chocolate Pear Flan

PREPARATION TIME: 25 minutes, plus chilling

SERVES: 4-6 people.

75g (3oz) butter
225g (8oz) plain chocolate digestive biscuits, crushed
425g (14½oz) can of pear halves
10ml (2 tsp) arrowroot

To Decorate
Grated chocolate

Melt the butter in a saucepan and mix with the crushed biscuits. Press the crumb mixture into the base and up the sides of an 18cm (7 inch) loose-bottomed fluted flan tin. Place in the refrigerator to set. Carefully remove the crumb case from the flan tin; leave it on the base, as this will make serving easier. Drain the juice from the pears and reserve it. Arrange the pear halves in the flan case. Mix the arrowroot with half of the pear juice in a small saucepan and bring to the boil. Stir gently until the mixture thickens and clears. Cool slightly and then spoon over the pears. Chill briefly. Sprinkle with grated chocolate and serve with cream.

Chocolate Orange Pudding

PREPARATION TIME: 25 minutes

COOKING TIME: about 1¾ hours

SERVES: 4-6 people

1 recipe Steamed Chocolate Pudding mixture (see recipe)
2 oranges

Make the chocolate pudding mixture as directed. Finely grate the rind of 1 orange and add this to the mixture. Thinly slice the second orange and press the orange circles around the inside of a greased 1 litre (2 pint) pudding basin; put one orange slice in the base. Fill with the pudding mixture. Cover and steam the pudding for about 1¾ hours. Serve with orange sauce or chocolate sauce.

Chocolate Mousse

PREPARATION TIME: 20 minutes, plus chilling time

SERVES: 4-6 people

100g (4oz) plain chocolate, grated
30ml (2 tblsp) water
15ml (1 tblsp) instant coffee

4 egg whites
100g (4oz) caster sugar

To Decorate
A little reserved chocolate

Put most of the chocolate, and the water and coffee into a bowl; stand it over a pan of hot water. Stir the mixture occasionally until the

This page: Chocolate Brandy Cheesecake (top left), Chocolate Orange Pudding (top right) and Chocolate Pear Flan (bottom)

Facing page: Chocolate Eclairs (top) and Chocolate Strudel (bottom).

chocolate has melted and the mixture is smooth. Whisk the egg whites until stiff but not dry, gradually whisking in half the sugar. Mix the remaining sugar into the chocolate mixture and fold in the meringue. Divide the mixture among 4-6 glasses and sprinkle with remaining grated chocolate. Chill briefly.

Strawberry Box

PREPARATION TIME: 50 minutes, plus chilling

SERVES: 6 people

Chocolate Case
225g (8oz) plain chocolate, chopped or grated
15g (½oz) vegetable oil

Filling
175g (6oz) plain chocolate, chopped or grated
15ml (1 tblsp) kirsch
2 egg yolks
150ml (¼ pint) double cream
150ml (¼ pint) single cream

Topping
225g (8oz) strawberries, hulled and halved
45ml (3 tblsp) strawberry jam, sieved
15ml (1 tblsp) kirsch
25g (1oz) plain chocolate, chopped or grated
150ml (¼ pint) double cream

Line either a 15cm (6 inch) square cake tin or an 18cm (7 inch) round cake tin, with a double thickness of foil. (Make sure that the foil comes above the top of the tin to make removal of the set chocolate case easy.) For the chocolate case: melt the chocolate with the vegetable oil; pour two-thirds into the prepared tin and turn and tilt the tin so that the sides and base are coated evenly. Allow the chocolate to set slightly and then repeat the process with the remaining melted chocolate. Leave it in a cool place until the chocolate has set completely. Remove the chocolate case from the tin by pulling the foil lining gently; peel the foil away carefully from the chocolate case. To make the filling: melt the chocolate. Remove from the heat and beat the kirsch and the egg yolks into the chocolate. Whip the double and single creams together until thick and then fold into the chocolate. Pour the chocolate cream into the prepared chocolate case. Chill until set. Arrange the stawberries on the top of the filled case. Bring the jam and the kirsch to the boil together and remove from the heat; allow to cool slightly. Spoon the topping glaze over the strawberries, but do not allow the hot jam to run to the edge of the chocolate case or it will melt. The glaze will set in about 5 minutes. Melt the chocolate and allow it to cool. Whip the double cream until thick and beat in the chocolate. Pipe the chocolate mixture decoratively around the case.

Chocolate Eclairs

PREPARATION TIME: 20 minutes

COOKING TIME: 20-25 minutes

OVEN TEMPERATURE: 220°C, 425°F, Gas Mark 7

MAKES: 10-12

50g (2oz) butter or margarine
150ml (¼ pint) water
65g (2½oz) plain flour, sieved
2 eggs, beaten
175ml (6 fl oz) double cream, whipped

Icing
100g (4oz) plain chocolate, chopped or grated
15g (½oz) butter

Melt the butter (or margarine) in a saucepan over a gentle heat. Add the water and bring it just to the boil. Remove the pan from the heat and add the flour. Beat the mixture well until it leaves the sides of the pan clean. Cool the mixture slightly, and beat in the eggs gradually, beating between each addition. Spoon the mixture into a piping bag fitted with a 1cm (½ inch) plain nozzle. Pipe 7.5cm (3 inch) lengths onto a lightly dampened baking sheet. Bake in a preheated oven for 20-25 minutes until crisp and golden brown. Make a slit in the side of each eclair to allow the steam to escape and cool on a wire rack. Fit a piping bag with a 1cm (½ inch) plain nozzle and spoon the whipped cream into the bag. Pipe the cream into each of the eclairs. Melt the chocolate and butter on a plate over a pan of hot water, stirring until smooth. Dip each eclair into the chocolate to give an even top coating and place on a wire rack to set.

Chocolate Strudel

PREPARATION TIME: 1 hour 30 minutes

COOKING TIME: 40 minutes

OVEN TEMPERATURE: 190°C, 375°F, Gas Mark 5

MAKES: a 36cm (14 inch) strudel

100g (4oz) plain flour
½ a beaten egg
2.5ml (½ tsp) salt
65ml (2½ fl oz) water
A few drops of vinegar
75g (3oz) butter, melted and cooled

Filling
40g (1½oz) butter
50g (2oz) vanilla sugar
2 eggs, separated
40g (1½oz) raisins
65ml (2½ fl oz) double cream
A pinch of ground cinnamon
22ml (1½ tblsp) caster sugar
50g (2oz) plain chocolate, grated
65g (2½oz) chopped walnuts
Icing sugar

Sieve the flour into a large mixing bowl and make a well in the centre. Beat together the egg, salt, water, vinegar and 15ml (1 tblsp) of the melted butter. Pour this mixture into the well. Mix all the ingredients together to a dough. Knead the dough on a well-floured board until smooth and elastic (this will take about 15 minutes). Put the dough into a floured bowl and cover with a cloth. Leave for 15 minutes. While the dough is resting make the filling. Beat together the butter and vanilla sugar until light and fluffy. Add the egg yolks one at a time, beating after each addition. Add the walnuts, cream, cinnamon, chocolate and raisins and mix well. Whisk the egg whites until stiff but not dry, and then gradually whisk in the caster sugar. Fold this mixture gently into the chocolate mixture. Cover the work surface with a large, clean cloth and dust the cloth with flour. Put the dough into the middle of the cloth and brush the top with melted butter. Working around the dough, roll it out to a thickness of 3mm (⅛ inch). Brush it with more butter and, using four hands (you'll need to enlist help!), stretch the dough outwards as thinly as possible. Try to work around the dough so it does not tear. Cut the dough into a rectangle measuring 36x18cm (14x18 inches). Butter a large baking sheet. Spoon the filling onto the strudel pastry, leaving a margin of 5cm (2 inches) around three of the edges. Fold the margins over the filling and brush the remaining pastry with the melted butter. Gently lift the cloth so that the dough rolls itself up. Roll the dough onto the prepared baking sheet. Bake for 40 minutes, basting with melted butter once or twice, until golden and crisp. Remove the strudel from the oven and dust with icing sugar. Serve warm or cold. (Do not be put off by the thought of handling strudel pastry. Although a professionally thin pastry is needed for good results, it is not as difficult to achieve as its reputation would suggest.)

Strawberry Box (top right) and Chocolate Mousse (right).

Chiffon Pie

PREPARATION TIME: 40 minutes, plus chilling

COOKING TIME: 1 hour

OVEN TEMPERATURE: 190°C, 375°F, Gas Mark 5

MAKES: 1 pie, 23cm (9 inches) in diameter

Shortcrust Pastry
225g (8oz) plain flour
30ml (2 tblsp) caster sugar
5ml (1 tsp) salt
50g (2oz) ground almonds
150g (5oz) unsalted butter, cut into pieces
1 egg yolk

Filling
250ml (8 fl oz) milk
120g (4½oz) caster sugar
200g (7oz) plain chocolate, broken into pieces
2 eggs, separated
15ml (1 tblsp) powdered gelatine
45ml (3 tblsp) strong black coffee
350ml (12 fl oz) double cream, whipped

Topping
250ml (8 fl oz) double or whipping cream, whipped
Grated chocolate

To make the pastry: sieve the flour, sugar and salt and add the almonds. Make a well in the centre of the dry ingredients and add the butter and egg yolk. Working quickly, use the fingertips to mix all the ingredients together. Shape the dough into a ball and wrap in foil or cling film. Leave to chill for 1 hour. Roll out the pastry on a floured work surface to a thickness of 3-5mm (⅛-¼ inch) and use to line a 23cm (9 inch) fluted deep pie tin. Cover the pastry with a sheet of greaseproof paper and weight it down with rice or beans. Bake blind in a pre-heated oven for 15 minutes, or until the edges begin to colour. Remove the paper and beans and bake for a further 15 minutes. Leave to cool on a wire rack before removing from the tin. To make the filling: mix the milk, 75g (3oz) of the sugar and the chocolate pieces in a saucepan; cook over a moderate heat. Stir constantly until the chocolate melts. The chocolate mixture should be thick and smooth when removed from the heat. Leave to cool. Whisk the egg yolks into the chocolate mixture. Dissolve the gelatine in the coffee, over a low heat, and stir into the warm

chocolate mixture. Chill until it begins to set. Whisk the egg whites until stiff but not dry. Whisk the remaining sugar into the beaten egg whites until stiff and glossy. Gently fold the egg whites into the chocolate mixture, followed by the whipped cream. Pour the mixture into the pie shell. Decorate with whipped cream and grated chocolate.

Chocolate Terrine with Cherry Sauce

PREPARATION TIME: 40 minutes, plus freezing

COOKING TIME: about 8 minutes

MAKES: 1 1¼kg (3lb) terrine

225g (8oz) plain chocolate, chopped or grated
225g (8oz) unsalted butter
100g (4oz) caster sugar
50g (2oz) icing sugar
50g (2oz) cocoa powder
100g (4oz) granulated sugar
150g (¼ pint) water
4 egg yolks, beaten
300ml (½ pint) double cream
100g (4oz) pitted black cherries

Sauce
30ml (2 tblsp) cornflour
300ml (½ pint) water
450g (1lb) pitted black cherries
100g (4oz) granulated sugar
60ml (4 tblsp) kirsch

Grease a 1¼kg (3lb) loaf tin, and line with greased greaseproof paper. Melt the chocolate in a bowl over a pan of hot water; remove from the heat and cool. Cream the butter and caster sugar until light and fluffy. Sieve the icing sugar and cocoa together and beat into the butter mixture; beat in the cooled melted chocolate. Put the granulated sugar and water into a small, heavy-based pan and stir over a gentle heat until the sugar has dissolved. Boil quickly to 110°C (225°F) on a sugar thermometer. Beat the egg yolks in a basin and add the sugar syrup; whisk into a mousse-like consistency. Beat into the butter and chocolate mixture. Whip the cream and lightly fold it into the mixture. Fold in the pitted cherries and turn the mixture into the prepared tin. Freeze for 6 hours or until firm.

Cherry Sauce
Blend the cornflour with 45ml (3

tblsp) water in a small bowl. Put the cherries into a pan with the remaining water and sugar and bring to the boil. Remove the pan from the heat and stir in the cornflour mixture. Bring back to the boil, stirring continuously. Remove from the heat and add the kirsch. Serve the Chocolate Terrine in slices, accompanied by the hot cherry sauce.

Banana and Chocolate Trifle

PREPARATION TIME: 30 minutes

SERVES: 6 people

1 packet pineapple jelly
3 bananas
1 chocolate Swiss roll
15ml (1 tblsp) cornflour
30ml (2 tblsp) caster sugar
600ml (1 pint) milk
30ml (2 tblsp) cocoa powder
150ml (¼ pint) double cream

To Decorate
4 glace cherries

Make up the jelly, following the instructions on the packet. As the jelly is about to set, slice two bananas and stir them into the jelly. Pour into a pretty glass dish. When the jelly has cooled (but not set), cut the Swiss roll into eight pieces and arrange the slices around the sides of the dish, standing up in the jelly. Mix the cornflour and the sugar with a little of the milk; add the cocoa powder and mix well. Add the remaining milk. Put the chocolate mixture into a small saucepan and boil for a few minutes, stirring until it thickens. Leave to cool. Lightly whip the cream and fold into the cold custard. Pour the mixture into the dish on top of the jelly. Before serving, decorate the top of the trifle with slices of the remaining banana and the glace cherries.

This page: Chocolate Terrine with Cherry Sauce (top) and Tarte au Chocolat (bottom).

Facing page: Banana and Chocolate Trifle (top) and Chiffon Pie (bottom).

Chocolate Rum Fool

PREPARATION TIME: 20 minutes, plus chilling

SERVES: 4-6 people

75g (3oz) raisins
60ml (4 tblsp) dark rum
225g (8oz) cold cooked potato
50g (2oz) caster sugar
200g (7oz) plain chocolate cake
  covering
225g (8oz) butter
150ml (¼ pint) double cream

Soak the raisins in the rum for one hour. Sieve the potato and beat in the rum-soaked raisins and the sugar. Melt the chocolate and the butter together. Remove from the heat and beat into the potato mixture. Whip the cream until thick, and gently fold two-thirds of it into the mixture. Turn the mixture into a serving dish and chill in the refrigerator for at least one hour. Decorate with the remaining cream when ready to serve.

Chocolate and Cherry Mousse

PREPARATION TIME: 35-40 minutes, plus chilling

SERVES: 6 people

Cherry Mousse
350g (12oz) pitted cherries, fresh or
  canned
7.5ml (1½ tsp) gelatine powder
30ml (2 tblsp) cold water
50g (2oz) caster sugar
2 eggs, separated
150ml (¼ pint) double or whipping
  cream

Chocolate Mousse
175g (6oz) plain chocolate, chopped
  or grated
10ml (2 tsp) instant coffee
15ml (1 tblsp) water
4 eggs, separated
150ml (¼ pint) double or whipping
  cream

To Decorate
150ml (¼ pint) whipped cream
A few whole cherries

Rub the cherries through a sieve, or puree them in a blender or food processor. Sprinkle the gelatine over the cold water and leave in a basin to soften for a few minutes; dissolve the gelatine over a pan of simmering water. Remove from the heat and cool. Whisk the sugar and egg yolks together until thick and creamy and then whisk in the gelatine; stir in the cherry puree

and mix well. Whisk the egg whites in a dry bowl until stiff but not dry. Whip the cream lightly until it holds its shape and then fold the cream gently into the cherry mixture. Fold the egg whites into the cherry mixture lightly but thoroughly. Pour into 6 individual serving dishes and chill for 30 minutes. For the chocolate mousse: melt the chocolate with the coffee and the water. Remove from the heat and beat in the egg yolks. Whip the cream lightly until it holds its shape, then whisk the egg whites in a separate bowl until stiff but not dry. Fold the cream into the chocolate mixture and then the egg whites. Pour the chocolate mousse over the chilled cherry mousse and chill for at least an hour. Decorate with whipped cream and cherries before serving.

Chocolate Quiche

PREPARATION TIME: 30 minutes, plus chilling time

COOKING TIME: about 1 hour

OVEN TEMPERATURE: 190°C, 375°F, Gas Mark 5 and then 180°C, 350°F, Gas Mark 4

SERVES: 10 people

100g (4oz) self-raising flour
Pinch of salt
100g (4oz) ground almonds
150g (5oz) butter
1 egg yolk
Cold water

Filling
500g (1lb 2oz) cooking chocolate,
  grated
750ml (1¼ pints) double cream
7 egg yolks

Mix the flour, salt and almonds in a bowl. Add the butter in small pieces and rub into the texture of crumbs. Beat the egg yolk with 30ml (2 tblsp) of water. Add to the crumble mixture and mix to a firm dough, adding a little extra water if required. Shape the dough into a ball; wrap and chill in the refrigerator. Flour a pastry slab or work surface and roll out the dough; use to line a large loose-bottomed flan tin, 30cm (12 inches) in diameter. Line the pastry with greaseproof paper and beans and bake "blind" at the higher temperature for 10 minutes. Remove the paper and beans and bake for a further 3 minutes. Leave to cool. Melt the chocolate and cool slightly. Beat the cream and the egg yolks until they are well blended, and add the melted chocolate. Pour into the pastry case. Bake for 45 minutes, at the

lower temperature, until the top is firm to the touch. Allow the quiche to cool a little, and then serve in small portions with whipped cream and/or fruit.

Nouvelle – Truffle Cakes

PREPARATION TIME: 40 minutes

COOKING TIME: 18-20 minutes

OVEN TEMPERATURE: 190°C, 375°F, Gas Mark 5

MAKES: 6

This is a very rich, sophisticated dessert, ideal for special occasions.
5 eggs, separated
40g (1½oz) granulated sugar
40g (1½oz) self-raising flour
25g (1oz) cocoa powder
5ml (1 tsp) baking powder
Pinch salt
30ml (2 tblsp) melted unsalted butter
75g (3oz) dark plain chocolate,
  melted
Cocoa powder
Rum, Grand Marnier or Amaretto
  liqueur
150ml (¼ pint) double cream, well
  chilled
Icing or vanilla sugar
1 recipe Nouvelle Chocolate Sauce
  (see recipe)
100g (4oz) split almonds, lightly
  toasted, and broken into pieces

To make the cake mixture: butter and flour six 10cm (4 inch) individual souffle dishes. Line the base of each dish with buttered greaseproof paper. Put the egg yolks and half the sugar into a bowl and beat well, preferably with an electric beater, until the eggs are thick and pale. Sieve the flour, cocoa, baking powder and salt together. Whisk the egg whites until stiff but not dry, gradually adding the remaining sugar. Fold the flour and melted butter alternately into the egg yolk mixture. Fold in the whisked egg whites lightly but thoroughly. Divide the mixture among the prepared dishes. Stand them on a baking sheet and bake for 18-20 minutes, or until a skewer inserted in the centre comes out clean. Take the cakes out of the oven and let them cool in their dishes. Remove them from their dishes, right way up, and cool on a wire rack. Trim the cakes a little so that they are rounded. Brush the tops and sides of the cakes with the melted chocolate and let it harden slightly before rolling them in the cocoa powder. Dig a little hole in the top of each cake. Sprinkle the inside of each cake with some of the liqueur

you have chosen. About 30 minutes before serving, whip the cream until thick and flavour it with icing or vanilla sugar and more of the chosen liqueur. Fit a piping bag with a small rosette nozzle and fill with the cream. Fill the little hole in each cake with the cream and place the truffle cake hole side down on a small plate. Pipe a small rosette of cream to decorate each cake. Mix the Nouvelle Sauce with the almonds: spoon it around the bottom of each cake, and a little over the top.

Chocolate and Cherry Mousse (right) and Chocolate Quiche (below).

Tarte au Chocolat

PREPARATION TIME: 25 minutes, plus chilling

COOKING TIME: 45 minutes

OVEN TEMPERATURE: 190°C, 375°F, Gas Mark 5

MAKES: 1 tart, 25cm (10 inches) in diameter

225g (8oz) plain flour
5ml (1 tsp) salt
50g (2oz) ground almonds
30ml (2 tblsp) caster sugar
150g (5oz) unsalted butter
1 egg yolk

Filling
200ml (⅓ pint) double cream
22ml (1½ tblsp) brandy
200g (7oz) plain chocolate, chopped or grated
2 egg whites, beaten
50g (2oz) caster sugar

Topping
300ml (½ pint) double cream
22ml (1½ tblsp) caster sugar
Praline (see recipe) or grated chocolate

Grease and line a 25cm (10 inch) flan tin with greaseproof paper. Sieve together the flour and salt and add the almonds and sugar; make a well in the centre. Add the butter and egg yolk. Mix all the ingredients together, using the fingertips, to form a dough. Shape the dough into a ball and wrap in foil or cling film. Chill for 1 hour. Roll the dough out on a floured work surface to about 3-5cm (⅛-¼ inch) thick. Use the dough to line the prepared flan tin. Cover with greaseproof paper and weight it down with rice or beans. Bake "blind" for 10-15 minutes until it begins to turn pale golden. Remove the paper and beans and bake for a further 15 minutes. Leave the flan case to cool in its tin. To make the filling: put the cream and brandy into a saucepan and bring just to the boil. Add the chocolate and stir until the mixture is thick and smooth. Leave to cool for at least 1 hour. Whisk until fluffy. Whisk the egg whites until stiff but not dry, adding the sugar slowly. Fold the meringue into the chocolate mixture. Remove the pastry case from its tin and fill it with the chocolate mixture. For the topping: whisk the cream with the sugar until it is light and fluffy, and then spread it over the chocolate filling. Decorate with crushed praline or chocolate.

Chocolate Honeycomb

PREPARATION TIME: 20 minutes, plus chilling

SERVES: 4-6 people

15g (½oz) gelatine
3 eggs, separated
50g (2oz) caster sugar
450ml (¾ pint) milk
75g (3oz) plain dark chocolate, grated
Vanilla essence

Put the gelatine, sugar and egg yolks into a basin and beat until creamy. Heat the milk in a small saucepan; add the grated chocolate to it and stir until dissolved. Pour the chocolate milk over the beaten egg yolk and gelatine mixture; put the bowl over a pan of gently simmering water and stir continuously until the mixture is thick. Leave the mixture to cool. Add a few drops of vanilla essence to the thickened chocolate mixture. Whisk the egg whites until stiff but not dry and fold in. Turn the mixture into a dampened mould and chill until set. Unmould carefully before serving.

Marbled Rum Cream Pie

PREPARATION TIME: 35 minutes, plus chilling

COOKING TIME: 10 minutes

SERVES: 6-8 people

225g (8oz) caster sugar
A pinch of salt
60ml (4 tblsp) water
15ml (1 tblsp) gelatine
2 eggs, separated
175ml (6 fl oz) milk
60ml (4 tblsp) dark rum
350g (12oz) plain chocolate, finely chopped
250ml (8 fl oz) double or whipping cream
5ml (1 tsp) vanilla essence
1 baked sweet shortcrust pastry flan case, 23cm (9 inches) in diameter

Mix 50g (2oz) of the sugar with the salt, water and gelatine in a small, heatproof bowl; stand over a pan of simmering water and stir until the gelatine has dissolved. Remove the bowl from the heat and beat in the egg yolks, milk and rum. Return to the heat, and continue to beat until

the mixture has thickened slightly. Remove from the heat and stir in the chocolate until it has melted. Chill until thickened but not set. Beat the egg whites until stiff but not dry and gradually beat in 100g (4oz) of the remaining sugar. Fold the meringue mixture into the chilled chocolate mixture. Whip the cream with the remaining sugar and vanilla essence until thick. Pile alternate spoons of cream and chocolate mixture into the cold cooked pastry flan case. Cut through the layers with a knife, to give a marbled effect. Chill well until firm.

Sherry Cream Pie

PREPARATION TIME: 30 minutes, plus chilling time

COOKING TIME: 35 minutes

OVEN TEMPERATURE: 190°C, 375°F, Gas Mark 5

MAKES: 1 flan, 20cm (8 inches) in diameter

150g (5oz) plain flour
50g (2oz) caster sugar
75g (3oz) butter
1 egg yolk

Filling
225g (8oz) plain dark chocolate, chopped or grated
45ml (3 tblsp) medium sherry
5ml (1 tsp) gelatine
4 eggs, separated

To Decorate
50g (2oz) plain dark chocolate, melted
150ml (¼ pint) double cream
15ml (1 tblsp) sherry

Put the flour and the sugar into a bowl; add the butter, cut into small pieces, and egg yolk. Knead to a smooth dough. Wrap the dough and chill for 30 minutes. Lightly flour the work surface and roll out the dough; use to line a 20cm (8 inch) loose-bottomed flan tin. Prick the base of the flan with a fork. Line with greaseproof paper and baking beans. Bake for 15 minutes; remove the paper and beans and bake for a further 15 minutes. Remove the pastry case from the tin and cool on a serving plate or platter. Put the chocolate into a small, heavy-based saucepan with the sherry and 30ml (2 tblsp) cold water. Sprinkle the gelatine over the top and stir over a low heat until the gelatine has dissolved. Beat the egg yolks into the sauce,

one at a time, and cool the mixture. Whisk the egg whites until stiff but not dry and then fold it into the sauce. Pour the mixture into the prepared flan case and chill until set. Melt the chocolate. Lightly whip the double cream. Divide the cream in half; stir the sherry into one half, and the chocolate into the other. Fit two piping bags with star nozzles and fill each bag with a different cream. Decorate the top of the pie with alternate stars of the different creams.

Steamed Chocolate Pud

| **PREPARATION TIME:** 25 minutes |
| **COOKING TIME:** 1¾-2 hours |
| **SERVES:** 6 people |

225g (8oz) caster sugar
225g (8oz) butter
4 eggs, beaten
175g (6oz) self-raising flour
50g (2oz) cocoa powder
30ml (2 tblsp) rum

Butter a 1 litre (2 pint) pudding basin. Beat the sugar and butter together until light and fluffy. Add the eggs gradually, beating well after each addition. Fold in the sieved flour and cocoa and the rum and mix well. Turn the mixture into the greased pudding basin. Cover the top with a double thickness of greaseproof paper or foil, making a pleat in the top to give room for the pudding to rise. Tie round with string. Steam for 1¾-2 hours until well risen and spongy to the touch.

Unmould the pudding and serve hot with a sauce of your choice.

Facing page: Marbled Rum Cream Pie (top) and Chocolate Honeycomb (bottom).

This page: Steamed Chocolate Pud (top) and Chocolate Rum Fool (bottom).

COOKING WITH CHOCOLATE

Fruits and Fantasies

Chocolate Dipped Pineapple with Melba Sauce

PREPARATION TIME: 40 minutes, plus chilling	
SERVES: 6-8 people	

1 good sized fresh pineapple
Rum
100g (4oz) granulated sugar
450g (1lb) raspberries
175g (6oz) bitter chocolate, chopped or grated

Peel and slice the pineapple into rings, 1cm (½ inch) thick. Sprinkle the slices first with the rum, and then with a little sugar. Cover and chill for at least one hour. Puree the raspberries and sieve them to remove the seeds. Sweeten with a little sugar to taste and add a little rum. Chill until needed. Melt the chocolate in a bowl over a saucepan of hot water. Remove the pineapple from the refrigerator and pat dry with absorbent paper. Cover a baking sheet with waxed paper and partially dip each ring of pineapple into the melted chocolate. Leave on the waxed paper to harden (you can put them in the refrigerator). Put each pineapple ring onto an individual plate and pour a pool of melba sauce over just before serving.

Chocolate Souffle with Sour Cherries

PREPARATION TIME: 40 minutes	
COOKING TIME: 10-12 minutes	
OVEN TEMPERATURE: 200°C, 400°F, Gas Mark 6	
SERVES: 6 people	

100g (4oz) caster sugar
3 eggs, separated
Vanilla essence
Grated rind of half a lemon
5 egg whites
5ml (1 tsp) instant mashed potato powder
Melted butter for greasing
Sugar to dust
5ml (1 tsp) arrowroot
375g (13oz) can sour cherries

Beat 25g (1oz) of the sugar with the egg yolks, vanilla essence and lemon rind. Whisk the egg whites with the remaining sugar until stiff but not dry; whisk in the potato powder. Fold the snowy egg whites into the egg yolk mixture. Brush the surface of a metal serving dish with melted butter and sprinkle with a little sugar. Put ¾ of the souffle mixture into the dish with a spatula and smooth it out into a boat shape, hollowing out the middle. Fit a piping bag with a star nozzle and fill with the remaining souffle mixture. Pipe a border around the top and bottom of the boat. Bake in the oven for 10-12 minutes. Drain the canned cherries and keep the juice. Mix the juice

This page: Locksmiths Lads (top) and Banana Fritters with Chocolate Rum Sauce (bottom).

Facing page: Chocolate Souffle with Sour Cherries (top) and Chocolate Dipped Pineapple with Melba Sauce (bottom).

with the arrowroot and stir over a low heat until it thickens. Add most of the cherries. Fill the top of the souffle with the reserved cherries. Serve the cherry sauce separately. Note: the metal of the dish will conduct the heat evenly through the souffle.

Chocolate Waffles and Fruit Kebabs

PREPARATION TIME: 15 minutes

COOKING TIME: 15 minutes

SERVES: 4 people

50g (2oz) plain chocolate, chopped or grated
50ml (2 fl oz) water
75g (3oz) unsalted butter
2 eggs
75-90g (3-3½oz) sugar
175g (6oz) plain flour
10ml (2 tsp) baking powder
120ml (4 fl oz) milk
75g (3oz) chopped walnuts
Whipped cream or ice cream to serve

Stir the chocolate and water together in a small, heavy-based saucepan until the chocolate melts. Remove the pan from the heat when the chocolate forms a paste. Beat the butter into the melted chocolate, and then add the eggs and the sugar. Sieve the flour and baking powder onto a sheet of greaseproof paper. Add the sieved flour and milk alternately to the chocolate mixture. Stir in the walnuts. Pour the batter into a hot, oiled waffle iron. Bring the cover down and cook for 2-3 minutes on either side. Serve with whipped cream, ice cream, and cocktail sticks threaded with pieces of fresh fruit.

Banana Fritters with Chocolate Rum Sauce

PREPARATION TIME: 20 minutes, plus standing time

COOKING TIME: 14-15 minutes

SERVES: 6 people

Almost any kind of fruit can be battered, and the accompanying sauces that can be used range from fruit purees to liqueured sauces, like the rum sauce in this recipe.

150g (5oz) flour
150ml (¼ pint) white wine
2 eggs, separated
15g (½oz) drinking chocolate
15g (½oz) caster sugar
6 bananas
Oil for deep frying
Icing sugar for dusting

Sauce
100g (4oz) butter
100g (4oz) caster sugar
A pinch of salt
30ml (2 tblsp) dark rum
50g (2oz) cocoa powder
150ml (¼ pint) double cream
5ml (1 tsp) vanilla essence

Sieve the flour into a bowl and whisk in the wine, egg yolks and drinking chocolate. Beat until smooth and let the batter stand for 15 minutes. Whisk the egg whites and sugar until fluffy. Fold the fluffy egg whites into the batter. Slice the bananas into bite-sized pieces. Put each piece onto a fork and dip into the batter. Lower immediately into the hot oil, frying until the batter is golden brown. Lift out of the oil with a slotted spoon and leave to drain on a piece of absorbent paper. Dust with icing sugar and serve with the sauce. To make the sauce: melt the butter in a small saucepan. Stir in the sugar, salt, rum and cocoa powder. Mix well over a low heat. Add the cream and bring to the boil. Simmer very gently for 5 minutes. Remove from the heat and add the vanilla essence. Note: you can use fresh butter to fry the fritters and this will give a very rich flavour, unlike lard or vegetable oil, which are usually well refined, and will not alter the natural flavour of the ingredients. The crisper the better, but be careful not to burn the fritters. You may have a tempura set which can be used when entertaining informally, or a thermostatically controlled deep fat fryer which will give you perfect results.

Locksmiths Lads
Beignets De Prunes Au Chocolat

PREPARATION TIME: 35 minutes

COOKING TIME: about 4 minutes

SERVES: 4 people

150g (5oz) plain flour
2 eggs, separated
150ml (¼ pint) white wine
A pinch of salt
30ml (2 tblsp) cooking oil
25g (1oz) caster sugar
16 large tenderised prunes
16 blanched almonds
Oil for deep frying
50g (2oz) grated chocolate
Icing sugar to dust

Zabaione Sauce
3 egg yolks
1 whole egg
120g (4½oz) caster sugar
90ml (6 tblsp) marsala

Sieve the flour into a mixing bowl; make a well in the centre and pour in the egg yolks, white wine, salt and the oil. Mix well using a wire whisk, and leave the batter to stand for 20 minutes. Whisk the egg whites until stiff and fold in the sugar. Fold the egg whites into the batter. Carefully remove the stone from each prune and replace it with an almond. Spike the prunes with a fork and dip them into the batter. Fry the coated prunes in hot oil until they are golden brown; remove and drain them on absorbent paper. Scatter the grated chocolate over the prunes when they are nearly cold. Dust with icing sugar. To make the sauce: cream the egg yolks, whole egg and sugar together in a heatproof bowl over a saucepan of simmering water. Add the marsala to the

mixture and beat it with a balloon whisk until it doubles in volume, and is foamy. Serve immediately with the Locksmiths Lads.

Strawberry Shortcake

PREPARATION TIME: 15 minutes

COOKING TIME: 7-10 minutes

OVEN TEMPERATURE: 230°C, 450°F, Gas Mark 8

SERVES: 6 people

A wonderful dessert for the summer, with a luxurious topping.

225g (8oz) plain flour
10ml (2 tsp) baking powder
50g (2oz) butter
25g (1oz) caster sugar
1 egg, lightly beaten
Milk
350g (12oz) strawberries, hulled
300ml (½ pint) double cream
1 recipe Chocolate Fudge Sauce (see recipe)

Chocolate Waffles and Fruit Kebabs (top right) and Strawberry Shortcake (right).

Sieve the flour and baking powder into a mixing bowl. Rub the butter into the mixture until it resembles breadcrumbs. Stir in the sugar. Add the beaten egg, and enough milk to bind the mixture into a stiff scone dough. Roll out the dough to a thickness of approximately 1cm (½ inch) and cut out two circles. Put the circles of dough onto greased baking sheets. Bake for 10 minutes (the shortcakes should be pale golden). Cool on a wire rack. Slice 225g (8oz) of the strawberries and whip the cream. Place one circle of the shortcake on a plate. Spoon half of the cream onto it and top with the sliced strawberries. Add a little more cream and place the second shortcake on top. Top the shortcake with spoonfuls of the remaining cream and the remaining strawberries. Drizzle over a little chocolate fudge sauce. Serve the remaining sauce separately.

Strawberry Fondue

PREPARATION TIME: 50 minutes

COOKING TIME: 20 minutes

SERVES: 6 people

Stand
*Oasis cone (from a florist) 30-38cm
    (12-15 inches) high
Kitchen foil
Dress net
Ribbon bows*

*1kg (2lb) large strawberries, washed
    and hulled
Cocktail sticks*

Vanilla Fondue
*375g (12oz) white chocolate, grated
85ml (3 fl oz) evaporated milk
1.25ml (¼ tsp) vanilla essence*

Grand Marnier Fondue
*175g (6oz) plain chocolate, grated
175g (6oz) milk chocolate, grated
200ml (7 fl oz) double cream
30ml (2 tblsp) Grand Marnier*

To make the stand: cover the oasis with kitchen foil and then cover it with the dress net (use a colour that will go with the strawberries and with your table decoration). Place ribbon bows at random, fixing them into the oasis. Stick the strawberries into the stand, using cocktail sticks, so that they almost cover the cone completely. To make the vanilla fondue: melt the white chocolate with ⅔ of the evaporated milk in a pan over a low heat. Add the vanilla essence and then add the remaining evaporated milk as required. (The fondue should coat the back of a spoon.) To make the Grand Marnier fondue: melt together the chocolates and then add the cream. Stir well and remove from the heat. Finally add the liqueur. Pour the two fondues into separate warmed bowls. Keep these on a warming tray, or fondue tray, or on stands with night light candles beneath. Your guests can then pick strawberries and dip them into the fondues.

Chocolate Apricot Horns

PREPARATION TIME: 15 minutes

COOKING TIME: 15-20 minutes

OVEN TEMPERATURE: 220°C, 425°F, Gas Mark 7

MAKES: 10

*225g (8oz) puff pastry
Beaten egg to glaze
100g (4oz) plain chocolate
15g (½oz) butter
30ml (2 tblsp) brandy
175ml (6 fl oz) apricot puree
175ml (6 fl oz) double cream,
    whipped*

To Decorate
Chocolate curls

Roll out the pastry into a rectangle about 25x33cm (10x13 inches) and trim the edges. Cut into strips 2.5cm (1 inch) wide. Dampen one long edge of each strip with water and wind round a metal cornet mould (start at the point and overlap the dampened edge as you go). Put the horns on a lightly dampened baking sheet and chill for 15 minutes. Brush the horns with beaten egg and bake for 15-20 minutes until golden brown. Leave for 5 minutes, before carefully removing the moulds; cool the pastry horns on a wire rack. Melt the chocolate with the butter on a plate, over a pan of hot water; dip each of the horns into the chocolate. Mix the brandy with the apricot puree and spoon a little into each of the horns. Fit a star nozzle to a piping bag and fill the piping bag with the whipped cream. Pipe the cream into the horns. Decorate with chocolate curls.

Profiteroles Vine

PREPARATION TIME: 30 minutes, plus cooling

COOKING TIME: 25-30 minutes

OVEN TEMPERATURE: 200°C, 400°F, Gas Mark 6

SERVES: 4-6 people

Choux Pastry
*150ml (¼ pint) water
50g (2oz) butter
65g (2½ oz) flour, sieved
2 eggs, beaten*

Filling
*30ml (2 tblsp) instant custard
    powder
15ml (1 tblsp) cocoa powder
15ml (1 tblsp) caster sugar*

*300ml (½ pint) milk
150ml (¼ pint) double cream,
    whipped
175g (6oz) plain chocolate, melted
Chocolate Butter Sauce (see recipe)*

For the pastry: heat the water and butter in a small saucepan until the butter melts. Bring to the boil; remove the pan from the heat and beat in the flour. Beat with a wooden spoon until it leaves the sides of the pan clean. Cool the mixture slightly, and gradually beat in the eggs, beating between each addition. (The mixture should be smooth and glossy.) Fill a piping bag fitted with a large plain nozzle with the choux pastry. Pipe 20 even-sized balls onto two dampened baking sheets. Bake in a pre-heated oven for 20-25 minutes, until well risen. Split each of the choux balls and let the steam escape; return to the oven for a further 2 minutes. To make the filling: mix the custard powder, cocoa and sugar with a little of the milk. Boil the remaining milk and stir it into the custard powder. Rinse the saucepan. Return the custard to the pan and cook for a few minutes. Beat the custard well with a wooden spoon, and pour it into a bowl to cool (cover the bowl with cling film so that a skin does not form as the custard cools). Stir the cream into the custard, making sure that there are no lumps (whisk if necessary). Fill a large piping bag, fitted with a plain nozzle, with the custard cream and fill the choux buns. To decorate and serve: coat a large leaf with melted chocolate; pipe a few curls and a stem onto a sheet of silicone paper. Leave them to set; gently peel off the paper and the leaf. Arrange the profiteroles to look like a bunch of grapes on a large serving tray or dish; add the chocolate leaf, stem and curls. Finally pour over the chocolate sauce.

This page: Strawberry Fondue (with Grand Marnier Fondue).

Facing page: Profiteroles Vine (top) and Chocolate Apricot Horns (bottom).

COOKING WITH CHOCOLATE
Frozen Desserts

Mocha Ice Cream

PREPARATION TIME: 25 minutes, plus freezing

SERVES: 6 people

30ml (2 tblsp) instant coffee granules
50g (2oz) butter
100g (4oz) soft brown sugar
60ml (4 tblsp) cocoa powder
75ml (5 tblsp) water
450ml (¾ pint) canned evaporated milk, chilled

Put the coffee, butter, sugar, cocoa and water into a saucepan, and heat gently. Stir the mixture until melted, and bring it to the boil. Cool. Whisk the chilled evaporated milk in a bowl, until it is thick and frothy. Mix it into the cooled mixture, whisking until it is well blended. Turn the mixture into a freezer container and freeze uncovered until slushy. Beat the ice cream well and re-freeze until firm.

Rum Ice Cream Gateau

PREPARATION TIME: 30 minutes, plus freezing

COOKING TIME: 1 hour

OVEN TEMPERATURE: 150°C, 300°F, Gas Mark 2

SERVES: 6-8 people

Oil for greasing
225g (8oz) caster sugar
3 egg whites
15ml (1 tblsp) instant coffee
30ml (2 tblsp) boiling water
450ml (¾ pint) double cream
30ml (2 tblsp) dark rum
150ml (5 fl oz) chocolate ice cream

Lightly oil a baking sheet and line the base of an 18cm (7 inch) round loose-bottomed cake tin with greased greaseproof paper. Whisk 50g (2oz) of the caster sugar into the egg whites and continue to whisk until stiff. Add the remaining sugar and whisk until it peaks. Fill a piping bag, fitted with a star nozzle, with the meringue mixture. Pipe small rosettes onto the baking sheet, keeping them well apart. Bake them in a pre-heated oven for 1 hour; leave in the oven for a

further 20 minutes, with the oven turned off. Remove the meringues from the oven and allow them to cool. Mix the coffee with the water in a small bowl. Whisk the cream until thick; fold in all but 4 of the meringues. Add the coffee and the rum, taking care not to crush the meringues. Use the mixture to fill the prepared cake tin. Cover and freeze until firm. Soften the ice

cream. When the gateau is hard enough, remove it from the tin. Beat the ice cream and use it to fill a piping bag fitted with a 1cm (½ inch) star nozzle. Quickly pipe rosettes on top of the gateau. Return the gateau to the freezer and leave until firm. Put the reserved meringues in the centre of the gateau. Refrigerate for 10 minutes before serving.

This page: Mocha Ice Cream (top) and Rum Ice Cream Gateau (bottom).

Facing page: Chocolate Chip Ice Cream (top) and Chocolate Ice Box Cake (bottom).

Chocolate Ice Cream

PREPARATION TIME: 1 hour 40 minutes, plus freezing time

COOKING TIME: 15-20 minutes

SERVES: 8 people

100g (4oz) plain chocolate, chopped or grated
600ml (1 pint) milk
7 egg yolks
100g (4oz) caster sugar

Put the chopped chocolate into a saucepan with a little milk. Stir over a low heat until the chocolate melts and forms a smooth paste. Add the remaining milk. Whisk the egg yolks and sugar together until thick and light. Whisk into the chocolate milk. Whisk continuously over a low heat until thick. Pour the mixture into a bowl and stand over ice. (If you do not have a lot of ice, chill in the refrigerator.) Either pour into an ice cream churn, and follow the manufacturer's instructions, or pour into ice trays and freeze for 30 minutes. Tip the par-frozen ice cream into a bowl and whisk until smooth. Return to the freezer. Repeat this process every 30 minutes, until the ice cream is really thick. Freeze until ready to serve.

Nougat Ice Cream Cake

PREPARATION TIME: 40 minutes, plus freezing

SERVES: 6-8 people

50g (2oz) ground hazelnuts
16 small wafer biscuits
425g (15½oz) can pineapple chunks, or
225g (8oz) crystallised pineapple
450ml (¾ pint) vanilla ice cream
450ml (¾ pint) chocolate ice cream
100g (4oz) plain chocolate, finely chopped
100g (4oz) nougat
450ml (¾ pint) whipping cream, whipped

Grease a 450g (1lb) loaf tin and sprinkle the inside with ground hazelnuts. Put 12 of the wafer biscuits around the sides and base of the tin. Drain the pineapple chunks (or chop the crystallised pineapple). Soften the ice creams by placing them in the refrigerator. Spoon the vanilla ice cream into the tin and smooth it down. Add the chopped chocolate to the chocolate ice cream, and ¾ of the chopped pineapple. Spoon this mixture on top of the vanilla ice

cream. Chop the nougat into small pieces and sprinkle it on top of the chocolate ice cream. Cover the chocolate ice cream with the remaining 4 wafer biscuits. Freeze for 3-4 hours, until firm. Spoon or pipe the whipped cream over the unmoulded ice cream cake. Decorate with the reserved pineapple. Serve cut into slices

Chocolate Ice Box Cake

PREPARATION TIME: 1 hour, plus freezing

COOKING TIME: 25-30 minutes

OVEN TEMPERATURE: 190°C, 375°F, Gas Mark 5

SERVES: 8 people

Melted butter for greasing
7 eggs, separated
75g (3oz) vanilla sugar
75ml (5 tblsp) plain flour
Pinch of salt
Caster sugar

Filling
350g (12oz) plain chocolate, chopped or grated
30ml (2 tblsp) strong black coffee
50ml (2 fl oz) brandy
2 egg yolks
5 egg whites, stiffly beaten
120ml (4 fl oz) double or whipping cream, lightly whipped

Icing
150ml (¼ pint) double cream
150g (5oz) plain chocolate, chopped or grated

Grease and line two 23x30cm (9x12 inch) Swiss roll tins with greaseproof paper. Brush the paper with melted butter and dust with flour. Whisk the egg yolks and vanilla sugar together until thick and light; fold in the flour and salt. Whisk the egg whites until stiff but not dry. Gently fold the whisked egg whites into the mixture. Divide the mixture between the two tins. Bake in a pre-heated oven for 15-20 minutes, or until golden. When the sponges are baked, spread two tea towels on a work surface and cover each one with a sheet of greaseproof paper. Sprinkle with caster sugar and turn the sponges out onto the sugared paper. Peel off the lining paper and leave the sponges to cool. Line the bottom of a 20cm (8 inch) spring form cake tin with greased greaseproof paper. Cut a circle of sponge from each rectangular sponge to fit the tin. Put one on top of the paper lining. Reserve the other. Cut three strips of sponge, 5cm (2 inches) wide, to line the sides of the tin. Place in position. To make the filling: put

the chocolate, coffee and brandy into a saucepan and stir over a low heat until the chocolate has melted. Leave to cool. Beat in the egg yolks, and then gently fold in the whisked egg whites, taking care not to over-mix. Finally, fold in the whipped double cream. Pour the mixture into the sponge-lined cake tin and put the remaining sponge circle on top as a lid. Cover the top of the tin with a plate 20cm (8 inches) in diameter, weighted down lightly. Put the cake tin into the freezer for 2-3 hours, or chill in the refrigerator for at least 5 hours. To make the icing: pour the cream into a pan and bring to the boil. Stir in the chocolate until it melts, and the mixture thickens. Carefully take the set cake out of its tin and pour icing over it. Open freeze, or refrigerate, until the icing has set.

Chocolate Chip Ice Cream

PREPARATION TIME: 30 minutes, plus freezing time

COOKING TIME: 6-8 minutes

SERVES: 8 people

90g (3½oz) plain chocolate, chopped or grated
300ml (½ pint) milk
3 egg yolks
75g (3oz) caster sugar
300ml (½ pint) double or whipping cream, lightly whipped
65g (2½oz) finely chopped chocolate

Stir the chopped or grated chocolate into the milk in a small, heavy-based saucepan; stir over a gentle heat until the chocolate melts. Put the egg yolks into a bowl with the sugar and whisk until thick and creamy. Add the chocolate milk and whisk. Return the chocolate mixture to the saucepan and stir continuously over a moderate heat until the mixture is thick, and will coat the back of a spoon. Strain the chocolate custard into a bowl and cool in the refrigerator. When quite cold, fold in the whipped cream. (If you are using a churn, pour in the mixture and follow the manufacturer's instructions, adding the chopped chocolate at the appropriate stage.) Pour into ice trays and freeze until the mixture begins to set around the edges. Pour into a bowl and whisk. Stir in

Chocolate Ice Cream (above right) and Nougat Ice Cream Cake (right).

the chopped chocolate. Return the ice cream to the ice trays and freeze for 30 minutes. Repeat the whisking and freezing method every 30 minutes, until the ice cream is really thick. Freeze until firm.

Luxury Lacé Ice Cream

PREPARATION TIME: 50 minutes, plus freezing

COOKING TIME: 6-8 minutes

SERVES: 6-8 people

300ml (½ pint) single cream
150g (5oz) plain chocolate, chopped
  or grated
5ml (1 tsp) instant coffee powder
4 egg yolks
100g (4oz) caster sugar
300ml (½ pint) double cream

To Decorate

100g (4oz) plain chocolate, chopped or grated

Put the single cream into a saucepan and heat gently. Add the chocolate and coffee powder and stir until the mixture is smooth, and the chocolate has melted. Whisk the egg yolks and sugar until thick, pale and creamy. Continue whisking, and slowly pour in the chocolate cream mixture. Return the mixture to the saucepan and stir it over a gentle heat until it reaches coating consistency. Remove from the heat and cool. Whip the cream lightly and fold it into the chocolate mixture. Pour the mixture into a shallow container and freeze it until firm. To make the chocolate lace decoration: put a large bun tray upside down. Smooth a piece of cling film over alternate domed shapes. Melt the plain chocolate and use it to fill a greaseproof piping bag fitted with a writing nozzle. Pipe around the edge of each dome and then pipe parallel lines in every direction over the dome, joining up all the lines with circles. Repeat the pattern so that it is "double" in thickness. Chill the chocolate domes until set. Carefully lift them off the bun tray. Keep them chilled until you are ready to serve the ice cream. To serve: put a generous scoop of ice cream into each chocolate lace cup and top it with another cup.

Frozen Chocolate Souffle

PREPARATION TIME: 30 minutes, plus freezing time

COOKING TIME: 15 minutes

SERVES: 6-8 people

This delicate and light chocolate dessert makes an unusual end to a meal.

50g (2oz) caster sugar
3 eggs, separated
90g (3½ oz) plain chocolate, melted and cooled
350ml (12 fl oz) double cream, lightly whipped

To Decorate
Chocolate scrolls
Icing sugar

Tie a collar of greased greaseproof paper around a 600ml (1 pint)

souffle dish, making sure that it extends at least 5cm (2 inches) above the rim of the dish. Whisk the sugar and egg yolks in a bowl over a pan of simmering water, until thick and light. The mixture should fall off the whisk in ribbons). Remove from the heat and beat in the melted chocolate. Whisk until the mixture has cooled. Fold the lightly whipped cream into the chocolate mixture. Whisk the egg whites until stiff but not dry; fold lightly into the mixture. Pour the mixture into the prepared souffle dish. Freeze for at least 4 hours. Just before serving, remove the paper collar by gently easing it off. Decorate the top with chocolate scrolls and dust lightly with icing sugar.

Minted Chocolate Chip Gateau

PREPARATION TIME: 25 minutes, plus freezing

COOKING TIME: 20 minutes

OVEN TEMPERATURE: 200°C, 400°F, Gas Mark 6

SERVES: 6 people

3 large eggs
75g (3oz) caster sugar
75g (3oz) self-raising flour, sieved
Filling
6 scoops chocolate chip ice cream

To decorate
1 box chocolate mint sticks

To make the sponge: whisk the eggs and sugar together until they are thick and light in colour. Fold the sieved flour lightly but thoroughly into the mixture. Put into a greased and lined shallow loaf tin. Bake in the oven for 20 minutes. Turn out and cool. Slice the cake through into layers; sandwich together with 4 scoops of the ice cream. Spread the remaining ice cream over the sides of the cake, omitting the top; stick on the chocolate mint sticks (you may have to use a piece of string or ribbon to hold them in position). Freeze the cake until firm. Cut the cake into slices to serve.

Iced Lake

PREPARATION TIME: 35 minutes, plus freezing

COOKING TIME: 10-15 minutes

OVEN TEMPERATURE: 180°C, 350°F, Gas Mark 4

SERVES: 6 people

Lemon Ice Cream
Grated rind of 2 lemons
Juice of 3 lemons
175g (6oz) caster sugar
300ml (½ pint) double cream
300ml (½ pint) milk

Chocolate Biscuits
50g (2oz) butter
50g (2oz) caster sugar
1 egg yolk
50g (2oz) plain flour
25g (1oz) rice flour
5ml (1 tsp) cocoa powder

To Serve
Nouvelle Chocolate Sauce (see recipe)

To make the ice cream: put the lemon rind, juice and sugar into a bowl and stir well. Add the cream and whisk until thick. Whisk in the milk slowly. Pour the mixture into a large freezer container and freeze it until slushy. Tip the ice cream into a bowl and whisk it until smooth. Re-freeze in its container until firm. To make the biscuits: lightly grease a baking sheet. Cream the butter and sugar together. Add the egg yolk, beat the mixture well. Add the plain flour, rice flour and cocoa and work them well into the mixture. Lightly flour the work surface and roll out the dough. Cut out shapes with animal cutters. Place on a baking sheet. Bake for 10-15 minutes. Cool on a wire rack. To serve: place scoops of ice cream onto small serving plates and top each one with an animal biscuit. Spoon Nouvelle Chocolate Sauce around each portion.

This page: Iced Lake (top) and **Minted Chocolate Chip Gateau (bottom).**

Facing page: **Frozen Chocolate Souffle (top) and Luxury Lace Ice Cream (bottom).**

COOKING WITH CHOCOLATE
Cookies and Confections

Chocolate Ravioli

PREPARATION TIME: 30 minutes, plus chilling

MAKES: 25 pieces

100g (4oz) roasted hazelnuts
15ml (1 tblsp) granulated sugar
30ml (2 tblsp) melted butter
50g (2oz) plain chocolate melted
15ml (1 tblsp) brandy
250g (9oz) white chocolate, melted

Line a square baking sheet with a rim of tinfoil, making sure that it is smooth and even, with neat corners. Crush the hazelnuts and mix them with the sugar and butter. Stir in the melted dark chocolate and brandy to form a paste. Form into 25 small balls and arrange them in rows over the bottom of the baking sheet, pressing the balls flat. Pour the melted white chocolate evenly over the small balls, so as to cover them completely. Place the tray in the refrigerator until firm. Cut the ravioli into rows with a knife or ravioli cutter, and then separate each one.

Chocolate Meringues

PREPARATION TIME: 35 minutes

COOKING TIME: 15-20 minutes

OVEN TEMPERATURE: 180°C, 350°F, Gas Mark 4

MAKES: about 8

2 egg whites
100g (4oz) icing sugar, sieved
50g (2oz) nuts

Filling
100g (4oz) plain chocolate, chopped
    or grated
60ml (4 tblsp) water
15ml (1 tblsp) strong black coffee
50g (2oz) butter
2 egg yolks
15ml (1 tblsp) dark rum

Whisk the egg whites until stiff and dry. Add the icing sugar a spoonful at a time and continue to whisk until very thick. Carefully fold in the chopped nuts; spoon or pipe small mounds onto a baking sheet lined with silicone paper. Bake for 15-20 minutes. Leave to cool slightly and then transfer onto a wire rack. Gently spoon out a little meringue from the underside of each of the meringues. For the filling: melt the chocolate and stir in the coffee and water; boil the mixture, stirring continuously for 2 minutes. Remove the pan from the heat and allow the mixture to cool; beat the butter into the cooled mixture, and blend in the egg yolks and the rum. Refrigerate until the mixture thickens. When cool, spoon it into a piping bag fitted with a plain nozzle, and pipe the filling into the meringues. Sandwich them together in pairs.

This page: **Toffee Bars (top left), Chocolate Fudge (top right) and Chocolate Ravioli (bottom).**

Facing page: **Florentines (top) and Chocolate Meringue Biscuits (bottom).**

Chocolate Eggs

PREPARATION TIME: 50 minutes

COOKING TIME: 12-15 minutes

MAKES: 6

6 small eggs
Food colouring
175ml (6 fl oz) double cream
257g (10 oz) plain or milk chocolate, melted
60ml (4 tblsp) white rum
Sticking plaster or tape

Using a needle, make a small hole in one end of each egg; carefully make a larger hole in the other end. Blow the egg contents out into a bowl. Pour running water into the egg shells and shake them well until clean. Put a little food colouring of your choice into a saucepan of water and boil the egg shells until they take on the colour. Dry the shells in a low oven for 5 minutes. Boil the cream and stir it into the melted chocolate. Stir in the rum. Put a small piece of plaster over the smallest hole in each egg shell; fill a piping bag fitted with a plain nozzle with the chocolate cream. Fit the nozzle gently into the egg shell and pipe in the chocolate cream until full. Clean off any chocolate on the shell and chill. Remove the plasters. These eggs are fun to give as gifts, or use uncoloured, as a joke for a chocolate breakfast. Note: stand the eggs in their box to make filling and chilling easier.

Artichoke

PREPARATION TIME: 1 hour 30 minutes, plus setting overnight

MAKES: 1 artichoke, serving 8-10 people

After dinner mints with a difference.

450g (1lb) plain chocolate, chopped or grated
30ml (2 tblsp) oil
Few drops of peppermint oil
1 globe artichoke

To Make the Artichoke

25g (1oz) caster sugar
25g (1oz) butter
30ml (2 tblsp) water
50g (2oz) icing sugar, sieved
25g (1oz) cocoa powder
A piece of cake the size of the artichoke

Artichoke (above), Chocolate Eggs (right) and Truffles (far right).

Melt the plain chocolate with the oil and stir occasionally until melted. Cool this mixture slightly and stir in the peppermint oil. Take the leaves off the artichoke; dip the front of each leaf into the melted chocolate and lay them on silicone paper. Leave overnight to set, before peeling off the artichoke leaves. To make the icing: dissolve the caster sugar in the butter and water over a low heat; remove from the heat and stir in the icing sugar and the cocoa powder. Cut the cake into a pyramid shape and cover it with some of the cooled icing. Stick the chocolate artichoke leaves around the cake, in the same order as the real artichoke was assembled. You will need to use some of the icing to help them to stick. Serve with the peppermint creams at the end of the meal.

Chocolate Fudge

PREPARATION TIME: 35 minutes
COOKING TIME: 10-15 minutes
MAKES: about 750g (1½lbs)

This fudge is much easier to make if you have a sugar thermometer, but do not worry if one is not available; the temperature of the fudge can be tested without one.

25g (1oz) butter
225g (8oz) plain chocolate, melted
225g (8oz) granulated sugar
450ml (¾ pint) canned evaporated milk

To Decorate
25g (1oz) cocoa powder, or drinking chocolate

If you have a sugar thermometer put it in your saucepan before you start the fudge. Heat the butter, sugar and evaporated milk in the saucepan, stirring continuously, until the sugar has dissolved. Boil the mixture until the thermometer reads 116°C, 240°F (if you do not have a thermometer, take out a little of the fudge with a small spoon and drop it into a jug of cold water; if it stays in a ball it is ready). Remove the saucepan from the heat and plunge the bottom of the pan into cold water to stop it cooking. After a few minutes beat the fudge until it is thick and grainy. Beat in the melted chocolate. Butter a shallow 30x18cm (12x7 inch) cake tin and pour in the fudge. Cool until set. Cut the fudge into squares. Dust the fudge in either cocoa powder or drinking chocolate.

Truffles

PREPARATION TIME: 15 minutes
MAKES: about 10

100g (4oz) plain chocolate, chopped or grated
15ml (1 tblsp) dark rum
25g (1oz) unsalted butter ·
1 egg yolk
100g (4oz) ground almonds
100g (4oz) cake crumbs
50g (2oz) chocolate vermicelli

Melt the chocolate with the rum in a small bowl over a saucepan of hot water. Beat in the butter and egg yolk and remove the mixture from the heat. Stir in the ground almonds and cake crumbs to make a smooth paste. Divide it into balls; roll them in the vermicelli until evenly coated.

Dipped Fruit

PREPARATION TIME: 10 minutes, plus drying

MAKES: 750g (1½lb) dipped fruit

750g (1½lb) prepared fruit (grapes, strawberries, etc.)
Melted plain chocolate

Wash the fruits, but leave the stems on them if possible. Holding each piece of fruit by the stem, dip into the melted chocolate, leaving the top section uncovered. Allow any excess to run off and leave to set on a tray lined with silicone paper.

Chocolate Meringue Biscuits

PREPARATION TIME: 20 minutes

COOKING TIME: 15-20 minutes

OVEN TEMPERATURE: 180°C, 350°F, Gas Mark 4

MAKES: about 10

100g (4oz) butter or margarine
50g (2oz) caster sugar
1 egg yolk
50g (2oz) ground almonds
175g (6oz) plain flour

Filling
100g (4oz) plain chocolate
15g (½oz) butter

Meringue Topping
For meringue ingredients see
  Chocolate Meringues recipe

Grease a baking sheet and line with silicone paper. Cream the butter or margarine and sugar together; add the egg yolk and beat well. Add the ground almonds and flour and mix well. Knead the mixture and roll it out thinly. Cut into rounds using a 6cm (2½ inch) cutter. Place the rounds on the prepared baking sheet and bake for 15-20 minutes. Make up the meringue mixture. Pipe into 2.5cm (1 inch) swirls on a baking sheet lined with silicone paper. Follow the baking instructions for chocolate meringues. When cool, gently ease them off the baking sheet. To make

up the filling: melt the chocolate with the butter over a gentle heat. Mix them well and spread over the top of each of the almond biscuits. Top each one with a meringue and leave until set.

Florentines

PREPARATION TIME: 15 minutes

COOKING TIME: 8-10 minutes

OVEN TEMPERATURE: 180°C, 350°F, Gas Mark 4

MAKES: 12

75g (3oz) butter
75g (3oz) golden syrup
75g (3oz) flaked almonds, chopped
25g (1oz) plain flour
25g (1oz) chopped mixed peel
50g (2oz) glace cherries, chopped
5ml (1 tsp) lemon juice
100g (4oz) plain chocolate, chopped
  or grated

Line a baking sheet with silicone paper. Melt the butter and syrup together in a small saucepan. Stir in the almonds, flour, mixed peel, cherries and lemon juice. Put small spoonfuls of the mixture onto the prepared baking sheet. Keep them well apart and flatten with a fork. Bake in a pre-heated oven for 8-10 minutes. Remove the Florentines carefully to a wire rack to cool.

Melt the chocolate in a bowl over a pan of hot water. Spread over the flat side of each Florentine. Place the biscuits chocolate sides uppermost, and mark the liquid chocolate with wavy lines, using a fork. Leave until set.

Toffee Bars

PREPARATION TIME: 40 minutes

COOKING TIME: 25-30 minutes

OVEN TEMPERATURE: 180°C, 350°F, Gas Mark 4

MAKES: 15 bars

Biscuit Base
100g (4oz) butter
50g (2oz) caster sugar
175g (6oz) plain flour, sieved

Toffee Caramel
100g (4oz) butter or margarine
50g (2oz) caster sugar
30ml (2 tblsp) golden syrup
150ml (5 fl oz) condensed milk

Chocolate Topping
100g (4oz) plain chocolate
15g (½oz) butter

For the biscuit base: cream the butter and sugar together until light and fluffy. Add the flour and knead until smooth. Press the dough into a greased 20cm (8 inch)

square shallow cake tin, and prick with a fork. Bake in a pre-heated oven for 25-30 minutes. Cool. Put the ingredients for the toffee caramel into a small saucepan and stir until dissolved; bring slowly to the boil, and cook stirring for 5-7 minutes. Cool slightly and then spread over the biscuit base. Leave to set. For the topping: melt the chocolate with the butter over a low heat; spread it carefully over the toffee. Leave it to set and cut into fingers.

Chocolate Muesli

PREPARATION TIME: 25 minutes

COOKING TIME: 10-12 minutes

OVEN TEMPERATURE: 190°C, 375°F, Gas Mark 5

MAKES: about 12

100g (4oz) margarine or butter
100g (4oz) caster sugar
1 egg, beaten
Few drops vanilla essence
100g (4oz) plain flour, sieved
2.5ml (½ tsp) bicarbonate of soda
50g (2oz) rolled oats
50g (2oz) cocoa powder

Chocolate Coating
100g (4oz) plain chocolate, chopped
  or grated
15g (½oz) butter

Beat the margarine or butter with the sugar until light and fluffy. Beat in the egg, adding the essence, flour and bicarbonate of soda. Stir in the oats and the cocoa powder. Spread the mixture onto a lightly greased baking sheet, and mark out into bars with a knife. Bake for 10-12 minutes until lightly browned. Re-mark with a sharp knife and cool on a wire rack. To make the chocolate coating: melt the chocolate and butter together and pour evenly over the bars. Separate the bars when set.

This page: Chocolate Meringues (top) and Dipped Fruit (bottom).

Facing page: Praline Orange Log (top), Chocolate Muesli (centre right) and Mint Creams (bottom left).

Chocolate Chip Cookies

PREPARATION TIME: 15 minutes, plus chilling

COOKING TIME: 10-12 minutes

OVEN TEMPERATURE: 180°C, 350°F, Gas Mark 4

MAKES: about 30

225g (8oz) self-raising flour
Pinch of salt
150g (5oz) butter
100g (4oz) caster sugar
1 egg, lightly beaten
50g (2oz) plain chocolate, grated

Sieve the flour and salt into a mixing bowl. Cut the butter into the flour and rub in until the mixture looks like breadcrumbs. Stir the sugar into the mixture. Add the egg and mix to a stiff dough. Knead the grated chocolate into the dough. Chill the dough for 30 minutes. Roll out the dough and cut into 5cm (2 inch) rounds with a plain cutter. Grease a baking sheet and put the rounds on it, placing them well apart. Prick the rounds with a fork. Bake in a pre-heated oven for 10-12 minutes until golden. Cool on a wire rack.

Chocolate Crunch

PREPARATION TIME: 20 minutes, plus chilling

MAKES: 1 450g (1lb) loaf

100g (4oz) chocolate shortbread finger biscuits
50g (2oz) whole hazelnuts
100g (4oz) firm margarine
75g (3oz) caster sugar
30ml (2 tblsp) cocoa powder
1 egg, beaten
50g (2oz) sultanas

To Decorate
Icing sugar

Line a 450g (1lb) loaf tin with cling film. Chop up the shortbread fingers. Brown the hazelnuts and rub off the skins. Put the margarine and sugar into a small saucepan and stir over a low heat until the sugar dissolves. Stir the cocoa into the mixture, and remove from the heat. Stir in the egg, hazelnuts, sultanas and chopped biscuits. Pour the mixture into the lined tin and smooth it level. Chill until set. Dust with icing sugar and serve cut in slices.

Chocolate Palmiers

PREPARATION TIME: 30 minutes

COOKING TIME: 12-15 minutes

OVEN TEMPERATURE: 220°C, 425°F, Gas Mark 7

MAKES: 6

225g (8oz) puff pastry
Caster sugar
75g (3oz) plain chocolate, coarsely grated

To decorate
175ml (6 fl oz) double cream, whipped
50g (2oz) strawberries, halved
Icing sugar for dusting

Roll out the pastry on a well-sugared surface to a rectangle measuring approximately 30x20cm (12x10 inches). Sprinkle with the chocolate and press down with a rolling pin. Take the shorter edge of the pastry and roll it up to the centre. Roll the opposite side to meet it at the centre. Moisten with water and press together the adjoining rolls. Cut into 1cm (½ inch) slices and place them cut side down on a dampened baking sheet. Keep them well apart and flatten them a little. Bake in a pre-heated oven for 12-15 minutes, until puffed and golden. (Turn the palmiers over once they begin to brown.) Cool them on a wire rack. Whip the cream and use it to fill a piping bag fitted with a 1cm (½ inch) fluted nozzle. Pipe swirls of cream on half of the palmiers and arrange the fruit on top of the cream. Use the other palmiers to sandwich the fruit. Sprinkle with icing sugar.

Praline Orange Log

PREPARATION TIME: 20-25 minutes, plus chilling

COOKING TIME: 30-35 minutes

OVEN TEMPERATURE: 180°C, 350°F, Gas Mark 4

MAKES: 30 slices

175g (6oz) plain chocolate, chopped or grated
15ml (1 tblsp) strong black coffee

25g (1oz) caster sugar
15ml (1 tblsp) orange liqueur
75g (3oz) butter
2 egg yolks

Praline
175g (6oz) shelled nuts (see below)
225g (8oz) granulated sugar
65ml (2½ fl oz) water
1 egg white, beaten

Use either almonds, hazelnuts, walnuts or pistachio nuts. Use the nuts chopped or whole, with or without the skins, toasted or plain. For praline powder, the nuts must be peeled.

Melt the chocolate in a bowl with the coffee, sugar, orange liqueur and butter, over a low heat. Remove from the heat and allow to cool thoroughly. Stir in the egg yolks. Chill for 3½-4 hours. To make the praline: put the nuts on a baking sheet and warm them in the oven for 10 minutes. Butter a marble slab or large baking sheet. Put the sugar and water into a small, heavy saucepan, stirring until the sugar has dissolved. Bring to the boil and boil until the sugar caramelizes; remove from the heat and plunge the base of the pan into cold water to halt the cooking process. Stir in the nuts. Pour onto the marble or onto a baking sheet. Spread out and leave until set and hard. Put the praline into a strong plastic bag and crush with a rolling pin. To make praline powder, grind it in a coffee grinder. Shape the chilled chocolate mixture into a log, 5cm (2 inches) in diameter. Brush the log with the beaten egg white and roll gently in the crushed praline, pressing firmly with the hands to help the praline stick. Chill the log until very firm. Cut into slices about 5mm (¼ inch) thick.

Chocolate Crunch (top right), Chocolate Palmiers (centre left) and Chocolate Chip Cookies (bottom).

Mint Creams

PREPARATION TIME: 20 minutes, plus setting overnight

MAKES: about 16

The white of 1 egg
1.25ml (¼ tsp) peppermint essence
350g (12oz) icing sugar
100g (4oz) plain or milk chocolate, chopped or grated

Beat the egg white and essence together in a bowl and gradually add the icing sugar. Lightly dust the work surface with extra icing sugar and knead the peppermint icing until smooth. Using plenty of extra icing sugar, roll out the icing to a thickness of about 5mm (¼ inch) and cut out shapes with a 4cm (1½ inch) cutter, either fluted or plain. Place the shaped mints on a baking sheet lined with greaseproof paper, and leave them in a warm place to dry out, preferably overnight. Melt the chocolate; dip the mints in so that half is coated in chocolate. Shake off any excess chocolate and place the mints on a sheet of buttered greaseproof paper or foil until set.

Dominoes

PREPARATION TIME: 25 minutes

COOKING TIME: 10-15 minutes

OVEN TEMPERATURE: 180°C, 350°F, Gas Mark 4

MAKES: about 14

100g (4oz) butter or margarine
100g (4oz) caster sugar
1 egg, beaten
250g (9oz) plain flour
25g (1oz) cocoa powder
Salt

Butter Icing
75g (3oz) butter
175g (6oz) icing sugar, sieved
Few drops of vanilla essence

Cream the butter and sugar together and add the egg. Sieve the flour, cocoa powder and salt together and work into the butter mixture. Knead the dough and roll it out between two sheets of greaseproof paper. Cut out rectangles, about 3x7cm (1¼x2¾ inches). Mark a line across the centre of the biscuits using a

skewer. Bake the biscuits on a greased baking sheet for 10-15 minutes. Cool them on a wire rack. To make the icing: soften the butter and beat in the icing sugar. You may need to add a few drops of hot water if the icing is too firm. Add vanilla essence to taste. If you want to sandwich the biscuits together, do so with a little of the butter icing. Pipe the top of the dominoes with dots, using a piping bag fitted with a plain nozzle and filled with the remaining butter icing.

Zigzag Shortbread

PREPARATION TIME: 20 minutes

COOKING TIME: 30-35 minutes

OVEN TEMPERATURE: 160°C, 325°F, Gas Mark 3

MAKES: about 14 fingers

150g (5oz) plain flour
50g (2oz) caster sugar
100g (4oz) butter
15ml (1 tblsp) cocoa powder
15ml (1 tblsp) drinking chocolate

Grease an 18cm (7 inch) square cake tin. Sieve the flour into a bowl, reserving 15g (½oz). Add the

sugar. Rub in the butter until it forms a crumble texture. Divide the mixture in half; add the cocoa and the drinking chocolate to one half. Add the remaining flour to the other half. Knead both mixtures to doughs. Turn the chocolate dough onto a lightly floured surface. Roll out and cut into strips 4cm (1½ inches) wide. Do the same with the plain dough. Lay the strips alternately in the tin, in a diagonal pattern, easing them in so that they fit. Bake until lightly crisp but not brown, for 30-35 minutes. Mark out into fingers and leave to cool in the tin. Note: the shortbread trimmings can be cut into small shapes and baked separately for 5 minutes.

Chocolate Whirls

PREPARATION TIME: 10 minutes

COOKING TIME: 15 minutes

OVEN TEMPERATURE: 180°C, 350°F, Gas Mark 4

MAKES: 10

50g (2oz) butter or margarine
25g (1oz) brown sugar
15ml (1 tblsp) black treacle
5ml (1 tsp) cocoa powder

Pinch of salt
100g (4oz) self-raising flour
10 hazelnuts

Grease a baking sheet. Put the butter and sugar into a mixing bowl and beat until soft and creamy. Add the treacle and stir well. Sieve the cocoa powder, flour and salt together and knead into the treacle mixture. Spoon the mixture into small balls on a floured work surface. Roll the balls into long sausage shapes; curve round one end and continue winding the rest of the sausage round so you have a Catherine wheel shape. Place the "wheels" on the baking sheet; push a hazelnut into the centre of each one. Bake for 15 minutes. Cool on a wire rack.

This page: Chocolate Whirls (left), Zigzag Shortbread (centre) and Dominoes (right).

Facing page: Iced Chocolate (left) and Chocolate Egg Cream Soda (right).

COOKING WITH CHOCOLATE

Drinks and Sauces

Iced Chocolate

PREPARATION TIME: 5 minutes,
plus chilling

COOKING TIME: 15 minutes

MAKES: 8-10 drinks

175g (6oz) granulated sugar
200ml (⅓ pint) water
40g (1½oz) cocoa powder
Chilled milk

Put the sugar and water into a
heavy-based saucepan and stir over
a moderate heat until the sugar
dissolves. Brush off any sugar
crystals that may form on the
inside of the pan with a pastry
brush dipped in cold water. Raise
the heat and boil the syrup until it
spins fine threads from a spoon or
fork. Remove from the heat. Add
the cocoa powder and stir until
well mixed over a low heat. Cool
the chocolate syrup and chill in the
refrigerator until required. To make
the drink: put 15ml (1 tblsp) chilled
syrup into a jug or blender with
300ml (½ pint) chilled milk and stir
or whisk until blended. Pour the
chocolate drink over ice cubes in
chilled glasses.

Bittersweet Butter Cream

PREPARATION TIME: 15 minutes

MAKES: 400ml (14 fl oz)

300g (10oz) bitter chocolate
350g (12oz) butter softened
350g (12oz) caster sugar
10ml (2 tsp) vanilla essence
3 eggs
45ml (3 tblsp) cocoa powder
5ml (1 tsp) instant coffee powder
10ml (2 tsp) dark rum
Pinch of salt

Melt the chocolate. Beat the butter
until creamy and add the sugar and
vanilla. Add the eggs, one at a time,
beating well after each addition.
Stir cocoa and coffee powder into
the melted chocolate and add it to
the buttercream. Stir in the rum
and salt, making sure that all the
ingredients are well incorporated.
Use to fill Chocolate Raspberry
Torte, or other chocolate recipe.

Banana Shake

PREPARATION TIME: 10 minutes

MAKES: 1 drink

45ml (3 tblsp) chocolate ice cream
30ml (2 tblsp) drinking chocolate
  powder
150ml (¼ pint) milk
1 banana
Ice cubes

Blend together all the ingredients in a blender or food processor, or whisk with a hand whisk (if using a hand whisk, mash the banana first). Serve in a tall glass with ice cubes.

Chocolate Butter Sauce

PREPARATION TIME: 5 minutes

COOKING TIME: 10 minutes

MAKES: 450ml (¾ pint)

250ml (8 fl oz) water
225g (8oz) plain chocolate, chopped
  or grated
15ml (1 tblsp) brandy
90g (3½oz) butter, cut into small
  pieces

Put the water, chocolate and brandy into a saucepan. Stir over a low heat until the chocolate has melted. The mixture should be smooth. Remove from the heat and slowly stir in the butter until it melts. The sauce should then become thick and glossy. This sauce can be served hot or cold.

Praline Sauce

PREPARATION TIME: 40 minutes, including making of praline

MAKES: about 300ml (½ pint)

15ml (1 tblsp) cocoa powder
175ml (6oz) canned evaporated milk
75g (3oz) plain chocolate, chopped or
  grated
60ml (4 tblsp) crushed praline (see
  recipe)

Whisk together the cocoa and evaporated milk in a small saucepan. Heat the mixture and bring it to the boil. Remove the pan from the heat and stir in the chocolate. Return to the heat and continue stirring over a gentle heat until the chocolate has melted. Add the praline.

Chocolate Toffee Sauce

PREPARATION TIME: 10 minutes

COOKING TIME: 15 minutes

MAKES: about 300ml (½ pint)

100g (4oz) plain chocolate, chopped
  or grated
85ml (3 fl oz) water
50g (2oz) granulated sugar
45ml (3 tblsp) chilled unsalted butter
5ml (1 tsp) vanilla essence
225g (8oz) nut brittle, broken into
  small chunks

Using a small, heavy-based saucepan, gently heat the chocolate and water until the chocolate has melted. Stir continuously. Stir in the sugar and continue to heat gently for 2 minutes, until the sugar has dissolved and the mixture has thickened. Remove the sauce from the heat and beat in the butter. Stir in the vanilla and the broken nut brittle. Serve hot. This sauce can be kept in the refrigerator for a few days. To serve warm, heat it gently to a pouring consistency.

Peppermint Sauce

PREPARATION TIME: 15 minutes

MAKES: about 200ml (⅓ pint)

75g (3oz) chocolate covered
  peppermint creams
150ml (¼ pint) single cream

Break up the peppermint creams and melt over a pan of hot water. Remove from the heat and slowly stir in the cream. Serve the sauce hot or cold with ice cream.

This page: Praline Sauce – shown with Nougat Slice – (top), Bitter Chocolate Sauce – shown with Cherries – (centre right) and Chocolate Butter Sauce (bottom left).

Facing page: Hot Fudge Sauce (left) and Chocolate Toffee Sauce (right).

Chocolate Custard

PREPARATION TIME: 10 minutes
COOKING TIME: 3 minutes
MAKES: about 600ml (1 pint)

45ml (3 tblsp) custard powder
15ml (1 tblsp) caster sugar
600ml (1 pint) milk
100g (4oz) milk chococlate, chopped
or grated

Put the custard powder and sugar
into a bowl with 30ml (2 tblsp) of
the milk; stir it into a paste. Boil the
remaining milk and add it to the
custard paste, stirring continuously.
Return the custard to the saucepan
and cook for 1 minute, stirring. Stir
in the chocolate until it melts.
Serve hot.

Bitter Chocolate Sauce

PREPARATION TIME: 5 minutes
COOKING TIME: 15 minutes
MAKES: 250ml (8 fl oz)

45ml (3 tblsp) strong black coffee
100g (4oz) plain dark chocolate,
chopped or grated
120ml (4 fl oz) double cream
85ml (3 fl oz) apricot jam

Put all the ingredients into a small,
heavy-based pan. Stir continuously
over a low heat until smooth.

**Honey Nut Spread (above),
Chocolate Custard – shown
with Steamed Pudding – (centre
right) and Bittersweet Butter
Cream (far right).**

Nouvelle Sauce

PREPARATION TIME: 10 minutes
COOKING TIME: 5 minutes
MAKES: 450ml (¾ pint)

This is a thin chocolate sauce which is served slightly cooled.

225g (8oz) plain chocolate, chopped or grated
100g (4oz) granulated sugar
350ml (15 fl oz) water
10ml (2 tsp) brandy

Melt the chocolate with the sugar and water; simmer for 4-5 minutes, stirring continuously. Remove the pan from the heat and let the chocolate mixture cool. Stir in the brandy. Strain the sauce and serve.

Honey Nut Spread

PREPARATION TIME: 10 minutes
MAKES: about 175g (6oz)

50g (2oz) butter, softened
15ml (1 tblsp) cocoa powder
10ml (2 tsp) orange liqueur
30ml (2 tblsp) honey
25g (1oz) icing sugar
50g (2 oz) nuts, chopped

Cream the butter with the cocoa powder and the orange liqueur; beat in the honey and the icing sugar, and then fold in the nuts. This spread is now ready to serve on hot toasted crumpets, or muffins, and is delicious with pancakes.

Chocolate Cream Sauce

PREPARATION TIME: 5 minutes
COOKING TIME: 10-15 minutes
MAKES: 450ml (¾ pint)

300ml (½ pint) double cream
15ml (1 tblsp) brandy
15ml (1 tblsp) strong black coffee
225g (8oz) plain chocolate, chopped or grated

Pour the cream, brandy and coffee into a small, heavy-based saucepan and bring to the boil. Remove from the heat and add the chopped chocolate. Stir the chocolate until it melts and the sauce is smooth. Serve this sauce hot or cold.

Cocoa Rum

PREPARATION TIME: 5 minutes
MAKES: 1 drink

15g (½oz) plain chocolate, chopped or grated
150ml (¼ pint) milk
15ml (1 tblsp) rum
15ml (1 tblsp) whipped cream
Grated nutmeg

Put the chocolate and milk into a saucepan and bring it to the boil. Stir the chocolate milk a few times, and then remove it from the heat. Whisk in the rum and pour into a heatproof glass. Put a spoonful of cream on the top and sprinkle with grated nutmeg.

Malted Chocolate Shake

PREPARATION TIME: 10 minutes, plus chilling

COOKING TIME: 5 minutes

MAKES: 2 drinks

50g (2oz) soft brown sugar
40g (1½oz) cocoa powder
300ml (½ pint) milk
30ml (2 tblsp) vanilla ice cream
15ml (1 tblsp) whisky

Put all the ingredients except the whisky and ice cream into a saucepan and mix well. Bring gently to the boil. Cook gently for 5 minutes, stirring frequently. Remove from the heat and leave to cool. Whisk in the ice cream. Cover and chill in the refrigerator until required. Pour into two glasses and add the whisky.

Chocolate Egg Cream Soda

PREPARATION TIME: 8 minutes

MAKES: 2 drinks

50g (2oz) plain chocolate, melted
1 egg
300ml (½ pint) full cream milk
2 scoops chocolate ice cream
Chilled soda water
2 scoops vanilla ice cream

Put two tall glasses in the freezer until they are frosted. Put the melted chocolate, egg, milk and chocolate ice cream into the liquidiser; blend for 1 minute. Divide this mixture between two glasses; add a scoop of vanilla ice cream to each one and top up with chilled soda water. Serve while it is still frothing.

Hot Fudge Sauce

PREPARATION TIME: 10 minutes

COOKING TIME: 10 minutes

MAKES: about 450ml (¾ pint)

150g (5oz) unsalted butter
50g (2oz) cocoa powder
50g (2oz) plain chocolate, chopped or grated
75g (3oz) granulated sugar
120ml (4 fl oz) evaporated milk
Pinch of salt
A few drops of vanilla essence

Melt the butter in a small, heavy-based saucepan. Remove from heat and add the cocoa powder. Whisk until smooth. Stir in the chopped chocolate, sugar and evaporated milk; bring to the boil over a moderate heat, stirring continuously. Remove the sauce from the heat and stir in the salt and vanilla essence. This sauce will keep in the refrigerator for 2-3 days.

Coffolate

PREPARATION TIME: 10 minutes, plus chilling time

COOKING TIME: about 15 minutes

MAKES: 4 drinks

15ml (1 tblsp) cornflour
450ml (¾ pint) boiling coffee
450ml (¾ pint) hot milk
50g (2oz) plain chocolate, chopped or grated
2.5ml (½ tsp) ground cinnamon
100g (4oz) caster sugar

To Decorate
Whipped cream

Mix the cornflour to a paste with a little of the coffee. Place the hot milk in a bowl over a pan of simmering water (or into a double boiler). Mix in the cornflour paste and stir well. Add the chocolate, cinnamon, sugar and remaining coffee. Simmer the mixture for 15 minutes, beating with a whisk; cool and chill. Serve in tall glasses with the cream to decorate.

This page, top picture: Cocoa Rum (left) and Coffolate (right). Bottom picture: Nouvelle Sauce (top left), Chocolate Cream Sauce (top right) and Peppermint Sauce – shown with Pear Flan – (bottom).

Facing page: Malted Chocolate Shake (left) and Banana Shake (right).

SWEET SURPRISE

Chocolate Lime Flan

PREPARATION TIME: 20 minutes

225g (8oz) digestive biscuits
75g (3oz) plain chocolate
25g (1oz) butter
350g (12oz) white marshmallows
150ml (¼ pint) milk
2 limes
150ml (5 fl oz) double cream
50g (2oz) plain chocolate, grated
The grated rind of 1 lemon
150ml (5 fl oz) double cream,
   whipped for decoration

Crush the biscuits. Melt the chocolate and butter together and mix in the biscuits. Lightly grease the sides and base of a 23cm (9 inch) flan dish. Press the biscuit mixture onto the base and sides of the dish. Melt the marshmallows in a basin over hot water and add the milk. Stir in the juice from one lime and grate the rind. Mix in the lemon rind, whip the double cream and fold into the marshmallow mixture. Pour into the crumb base and leave to set. Decorate the flan with the remaining cream, grated chocolate and slices of the second lime.

Cointreau and Mandarin Mousse

PREPARATION TIME: 10 minutes

290g (10½oz) tin of mandarin
   oranges
1 tablespoon gelatine
4 tablespoons Cointreau or orange
   liqueur
3 egg yolks
2 tablespoons caster sugar

Strain the mandarins, reserving the juice. Sprinkle the gelatine over the juice. Pour two tablespoons of Cointreau over the mandarins and leave them to soak. Add the remaining Cointreau, egg yolks and sugar to the gelatine. Whisk the egg mixture over a bowl of hot water until thick and frothy (with an electric whisk this should take 4 minutes). Pour into individual glass dishes and chill until set. Spoon the soaked mandarins on top. Serve.

Cheese Mousse with Strawberries

PREPARATION TIME: 45 minutes

200g (7oz) cottage cheese
150g (5oz) strawberries
25g (1oz) icing sugar
2 tablespoons Cointreau or orange
   liqueur
2 tablespoons lemon juice
2 tablespoons orange juice
1 tablespoon gelatine
150ml (5 fl oz) double cream
6 meringue rosettes

Chocolate Sauce

215g (8oz) plain chocolate
2 tablespoons milk
25g (1oz) butter

Put the cottage cheese into a bowl and add the strawberries, reserving a few strawberries for decoration. Sift the icing sugar over the cheese and sprinkle over the Cointreau. Cover and leave to stand in the fridge for about half an hour. Heat the orange and lemon juice and dissolve the gelatine in it. Whilst the gelatine is still warm, stir in the cheese mixture. Stiffly whip the cream and fold it in. Serve the mousse on the plate and decorate with the reserved strawberries. Serve with some chocolate sauce and meringue rosettes.

Chocolate Sauce

Melt the chololate, milk and butter in a bowl over hot water. Stir rapidly. Serve.

This page: Chocolate Lime Flan.

Facing page: Cointreau and Mandarin Mousse (top) and Cheese Mousse with Strawberries (bottom).

Special Desserts

Ginger Rum Trifle

PREPARATION TIME: 20 minutes

300g (12oz) ginger cake, sliced
300g (12oz) tinned pear quarters
9 tablespoons rum
450ml (¾ pint) cold thick custard
300ml (½ pint) double cream
2-3 teaspoons icing sugar
Toasted flaked almonds
Stem ginger cut into strips

Line the bottom of a glass dish with half the ginger cake. Drain the tinned pears and mix the rum with the juice. Sprinkle half over the cake. Place the pears on the top of the cake and cover with the remaining slices. Pour over a little more rum mixture. Spoon the custard over the cake. Whip the cream and gradually add icing sugar until it peaks. Spoon the cream over the custard and decorate with lightly toasted almond flakes and stem ginger strips.

Lemon Brandy Cream

PREPARATION TIME: 15 minutes

300ml (½ pint) single cream
300ml (½ pint) double cream
75g (3oz) soft brown sugar
2 large lemons
75g (3oz) sponge cake
30ml (2 tablespoons) brandy
25g (1oz) toasted flaked almonds

Mix the single and double cream in a small saucepan and add the sugar. Stir over a low heat until the cream begins to bubble. Grate the rind of the lemons and gently stir into the cream. Leave the mixture to cool and crumble the cake crumbs into glasses or serving dish. Stir the brandy into the cream mixture with the juice from both lemons. Pour the mixture into the glasses or dish over the cake crumbs and refrigerate for 30 minutes. Decorate with toasted almond flakes.

Exotic Fruit Salad Basket

PREPARATION TIME: 15 minutes

1 large melon
1 persimmon
3 kiwi fruit, washed
100g (4oz) blackberries, washed
175g (6oz) raspberries, washed
175g (6oz) redcurrants, washed
175g (6oz) strawberries, washed
175g (6oz) blackcurrants, washed
175g (6oz) grapes, red and green
1 mango, peeled and sliced
Strawberry leaves
Use as many fruits in season as are
    available
Sugar syrup (see Sauces)

Hollow out a melon and reserve the pulp. Slice the persimmon and kiwi fruit, and make melon balls using the reserved melon. Arrange the fruit in the melon basket and spoon over with sugar syrup (see Sauces).

Inset illustration: Lemon Brandy Cream (left), Berry Whip (right).

These pages: Exotic Fruit Salad (top left), Cranberry Fool (top right) and Ginger Rum Trifle (bottom).

Cranberry Fool, Chilled

PREPARATION TIME: 30 minutes

450g (1lb) cranberries
125g (5oz) sugar
2 tablespoons lemon juice
150ml (5 fl oz) carton soured cream

Bring the cranberries to the boil in 450ml (¾ pint) water in a saucepan, then simmer for about 15 minutes. Cool and stir in the sugar until dissolved. Purée the mixture until most of it is smooth by rubbing it through a sieve to remove the cranberry skins. Make sure the mixture is cool, stir in the lemon juice, cover and chill. Spoon into serving dish and serve with sour cream.

Berry Whip

PREPARATION TIME: 15 minutes

3 egg whites
A few grains of salt
150g (6oz) icing sugar
200g (8oz) blackberries
Sponge fingers

In a deep bowl whisk the egg whites. Add the sugar and salt and beat until very stiff. Fold in the berries. Spoon into glasses and chill. Serve with sponge fingers.

Cremets

PREPARATION TIME: 10 minutes

300g (12oz) curd cheese
25g (1oz) vanilla sugar or caster sugar with a few drops of vanilla essence
300ml (½ pint) double cream

Beat the curd cheese until smooth. Add the sugar and gradually beat in the cream. Pile into a bowl and chill.

Almond Galette

PREPARATION TIME: 1 hour
COOKING TIME: 10 minutes for each batch of rounds
OVEN: 190°C (375°F) Gas Mark 5

350g (12oz) butter
450g (1lb) caster sugar
2 eggs
300g (11oz) plain flour
2 tablespoons ground almonds
900ml (1½ pints) double or whipping cream, whipped
Icing sugar
Double cream
Whole almonds

Cut out 12 22cm (9 inch) circles of non-stick baking paper. Cream the sugar and butter together and beat in the eggs. Fold in the sifted flour and ground almonds. Divide the mixture into 12 and using a large palette knife coat the individual paper rounds with the mixture. Work from the centre outwards with smooth strokes. Wet a baking sheet and bake the rounds. Leave until cool and carefully peel off the paper. When all the rounds are cooked use them to form layers spreading each one with whipped

cream. Reserve 150ml (5 fl oz) of cream for decoration. Dust the top with icing sugar and decorate with almonds and cream.

Blackberry, Raisin and Walnut Jelly

PREPARATION TIME: 10 minutes
Note: In order that the fruit should be plump, soak overnight.

100g (4oz) seedless raisins
2 tablespoons rum
1 packet blackberry jelly
300ml (½ pint) port
400g (1lb) frozen blackberries (keep frozen)
6 walnuts halved
Cream
Flowers

Soak the raisins in the rum for a few hours, preferably overnight. Dissolve the jelly in 300ml (½ pint) of boiling water. Add the port and cool, making sure the jelly does not set. Put the fruit and nuts in individual glasses or a mould making sure they are quite full. Spoon over the jelly and leave to set. Decorate with flowers and/or cream.

French Plum Pudding

PREPARATION TIME: 20 minutes
COOKING TIME: 40 minutes
OVEN: 200°C (400°F) Gas Mark 6

175g (6oz) plain flour
175g (6oz) butter
75g (3oz) caster sugar
50g (2oz) ground almonds
1 egg yolk
1 tablespoon cold water
750g (1½lb) plums, halved and stoned

Sift the flour into a mixing bowl. Rub in two-thirds of the butter and 25g (1oz) of the sugar. Add the ground almonds and mix into a firm dough with the egg yolk and water. Chill. Melt the reserved butter in a 23cm (9 inch) round ovenproof dish. Add the remaining sugar until caramelised. Remove from heat. Arrange the plums, skin side down, in the ovenproof dish. On a lightly floured surface roll out the dough into a round slightly bigger than the dish. Place the dough on top of the plums and gently press down, tucking in the edges as you go. Bake in the oven until golden. To serve turn out onto a serving dish. Serve instantly.

Chocolate Meringues

PREPARATION TIME: 40 minutes
COOKING TIME: 2 hours
(leave the meringues to cool for as long as necessary)
OVEN: 120°C (250°F) Gas Mark ½

4 egg whites
225g (8oz) caster sugar
50g (2oz) hazelnuts, finely ground
300ml (10 fl oz) double or whipping cream
1 tablespoon cocoa powder
Chocolate curls

Whisk the egg whites until stiff. Gently whisk in the sugar a little at a time and fold in the hazelnuts with a metal spoon. Spoon out rounds of meringue onto a baking sheet lined with non-stick silicone paper or lightly oiled greaseproof paper. Bake until well dried out. Cool on wire racks. Whip the cream until stiff and fold in the cocoa powder. Use the cream to sandwich the meringues and decorate with chocolate shavings or curls.

Coconut Cup

PREPARATION TIME: 35 minutes

3 coconuts sawed in half
3 scoops soft-scoop vanilla ice cream per half coconut
3 tablespoons dark rum
450g (1lb) dried mixed fruit

Soak fruit in rum overnight. Saw coconuts in half and remove the flesh. Grate half the flesh, and incorporate in the ice cream along with the fruit, reserving some of the fruit for decoration. Fill coconut halves with mixture and place in freezer until firm. To serve, top with remaining fruit and grated coconut.

This page: Cremet (left), Almond Galette (right).

Facing page: Blackberry, Raisin and Walnut Jelly (top right), French Plum Pudding (centre left) and Chocolate Meringues (bottom).

Blackberry Ice Cream Dessert

PREPARATION TIME: 20 minutes plus freezing time

75g (3oz) sugar
1½ tablespoons Curaçao
300g (11oz) blackberry purée
175ml (6 fl oz) low-fat plain yogurt
Generous pinch of cinnamon
150ml (¼ pint) double or whipping
    cream, whipped
150ml (5 fl oz) water

Boil the sugar with the water for a minute and add the Curaçao. Stir in the blackberry purée (rub the fruit through a nylon sieve). Stir in the yogurt and cinnamon, and lastly fold in the whipped cream. Freeze until creamy and serve.

Kiwi Cheesecake

PREPARATION TIME: 45 minutes
COOKING TIME: 20 minutes
OVEN: 180°C (350°F) Gas Mark 4

Base
50g (2oz) soft margarine
50g (2oz) caster sugar
1 egg
65g (2½oz) self raising flour
½ level teaspoon baking powder
Finely grated rind of ½ medium
    orange

Filling
150g (6oz) cream cheese
50g (2oz) caster sugar
3 eggs, separated
Juice of 1 medium orange
Finely grated rind of ½ medium
    orange
15g (½oz) gelatine
4 tablespoons cold water
125g (5oz) natural yogurt
150ml (¼ pint) whipping cream

To decorate
150ml (¼ pint) whipped cream
3 kiwi fruit, peeled and sliced
Nuts

Base
Grease and line the base and sides of a 20cm (8 inch) loose bottom cake tin with greaseproof paper. Note: The paper should come over the top of the tin. In a mixing bowl add the margarine, egg and caster sugar and cream the mixture until fluffy. Sieve the flour and baking

powder into the bowl and beat. Add the orange rind. Use either a wooden spoon or electric whisk for two or one minute respectively. Spoon the mixture into the cake tin and cook for 20 minutes, 180°C (350°F) Gas Mark 4. Leave in tin when cooked and allow to cool.

Filling
While the base is cooking, beat the sugar with cream cheese and add the egg yolks, orange juice and rind. Beat until very smooth. In a heatproof basin put the cold water and sprinkle in the gelatine, leaving it to stand for 10 minutes until soft. Stand the basin in a pan of simmering water until gelatine dissolves. Stir constantly. Leave to cool but not set. Pour the gelatine in a constant stream into the cheese mixture and stir. Whisk in the yogurt. Whip the cream and fold carefully into the mixture using a metal spoon. Whisk the egg whites in a clean bowl until stiff

and fold into cheese mixture. Pour the cheese mixture over the base and smooth the top. Leave to set in the fridge for several hours.

To decorate
Remove from the tin and carefully peel off the paper, serve decorated with cream, kiwi fruit and nuts (an alternative could be orange segments). Serve chilled.

Poached Minty Pears

PREPARATION TIME: 40 minutes
                        plus chilling

6 large pears, peeled
6 tablespoons sugar
Fresh mint leaves
6 tablespoons clear honey
3 tablespoons Creme de Menthe
    liqueur

Put the pears in a saucepan. Stand upright and pour water over. Cover all the pears. Boil and then simmer for 30 minutes. Pour off half the water and sprinkle over with sugar. Add the fresh mint and simmer for 10 minutes. Transfer the pears to a bowl. Reserve 150ml (¼ pint) water from the pan and stir in the honey and liqueur. Pour this mixture over the pears and allow it to cool. Cover the pears and chill for 2 hours. Stand each pear on an individual serving dish and spoon over the mint sauce.

This page: Blackberry Ice Cream Dessert (top), Coconut Cups (bottom).

Facing page: Kiwi Cheesecake (top), Poached Minty Pear (bottom).

Coffee Truffles

PREPARATION TIME: 10 minutes

200-225g (8oz) cake crumbs
25g (1oz) ground almonds
¼ teaspoon coffee powder
Heaped tablespoon apricot jam, melted
2-3 tablespoons coffee liqueur
50g (2oz) chocolate vermicelli

Put the crumbs and ground almonds into a bowl. Mix in the jam and coffee liqueur and mix together to form a stiff paste. Shape into small balls and roll in chocolate vermicelli.

Crystal Fruits

1 egg white
200g (8oz) bunch of grapes
2 large red apples
2 large pears
100g (4oz) plums
Any other soft fruit in season

Whisk up the egg white well and brush onto the fruit. Leave for a few minutes but not until dry. Dip the fruit into caster sugar and place on greaseproof paper until dry. Arrange in fruit bowl or stand.

Apricot Mountain

PREPARATION TIME: 20 minutes

COOKING TIME: 4 minutes or until meringue is brown

OVEN: 230°C (450°F) Gas Mark 8

About 350g (¾lb) tinned apricot halves
4-6 tablespoons Marsala or sweet sherry
3 egg whites
100g (4oz) caster sugar
1 x 20cm (8 inch) sponge flan case
450ml (¾ pint) vanilla ice cream

Strain the apricots and sprinkle them with the sherry. Whisk the egg whites until stiff and fold in the sugar. Whisk again until the meringue peaks. Stand the flan case on a heatproof dish and sprinkle with a little more sherry. Pile the apricots into the flan case. Cover the apricots with a mountain shape of ice cream. Using the meringue mixture, quickly cover the ice cream and the sponge base. Bake immediately until the meringue is

light brown. Serve from the oven. For a very special effect bury half an egg shell at the top of the mountain before baking the meringue. As you serve fill it with warmed brandy, ignite and serve flaming.

Petits Fours

PREPARATION TIME: 40 minutes
OVEN: 200°C (400°F) Gas Mark 6

Sponge
3 eggs
125g (4oz) caster sugar
75g (3oz) plain flour
1 tablespoon hot water

Topping
Fruits in season
Apricot jam to glaze

Sponge
Whisk eggs and sugar until thick and creamy. Sift in flour and fold in with the hot water. Place mixture in a greased and floured swiss roll tin. Bake for 8 to 10 minutes until cake springs back when pressed. Turn out and cool. Cut shapes out of the sponge using pastry cutters.

Topping
Place sponge shapes on a wire rack and top with attractively arranged fruit. Melt apricot jam on low heat and spoon over shapes to glaze. When surplus has dripped off and jam has set remove and place on serving plate.

Chocolate Leaf, Filled with Orange Mousse

PREPARATION TIME: 1 hour
plus chilling

For the Leaf
175g (6oz) plain chocolate
1 cabbage leaf (with veins)

Mousse
3 whole eggs plus 2 yolks
50g (2oz) caster sugar
Juice of ½ lemon
15g (½oz) powdered gelatine
150ml (¼ pint) double cream
150ml (¼ pint) freshly squeezed orange juice
Finely grated rind of 2 oranges

Leaf
Put the chocolate in a basin over

simmering water and stir until smooth. With a pastry brush, paint the chocolate over a well-veined cabbage leaf and leave to cool and harden. Repeat the process until there is a thick build up of chocolate on the leaf. When hard the cabbage leaf can be easily removed.

Mousse
Put the eggs and yolks in a basin with the caster sugar. Whisk until pale and frothy. This can be done over a saucepan of simmering water, but make sure that the basin doesn't touch the water. Beat until thick. Remove from the heat and whisk until cold. Put the lemon juice and a little water into a small saucepan and sprinkle in the gelatine and leave it to soak for a few minutes. Whip the cream and stir it into the egg mixture, gradually adding the orange juice and grated rind. Gently heat the gelatine until clear and stir it quickly into the mixture. Fill the serving dish and refrigerate until set. This mousse can either be served with one leaf or several small leaves to go with each portion of mousse.

Crystal Fruits (left), Coffee Truffles (bottom left)
and Petits Fours (bottom right).

Fruit Salad with Mango Purée

PREPARATION TIME: 20 minutes plus 1 hour chilling in the refrigerator

3 peaches
3 tamarillos (tree tomatoes)
3 kiwi fruit
1½ tablespoons lemon juice
3 tablespoons sugar syrup

Mango Purée
2 well-ripened mangoes weighing about 300g (12oz)
Juice of ½ a lime, or lemon
3 teaspoons honey
125g (5oz) redcurrants
Strawberry leaves for decoration

Blanch the peaches briefly and peel. Halve and remove stones and cut into delicate wedges. Peel and slice the tamarillos, nectarines and kiwi fruit, arrange in serving dish and scatter over with redcurrants. Pour over the lemon juice mixed with sugar syrup. Leave the fruits to stand in syrup for 1 hour in a cool place.

Mango Purée
Either liquidise or rub through a wire sieve the flesh of the mangoes and mix with the lime juice. Mix in the honey and pour the mixture over the fruit. Decorate with strawberry leaves.

Pineapple Malibu

PREPARATION TIME: 30 minutes

1 medium ripe pineapple
450ml (15 fl oz) double cream
75g (3oz) macaroons, roughly crushed
3 tablespoons coconut liqueur

Cut the pineapple a few inches below the top. Scoop out as much of the fruit as possible, discarding the core if hard. Chop the fruit into bite-size pieces. Whip two-thirds of the cream until it begins to stiffen and fold in the macaroons, having first soaked them in the coconut liqueur. In another bowl whip up the remaining cream and fold into the coconut cream. Spoon alternate spoonfuls of diced pineapple and cream mixture into the hollowed pineapple and chill. Serve straight from the fridge.

Chocolate Ginger Flan

PREPARATION TIME: 30 minutes

100g (4oz) plain chocolate
300ml (½ pint) milk
100g (4oz) caster sugar
3 tablespoons flour
100g (4oz) butter
2 egg yolks
150g (6oz) ginger nut biscuits
Whipped cream
100g (4oz) stem ginger cut into thin slices

Melt the chocolate in the milk in a saucepan, stirring constantly.

Remove pan from heat. Mix the caster sugar, flour and 50g (2oz) butter into the chocolate milk and stir in the egg yolks. Put on a low heat and slowly bring to the boil. Simmer for 5 minutes until the mixture begins to thicken, stir until smooth. Remove from heat and cool. While the filling is cooling, melt the remaining 50g (2oz) of butter and crush the ginger nut biscuits. Mix the biscuits with the melted butter and press in a greased pie mould. When the filling is cool, pour onto the ginger nut base. Chill and decorate with whipped cream and sprinkle with stemmed ginger cut into thin slices

(an alternative decoration is chocolate vermicelli).

Coffee Charlotte

PREPARATION TIME: 1½ hours
COOKING TIME: 12 minutes
OVEN: 220°C (475°F) Gas Mark 7

Sponge
4 egg yolks
50g (2oz) sugar
Generous pinch of salt
3 egg whites
60g (2½oz) flour mixed with 2 teaspoons coffee powder

tablespoon of brandy. Add to the custard mixture and stir well. Cool the custard. Meanwhile stiffly whip the cream, adding the remaining sugar. When the custard begins to set, carefully fold in the cream and fill the sponge-lined mould. Stir in the marinated apricot and cover the top of the mould with slices from the sponge roll. Let the charlotte set for three hours in the refrigerator and turn onto a serving dish. Brush with the apricot glaze.

Orange Campari Mousse

PREPARATION TIME: 45 minutes
plus chilling

1 teaspoon powdered gelatine
2 medium oranges, washed and dried
75g (3oz) caster sugar
2 eggs, separated
3 tablespoons Campari
150ml (¼ pint) double cream
1 tablespoon cold milk
Red grapes

Add gelatine to two tablespoons of water in a saucepan. Leave to one side. Grate peel of 1 orange. Squeeze oranges and if necessary make up juice to 175ml (6 fl oz) with water. Melt gelatine and water over a low heat. Stir in orange juice. Pour mixture into a bowl, whisk in sugar, egg yolks, Campari and orange peel. Place in fridge until the mixture begins to thicken and set. In one bowl beat egg whites until stiff. In another whisk milk and cream together thick. Gradually mix egg whites and cream alternately into the orange mixture until totally incorporated. Pour into a bowl and place in refrigerator until firm and set. Serve in glasses decorated with sliced red grapes.

175g (6oz) apricot jam
3 tablespoons brandy
2 tablespoons cornflour

Charlotte
6 apricot halves
1 tablespoon vanilla sugar
1 tablespoon brandy
4 egg yolks
100g (4oz) sugar
Plus 1 tablespoon sugar
250ml (8 fl oz) milk
½ vanilla pod
15g (½oz) powdered gelatine
250ml (8 fl oz) double or whipping
   cream
75ml (2½ fl oz) apricot glaze
   (warmed apricot jam)

Sponge
Beat the egg yolks with a spoonful of sugar and the salt. Whisk the egg whites and fold the egg yolk mixture into the meringue. Sift together the cornflour and flour and stir them in. Line a swiss roll tin with non-stick silicone paper or greaseproof paper. Spread the sponge mixture evenly in the swiss roll tin using a spatula. Bake until golden. Turn it out at once onto a damp tea towel and peel off the paper. Blend the jam with the brandy and spread the sponge cake with it. Roll it up. Let it cool and cut into thin slices 5mm (¼ inch) thick. Line the mould with the

slices as close together as possible.

Charlotte
Place the apricot halves in a dish and sprinkle them with vanilla sugar. Pour over the brandy. Leave them to marinate in the refrigerator for half an hour. Cream the egg yolks and sugar together in a mixing bowl and put the milk in a small saucepan with the vanilla pod. Heat the milk and bring to the boil and pour into the egg yolks. Return the custard mixture to the saucepan and stir until it is thick enough to coat the spoon. Remove from heat. Dissolve the gelatine in warm water and stir in the

Facing page: Apricot Mountain (left), Orange Campari Mousse (right).

This page: Chocolate Leaf, Filled with Orange Mousse (top), Chocolate Ginger Flan (centre left) and Fruit Salad with Mango Purée (bottom right).

Strawberry Shortcake

PREPARATION TIME: 1 hour

COOKING TIME: 25 minutes

OVEN: 220°C (425°F) Gas Mark 7

Shortcake
225g (8oz) plain flour
Pinch of salt
4 teaspoons baking powder
75g (3oz) butter
1 large egg
40g (1½oz) caster sugar
3 tablespoons milk
1 tablespoon melted butter

Filling
1 tablespoon custard powder
300ml (½ pint) milk
2 tablespoons sugar
150ml (¼ pint) double cream
450g (1lb) fresh or thawed, frozen
    strawberries
8 toasted almonds

Shortcake
Sift the flour, salt and baking powder into a bowl. With a knife mix in the butter. Beat in the egg, sugar and milk and pour into the centre of the dry ingredients. Mix into a dough. On a lightly floured surface knead gently and divide into two. Brush a 20cm (8 inch) sandwich tin with melted butter and shape half the dough into a circle to fit. Place the second circle on top and bake until risen and golden brown. Cool and separate the two halves.

Filling
Make up the custard using the milk and sugar. Cover and leave to cool. Whisk the cream until just stiff. Fold the cream into the cooled custard, reserving two tablespoons for decoration. Reserving 8 whole strawberries and one-third of the custard mixture, halve the remaining strawberries and mix into the custard cream. Spread the strawberry custard on the bottom layer of the shortbread and sandwich with the top layer. Spread the top with the reserved custard mixture and decorate with whole strawberries and almonds.

Green Devils

PREPARATION TIME: 20 minutes
    plus chilling

600g (1½lb) dessert gooseberries
150g (6oz) caster sugar
600ml (1 pint) water
3 tablespoons grenadine
Juice ½ lemon
1 level tablespoon cornflour
Cream

Rinse and top and tail the gooseberries. Put the caster sugar in a small saucepan and dissolve it in the water. Simmer and bring to the boil. Take off heat and stir in the grenadine, lemon juice and gooseberries and bring back to simmer. Cook very gently for five minutes until the fruit is tender. Remove from heat. Lift out the fruit and put into the serving dish. Mix the cornflour with a little water to make a thin paste. Stir into the fruit juice till it begins to thicken. Stir all the time. When the syrup is clear, pour over the fruit. Chill, preferably overnight, and serve with thick pouring cream.

Chestnut Parfait

PREPARATION TIME: 40 minutes
    plus freezing

4 egg yolks
150g (5oz) sugar
150ml (¼ pint) milk, warmed and
    flavoured with a vanilla pod
200g (7oz) unsweetened chestnut
    purée
2 tablespoons dark rum
2 egg whites
50g (2oz) sugar
500ml (17 fl oz) double cream
Chocolate leaves
A few cranberries
Whipped cream

Beat the egg yolks with the sugar and add the warmed milk flavoured with the vanilla pod and cook until thickened, stirring gently. The mixture should coat the spoon. Transfer to a mixing bowl. Add the chestnut purée and rum while the mixture is still lukewarm. Chill well. Whip the egg whites with the sugar until very stiff. Whisk the cream until it peaks. Fold the egg white into the chestnut custard and carefully fold in the whipped cream. Pour into a 1.5 litre (2¾ pint) mould and freeze for 4 hours. Decorate with small rounds of sweetened chestnut purée dusted with chocolate powder or melted chocolate sauce.

Facing page: Pineapple Malibu (top), Coffee Charlotte (centre right) and Chestnut Parfait (bottom).

This page: Green Devils (top), Strawberry Shortcake (bottom).

CAKES
AND
CAKE DECORATION

Introduction

Cake decorating is both rewarding and interesting. It is hoped that this section of the book will show how simple it can be and encourage those who use it to improve on their basic skills.

Starting with the simplest icings, such as butter icing, which is easy to use and can create elaborate novelty cakes, the more complex techniques required to master the icing and decoration of wedding and other celebration cakes are gradually introduced.

Always try to avoid last-minute rushes; many of the decorations can be made in advance and stored. Try to plan ahead when you know that you will be making a special cake and remember that icing and decorating can take time and patience. If you have not had much

practice, start with the simpler designs before trying to tackle a royal-icing celebration cake. You will be anxious that the result should be stunning, so practice first!

Never pipe the design straight onto the cake, as you may ruin the surface you have created. If you are using a complex design, pipe first in white icing then overpipe in colour. This way, if you make a mistake, you have not stained the surface of the cake. The cakes described here will certainly give you some new ideas and may encourage you to design versions of your own.

Cakes and their decoration is an absorbing hobby. By following and practising some of the designs suggested, it is hoped you will be able to produce a highly professional result – cakes for every occasion.

Note:
All eggs are size 2.
All spoon measures are level in both imperial and metric sizes.
Some spoon measures even supply a spoon equivalent to a pinch. Metric and imperial measurements have been calculated separately. Only use one set of measurements – they are not interchangeable.

Cooking times may vary as they depend upon the efficiency of your oven. Dishes should always be placed in the centre of the oven unless otherwise stated.

Fan-assisted ovens may cook slightly quicker, so follow the manufacturer's instructions. Always preheat the oven to the specified temperature.

CAKES AND CAKE DECORATION

Basic Cakes and Icing

Lining Cake Tins
All tins must be greased and lined unless you are using a non-stick cake tin, in which case follow the manufacturer's instructions.
If using a shallow tin, only the base needs to be lined for whisked sponges and the quick cake mixture.
If you are making a fruit cake, which will take longer to bake, then the sides as well as the base need lining using a double thickness of greaseproof paper.

To Grease the Tin
Brush with melted lard, margarine or oil. Grease the greaseproof paper with melted fat or oil; if you are using non-stick silicone paper do not grease it. In the preparation of tins, it is necessary to grease and dust them with flour if you are not lining them.

Round Tins
To line a deep, round tin, draw with a pencil round the edge of the cake tin on double thickness greaseproof paper and cut the resulting shape out.
Using a piece of string, measure round the tin. Use another piece of string to measure the height plus 2.5cm (1 inch). Cut out one long strip or two shorter lengths of greaseproof paper to the equivalent of these measurements. If making two lengths, add on a little extra for them to overlap. Make a fold 5mm (¼ inch) deep along one edge and cut into the fold at regular intervals at a slight angle. Place one of the circles of paper in the bottom of the tin, followed by the side pieces and, finally, the second paper circle which will cover the slashed edges.

Square Tins
To line a deep, square tin follow the instructions above for a round tin, but fold the long strips so they fit into the corners of the tin.

Rich Fruit Cake

CAKE SIZES	12cm (5in) round 10cm (4in) square	15cm (6in) round 12cm (5in) square	18cm (7in) round 15cm (6in) square	20cm (8in) round 18cm (7in) square	23cm (9in) round 20cm (8in) square	25cm (10in) roun 23cm (9in) squar
APPROX COOKING TIME:	2½ hours	2¾ hours	3¼ hours	3¼ hours	4 hours	4¼-4½ hours
OVEN:	140°C/275°F Gas Mark 1	140°C/275°F Gas Mark 1	140°C/275°F Gas Mark 1	140°C/275°F Gas Mark 1	140°C/275°F Gas Mark 1	140°C/275°F Gas Mark 1
Note for all recipes: First ⅔ of cooking time at 150°C/300°F Gas Mark 2						
Butter	65g/2½oz	75g/3oz	125g/4oz	150g/5oz	200g/7oz	250g/9oz
Eggs	2	2	3	4	5	6
Plain flour	75g/3oz	125g/4oz	175g/6oz	200g/7oz	250g/9oz	300g/11oz
Dark soft brown sugar	75g/3oz	90g/3½oz	150g/5oz	175g/6oz	225g/8oz	275g/10oz
Black treacle	½ tblsp	½ tblsp	1 tblsp	1 tblsp	1 tblsp	1 tblsp
Ground almonds	25g/1oz	25g/1oz	40g/1½oz	50g/2oz	65g/2½oz	75g/3oz
Ground mixed spice	½ tsp	½ tsp	¾ tsp	1 tsp	1¼ tsp	1½ tsp
Grated lemon rind	½ lemon	½ lemon	1 lemon	1 lemon	1 lemon	2 lemons
Grated orange rind	½ orange	½ orange	1 orange	1 orange	1 orange	2 oranges
Grated nutmeg	¼ tsp	¼ tsp	¼ tsp	½ tsp	½ tsp	¾ tsp
Chopped almonds	25g/1oz	40g/1½oz	50g/2oz	65g/2½ oz	90g/3½oz	125g/4oz
Currants	150g/5oz	175g/6oz	225g/8oz	275g/10oz	375g/13oz	450g/1lb
Raisins	25g/1oz	50g/2oz	75g/3oz	125g/4oz	150g/5oz	175g/6oz
Sultanas	75g/3oz	125g/4oz	150g/5oz	200g/7oz	250g/9oz	300g/11oz
Chopped mixed peel	25g/1oz	40g/1½oz	50g/2oz	65g/2½oz	90g/3½oz	125g/4oz
Glacé cherries	25g/1oz	40g/1½oz	50g/2oz	65g/2½oz	90g/3½oz	125g/4oz
Orange juice	1 tblsp	1 tblsp	1 tblsp	1 tblsp	2 tblsp	2 tblsp
Brandy	1 tblsp	1 tblsp	1 tblsp	2 tblsp	2 tblsp	3 tblsp

Swiss Roll Tins (Long, Shallow Tins)

Grease and line a shallow tin so that the cake may be easily removed. Line the sides of the tin with paper at least 4cm (1½ inches) longer than the tin, cutting into each corner.

Loaf Tins

When lining a loaf tin the method is again the same, but the paper should be 15cm (6 inches) larger than the top of the tin.

28cm (11in) round 25cm (10in) square	30cm (12in) round 28cm (11in) square
5-5¼ hours	6 hours
140°C/275°F Gas Mark 1	140°C/275°F Gas Mark 1
See note opposite	
300g/11oz	375g/13oz
7	8
400g/14oz	450g/1lb
350g/12oz	400g/14oz
1½ tblsp	2 tblsp
90g/3½oz	125g/4oz
1½ tsp	2 tsp
2 lemons	2 lemons
2 oranges	2 oranges
¼ tsp	1 tsp
150g/5oz	175g/6oz
575g/1¼lb	675g/1½lb
200g/7oz	225g/8oz
375g/13oz	450g/1lb
150g/5oz	175g/6oz
150g/5oz	175g/6oz
3 tblsp	3 tblsp
3 tblsp	4 tblsp

Rich Fruit Cake

This is a traditional recipe which cuts well and is rich, dark and moist. Traditional fruit cake improves with keeping and is used for celebration cakes – weddings, birthdays and Christmas – marzipanned and royal iced. Prepacked dried fruit is ready washed, but if you are buying your fruit loose, rinse it through with cold water and dry it well with kitchen paper or clean cloths. Then spread it out on a tea towel placed on a baking sheet in a warm (not hot) place for 24 hours. Do not use wet fruit in a cake as the fruit will sink.

Mix the sultanas, currants and raisins together. Cut the glacé cherries into quarters, rinse in warm water and dry with kitchen paper. Add the cherries to the fruit together with mixed peel, almonds, and grated orange and lemon rind.

Oiling and lining cake tins.

Sift the flour with a pinch of salt, ground cinnamon and mixed spice. Cream the butter until soft, then add the sugar and cream until light and fluffy (do not overbeat). Add the eggs one at a time, beat well and after each egg add a spoonful of flour. Add the black treacle, orange juice and brandy, if desired. Spread the mixture evenly into a greased and double-lined tin. Use the back of a spoon to make a slight hollow in the centre of the cake so it will be flat when cooked. Tie two thicknesses of brown paper round the tin then bake in the centre of the oven at 150°C, 300°F, Gas Mark 2 (see chart for

the suggested time). With large cakes turn the oven down to 140°C, 275°F, Gas Mark 1, after two-thirds of the cooking time. To test the cake, push a skewer into the centre. It should come out clean if the cake is cooked. When the cake is cooked, remove the tin from the oven and leave the cake in the tin to cool. Turn the cake onto a wire rack and remove the lining paper. Spike the top of the cake with a skewer and spoon a few tablespoons of brandy or other spirit over the top. To store the cake, wrap it in greaseproof paper and foil. If possible, repeat the spooning over of brandy or spirit every few weeks. The cake can be allowed to mature for 2-3 months.

Quick Mix Cake

This is a quick cake, which is ideal for novelty cakes, and the mixture is firm enough to cut into any shape; it is moist and crumbly and can be filled with cream, butter or jam.

Put the margarine, sugar, eggs, sifted flour and baking powder in a bowl. Mix together all the ingredients with either a wooden spoon or electric mixer. Beat for 1-2 minutes until the mixture is smooth and glossy. In a food processor this will take 30 seconds-1 minute. Put the mixture in a prepared tin. Level the top with the back of a spoon and bake in the centre of the oven at 160°C, 325°F, Gas Mark 3 (see chart for the suggested time). When baked, the cake will be firm to the touch and shrink away from the sides of the tin. Loosen the sides of the cake from the tin and leave it to cool on a wire rack. Turn the cake right way up onto another wire rack.

Whisked Sponge Cake

This cake mixture is ideal for afternoon tea and the cake may be filled with cream, butter icing or fruit. It does not keep well and is best eaten the same day it is made, although it can be kept in the freezer for up to 2 months.

Put the eggs and sugar in a

heatproof bowl over a saucepan of hot, not boiling, water. The bowl must not touch the water. Whisk the mixture until it becomes thick enough to leave a trail when lifted. Sift the flour and baking powder together and fold into the egg mixture with a metal spoon, taking care not to knock the air out. Pour the mixture into a prepared tin and gently shake the mixture level. Bake in the centre of the oven (see chart for oven temperature and suggested time). Remove from the tin and cool on a wire rack. When making a Swiss roll, turn out the cake onto a sheet of greaseproof paper sprinkled with caster sugar. Quickly peel off the lining paper and trim the cake edges. Fold and roll the cake up without cracking it. Let it cool a little, then unroll and remove the greaseproof paper. Fill and re-roll the cake.

Madeira Cake

Madeira cake is a moist cake that can be covered with marzipan and then iced with royal icing or any other icing.

PREPARATION TIME: 15 minutes

COOKING TIME: 1 hour 15 minutes to 1 hour 30 minutes

OVEN TEMPERATURE: 160°C, 325°F, Gas Mark 3

175g (6oz) butter
175g (6oz) caster sugar
Grated rind of 1 lemon
3 eggs
225g (8oz) plain flour
7.5ml (1½ tsp) baking powder
30ml (2 tblsp) warm water

Cream the butter and sugar until they are light and fluffy. Beat the eggs in one at a time, then after each egg add a spoonful of flour. Sift in the remaining flour and fold it into the flour with lemon rind and juice. Turn into a prepared cake tin and bake in the oven for 1¼-1½ hours. When cooked, the cake should be firm to the touch. Leave it in the tin to cool for 5-10 minutes, then turn onto a wire rack and remove the lining paper.

Whisked Sponge Cake

CAKE SIZES	2 x 18cm (7in) sandwich tins	20cm (8in) sandwich tin 18cm (7in) square tin	28 x 18cm (11 x 7in) Swiss roll tin	18 sponge drops	20cm (8in) round cake tin	2 x 20cm (8in) sandwich tins
APPROX COOKING TIME:	20-25 minutes	25-30 minutes	10-12 minutes	5-10 minutes	35-40 minutes	20-25 minutes
OVEN:	180°C/350°F Gas Mark 4	180°C/350°F Gas Mark 4	190°C/375°F Gas Mark 5	190°C/375°F Gas Mark 5	180°C/350°F Gas Mark 4	180°C/350°F Gas Mark 4
Eggs (sizes 1-2)	2	2	2	2	3	3
Caster sugar	50g/2oz	50g/2oz	50g/2oz	50g/2oz	75g/3oz	75g/3oz
Plain flour	50g/2oz	50g/2oz	50g/2oz	50g/2oz	75g/3oz	75g/3oz
Baking powder	½ tsp	½ tsp	½ tsp	½ tsp	½ tsp	½ tsp

Quick Mix Cake

CAKE SIZES	2 x 18cm (7in) sandwich tins	18 paper cake cases or patty tins	20cm (8in) sandwich tin 20cm (8in) ring mould 18cm (7in) deep square tin	*900ml (1½ pint) pudding basin *add 25g/1oz cornflour sifted with the flour	About 26 paper cake cases or patty tins	2 x 20cm (8in) sandwich tins
APPROX COOKING TIME:	25-30 minutes	15-20 minutes	35-40 minutes	about 50 minutes	15-20 minutes	30-35 minutes
OVEN:	160°C/325°F Gas Mark 3	160°C/325°F Gas Mark 3	160°C/325°F Gas Mark 3	160°C/325°F Gas Mark 3	160°C/325°F Gas Mark 3	160°C/325°F Gas Mark 3
Soft tub margarine, chilled	100g/4oz	100g/4oz	100g/4oz	100g/4oz	175g/6oz	175g/6oz
Caster sugar	100g/4oz	100g/4oz	100g/4oz	100g/4oz	175g/6oz	175g/6oz
Eggs (sizes 1-2)	2	2	2	2	3	3
Self-raising flour	100g/4oz	100g/4oz	100g/4oz	100g/4oz	175g/6oz	175g/6oz
Baking powder	1 tsp	1 tsp	1 tsp	1 tsp	1½ tsp	1½ tsp
Vanilla essence	4 drops	4 drops	4 drops	4 drops	6 drops	6 drops

For Victoria Sponge see 'Tea Time Treats'.

Variations

Chocolate Victoria Sponge
Replace 25g (1oz) flour with 25g (1oz) sifted cocoa powder. Add this to the other flour.

Coffee Victoria Sponge
Replace the water with coffee essence, or dissolve 10ml (2 tsp) instant coffee powder in 15ml (1 tblsp) boiling water.

Lemon Victoria Sponge
Add the very finely grated rind of 1 lemon.

28 x 18 x 4cm (11 x 7 x 1½in) slab cake	30 x 23cm (12 x 9in) Swiss roll tin
30-35 minutes	12-15 minutes
180°C/350°F Gas Mark 4	200°C/400°F Gas Mark 6
3	3
75g/3oz	75g/3oz
75g/3oz	75g/3oz
½ tsp	½ tsp

23cm (9in) sandwich tin	28 x 18 x 4cm (11 x 7 x 1½in) slab cake / 20cm (8in) round tin / 20cm (8in) square tin	1 litre (2 pint) pudding basin	29 x 21 x 4cm (11½ x 8½ x 1½in) slab cake	23cm (9in) round tin / 23cm (9in) square tin	30 x 25 x 5cm (12 x 10 x 2in) slab cake
about 25 minutes	35-40 minutes	about 1 hour	about 40 minutes	about 1 hour	50-60 minutes
160°C/325°F Gas Mark 3	160°C/325°F Gas Mark 3	160°C/325°F Gas Mark 3	160°C/325°F Gas Mark 3	160°C/325°F Gas Mark 3	160°C/325°F Gas Mark 3
175g/6oz	175g/6oz	175g/6oz	200g/8oz	200g/8oz	275g/10oz
175g/6oz	175g/6oz	175g/6oz	200g/8oz	200g/8oz	275g/10oz
3	3	3	4	4	5
175g/6oz	175g/6oz	175g/6oz	200g/8oz	200g/8oz	275g/10oz
1½ tsp	1½ tsp	1½ tsp	2 tsp	2 tsp	2½ tsp
6 drops	6 drops	6 drops	8 drops	8 drops	10 drops

Basic Icing Recipes and Their Uses

Quick Frosting

This is an easy white frosting which is a quick version of the traditional American frosting. A sugar thermometer is not required for this recipe, but the icing must be used very quickly before it sets.

PREPARATION TIME: 7-10 minutes

1 egg white
150g (6oz) caster sugar
Pinch of salt
30ml (2 tblsp) water
Pinch of cream of tartar

Put all the ingredients into a heatproof bowl and mix. Put the bowl over a pan of simmering hot water and beat the mixture. If possible, use an electric mixer until the icing peaks. Remove the icing from the heat and pour it over the cake, spreading it quickly. This will cover an 18cm (7 inch) cake.

Chocolate Fudge Icing

PREPARATION TIME: 10 minutes

This is a delicious chocolate icing which is quick and easy to make.

50g (2oz) butter
45ml (3 tblsp) milk
250g (8oz) icing sugar, well sifted
30ml (2 tblsp) cocoa powder, sifted

Melt the butter in a small saucepan with the milk. Add the icing sugar and cocoa and beat well until smooth and very glossy. Cool until lukewarm and pour over cake. This is enough to fill and ice the top of a 20cm (8 inch) cake.
NB: if the icing is too thick to pour, reheat gently to thin. This icing can also be made in a small bowl over a pan of gently simmering water.

Sponges: Whisked Sponge, Madeira Cake.

Marzipan or Almond Paste

This is a paste which is made firm and rollable, and is traditionally used as a base cover for fruit cakes before coating with royal icing or any other decorative icing. Prepare the cake by levelling the top, if necessary. Dust a work surface with icing sugar and roll out half the almond paste 2.5cm (1 inch) larger than the top of the cake. Brush the top of the cake with the apricot glaze, or the egg white and brandy. Invert the cake onto the almond paste and, using a palette knife, draw up the top of the almond paste around the cake. Put the top of the cake down on a board and brush the sides of the cake with apricot glaze. Cut two pieces of string or thread, one the height of the cake and the other equal in length to the circumference. Roll out the remaining almond paste into a strip, equal in height and length of circumference of the cake, using the strings as a guide, or cut two short strips of paste instead. Carefully wrap the almond paste round the cake, pressing firmly round the sides and joins. For a square cake, cut the string into four lengths, equal to the sides of the cake and cut the paste to match. Press lightly on the paste when it is placed round the cake in order to produce sharp corners. When covered, leave the cake for 24 hours to dry. Wedding cakes should be left for up to 1 week before icing, otherwise almond oil will stain the icing if the cake is kept after the wedding.

Marzipan or Almond Paste

PREPARATION TIME: 15 minutes

100g (4oz) caster sugar
100g (4oz) icing sugar
200g (8oz) ground almonds
5ml (1 tsp) lemon juice
A few drops almond essence
1 or 2 egg yolks, beaten

Mix the sugars and the ground almonds in a bowl. Make a well in the centre and add the lemon juice, almond essence and egg yolk or yolks to the mixture and form into a pliable dough. Lightly dust the work surface with icing sugar and

Guide to Almond Paste Quantities Required for Cakes

Square	Round	Paste / marzipan
12.5cm (5 inch)	15cm (6 inch)	350g (12oz)
15cm (6 inch)	18cm (7 inch)	550g (1lb 4oz)
18cm (7 inch)	20cm (8 inch)	675g (1½lb)
20cm (8 inch)	23cm (9 inch)	675g (1½lb)
23cm (9 inch)	25cm (10 inch)	900g (2lb)
25cm (10 inch)	28cm (11 inch)	1kg (2¼lb)
28cm (11 inch)	30cm (12 inch)	1.25kg (2½lb)
30cm (12 inch)		1.5kg (3lb)

turn out the dough. Knead until smooth. The marzipan can be stored in a polythene bag or wrapped in foil for 2-3 days before use. Makes 450g (1lb).

Apricot Glaze

PREPARATION TIME: 10 minutes

This glaze can be stored in an airtight container for up to 1 week, if kept in the refrigerator. Re-boil the glaze and cool before applying to the cake.

175-225g (6-8oz) apricot jam
30ml (2 tblsp) water

Put the jam and water in a saucepan and heat until the jam has melted, stirring occasionally. Pour the jam through a sieve and return it to a clean saucepan. Re-boil and simmer until you have a slightly thickened consistency. Cool before applying to the cake.

How to Royal Ice

It does not matter whether you ice the top or the sides first. The important point to remember is that the icing should be applied in several thin coats. Try icing a section first, rather than doing all of it in one go. Your aim is to achieve a smooth surface and you must let each coat dry before applying another. Most cakes require 2 coats on the top and sides, with maybe 3 on the top for a very smooth finish. Wedding cakes require three coats all over and the bottom tiers need 4 coats. For a 2 or 3-tier cake apply 4 coats to the bottom tier; for a 4-tier cake apply 4 coats to the bottom 2 tiers.

Method for Icing a Cake – Icing the Sides of a Round Cake

A flat-sided scraper is essential for producing smooth sides. Put plenty of icing on the side of the cake and, using a small palette knife, move it back and forth to get a relatively smooth surface and to remove little air pockets. For round cakes, put your arm round the back of the cake and move the scraper forwards on the cake as you can try to get a smooth, sweeping movement without stopping. The scraper should be upright against the side of the cake. Move the scraper off the cake at an angle so the join is not noticeable. If you use a turntable, it will make icing larger cakes easier. Hold the scraper to the side of the cake and use the other hand round the cake so the turntable moves round quickly and smoothly in one revolution. Scrape off any extra icing with a small palette knife. Wipe the cake board and allow each coat to dry for 2-3 hours or overnight before icing the top.

Icing the Top

When icing the base tier of a wedding cake, remember not to add glycerine. Spread the icing on the cake and, using a metal, or firm, plastic, ruler held at a 30° angle, draw it gently across the cake with a positive movement. Try not to press down too hard or the icing will be too thin. Remove any surplus icing from the sides of the cake with a clean palette knife. Leave the icing for at least a day to dry. Remove any rough edges round the joins with clean, fine-graded sandpaper. If the coating is not enough, repeat this 2-3 times. Wait 24 hours before piping decoration onto the cake.

Icing a Square Cake

Ice 2 opposite sides first, then the other 2 sides to produce sharp corners. Hold the palette knife parallel with the side of the cake when icing.

Royal Icing

The consistency of royal icing depends upon its use. For rosettes and flat icing it should be quite firm, whereas for piping latticework and writing it should be a little thinner. When icing is required for any flooding and runouts, it should be thin and smooth. Royal icing can be made in any quantity in the proportion of 1 egg per 225g (8oz) of sieved icing sugar. Keep the icing bowl covered with a damp cloth to keep it moist. As an egg substitute, egg albumen (white) can be bought in specialist cake decoration shops and the instructions for use are given on the packet. The addition of glycerine will aid the softening of the icing when it is dry. This makes it easier to cut.

Wedding Cakes

When icing wedding cakes, do not add glycerine to the two top layers of icing on the bottom tier, so the cake can support the other tiers. Made icing can be stored in an airtight container in a cool atmosphere for 2 days. Before use the stored icing should be stirred well.

Beat the egg whites until frothy with a wire whisk, making sure that the bowl is clean and dry first. Gradually beat in half the icing sugar using a wooden spoon. Beat in the remaining half of the icing sugar with the glycerine and, if using lemon juice, add it now. Beat the mixture thoroughly until smooth and white. Beat in enough icing sugar to give the mixture a consistency which is stiff and stands in peaks. Add the colour, if required. Cover the bowl with a damp cloth and leave the icing to stand for several hours. This allows any air bubbles to rise to the surface of the icing and burst. Before using, stir well with a wooden spoon. Do not overbeat. Note: if you are using an electric mixer, use the slowest speed and leave the icing for 24 hours. It will incorporate more air and will need longer to stand.

Facing page: covering with marzipan, and using apricot glaze.

Guide to Royal Icing Quantities Required to Flat Ice in Two Thin Coats

Square	Round	Icing Sugar
12.5cm (5 inch)	15cm (6 inch)	675g (1½lb)
15cm (6 inch)	18cm (7 inch)	900g (2lb)
18cm (7 inch)	20cm (8 inch)	1.25kg (2½lb)
20cm (8 inch)	23cm (9 inch)	1.5kg (3lb)
23cm (9 inch)	25cm (10 inch)	1.6kg (3½lb)
25cm (10 inch)	28cm (11 inch)	1.6kg (3½lb)
28cm (11 inch)	30cm (12 inch)	2kg (4½lb)
30cm (12 inch)	2kg (4½lb)	

Moulding Icing

PREPARATION TIME: 20 minutes

This is also known as kneaded fondant. It is very easy to use and can be rolled out like pastry. It is ideal for covering novelty cakes and even rich fruit cake. The icing sets and becomes firm. Moulding icing can be used to cover a cake directly or over almond paste or marzipan. If using marzipan first, allow the paste to dry before covering with the icing, which can also be used to make flowers and other decorations.

450g (1lb) icing sugar
1 egg white
50g (2oz) liquid glucose
Food colouring or flavouring, if
  desired

Sift the icing sugar into a mixing bowl and add the egg white and the liquid glucose to the centre of the sugar. Beat the ingredients with a wooden spoon, gradually incorporating the icing sugar to result in a stiff mixture. Knead the icing until you have a pliable paste. This icing can be stored by placing it into a bag, or wrapping it in cling film, or sealing it in a plastic container and storing it in a cool place for up to 3 days. If adding a colour, sprinkle with a little more sifted icing sugar to keep the icing the same consistency.

To Apply Moulding or Gelatine Icing
Attach the icing by first brushing either the cake with apricot glaze or the marzipan with egg white. Roll out the icing on a surface dusted with icing sugar or cornflour, or between two sheets of dusted polythene. Roll out the icing at least 7.5cm (3 inches) larger than the top of the cake. Support the icing on a rolling pin and drape it over the cake. Dust your hands with cornflour or icing sugar and rub the surface of the cake, working in circular movements with the palms of your hands to make the icing thinner and ease down the sides of the cake. Smooth out any folds in the icing and cut off the excess. If icing a square cake, mould the corners so that the square keeps it shape. Leave to dry.
NB: liquid glucose is available from chemists.

Gelatine Icing

PREPARATION TIME: 20 minutes

This icing can be used in the same way as moulding icing, but when it dries it becomes quite brittle. The icing can be used to make decorations such as flowers and leaves.

10ml (2 tsp) gelatine powder
30ml (2 tblsp) water to dissolve the
  gelatine
450g (1lb) icing sugar
1 egg white

Put the gelatine powder into the water, which is contained in a small heatproof basin held over a saucepan of hot water. Stir until the gelatine has dissolved. Sift the icing sugar into another bowl and add the dissolved gelatine and egg white. Stir well until firm, then knead with the fingers until smooth. Dust with extra icing sugar, if necessary. If adding food colouring, sprinkle with more icing sugar to keep the icing to the same consistency. This icing can be stored for 2 to 3 days before use. To do so, wrap it in cling film or a polythene bag and keep it in a sealed container. If it begins to dry, place or keep the icing in its sealed polythene bag and dip briefly in hot water. Leave for 1 hour and knead well before use.

Glacé Icing

PREPARATION TIME: 10 minutes

Probably the quickest icing to make, it is used on sponges, small cakes and biscuits. To keep the icing liquid, place the bowl over a pan of hot water.

250g (8oz) icing sugar
30ml (2 tblsp) warm water
Various flavourings and colourings

Sift the icing sugar into a mixing bowl and gradually add the water. The icing should be thick enough to coat the back of a spoon when it is withdrawn from the mixture. Add the flavouring and the colouring, if desired. This quantity will ice 18 small cakes and half the amount will ice the top of a 20cm (8 inch) cake.

Variations

Coffee
Replace 15ml (1 tblsp) warm water with 15ml (1 tblsp) coffee essence.

Orange or Lemon
Replace 15ml (1 tblsp) warm water with 15ml (1 tblsp) orange or lemon juice. Add the grated rind of one orange or lemon and a few drops of food colouring.

Chocolate
Sift 45ml (3 tblsp) cocoa powder with the icing sugar.
NB: you must be careful not to keep the icing in too hot a bowl of water, otherwise it will lose its gloss. Also, if a newly-iced cake is moved around without being given a chance to set, the glacé icing could crack and spoil the smooth surface.

Buttercream Icing

This icing is good for covering sponge and quick cake mixture cakes. Butter icing is ideal for covering novelty cakes, as it can be flavoured and coloured easily and is no problem to pipe.

PREPARATION TIME: 10 minutes

125g (4oz) butter
225g (8oz) sifted icing sugar
30ml (2 tblsp) milk
Flavourings (see 'Variations')

Beat the butter and some of the icing sugar until smooth. Add the remaining icing sugar with the milk and flavouring. Beat until creamy. This icing will cover and fill a 20cm (8 inch) sandwich cake. Store in an airtight container in the refrigerator, for several weeks if necessary.

Variations

Lemon or Orange
Add the grated rind of 1 lemon or orange to the butter. Replace the milk with lemon or orange juice. Add a few drops of orange or lemon colouring.

Moulding icing, Royal icing, Butter icing, American frosting and Buttercream icing.

Chocolate

Blend 30ml (2 tblsp) cocoa powder with 30ml (2 tblsp) boiling water. Cool, then add to the mixture with 15ml (1 tblsp) milk.

Coffee

Replace 15ml (1 tblsp) milk with 15ml (1 tblsp) coffee essence.

Crème au Beurre

PREPARATION TIME: 15 minutes

2 egg whites
125g (4oz) icing sugar, sifted
125g (4oz) unsalted butter
Flavourings (see 'Variations')

Place the egg whites and icing sugar in a bowl over a pan of simmering water. Whisk until the mixture holds its shape. Cool. Cream the

butter until soft then beat into the egg white mixture, a little at a time. Flavour or colour as required.

Variations

Chocolate

Melt 50g (2oz) plain chocolate in a bowl over a pan of hot water. Cool and beat into the egg white mixture.

Coffee

Add 15ml (1 tblsp) coffee essence to the egg white mixture.

Praline

Gently heat 50g (2oz) of both caster sugar and blanched almonds in a small pan until the sugar turns brown round the nuts. Turn the mixture onto an oiled baking sheet, cool and crush with a rolling pin. Add the 45ml (3 tblsp) of this crushed praline to the egg white mixture.

NB: this icing can be stored in an airtight container in the refrigerator for several weeks.

Confectioner's Custard

PREPARATION TIME: 10-15 minutes

3 egg yolks
50g (2oz) caster sugar
25g (1oz) plain flour
300ml (½ pint) milk
25g (1oz) butter
10ml (1 dsp) sherry

Put the egg yolks and sugar in a bowl and beat until smooth and creamy. Stir in flour and mix well. Heat the milk until hot, but not boiling, and stir into the egg mixture. Return the mixture to the pan and stir, bringing it gently to the boil. Remove from the heat

and beat in the butter and the sherry. Pour into a bowl, stirring occasionally to prevent a skin forming. Makes 450ml (¾ pint) of custard.

NB: the custard can be stored in the refrigerator for up to 48 hours.

Basic Equipment and Practising Skills

You will probably have most of the basic pieces of equipment needed for decorating simple cakes: various-sized bowls and basins, measuring jugs, measuring spoons, wooden spoons, spatula, pastry brush, rolling pin, kitchen scales, airtight containers, cocktail sticks, artist's brush and a skewer, to name but a few. However, special icing equipment is often required, so it is wise to invest in a good, basic selection. You can extend your range as the need arises. Palette knives are ideal for smoothing and spreading icing. They come in various sizes and one would prove most useful. An icing ruler is essential for flat icing the tops of cakes. Choose a firm, not flexible, ruler – at least 30cm (12 inches) long, but preferably 36cm (14 inches). An icing rule is even better. An icing turntable is invaluable for icing and decorating large cakes. There are several types of icing scrapers and these are used for pulling round the sides of the cake until it is smooth. Icing cones come into the same category and have serrated teeth of various sizes.

Piping Nozzles

Piping nozzles come in various forms, the metal types giving the best definition. Try to start with a few basic nozzles. The range available starts from size 00. A basic icing-nozzle kit should consist of a fine, a medium and a thick writing nozzle; a shell nozzle; a leaf and a scroll nozzle; a ribbon nozzle (which is also used for basketwork); a forget-me-not and an 8-point and 10-point star nozzle.

Nozzles are available in two styles: plain or screw-on types. Screw-on nozzles are used in conjunction with nylon piping bags and a screw connector. Plain nozzles can be used with paper or nylon icing bags. With this type of nozzle remember that the icing has to be removed in order to change a nozzle. You can either make your own, or use a nylon piping bag or icing pump.

To make a paper icing bag, cut a piece of good quality greaseproof paper or non-stick silicone paper into a 25cm (10 inch) square. Fold in half to form a triangle. Fold the triangle in half to make a yet smaller triangle. Open out the smaller triangle and re-shape into a cone. Turn over the points of the cone so that it stays conical. Secure the join with a little sticky tape. Cut about 1cm (½ inch) off the tip of the bag and push in a nozzle.

Nylon Piping Bags

Nylon bags are sold in various sizes and can be easily filled. These bags are used with a screw connector. The connector is pushed into the bag and protrudes through the hole at the tip of the bag. This allows the nozzle to be placed at the end and secured with a screw-on attachment, allowing the nozzle

to be changed without emptying the piping bag.

Nylon piping bags are most useful for gâteaux as they can be filled with cream, and a meringue nozzle (a large decorative nozzle) can be attached to pipe rosettes.

Icing Pumps

These are bought as part of an icing set; some are made of metal and others of plastic. They consist of a tube with a screw attachment for the screw-on type of nozzle. The icing is controlled with a plunger and is unscrewed to refill the tube. Unfortunately, they are difficult to use for delicate work and you cannot feel the movement of the icing to help control it.

Piping Decorations

Stars

Stars, for example, can be piped with various-shaped nozzles ranging from 5 to 8, or more, points. With the 5-point star, use a nozzle number 13 or 8. These are the most useful sizes. Place the star nozzle in the bag and fill with icing. Hold the bag upright and pipe out enough icing to form a star. Remove the nozzle from the surface of the piped star swiftly. Stars should be fairly flat without a point in the centre.

Rosettes

These are piped with a star nozzle, but using a circular movement. Start at one side of the circle and finish slightly higher than the surface of the icing in the middle of the circle.

Shell

Use either a star nozzle or a special shell nozzle No. 12. Shell nozzles give fatter shells. Hold the icing bag at an angle to the surface on which the shell is required and start piping towards the centre of where the shell will rest. First move the nozzle away from you and then towards you. Push out more icing for the thicker parts of the shell. Link the shells together by starting the second shell over the tail of the first.

Leaves

Use a leaf nozzle, which is No. 10 and has a pointed tip, or sometimes an indentation in the centre of the point. Leaves can be piped straight onto the cake, or on non-stick silicone paper, left to dry

and then placed onto the cake for decoration. When piping you can make two or three overlapping movements to give the leaf some form.

Basket Weaving

See 'Tracy Rose Wedding Cake'.

Templates

These are patterns made of paper or card which are used to transfer the pattern onto the top of a cake. It is easy to create your own or, for simple decorations, i.e. circles and squares, draw round a saucepan lid or plastic storage container. On the 21st birthday cake we use a round template. Draw a circle the size required onto a piece of greaseproof paper and cut it out with a pair of scissors. Fold the circle in half, into quarters and into eighths, ending with a flattened cone shape. Draw a line in a concave shape from one point to another and cut it out. When the circle is opened, the edge of it will be scallop shaped.

Piped Flowers

Use a large, medium or fine petal nozzle, depending on the size of flower required, and an icing nail, or a piece of waxed paper cut into squares and attached to a cork. Once piped, leave the flowers to dry for at least 1 day before transferring them to a cake.

Rose

Hold the piping bag with the thin part of the nozzle upright. Pipe a cone of icing, twisting the nail quickly through the fingers and thumb. Pipe three, four or five petals round the centre of the rose by curving them outwards.

Forget-me-nots

Pipe these straight onto the cake, using a No. 2 writing nozzle for the petals, by joining five or six dots together round the edge of the piping nail and piping a curved petal in the centre. Alternatively use a forget-me-not nozzle.

Holly Leaves

Colour some marzipan green and roll out onto waxed paper and cut into rectangles. Using an icing nozzle, cut each holly leaf into shape by cutting first two corners of the rectangle and working your way down the sides until you have a holly leaf shape. Mark the 'veins' with a knife point. Roll out a little more marzipan and colour it red for the holly berries.

Christmas Roses

Cover the top of an essence bottle with a little foil and take a piece of moulding icing the size of a pea and dip it into cornflour and roll it into a ball. Shape another piece into a petal (see 'Moulded Roses'). Repeat until you have five petals. Place the small ball in the foil and surround it with the petals, overlapping them. Leave to dry. Remove from the foil and paint the centre yellow with a little food colouring.

Mistletoe

Roll out a little moulding icing, or marzipan, coloured green. Cut into tongue shapes and round the ends. Mark a definite vein down the middle of the leaf with a knife and leave it to dry. Make small, pea-sized balls out of either natural marzipan or white moulding icing.

Moulded Roses

Make a cone with a little coloured, moulded icing and press it out at the base so that it stands. Place a piece of icing the size of a pea in a little cornflour and roll it into a ball. Using a hard-boiled egg, flatten the icing in your hand with quick strokes. Use more cornflour if it gets too sticky. Gently try to get the icing very thin. Carefully wrap the petals round the cone and turn the edges outwards. Repeat the process until a fully shaped rose is achieved. Leave the rose to dry and cut off the base. It may be necessary to use a cocktail stick to curl the petals.

Chocolate Leaves

Break the chocolate into small pieces and place in a bowl over a pan of hot water. Gently heat until the chocolate melts. Do not overheat the chocolate or let any water dilute it. With an artist's small paintbrush, making sure that the chocolate spreads evenly over the surface of the leaf, paint the underside of the freshly-picked, undamaged and washed rose leaf. Allow the chocolate to set and, when hard, carefully peel the leaf away from the chocolate, starting from the tip.

Facing page: a variety of cake decorations.

CAKES AND CAKE DECORATION
Novelty Cakes

(4oz) of moulding icing and cover the white side of a thin, rectangular, silver cake board (the same size as the top of the cake). Fit a piping bag with a small star nozzle and fill with royal icing. Pipe shells round the bottom edge of the cake. Put the lid on a basin and pipe shells round the edge of the lid. Decorate the lid with either fresh or piped flowers and a bow secured with royal icing. Place the sweets on top of the cake and put the lid on, leaving them partially revealed.

Clown

450g (1lb) moulding icing
  75g (3oz) coloured pale orange
  175g (6oz) coloured yellow
  150g (5oz) coloured red
  50g (2oz) coloured green
1 large Swiss roll
4 small Swiss rolls
2 sponge fingers (boudoir biscuits)
1 marshmallow
1 recipe apricot glaze
1 recipe royal icing, coloured red

Using the orange moulding icing, break off 2 small rounds and gently flatten them. Make 4 cuts halfway into the balls, to make fingers. Roll out the remaining orange icing into a strip which is 20.5x7.5cm (8x3 inches). Brush the end of the Swiss roll with the apricot glaze and use the orange strip to cover the ends of the Swiss roll. Brush the rest of the Swiss roll with the glaze and with a third of the yellow icing rolled out into a strip 20.5x12.5cm (8x5 inches), cover the glazed area of the Swiss roll. Squeeze the join of the yellow and orange icing so it forms a head and body. Stand the Swiss roll upright on a cake board with something for support. Put the small Swiss rolls lengthways for the legs and brush with glaze. Take a small ball of yellow moulding icing and roll it out into a

These are fun cakes enjoyed by all ages, but particularly by children. There follows a variety of designs which can be used for every occasion. It is suggested that you use the quick cake mixture or maderia cake for these. Hopefully this will inspire you to design your own novelty cakes which might be more appropriate for a specific occasion. If you find it difficult to find a cake board for an unusual cake, make your own by covering a sheet of thick card with silver foil.

Birthday Box

30x25x5cm (12x10x2 inch) quick mix cake
Recipe apricot glaze
225g (8oz) marzipan (optional) – this makes the cake a little smoother
Recipe moulding icing
Thin 30x25cm (12x10 inch) cake board or piece of thick card
Food colouring – yellow
225g (8oz) sweets
225g (8oz) royal icing

Egg white, beaten, for attaching moulding icing

Put the cake on a larger cake board. Brush with apricot glaze and cover, if desired, with a thin layer of marzipan. Colour the moulding icing and save 100g (4oz) in a plastic bag. Brush the cake with egg white, roll out the moulding icing and use it to cover the marzipanned cake. With a knife or ruler press lines diagonally into the icing. Roll out the reserved 100g

This page: Birthday Box.

Facing page: Clown.

10x2.5cm (4x1 inch) width. Divide it into 2 and cut slashes in each halfway up. These will be used for the hair (reserve). Brush the sponge fingers with glaze and cover them with yellow fondant. Stick them with jam onto the sides of the body. Roll out the remaining yellow icing into a strip 20.5x12.5cm (8x5 inches) and cut it down the middle. Use each strip to cover the legs. Roll out a small piece of red icing and mould it over the marshmallow and leave to dry. Roll out 2 pea-sized balls of red icing and use them as buttons. Roll out another small piece of red icing and cut with a pastry cutter. Divide the green icing into two balls, rolling out one and cutting with the same round pastry cutter. Using a cocktail stick, create folds in the circles which radiate from the centre. Work your way round. Cut one of the circles in two and the other into four. Roll out the red icing into an oblong 18x7.5cm (7x3 inches) and attach it to the legs in thin strips. Using the reserved green icing, flatten it a little and cut it into two, shaping each half into an oval. Stick them upright on to the end of the legs as boots. Put half red and half green frills round the neck of the clown, securing them with a little apricot glaze. Put quarter frills round his

wrists and ankles, with a little glaze to attach them to the hands. Secure the hair to his head with glaze. Do the same with the hat. Fill a piping bag fitted with a writing nozzle with the red icing and pipe his features onto his face. Surround him with sweets or put ballons in his hand.

Giant Sandwich Cake

30x25x5cm (12x10x2 inch) quick mix cake
Food colourings – brown, green, yellow, pink, red
Recipe moulding icing
Egg white to brush marzipan
½ x recipe butter cream icing
225g (8oz) marzipan, if required

Cut the cake diagonally so you have 2 triangles. Colour half of the icing pale brown. Divide a further quarter into four and colour the pieces green, yellow, salmon pink and red. Remember to keep icing in a plastic bag when you are not using it to prevent it drying out. For the lettuce, roll out an irregular shape with the green icing and crinkle it up using a cocktail stick so it looks like ruched material. Reserve on a sheet of non-stick silicone paper. To make the ham, roll out the pink icing with a pinch of white icing, making sure the colours stay separate. Roll out into an oval shape and reserve. For the cheese, roll the yellow icing into a 10cm (4 inch) square and reserve. For the tomato slices, roll the red icing into a 10cm (4 inch) square and with a small, plain round

pastry cutter cut rounds. Roll out the pale brown icing into 6 strips all 5cm (2 inches) wide: two 30cm (12 inches) long, two 25cm (10 inches) long, two 40cm (16 inches) long. Use the egg white and brush the sides of the triangles. Stick the brown strips onto the appropriate length sides. The longest strips go along the cut diagonally. Roll out the remaining white icing into a triangle large enough to cover the top of one triangular cake piece. Brush the top of the cake triangle and fix on the moulding icing triangle. Spread the top of the other cake, the one without white moulding icing, with a little butter icing to make the bottom half of the sandwich and make sure it is on either a presentation plate or a cake board. Round the edges of the bottom triangle lay the lettuce, ham, tomato and cheese so they spill out of the cake. Sandwich together with the iced triangle. Fit a piping bag with a star nozzle and fill with the remaining butter icing. Pipe irregular swirls in between the lettuce, tomato, cheese and ham. Dust the top of the triangular cake with a little icing sugar.

Birthday Breakfast

Rich fruit cake (measure the size of your frying pan and bake a cake that will fit)
Recipe apricot glaze
100g (4oz) white moulding icing
Food colourings – brown, pink
425g (15oz) tin apricot halves

Transfer the fruit cake to the frying pan. Brush the top with apricot glaze. Roll out the white moulding icing and cut into several irregular shapes, rounding off any sharp corners. Roll the remaining icing into sausage shapes and brush them with a little brown and pink food colouring. Drain the tin of apricot halves. Place the irregular white moulding icing shapes on top of the cake, putting an inverted apricot half on each one. Put the sausages in the pan. Brush the sausages and the apricot halves with a little apricot glaze.

Camelot Castle

20cm (8 inch) square 6-egg Victoria sponge
Recipe butter cream icing
Recipe apricot glaze
4 ice-cream cones
4 miniature Swiss rolls
1 rectangular plain biscuit
1 water biscuit
100g (4oz) granulated sugar
100g (4oz) moulding icing
Recipe royal icing
Sugar flowers
Silver balls
3 or 4 small sandwich flags
Food colourings – pink, green, red

Toffee Water (To Fill Moat)
225g (8oz) granulated sugar
150ml (5 fl oz) water
Blue food colouring
Sugar thermometer, if available

Cut a 5cm (2 inch) wide slice from a cake. Put the other cake towards the back of the cake board. Sandwich the large section of cake to the cake on the board with some butter icing. Make sure it sits towards the back of the base cake. With apricot glaze, secure the 5cm (2 inch) slice on the front edge of the cake board. Using apricot glaze, brush the ends of the small Swiss rolls and place them in the four corners of the cake, placing the ice-cream cones on top. Cover the small Swiss rolls, ice-cream cones and the top and sides of the cake with butter icing. Also ice the 5cm (2 inch) slice. Put the water biscuit on the front side of the cake between the 2 Swiss roll towers. Put the granulated sugar, with a few drops of pink food colouring, in a bowl and stir well until the sugar takes up the colour. Sprinkle the coloured sugar over the ice-cream cones, the top of the castle and the grounds. Fit a star nozzle to a piping bag and fill with royal icing. Pipe round the top of the castle walls and over the front surface of the water biscuit. When the piped stars are just drying, go round the top of the walls and pipe another row of stars on top of each alternate star. Put a silver ball in the centre of each of the stars round the edge of the door and 2 for doorknobs. Colour a little of the royal icing green, and a little red, and pipe the green vine with red stars for flowers. You can also use sugar flowers.

To Make the Water to Fill the Moat
Colour the moulding icing green and roll it out to form a long sausage which will go round the

Giant Sandwich Cake (top left) and Birthday Breakfast (bottom left).

edge of the board. Use the icing to form a wall and stick it down by smoothing it onto the board, then leave it to dry for one hour. Heat the sugar and water so the sugar dissolves and boils. Continue to boil the mixture until it reaches 'soft crack' point, that is, just before it starts to colour. If a sugar thermometer is available, the reading should be 132-143ºC, 270-290ºF. Pour the sugar mixture into the moat. Put the sugar flowers on the green banks of the moat and lay the biscuit across from the castle to the land to form a drawbridge. Use the flags to decorate.

Ballet Shoes

2 Swiss rolls
30cm (12 inch) square cake board
900g (2lb) fondant icing
Food colouring – pink
Recipe apricot glaze
Cornflour to dust
60ml (4 tblsp) jam
1 metre (1 yard) pink satin ribbon (as an alternative to fondant ribbons)

To Make Shoes

Cut the edge of one end of the cake into a point. Then cut the tip of the point. This will be the toe end of the shoe. Repeat for the

other shoe and place them both on the cake board. Cut the other end of the cake, rounding it slightly. Cut out a long oval towards the heel end of the cake. Press the cake in firmly, but gently, to create an instep. Colour all the fondant pale pink. Brush the cake with the glaze. Roll out the fondant on the cornflour-dusted work surface. Press the fondant down and smooth out any cracks. Mould it gently round the toe and take special care to squeeze and tuck it into the inside of the shoe. Cut off any excess and re-mould it into a ball. Roll out. Cut 4 long strips 2.5cm (1 inch) wide and cut the

shortest ends with pinking shears or cut with a pastry wheel. With a little water attach the ribbons of fondant to the inside of the shoes approximately halfway between the toe and heel. With a cocktail stick, gently mark round the top of the shoe, then the sole. Cut two 15cm (6 inch) long, string-width strips of fondant and make a little bow out of each and put them in place. As an alternative, pink satin ribbon can be used in place of fondant. Fill the shoes with sweets.

Football Boot

25x20cm (10x8 inch) quick mix cake
Jam for filling
Recipe apricot glaze
Recipe moulding icing
Recipe butter icing
50g (2oz) desiccated coconut
50g (2oz) chocolate dots
Food colouring – red, yellow, black and green
Medium star nozzle and piping bag
2 liquorice laces
30cm (12 inch) square cake board
1 cocktail stick

Cut the cake horizontally and sandwich with jam for filling. Put the cakes on the board. With a cocktail stick mark out the outline of the boot. When you are happy with the outline, cut it out with a sharp knife and brush with apricot glaze. Divide the moulding icing into two, remembering to keep the icing in a plastic bag when not in use. Roll out half the icing into an oblong and cover the boot shape (top and sides). Do not ice the leg. Cut the icing at the ankle to indicate the top of the boot. Divide the remaining icing into two, colouring half red and the rest yellow. Draw out the shapes for the patches, tongue of the boot and the flash on some greaseproof paper. Draw a large 'E' with a double line and cut it out. This should be used as a template to guide you when you roll out the red icing to cover the ankle and the

This page: Camelot Castle.

Facing page: Ballet Shoes (top) and Football Boot (bottom).

flash for the side of the boot. Roll out the yellow moulding icing and cut the same shapes, but smaller, to go on top of the red. Cut the liquorice laces and tie into a bow. With a little icing place it at the ankle. Mix half of the butter icing yellow and half red. Fill a piping bag with the red butter icing and pipe a band about 6 stripes wide, then repeat with the yellow icing. Work your way up the leg until you have 3 red bands and 2 yellow. Put rows of chocolate drops on the side of the boot to represent studs. Put the desiccated coconut in a bowl and add a few drops of green food colour. Stir in and use to sprinkle on the board to represent grass.

Shirt and Tie

13x9x2cm (15x3½x¾ inch) quick mix cake
2 x recipe butter cream icing
100g (4oz) coloured fondant, if using design with tie
1 small packet round sweets, e.g. jellies, fruit gums or milk drops
Food colouring – red

In a clean bowl reserve ¼ of the butter cream icing and with the food colouring make up a darker shade of the colour previously used. Wash the tin used for baking the cake and, if the tin is old or marked, line with foil so that the tin is totally covered both inside and out. You could otherwise find or make an old shirt box. Put the cake into the cake tin or box, and spread with the lighter icing. If the cake fits snugly into its box or tin, only ice the top; if not, ice all the visible cake. Make the neck and collar shaping by first marking it out. Draw a line in the icing with a cocktail stick 7.5cm (3 inches) from one end of the cake. (The 23cm (9 inch) sides are top and bottom). This marks the shoulder line, so use this line to guide you when building up the collar with more icing. Half the collar (front and back) should be on either side of the faint line. Fill the piping bag with the darker icing and with a writing nozzle outline the collar and shoulder seam. Roll out a thin strip of fondant 4cm (1½ inches) wide and 35cm (14 inches) long, pinch it in to form the knot and place on the cake. If you are using the design with centre placket (shirt front) pocket and sleeves use the darker icing in the piping bag and pipe the shirt front, pocket and sleeves. Put the sweets in position as buttons.

Artist's Palette

23cm (9 inch) square quick mix cake
Recipe apricot glaze
350g (¾lb) moulding icing
100g (4oz) granulated sugar
Food colourings – red, blue, green, yellow, orange, violet and brown

Cut a kidney shape out of the cake and carefully cut a circle slightly off centre. Place the cake on the cake board and brush with apricot glaze. Colour all except 50g (2oz) of the moulding icing pale brown. Roll out and use to cover the palette, pushing in gently at the hole so that the icing coats the inner wall of the circle. Push down to reveal the cake board. Using a dry brush, dip gently into the brown food colouring and drag hesitantly across the palette. Wipe the brush with kitchen paper to absorb some of the food colouring and continue to cover the palette with the wood grain. Leave to dry. Colour 15ml (1 tblsp) of granulated sugar with each of the food colourings. This is done by adding a few drops and stirring until the sugar absorbs the colour. Roll out the remaining moulding icing into a long sausage shape and cut into half. Make a point at the end of one sausage and leave to dry and gently flatten the end of the other.

To Make the Pencil and Paintbrush

When the moulding icing shapes are dry, copying a pencil, colour the one with the pointed end by painting in the lead and the outside. Copy the brush you are using and place them next to the palette. When the palette is dry, put little mounds of the coloured sugar on the top.

Artist's Palette (left) and Shirt and Tie (below).

Celebration Cakes

Pipe a row of stars round the bottom of the cake. With a medium, plain nozzle pipe bulbs between each of the stars on the inner edge of the cake. Pipe another row of bulbs on the side of the cake above the stars. Colour a little of the icing pink and fit a piping bag with a writing nozzle. Pipe a row of dropped loops from each of the bulbs on the top of the cake. From the point of alternate stars on the top edge of the cake, pipe a row of dropped loops. Go round the cake again piping loops on the stars omitted on the first round. Pipe a bulb on the point of each of the stars. With the pink icing, pipe a scallop on the cake board round the stars. Pipe the message with swirls round it in the shape of 'S's and 'C's on the top of the cake and place the flowers, a little fern and the ribbon in position.

Boy's Birthday Cake

20cm (8 inch) square, rich fruit cake
Recipe apricot glaze
800g (1¾lb) marzipan
Royal icing, made with 1.4kg (3lb)
  icing sugar
Food colouring – blue
8 silver leaves for the top
16 silver leaves for the side panels

Brush the top of the cake with the apricot glaze. Cover the cake with the marzipan and leave it to dry. Attach the cake to the board with a little icing. Flat ice the sides and the top of the cake and let it dry. Fit a piping bag with a large nozzle and pipe a continuous 'S' pattern on the top edge and the base of the cake. Pipe 4 bars horizontally

Mother's Day Cake

18cm (7 inch) or 20cm (8 inch)
  square or round cake
Recipe apricot glaze
675g (1½lb) marzipan
Royal icing, made with 900g (2lb)
  icing sugar
Food colourings – green, yellow
Green ribbon
Piped flowers

Brush the top and sides of the cake with apricot glaze and cover with marzipan; leave to dry. With a little icing, attach the cake to the cake board and flat ice the top and sides; leave to dry. Using a piping bag fitted with a leaf nozzle, pipe a row of leaves in white icing facing outwards around the bottom of the cake. Then pipe an overlapping circle of white leaves around the top edge of the cake. Fill another piping bag with green-coloured icing and pipe a row of leaves facing outwards on top. Finally, pipe an overlapping circle of green leaves on the top. Fill a piping bag with a little yellow-coloured icing and fit a medium writing nozzle and write 'Mother' on the top surface of the cake. Attach the piped flowers on the top surface with a dab of icing and, using the piping bag with green icing and the leaf nozzle again, pipe a few leaves around the flowers to finish. Decorate with the green ribbon.

Girl's Birthday Cake

20cm (8 inch) round, rich fruit cake
Recipe apricot glaze
800g (1¾lb) marzipan
Royal icing, made with 1.4kg (3lb)
  icing sugar
3 piped flowers
Food colouring – pink
Pink ribbon
Frond of asparagus fern

Brush the top and the sides of the cake with apricot glaze. Cover the cake with the marzipan. Attach the cake to the board with a little icing. Flat ice the top and the sides of the cake. Fit a piping bag with a large star nozzle and pipe a circle of stars round the top edge of the cake.

This page: Girl's Birthday Cake and Boy's Birthday Cake.

Facing page: Mother's Day Cake.

across and down the corners of the cake. At each of the 4 corners, and on the top of the cake, pipe a single line from the flat surface of the cake crossing the continuous 'S' and ending in the corner. Fit a small star nozzle and pipe vertically down the corners of the cake, covering the ends of the bars. Pipe the decorative lines on the top of the cake, starting with a long line with a dot at each end and working out and down with shorter lines towards the outer edge. Write the name in the centre of the cake. Colour a little of the icing blue and fit a writing nozzle onto the piping bag. Pipe 2 rows of scallops on the top edge of the cake, a row on each side of the continuous 'S', ending at the corner where the corner bars start. Overpipe the name in blue. Pipe a dropped loop round the base of the cake, with the point of the loops at each of the corners. Attach 2 silver leaves at the base corners of each of the 4 side panels, and 2 silver leaves on the top of the cake at each of the 4 corners, attached to the flat surface of the cake.

Silver Wedding Anniversary Cake

20 or 23cm (8 or 9 inch) square, rich fruit cake
Recipe apricot glaze
800-900g (1¾-2lb) marzipan
Royal icing, made with 1.25kg (2½lb) icing sugar
8 silver leaves
Silver non-toxic colouring

Brush the top and the sides of the cake with apricot glaze and cover with marzipan. Leave the cake to dry. Attach the cake to the board with a little icing. Flat ice the top and sides of the cake, giving 2 or 3 coats. Fit your piping bag with a medium writing nozzle. Using a saucepan lid or a round template, draw a circle in the centre of the top of the cake. Using a medium-sized five-star nozzle, pipe a continuous swirl round the bottom edge of the cake and finish off each corner with a shell. With a smaller star nozzle, pipe a small dot on the top edge of the cake in the centre of the top edge of each of the side panels and divide the space

between the original dot and the corner of the cake with a further dot. You should have 3 dots on each of the top sides of the cake. Using these as a guide, join them together by piping a scallop, with the dots marking the points of the scallop. Using a writing nozzle, pipe with a scribbling line between the scallop on the sides of the cake and the template circle drawn on the top of the cake. The scribbling should be done with a continuous line that never crosses itself. Using the same nozzle, overpipe the template-drawn circle with a continuously twisting line. On the side panels and on the corners of

the cake, pipe three beads in descending size below each of the points of the scallop. Overpipe the continuous swirls round the bottom of the cake with a plain, continuous swirl beginning and ending with an 'S' shape. Pipe the '25' in the circle on top of the cake, then – when dry – overpipe this again with white. Fit your piping bag with a medium star nozzle and, having positioned the silver leaves, secure them with a piped rosette. Using a fine paintbrush, gently paint the continuous swirl overpiped on the circle on the top surface of the cake and also the top of the '25' with a single silver line.

It is most important that a celebration cake should feed the desired number of guests, so here is a guide:

Round	Square	Portions
15cm (6 inch)	13cm (5 inch)	20-30
20cm (7½-8 inch)	18cm (7 inch)	40-45
25cm (10 inch)	23cm (9 inch)	70-80
28cm (11 inch)	25cm (10 inch)	100-110
30cm (12 inch)	30cm (12 inch)	130-140

NB: for decorating simple cakes, sweets can be utilised and are easily applied to butter icing. These are much used in novelty cake designs.

Silver Wedding Anniversary Cake.

Golden Wedding Cake

25cm (10 inch) round, rich fruit cake
Recipe apricot glaze
1kg (2¼lb) marzipan
Royal icing, made from 1.4kg (3lb)
  icing sugar
Food colouring – yellow
6 gold leaves
Yellow ribbon

Brush the sides and top of the cake with the apricot glaze. Cover the cake with the marzipan and leave to dry. Attach the cake to the board with a little icing. Flat ice the top and sides of the cake. Fit a piping bag with a large star nozzle and pipe a row of shells round the top of the cake. Pipe a row of shells round the bottom of the cake. Fit the piping bag with a smaller star nozzle and pipe continuous 'C's on the shells on the top of the cake. Fit the piping bag with a medium-sized plain nozzle and pipe a scallop on the top of the cake round the shells. Round the bottom of the cake, on the board, pipe a scallop round the shells. Repeat the scallop on the side of the cake under the shells on the top edge of the cake. Colour a little of the icing yellow and, using a writing nozzle, repeat the pattern of continuous 'C's on the top edge of the cake. Pipe a dropped loop on top of the shell at the base of the cake. Fit the same piping bag with a leaf nozzle and pipe inverted leaves between the shells at the base of the cake, with the point of the leaves creeping up the sides of the cake. With a writing nozzle, pipe the words and surround them with 'S's and 'C's. Decorate with a real rose or any other flower, or piped flowers and/or gold leaves.

Diana Wedding Cake

Two-Tier Round Cake
25cm (10 inch) round, rich fruit cake
15 or 18cm (6 or 7 inch) round, rich
  fruit cake
2 x recipe apricot glaze
1.4kg (3lb) marzipan
Royal icing, made from 1.6kg (3½lb)
  icing sugar
Silver cake boards: 33cm (13 inch)
  and 20 or 23cm (8 or 9 inch)
32 silver leaves
8 piped flowers
4 round pillars

Brush the top and sides of the cake with apricot glaze and cover with

marzipan. Leave the cake to dry. Attach the cake to the board with a little icing. Flat ice the top and sides of the cake, giving three coats and an extra coat on the base cake. Fit a piping bag with a large star nozzle and pipe shells round the bottom of each of the cakes. Using the same nozzle, mark the cake surface lightly at the edge as though it were square. That is, treat it as though it had four corners, putting a dab of icing in each of the four corners and a smaller dab at the centre of each of the four sides. From each of the

dabs which mark the centre of the sides pipe an inverted 'S', finishing at the corner mark. Repeat this from where you started and mirror the original shape towards the other corner point. Repeat this round the cake. Pipe a 'C' facing the centre of the cake, with its back marking the centre point of the side. Overpipe all the decorative swirls, the 'S's and 'C's twice. Fit a piping bag with a medium-sized plain nozzle and pipe a continuously twisting scallop on the upper edge of the sides of the cakes. Repeat this pattern on the

cake board around the shells. With the same nozzle overpipe the decorative swirls, 'S's and 'C's on the tops of the cakes. Pipe a scallop on the top surface of the cake, encompassing the 'C's in the curves; three curves to each

This page: Golden Wedding Cake. Facing page: Diana Wedding Cake.

Lindsey Jane
Wedding Cake.

imaginary side. Pipe dropped loops under the continuously twisting scallop on the sides of cakes. On the sides of the cake below the loops, attach the flowers and leaves with a little icing, four flowers per cake below each 'C' and an icing rosette to attach the other leaves between each of the flowers. Assemble the cake using the pillars and decorate the top with flowers.

Lindsey Jane Wedding Cake

Two-Tier Square Cake
15cm (6 inch) square, rich fruit cake
25cm (10 inch) square, rich fruit cake
2 x recipe apricot glaze
1.5kg (3¼lb) marzipan
Royal icing made with 1.75kg (4lb) icing sugar
28 pink piped roses, to decorate
Asparagus fern, to decorate
Silver cake boards, 20cm (8 inch) and 30cm (12 inch)
4 square pillars
2 narrow ribbon bows

This design is suitable for a 1, 2 or 3-tier cake. The roses are chosen to match the bridal attire.
Brush the sides and tops of the cakes with apricot glaze and cover with marzipan. Leave to dry. Attach the cakes to the cake boards with a dab of icing. Flat ice the cakes, giving two or three coats all over. Fit a piping bag with a medium-sized shell nozzle and pipe shells on the top edge, the bottom edge and up each of the corners of the cakes. Pipe on the top of the cakes in each corner 2 shells facing each other. Fit the piping bag with a medium-sized plain nozzle and pipe a shallow scallop round the top side of the cake. Pipe with an 'S'-shaped swirl, filling each of the small scallops. On the bottom tier, put a cluster of roses in the middle of the cake, surrounded by fern,

two roses in each of the corners and one rose at the base of each of the corners. On the top tier, repeat but with a single rose at the top of each corner and the ribbon bows on top of the cake. Assemble the cake using the pillars.

Christening Cake

20cm (8 inch) round, rich fruit cake
Recipe apricot glaze
800g (1¾lb) marzipan
Royal icing, made with 1.4kg (3lb) icing sugar
Food colouring – blue
15g (½oz) marzipan
1 narrow, white ribbon bow

Brush the top and sides of the cake with the apricot glaze. Cover the cake with the marzipan and leave it to dry. Attach the cake to the board with the royal icing. Fit a piping bag with a large star nozzle. With an icing comb, comb the sides of the cake with a swirling line and pipe a row of shells round the top of the cake. Fit a piping bag with a small star nozzle and pipe a scallop round the top of the shells. Pipe a graduated rope round the bottom of the cake, with a large, dropped loop round the rope. Fit the piping bag with a small, plain nozzle and pipe a scallop on the top of the cake next to the shells. Pipe the name of the baby on the top of the cake. Colour a little royal icing blue. Using a writing nozzle, pipe beads at the points of each of the nozzles. Pipe another scallop onto the silver board. Pipe over the name with the blue, piping small 'C's and scrolls. To make the bootees, colour a little moulding icing pale blue and shape into two. Press a small hole towards the end of each of the oval shapes. With a writing nozzle, pipe round the holes, making a little bow at the front. Decorate with a silver ball and put the small bow between the bootees.

Tracy Rose Wedding Cake

Three-Tier Square
13cm (5 inch) square, rich fruit cake
20cm (8 inch) square, rich fruit cake
28cm (11 inch) square, rich fruit cake
3 x recipe apricot glaze
2.25kg (5lb) marzipan
Royal icing, made with 3.3kg (8lb) icing sugar
2 x recipe moulding icing, peach colour (to make 60 moulded roses)
3 cake boards: 18cm (7 inch), 25cm (10 inch) and 35cm (14 inch)
Food colourings – green, peach (brown)
8 square cake pillars
2 rectangular silver boards

Brush the top and sides of the cakes with apricot glaze and cover with marzipan; leave to dry. Attach the cakes to the silver cake boards with a dab of icing. Flat ice the tops of the cakes with the royal icing, which is tinted peach in colour. Cut the thin, rectangular cake boards lengthways down the middle and then cut each widthways with a sharp knife. Cut the corners off each piece diagonally so that they will go together to form a square with a square hole in the centre. Place each on a sheet of greaseproof paper and flat ice onto the white side with a palette knife; leave to dry. Fill a piping bag with a medium writing nozzle and the other with a basket weave nozzle. Hold the basket weave nozzle sideways and on the side of the first cake pipe 3 lines, evenly spaced, one above the other and all of the same length. Pipe a vertical line using the writing nozzle along the edge of the basket weaving. Continue this process until the cake is covered. Repeat the basket weave method on each of the cardboard lids. To make the moulded flowers see chapter on decorations. Colour a little of the royal icing green and fit a piping bag with a leaf nozzle. Colour a little more royal icing a dark peach and use it to fill a bag fitted with a star nozzle. Continue to use the writing nozzle filled with the tinted peach royal icing as used in the basket weave. Position the moulded icing roses facing outward round the top edges of the 2 bottom tiers and in a radiating pattern on the small top tier. Pipe dark peach stars between each of the roses and dot the centre of each star using the tinted

peach royal icing. Pipe leaves at random round the flowers. Place the pillars on a tray and pipe small stars dotted with tinted peach for the centre of the flower. Again, pipe leaves at random and leave to dry.

To Assemble the Cake
Place the basket lids round the outer edge of each of the cake's bottom two tiers and, with a little icing, secure them to the top of the cake. Make sure that there is enough room in the square at the centre of each cake for the four pillars.
Note: the cake board can be iced with a palette knife to surround each of the cakes, if required.

This page: Christening Cake.

Facing page: Tracy Rose Wedding Cake.

BARBECUES & SALADS

Before gas and electricity were harnessed for our cooking convenience, our ancestors employed barbecue cooking, although they didn't know it by that name. Flaming food, however, seemed to go out of fashion for a time in northern Europe, except in chafing dishes in expensive restaurants. Countries with sunnier climates kept up the art and the United States, where informality is the spirit of entertaining, adopted barbecue cooking as its own.

A barbecue grill can be a very primitive arrangement of a firebowl – a place to hold charcoal or wood – and a rack, or some support to hold the food. Modern design has added several different interpretations:

Portable barbecue grills – These are small and are often called picnic barbecues. They have folding or telescopic legs. Table-top models with short legs and hibachis in various sizes are popular styles.

Semi-portable grills – These are slightly larger and have fixed legs, sometimes with wheels for easy movement. They are often round with rotating racks, good for moving food quickly off hot-spots, or adjustable shelves. Rotisseries can be fixed to these grills and most have windshields along the back.

Hooded grills – These keep the food at an even temperature and the smoke out of the cook's eyes! With practice, whole meals can be cooked, and food can be smoked over aromatic wood chips for extra flavour.

Home-made grills – Barbecues can be built of brick or stone with oven shelves for racks.

Electric and gas grills – These use special rocks that radiate heat from electric coils or gas flames. They give the taste and appearance of charcoal-grilled food along with control over the intensity of heat. A dial with a number of settings allows more delicate foods to be cooked through without charring on the outside. These grills are cleaner and heat much faster than charcoal or wood-fired grills, which must be lit at least 1 hour before cooking. They are also nearly self-cleaning. The recipes in this book were cooked on an electric grill from Redring Electric Company.

When choosing a fuel for barbecueing, you should bear in mind that charcoal compressed into briquettes will burn for twice as long with more uniform heat than lumpwood charcoal – irregular-sized pieces of kiln-charred hardwood. However, lumpwood charcoal is easier to light than briquettes. Vine wood cuttings are an alternative to charcoal, but do not burn as long. Hardwood, such as birch or cherry can be used, but takes a long time to light and is expensive.

Firelighters, either liquid or solid, get the fire going faster. Use them to start a fire, but never, for safety reasons, on coals that are already hot. With any grill that uses charcoal or wood, be sure the fire bowl has perforations in the bottom and sides, or that the coals can sit on a perforated rack inside. This allows air to circulate underneath and makes the fire easier to light and keep going.

Special equipment is not necessary, but long-handled cooking utensils are easiest and safest to use. When grilling fish, a hinged wire rack, specially shaped for both small or large fish, is a great help. So, too, are square hinged racks for turning a number of hamburgers, sausages or steaks at the same time.

Cooking times for barbecued food cannot be very exact. There is room for variation depending on the type of grill and source of heat. For grills without adjustable shelves, results are better if the food is cooked in the oven for about half to three-quarters of the cooking time and the remaining time on the barbecue grill for colour and flavour. Similarly, larger cuts of meat, such as Butterflied Lamb, will cook faster and be juicer if pre-cooked in the oven. In fact, employ this method with any food cooked for a large group and you will avoid the problem of eating in shifts.

Salads are a natural accompaniment to barbecued food. On a warm summer's day or evening they can also be a light and refreshing meal in themselves. So when summer arrives, abandon your oven occasionally and try barbecues and salads and discover why food tastes so much better when cooked and eaten outdoors.

BARBECUES & SALADS

Starters and Side Salads

Satay

PREPARATION TIME:	25 minutes
COOKING TIME:	10-15 minutes
SERVES:	4 people

450g/1lb chicken, skinned, boned and cut
  into 2.5cm/1 inch cubes

MARINADE
30ml/2 tbsps soy sauce
30ml/2 tbsps oil
30ml/2 tbsps lime juice
5ml/1 tsp ground cumin
5ml/1 tsp turmeric
10ml/2 tsps ground coriander

SAUCE
30ml/2 tbsps oil
1 small onion, finely chopped
5ml/1 tsp chili powder
120g/4oz/1 cup peanut butter
5ml/1 tsp brown sugar
Remaining marinade

GARNISH
Lime wedges
Coriander leaves

Combine the marinade ingredients in
a deep bowl. Put in the meat and stir
to coat. Leave covered in the
refrigerator for 1 hour. Drain and
thread the meat on 4 large or 8 small
skewers. Grill about 10-15 minutes,
turning frequently to cook all sides.
Baste often. Meanwhile heat the oil
in a small saucepan. Add the onion
and the chili powder. Cook until the
onion is slightly softened. Take off
the heat and set aside. When the
meat is nearly cooked combine the
marinade with the oil and onion and
chili powder. Stir in the remaining
sauce ingredients, thinning with
water if necessary. Brush the Satay
with the sauce 1 to 2 minutes before
the end of cooking time. Spoon over
a bit more sauce and serve the rest
separately. Garnish each serving with
lime wedges and coriander leaves.

This page: **Rumaki (left)** and **Satay
(right). Facing page: Grilled Garlic
Prawns/Shrimp (left) aand Smoked
Fish Kebabs with Horseradish
Sauce (right).**

Rumaki

PREPARATION TIME: 15 minutes

COOKING TIME: 10-15 minutes

SERVES: 4 people

180ml/6 fl oz/¾ cup soy sauce
450g/1lb chicken livers, trimmed and cut
*   into 5cm/2 inch pieces*
1 200g/7oz can water chestnuts, drained
8 slices smoked streaky bacon
1 red pepper, cut in 2.5cm/1 inch pieces
Brown sugar

Combine half the soy sauce and all the chicken livers in a deep bowl. Leave to marinate in the refrigerator for 1 hour. Place the bacon slices on a wooden board. Stretch the bacon by running the back of knife backwards and forwards over each slice. Cut the slices in half across. Drain the chicken livers and discard the soy sauce. Put a piece of liver and a water chestnut on each slice of bacon and roll up. Thread on skewers, alternating with a piece of red pepper. Grill on an oiled rack above hot coals for 10-15 minutes, basting with the remaining half of the soy sauce and turning frequently. One minute before the end of cooking, sprinkle lightly with brown sugar and allow to glaze. Garnish serving dishes with parsley if desired.

Greek Salad

PREPARATION TIME: 15 minutes

SERVES: 4 people

1 head cos/romaine lettuce
16 black olives, stoned
120g/4oz/1 cup crumbled feta cheese
1 small can anchovies, drained
8 mild pickled peppers
60g/2oz cherry tomatoes, halved
½ cucumber, cut in small dice
30ml/2 tbsps chopped fresh oregano or
*   15ml/1 tbsp dried oregano*

DRESSING
120ml/4 fl oz/½ cup olive oil
45ml/3 tbsps red wine vinegar
1 clove garlic, finely minced
Salt and pepper

Wash and dry the cos/romaine lettuce and tear the leaves into bite-size pieces. Place the leaves in a large salad bowl and arrange or scatter all the other ingredients on top of the lettuce. If the anchovies are large, cut them into thinner strips or chop into small pieces. Sprinkle the fresh or dried oregano over all the ingredients in the salad bowl. Mix the dressing together well and pour over the salad just before serving.

Caesar Salad

PREPARATION TIME: 20 minutes

COOKING TIME: 3 minutes

SERVES: 4-6 people

1 large or two small heads cos/romaine
*   lettuce*
8 slices white bread, crusts removed
120ml/4 fl oz/½ cup oil
1 clove garlic, peeled
1 small can anchovies
90g/3oz fresh Parmesan cheese

DRESSING
1 egg
120ml/4 fl oz/½ cup olive oil
Juice of 1 lemon
1 clove garlic, finely minced
Salt and pepper

Wash the lettuce and dry well. Tear the lettuce into bite-size pieces and place in a large salad bowl, or four individual bowls. Cut the slices of bread into 1.25cm/½ inch dice. Heat the vegetable oil in a small frying pan. When the oil is hot put in the clove of garlic and the cubes of bread. Lower the heat slightly and, using a metal spoon, keep stirring the cubes of bread to brown them evenly. When they are golden brown and crisp, remove them to paper towels to drain. Add the anchovies to the lettuce in the salad bowl and sprinkle on the fried bread croûtons. To prepare the dressing, place the egg in boiling water for 1 minute. Break into a small bowl and combine with remaining dressing ingredients, whisking very well. Pour the dressing over the salad and toss. Using a cheese slicer, shave off thin slices of Parmesan cheese and add to the salad. Alternatively, grate the cheese and add to the salad with the dressing.

Smoked Fish Kebabs with Horseradish Sauce

PREPARATION TIME: 15 minutes

COOKING TIME: 6 minutes

SERVES: 4 people

1 smoked kipper fillet, skinned and cut
*   into 2.5cm/1 inch pieces*
1 smoked haddock fillet, skinned and cut
*   into 2.5cm/1 inch pieces*
8 bay leaves
1 small red onion, quartered
Oil
SAUCE
30ml/2 tbsps grated fresh or bottled
*   horseradish*
280ml/½ pint/1 cup sour cream
10ml/2 tsps fresh dill, chopped
Salt and pepper
Squeeze of lemon juice
Pinch sugar

Thread the fish, bay leaves and slices of onion on skewers, alternating ingredients and types of fish. Brush with oil and place on an oiled grill rack above hot coals. Mix the sauce ingredients together and divide onto side plates. Grill the kebabs for about 6 minutes, turning and basting with oil frequently. When the onion is cooked, remove to serving dishes. Place kebabs on lettuce leaves, if desired, for serving.

Grilled Garlic Prawns/Shrimp

PREPARATION TIME: 15 minutes

COOKING TIME: 8-10 minutes

SERVES: 4 people

900g/2lbs uncooked king prawns/jumbo
*   shrimp*
60g/2oz/4 tbsps melted butter

Facing page: Greek Salad (top) and Caesar Salad (bottom).

30ml/2 tbsps double/heavy cream
Salt and pepper
15ml/1 tbsp sugar

Place the carrots in iced water for 1 hour. Dry them and grate coarsely into a bowl. Add the raisins, nuts and sesame seeds. Mix the dressing ingredients together, adding more cream if the dressing appears too thick. If dressing separates, whisk vigorously until it comes together before adding additional cream. Toss with the carrot salad and serve.

Curried Rice Salad

PREPARATION TIME: 20 minutes

COOKING TIME: 12 minutes

SERVES: 6 people

180g/6oz/¾ cup long grain rice
15ml/1 tbsp curry powder, hot or mild as desired
4 spring/green onions, sliced
2 sticks celery, sliced
1 small green pepper, diced
10 black olives, halved and stoned
60g/2oz/¼ cup sultanas/golden raisins
60g/2oz/¼ cup toasted flaked/sliced almonds
60ml/4 tbsps flaked coconut
2 hard-boiled eggs, chopped

DRESSING
140ml/¼ pint/½ cup mayonnaise
15ml/1 tbsp mango chutney
Juice and grated rind of ½ a lime
60ml/4 tbsps natural yogurt
Salt

GARNISH
2 avocados, peeled and cut in cubes
Juice of ½ lemon or lime

Cook the rice in boiling salted water for about 12 minutes or until tender. During the last 3 minutes of cooking time drain away half the water and stir in the curry powder. Leave to continue cooking over a gentle heat until the rice is cooked and the water

MARINADE
3 cloves garlic, finely chopped
60ml/4 tbsps oil
120ml/4 fl oz/½ cup lemon juice
60ml/4 tbsps chopped basil
Salt
Coarsely ground black pepper

Shell and de-vein the prawns/shrimp. Leave the shell on the ends of the tails. Combine the marinade ingredients in a plastic bag. Put in the prawns/shrimp and seal the bag. Refrigerate for 1 hour, turning frequently. Place the bag in a bowl to catch possible drips. Drain the prawns/shrimp and thread onto 4 skewers. Mix the marinade with the melted butter and brush the prawns/shrimp with the mixture. Grill for 8-10 minutes about 10-15cm/4-6

inches above the coals. Brush frequently with the marinade while the prawns/shrimp cook. Pour over remaining marinade before serving.

Carrot Salad with Creamy Sesame Dressing

PREPARATION TIME: 1 hour

SERVES: 4 people

4 large carrots, peeled
120g/4oz/1 cup raisins
120g/4oz/1 cup chopped walnuts
30ml/2 tbsps sesame seeds
30ml/2 tbsps oil
15ml/1 tbsp lemon juice
90ml/6 tbsps sesame paste (tahini)
90ml/6 tbsps warm water

This page: Carrot Salad with Creamy Sesame Dressing. Facing page: Curried Rice Salad.

is evaporated. Leave covered to stand for about 5 minutes. Toss the rice with a fork, drain away any excess water and leave to cool. Combine with the remaining salad ingredients, stirring carefully so that the hard-boiled eggs do not break up. Mix the dressing ingredients together thoroughly. Chop any large pieces of mango in the chutney finely. Stir the dressing into the salad and toss gently to coat. Arrange the rice salad in a mound on a serving dish. Sprinkle the cubed avocado with the lemon juice to keep it green and place around the rice salad before serving.

Cheese and Vine Leaves

PREPARATION TIME: 20 minutes	
COOKING TIME: 6 minutes	
SERVES: 4 people	

4 pieces goat's, feta or haloumi cheese
280ml/½ pint/1 cup olive oil
60ml/4 tbsps chopped fresh herbs such as
    basil, tarragon, oregano, marjoram,
    parsley
2 cloves garlic, peeled and crushed
    (optional)
1 bay leaf
Squeeze lemon juice

TO SERVE
4 fresh vine leaves, washed, or 4 brine-
    packed vine leaves, soaked 30 minutes
1 head radicchio
8 leaves curly endive, washed and torn in
    bite-size pieces

If using goat's cheese, make sure it is not too ripe. Lightly score the surface of whichever cheese is used. Mix together the oil, herbs, garlic and lemon juice. Place the cheese in a small, deep bowl or jar and pour over the oil mixture. If cheese is not completely covered, pour on more oil. Leave, covered, overnight in the refrigerator. Drain the cheese and place in a hinged wire rack. Grill the cheese over hot coals until light golden brown and just beginning to melt. Drain and dry the vine leaves. Wash the radicchio and break apart the leaves. Arrange radicchio and endive leaves on 4 small plates and

place a vine leaf on top. Place the cooked cheese on top of the vine leaf and spoon some of the oil mixture over each serving.

Gorgonzola and Bean Salad with Pine Nuts

PREPARATION TIME: 20 minutes	
COOKING TIME: 4-5 minutes	
SERVES: 4 people	

340g/12oz French/green beans, ends
    trimmed
60g/2oz/½ cup pine nuts, toasted if
    desired
120g/4oz/1 cup crumbled gorgonzola or
    other blue cheese
30ml/2 tbsps red wine vinegar
90ml/6 tbsps olive oil
½ clove garlic, finely minced
Salt and pepper
2 heads radicchio

This page: Cheese and Vine Leaves. Facing page: Gorgonzola and Bean Salad with Pine Nuts (top), and Spinach Salad with Bacon, Hazelnuts and Mushrooms (bottom).

If the beans are large, cut across in half or thirds. Place in boiling salted water and cook for 4-5 minutes or until tender-crisp. Rinse under cold water and leave to drain. Toast pine nuts, if desired, at 180°C, 350°F, Gas Mark 4 for 10 minutes. Allow to cool. Mix the vinegar, oil, garlic, salt and pepper until well emulsified. Toss the beans in the dressing and add the cheese and nuts. Separate the leaves of radicchio, wash and dry. Arrange on salad plates and spoon the bean salad on top. Alternatively, tear radicchio into bite-size pieces and toss all the ingredients together.

Beetroot and Celeriac Salad

PREPARATION TIME: 25 minutes

COOKING TIME: 20 minutes

SERVES: 4 people

1 large celeriac root, peeled
4-6 cooked beets/beetroot
4 spring/green onions chopped
Juice of ½ a lemon

DRESSING
430ml/¾ pint/1½ cups sour cream
10ml/2 tsps white wine vinegar
Pinch sugar
10ml/2 tsps celery seed
25ml/1½ tbsps parsley

Cut the celeriac into 1.25cm/½ inch dice. Cook in boiling salted water with the juice of half a lemon for about 20 minutes or until tender. Drain and set aside to cool. Dice the beets/beetroot the same size as the celeriac. Mix the beets/beetroot with the spring/green onions and carefully combine with the celeriac. Mix the dressing ingredients together, reserving half of the parsley. Combine the dressing with the celeriac and the beets/beetroot, taking care not to over mix. Sprinkle the remaining parsley over the salad before serving.

Red Cabbage, Celery and Carrot Salad

PREPARATION TIME: 15 minutes

SERVES: 6-8 people

1 small head red cabbage
4-6 carrots, peeled
4-6 sticks celery

DRESSING
120ml/4 fl oz/½ cup oil
15ml/1 tbsp white wine vinegar
30ml/2 tbsps lemon juice
15ml/1 tbsp honey
15ml/1 tbsp celery seed
10ml/2 tsps chopped parsley
Salt and pepper

Cut the cabbage in quarters and remove the core. Grate coarsely or

Parsley Salad Vinaigrette

PREPARATION TIME: 20 minutes

COOKING TIME: 2 minutes

SERVES: 4 people

2 large bunches parsley (preferably flat Italian variety)
225g/8oz tomatoes, quartered and seeded
120g/4oz/1 cup stoned black olives, sliced
140ml/¼ pint/½ cup vegetable oil
1 clove garlic, finely minced
45ml/3 tbsps white wine vinegar
5ml/1 tsp dry mustard
Pinch sugar
Salt and pepper
60g/2oz/½ cup grated fresh Parmesan cheese

This page: Red Cabbage, Celery and Carrot Salad. Facing page: Parsley Salad Vinaigrette (top), and Beetroot and Celeriac Salad (bottom).

Pick over the parsley and discard any yellow and thick stems. Break parsley into individual leaves. Cut the tomatoes into 1.25cm/½ inch dice. Use 30ml/2 tbsps of measured oil and heat in a small frying pan. Add the finely chopped garlic and cook slowly to brown lightly. Combine with the remaining oil, vinegar, mustard, sugar, salt and pepper and beat well. Toss the dressing with the parsley, tomatoes and olives before serving. Sprinkle over the Parmesan cheese.

slice finely. Grate the carrots coarsely. Cut the celery into very fine strips. Combine all the vegetables in a large salad bowl or in individual bowls. Mix the salad dressing ingredients very well. This can be done by hand with wire whisk or in a blender. Once the dressing is well emulsified, add the celery seeds and whisk again. Pour over the salad and toss before serving.

Three Bean Salad

PREPARATION TIME: 15 minutes, plus marinating time

SERVES: 6-8 people

1 225g/8oz can chickpeas
1 225g/8oz can red kidney beans
1 225g/8oz can green flageolet beans
6-8 tomatoes, quartered

DRESSING
140ml/¼ pint/½ cup olive oil and
    vegetable oil mixed
60ml/4 tbsps white wine vinegar
30ml/2 tbsps chopped parsley
15ml/1 tbsp chopped basil
1 shallot, finely chopped
1 clove garlic, finely minced
Salt and pepper

Drain and rinse all the beans. Mix the dressing ingredients together thoroughly and combine with the beans. Allow to marinate for 2 hours. Mound the beans into a serving dish and surround with the quartered tomatoes to serve.

Pea, Cheese and Bacon Salad

PREPARATION TIME: 20 minutes

COOKING TIME: 15-20 minutes

SERVES: 6 people

6 strips bacon/smoked streaky bacon,
    rind and bones removed
450g/1lb fresh or frozen shelled peas
120g/4oz Red Leicester/Colby cheese
4 sticks celery, diced
4 spring/green onions, sliced thinly or
    1 small red onion, diced
1 red pepper, cored, seeded and diced

1 head Buttercrunch lettuce
180ml/6 fl oz/¾ cup sour cream or
    natural yogurt
15ml/1 tbsp chopped fresh mixed herbs
5ml/1 tsp white wine vinegar
5ml/1 tsp sugar
Salt and pepper

Dice the bacon and cook gently in a small frying pan until the fat runs. Turn up the heat and fry the bacon until brown and crisp. Remove to paper towels to drain. Meanwhile cook the peas in boiling salted water for 15-20 minutes for fresh peas and 5 minutes for frozen peas. When the peas are cooked, drain and refresh under cold water and leave to drain dry. Cut the cheese into dice slightly larger than the peas. Dice the celery and red pepper to the same size as

This page: Tomato and Mozzarella Salad with Fresh Basil. Facing page: Three Bean Salad (left), and Pea, Cheese and Bacon Salad (right).

the cheese. Combine the peas, cheese, celery, spring/green onions, red pepper and bacon in a bowl. Mix the dressing ingredients together, reserving half of the chopped mixed herbs. Combine the vegetables and bacon with half of the dressing. Separate the leaves of the lettuce and wash well. Pat dry and arrange on serving dishes. Spoon on the salad mixture and top with the remaining dressing. Sprinkle the reserved chopped herbs on top of the dressing.

Tomato and Mozzarella Salad with Fresh Basil

PREPARATION TIME: 15 minutes

SERVES: 4 people

3 large beefsteak tomatoes, sliced 6mm/
¼ inch thick
180g/6oz mozzarella cheese, drained,
dried and sliced 6mm/¼ inch thick
60ml/4 tbsps coarsely chopped fresh basil
leaves

DRESSING
90ml/6 tbsps olive oil and vegetable oil
mixed
30ml/2 tbsps balsamic vinegar or white
wine vinegar
1.25ml/¼ tsp Dijon mustard
Salt and pepper

GARNISH
Fresh basil leaves

Arrange the tomato slices and mozzarella cheese slices in overlapping circles on four individual salad plates. Sprinkle the fresh chopped basil leaves on top and garnish in the centre with the whole basil leaves. Mix all the dressing ingredients together very well and spoon some over the salads before serving. Serve the rest of the dressing separately.

Cracked Wheat Salad

PREPARATION TIME: 20 minutes

SERVES: 4-6 people

225g/8oz/2 cups bulgur wheat, washed
and drained
4 spring/green onions, chopped
1 cucumber, cut in small cubes
Juice and rind of 1 lemon
4 tomatoes, cubed
4 sticks celery, diced
60g/2oz/½ cup toasted sunflower seeds
120g/4oz/1 cup crumbled feta cheese
140ml/¼ pint/½ cup olive oil
1 clove garlic, minced
Salt and pepper
60ml/4 tbsps chopped mixed herbs

Place the washed bulgur wheat in clean water and leave to soak for 5 minutes. Drain and squeeze as much moisture out as possible. Spread the wheat out onto a clean towel to drain and dry. When the wheat is dry put into a large bowl with all the remaining ingredients and toss together carefully so that the cheese does not break up. Allow the salad to chill for up to 1 hour before serving. If desired, garnish the salad with whole sprigs of herbs.

Spinach Salad with Bacon, Hazelnuts and Mushrooms

PREPARATION TIME: 20 minutes

COOKING TIME: 2-3 minutes

SERVES: 4 people

675g/1½ lbs spinach, stalks removed,
washed and dried
6 strips bacon/smoked streaky bacon,
bones and rind removed
225g/8oz mushrooms, sliced
120g/4oz/1 cup hazelnuts, roasted,
skinned and roughly chopped

DRESSING
140ml/¼ pint/½ cup oil
45ml/3 tbsps white wine vinegar
5ml/1 tsp Dijon mustard
1 shallot, finely chopped
Salt and pepper
Pinch sugar (optional)

Tear the spinach leaves into bite-size pieces and put into a serving bowl. Fry or grill/broil the bacon until brown and crisp. Crumble the bacon and sprinkle over the spinach. Add the hazelnuts and mushrooms to the spinach salad and toss. Mix all the dressing ingredients very well and pour over the salad just before serving.

Cucumber and Mint Salad

PREPARATION TIME: 30 minutes

SERVES: 4 people

1 large or 2 small cucumbers, peeled for a
striped effect or scratched with the prongs of a fork lengthwise along the
skin
Salt

DRESSING
280ml/½ pint/1 cup sour cream or
natural yogurt
30ml/2 tbsps chopped fresh mint
15ml/1 tbsp chopped parsley
Pinch sugar
Squeeze lemon juice
Salt and pepper

GARNISH
Whole sprigs of mint

Slice the cucumber thinly in rounds. Place the cucumber in a colander and sprinkle lightly with salt. Leave for 30 minutes to drain. Rinse the cucumber under cold water to remove the salt and pat dry. Mix the sour cream or yogurt with the sugar, lemon juice, salt, pepper, mint and parsley. Pour over the drained cucumber and toss. Leave refrigerated for 30 minutes before serving, and garnish with whole sprigs of mint.

Potato Salad with Mustard-Chive Dressing

PREPARATION TIME: 25 minutes

COOKING TIME: 20 minutes

SERVES: 6 people

1.5kg/3lbs potatoes, new or red variety
6 sticks celery, thinly sliced
1 red pepper, seeded, cored and diced
3 hard-boiled eggs

DRESSING
280ml/½ pint/1 cup prepared
mayonnaise
280ml/½ pint/1 cup natural yogurt
60ml/4 tbsp Dijon mustard and mild
mustard mixed half and half
1 bunch chives, snipped
Salt and pepper

Facing page: Cucumber and Mint Salad (top), and Cracked Wheat Salad (bottom).

Cook the potatoes in their skins for about 20 minutes in salted water. When the potatoes are tender, drain and peel while still warm. Cut the potatoes into cubes and mix with the celery and red pepper. Set the potato salad aside to cool while mixing the dressing. Combine the mayonnaise, yogurt, mustard, half the chives, salt and pepper and mix well. Toss carefully with the potato salad so that the potatoes do not break up. Spoon the salad into a serving dish and slice the hard-boiled eggs into rounds, or chop roughly. Arrange the hard-boiled eggs in circles on top of the potato salad or scatter over, if chopped. Sprinkle over reserved chives and refrigerate for about 1 hour before serving.

Red, Green and Yellow Pepper Salad

PREPARATION TIME: 20 minutes

SERVES: 6 people

3 sweet red peppers
3 green peppers
3 yellow peppers
Oil
60g/2oz/½ cup small black olives, stoned
30ml/2 tbsps finely chopped coriander
  leaves
3 hard-boiled eggs

DRESSING
90ml/6 tbsps oil
10ml/2 tsps lemon juice
30ml/2 tbsps white wine vinegar
1 small clove garlic, finely minced
Pinch salt
Pinch cayenne pepper
Pinch sugar (optional)

Cut all the peppers in half and remove the seeds and cores. Press lightly with palm to flatten. Brush the skin side of each pepper with oil and place under a preheated grill/broiler about 15cm/6 inches from the heat. Cook until the skin chars. Remove and wrap the peppers in a clean towel. Leave them to cool 10-15 minutes. Mix the dressing ingredients and quarter the eggs. Unwrap the peppers and peel off the skin. Cut the peppers into strips about 2.5cm/

1 inch wide and arrange in a circle, alternating colours. Arrange the olives and quartered egg in the centre. Sprinkle the coriander leaves over the peppers and spoon over the dressing. Leave the salad, covered, in the refrigerator for 1 hour before serving. Peeled peppers will keep covered in oil up to 5 days in the refrigerator.

Coleslaw

PREPARATION TIME: 25 minutes

SERVES: 6 people

DRESSING
280ml/½ pint/1 cup prepared
  mayonnaise
4 spring/green onions finely chopped
280ml/½ pint/1 cup sour cream
60g/2oz Roquefort or blue cheese

This page: Zanzibar Prawns/ Shrimp. Facing page: Coleslaw (top), and Potato Salad with Mustard-Chive Dressing (bottom).

1.25ml/¼ tsp Worcestershire sauce
5ml/1 tsp vinegar
30ml/2 tbsps chopped parsley
Pinch sugar
Salt and pepper

SALAD
1 medium size head white cabbage,
  shredded
6 carrots, peeled and coarsely grated
1 green pepper, cut into thin short strips
120g/4oz/1 cup roasted peanuts or
  raisins

Combine all the dressing ingredients, reserving half the parsley, and refrigerate in a covered bowl for about 1 hour to allow the flavours to blend. Combine the dressing with the salad ingredients and toss to serve. Sprinkle on reserved chopped parsley.

Zanzibar Prawns/Shrimp

PREPARATION TIME: 25 minutes

COOKING TIME: 18-23 minutes

SERVES: 4 people

450g/1lb king prawns/jumbo shrimp, shelled and de-veined
1 large fresh pineapple, peeled, cored and cut into chunks
Oil

SAUCE
140ml/¼ pint/½ cup orange juice
15ml/1 tbsp vinegar
15ml/1 tbsp lime juice
5ml/1 tsp dry mustard
15ml/1 tbsp brown sugar
Remaining pineapple

GARNISH
Flaked coconut
Curly endive

Thread the prawns/shrimp and pineapple pieces on skewers, alternating each ingredient. Use about 4 pineapple pieces per skewer. Place the remaining pineapple and the sauce ingredients into a food processor and purée. Pour into a small pan and cook over low heat for about 10-15 minutes to reduce slightly. Place the kebabs on a lightly oiled rack above the coals and cook about 6 minutes, basting frequently with the sauce. Sprinkle cooked kebabs with coconut and serve on endive leaves. Serve remaining sauce separately.

Egg Mayonnaise with Asparagus and Caviar

PREPARATION TIME: 25 minutes

COOKING TIME: 10 minutes

SERVES: 4-6 people

12 asparagus spears, trimmed and peeled
6 hard-boiled eggs
430ml/¾ pint/1½ cups prepared mayonnaise
15ml/1 tbsp lemon juice
Hot water
Red caviar

Tie asparagus in a bundle and cook in a deep saucepan of boiling salted water, keeping the asparagus tips out of the water. The tips will cook in the steam and the thick stalks will cook in the water, thus helping the asparagus to cook evenly. Cook about 5-8 minutes or until just tender. Rinse under cold water and

This page: Red, Green and Yellow Pepper Salad. Facing page: Egg Mayonnaise with Asparagus and Caviar.

drain. Meanwhile, place eggs in boiling water. Bring water back to the boil and cook eggs for 10 minutes. Cool completely under cold running water and peel. Combine mayonnaise and lemon juice. If very thick, add enough hot water until of coating consistency. Arrange eggs cut side down on a plate and coat with the mayonnaise. Surround with asparagus and garnish the eggs with caviar.

BARBECUES & SALADS

Meat and Poultry

Kashmiri Lamb Kebabs

PREPARATION TIME: 20 minutes	
COOKING TIME: 10 minutes	
SERVES: 4 people	

675g/1½ lbs lamb shoulder or leg
30ml/2 tbsps oil
1 clove garlic, finely minced
15ml/1 tbsp ground cumin
5ml/1 tsp turmeric
5ml/1 tsp grated gresh ginger
Chopped fresh coriander or parsley leaves
Salt and pepper
1 red pepper, cut in 2.5cm/1 inch pieces
1 small onion, cut in rings

Cut the lamb in 2.5cm/1 inch cubes. Heat the oil and cook the garlic, cumin, turmeric and ginger for 1 minute. Add the coriander, salt and pepper. Allow to cool and then rub the spice mixture over the meat. Leave covered in the refrigerator for several hours. Thread the meat on skewers, alternating with the pepper slices. Cook about 10 minutes, turning frequently. During the last 5 minutes of cooking, thread sliced onion rings around the meat and continue cooking until the onion is cooked and slightly browned and meat has reached desired doneness.

Minced Lamb Kebabs with Olives and Tomatoes

PREPARATION TIME: 20 minutes	
COOKING TIME: 10 minutes	
SERVES: 4 people	

30g/1oz/4 tbsps bulgur wheat, soaked
and drained

550g/1¼lbs minced/ground lamb
1 clove garlic, finely minced
10ml/2 tsps ground cumin
Pinch cinnamon
Salt and pepper
1 egg, beaten
Oil
16 large green olives, stoned
16 cherry tomatoes

This page: Mustard Grilled Pork with Poppy Seeds. Facing page: Kashmiri Lamb Kebabs (left) and Minced Lamb Kebabs with Olives and Tomatoes (right).

SAUCE

280ml/½ pint/1 cup yogurt
30ml/2 tbsps chopped fresh mint
Salt and pepper

Soak the bulgur wheat until soft. Wring out and spread on paper towels to drain and dry. Mix with the remaining ingredients and enough of the beaten egg to bind together. The mixture should not be too wet. Form into small balls about 3.75cm/ 1½ inches in diameter. Thread onto skewers with the olives and tomatoes. Brush with oil and grill about 10 minutes, turning frequently. Mix the yogurt, mint, salt and pepper and serve with the kebabs.

Mustard Grilled Pork with Poppy Seeds

PREPARATION TIME: 20 minutes plus marinating time

COOKING TIME: 45 minutes to 1 hour

SERVES: 4-6 people

4 175-200g/6-7oz whole pork fillets/ tenderloin
30ml/2 tbsps black poppy seeds

MARINADE

15ml/1 tbsp mild mustard
60ml/4 tbsps oil
60ml/4 tbsps unsweetened apple juice
1 clove garlic, finely minced
Salt and pepper

SWEET MUSTARD SAUCE

280ml/½ pint/1 cup mild mustard
60g/2oz/¼ cup brown sugar
60ml/2 fl oz/¼ cup dry cider or unsweetened apple juice
10ml/2 tsps chopped fresh or crumbled dried tarragon
Pinch cayenne pepper
Salt

Mix the marinade and rub into the pork. Place the pork in a dish or pan and cover. Refrigerate for 4 hours or overnight. Using a grill with an adjustable rack, place the pork over the coals on the highest level or set an electric or gas grill to a medium temperature. Cook the pork for 45 minutes-1 hour, basting with the marinade and turning frequently. Lower the shelf or raise the temperature. Baste frequently with the sauce during the last 10 minutes of cooking time. During the last 5 minutes, sprinkle the pork fillets with the poppy seeds. Serve the pork sliced thinly with the remaining sauce.

Turkey and Pancetta Rolls

PREPARATION TIME: 30 minutes

COOKING TIME: 20-30 minutes

SERVES: 4-6 people

2 turkey breasts, 450g/1lb each, skinned
90g/3oz/⅓ cup butter softened
1 clove garlic, minced
15ml/1 tbsp oregano leaves
16 slices pancetta or prosciutto ham
Salt and pepper
Oil

Cut the turkey breasts in half, lengthwise. Place each piece between two sheets of clingfilm/plastic wrap and bat out each piece with a rolling pin or meat mallet to flatten. Mix the butter, garlic, oregano, salt and pepper together. Spread half of the mixture over each slice of turkey. Lay 4 slices of pancetta on top of each piece of turkey. Roll up, tucking in the sides and tie with fine string in 3 places. Spread the remaining butter on the outside of each roll. Cook the rolls over medium hot coals until tender. Insert a meat thermometer into each roll to check doneness. The temperature should read 90°C/ 190°F. Cooking should take approximately 20 to 30 minutes. Slice each roll into 1.25cm/½ inch rounds to serve.

Niçoise Chicken

PREPARATION TIME: 30 minutes

COOKING TIME: 20 minutes

SERVES: 4 people

4 boned chicken breasts, unskinned
60ml/4 tbsps oil
30ml/2 tbsps lemon juice

TAPENADE FILLING

450g/1lb large black olives, stoned
60ml/2 tbsps capers
1 clove garlic, peeled and roughly chopped
4 anchovy fillets
30ml/2 tbsps olive oil
Raw tomato sauce

450g/1lb ripe tomatoes, peeled, seeded and chopped
1 shallot, very finely chopped
30ml/2 tbsps chopped parsley
30ml/2 tbsps chopped basil
30ml/2 tbsps white wine vinegar
30ml/2 tbsps olive oil
15ml/1 tbsp sugar
Salt and pepper
15ml/1 tbsp tomato purée/paste (optional)

Cut a pocket in the thickest side of the chicken breasts. Combine half the olives, half the capers and the remaining ingredients for the tapenade in a blender or food processor. Work to a purée. Add the remaining olives and capers and process a few times to chop them roughly. Fill the chicken breasts with the tapenade. Chill to help filling to firm. Baste the skin side with oil and lemon juice mixed together. Cook skin side down first for 10 minutes over medium hot coals. Turn over, baste again and grill for another 10 minutes on the other side. Meanwhile, combine the sauce ingredients and mix very well. Serve with the chicken.

Orange Grilled Duck with Sesame and Spice

PREPARATION TIME: 20 minutes, plus marinating time

COOKING TIME: 40 minutes

SERVES: 4 people

4 boned duck breasts
60ml/4 tbsps sesame seeds

Facing page: Turkey and Pancetta Rolls (top) and Niçoise Chicken (bottom).

minutes before the duck is cooked, sprinkle the orange slices with brown sugar and grill on both sides to glaze. Serve with the duck.

Herb and Onion Grilled Lamb Chops

PREPARATION TIME: 10 minutes

COOKING TIME: 15 minutes

SERVES: 4 people

4 leg chops, cut 2cm/¾ inch thick

MARINADE
1 large onion, finely chopped
15ml/1 tbsp parsley, finely chopped
15ml/1 tbsp fresh thyme or mint leaves, roughly chopped
2 fresh bay leaves, cut in thin shreds with scissors
1 clove garlic, finely minced
45ml/3 tbsps oil
Juice of ½ lemon
Salt and pepper

Combine all the marinade ingredients and pour over the chops in a dish. Leave, covered, 2 hours in the refrigerator. Place on a rack over hot coals and cook the chops 15 minutes, turning often and basting frequently with the remaining marinade.

Barbecued Flank Steak

PREPARATION TIME: 25 minutes

COOKING TIME: 45-55 minutes

SERVES: 6 people

1.5kg/3½ lbs skirt steak/flank steak, in one piece

BARBECUE SEASONING
60ml/4 tbsps salt
7.5ml/1½ tsp freshly ground pepper
7.5ml/1½ tsp cayenne pepper (or paprika for a milder tasting mixture))

This page: Orange Grilled Duck with Sesame and Spice. Facing page: Herb and Onion Grilled Lamb Chops (top), and Barbecued Flank Steak (bottom).

MARINADE
60ml/4 tbsps soy sauce
120ml/4 fl oz/½ cup dry white wine
45ml/3 tbsps oil
Pinch ground nutmeg
Pinch ground ginger
Pinch ground mustard
Salt and pepper

SAUCE
Reserved marinade
180ml/6 fl oz/¾ cup orange juice
1 shallot, finely chopped
10ml/2 tsps cornflour/cornstarch

GARNISH
1 orange, peeled and thinly sliced in rounds
Brown sugar

Score the fat side of each duck breast with a sharp knife. Mix the marinade ingredients together and pour over the duck in a shallow dish. Cover and refrigerate for 2 hours. Turn the duck frequently. Place the duck breasts fat side down on grill. Cook for 20 minutes per side, basting frequently. If the duck appears to be cooking too quickly, turn more often. Combine the sauce ingredients and add any remaining marinade. Cook 1 to 2 minutes over moderate heat until boiling and, just before the duck is finished cooking, brush the fat side lightly with the sauce and sprinkle on the sesame seeds. Turn fat side down onto the grill for 1 minute. Serve remaining sauce with the duck. Five

Barbecued Ribs

PREPARATION TIME: 15 minutes

COOKING TIME: 2 hours

SERVES: 4-6 people

2-3 racks pork spare ribs (about 2.5kg/ 5lbs)
Barbecue Sauce (see recipe for Barbecued Flank Steak)
or
Sweet Mustard Sauce (see recipe for Mustard Grilled Pork with Poppy Seeds)

Leave the ribs in whole racks. Combine the ingredients for either sauce and pour over the meat in a roasting pan. Cover with foil and bake, turning and basting frequently, for 1 hour in a 150°C/325°F/ Gas Mark 3 oven. Uncover and bake 30 minutes more in the oven. Finish on a barbecue grill over moderately hot coals for about 30 minutes, basting frequently with the sauce. Cut between the bones into pieces. Serve with the remaining sauce.

Javanese Pork

PREPARATION TIME: 20 minutes

COOKING TIME: 30-45 minutes

SERVES: 4 people

4 pork rib or loin chops cut 2.5cm/1 inch thick
60ml/4 tbsps dark soy sauce
Large pinch cayenne pepper
45ml/3 tbsps lime or lemon juice
15ml/1 tbsp ground coriander
30ml/2 tbsps oil
30ml/2 tbsps brown sugar
4 medium-sized sweet red peppers
Oil
1 bunch fresh coriander

Snip the fat around the edges of the chops at 1.25cm/½ inch intervals to prevent curling. Mix soy sauce, cayenne pepper, lemon juice, coriander and oil together in a dish or pan. Place the pork chops in the

BARBECUE SAUCE
60ml/4 tbsps oil
340ml/12 fl oz/1¼ cups tomato ketchup
45ml/3 tbsps Worcestershire sauce
90ml/6 tbsps cider vinegar
60ml/4 tbsps soft brown sugar
60ml/4 tbsps chopped onion
1 clove garlic, crushed (optional)
1 bay leaf
60ml/4 tbsps water
10ml/2 tsps dry mustard
Dash tabasco
Salt and pepper

First prepare the barbecue sauce. Combine all the ingredients, reserving salt and pepper to add later. Cook in a heavy saucepan over low heat for 30 minutes, stirring frequently and adding more water if the sauce reduces too quickly.

Remove the bay leaf and add salt and pepper to taste before using. The sauce should be thick. Use the sauce for basting while cooking, or serve hot to accompany cooked meat and poultry. Score the meat across both sides with a large knife. Mix together the barbecue seasoning and rub 30ml/2 tbsps over the meat, reserving the rest of the seasoning for other use. Sear the meat on both sides over hot coals. Raise the grill rack or lower the temperature on a gas or electric grill/broiler. Baste with the sauce and grill the meat slowly. During last 5 minutes, lower the rack or raise the temperature and grill the meat quickly on both sides, basting with the sauce. Slice the meat thinly across the grain and serve with any remaining sauce.

This page: Javanese Pork. Facing page: Chinese Pork and Aubergine/ Eggplant Kebabs (left), and Barbecued Ribs (right).

**This page: Stuffed Hamburgers.
Facing page: Butterflied Lamb.**

marinade and leave, covered, in the refrigerator for 1 hour. Turn over after 30 minutes. Place on grill over medium hot coals or on a middle rack. Mix sugar into remaining marinade. Cook chops for 15-20 minutes on each side until well done. Baste with the marinade frequently during the last 10-15 minutes of cooking. Meanwhile, wash and dry the peppers and brush with oil on all sides. Place alongside pork for half of its cooking time. Turn the peppers often. They will soften and char on the outside. Serve the pork chops with peppers and garnish with coriander leaves.

Butterflied Lamb

PREPARATION TIME: 30 minutes, plus marinating time

COOKING TIME: 40-50 minutes

SERVES: 6-8 people

1.8kg/4lbs leg of lamb
75ml/5 tbsps oil
Juice and rind of one lemon
Small bunch mint, roughly chopped
Salt and coarsely ground black pepper
1 clove garlic, crushed

To butterfly the lamb, cut through the skin along the line of the main bone down to the bone. Cut the meat away from the bone, opening out the leg while scraping against the bone with a small, sharp knife. Take out the bone and remove excess fat. Flatten thick places by batting with a rolling pin or meat mallet.

Alternatively, make shallow cuts halfway through the thickest parts and press open. Thread two or three long skewers through the meat – this will make the meat easier to handle and turn on the grill. Place in a plastic bag or large, shallow dish. Mix the other ingredients together and pour over the lamb, rubbing it in well. Cover the dish or seal the bag and leave at room temperature for 6 hours or overnight in the refrigerator. Turn the lamb frequently. Remove from the dish or the bag and reserve the marinade. Grill at least 15cm/6 inches away from the coals on the skin side first. Grill 20 minutes per side for pink lamb and 30-40 minutes per side for more well done lamb. Baste frequently during grilling. Remove the skewers and cut the slices across the grain. If fresh mint is unavailable, use rosemary, fresh or dried. Alternatively, roast lamb in a 180°C/350°F/Gas Mark 4 oven for half of the cooking time and grill for the last half of cooking.

Stuffed Hamburgers

PREPARATION TIME: 30 minutes

COOKING TIME: 20 minutes

SERVES: 4-8 people

900g/2lbs minced/ground beef
1 onion, finely chopped
60ml/4 tbsps Worcestershire sauce
Salt and pepper
8 hamburger buns

GUACAMOLE BURGERS

FILLING
120g/4oz Tilsit or Monterey Jack cheese, cubed
1 mild chili pepper, thinly sliced and seeds removed

TOPPING
1 avocado, peeled and mashed
1 small clove garlic, crushed
10ml/2 tsps lemon or lime juice
1 tomato, peeled, seeded and finely chopped
Salt and pepper

BLUE CHEESE BURGERS
FILLING
120g/4oz blue cheese, crumbled
30g/1oz/¼ cup chopped walnuts

TOPPING
15ml/1 tbsp brown/steak sauce
75ml/5 tbsps prepared mayonnaise
90ml/6 tbsps sour cream or yogurt
Salt and pepper

GRUYÈRE AND MUSHROOM BURGERS
FILLING
60g/2oz mushrooms, roughly chopped
120g/4oz Gruyère or Swiss cheese, cubed

TOPPING
450g/1lb tomatoes
1 clove garlic, finely minced
30ml/2 tbsps tarragon, chopped
15ml/1 tbsp tarragon vinegar
Pinch sugar
30ml/2 tbsps oil
Salt and pepper

Mix the hamburger ingredients well, mould the meat around the chosen fillings and press carefully into patties. Mix the guacamole topping ingredients together and set aside while grilling the hamburgers. Mix the topping for the blue cheese burgers and refrigerate until needed. For the Gruyère burger topping, roughly chop tomatoes and then finely chop in a blender or food processor. Sieve to remove the seeds and skin, combine with the remaining tomato sauce ingredients and mix well. Grill hamburgers over hot coals 10 minutes per side. Quickly grill cut sides of the hamburger buns to heat through and place the hamburgers inside. Spoon on the appropriate toppings for each filling.

Chicken Tikka

PREPARATION TIME: 20 minutes

COOKING TIME: 10-15 minutes

SERVES: 4 people

1.5kg/3lb chicken, skinned and boned

MARINADE
140ml/¼ pint/½ cup natural yogurt
1 small piece ginger, grated
1 clove garlic, finely minced
5ml/1 tsp chili powder, hot or mild
2.5ml/½ tsp ground coriander
2.5ml/½ tsp ground cumin
1.25ml/¼ tsp turmeric

1.25ml/¼ tsp red food colouring (optional)
Juice of one lime
Salt and pepper

Half head Iceberg lettuce, shredded
4 lemon wedges
4 small tomatoes, quartered

Cut chicken into 2.5cm/1 inch pieces. Mix all the marinade ingredients together. Pour over the chicken and stir well. Cover and leave for several hours in the refrigerator. Thread chicken on skewers and grill 10-15 minutes, turning frequently. Baste with any remaining marinade. Serve on a bed of shredded lettuce with tomatoes and lemon wedges.

Indian Chicken

PREPARATION TIME: 15 minutes plus marinating time

COOKING TIME: 45 minutes to 1 hour

SERVES: 4-6 people

1 1.5kg/3lbs chicken, cut into 8 pieces
570ml/1 pint/2 cups natural yogurt
10ml/2 tsps ground coriander
10ml/2 tsps paprika
5ml/1 tsp ground turmeric
Juice of 1 lime
15ml/1 tbsp honey
½ clove garlic, finely minced
1 small piece ginger, peeled and grated

Pierce the chicken all over with a fork or skewer. Combine all the remaining ingredients and spread half the mixture over the chicken, rubbing in well. Place the chicken in a shallow dish or a plastic bag and cover or tie and leave for at last 4 hours or overnight in the refrigerator. If your barbecue has adjustable shelves, place on the level furthest from the coals. Arrange the chicken skin side down and grill until lightly browned, turn over and cook again until lightly browned. Baste frequently with remaining marinade. Lower the grill for the last 15 minutes and cook, turning and basting frequently, until the chicken is brown and the skin is crisp. Alternatively, cook the chicken

in a covered pan in the oven at 150°C/325°F Gas Mark 4 for 45 minutes to 1 hour and grill for the last 15 minutes for flavour and colour. Serve any remaining yogurt mixture separately as a sauce.

Chinese Pork and Aubergine/Eggplant Kebabs

PREPARATION TIME: 20 minutes

COOKING TIME: 15-20 minutes

SERVES: 4 people

450g/1lb pork fillet/tenderloin, cut in 2.5cm/1 inch cubes
2 medium onions, cut in 2.5cm/1 inch pieces
1 large aubergine/eggplant, cut in 3.75cm/1½ inch cubes
30ml/2 tbsps Hoisin sauce
45ml/3 tbsps soy sauce
60ml/4 tbsps rice wine or dry sherry
1 clove garlic, finely minced
Sesame seeds
Salt

Sprinkle the aubergine/eggplant cubes with salt and leave in a colander to drain for 30 minutes. Rinse well and pat dry. Pre-cook in 30ml/2 tbsps oil to soften slightly. Thread the pork, onion and aubergine/eggplant on skewers, alternating the ingredients. Mix the hoisin sauce, soy sauce, rice wine or sherry and garlic together. Brush the kebabs with the mixture and place them on a lightly-oiled grill. Cook about 15-20 minutes, turning and basting frequently. During the last 2 minutes sprinkle all sides with sesame seeds and continue grilling to brown the seeds. Pour over any remaining sauce before serving.

Facing page: Indian Chicken (top), and Chicken Tikka (bottom).

Burgundy Beef Kebabs

PREPARATION TIME: 20 minutes, plus marinating time

COOKING TIME: 10 minutes

SERVES: 4 people

120g/4oz shallots or button onions, parboiled 3 minutes and peeled
670g/1½ lbs sirloin or rump steak, cut in 2.5cm/1 inch thick cubes

MARINADE
280ml/½ pint/1 cup burgundy or other dry red wine
45ml/3 tbsps oil
1 bay leaf
1 clove garlic, peeled
1 sliced onion
6 black peppercorns
1 sprig fresh thyme
Pinch salt

SAUCE
280ml/½ pint/1 cup sour cream
30g/2 tbsps chopped fresh mixed herbs (such as parsley, thyme, marjoram and chervil)
15ml/1 tbsp red wine vinegar
Pinch sugar
10ml/2 tsps Dijon mustard
Salt and pepper

Bring the marinade ingredients to the boil in a small saucepan. Remove from the heat and allow to cool completely. When cold, pour over the meat in a plastic bag. Seal the bag well, but place it in a bowl to catch any drips. Marinate overnight in the refrigerator, turning the bag occasionally. Thread the meat onto skewers with the onions and grill 10 minutes, turning and basting frequently. Mix the sauce ingredients together and serve with the kebabs.

Smoked Sausage and Apple Kebabs

PREPARATION TIME: 20 minutes

COOKING TIME: 6 minutes

SERVES: 4 people

Two rings smoked pork or beef sausage, cut in 2.5cm/1 inch thick slices

4 small apples, quartered and cored
8 sage leaves
Lemon juice
Quarter quantity sweet mustard sauce (see recipe for Mustard Grilled Pork with Poppy Seeds)

Brush the apples with lemon juice. Thread onto skewers, alternating with sausage pieces and bay leaves.

Brush with the mustard sauce and grill 10 minutes, turning frequently and basting with the sauce. Serve any remaining sauce with the kebabs if desired.

Ham and Apricot Kebabs

PREPARATION TIME: 15 minutes

COOKING TIME: 12 minutes

SERVES: 4 people

*675g/1½ lbs cooked gammon/ham cut in
5cm/2 inch cubes*
*225g/8oz canned or fresh apricots,
halved and stoned*
1 green pepper, cut in 5cm/2 inch pieces

APRICOT BASTE
180g/6oz/¾ cup light brown sugar
60g/4 tbsps apricot jam, sieved
90ml/6 tbsps wine or cider vinegar
5ml/1 tsp dry mustard
45ml/3 tbsps light soy sauce
Salt and pepper

Thread ham, apricots and pepper
pieces onto skewers, alternating the
ingredients. Mix the apricot baste
ingredients together and cook over
gentle heat to dissolve the sugar.
Brush over kebabs as they cook. Turn
and baste several times for about
12 minutes over hot coals. If using
canned apricots, reserve the juice and
add to any baste that remains after
the kebabs are cooked. Bring this
mixture to the boil to reduce slightly
and serve as a sauce with the kebabs.

Spicy Madeira Steaks

PREPARATION TIME: 20 minutes

COOKING TIME: 15 minutes

SERVES: 4 people

4 rump/butt steaks about 180g/6oz each

MARINADE
60ml/4 tbsps oil
140ml/¼ pint/½ cup ketchup
180ml/6 fl oz/¾ cup red wine vinegar
1 clove garlic, crushed
5ml/1 tsp pepper
5ml/1 tsp ground cloves
2.5ml/½ tsp cinnamon
2.5ml/½ tsp thyme leaves

SAUCE
140ml/¼ pint/½ cup reserved marinade
30ml/2 tbsps flour
140ml/¼ pint/½ cup beef stock
140ml/¼ pint/½ cup Madeira
Salt

Combine marinade ingredients and

pour over steaks in a dish. Cover and
refrigerate at least 4 hours. Remove
from marinade and place over hot
coals. Grill, basting frequently, until
of desired doneness. Combine flour
with reserved marinade, beating well
to mix to a smooth paste. Gradually
beat in stock. Bring to the boil in a
small saucepan, stirring constantly.
Cook until thickened, about 1
minute. Reduce heat and simmer 5
minutes. Stir in Madeira and add salt
to taste. Serve with the steak.

**Facing page: Spicy Madeira Steaks
(left), and Burgundy Beef Kebabs
(right). This page: Ham and
Apricot Kebabs (left), and Smoked
Sausage and Apple Kebabs (right).**

Fish and Seafood

Marsala Fish

PREPARATION TIME: 25 minutes

COOKING TIME: 10-15 minutes

SERVES: 4 people

4 medium sized mackerel, trout or similar
    fish
Juice of 1 lemon
10ml/2 tsps turmeric
2 green chili peppers, finely chopped
1 small piece ginger, grated
1 clove garlic, finely minced
Pinch ground cinnamon
Pinch ground cloves
60ml/4 tbsps oil
Salt and pepper
Fresh coriander leaves

ACCOMPANIMENT
½ cucumber, finely diced
140ml/¼ pint/½ cup thick natural yogurt
1 spring/green onion, finely chopped
Salt and pepper

Clean and gut the fish. Cut three slits
on each side of the fish. Combine
spices, lemon juice, oil, garlic and
chili peppers and spread over the fish
and inside the cuts. Place whole
sprigs of coriander inside the fish.
Brush the grill rack lightly with oil or
use a wire fish rack. Cook the fish 10-
15 minutes, turning often and basting
with any remaining mixture.
Combine the accompaniment
ingredients and serve with the fish.

Scallops, Bacon and Prawn/Shrimp Kebabs

PREPARATION TIME: 25 minutes

COOKING TIME: 20-25 minutes

SERVES: 4 people

12 large, raw scallops
12 raw king prawns/jumbo shrimp,
    peeled and de-veined
12 slices smoked streaky bacon/bacon
Juice of 1 lemon
60ml/2 tbsps oil
Coarsely ground black pepper

**This page: Scallops, Bacon and
Prawn/Shrimp Kebabs. Facing
page: Marsala Fish.**

RED CHILI YOGURT SAUCE
2 cloves garlic, finely chopped
1 red pepper, grilled and peeled
1 red chili pepper, chopped
3 slices bread, crusts removed, soaked in
  water
45ml/3 tbsps olive oil
140ml/¼ pint/½ cup natural yogurt

Wrap each scallop in a slice of bacon and thread onto skewers, alternating with prawns/shrimp. Mix the lemon juice, oil and pepper and brush over the shellfish as they cook. Turn frequently and cook until the bacon is lightly crisped and the scallops are just firm. Meanwhile, prepare the sauce. Squeeze the bread to remove the water and place the bread in a blender. Add the finely chopped garlic, the chopped red chili pepper and peeled red pepper and blend well. With the machine running, pour in the oil through the funnel in a thin, steady stream. Keep the machine running until the mixture is a smooth, shiny paste. Combine with the yogurt and mix well. Serve with kebabs.

Grilled Sardines with Lemon and Oregano

PREPARATION TIME: 15 minutes

COOKING TIME: 6-8 minutes

SERVES: 4-6 people

8-12 fresh sardines, gutted, scaled, washed
  and dried
8-12 sprigs fresh oregano
90ml/3 fl oz/⅓ cup olive oil
Juice and rind of 2 lemons
Salt and pepper
15ml/1 tbsp dried oregano

Place one sprig of oregano inside each fish. Mix oil, lemon juice and rind, salt and pepper together. Make two slits on each side of the fish. Brush the fish with the lemon mixture and grill over hot coals for 3-4 minutes per side, basting frequently. When the fish are nearly done, sprinkle the dried oregano on the coals. The smoke will give the fish extra flavour. May be served as a starter/appetizer or main course.

Grey Mullet with Fennel

PREPARATION TIME: 15 minutes

COOKING TIME: 18-22 minutes

SERVES: 4 people

2-4 grey mullet, depending upon size,
  gutted and cleaned

MARINADE
90ml/3 fl oz/⅓ cup oil
15ml/1 tbsp fennel seeds, slightly crushed
1 clove garlic, finely minced
Juice and rind of one lemon
30ml/2 tbsps chopped fennel tops
Salt and pepper

Heat oil and add the fennel seeds. Cook for one minute. Add the garlic and remaining ingredients except the fennel tops. Leave the mixture to cool completely. Pour over the fish in a shallow dish. Cover and refrigerate for 1 hour. Grill over hot coals 10–12 minutes per side. Sprinkle over fennel tops half way through cooking. Tops may also be placed directly on the coals for aromatic smoke.

Swordfish Steaks with Green Peppercorns and Garlic Oregano Sauce

PREPARATION TIME: 25 minutes

COOKING TIME: 15 minutes

SERVES: 4 people

30ml/2 tbsps fresh green peppercorns
  (substitute well rinsed canned green
  peppercorns)
90ml/6 tbsps lemon juice
60ml/4 tbsps olive oil
Salt
4 swordfish steaks (tuna steaks may also
  be used)

SAUCE
1 egg
1 clove garlic, roughly chopped
140ml/¼ pint/½ cup oil
15ml/1 tbsp lemon juice
2 sprigs fresh oregano
Salt and pepper

Crush the green peppercorns slightly

and mix with lemon juice, oil and salt. Place the swordfish steaks in a shallow dish and pour over the lemon oil mixture. Cover and refrigerate several hours, turning frequently. Process the egg and garlic in a blender or food processor. With the machine running, pour oil through the funnel in a thin, steady stream. When the sauce is thick, strip the leaves off the oregano and process to chop them finely. Add lemon juice, salt and pepper. Grill the swordfish over hot coals for 15 minutes, basting frequently and turning once. Serve with the sauce. (Peppercorns will pop when exposed to the heat of the grill.)

Grilled Red Mullet with Tarragon

PREPARATION TIME: 15 minutes

COOKING TIME: 10-16 minutes

SERVES: 4 people

4 large or 8 small red mullet, gutted,
  scaled, washed and dried
4 or 8 sprigs fresh tarragon

MARINADE
60ml/4 tbsps oil
30ml/2 tbsps tarragon vinegar
Salt and pepper

SAUCE
1 egg
140ml/¼ pint/½ cup oil
5ml/1 tsp Dijon mustard
15ml/1 tbsp chopped tarragon
15ml/1 tbsp chopped parsley
15ml/1 tbsp tarragon vinegar
30ml/2 tbsps double/heavy cream
5ml/1 tsp brandy
Salt and pepper

Place a sprig of tarragon inside each fish. Cut two slits on the side of each fish. Mix the marinade ingredients together, pour over the fish in a shallow dish and refrigerate for 30 minutes, covered. Put the egg in a

Facing page: Swordfish Steaks with Green Peppercorns and Garlic Oregano Sauce (top), and Grilled Sardines with Lemon and Oregano (bottom).

blender or food processor. Add the mustard, salt and pepper and process to mix. Add the oil through the funnel, with the machine running, in a thin, steady stream. When all the oil has been added, add the herbs, vinegar and brandy and process to mix well. Fold in the double/heavy cream and pour into a serving dish. Keep in the refrigerator until ready to use. Cook the fish for 5 to 8 minutes per side, depending upon size of fish. Baste frequently with the marinade while cooking. Serve with the sauce.

This page: Grey Mullet with Fennel (top), and Grilled Red Mullet with Tarragon (bottom). Facing page: Monkfish and Pepper Kebabs with Bernaise Butter Sauce.

Monkfish and Pepper Kebabs with Bernaise Butter Sauce

PREPARATION TIME: 30 minutes

COOKING TIME: 25 minutes

SERVES: 4 people

450g/1lb monkfish, cut into 5cm/2 inch pieces
8 strips bacon/streaky bacon, rind and bone removed
2 pieces lemon grass
1 green pepper, cut in 5cm/2 inch pieces
1 red pepper, cut in 5cm/2 inch pieces
12 mushroom caps
8 bay leaves
Oil

BERNAISE BUTTER SAUCE
120ml/4 fl oz/½ cup dry white wine
60ml/4 tbsps tarragon vinegar
2 shallots, finely chopped
15ml/1 tbsp chopped fresh tarragon
15ml/1 tbsp chopped fresh chervil or parsley
225g/8oz/1 cup butter, softened
Salt and pepper

Cut the bacon in half lengthwise and again in half across. Peel the lemon grass and use only the core. Cut into small pieces. Place a piece of fish on each strip of bacon and top with a piece of lemon grass. Roll up. Thread the rolls of fish on skewers, alternating with peppers, mushrooms and bay leaves. Brush with oil and grill 15 minutes, turning and basting often. While the fish cooks, heat the white wine, vinegar and shallots in a small saucepan until boiling. Cook rapidly to reduce by half. Add the herbs and lower the heat. Beat in the softened butter a bit at a time until the sauce is the thickness of hollandaise sauce. Season with salt and pepper to taste and serve with the fish kebabs.

Barbecued Vegetables

Grilled Fennel

PREPARATION TIME: 15 minutes

COOKING TIME: 20 minutes

SERVES: 4 people

4 small bulbs fennel
Juice and rind of 1 lemon
60ml/4 tbsps oil
1 shallot, finely chopped
Salt and pepper

Remove the fennel tops and reserve them. Cut the fennel bulbs in half and remove the cores. Parboil the fennel for 5 minutes. Combine the juice and rind of the lemon, salt, pepper, oil and shallot. Pour over the fennel and set aside for 15 minutes. Place the fennel bulbs on hot coals and cook 15 minutes, turning often and brushing with the lemon mixture. Chop the fennel tops finely and sprinkle over the grilled fennel. Pour over any remaining lemon juice mixture to serve.

Grilled Tomatoes

PREPARATION TIME: 15 minutes

COOKING TIME: 6 minutes

SERVES: 4 people

4 beefsteak tomatoes cut in half
15ml/1 tbsp oregano, fresh or dried
30ml/2 tbsps olive oil
15ml/1 tbsp lemon juice
Salt and pepper
120g/4oz feta cheese, crumbled

Mix the oil, lemon juice, salt, pepper and oregano together. Brush over the cut side of the tomatoes and grill that side first for 3 minutes over hot coals. Brush the skin side of the tomatoes and turn them over. Grill 3 minutes more on skin side and remove the tomatoes to a serving dish. Sprinkle over the crumbled feta cheese and pour over the remaining basting mixture to serve.

Grilled Corn-on-the-Cob

PREPARATION TIME: 20 minutes

COOKING TIME: 15 minutes

SERVES: 4 people

4 large ears of corn, husks and silk
  removed, parboiled 5 minutes
120g/4oz/½ cup butter, melted
Salt and pepper
Chili powder or paprika (optional)

Brush the drained corn liberally with melted butter. Sprinkle with salt and pepper. Chili powder or paprika can be substituted for the pepper, if desired. Grill over medium hot coals for 15 minutes, turning often and basting frequently with butter. To serve, pour over any remaining butter.

Grilled Aubergine/Eggplant

PREPARATION TIME: 30 minutes

COOKING TIME: 20-24 minutes

SERVES: 4 people

2 aubergines/eggplants
180ml/6 fl oz/¾ cup olive oil
90ml/6 tbsps lemon juice
15ml/1 tbsp cumin seed
1 clove garlic, finely chopped
30ml/2 tbsps parsley, chopped
Salt and pepper

Cut the aubergine/eggplant into rounds about 2.5cm/1 inch thick. Score the surface of each round lightly with a sharp knife, sprinkle with salt and leave to stand for 30 minutes. Heat oil for 1 minute and add the cumin seed and cook for the 30 seconds. Add the garlic and cook for a further 30 seconds. Add the lemon juice. Rinse the salt from the aubergine/eggplant slices and pat dry. Brush one side of the slices with the basting mixture. Grill on a lightly oiled rack or place in a hinged wire rack. Cook for 10-12 minutes per side until soft, basting frequently. Place the slices in a serving dish and pour over the remaining basting mixture. Sprinkle with parsley just before serving.

Grilled Mushrooms

PREPARATION TIME: 10 minutes

COOKING TIME: 15-20 minutes

SERVES: 4 people

450g/1lb large mushrooms, cleaned

MARINADE
15ml/1 tbsp chopped tarragon, fresh or
  dried
Grated rind and juice of 1 orange
15ml/1 tbsp tarragon vinegar
30ml/2 tbsps oil
Salt and pepper

**Facing page: Grilled Tomatoes
(top), and Grilled Fennel (bottom).**

Mix together the marinade ingredients. Cut the stalks from the mushrooms and place the mushroom caps in a shallow dish. Pour over the marinade and leave the mushrooms for 15-20 minutes. Place the mushrooms in a wire rack and cook 15-20 minutes over hot coals. Brush the mushrooms frequently with the marinade and turn them once or twice. Remove to a serving dish and pour over the remaining marinade to serve.

Courgette/Zucchini, Pepper and Onion Kebabs

PREPARATION TIME: 20 minutes

COOKING TIME: 10-12 minutes

SERVES: 4 people

4-6 courgettes/zucchini, ends trimmed
1 large onion
1 large green pepper
1 large red pepper
Oil
60ml/4 tbsps dry white wine
5ml/1 tsp thyme
10ml/2 tsps chopped parsley
5ml/1 tsp chopped chives
120g/4oz/½ cup melted butter

Peel the courgettes/zucchini with swivel peeler for a striped effect. Parboil 4 minutes. Refresh under cold water. Cut in 5cm/2 inch pieces. Quarter the onion and cut in large pieces, separating the layers. Cut the peppers in half and remove the core and seeds. Cut into pieces the same size as the onion. Thread the vegetables onto skewers. Melt the butter and add the wine and cook 1 minute. Add the herbs, salt and pepper. Brush the kebabs lightly with oil and grill 5-6 minutes per side. Brush frequently with the butter mixture. When the courgettes/zucchini are tender, remove to a serving dish. Pour over the remaining butter.

Barbecued Baked Potatoes

PREPARATION TIME: 15 minutes

COOKING TIME: 25 minutes

SERVES: 4-6 people

4 large potatoes, scrubbed but not peeled
Salt and pepper
Paprika
120g/4oz/½ cup melted butter

SAUCE
280ml/½ pint/1 cup sour cream
10ml/2 tsps red wine vinegar

This page: Courgette/Zucchini, Pepper and Onion Kebabs. Facing page: Grilled Aubergine/Eggplant and Grilled Mushrooms.

5ml/1 tsp sugar
5ml/1 tsp mustard powder
5ml/1 tsp celery salt
5ml/1 tsp chopped fresh herbs

Parboil the potatoes for 10 minutes in their skins. Cut the potatoes in quarters lengthwise. Brush the potatoes with a mixture of butter, paprika, salt and pepper on all surfaces. Grill the potatoes for 15 minutes, basting frequently with the remaining butter. Meanwhile, combine all the sauce ingredients and set aside in the refrigerator until ready to serve with the potatoes.

This page: Grilled Corn-on-the-Cob (top), and Barbecued Baked Potatoes (bottom). Facing page: Hungarian Sausage Salad.

BARBECUES & SALADS

Main Dishes and Pasta Salads

Hungarian Sausage Salad

PREPARATION TIME: 25 minutes

COOKING TIME: 20-25 minutes

SERVES: 4-6 people

4 small potatoes
140ml/¼ pint/½ cup oil
45ml/3 tbsps wine vinegar
5ml/1 tsp Dijon mustard
5ml/1 tsp dill seeds, slightly crushed
15ml/1 tbsp chopped parsley
5ml/1 tsp chopped dill
Pinch hot paprika
Salt
450g/1lb sausage such as kielbasa,
    smoked pork sausage, knockwurst or
    bratwurst
1 large red onion, thinly sliced
2 green peppers, cored and sliced
4 tomatoes, quartered

Scrub and peel potatoes and cook in salted water in a covered saucepan for 20 minutes or until soft. Mix all the dressing ingredients together in a medium-sized bowl. Dice the potatoes while still warm and coat with the dressing. Leave the potatoes to cool in the dressing. If using knockwurst boil for 5 minutes. Grill/broil the bratwurst until evenly browned on all sides. Slice the sausage in 2.5cm/½ inch slices and combine with the onion, pepper and tomatoes. Carefully combine with the potatoes in the dressing, taking care not to over mix and break up the potatoes. Pile into a large serving dish and allow to stand for 1 hour before serving.

Salade Niçoise

PREPARATION TIME: 20 minutes

COOKING TIME: 15-20 minutes

SERVES: 4 people

2 large potatoes, or 6 small new potatoes
180g/6oz French/green beans
4 hard-boiled eggs
1 can tuna
120g/4oz prawns/shrimp

1 can anchovies
4 ripe tomatoes
90g/3oz/¾ cup black olives, stoned
1 small cucumber, diced

DRESSING
90ml/6 tbsps olive oil
30ml/2 tbsps white wine vinegar

1 head radicchio, leaves separated and
　washed
1 head cos/romaine lettuce, washed
4 chicken breasts, cooked, skinned and
　thinly sliced
120g/4oz Bresse Bleu or other blue
　cheese, cut in small pieces
16 cornichons (small pickled gherkins)
　thinly sliced
120g/4oz cherry tomatoes, halved and
　cored
60g/2oz/½ cup walnut halves

DRESSING
30ml/2 tbsps vegetable and walnut oil
　mixed
10ml/2 tsps white wine vinegar
180ml/6 fl oz/¾ cup crème frâiche
10ml/2 tsps chopped fresh tarragon
Salt and pepper

Tear the radicchio and cos/romaine
lettuce into bite-size pieces. Leave
the lamb's lettuce in whole leaves.
If using watercress, remove the thick
stems and yellow leaves. Toss the
lettuces together and pile onto a
salad plate. Place the chicken, cheese,
cornichons, tomatoes and walnuts on
top of the lettuce. Mix the oils and
vinegar together and whisk well to
emulsify. Fold in the crème frâiche
and add the tarragon, salt and
pepper. Drizzle some of the dressing
over the salad to serve and hand the
rest of the dressing separately.

Pasta and Vegetables in Parmesan Dressing

PREPARATION TIME: 25 minutes

COOKING TIME: 13-15 minutes

SERVES: 6 people

450g/1lb pasta spirals or other shapes
225g/8oz assorted vegetables such as:
Courgettes/zucchini, cut in rounds or
　matchsticks
Broccoli, trimmed into very small
　flowerets

**This page: Salade Niçoise (top),
and Salade Bresse (bottom). Facing
page: Pasta and Vegetables in
Parmesan Dressing.**

45ml/3 tbsps chopped mixed fresh herbs
10ml/2 tsps French mustard
Salt and pepper

Peel and cook the potatoes (skins
may be left on new potatoes if
desired) until tender. If using old
potatoes, cut into 1.25cm/½ inch
dice (new potatoes may be sliced into
6mm/¼ inch rounds). Trim the ends
of the beans, put into boiling salted
water for about 3-4 minutes or until
just barely cooked. Drain and rinse
under cold water, then leave to drain
dry. Quarter the tomatoes, or if large
cut into eighths. Quarter the hard-
boiled eggs. Cut the anchovies into

short strips. Mix the dressing
ingredients together and blend well.
Drain oil from the tuna and mix the
tuna and all the salad ingredients
together. Pour over the dressing and
toss carefully, so that the potatoes do
not break up. Serve the salad on top
of lettuce leaves if desired.

Salade Bresse

PREPARATION TIME: 20 minutes

SERVES: 4-6 people

1 bunch lamb's lettuce or watercress,
　washed

Mangetout/pea pods, ends trimmed
Carrots, cut in rounds or matchsticks
Celery, cut in matchsticks
Cucumber, cut in matchsticks
Spring/green onions, thinly shredded or
    sliced
Asparagus tips
French/green beans, sliced
Red or yellow peppers, thinly sliced

DRESSING
140ml/¼ pint/½ cup olive oil
45ml/3 tbsps lemon juice
15ml/1 tbsp sherry pepper sauce
15ml/1 tbsp chopped parsley
15ml/1 tbsp chopped basil
60g/2oz/¼ cup freshly grated Parmesan
    cheese
30ml/2 tbsps mild mustard
Salt and pepper
Pinch sugar

Cook pasta in a large saucepan of boiling salted water with 15ml/1 tbsp oil for 10-12 minutes or until just tender. Rinse under hot water to remove starch. Leave in cold water. Place all the vegetables except the cucumber into boiling salted water for 3 minutes until just tender. Rinse in cold water and leave to drain. Mix the dressing ingredients together very well. Drain the pasta thoroughly and toss with the dressing. Add the vegetables and toss to coat. Refrigerate for up to 1 hour before serving.

Cob Salad

| **PREPARATION TIME:** 25 minutes |
| **SERVES:** 4-6 people |

1 large head cos/romaine lettuce, washed
2 avocados, peeled and chopped
3 tomatoes, cut in small dice
1 cucumber, cut in small dice
120g/4 oz/1 cup blue cheese, crumbled
4 spring/green onions, chopped or 1 small
    red onion, chopped
120g/4 oz cooked chicken breasts, cut in
    small pieces
2 hard-boiled eggs, chopped

GREEN GODDESS DRESSING
½ can anchovies
60ml/4 tbsps chopped parsley
30ml/2 tbsps chopped basil or tarragon

30ml/2 tbsps chopped chives
Small bunch watercress, leaves only
430ml/¾ pint/1½ cups mayonnaise
15ml/1 tbsp white wine vinegar

Dry the lettuce and cut it into strips. Tear the strips into small pieces and put into a salad bowl. Arrange all the ingredients on top. To prepare the dressing, combine all the ingredients in the blender or food processor and purée until smooth and very green. Serve the dressing separately with the salad.

Crab Louis

| **PREPARATION TIME:** 20 minutes |
| **SERVES:** 4 people |

DRESSING
280ml/½ pint/1 cup mayonnaise
120ml/4 fl oz/½ cup yogurt
60ml/4 tbsps tomato chutney/chili sauce
2 spring/green onions, finely chopped
½ green pepper, finely diced
5ml/1 tsp lemon juice
Salt and pepper

450g/1lb crabmeat, flaked
1 head Buttercrunch or ½ head Iceberg
    lettuce
4 hard-boiled eggs, quartered
120g/4oz/1 cup black olives, stoned

Combine all the dressing ingredients and mix half with the flaked crabmeat. Arrange a bed of lettuce on a serving dish and mound on the crabmeat. Coat the crabmeat with the remaining dressing. Arrange the quartered egg and black olives around the salad.

Julienne Salad

| **PREPARATION TIME:** 25 minutes |
| **SERVES:** 4-6 people |

1 small head Iceberg lettuce
1 small Buttercrunch lettuce
4 tomatoes, quartered
1 small red onion, chopped
½ cucumber, sliced
6 radishes, sliced
60g/2oz cooked ham
60g/2oz cooked tongue

120g/4oz cooked chicken
60g/2oz Gruyère or Swiss cheese
60g/2oz Red Leicester/Colby cheese

CREAMY HERB DRESSING
280ml/½ pint/1 cup natural yogurt
120ml/4 fl oz/½ cup double/heavy
    cream
45ml/3 tbsps fresh mixed herbs, chopped
    (use chervil, tarragon, basil, dill or
    parsley)
30ml/2 tbsps prepared mayonnaise
Salt and pepper

Tear the lettuce into bite-sized pieces and mix with the remaining vegetables. Divide into four salad bowls. Slice the meats and the cheeses into thin strips. Arrange on top of the salad ingredients. Mix the dressing thoroughly and serve separately.

Lobster and Cauliflower Salad

| **PREPARATION TIME:** 30 minutes |
| **SERVES:** 4-6 people |

1 large cauliflower, washed
140ml/¼ pint/½ cup vegetable oil
45ml/3 tbsps lemon juice
5ml/1 tsp dry mustard
Salt and pepper
1 large cooked lobster
280ml/½ pint/1 cup prepared
    mayonnaise
10ml/2 tsps Dijon mustard
4 hard-boiled eggs
16 black olives, halved and stoned
2 bunches watercress, washed
Red caviar

Break the cauliflower into small flowerets and mix with the vegetable oil, lemon juice, mustard and salt and pepper. Leave for at least 2 hours in a cool place. Crack the lobster and remove all the meat from the shell and set aside in a small bowl. Mix the mayonnaise and Dijon mustard. Thin if necessary with a spoonful of hot water. Add half the dressing to the

Facing page: Julienne Salad (top), and Cob Salad (bottom).

lobster and mix carefully. Combine the cauliflower with the eggs and olives. Stir to coat the eggs with dressing but do not over-mix or break up the eggs. Remove the thick stems from the watercress and any yellow leaves. Arrange beds of watercress on four small plates. Spoon in equal portions of the cauliflower salad onto the watercress and top with an equal portion of the

lobster. Coat the lobster salads with the remaining mustard mayonnaise and spoon some red caviar over the dressing.

Tuna and Pasta with Red Kidney Beans

PREPARATION TIME: 20 minutes

This page: Tuna and Pasta with Red Kidney Beans. Facing page: Crab Louis (top), and Lobster and Cauliflower Salad (bottom).

| **COOKING TIME:** 10 minutes |
| **SERVES:** 4-6 people |

225g/8oz/1½ cups small pasta shells
1 225g/8oz can red kidney beans,
  drained and rinsed

120g/4oz small mushrooms, quartered
1 can tuna, drained and flaked
4 spring/green onions, sliced
30ml/2 tbsps chopped mixed herbs

DRESSING
140ml/¼ pint/½ cup olive oil
45ml/3 tbsps white wine vinegar
Squeeze lemon juice
15ml/1 tbsp Dijon mustard
Salt and pepper

Cook the pasta shells in boiling salted water with 15ml/1 tbsp oil for 10 minutes or until just tender. Rinse under hot water and then place in cold water until ready to use. Mix the dressing ingredients together thoroughly and drain the pasta shells. Mix the pasta with the beans, mushrooms, tuna, spring/green onions and chopped mixed herbs. Pour over the dressing and toss to coat. Chill up to 1 hour in the refrigerator before serving.

Mariner's Salad

PREPARATION TIME: 25 minutes

COOKING TIME: 15 minutes

SERVES: 6 people

450g/1lb pasta shells, plain and spinach
4 large scallops, cleaned
280ml/½ pint/1 cup frozen mussels, defrosted
140ml/¼ pint/½ cup lemon juice and water mixed
120g/4oz shelled and de-veined prawns/ shrimp
140ml/¼ pint/½ cup cockles or small clams, cooked
4 crab sticks, cut in small pieces
4 spring/green onions, chopped
15ml/1 tbsp chopped parsley

DRESSING
Grated rind and juice of ½ lemon
280ml/½ pint/1 cup mayonnaise
10ml/2 tsps paprika
90ml/3 fl oz/⅓ cup sour cream or natural yogurt
Salt and pepper

Cook the pasta for 10 minutes in a large pan of boiling salted water with 15ml/1 tbsp oil. Drain and rinse under hot water. Leave in cold water

until ready to use. Cook the scallops and mussels in the lemon juice and water mixture for about 5 minutes or until fairly firm. Cut the scallops into 2 or 3 pieces, depending upon size. Mix the dressing and drain the pasta thoroughly. Mix all ingredients together to coat completely with dressing. Stir carefully so that the shellfish do not break-up. Chill for up to 1 hour before serving.

Italian Pasta Salad

PREPARATION TIME: 25 minutes

COOKING TIME: 10 minutes

SERVES: 4-6 people

450g/1lb pasta shapes
225g/8oz assorted Italian meats, cut in strips: salami, mortadella, prosciutto, coppa, bresaola
120g/4oz provolone or fontina cheese, cut in strips
15 black olives, halved and stoned
60g/4 tbsp small capers
120g/4oz peas
1 small red onion or 2 shallots, chopped
160g/6oz oyster mushrooms, stems trimmed and sliced

DRESSING
45ml/3 tbsps white wine vinegar
140ml/¼ pint/½ cup olive oil
½ clove garlic, minced
5ml/1 tsp fennel seed, crushed
15ml/1 tbsp chopped parsley
15ml/1 tbsp chopped basil
15ml/1 tbsp mustard
Salt and pepper

Cook the pasta in a large saucepan of boiling water with a pinch of salt and 15ml/1 tbsp oil. Cook for about 10 minutes or until just tender. Add the frozen peas during the last 3 minutes of cooking time. Drain the pasta and peas and rinse under hot water. Leave in cold water until ready to use. Mix the dressing ingredients together well and drain the pasta and peas thoroughly. Mix the pasta and peas with the Italian meats and cheeses, olives, capers, chopped onion or shallot and sliced mushrooms. Pour the dressing over the salad and toss all the ingredients together to coat. Do not over-mix.

Leave the salad to chill for up to 1 hour before serving.

Shrimp and Cashews in Pineapples with Tarragon Dressing

PREPARATION TIME: 30 minutes

COOKING TIME: 10 minutes

SERVES: 4 people

2 small fresh pineapples
225g/8oz small cooked shrimp
120g/4oz/1 cup roasted unsalted cashew nuts
2 sticks celery, thinly sliced
60ml/4 tbsps lemon juice

DRESSING
1 egg
30ml/2 tbsps sugar
15ml/1 tbsp tarragon vinegar
120ml/4 fl oz/¼ pint whipping cream
10ml/2 tsps chopped fresh tarragon or 5ml/1 tsp dried tarragon, crumbled

Cut the pineapples carefully in half lengthwise, leaving the green tops attached. Carefully cut out the flesh and remove the cores. Cut the flesh into bite-size pieces. Combine the shrimp, cashews and celery and toss with the lemon juice. Spoon the mixture into the pineapple shells and refrigerate to chill. To prepare the dressing, beat the egg and sugar together until light in a heat-proof bowl. Add the vinegar and tarragon, place the bowl over hot water. Whip with a wire whisk until thick. Take off the heat and allow to cool, whisking occasionally. When cold, lightly whip the cream and fold into the dressing. Spoon over the salad and serve in the pineapple shells.

Facing page: Italian Pasta Salad (top), and Mariner's Salad (bottom).

Oriental Salad

PREPARATION TIME: 25 minutes

COOKING TIME: 2 minutes

SERVES: 4-6 people

1 cake tofu, cut in small cubes
140ml/¼ pint/½ cup vegetable oil
120g/4oz mangetout/pea pods, ends
 trimmed
60g/2oz mushrooms, sliced
60g/2oz broccoli flowerets
2 carrots, peeled and thinly sliced
4 spring/green onions thinly sliced
2 sticks celery, thinly sliced
60g/2oz/½ cup unsalted roasted peanuts

120g/4oz bean sprouts
½ head Chinese leaves/cabbage, shredded

DRESSING
45ml/3 tbsps lemon juice
10ml/2 tsps honey
5ml/1 tsp grated ginger
45ml/3 tbsps soy sauce
Dash sesame oil

Drain tofu well and press gently to remove excess moisture. Cut into 1.25cm/½ inch cubes. Heat 30ml/2 tbsps from the 140ml/¼ pint/½ cup oil in the wok or frying pan. Save the remaining oil for the dressing. Cook the mangetout/pea pods, mushrooms, broccoli, carrots and celery for 2 minutes. Remove the vegetables and set them aside to cool. When cool mix them together with the onions, peanuts and bean sprouts. Mix the dressing and pour over the vegetables. Add the tofu and toss carefully. Arrange a bed of Chinese leaves/cabbage on a serving dish and pile the salad ingredients on top to serve.

This page: **Oriental Salad.** Facing page: **Shrimps and Cashews in Pineapple with Tarragon Dressing.**

Salads with Fruit

Waldorf Salad

PREPARATION TIME: 20 minutes

SERVES: 6 people

4 sticks celery, diced
4 apples, mixture of red-skinned and
green-skinned, diced
180g/6oz grapes, black and white, halved
and seeded
120g/4oz/1 cup walnuts or pecans,
roughly chopped
280ml/½ pint/1 cup prepared
mayonnaise
60ml/4 tbsps heavy cream
Juice of half a lemon

Mix the celery, apples, grapes and nuts together and toss with the lemon juice. Lightly whip the cream, fold into the mayonnaise. Fold the dressing into the salad and serve chilled. If desired, substitute raisins for the grapes and garnish with 30ml/2 tbsps chopped parsley.

Fruit Salad with Coconut Cream Dressing

PREPARATION TIME: 30 minutes

SERVES: 6-8 people

900g/2lb fresh assorted fruit, such as:
Pineapple, peeled, cored and cut in
wedges
Melon, skinned and sliced
Bananas, peeled, cut in thick rounds and
sprinkled with lemon juice
Apricots, halved and stoned and sprinkled
with lemon juice
Peaches, peeled and sliced and sprinkled
with lemon juice
Strawberries, hulled and washed
Raspberries or blackberries washed

Papaya, peeled and sliced
Currants, stems removed
Blueberries/bilberries, washed
Kiwi, peeled and sliced
Kumquats, thinly sliced, seeds removed
Fresh figs, quartered
Pears, peeled, cored and sliced

DRESSING
280ml/½ pint/1 cup natural yogurt
140ml/¼ pint/½ cup coconut cream
30-45ml/2-3 tbsps lime juice
Seeds of 1 fresh pomegranate

Arrange assortment of fruit on plates. Mix together the ingredients for the dressing and drizzle over the fruit. Sprinkle on the pomegranate seeds.

Green and Gold Sunflower Salad

PREPARATION TIME: 15 minutes

SERVES: 4 people

2 large ripe avocados
8 ripe apricots

DRESSING
45ml/3 tbsps sunflower oil
15ml/1 tbsp lemon juice
Salt and pepper

YOGURT DRESSING
140ml/¼ pint/½ cup natural yogurt
10ml/2 tsps honey
Grated rind of 1 lemon
10ml/2 tsps chopped parsley
60g/4 tbsps toasted sunflower seeds
1 small Buttercrunch lettuce, washed and
separated into leaves

Prepare the oil and lemon juice dressing. Cut avocados in half and remove the stones. Peel and cut into slices. Cut apricots in half and

remove the stones. If the apricots are large cut in half again. Add the apricots to the avocados, spooning over the dressing. Mix all the ingredients for the yogurt dressing together except the sunflower seeds. Place the lettuce leaves on salad plates and arrange the avocado and apricots on top. Spoon over some of the yogurt dressing and sprinkle the sunflower seeds onto the dressing. Serve immediately and hand extra dressing separately.

Watercress and Orange Salad

PREPARATION TIME: 20 minutes

SERVES: 4-6 people

3 large bunches watercress, well washed
and thick stalks removed
4 oranges, peeled and segmented

DRESSING
90ml/6 tbsps vegetable oil
Juice and rind of 1 orange
Pinch sugar
Squeeze lemon juice
Salt and pepper

Break watercress into small sprigs and discard any yellow leaves. Arrange the watercress with the orange segments on plates or toss in one large salad bowl. Mix the dressing ingredients together very well and pour over the salad just before serving.

Facing page: Watercress and Orange Salad (top), and Waldorf Salad (bottom).

Fennel, Orange and Tomato Salad

PREPARATION TIME: 25 minutes

COOKING TIME: 3-4 minutes

SERVES: 4 people

2 bulbs fennel, green top trimmed and
reserved
2 large, ripe tomatoes
2 oranges

DRESSING
30ml/2 tbsps orange juice
25ml/1½ tbsps lemon juice
Zest of 1 orange
90ml/3 fl oz/⅓ cup olive oil and
vegetable oil mixed half and half
5ml/1 tsp chopped fresh oregano or basil

Pinch sugar
Salt and pepper

Choose fennel with a lot of feathery green top. Reserve the tops. Cut the cores out of the bottom of the fennel bulbs and discard. Bring water to the boil in a large saucepan. Slice the fennel thinly, lengthwise, and place the slices in the boiling water. Cook until becoming translucent and slightly softened, about 3-4 minutes. Carefully remove the slices to a colander and rinse under cold water. Leave to drain. Place the tomatoes into the boiling water for 5-10 seconds. Put immediately into cold water. Peel and slice into 6mm/¼ inch rounds. Grate or use a zester to remove the peel from 1 orange.

This page: Fruit Salad with Coconut Cream Dressing. Facing page: Green and Gold Sunflower Salad (top), and Fennel, Orange and Tomato Salad (bottom).

Peel off the pith with knife and peel the remaining orange. Slice both oranges into 6mm/¼ inch rounds. Prepare the dressing by whisking all the ingredients very well and reserving the orange zest. Arrange the fennel, tomato and orange slices in circles on a round serving dish. Pour over the dressing and sprinkle on the orange zest. Chop the fennel tops and sprinkle over or use whole to garnish the salad.

JAPANESE COOKING

The words simplicity and elegance define Japanese cooking best. With no complicated sauces to distract from the main ingredients, Japanese cooking calls for a few perfect ingredients, exquisitely prepared. Garnishes are kept to a minimum, but they are like miniature sculptures. The Japanese love of pure ingredients stems from the people's love and reverence for nature and all that comes from it. Often, food is garnished with leaves, pine needles or sea plants to remind each person of its origins. Study the artistic arrangement of a Japanese dish and you will see the roots of nouvelle cuisine.

The chapters in this book follow the order of courses at a formal Japenese banquet. Each of the following courses illustrates an important technique in Japanese cooking:

1 Zensai – hors d'oeuvres
2 Sumashi-jiru – clear soups (we have combined this course with miso soups, which normally appear later in the meal)
3 Sashimi – raw fish and garnishes
4 Yakimono – grilled/broiled and pan-fried food
5 Mushimono – steamed and baked food
6 Nimono – simmered food
7 Agemono – deep-fried food (Nabemono, one pot dishes such as Sukiyaki, are included in the chapter on simmered food, and sometimes take the place of courses 4-7)

8 Sunomo or Aemono – vinegared food and salads
9 Gohan – rice
10 Miso-shiru – miso soups
11 Tsukemono – pickles
12 Green tea
13 Fresh fruit or desserts

If the number of courses seems daunting, remember that each course is a small serving by Western standards, and that two or three courses can make an excellent meal on their own. Also, don't imagine that you need a vast kitchen filled with specialised equipment – average kitchens in Japan are small, with very basic appliances – everyday kitchen utensils are quite adequate, and sharp knives are an absolute must. Woks are not traditional Japanese cookware, but they adapt well for steaming or frying. Ingredients do not have to be unusual, merely as fresh and good looking as possible, to maintain the Japanese standard. It is, however, useful to have a basic understanding of the following Japanese ingredients:

Adzuki beans – Small dried red beans. Used in rice dishes and sweets.
Agar-agar – Vegetable gelatine sold in blocks or powder. Needs soaking in liquid before use. Use normal gelatine.
Bamboo shoots – First shoots of the bamboo plant. Fresh shoots are best, but the canned variety is more readily available. Rinse canned shoots before use.

Bonito flakes, dried – Used to make dashi, the basic stock for soups and simmering. Also sprinkled on food to garnish. Sold pre-packaged, the flakes are made from fillets of a mackerel-like fish.

Daikon – A large, white radish, used cooked or raw. Often used grated as a garnish or ingredient in a dipping sauce. Do not substitute pink or red radishes.

Ginger – Knobbly root with a spicy, hot taste. Peel and grate for use. Pickled ginger is often used as a garnish, grated or sliced, for grilled/broiled meats. Red or pink in its pickled form.

Glutinous rice – A round-grain variety which cooks to a sticky consistency essential for sushi or vinegared-rice dishes and for picking up with chopsticks. Short-grain rice can be substituted. Rice is so important in Japanese cooking that it is used as a course in itself. For plain boiled rice use long-grain or Patna rice.

Kamaboko – Fish paste sold in a rectangular cake, tinted pink or light green with a white centre.

Konbu – A greenish-brown kelp and an important flavouring in dashi. Sold dried, it should be stored tightly covered.

Konnyaku – Gelatinous vegetable paste formed into a cake. It absorbs tastes and colours of foods it is cooked with. Stored in water, it will keep for up to two weeks if the water is changed every day.

Lotus root – Root of the waterlily. Cross-section slice looks like a flower. Available fresh or canned from Japanese groceries.

Mirin – Fermented soy bean paste. Used as a soup base, condiment, sauce ingredient or salad dressing. It comes in a light or white variety, or dark, reddish colour. A yellow variety is the most common.

Noodles – Harusame are transparent noodles made from rice. Shirataki noodles are made from devil's tongue root. Both are often called cellophane noodles. Soba are buckwheat noodles. Udon are white noodles made from wheat flour and vary in length and thickness. Somen noodles are the thinnest. Both buckwheat and udon noodles are available dried or fresh in vacuum-sealed packs.

Nori – Laver (seaweed) used to wrap sushi, or shredded to use as a garnish. Sold in thin sheets.

Sesame seeds – Both black and white varieties are used.

Seven-taste (or spice) pepper – A combination of red pepper, sanso pepper, ground orange peel, sesame seed, hemp seed, poppy seed and ground nori seaweed. Usually used to season food at the table.

Shiitake mushroom – Available fresh or dried, the latter being the more common form. Dried mushrooms must be soaked in water for 30 minutes before use, and the stems are removed before cooking.

Shiso leaves – Bright green leaves from a small herb plant. Used as a garnish and available fresh from Japanese groceries. They have a mint-like flavour.

Soy sauce – Japanese type is lighter and sweeter than Chinese. Light variety is saltier than the dark.

Tofu – White cake made from soy bean curd, and custard-like in texture. Usually sold in water-packed cartons, it needs to be thoroughly drained before use. Can be stored in the refrigerator if kept in water that is changed daily.

Trefoil – A herb related to parsley. Use salad cress as a substitute.

Vinegar – Made from rice and pale yellow in colour.

Wasabi horseradish – Pale green powdered root with a very hot, pungent taste. Mix with water to a smooth paste and shape into mounds or small leaf shapes. Use as an accompaniment to sashimi or an addition to dipping sauce.

Japanese garnishes are beautiful and, with practice, not difficult to make. The following are the easiest and the ones used in these recipes:

Carrot spurs – Cut a carrot into 7.5cm/3 inch sections and peel. Place in boiling water for about 4 minutes. Carve lengthwise with a sharp knife or dannelle knife. Cut triangular grooves down the length of each carrot. Cut crosswise into slices.

Carrot twists – Cut carrot into 7.5cm/3 inch sections and peel. Slice thinly, lengthwise. Make a 2.5cm/1 inch slit in the centre of each slice. Soak the pieces in salt water for at least 10 minutes. Rinse. When pieces are pliable, slip one end of each piece through the slit in the middle and pull back.

Carrot blossoms – Cut carrot in 7.5cm/3 inch sections. Slice five sides to form a pentagon. with a knife or cannelle knife make five lengthwise triangular cuts on all five sides. Trim the top of the carrot so that one end is higher than the other. Slice the flowers thinly, turning as you slice. Go around twice to make double flowers.

Cucumber twigs – Cut 5cm/2 inch sections from an unpeeled cucmber. Slice one side lengthwise off this section, about 6mm/¼ inch thick. Cut a centre section from this piece about 5cm/2 inches wide. In this section, make two lengthwise cuts from either end. Do not cut all the way through. Each cut should end 6cm/¼ inch from the opposite end. Twist the two outer strips so that they cross over. The same thing can be done with a thick piece of lemon rind.

Courgette/zucchini fan or comet – cut the ends off. Slice in half, lengthwise. Make a series of cuts, close together down the length of one half, leaving a spine along the side to hold the slices together. Soak in salt water for at least 10 minutes. Rinse. Spread out on a serving plate. Add a carrot spur.

Radish flowers – Cut stems and tips from radishes. Make two cuts in each of the four sides. Tip should be uppermost. Cut a cross in the top. Soak in ice water until the slice opens.

Radish fans – Choose radishes with leaves. Cut the tip off the radish and cut lengthwise, but not quite through to the leaf end. Soak in salt water and spread out on a plate.

Radish jacks – Slice a radish into thin rounds, Cut a notch in each slice. Slide one slice into the notch of the other.

Lemon and cucumber whirls – Thinly slice lemons and cucumbers. Notch each slice and twist.

Scored mushrooms – Soak dried shiitake mushrooms in hot water for 30 minutes. Cut off the stems and make a cross in the middle of the top of each cap.

JAPANESE COOKING

Hors d'Oeuvres

Lemon-Ikura

PREPARATION TIME: 5 minutes

SERVES: 4 people

20g/4 rounded tsps salmon roe (large grain)
4 thin slices lemon
2 chives, very finely shredded

Arrange the lemon slices on a serving dish. Mound a spoonful of roe on top of each slice. Garnish each with a few shreds of chive. Serve cold as part of a selection of hors d'oeuvres.

Fresh Vegetables with Sauces

PREPARATION TIME: 30 minutes

COOKING TIME: 2 minutes

SERVES: 4 people

Selection of the following:
Mangetout/pea pods (2 per person, stems trimmed)
Courgettes/zucchini (if small, 1 per person, sliced in half. If large, cut 1 into thin strips)
Carrots (as for courgettes/zucchini)
French/green beans (2 per person, stems trimmed)
Shiitake mushrooms, dried (1 per person, cut in quarters if large)
Daikon radish (as for carrots)
Turnips (1 large or 2 small, peeled, quartered and sliced)
Leeks (1 small thin one cut into 2.5cm/ 1 inch pieces)

SOY AND LEMON SAUCE
90ml/6 tbsps soy sauce
60ml/4 tbsps fresh lemon juice

SESAME SAUCE
45ml/3 tbsps white sesame seeds

30ml/2 tbsps mirin
90ml/6 tbsps soy sauce
60ml/4 tbsps dashi

Fresh Vegetables with Sauces.

Place the vegetables in a steamer or on a rack above boiling water. Cover well and cook 2 minutes. Mix the ingredients for each sauce and divide the mixture among 8 small bowls. Arrange the vegetables attractively on 4 serving plates and serve with the dipping sauces.

Prawns/Shrimp in Nori Packages

PREPARATION TIME:	20 minutes
COOKING TIME:	2 minutes
SERVES:	4 people

This page: Lemon-Ikura. Facing page: Pink, White and Green Rolls (top) and Prawns/Shrimp in Nori Packages (bottom).

4 king prawns/jumbo shrimp
1 square nori
4 chives

GRILLING SAUCE
30ml/2 tbsps soy sauce
15ml/1 tbsp mirin
15ml/1 tbsp grated ginger squeezed for
  juice

GARNISH
Courgette/zucchini fan (see introduction)

Shell and de-vein the prawns/shrimp, but leave on the tail ends. Pass the sheet of nori over a gas flame on both sides to freshen it. Cut it into 4 strips. Mix all the sauce ingredients together and brush the prawns/shrimp. Brush the nori strips and wrap one around each prawn/shrimp, but do not completely cover. Place under a pre-heated grill/broiler and cook for 1 minute on each side, brushing with the remaining sauce. Tie each with 1 chive. If desired, prepare double quantity sauce and use some for dipping. Garnish with prepared courgette/zucchini fan.

Tofu-Dengaku

PREPARATION TIME: 20 minutes

COOKING TIME: 5-6 minutes

SERVES: 4 people

90g/3oz tofu, well drained, pressed for
  15 minutes and sliced into rectangles
  5cm/2 inches long and 1.25cm/½ inch
  thick
25g/1½ tbsps miso
25ml/1½ tbsps mirin
25ml/1½ tbsps dashi
15g/½ oz spinach, cooked and puréed or
  defrosted and well drained
15g/1 tbsp white sesame seeds

GARNISH
Radish flower (see introduction)

Prepare the garnish. Place the tofu in a steamer or on a rack above boiling water. Cover and cook for 5-6 minutes. Combine the remaining ingredients, except spinach and sesame seeds, in a small pan and cook slowly until very thick. Add the

spinach and mix well. Place tofu on serving dishes and insert small bamboo skewers lengthwise. Spread the spinach mixture evenly over each piece of tofu and sprinkle with sesame seeds. Garnish with radish flower.

Chicken Livers with Cucumber

PREPARATION TIME: 25 minutes

COOKING TIME: 5-6 minutes

SERVES: 4-6 people

15ml/1 tbsp oil
180g/6oz chicken livers, picked over and
  trimmed
10ml/2 tsps grated ginger, squeezed for
  juice
10ml/2 tsps mirin
10ml/2 tsps soy sauce
½ cucumber, peeled in stripes
15ml/1 tbsp white sesame seeds

Heat the oil in a frying pan. Cut the chicken livers into even-sized pieces, but not too small. Put into the hot oil and cook over high heat, turning frequently to brown on the outside. Pour in the soy sauce, mirin and ginger juice and continue to cook 1-2 minutes over medium heat. Livers may be served slightly pink inside. Toss half the livers with sesame seeds to coat. Cut the cucumber half in quarters, lengthwise, and then into pieces the size of the livers. Thread one sesame-seed-coated liver, one piece of cucumber and one plain liver onto small bamboo skewers to serve.

Pink, White and Green Rolls

PREPARATION TIME: 30 minutes,
plus chilling time

COOKING TIME: 2 minutes

SERVES: 8 people

8cm/3 inch piece of daikon (white)
  radish, peeled
8 large or 16 small spinach leaves
120g/4oz smoked salmon, thinly sliced
Pinch salt

45ml/3 tbsps rice vinegar
45g/3 tbsps sugar

Trim the piece of daikon radish into a large cube. Cut the cube into 16 very thin slices. Soak in 570ml/1 pint/2 cups water with 10ml/2 tsps salt for about 20 minutes to soften. Wash spinach leaves well and remove thick stalks. Cook 2 minutes in a covered saucepan with a pinch of salt until just wilted. Rinse in cold water and pat dry. Place the salmon slices in 4 rows. Place the spinach leaves, evenly divided, on top of the salmon. Divide the radish slices evenly among the four rows and place on top of the spinach. Roll up and secure with cocktail sticks/wooden picks. Mix the vinegar and sugar and pour over the rolls. Refrigerate for 2-3 hours, turning once or twice. When ready to serve, remove the sticks/picks and slice each roll in half, crosswise. Serve cut side up so that a spiral of pink, white and green shows.

Beef and Scallion Rolls

PREPARATION TIME: 25 minutes

COOKING TIME: 12-15 minutes

SERVES: 4 people

4-6 spring/green onions, trimmed and cut
  into 5cm/2 inch lengths
120g/4oz sirloin, fat trimmed, sliced very
  thin and cut into 12 x 5cm/5 x 2 inch
  pieces
15ml/1 tbsp oil
30ml/2 tbsps soy sauce
15ml/1 tbsp sugar
15ml/1 tbsp saké
15ml/1 tbsp dashi
15ml/1 tbsp mirin

GARNISH
Carrot blossoms (see introduction)
Cucumber twigs (see introduction)

Prepare the garnishes. Divide onions equally into 4-6 groups. Roll 1 slice of beef around 1 group of onions. Tie

Facing page: Tofu-Dengaku (top) and Chicken Livers with Cucumber (bottom).

rolls with string. Repeat with remaining onions and beef. Heat oil in a large heavy-based frying pan. Add the beef rolls, seam side down, and cook about 1 minute over moderate heat. Turn the rolls several times to brown evenly. Reduce the heat and add all remaining

ingredients except the mirin. Cook a further 3 minutes and remove the meat with a slotted spoon. Turn up the heat and cook the pan juices to reduce by half. Add the mirin. Remove the string from the rolls and return them to the pan. Cook the rolls, turning them often, until well

This page: Beef and Scallion Rolls.

glazed. Cut each roll into 1.25cm/ ½ inch thick rounds. Thread the rounds on skewers and garnish.

JAPANESE COOKING

Soups

Summer Chilled Miso Soup

PREPARATION TIME: 25 minutes plus chilling time

COOKING TIME: 25 minutes – 1 hour

SERVES: 4 people

1150ml/2 pints/4 cups chicken stock or dashi
90g/3oz miso
½ small cucumber, thinly sliced
1-2 tomatoes, skinned and sliced
15g/½ oz trefoil (salad cress)

Make the stock as for Sumashi Jiru or dashi as for Butaniku no Dango. Chill thoroughly. Cream the miso with about 280ml/½ pint/1 cup of the stock and add to the remaining stock with all the remaining ingredients.

Butaniku no Dango

PREPARATION TIME: 20 minutes

COOKING TIME: 15 minutes

SERVES: 4 people

DASHI
1.7 litres/3 pints/6 cups water
15g/½ oz konbu seaweed
15g/½ oz shaved, dried bonito fillet

225g/8oz minced/ground pork
2.5ml/½ tsp ground ginger
30ml/2 tbsps soy sauce
15g/½ oz somen noodles
4 spring/green onions shredded

This page: Sumashi Jiru (Basic Clear Soup) (top) and Butaniku no Dango (bottom).

Bring the water to the boil in a heavy-based pan, add the seaweed and simmer gently 1-2 minutes. Remove the seaweed and add the bonito flakes. Bring back to the boil and then remove from the heat. Allow the bonito flakes to sink to the bottom of the pan and then strain the stock through muslin/ cheesecloth, or a very fine meshed strainer. Combine the pork and ginger and form into small balls. Return the stock to the rinsed-out pan. Add the soy sauce and bring the stock back to the boil. Add the pork balls, cover and simmer gently for 5 minutes. Add the noodles and continue simmering for 5 minutes, until the meat balls and noodles are cooked. Add the spring/green onions and serve.

This page: Summer Chilled Miso Soup. Facing page: Soup with Fish Dumplings (top) and Prawn/ Shrimp Noodle Soup (bottom).

Prawn/Shrimp Noodle Soup

PREPARATION TIME:	20 minutes
COOKING TIME:	25-35 minutes
SERVES:	4 people

STOCK
225g/8oz fish trimmings (head, bones and skin)
1 small onion, studded with 6 cloves
1 small piece ginger root
1.3 litres/2½ pints/5 cups water

SOUP
Strained stock
30g/1oz soba noodles
225g/8oz cooked, peeled prawns/shrimp

GARNISH
Parsley sprigs

Place all the stock ingredients into a heavy-based pan. Bring to the boil and simmer gently for 20-25 minutes. Do not over-boil or stock will taste bitter. Remove scum from the surface and strain through muslin/cheesecloth, or a fine-meshed strainer. Return the stock to the rinsed-out pan. Add the noodles and simmer for 5-10 minutes until noodles are cooked. Add the prawns/shrimp to the hot soup and pour into individual dishes to serve. Garnish with small sprigs of parsley.

Vegetable Miso Soup

PREPARATION TIME:	30 minutes
COOKING TIME:	25 minutes – 1 hour
SERVES:	4 people

1150ml/2 pints/4 cups dashi or chicken stock
30ml/2 tbsps oil
120g/4oz daikon radish, cut into matchsticks
2 carrots, peeled and cut into matchsticks
1 small onion, diced
4 whole okra, stems removed and cut into rounds
4 dried mushrooms, soaked 30 minutes, stalks removed
120g/4oz miso

Make stock as for Sumashi Jiru or dashi as for Butaniku no Dango. Heat oil in a heavy-based pan and sauté radish, carrot and onion. When soft, add the okra, mushrooms, with caps scored if desired, and stock or dashi. Bring almost to the boil and mix about 280ml/½ pint/1 cup of the hot stock with the miso. Add this slowly back to the soup. Remove from heat and serve.

Sumashi Jiru (Basic Clear Soup)

PREPARATION TIME:	20 minutes
COOKING TIME:	55 minutes – 1 hour 10 minutes
SERVES:	4 people

STOCK
1 chicken carcass or about 450g/1lb chicken trimmings (bones, giblets, skin etc.)
1 carrot, peeled and roughly chopped
1 small onion, peeled and roughly chopped
2 sticks celery
1150ml/2 pints/4 cups water

SOUP
Stock (as above), strained
15ml/1 tbsp sherry
30ml/2 tbsps soy sauce
120g/4oz diced, cooked chicken
1 medium carrot
4 sprigs watercress

Break the chicken bones into small pieces and add with the remaining stock ingredients to a heavy-based pan. Bring to the boil and then simmer gently for 45 minutes to 1 hour, occasionally skimming off fat if necessary. Strain through muslin/cheesecloth, or a very fine meshed strainer. Return to the rinsed out pan. Peel the carrot for the soup and pare off small strips with a cannelle knife, or small paring knife, down the length of the carrot. Cut the carrot into slices to form "flowers". Bring the stock to the boil and add the sherry and soy sauce. Season with salt and pepper, if necessary. Add the carrot flowers and chicken and cook gently for 5-10 minutes until the chicken is hot and carrot is just tender. Pour into individual bowls and garnish with watercress.

Miso Soup with Prawns/Shrimp and Fried Tofu

PREPARATION TIME:	25 minutes
COOKING TIME:	25 minutes – 1 hour
SERVES:	4 people

1150ml/2 pints/4 cups chicken stock or dashi
30ml/2 tbsps oil
120g/4oz tofu, drained and cubed
60g/4 tbsps miso
120g/4oz prawns/shrimp
2 spring/green onions, sliced diagonally

GARNISH
4 unshelled prawns/shrimp

Make stock as for Sumashi Jiru or dashi as for Butaniku no Dango. Heat the oil in a frying pan and fry the tofu 2 minutes. Remove from the pan and pour over boiling water to remove excess oil. Drain. Heat most of the stock or dashi in a heavy-based pan until just boiling. Remove from the heat. Mix the remaining stock or dashi with miso and add gradually to the pan. Add the tofu and prawns/shrimp and garnish with sliced spring/green onion and whole prawns/shrimp.

Soup with Fish Dumplings

PREPARATION TIME:	25 minutes
COOKING TIME:	25-35 minutes
SERVES:	4 people

STOCK
340-450g/12oz-1lb whole whitefish (to give 120g/4oz fillets)
1 small onion, studded with 6 cloves
1 small piece ginger root
1.3 litres/2½ pints/5 cups water

Facing page: Miso Soup with Prawns/Shrimp and Fried Tofu (top) and Vegetable Miso Soup (bottom).

1.25ml/¼ tsp ground ginger
2 spring/green onions
1 egg white
60-75ml/4-5 tbsps (approx) plain/
  all-purpose flour
30ml/2 tbsps oil
4 spears asparagus cut diagonally into
  1 inch pieces
Salt and pepper
Rind and juice of 1 lemon
15ml/1 tbsp soy sauce

Fillet and skin the fish, using the trimmings to make stock as for Prawn Noodle Soup. Mince the fish fillets in a food processor with the ground ginger, spring/green onions, egg white, salt and pepper. Gradually blend in flour until mixture is stiff enough to shape into small balls. The mixture will be sticky. Heat the oil in a heavy-based pan and sauté the asparagus until just tender. Add the stock and return to the boil gently. Carefully add the fish dumplings, lemon rind and juice and soy sauce, and simmer for 5-10 minutes until cooked. Serve immediately.

Clear Tofu Soup

| **PREPARATION TIME:** 20 minutes |
| **COOKING TIME:** 55 minutes – 1 hour |
| **SERVES:** 4 people |

1150ml/2 pints/4 cups chicken stock or
  dashi
45ml/3 tbsps soy sauce

This page: Clear Tofu Soup. Facing page: Salmon or Tuna Sashimi.

120g/4oz tofu, drained and cubed
2 small leeks, washed, trimmed and sliced
60g/2oz bean sprouts

Make up stock as for Sumashi Jiru (Basic Clear Soup) or dashi as for Butaniku no Dango. Bring to the boil in a heavy-based pan and add soy sauce and leek slices. Simmer until leeks are tender. Divide between individual dishes and add the tofu and bean sprouts to the hot soup. Serve immediately.

JAPANESE COOKING

Raw Fish

Tuna Sashimi

PREPARATION TIME: 50 minutes

SERVES: 4 people

225g/8oz tuna fillet
120ml/4 fl oz/½ cup light soy sauce

GARNISH
Carrot twists (see introduction)
Cellophane noodles

Prepare the carrot twists. Skin the fillets and treat as in Salmon Sashimi. Slice the tuna across the grain. Place in shallow serving bowls. Cover cellophane noodles with hot water and soak for 5 minutes. Drain and leave to cool. Arrange carrot twists and a portion of cellophane noodles next to the tuna on each plate.

Salmon or Tuna Sashimi

PREPARATION TIME: 50 minutes

SERVES: 4 people

225g/8oz raw salmon or tuna fillet
½ daikon radish, finely grated

SAUCE
90ml/6 tbsps soy sauce
45ml/3 tbsps lemon juice

GARNISH
4 courgette/zucchini fans (see introduction)
4 carrot spurs (see introduction)

Skin the fish fillet, place in a colander and pour over boiling water. This will not cook the fish. Place immediately into ice-cold water. Pat the fish dry and slice across the grain into 1cm/ ⅜ inch thick strips. Arrange daikon radish in mounds in 4 serving bowls. Place the slices of fish against the daikon radish mounds. Mix the soy sauce and lemon juice and divide into 4 small bowls. Garnish with prepared courgette/zucchini fans and carrot spurs arranged to look like a comet.

Scallop Sashimi

PREPARATION TIME: 50 minutes

SERVES: 4 people

4 large or 8 small, fresh scallops with roe, if possible
4 shiso leaves
4 lemon twigs (see introduction)
30g/2 tbsps wasabi horseradish powder mixed with water to a thick paste

SAUCE
90ml/6 tbsps light soy sauce
30ml/2 tbsps lemon juice

Wash the scallops in cold, salted water. Pat dry and slice into very thin rounds, leaving the roe in one piece. Overlap slices of scallops in serving dish or place roe on one side. Decorate with shiso leaves and lemon twigs. Mix the soy sauce and lemon juice together and serve one bowl of the sauce with each serving of sashimi.

Squid Sashimi

PREPARATION TIME: 50 minutes

SERVES: 4 people

1 squid (prepared squid are available from fishmongers and Japanese markets)
1 carrot, finely grated

SAUCE
120ml/4 fl oz/½ cup soy sauce
Pinch wasabi powder

GARNISH
Fennel or dill fronds
4 radish fans (see introduction)

Prepare the radish fans. Wash the squid in cold, salted water and pat dry. Lightly score one side of the squid and then cut into 1cm/⅜ inch thick strips, crosswise. Place a mound

of carrot on each serving dish. Place the squid against the mound of carrot. Mix the soy sauce and the wasabi and pour into 4 small bowls. Garnish with fennel or dill and prepared radish fans.

This page: Tuna Sashimi. Facing page: Scallop Sashimi (top) and Squid Sashimi (bottom).

JAPANESE COOKING

Grilling and Pan Frying

Beef and Leek Skewers

PREPARATION TIME: 25 minutes

COOKING TIME: 8-10 minutes

SERVES: 4 people

450g/1lb rump/butt steak, cut in
   3.75cm/1½ inch cubes
4 leeks, cut in 3.75cm/1½ inch pieces,
   white and pale green part only
45ml/3 tbsps oil
60g/4 tbsps sugar
30ml/2 tbsps mirin
15ml/1 tbsp grated ginger
120ml/4 fl oz/½ cup soy sauce
Pinch black pepper

GARNISH
Lemon slices

Thread the leeks and beef alternately
onto bamboo skewers. This should
fill 2-3 skewers per person. Pour oil
into a large frying pan. When hot,
add 2 skewers at a time and brown all
sides well, about 1-2 minutes. Drain
off any excess oil and mix the
remaining ingredients. Pour over the
meat and cook a further 2-3 minutes.
Remove the meat and simmer until
the sauce is thick and syrupy, about
5 minutes. Pour over the meat and
garnish with lemon slices.

Chicken Yakitori

PREPARATION TIME: 30 minutes

COOKING TIME: 5-6 minutes

SERVES: 4 people

60ml/4 tbsps mirin
60ml/4 tbsps sake
140ml/¼ pint/½ cup soy sauce

Pinch cayenne pepper
1 clove garlic
1 small piece ginger
5ml/1 tsp sugar

**This page: Chicken Yakitori. Facing
page: Pork Kebabs with Vegetables
(top) and Beef and Leek Skewers
(bottom).**

1 chicken, skinned, boned and cut in
   2.5cm/1 inch pieces
2 large green peppers, cored, seeded and
   cut in 2.5cm/1 inch pieces
2-4 leeks, depending on size (substitute
   spring/green onions when leeks are out
   of season)

GARNISH
Radish jacks (see introduction)

Combine the first 7 ingredients in a small pan and bring to the boil. Remove from the heat and set aside to cool. Pour over the chicken and marinate for 30 minutes. Wash the leeks well and cut off the dark green tops. Cut the white and pale green parts into 2.5cm/1 inch pieces. If the leeks are very thick, cut in half. Thread 2 pieces of chicken onto bamboo or metal skewers, followed by a piece of pepper and leek until all the ingredients are used. This will make 2-3 skewers per person. Reserve the marinade. Pre-heat a grill/broiler and cook the chicken skewers 5-6 minutes per side, basting frequently with the marinade. May be cooked on a charcoal grill as well. Garnish with radish jacks.

Pork Kebabs with Vegetables

PREPARATION TIME: 30 minutes

COOKING TIME: 5-6 minutes

SERVES: 4 people

1 small aubergine/eggplant
2 green peppers
1 onion, cut in 2.5cm/1 inch pieces
340g/12oz pork fillet/tenderloin

SAUCE
30ml/2 tbsps oil
30ml/2 tbsps soy sauce
45ml/3 tbsps Worcestershire sauce
45ml/3 tbsps ketchup
15ml/1 tbsp grated ginger, squeezed for
   juice
1 clove garlic, finely minced

GARNISH
*Lemon and cucumber twists (see
   introduction)*

Slice the aubergine/eggplant in half and score lightly. Sprinkle with salt and leave to stand 30 minutes. Cut the peppers in half and remove seeds. Cut into 2.5cm/1 inch pieces. Cut the pork into 2.5cm/1 inch pieces. Squeeze the juices from the aubergine/eggplant and rinse well. Pat dry and cut into pieces the size of the pork. Thread the ingredients onto bamboo or metal skewers, beginning with pork and alternating between pork and vegetables, ending with pork. This should make 2-3 kebabs per person. Mix the sauce ingredients thoroughly. Brush the kebabs and place under a pre-heated grill/broiler. Cook 5-6 minutes, turning every 2 minutes, until the pork is cooked. Brush frequently with the sauce. Serve remaining sauce in separate bowls. Garnish with lemon and cucumber twists.

Beef Teriyaki

PREPARATION TIME: 30 minutes

COOKING TIME: 12-14 minutes

SERVES: 4 people

*Light cooking oil, such as soya or
   groundnut/peanut oil
1 large onion, sliced
4 very small courgettes/zucchini, ends
   trimmed
8 small or 4 large mushrooms, halved and
   scored
4 rump/butt steaks about 120g/4oz in
   weight*

SAUCE
60ml/4 tbsps dark soy sauce
60ml/4 tbsps sake
45ml/3 tbsps mirin
1 clove garlic, finely chopped
1 small piece ginger, finely chopped

Pour about 30ml/2 tbsps oil into a large frying pan. When hot, place in the onion slices in one layer. Fry until golden brown on both sides, about 1-2 minutes. Remove and keep warm. Cut the courgettes/zucchini into thin rounds. Add 30ml/2 tbsps more oil to the pan and cook the courgettes/zucchini quickly over high heat. Set aside and add the mushrooms to the pan. Cook 1 minute and set aside. Keep all the vegetables warm while cooking the steaks. Add more oil to the pan and keep the heat high. Cook 1 steak at a time until both sides are brown, about 1 minute per side. Put all the steaks into the pan, pour over the sauce and cover. Cook over moderate heat 1-2 minutes. Divide all the vegetables evenly among 4 plates. Place steaks on the plates and cut in half, lengthwise, then into about 8 short strips. Pour the sauce over the steaks to serve.

Tuna Teriyaki

PREPARATION TIME: 20 minutes

COOKING TIME: 17 minutes

SERVES: 4 people

4 tuna fish steaks
30ml/2 tbsps oil
60ml/4 tbsps soy sauce
15ml/1 tbsp mirin
15ml/1 tbsp sugar
15ml/1 tbsp miso

GARNISH
*Radish flowers and leaves (see
   introduction)*

Heat the oil in a large frying pan. Add the tuna and cook until slightly browned, about 2 minutes. Drain away excess oil and add the soy sauce, mirin and sugar. Cook over very low heat to cook the fish, about 5 minutes. Remove the fish from the pan and keep warm. Cook liquid over high heat to reduce by half. Stir in the miso. Skin tuna steaks and separate carefully in half. Discard bones and skin. Pour sauce over the fish and garnish with radish flowers and leaves.

**Facing page: Beef Teriyaki (top)
and Tuna Teriyaki (bottom).**

Grilled/Broiled Green Peppers

PREPARATION TIME: 15 minutes

COOKING TIME: 4-5 minutes

SERVES: 4 people

4 medium-sized green peppers
30ml/2 tbsps oil
Sesame seeds
Pickled ginger

Quarter the peppers and remove the seeds and cores. Heat a grill/broiler and brush the peppers on all sides with oil. Cook for 4-5 minutes, turning the peppers every minute. During the last minute of cooking, turn the peppers skin side up and sprinkle over the sesame seeds. Allow the seeds to brown slightly and then remove the peppers to a serving dish. Serve with grated pickled ginger, if desired.

Flying Fish

PREPARATION TIME: 40 minutes

COOKING TIME: 4-10 minutes

SERVES: 4 people

4 fresh small sea bream, trout or red
*   mullet*
Salt
Soy sauce

GARNISH
4 shiso leaves
4 lemon twigs

Scale the fish and gut them through the gills (a fishmonger will prepare the fish in this way). Rinse the fish very well and pat dry. Place the fish with the heads all pointing to the right and the stomach in front of you. Starting just behind the eye area, thread one or two metal skewers 3 times through 1 side of the fish. Do not allow the skewers to penetrate both sides of the fish. Bend the fish slightly every time the skewers are threaded through. Rub salt into the fins to make them stand up. Coat the tail with salt as well. Make sure the salt coating is quite heavy. Pre-heat a grill/broiler and place the fish on a

rack, the side not penetrated by skewers uppermost. Grill/broil 2-5 minutes per side. Twist the skewers occasionally to make them easier to remove. Place the fish on individual serving plates with the side grilled first uppermost. Remove the skewers and garnish with the shiso leaves and lemon twigs. Serve the soy sauce in individual bowls for dipping.

Egg Roll

PREPARATION TIME: 20 minutes

COOKING TIME: 1-2 minutes

SERVES: 3 people

4 eggs, beaten
90ml/3 fl oz/⅓ cup dashi
Pinch salt
1.25ml/¼ tsp light soy sauce
2 spring/green onions, roughly chopped
1 shiitake mushroom, roughly chopped
1 sheet nori, finely shredded

GARNISH
½ daikon radish, finely grated

This is best made in a special oblong Japanese omelette pan. A large frying pan may be substituted. Mix the eggs with the dashi, salt and soy sauce. Brush the pan with a light film of oil. Heat until slightly smoking. Pour in enough of the egg to coat the bottom of the pan. Cook for a few seconds, until the egg is just set. Sprinkle over the onions and mushroom. Roll up the omelette and push to one side of the pan. Brush the pan again with oil and pour in more of the egg. Cook again until just set. Roll up the first omelette inside the second and repeat until all the egg is used. Lift out of the pan and cut into nine rolls. Pass the nori over a gas flame on both sides to freshen. Shred finely. Arrange nori strips on plates and place 3 rolls on top. Garnish with a little grated daikon radish.

**This page: Flying Fish. Facing page:
Egg Roll (top) and Grilled/Broiled
Green Peppers (bottom).**

Steaming and Baking

Prawn/Shrimp Egg Custard

PREPARATION TIME: 20 minutes

COOKING TIME: 20-25 minutes

SERVES: 4 people

STOCK
570ml/1 pint/2 cups dashi
5ml/1 tsp soy sauce
5ml/1 tsp mirin
Pinch salt

4 dried shiitake mushrooms, soaked
* 30 minutes, drained and scored*
4 king prawns/jumbo shrimp
4 mangetout/pea pods, blanched and cut
* in half*
30g/1oz bean sprouts
5 eggs, beaten

GARNISH
1 piece pickled ginger, grated

Bring stock ingredients to the boil.
Take off the heat and leave to cool.
Strain the stock and when cool mix
with the beaten eggs. Divide the
mixture evenly among 4 heat-
resistant cups or small bowls. Add
the bean sprouts and position the
prawns/shrimp so the tail shows.
Add the mangetout/pea pods and
float a mushroom on top of the
custard. Pour water into a steamer or
a large, deep saucepan and bring to
the boil. Place the cups on a steamer
or a rack above the boiling water.
Cover the pan or steamer and cook

**This page: Prawn/Shrimp Egg
Custard. Facing page: Steamed
Abalone (top) and Baked Stuffed
Trout (bottom).**

over high heat for about 2 minutes. Reduce the heat and steam until just set, about 15 minutes. A toothpick inserted into the middle of the custard should come out clean when the custard is cooked. Garnish with the pickled ginger.

Baked Stuffed Trout

PREPARATION TIME: 20 minutes

COOKING TIME: 16-19 minutes

OVEN TEMPERATURE:
400°F/200°C/Gas Mark 6

SERVES: 4 people

4 small trout, cleaned and boned

STUFFING
60g/4 tbsps red miso
2 spring/green onions, chopped
30g/2 tbsps sugar
15ml/1 tbsp mirin
15ml/1 tbsp dashi
15ml/1 tbsp grated ginger

GARNISH
Lime slices

Make sure the heads and tails of the fish are left on. Cut 4 pieces of foil large enough to enclose each fish. Brush lightly with oil. Combine stuffing ingredients in a saucepan. Cook over moderate heat 4 minutes to thicken. Place each fish on a piece of foil and spread the stuffing in the cavity. Fold the foil over the fish tightly and twist the ends. Bake 12-14 minutes. Partially open the foil to serve. Garnish with a slice of lime.

Beef Roasted with Vegetables

PREPARATION TIME: 25 minutes

COOKING TIME: 15 minutes

OVEN TEMPERATURE:
400°F/200°C/Gas Mark 6

SERVES: 4 people

450g/1lb sirloin or rib roast, sliced in very thin strips

8 shiitake mushrooms, quartered lengthwise
1 green pepper, cored, seeded and cut in 8 pieces, lengthwise
1 carrot, quartered
60ml/4 tbsps mirin
60ml/4 tbsps soy sauce
Seven spices pepper

DIPPING SAUCE
60ml/4 tbsps lemon juice
60ml/4 tbsps orange juice
120ml/4 fl oz/½ cup soy sauce
120ml/4 fl oz/½ cup dashi

GARNISH
1 small piece daikon radish
1 small red chili pepper
4 shiso leaves
4 orange slices

Cut 4 pieces of foil about 25cm/10 inches square. Brush with oil. Place an equal portion of beef, bamboo shoots, peppers, mushroom and carrot on the foil. Mix mirin, soy sauce and seven spice pepper together and pour over each portion. Wrap well and cook 15 minutes. Combine sauce ingredients and pour into 4 small bowls. Remove core from the radish with a vegetable peeler. Insert chili pepper and grate together, finely. Arrange a leaf on each serving plate. Add grated daikon radish and chili pepper and an orange slice. Open the foil packets and place one on each dish. Serve each person with a sauce bowl for dipping.

Steamed Abalone

PREPARATION TIME: 30 minutes

COOKING TIME: 20 minutes

SERVES: 4 people

4 fresh abalone in the shell, if possible
Salt
60ml/4 tbsps sake

MISO SAUCE
90ml/⅓ cup red miso
60ml/4 tbsps dashi
30ml/2 tbsps sugar
30ml/2 tbsps mirin

GARNISH
4 large pieces konbu seaweed
60g/2oz pickled ginger, sliced

Use a strong spatula to remove the abalone if in the shell. Scrub the shells well and reserve. Sprinkle the abalone liberally with salt and scrub to remove black portion. Peel off green edges with a knife. Lightly score the surface of the abalone and line the shells or serving dishes with the seaweed. Replace the abalone in the shell on top of the seaweed and put into a steamer or on a rack above boiling water. Spoon the sake over each abalone, cover and steam for 20 minutes on moderate heat. Brush with miso sauce after about 12 minutes steaming. Remove the abalone, cut in half horizontally and then into 1.25cm/½ inch strips. Replace in the shells. Garnish with cucumber and ginger. Use any remaining miso sauce as a dipping sauce.

Steamed Chicken

PREPARATION TIME: 25 minutes

COOKING TIME: 15 minutes

SERVES: 4 people

450g/1lb chicken breasts, boned
10ml/2 tsps salt
30ml/2 tbsps sake
15ml/1 tbsp light soy sauce
15ml/1 tbsp dark soy sauce

4 leaves of Chinese cabbage
1 piece daikon radish
1 small red pepper

Prick the skin of the chicken and salt lightly. Mix the sake and soy sauce and pour over the chicken. Rub in well. Place chicken in a steamer or in a dish on a rack over boiling water. Cover and cook 15 minutes on moderate heat. Cut into 1.25cm/½ inch strips. Meanwhile, insert a vegetable peeler lengthwise into the daikon radish and remove a core.

Facing page: Beef Roasted with Vegetables.

Push in the pepper. Grate the two together, finely. Place the Chinese leaves/cabbage on plate and arrange the chicken. Garnish with small mounds of grated daikon radish. Reduce the cooking liquid from the chicken by boiling rapidly in a small saucepan. Use as a sauce.

Steamed Fish Rolls

PREPARATION TIME:	25 minutes
COOKING TIME:	10-15 minutes
SERVES:	4 people

2 large sole or plaice/flounder to give
   4 whole fillets
4 spring/green onions, blanched
   2 minutes
180g/6oz prawns/shrimp
10ml/2 tsps cornflour/cornstarch
5ml/1 tsp sake
2 eggs, beaten
Salt

GLAZE
15ml/1 tbsp white miso
15ml/1 tbsp mirin

GARNISH
1 small piece pickled daikon radish,
   fanned
4 whole prawns/shrimp

Skin the fish fillets and lay them skin side up on a flat surface. Chop the prawns/shrimp finely and mix with cornflour/cornstarch and sake. Divide the prawn/shrimp filling between the 2 fillets and spoon into a mound across the middle of the fillet. Trim off the white part of the onions and use only the green. Place the onions next to the prawn/shrimp filling. Cook the eggs with a pinch of salt until softly scrambled. Place in a mound next to the onions. Roll up the fish fillets, folding the thicker end over the filling first. Secure with cocktail sticks/wooden picks. Place in the top part of a steamer. Boil water in the bottom part. Alternatively, use a large pan and place the fish on a rack over boiling water. Steam for 10-15 minutes, until the fish is cooked. Five minutes before the end of cooking, brush with

combined glaze ingredients. Cut in slices and serve garnished with pickled daikon radish cut in a fan shape and whole prawns/shrimp.

Hakata-Mushi (Steamed Minced Pork)

PREPARATION TIME:	30 minutes
COOKING TIME:	50 minutes
SERVES:	4 people

450g/1lb Chinese leaves/cabbage,
   parboiled 2 minutes
3 eggs, beaten
450g/1lb minced/ground pork
30g/2 tbsps plain/all-purpose flour
15ml/1 tbsp soy sauce
Pinch salt

SAUCE
570ml/½ pint/2 cups dashi
45ml/3 tbsps soy sauce
½ clove garlic, finely minced
15ml/1 tbsp cornflour/cornstarch

Line the bottom of a greased 450g/ 1lb loaf pan with ⅓ of the cabbage leaves. Mix ⅓ of the beaten egg with the meat, flour, soy sauce and salt. Pour half of the remaining egg into the pan over the cabbage leaves. Press half of the meat mixture on top of the egg. Cover with another ⅓ of the cabbage leaves and add another layer of meat. Pour remaining egg over the meat and cover with remaining cabbage leaves. Press the mixture down and cover the pan with foil. Bring water to the boil in a steamer or large, deep pan with a tight-fitting lid. Place the pan in the steamer or on a rack above the water and cook 50 minutes, covered. Mix the cornflour/cornstarch with 30ml/ 2 tbsps of dashi. Bring the remaining dashi to the boil and add the soy sauce and garlic. Gradually stir in the cornflour/cornstarch and cook, stirring constantly until the mixture

Facing page: Steamed Chicken (top) and Hakata-Mushi (Steamed Minced Pork) (bottom). This page: Steamed Fish Rolls.

thickens. Cover the surface of the sauce with greaseproof/wax paper to prevent a skin forming. Allow the sauce to cool. Cool the hakata-mushi to room temperature and cut into squares or slices. Serve with the cooled sauce for dipping.

Simmering and One Pot Cooking

Simmered Flounder

PREPARATION TIME: 35 minutes

COOKING TIME: 27 minutes

SERVES: 4 people

140ml/¼ pint/½ cup sake
430ml/¾ pint/1½ cups dashi
140ml/¼ pint/½ cup mirin
140ml/¼ pint/½ cup soy sauce
4 small plaice/flounder or sole

120g/4oz mangetout/pea pods, steamed
   2 minutes
1 cake konnyaku

GARNISH
Lemon Slices
Shredded chives

Pour sake into a small saucepan and warm gently. Ignite the fumes and allow to burn until the flames die off naturally. Keep a pan lid handy in case the flames shoot up. Add the dashi, mirin and soy sauce. Gut the fish or buy already prepared. Leave on the heads and tails. Score the white side of the fish with a sharp knife. Put the fish cut sides down into a large, shallow pan. Pour over the stock and cook gently on top of the heat for 15-20 minutes. Remove the fish to serving dishes and turn cut side up. Keep warm. Cut the konnyaku cake into rectangles about 6mm/¼ inch thick. Cut a slit in the middle and pull the end of the konnyaku through the slit, twisting as you pull. Place in the fish cooking liquid and cook 5 minutes on gentle heat. Arrange the blanched mangetout/pea pods and konnyaku against the fish and spoon some of the cooking liquid over each.

Simmered Vegetables

PREPARATION TIME: 30 minutes

COOKING TIME: 7 minutes

SERVES: 4 people

900g/2lbs of a selection of the following:
Shiitake mushrooms, soaked 30 minutes,
   stalks removed
Turnips, peeled and pared into thick
   barrel shapes
Carrots, peeled

This page: Simmered Flounder. Facing page: Simmered Vegetables (top) and Simmered Coltsfoot and Carrots (bottom).

Konnyaku cake, cut in 6mm/¼ inch
   slices
Courgettes/zucchini cut in 6mm/¼ inch
   diagonal slices
Mangetout/pea pods, strings removed if
   necessary, ends trimmed on the diagonal
Spring/green onions, cut in 2.5cm/1 inch
   diagonal pieces

BROTH
480ml/¾ pint/1½ cups dashi
10ml/2 tsps sake
60ml/4 tbsps soy sauce
45ml/3 tbsps mirin

Score the mushroom caps if desired. Use a sharp, small knife to cut the turnips into thick hexagonal shapes. Take strips off the carrots, lengthwise, with a cannelle knife or paring knife. Cut crosswise into "flower" shapes. Cut a lengthwise slit in the konnyaku cake slices. Pull one end through the slit, twisting as you pull. Bring the dashi and sake to the boil in a saucepan and add the turnip and konnyaku. Blanch 1 minute. Remove the vegetables and set aside. Put in the mangetout/pea pods and courgettes/zucchini. Blanch 30 seconds. Return the turnips and konnyaku to the pan and add the mushrooms and carrots. Add the sugar, soy sauce and bring to the boil. Allow to simmer 5 minutes. Add the spring/green onions during the last minute of cooking. Remove all the vegetables with a draining spoon and arrange in serving dishes. Allow the sauce to boil rapidly to reduce it. Add the mirin and cook 30 seconds. Allow to cool slightly and pour over the vegetables.

Chicken One Pot

PREPARATION TIME: 35 minutes

COOKING TIME: 30 minutes

SERVES: 6 people

30ml/2 tbsps oil
450g/1lb boned chicken, thinly sliced
280ml/½ pint/1 cup chicken stock
60ml/4 tbsp soy sauce
30ml/2 tbsps sugar
1 carrot, sliced diagonally
1 medium green pepper, cut in thin strips

225g/8oz fresh spinach leaves, well
   washed
8 shiitake mushrooms, soaked 30 minutes
1 piece tofu, sliced
1 small bunch coriander leaves
225g/8oz buckwheat noodles, cooked

SAUCE AND GARNISH
90ml/6 tbsps soy sauce
90ml/6 tbsps lemon juice
1 piece daikon radish, peeled and stuck
   with 1 small red chili pepper

Heat oil in an electric frying pan or chafing dish at the table. Start frying the chicken a few slices at a time. Mix stock, soy sauce and sugar. When chicken pieces are cooked, push to the side of the pan and add some of each vegetable and a small portion of noodles. Moisten all with stock mixture. Make a hole in the centre of the daikon radish with a vegetable peeler and push in the chili pepper. Grate the two together finely and serve in small mounds next to mounds of onion. Serve the soy sauce and lemon juice in individual bowls. As the ingredients are cooked, each person takes food from the pan. A bit of the radish and onion may be mixed into the dipping sauce. Dip food into the sauce and continue to cook ingredients as the meal goes on.

Simmered Chicken with Okra

PREPARATION TIME: 20 minutes

COOKING TIME: 12 minutes

SERVES: 4 people

430ml/¾ pint/1½ cups dashi or chicken
   stock
45ml/3 tbsps mirin
75ml/5 tbsps soy sauce
2 chicken breasts, boned and cut in slivers
140ml/½ pint/½ cup dashi or chicken
   stock
6 okra pods, stems trimmed and cut in
   rounds
1 piece tofu, cut in slices
Bamboo shoots cut in thin matchsticks

GARNISH
Carrot flowers (see introduction)

Prepare the garnish. Mix the first 3 ingredients and bring to the boil in a shallow pan. Add the chicken and cook 10 minutes on moderate heat. Take off the heat and set aside. Add remaining dashi to a small saucepan with the okra, tofu and bamboo shoots. Cook 2 minutes. Arrange the chicken and vegetables in shallow serving bowls. Pour over a small amount of chicken cooking liquid. Garnish with carrot flowers.

Simmered Coltsfoot and Carrots

PREPARATION TIME: 25 minutes

COOKING TIME: 14 minutes

SERVES: 4 people

2 coltsfoot stems (4 sticks celery may be
   substituted)
570ml/1 pint/2 cups dashi
15ml/1 tbsp sugar
30ml/2 tbsps mirin
30ml/2 tbsps soy sauce
1 small carrot, cut in thin ribbons
Bonito flakes

Cook the coltsfoot stems or celery sticks whole in 1150ml/2 pints/ 4 cups salted water. Cook 4 minutes. Rinse under cold water. Peel the stems from the bottom of the coltsfoot and drain. Cut coltsfoot or celery into 5cm/2 inch sticks. Combine dashi, sugar, mirin and soy sauce in a saucepan and bring to the boil. Add the coltsfoot and simmer 10 minutes. Simmer only 5 minutes for celery. Add the carrot ribbons 2 minutes before the end of cooking. Remove the vegetables and arrange in dishes. Allow the vegetables and cooking liquid to cool. Pour some of the liquid over each serving of vegetables and serve cold, garnished with bonito flakes.

Facing page: Simmered Chicken with Okra (top) and Chicken One Pot (bottom).

60g/2oz bamboo shoots, cut into
   matchsticks
430ml/¾ pint/1½ cups dashi
15ml/1 tbsp mirin
1 small piece ginger, peeled and left whole

Cut strips from the carrot lengthwise
with a cannelle knife or paring knife.
Cut the carrot crosswise into 6mm/
¼ inch "flower" slices. Trim the ends
of the beans on the diagonal. Slice
the daikon pieces into thin
rectangles. Cut the kamaboku paste
into slices and cut a lengthwise slit in
the middle of each. Pull one end of
the paste through the slit, twisting
gently. Place the paste and all the
vegetables, except the mushrooms, in
a shallow pan and cover with water.
Add a pinch of salt and cover the
pan tightly. Cook about 2 minutes on
high heat, until the carrots are almost
tender. Add the bamboo shoots
halfway through cooking time.
Meanwhile, bring the dashi, mirin
and ginger to the boil in a shallow
pan. Leave the shells on the very
ends of the tails of the prawns/
shrimp. Place them in the hot dashi
and cook 2 minutes or until just pink.
Do not allow them to boil. Arrange
all the ingredients attractively in
4 shallow bowls. Spoon over some of
the dashi mixture and serve
immediately.

Sukiyaki

PREPARATION TIME: 40 minutes

COOKING TIME: 30 minutes

SERVES: 6 people

6 eggs, beaten
45ml/3 tbsps oil
675g/1½ lbs sirloin, sliced paper thin
1 bunch spring/green onions, cut in
   1.25cm/½ inch diagonal pieces
8 shiitake mushrooms, soaked 30 minutes
   and scored
140g/5oz shirataki noodles, soaked
   5 minutes and cut in 12cm/5 inch
   lengths
140g/5oz udon noodles, cooked
225g/8oz Chinese leaves/cabbage
225g/8oz fresh spinach, leaves washed
   and stems removed
2 bamboo shoots, cut in triangular pieces
1 150g/5oz cake konnyaku, sliced

Simmered Prawns/Shrimp with Vegetables

PREPARATION TIME: 30 minutes

COOKING TIME: 2 minutes

SERVES: 4 people

225g/8oz prawns/shrimp or 450g/1lb
   king prawns/jumbo shrimp
2 medium carrots, peeled

**This page: Sukiyaki. Facing page:
Cod and Cabbage One Pot (top)
and Simmered Prawns/Shrimp
with Vegetables (bottom).**

16 French/green beans
1 small piece daikon radish, cut into
   matchsticks
1 piece kamaboku fish paste or konnyaku

1 150g/5oz cake tofu, sliced
Trefoil (salad cress) or watercress

BROTH
280ml/½ pint/1 cup dashi
140ml/¼ pint/½ cup soy sauce
45ml/3 tbsps mirin
15ml/1 tbsp sugar

Break one egg into each of 6 bowls and beat lightly. Arrange all the ingredients on a large tray. Heat oil in an electric frying pan or chafing dish at the table. Brown the meat a few pieces at a time. Add onions. Move meat to one side of the dish and add equal portions of the other ingredients. Mix broth ingredients together and add some to the pan. Each person takes some of the cooked food and dips it into the egg which quickly glazes the hot food. Keep adding ingredients and simmering liquid as the meal progresses.

Eternity Patties

PREPARATION TIME: 20 minutes

COOKING TIME: 13-15 minutes

SERVES: 4-5 people

340g/12oz minced/ground chicken
½ egg, beaten
30g/2 tbsps plain/all-purpose flour
2.5ml/½ tsp ground ginger
60g/2oz/½ cup plain/all-purpose flour
700ml/1¼ pints/2½ cups dashi
45ml/3 tbsps soy sauce
30ml/2 tbsps sugar
15ml/1 tbsp sake

GARNISH
Radish flowers and leaves

Combine the chicken, egg, 30g/ 2 tbsps flour, ginger and salt in a large bowl and mix well. Divide the mixture into 10 (mixture will be soft). Lightly flour hands and form mixture into patties. Coat the patties with the remaining flour mixed with a pinch of salt. Score a lattice on the top of each patty using the blunt side of a knife. Combine remaining ingredients in a large frying pan and bring to the boil. Add the patties to the pan,

scored side up, and swirl liquid over the tops. Reduce heat and simmer 3-4 minutes. Gently turn the patties over and cook 5-6 minutes. Turn again and increase the heat to bring the liquid up to a rapid boil. Quickly swirl the liquid over the patties for about 2 minutes. Transfer the patties to a serving dish and spoon over some of the cooking liquid. Garnish with radish flowers and leaves.

Cod and Cabbage One Pot

PREPARATION TIME: 40 minutes

COOKING TIME: 30 minutes

SERVES: 4 people

10 dried shiitake mushrooms, soaked 30 minutes
450g/1lb cod fillet, skinned and cut in 2.5cm/1 inch pieces
3 small leeks, washed and cut in 6cm/ 2½ inch lengths
225g/8oz Chinese leaves/cabbage
225g/8oz tofu, drained
45g/1½ oz cellophane noodles, soaked 5 minutes
1.3 litres/2½ pints/5 cups dashi

SAUCE
30ml/2 tbsps rice vinegar
30ml/2 tbsps soy sauce
60ml/4 tbsps mirin
30ml/2 tbsps lemon juice
60ml/4 tbsps sake
1 small piece konbu seaweed

GARNISH
2 spring/green onions, finely chopped
90g/3oz piece daikon radish, stuck with 1 red pepper, finely grated

Drain mushrooms and cut off stalks. Trim down spines of the cabbage leaves and cut the leaves into 3 irregular-shaped pieces. Cut the tofu into 10 pieces. Drain the noodles and arrange all the ingredients on a large tray. Bring the stock to the boil. Mix the sauce ingredients and pour into 4 small bowls. Arrange a mound of onion and one of grated daikon radish on 4 separate plates or trays. Put the pot of stock on an electric ring on the table. Add the fish, then

the mushrooms and then the cabbage leaves. Add the leeks, noodles and tofu. Each person mixes small amounts of onion and radish into the sauce and takes food from the main pot to dip into the sauce. A fondue pot may also be used for cooking.

Simmered Pork and Vegetable Casserole

PREPARATION TIME: 25 minutes

COOKING TIME: 1 hour

SERVES: 4 people

30ml/2 tbsps oil
450g/1lb pork spare ribs, cut in 2.5cm/ 1 inch pieces
30g/1oz piece ginger, sliced thinly
45ml/3 tbsps sake
60ml/4 tbsps soy sauce
30g/2 tbsps sugar
60g/2oz French/green beans, cut in 5cm/2 inch lengths
2 sticks celery, cut in 5cm/2 inch lengths
60g/2oz bamboo shoots, cut into strips

Heat the oil in a large sauté pan. Cook the sliced ginger briefly and remove. Add the pork to the pan, turn up the heat and brown on all sides. Pour in water to just barely cover. Return the ginger to the pan. Add the sake, cover and cook for 1 hour. Check the level of liquid and add more water if the meat begins to dry out. When the pork is tender, add the soy sauce, sugar and cook, uncovered, to reduce the sauce to syrupy consistency. Meanwhile put beans and celery into a small pan and barely cover with water. Add a pinch of salt and bring to the boil. Cook 2-3 minutes until tender-crisp. Add the bamboo shoots after about 2 minutes. Place the pork in individual serving dishes and scatter over the vegetables. Pour over any remaining sauce.

Facing page: Simmered Pork and Vegetable Casserole (top) and Eternity Patties (bottom).

JAPANESE COOKING

Deep Frying

Lemony Marinated Herring

PREPARATION TIME: 15 minutes

COOKING TIME: 10-20 minutes

SERVES: 4 people

4 herrings, cleaned and heads removed
45ml/3 tbsps rice vinegar
30ml/2 tbsps soy sauce
30ml/2 tbsps sake
15ml/1 tbsp lemon juice
Cornflour/cornstarch to dredge
Oil for frying

Score the fish diagonally 3 or 4 times on one side. Mix the vinegar, soy sauce, sake and lemon juice together and sprinkle over the fish. Leave in a cool place to marinate for 15 minutes. Heat oil to 350°F/180°C in a deep-fat fryer or wok. Dredge the fish with cornflour/cornstarch and fry in the hot oil, 2 fish at a time. Cook for 5-10 minutes. Drain on paper towels. Garnish with lemon and cucumber twigs, if desired.

Deep-Fried Pork

PREPARATION TIME: 15 minutes

COOKING TIME: 5 minutes per batch

SERVES: 4 people

4 slices pork loin or fillet/tenderloin,
*   about 1.25cm/½ inch thick*
Flour with salt and pepper
2 egg whites, lightly beaten
120g/4oz/1 cup fresh breadcrumbs
Oil for frying
½ head Chinese leaves/cabbage
1 lime, sliced

Clip the edges of the pork slices to prevent curling and dip in the

seasoned flour. Shake off excess flour and dip the pork into the egg white and then sprinkle with breadcrumbs. Heat the oil to 350°F/180°C in a deep-fat fryer or wok. Fry 1 or 2 slices

This page: Taksuta-Age (Deep-Fried Chicken) (top) and Deep-Fried Pork (bottom). Facing page: Snowy Fried Prawns/Shrimp (top) and Lemon Marinated Herring (bottom).

at a time for about 5 minutes. Remove the pork and drain on paper towels. Slice each piece diagonally into 1.25cm/½ inch thick strips. Serve assembled on a bed of shredded Chinese leaves/cabbage and garnish with lime slices.

Snowy Fried Prawns/ Shrimp

PREPARATION TIME: 20 minutes

COOKING TIME: 2 minutes per batch

SERVES: 4 people

675g/1½ lbs cooked king prawns/jumbo shrimp, peeled
60g/2oz harusame or saifan (soy flour noodles)
60g/2oz/½ cup flour with salt and pepper
2 egg whites
Oil for frying

De-vein the prawns/shrimp and score diagonally on the underside. Cut the noodles into 6mm-1.25cm/¼-½ inch pieces. Whisk the egg whites until foamy. Dip the prawns/shrimp into the seasoned flour and shake off surplus. Dip into egg white and then sprinkle on the noodles until each prawn/shrimp is completely covered. Heat oil in a deep-fat fryer or wok to 325°F/160°C. Add the prawns/shrimp to the hot oil and fry a few at a time until the noodles look opaque, about 2 minutes. Drain well before serving. They should not be allowed to brown.

Vegetable Tempura

PREPARATION TIME: 30 minutes

COOKING TIME: 2 minutes per batch

SERVES: 4 people

Selection of the following ingredients prepared as directed:
Celery, cut into sticks
Artichoke hearts, halved
Lotus root, sliced in rounds about 6mm/¼ inch thick
Mushrooms, whole fresh or dried, soaked 30 minutes, with stems removed
Green peppers, cut in 6mm/¼ inch thick rings or strips
Onions, cut in 6mm/¼ inch rings
Parsnips, peeled and cut into sticks
Asparagus tips
Turnips, peeled and cubed
Mangetout/pea pods, ends trimmed and strings removed if necessary
French beans/green beans, ends trimmed
Aubergine/eggplant, cut in half. Cut away flesh, leaving 3mm/⅛ inch clinging to the skin. Cut the skin into fan shapes about 3.75cm/1½ inches long
Courgettes/zucchini, cut in half lengthwise and then into thin slices across
Okra, stems removed and pods left whole
Broccoli, cut into flowerets
Cauliflower, cut into flowerets
Parsley, snipped into small bunches
Sweet potato, peeled and sliced into 1.25cm/½ inch rounds
Carrots, peeled and cut into diagonal slices
Cucumber, cut in quarters lengthwise and then into 2.5cm/1 inch wedges
Oil for frying

DIPPING SAUCE
120ml/4 fl oz/½ cups chicken stock
60ml/4 tbsps soy sauce
60ml/4 tbsps sherry or sake
Pinch sugar
Small piece daikon radish, grated
Small piece ginger, grated

BATTER
1 egg yolk
280ml/½ pint/1¼ cups iced water
120g/4 oz/1 cup plain/all-purpose flour

Prepare the vegetables as directed. Mix all the ingredients for the sauce except the radish and ginger. Pour the sauce into 4 small bowls. Place a small mound of grated radish and one of grated ginger on each of 4 plates. Heat oil in a deep-fat fryer to 350°F/180°C. A wok may also be used. Beat the egg yolk lightly and beat in the water. Sift in the flour and stir with a table knife. The batter should look lumpy and under-mixed. Dip each vegetable in the batter and shake off the excess. Lower ingredients carefully into the hot oil and cook for about 2 minutes, turning once or twice with a metal spoon. Fry only 3 or 4 pieces at a time and fry only 1 kind of vegetable at a time. Do not coat too many vegetables in advance. Drain fried vegetables on paper towels on a rack for a few seconds before serving. Serve while still hot and crisp. Each person may mix a desired amount of the grated radish and ginger into the dipping sauce to eat with the tempura.

Taksuta-Age (Deep-Fried Chicken)

PREPARATION TIME: 15 minutes, plus marinating time

COOKING TIME: 2-3 minutes per batch

SERVES: 4 people

4 chicken breasts
45ml/3 tbsps soy sauce
15ml/1 tbsp mirin or sweet sherry
15ml/1 tbsp rice vinegar
10ml/2 tbps sugar
1 clove garlic, minced
60g/2oz flour, with a pinch of salt and pepper
Oil for frying

Cut the chicken into 2.5cm/1 inch cubes and combine with all remaining ingredients except flour in a deep bowl and leave to marinate, covered, for about 1 hour in a cool place. Stir occasionally to coat the chicken evenly. Remove the chicken from the marinade with a draining spoon. Toss in the seasoned flour to coat. Heat the oil in a deep-fat fryer or wok to 350°F/180°C and fry the chicken, a few pieces at a time. Cook until golden brown and crisp, about 2-3 minutes per batch. Drain on paper towels a few seconds before serving. Serve with extra soy sauce for dipping, if desired.

Facing page: Vegetable Tempura.

Fish Tempura

PREPARATION TIME: 30 minutes

COOKING TIME: 2 minutes per batch

SERVES: 4 people

12 uncooked king prawns/jumbo shrimp
2 whitefish fillets, skinned and cut into
  5 x 2cm/2 x ¾ inch strips
Small whole fish such as smelt or
  whitebait
Squid, cleaned and cut into strips
  2.5 x 7.5cm/1 x 3 inches and dredged
  with flour
Oil for frying

DIPPING SAUCE
90ml/3 fl oz/⅓ cup soy sauce
Juice and zest of 1 lemon or lime
60ml/2 fl oz/¼ cup dashi

BATTER
1 egg yolk
240ml/8 fl oz/1 cup iced water
120g/4oz/1 cup plain/all-purpose flour,
  sifted

Shell the prawns/shrimp, leaving only the tail shell on the end of each. De-vein if necessary. Wash the whole fish and pat dry. Prepare other fish as directed. Mix the dipping sauce ingredients and pour into small bowls. Heat oil in a deep-fat fryer to 350°F/180°C. A wok may also be used. To make the batter, beat the egg yolk lightly and gradually beat in the iced water. Sift in the flour and stir the batter with a table knife. Batter will be lumpy and look under-mixed. Dip each piece of fish in the batter and shake off the excess. Lower ingredients carefully into the hot oil and cook for about 2 minutes, turning once or twice with a metal spoon. Fry only 3 or 4 pieces of fish at a time, and only 1 kind of fish at a time. Do not coat too many pieces of

1 inch cubes. Heat the oil in a deep-fat fryer or wok to 350°F/180°C. Reduce heat slightly and add the tofu cubes to the hot oil. Deep-fry 1-2 minutes or until cubes float to the surface. Turn them over and fry a further 1 minute. Remove from the oil with a draining spoon and drain on a rack or paper towels. Cook tofu in several batches. Meanwhile, bring the stock to the boil in a saucepan. Add the beans and bonito flakes and simmer gently for 5 minutes until the beans are just tender. Transfer the beans to a serving dish with a draining spoon. Arrange them in a circle and keep warm. Rapidly boil the cooking liquid to reduce by half and pour over the beans. Pile the deep-fried tofu into the centre of the beans to serve.

Chicken Croquettes

PREPARATION TIME: 20 minutes

COOKING TIME: 3-5 minutes per batch

SERVES: 4 people

225g/8oz minced/ground chicken
225g/8oz cooked, mashed potatoes
½ small onion, finely chopped
1 clove garlic, minced
30ml/2 tbsps chopped parsley
Salt
Pepper
15ml/1tbsp soy sauce
1 egg, beaten
225g/8oz/1 cup breadcrumbs
Oil for frying

Combine the chicken, potatoes, onion, garlic, parsley, salt, pepper and soy sauce together in a mixing bowl. Add the egg and mix well. Form the mixture into small cylinder shapes about 5 x1.25cm/2 x ½ inch. Roll in breadcrumbs and chill briefly. Heat oil to 350°F/180°C in a deep-fat fryer or wok. Lower the croquettes carefully into the hot oil and fry for about 3-5 minutes, until golden brown and crisp. Cook in small batches. Drain on paper towels on a rack for a few seconds before serving. Serve with soy sauce for dipping if desired.

fish in advance. Drain on a rack with paper towels for a few seconds before serving. Serve while still hot and crisp with the sauce for dipping.

Deep-Fried Tofu with Green Beans

PREPARATION TIME: 20 minutes

COOKING TIME: 5 minutes for beans, 1-2 minutes per batch for tofu

SERVES: 4 people

Facing page: Fish Tempura. This page: Deep-Fried Tofu with Green Beans (top) and Chicken Croquettes (bottom).

450g/1lb tofu
240ml/8 fl oz/1 cup chicken stock
225g/8oz French/green beans, trimmed
15ml/1tbsp bonito flakes
Oil for frying

Drain and press tofu to remove excess moisture and cut into 2.5 cm/

Vinegared Foods and Salads

Spinach and Bean Sprouts with Wasabi

PREPARATION TIME: 15 minutes

COOKING TIME: 1 minutes

SERVES: 4 people

*450g/1lb fresh spinach, washed well and
   stalks removed*
120g/4oz bean sprouts

DRESSING
30ml/2 tbsps rice vinegar
10ml/2 tbsps sugar
15ml/1 tbsp soy sauce
*2.5ml/½ tsp wasabi powder mixed to a
   paste with water*

Cook the spinach 1 minute in a
covered saucepan with only the
water that clings to the leaves after
washing. Refresh under cold water,
press to remove excess moisture and
leave to drain. Combine leaves with
bean sprouts. Mix dressing ingredients
very well and pour over salad. Toss
lightly and serve in individual bowls.

Daikon and Carrot Salad

PREPARATION TIME: 25 minutes

SERVES: 4 people

4 small oranges
*½ daikon radish, peeled and coarsely
   grated*
1 large carrot, peeled and coarsely grated
1 small piece ginger, grated
Rice vinegar
30g/2 tbsps sugar
Pinch salt

GARNISH
Radish flowers and leaves

Cut the oranges in half and squeeze
for juice. Measure the juice and add
an equal amount of vinegar. Add the
sugar and salt and mix well. Cook
over low heat to dissolve sugar and
evaporate vinegar fumes. Set the
dressing aside to cool. Cut a slice
from the rounded end of the orange
shells so that they stand level. Do
not cut completely through the base.
Scoop out the orange pulp and cut

**This page: Daikon and Carrot
Salad. Facing page: Bean Salad
with Sesame Dressing (top) and
Spinach and Bean Sprouts with
Wasabi (bottom).**

the edge in scallops or points if
desired. Mix radish, carrot and ginger
with the dressing. Leave to stand 30
minutes. Fill orange shells with the
salad and serve chilled.

Gold Salad

PREPARATION TIME: 20 minutes

COOKING TIME: 6-8 minutes

SERVES: 4 people

20 spears white asparagus, stalks trimmed
Salt

SAUCE
2 egg yolks
30ml/2 tbsps rice vinegar
10ml/2 tsps dry mustard
15ml/1 tbsp sugar
10ml/2 tsps cornflour/cornstarch
60ml/4 tbsps dashi
Chopped parsley

Cut the asparagus into 5cm/2 inch diagonal pieces, leaving the tips whole. Bring 570ml/1 pint/2 cups water to the boil. Add a pinch of salt and the asparagus. Cook 2-3 minutes. Asparagus should still be crisp. Rinse in cold water and drain.

Combine all ingredients for the sauce in a double boiler or in a small bowl in a bain marie. Stirring constantly, cook over boiling water to thicken. Remove and stir or wisk until the sauce cools. It should be the consistency of mayonnaise. Divide asparagus into 4 bowls, spoon over the sauce and sprinkle on chopped parsley.

GARNISH
3 spring/green onions, very finely chopped

Pre-heat a grill/broiler, or cook over charcoal. Dry mushrooms well. Cut stalks off and sprinkle caps with salt. Cut the tofu into 1.25cm/½ inch slices. Brush lightly with oil on both sides. Grill/broil with the mushrooms, about 3 minutes per side, turning once. Cut mushrooms and tofu into thin slices. Arrange on dishes and mix the sauce ingredients. Pour over the mushrooms and tofu. Garnish with the onion. Serve hot.

Okra with Garlic and Seven Spice Pepper

PREPARATION TIME: 15 minutes

COOKING TIME: 5 minutes

SERVES: 4 people

40 okra pods
15ml/1 tbsp soy sauce
2 cloves garlic, grated finely
Seven spice pepper

Wash the okra well. Keep stem end on and put okra into boiling, salted water. Cook 5 minutes. Refresh under cold water and drain well. Cut off the stem ends. If the pods are small, leave whole. If large cut on the diagonal into 1.25cm/½ inch lengths. Sprinkle over soy sauce, garlic and pepper. Toss and serve in small bowls.

Broad Beans in Tofu Dressing

PREPARATION TIME: 25 minutes

COOKING TIME: 5 minutes

SERVES: 4 people

900g/2lbs fresh broad/lima beans (weight when shelled)
Salt

DRESSING
1 225g/8oz cake tofu
30ml/2 tbsps sugar
Pinch salt
10ml/2 tsps sesame oil
2.5ml/½ tsp soy sauce

Facing page: Okra with Garlic and Seven Spice Pepper (top) and Broad Beans in Tofu Dressing (bottom). This page: Gold Salad (top) and Vinegared Mushroom Salad with Tofu (bottom).

Vinegared Mushroom Salad with Tofu

PREPARATION TIME: 30 minutes

COOKING TIME: 3 minutes

SERVES: 4 people

12 large shiitake mushrooms, soaked 30 minutes
1 225g/8oz cake tofu, drained
Salt
Oil

SAUCE
45ml/3 tbsps lemon juice
45ml/3 tbsps rice vinegar
90ml/6 tbsps soy sauce
Dash mirin

45ml/3 tbsps hot water
Black sesame seeds

Cook the beans in lots of boiling, salted water for about 5 minutes. Reserve the water. Rinse beans in cold water and peel off their outer skins, using only the bright green inner beans. Lower the cake of tofu carefully into the boiling water left from the beans. Leave tofu in the water about 5 seconds and remove with a draining spoon. Drain well and wrap in muslin/cheesecloth and press gently to extract all moisture. Blend in a food processor or blender with remaining dressing ingredients except sesame seeds. Pour over beans and sprinkle on sesame seeds.

Vinegared Crab

PREPARATION TIME: 25 minutes

COOKING TIME: 3 minutes

SERVES: 4 people

1 small cucumber, grated
1 large cooked crab
1 small piece ginger, grated

SAUCE
30ml/2 tbsps rice vinegar
30ml/2 tbsps dashi
60ml/4 tbsps mirin
15ml/1 tbsp soy sauce

GARNISH
Chinese leaves/cabbage
Grated pickled ginger

Sprinkle cucumber with salt and leave to stand 30 minutes. Bring sauce ingredients to the boil and set aside to cool. Pour into small bowls. Rinse and drain the cucumber. Press to remove excess moisture. Crack legs and claws off the crab. Remove the meat from the claws and leave the thin legs whole. Separate the underbody from the shell and remove the stomach sac and gills and discard. Scrape all the brown meat from the shell and crack the body into 4 pieces. Use a skewer to pick out the meat. Combine all meat with the ginger and cucumber and toss carefully. Arrange Chinese leaves/cabbage on plates or trays and pile

This page: Vinegared Crab. Facing page: Sushi.

salad on, leaving some of the leaves showing on each plate. Garnish with whole crab legs and pickled ginger. Serve the sauce for dipping.

Bean Salad with Sesame Dressing

PREPARATION TIME: 15 minutes

COOKING TIME: 2 minutes

SERVES: 4 people

225g/8oz French/green beans, trimmed
*   and cut in 5cm/2 inch lengths*
Salt

DRESSING
30ml/2 tbsps sesame paste
15ml/1 tbsp sugar
10ml/2 tsps soy sauce
10ml/2 tsps rice vinegar
Black sesame seeds

Bring water to the boil in a large pan with a pinch of salt. Add the beans and cook for 2 minutes after the water comes back to the boil. Drain and refresh under cold water. Leave to drain and dry. Mix all ingredients for the dressing except sesame seeds. Spoon over the beans and toss lightly. Sprinkle on seeds and serve in individual bowls.

JAPANESE COOKING

Rice, Noodles and Pickles

Sushi

PREPARATION TIME: 40 minutes

COOKING TIME: 18 minutes

SERVES: 6-8 people

RICE
600g/1¼ lbs/2½ cups short grain rice
Small piece konbu seaweed
1 litre/1¾ pints/3½ cups water
5ml/1 tbsp sake

ROLLED SUSHI
4 sheets nori
½ cucumber
2 pieces pickled red ginger
Wasabi horseradish

LAYERED SUSHI
2 sheets nori
½ cucumber
120g/4oz smoked salmon, thinly sliced

SWEET VINEGAR
120ml/8 tbsps rice vinegar
50ml/3 tbsps sugar
Pinch salt

Rinse raw rice until water is almost clear. Leave in a colander 1 hour to drain. Meanwhile toast sheets of nori over a gas flame for 1 minute to freshen. Mix wasabi with enough water to make a paste. Slice the cucumber in half lengthwise. Reserve one half and quarter the other half. Mix the sweet vinegar ingredients and heat slowly in a small saucepan until sugar is dissolved. Leave to cool completely. Bring the water to the boil in a large pan with the piece of konbu. Remove the seaweed as soon as the water reaches a rolling boil. Add the sake and rice. Bring back to the boil and cook for 30 seconds on high heat. Lower the heat and cook for a further 12 minutes, covered.

Turn up the heat again and cook for 5 minutes to evaporate excess moisture. Take the pan off the heat and leave to stand, covered, for 10-15 minutes. Transfer the hot rice to a clean bowl and toss with the sweet vinegar. Cover the bowl with a damp towel until ready to use. Place 1 sheet of nori on a clean towel or piece of greaseproof/wax paper. If you have

Japanese bamboo mats these are ideal to use. Divide rice mixture in half and reserve half, covered. Divide half the mixture in fourths and spread some on the sheet of nori across the end closest to you. Spread some of the wasabi carefully over the rice. Cut a quarter of the cucumber to fit the sheet of nori and place on top of the rice. Cover the cucumber with another layer of rice and press it around firmly. Fold the end of the nori over the rice and tuck in the sides. Roll up using the towel, paper or mat to help you. Roll tightly, tucking in the sides as you roll. Repeat with the remaining rice, the remaining quarter of cucumber and use the same method with the pickled ginger, leaving out the wasabi. Leave each roll to stand, seam side down, for at least 2 minutes before slicing into 4-6 pieces with a dampened knife.

To make the layered sushi, line 2 15 or 20cm/6 or 8 inch oblong pans with clingfilm/plastic wrap. Divide the remaining rice mixture in half. Press half of that into one of the pans. Place the nori on top of the rice and cover with another layer of rice. Slice the cucumber lengthwise into thin slices. Place on top of the rice. Cover with another sheet of clingfilm/plastic wrap and place another pan of the same size on top. Press down and weight lightly. Leave to stand 5-10 minutes before removing form the pan and slicing the sushi into 5cm/2 inch pieces. Use the same method with the remaining rice and top with smoked salmon. Arrange the rolled and layered sushi on a large serving plate and give each person a bowl of soy sauce for dipping if desired.

Chrysanthemum Rice

PREPARATION TIME: 30 minutes

COOKING TIME: 30 minutes

MAKES: 15 balls

225g/8oz/1 cup short grain rice
300ml/10 fl oz/1¼ cups water
45ml/3 tbsps soy sauce
½ sheet nori
15ml/1 tbsp toasted sesame seeds
1 piece ginger, grated
6 eggs
45ml/3 tbsps dashi
15ml/1 tbsp sugar
15ml/1 tbsp sherry or sake
Oil for frying
Red caviar to garnish

Cook rice as for Chicken Donbun. Sprinkle soy sauce over warm rice, toss and cover with a damp cloth. Pre-heat oven to 250°F/130°C, place a sheet of nori on a baking tray and let dry for 3-4 minutes. When dry, crumble the nori. Add to the rice with the toasted sesame seeds and ginger, and toss lightly. With dampened hands, divide rice into 15 balls. Place 1 ball in the centre of a piece of muslin/cheesecloth, gather up the ends and twist cloth to form a firm ball of rice. Remove rice ball from the cloth and repeat with all the remaining rice. Dampen fingers and flatten the rice balls slightly. Cover with a damp cloth and set aside. Combine eggs, dashi, sugar and

This page: Sekihan (Red Rice) (top) and Chicken Donbun (bottom). Facing page: Chrysanthemum Rice (top) and Onigiri (bottom).

sherry or sake in a bowl and beat well. Lightly oil a 6 inch omelette pan or frying pan and heat. Add about 60ml/4 tbsps of the egg mixture to the pan and cook over medium heat for 1½ minutes, until edges are dry. Turn omelette over and continue cooking until set, about 30 seconds-1 minute. Transfer to a plate and repeat with remaining egg mixture. Let cool completely and then cut into thin

strips, about 7.5-10cm/3-4 inch long. Lay the omelette strips over each rice ball to form "chrysanthemum petals." Make a slight indentation in the middle of each one and fill with a little red caviar.

Chicken Donbun

| PREPARATION TIME: 15 minutes |
| COOKING TIME: 40 minutes |
| SERVES: 4 people |

225g/8oz cooked chicken
225g/8oz/1 cup short grain rice
430ml/¾ pint/1½ cups water
240ml/8 fl oz/1 cup chicken stock
30ml/2 tbsps sweet sherry or mirin
30ml/2 tbsps soy sauce
225g/8oz fresh mushrooms, sliced
120g/4oz peas
3 eggs
5ml/1 tsp salt

Cut the chicken into bite-sized pieces and set aside. Rinse the rice under cold water until the water runs almost clear. Leave in a colander to drain. Put the rice and water into a heavy-based saucepan and bring to the boil. Reduce the heat and simmer, covered, for 15 minutes until the rice is tender and the water is just absorbed. Stir and leave to stand, covered for 10-15 minutes before using. Put the stock, sherry, soy sauce, mushrooms and peas into a saucepan and bring to the boil. Reduce heat and simmer for 1-2 minutes until vegetables are tender. Add the rice and chicken and stir gently. Beat the egg and salt together and add to the ingredients in the saucepan. Cook over low heat, stirring occasionally until egg is just set. Serve immediately.

Sekihan (Red Rice)

| PREPARATION TIME: 15 minutes plus soaking time |
| COOKING TIME: 55-57 minutes |
| SERVES: 4 people |

60g/2oz/¼ cup azuki beans (small red beans), soaked overnight

300g/10oz/1½ cups short grain rice
30ml/2 tbsps black sesame seeds

Rinse beans and place in a saucepan with 570ml/1 pint/2 cups water. Bring to the boil and then simmer, uncovered, for 10-12 minutes or until beans begin to soften. Drain and reserve the cooking liquid. Wash the rice until the water runs almost clear. Soak the rice in half the bean liquid for about 2 hours. Reserve remaining bean liquid. Drain the rice and mix with beans. Spread both out on a plate in an even layer. Place the plate in the top part of a steamer or on a rack above boiling water. Cover tightly and steam 15 minutes. Uncover and spoon over about ⅓ of the remaining bean liquid. Re-cover and steam a further 10 minutes. Repeat the procedure twice more during cooking. Rice and beans should steam about 45 minutes. Toss the red rice to fluff it up and sprinkle over sesame seeds to serve.

Garnished Noodles

| PREPARATION TIME: 25 minutes |
| COOKING TIME: 20 minutes |
| SERVES: 4 people |

SAUCE
45ml/3 tbsps white wine vinegar
45ml/3 tbsps soy sauce
10ml/2 tsps sugar
140ml/¼ pint/½ cup chicken stock or dashi
450g/1lb soba noodles
1150ml/2 pints/4 cups water

GARNISHES
Cucumber, diced
120g/4oz small, cooked and peeled shrimp
Celery leaves
2 sheets nori, toasted and crumbled or shredded

Combine vinegar, soy sauce, stock/dashi in a saucepan and bring to the boil. Remove from the heat and keep warm. Bring water to the boil and add the noodles. Stir once and bring back to the boil. Simmer gently until tender, about 5 minutes. Drain in a colander and rinse with hot water.

Divide the noodles among 4 serving dishes and arrange garnishes on top. Pour over the sauce and serve.

Five-Coloured Noodles

| PREPARATION TIME: 25 minutes |
| COOKING TIME: 18-20 minutes |
| SERVES: 4 people |

225g/8oz ubon or somen noodles
1150ml/2 pints/4 cups water
140ml/¼ pint/½ cup chicken stock
1 carrot cut into diagonal slices
1 small turnip, diced
4 dried shiitake mushrooms, soaked 30 minutes, drained and stalks removed, and sliced
120g/4oz French/green beans, cut into 3.75cm/1½ inch strips
10ml/2 tsps cornflour/cornstarch
45ml/3 tbsps soy sauce
20ml/4 tsps black sesame seeds

Cook noodles as for Garnished Noodles. Rinse under cold water and drain thoroughly. In a saucepan, bring the stock to the boil; add carrot, turnip, mushrooms and beans and cover the pan. Simmer 8-10 minutes until just tender. Blend cornflour/cornstarch and soy sauce together and add to the stock. Continue cooking until slightly thickened. Divide the noodles among 4 serving bowls and pour over the vegetables. Sprinkle with black sesame seeds and serve.

Onigiri

| PREPARATION TIME: 30 minutes |
| COOKING TIME: 25 minutes |
| SERVES: 6 people |

450g/1lb short grain rice
700ml/1¼ pints/2½ cups water
60ml/4 tbsps black sesame seeds
Seven spice pepper
2 sheets nori

Facing page: Five-Coloured Noodles (top) and Garnished Noodles (bottom).

Cook rice as for Chicken Donbun. Dampen hands with salt water and shape hot rice into cakes, triangles and oblongs. Rice moulds are available in various shapes and may be used instead of the hand-shaping method. Place the moulds on a flat surface and fill with rice. Use the pusher to press the rice firmly into shape and then remove the mould. Toast the nori sheets over a gas flame and cut into strips. Wrap a strip around each rice oblong. Decorate one of the other shapes with black sesame seeds and the other with the seven spice pepper. Serve warm. In Japan, these are often eaten as snacks.

Cauliflower and Broccoli Pickles

PREPARATION TIME: 20 minutes

COOKING TIME: 3 minutes

SERVES: 4 people

1 small head cauliflower, cut in flowerets
120g/4oz broccoli, cut in flowerets

DRESSING
15ml/1 tbsp wasabi horseradish
90ml/6 tbsps soy sauce
30ml/2 tbsps mirin
Black sesame seeds

Bring lots of salted water to the boil in a large saucepan and add the prepared vegetables. Mix the remaining ingredients and set aside. Cook vegetables about 3 minutes. Drain and refresh under cold water. Leave to dry. Toss with the dressing and refrigerate 3 hours before serving.

Cucumber Pickles

PREPARATION TIME: 30 minutes

SERVES: 4 people

10ml/2 tsps sesame seeds, mixed with
   15ml/1 tbsp oil
1 cucumber
30-60ml/2-4 tbsps soy sauce
Bonito flakes

Spread the sesame seeds over the bottom of a heavy frying pan and cook over gentle heat until lightly browned. Peel the cucumbers and cut into 2.5cm/1 inch irregular wedges. Combine all ingredients except the bonito flakes and leave to marinate 20 minutes in a cool place. Sprinkle bonito flakes on top before serving.

Lemon Turnips

PREPARATION TIME: 20 minutes plus chilling time

SERVES: 4 people

4 medium turnips
Juice and rind of ½ lemon

This page: Cauliflower and Broccoli Pickles. Facing page: Lemon Turnips (top) and Cucumber Pickles (bottom).

Salt
1 small piece nori, shredded

Peel turnips and cut into large dice. Combine all the ingredients except nori. Put into a large bowl. Press a smaller bowl on top and weight. Refrigerate overnight. When ready to serve, refresh nori over a gas flame and shred finely. Sprinkle over the top of the pickle.

Desserts

sugar until dissolved. Sprinkle on the agar-agar and whisk until dissolved. Dampen an 1150ml/2 pint/4 cup loaf pan and pour in the mixture. Leave in the refrigerator to set. Unmould onto a serving dish. Slice the kiwi fruit and arrange on top of the jelly.

Sweet Tempura

PREPARATION TIME: 20 minutes

COOKING TIME: 2-3 minutes per batch

SERVES: 4 people

Selection of the following prepared as directed:
Strawberries, hulled, washed and drained
Kiwi fruit, peeled and cut into 6mm/ ¼ inch slices
Apples, cored and cut into wedges, lightly sprinkled with lemon juice
Pears, peeled, cored and cut into wedges, lightly sprinkled with lemon juice
Pineapple, peeled, cored and cut in rings or pieces
Banana, peeled and sliced, lightly sprinkled with lemon juice
Plums, small ones left whole
Tangerine, peeled and segmented
Melon, peeled, seeded and cut into cubes or wedges

BATTER
1 egg
140ml/¼ pint/½ cup water
90g/3oz/¾ cup plain/all-purpose flour
60g/2oz/¼ cup cornflour/cornstarch

Clear honey

Orange and Kiwi Jelly

PREPARATION TIME: 20 minutes

SERVES: 4-6 people

430ml/¾ Pint/1½ cups orange juice
140ml/¼ pint/½ cup water

120g/4oz/½ cup sugar
10ml/2 tsps agar-agar
1 or 2 kiwi fruit, peeled

Put orange juice and water into a saucepan and heat until boiling. Remove from the heat and stir in the

This page: Sweet Tempura. Facing page: Orange and Kiwi Jelly.

Prepare fruit before preparing the batter. Pre-heat oil in a deep-fat fryer or wok to 350°F/180°C. Lightly beat egg and stir in the water. Sift in the flour and cornflour/cornstarch and stir in with a table knife. Do not overmix; batter should be lumpy. Dip the fruit into the batter and lower carefully into the hot oil. Cook for 2-3 minutes until lightly golden and crisp. Cook in small batches and cook only one kind of fruit at a time. Drain a few seconds on paper towels. Arrange on serving plates and drizzle with honey. Serve immediately.

Nishiki-Tamago (Brocade Eggs)

PREPARATION TIME: 15 minutes

COOKING TIME: 20 minutes

OVEN TEMPERATURE: 325°F/150°C/Gas Mark 3

10 eggs
200g/7oz/scant 1 cup sugar
Pinch salt

Bring a large saucepan of water to the boil. Carefully lower in the eggs and bring back to the boil. Cook the eggs 10 minutes from the time the water begins to boil. Run cold water over the eggs until they are completely cooled. If prepared in advance, leave in shells in cold water. To prepare, peel eggs and push the whites and yolks through a metal strainer, keeping them separate. Egg whites can be finely chopped in a food processor. Mix the whites with a pinch of salt and about 90g/3oz/⅓ cup of the sugar. Mix the egg yolks with remaining sugar. Place the whites in a square pan and press down lightly. Cover with the yolk mixture and press again. Bake for 10 minutes. Allow to cool completely and cut into 2.5-5cm/1-2 inch pieces.

Sweet Potato and Chestnut Pudding

PREPARATION TIME: 30 minutes

COOKING TIME: 30 minutes

SERVES: 6-8 people

300g/10oz sweet potatoes, peeled and
*   sliced*
120g/4oz can whole chestnuts in syrup
45ml/3 tbsps sugar
30ml/2 tbsps mirin or sherry
15ml/1 tbsp cornflour/cornstarch
60ml/4 tbsps water

Soak sweet potatoes in cold water for 30 minutes. Place in fresh water in a large saucepan. Cover and bring to the boil. Cook about 20 minutes, or until very soft. Drain and dry over low heat, mashing with a fork or potato masher until smooth. Meanwhile drain the chestnuts and reserve the syrup. Mix syrup with sugar and bring slowly to the boil in a heavy-based pan. Cook until the sugar dissolves and mixture thickens slightly. Mix half the syrup with the sweet potatoes. Cook the potatoes again over moderate heat, beating constantly with a wooden spoon until the potatoes thicken. Chop half the chestnuts roughly and add to the potatoes. Mound the pudding into a serving dish and decorate with whole chestnuts. Mix the remaining syrup with the mirin and the cornflour/

cornstarch dissolved in the water. Bring syrup to the boil. Stir and cook until thickened. Allow to cool completely and pour over the pudding to serve.

Almond Sesame Cookies

PREPARATION TIME: 15 minutes

COOKING TIME: 10-20 minutes

OVEN TEMPERATURE: 325°F/ 150°C/Gas Mark 3

MAKES: 20

30ml/2 tbsps sesame oil
120ml/4 fl oz/½ cup water
120g/4oz/1 cup raisins
225g/8oz/1 cup sesame seeds
1 egg, beaten
Few drops almond essence/extract
120g/4oz/½ cup sugar
120g/4oz/1 cup self-raising flour or
  plain/all-purpose flour and 5ml/1 tsp
  baking powder
120g/4oz/1 cup whole-wheat flour
20 whole almonds

Pre-heat oven. Place the sesame oil, water, raisins, sesame seeds, egg and almond essence/extract in a bowl

Facing page: Nishiki-Tamago (Brocade Eggs) (top) and Almond Sesame Cookies (bottom). This page: Sweet Potato and Chestnut Pudding.

and mix well. Sift in sugar, the flours and baking powder, if using and mix to a stiff dough. Divide the mixture into 20 portions and roll each into a ball. Arrange the balls on a greased baking sheet and press an almond into the top of each, flattening them slightly. Bake 10 minutes depending on the number of cookies. The cookies should be crisp and golden when done.

MICROWAVE ENTERTAINING

Introduction

Giving a party is supposed to be fun. Frequently, however, the thought fills some people with terror. The remedy for this is advance planning and dependable equipment, and one appliance that can help enormously is the microwave oven. It comes to the rescue in so many ways, from speedy preparation of sauces to last minute reheating of vegetables. Use it in combination with your labour-saving appliances, such as food processors and blenders, and really make entertaining easy.

Advance preparation is one of the best ways of insuring against that last-minute panic, and the following points are worth considering:

● Be flexible with the menu. Plan ahead, but be prepared to make final decisions depending on what is available and looks best when you are in the shops.

● Buy ingredients that will keep a few days in advance. Buy fresh ingredients the day before the party.

● Make a timetable. Write down the order in which you need to prepare, cook, reheat and serve dishes.

● Prepare starters/appetizers and puddings/desserts in advance and reheat in your microwave oven as necessary at the last minute. If one of the dishes can be served cold, so much the better.

● If the main course is to be accompanied by a sauce, choose one that can be made in advance, and then frozen and reheated successfully.

● Pre-cook main courses if they will not spoil with standing. In particular, poultry can be cooked and then reheated in a sauce, and meat can be browned in advance. One of the great advantages of the microwave is that it reheats without drying out the food.

● Pre-cook rice, potatoes and pasta. All of these reheat successfully in a microwave oven. Choose vegetables that can be parboiled and reheated, too.

● Reheat directly on serving dishes whenever possible, thus saving time and the chore of washing up. The microwave is perfect for this.

● If you forget to take cheese or butter out of the refrigerator, both can be softened by heating on a LOW or DEFROST setting for 15-20 seconds.

When planning your menu, keep colour, texture and shape in mind when choosing the food for each course, so that you have an interesting and varied meal. Also keep in mind the style of each dish; for example, don't choose an informal starter to precede a very formal main course and dessert.

While you are unlikely to forget that white wine goes with fish and white meats and that red wine should be served with red meats, you may be surprised at how pleasant the combination of a light red wine and salmon can be. Even though chicken and veal are white meats, if they are served in a dark, rich sauce they need a red wine. Smoked fish or spicy food can present a problem, but a Hock or Alsace wine is a good choice when a white wine is necessary. If choosing a dessert wine confuses you, remember that Champagne is always delicious!

With a well-planned menu and a microwave oven in the kitchen, you will have more time to enjoy yourself with your guests. Entertaining will be more "entertaining".

All the recipes in this book were prepared in an oven with a 700 watt maximum output. For 500 watt ovens add 40 seconds for each minute stated in the recipe. For 600 watt ovens add 20 seconds for each minute stated in the recipe. If using a 650 watt oven only a slight increase in overall time is necessary.

Dinner Party Menus

MENU 1

Garlic Vegetables

PREPARATION TIME: 15 minutes

MICROWAVE COOKING TIME:
11-14 minutes plus standing time

SERVES: 6 people

1 small head cauliflower, broken into
 small flowerets
120g/4oz broccoli
60g/2oz mangetout/pea pods
½ red pepper, seeded and finely sliced
½ yellow pepper, seeded and finely sliced
4 spring/green onions, thinly sliced on the
 diagonal

DRESSING
140ml/¼ pint/½ cup prepared
 mayonnaise
2 cloves garlic, crushed
15ml/1 tbsp chopped parsley and chives,
 mixed
Pinch salt and pepper

GARNISH
1 hard-boiled egg, finely chopped

Place the cauliflower flowerets in a casserole with 60ml/4 tbsps salted water. Cover and cook on HIGH for 6-8 minutes, cut the broccoli spears into flowerets the same size as the cauliflower and keep the stalks for other use or discard. Place in a casserole with 30ml/2 tbsps salted water and cover loosely. Cook on HIGH for 4-5 minutes. Top and tail the mangetout/pea pods and add to the broccoli 1-2 minutes before the end of cooking time. Drain all the vegetables and combine with the sliced red and yellow pepper and the

spring/green onions. Mix all the dressing ingredients together and stir carefully into the vegetables. Place the vegetables on serving plates and heat through for 1 minute on HIGH. Top with the chopped hard-boiled egg before serving. Surround with lettuce leaves or shredded lettuce if desired. Serve with French bread or melba toast.

Involtini alla Romana

PREPARATION TIME: 30 minutes

MICROWAVE COOKING TIME:
15-19 minutes

SERVES: 6 people

6 veal escalopes (about 120-180g/4-6oz
 each)
6 slices Parma ham
225g/8oz garlic cheese
15ml/1 tbsp chopped fresh oregano or
 basil or 7.5ml/½ tbsp dried
Salt and pepper

SAUCE
300g/14oz canned tomatoes
1 onion, roughly chopped
Salt and pepper
1 bay leaf
Pinch nutmeg
60ml/4 tbsps dry white wine
6 tomatoes, peeled, seeded and cut into
 thin strips
15ml/1 tbsp chopped parsley
Grated Parmesan cheese (optional)

Flatten the veal between 2 sheets of greaseproof/wax paper using a rolling pin or meat mallet. Place a slice of

Parma ham on top of each veal escalope. Mix the cheese and the marjoram together and divide evenly among the veal escalopes. Place the cheese in the middle and roll the veal and ham around the cheese. Arrange in a circle in a dish and cook, uncovered, on HIGH for 8-10 minutes. Set aside while preparing the sauce. Combine all the ingredients except the chopped parsley, the tomato strips and cheese in a small, deep bowl. Cook on HIGH, uncovered, for 6-8 minutes or until the onion has softened and the sauce has reduced. Purée in a food processor or blender and sieve out the seeds. Arrange veal in a serving dish, pour over the sauce and sprinkle on the chopped parsley and the tomato strips. Reheat for 1 minute on HIGH before serving. Sprinkle with cheese, if desired. Serve with pasta or Italian rice.

Zabaglione

PREPARATION TIME: 25 minutes

MICROWAVE COOKING TIME:
3½ minutes

SERVES: 6 people

140ml/¼ pint/½ cup marsala or sweet
 sherry
6 egg yolks
45g/3 tbsps sugar

**Menu 1: Zabaglione (top left),
Involtini alla Romana (top right)
and Garlic Vegetables (bottom).**

10ml/2 tsps grated lemon rind
4-6 large peaches, nectarines or apricots, peeled
Lemon juice

Microwave meringues, crushed

Peel the peaches or nectarines according to the recipe for Peches Melba. Crush 3 or 4 meringues coarsely or use ratafia biscuits. Place the meringues or biscuits in the bottom of each of 6 dessert glasses. Cut the fruit in half and remove the stones. Slice thinly, toss in lemon juice and divide the fruit among the glasses. To prepare the zabaglione pour the marsala into a glass measure and microwave on HIGH for 30-45 seconds. Whisk the egg yolks, sugar and lemon rind together in a large bowl and then gradually whisk in the hot liqueur. Microwave the mixture on LOW or DEFROST for 1½ minutes, remove and whisk well and then continue to cook on the same setting for a further 1½ minutes, whisking halfway through the cooking time. Whisk again briefly and then spoon the mixture on top of the fruit and meringues or biscuits. Sprinkle with grated nutmeg if desired.

MENU 2

Salmon Quenelles

PREPARATION TIME: 10-15 minutes

MICROWAVE COOKING TIME: 20-21 minutes

SERVES: 4 people

450g/1lb salmon
1 bay leaf
1 slice onion
1 blade mace
140ml/¼ pint/½ cup water
3 slices bread, crusts removed
45ml/3 tbsps double/heavy cream
2 egg whites
Salt and pepper

SAUCE
120g/4oz/½ cup butter
2 egg yolks
15ml/1 tbsp white wine vinegar
15ml/1 tbsp lemon juice
15ml/1 tbsp green peppercorns, drained and rinsed if packed in brine
30ml/2 tbsps double/heavy cream
Salt and pepper

Skin the salmon and remove any bones. Place the skin with the bones, bay leaf, onion slice, blade mace and water in a bowl. Cook, uncovered, on HIGH 2-3 minutes or until boiling. Reduce the setting and cook for 10 minutes on LOW. Strain the liquid and make-up to 90ml/6 tbsps with water if necessary. If the liquid exceeds 90ml/6 tbsps, continue cooking on HIGH until reduced. Cut up the fish and purée in a food processor with the bread, egg whites and fish cooking liquid. Blend in the cream by hand and season with salt and pepper. Pour 570ml/1 pint/ 2 cups of hot water into a large, shallow dish. Cook on HIGH for 2-3 minutes or until very hot or boiling. Divide the fish mixture into equal portions and shape into ovals using 2 spoons. Place spaced well apart into the hot water and cover the dish. Cook on HIGH for 6 minutes, repositioning the fish quenelles halfway through cooking. Leave to stand while preparing the sauce. Melt the butter for 1½ minutes on HIGH and beat the egg yolks with the remaining ingredients. Whisk the egg yolks into the hot butter and cook on MEDIUM for 1 minute, stirring after 15 seconds. Do not allow the sauce to boil. If the sauce begins to curdle, place the bowl in another bowl of iced water to stop the cooking. Continue cooking the sauce for the remaining 15 seconds or until thickened. Stir in the peppercorns and cream. Serve with the salmon quenelles.

Lemon Duckling

PREPARATION TIME: 30 minutes plus marinating time

MICROWAVE COOKING TIME: 30 minutes

SERVES: 6 people

6 duck breast fillets, about 180g/6oz each

MARINADE
30ml/2 tbsps vegetable oil
Juice of 2 lemons
1 clove garlic, crushed
2.5ml/½ tsp ground coriander
Salt and pepper
15ml/1 tbsp chopped parsley
1 bay leaf

SAUCE
Zest of 4 lemons
2 lemons segmented
10ml/2 tsps cornflour/cornstarch
25ml/1½ tbsps water
140ml/¼ pint/½ cup chicken stock
15ml/1 tbsp soy sauce
10ml/2 tsps honey
Pinch salt and pepper

Wipe the duck breasts with paper towels and then score the skin to make a diamond pattern. Combine the marinade ingredients in a shallow dish or plastic bag, add the duck and turn to coat well. Cover and leave in the refrigerator for 4 hours, turning occasionally. Drain and reserve the marinade, discarding the bay leaf. Heat a browning dish according to the manufacturer's directions. Place the duck breasts skin side down three at a time on the dish and cook on HIGH for 3 minutes. Turn over and cook for a further 10 minutes, rearranging the duck once or twice

Menu 2: Fig and Apricot Charlottes (top), Lemon Duckling (centre) and Salmon Quenelles (bottom).

during cooking. Leave to stand for 5 minutes while cooking the second batch. If desired, the duck may be browned under a preheated grill/broiler for 1-2 minutes for crisper skin. Mix cornflour/cornstarch and water in a small, deep bowl. Add the reserved marinade and stock and cook on HIGH for 2 minutes, stirring once or twice. Add the lemon segments, zest, soy sauce and honey. Pour the sauce over the duck to serve and garnish with lemon slices and fresh coriander if desired. Serve with rice.

Fig and Apricot Charlottes

PREPARATION TIME: 25 minutes

MICROWAVE COOKING TIME: 1-2 minutes plus standing time

SERVES: 6 people

225g/8oz dried figs
225g/8oz dried apricots
140ml/¼ pint/½ cup brandy
450g/1lb cream or curd cheese
140ml/¼ pint/½ cup thick natural yogurt
45ml/3 tbsps honey
Halved toasted almonds
140ml/¼ pint/½ cup double/heavy
  cream
Nutmeg

Place the figs and the apricots in a deep bowl with the brandy and heat for 30 seconds-1 minute on HIGH. Leave to stand, covered, 2-3 minutes. Drain off the brandy and reserve. Place a circle of greaseproof/wax paper in the bottom of 6 individual ramekins/custard cups. Cut the figs

in half and press them flat. Press the apricots to flatten slightly. Use the fruit to line the sides of the dishes, seed side of the fig inside. Soften the cream or curd cheese for 30 seconds-1 minute on MEDIUM. Stir in the yogurt, honey and the reserved brandy. Spoon the mixture into the moulds, pressing down firmly against the base and the fruit lining the sides. Fold any fruit ends over the cheese filling and chill or freeze. To serve from frozen, leave overnight in a refrigerator and then at room temperature for 1 hour before serving. Turn the charlottes out onto a serving plate and carefully pour cream around the base of each. Remove the paper circles from the top and decorate with toasted almonds. Sprinkle nutmeg on the cream.

MENU 3

Broad Beans, Scallops and Bacon

PREPARATION TIME: 25 minutes

MICROWAVE COOKING TIME: 17-20 minutes

SERVES: 6 people

675g/1½ lbs shelled fresh or frozen
  broad/lima beans
6 rashers bacon/smoked streaky bacon,
  rind and bones removed
12 scallops, roes attached if possible

DRESSING
60ml/4 tbsps oil
1 shallot, finely chopped
25ml/1½ tbsps white wine vinegar
10ml/2 tsps Dijon mustard
Pinch sugar
Salt and pepper
5ml/1 tsp chopped thyme, parsley or
  chervil

Combine the broad/lima beans with 90-120ml/6-8 tbsps hot water in a casserole. Cover and cook on HIGH for 5-6 minutes. Leave to stand,

covered, while preparing the remaining ingredients. Place the bacon on a microwave rack or between 2-3 layers of paper towels on a plate. Cook on HIGH for 4-5 minutes, turning over halfway through. Leave to stand and, when cool, crumble or chop coarsely. Place the scallops in a circle in a shallow dish or casserole and cover the top loosely. Cook on MEDIUM for 7-8 minutes or until just firm. In a medium size bowl combine the oil and the shallot and cook for 1 minute on HIGH, or until the shallot is just softened. Leave to cool and combine with the remaining dressing ingredients. If the broad/lima beans are old, peel off the outer skins. If they are young, tender beans the outer skin may be left on. Add the beans and the bacon to the dressing and set aside. Cut the scallops in half through the middle or cut the white muscles into quarters and leave the roes whole. Add to the broad/lima beans and the bacon in the dressing and cover the bowl. Heat through on HIGH for 1 minute and serve

immediately on a bed of lettuce, radicchio, curly endive or lambs lettuce (mache).

Chicken Veronique

PREPARATION TIME: 35 minutes

MICROWAVE COOKING TIME: 40-50 minutes

SERVES: 6 people

6 boned chicken breasts, skinned
250ml/7 fl oz/scant 1 cup white wine
1 bay leaf
6 black peppercorns
1 slice onion
30g/2 tbsps butter or margarine
25g/1½ tbsps flour
10ml/2 tsps chopped fresh tarragon or
  5ml/1 tsp dried tarragon
Salt and pepper
140ml/¼ pint/1 cup single/light cream
180g/6oz white/green seedless grapes
Salt and white pepper

Menu 3: Fruit Shortcake (top), Chicken Veronique (centre) and Broad Beans, Scallops and Bacon (bottom).

ALMOND RICE PILAF
30g/1oz/2 tbsps butter or margarine
60g/2oz/½ cup flaked/sliced almonds
1 medium onion, finely chopped
Pinch saffron
225g/8oz/1 cup long grain rice
430ml/¾ pint/1½ cups hot chicken stock or water

Place the chicken in a casserole with the wine, bay leaf, peppercorns and onion slice. Cover with pierced cling film/plastic wrap and cook on HIGH for 20-25 minutes or until the juices from the chicken run clear. Melt the butter for the sauce for 30 seconds on HIGH and stir in the flour. Strain on the chicken cooking liquid and stir in gradually. Add salt, pepper and tarragon and cook on HIGH for 3-5 minutes, or until thickened. Stir in the cream, add the grapes and leave the sauce to stand, covered, while preparing the pilaf. Melt the butter or margarine in a large bowl or casserole and add the almonds. Cook on HIGH for 1-2 minutes or until the almonds begin to brown. Add the onion and cook a further 2 minutes to soften the onion and to brown the almonds. Add the saffron, rice and hot stock or water. Stir well and cover the bowl. Cook on HIGH for 13-14 minutes, stirring occasionally. Leave to stand for 10 minutes before serving. To serve, place 1 chicken breast on each serving dish, loosely cover and reheat for 1-2 minutes on HIGH. Reheat the sauce for 1 minute on HIGH and coat some over each chicken breast. Serve the rest of the sauce separately and place a portion of almond rice pilaf on each serving plate. Garnish each serving with mint leaves and small bunches of grapes if desired.

Fruit Shortcake

PREPARATION TIME: 35 minutes	
MICROWAVE COOKING TIME: 9½ minutes	
SERVES: 6 people	

PASTRY
225g/8oz/2 cups plain/all-purpose flour
15ml/1 tbsp ground cinnamon
60g/4 tbsps icing/powdered sugar
150g/5oz/½ cup plus 2 tbsps butter or margarine, softened

TOPPING
280ml/½ pint/1 cup redcurrant jelly
450g/1lb strawberries, raspberries or blackberries
140ml/¼ pint/½ cup whipped cream
Shelled pistachio nuts or angelica, washed and cut into small diamonds

Sift the flour, cinnamon and sugar together, rub in the butter until the mixture is like fine breadcrumbs or work in a food processor. Place a circle of greaseproof/wax paper in the bottom of a 29cm/9 inch round dish. Press in the mixture and smooth down firmly. Cook on LOW or DEFROST for 8 minutes. If brown spots form, cover them with small pieces of foil and continue cooking. The shortcake is done when a skewer inserted into the centre of the cake comes out clean. Cool for at least 1 hour in the baking dish. Remove the shortcake and place on a serving plate. Melt the redcurrant jelly in a small bowl on HIGH for 1 minute. Stir and then push through a strainer into a clean bowl. Brush a thin layer of jelly to within 1.25cm/½ inch of the edge of the pastry and allow to set slightly. Arrange the fruit on top of the jelly. If the strawberries are large, cut in half and place cut side down on the jelly. Reheat the jelly 30 seconds on HIGH and stir. Brush the fruit with a thin layer of jelly, making sure the holes between the fruit are filled with jelly. Allow to set and cool completely. Pipe rosettes of cream around the outside edge of the fruit and decorate with nuts or angelica.

Menu 4: Petits Vacherins (top), Veal with Wild Mushrooms (centre) and Jerusalem Artichoke Soup (bottom).

MENU 4

Jerusalem Artichoke Soup

PREPARATION TIME: 25 minutes

MICROWAVE COOKING TIME:
8-9 minutes

SERVES: 6 people

225g/8oz Jerusalem artichokes, peeled
    and sliced
2 potatoes, peeled and sliced
1 litre/1¾ pints/3½ cups chicken or
    vegetable stock
Salt and pepper
30g/1oz/2 tbsps butter (optional)
140ml/¼ pint/½ cup whipping cream

GARNISH
1 small jar red caviar
90ml/6 tbsps thick yogurt
30ml/2 tbsps chopped fresh chives

Place the artichokes and potatoes in a large, deep bowl. Cover the bowl loosely with cling film/plastic wrap and cook on HIGH for 6 minutes or until soft. Add the stock, salt and pepper and the butter if using. Cover and cook 8 minutes on HIGH or until the stock just comes to the boil. Allow to cool slightly and pour into a food processor or blender and purée until smooth. Add the cream and adjust the seasoning. Reheat for 2-3 minutes on HIGH before serving and garnish each serving with a spoonful of yogurt, 2.5ml/½ tsp red caviar and some chives.

Veal with Wild Mushrooms

PREPARATION TIME: 25 minutes

MICROWAVE COOKING TIME:
14-15 minutes

SERVES: 6 people

900g/2lbs veal, cut in large chunks
12 oyster or other wild mushrooms
60g/2oz/4 tbsps butter or margarine
60g/2oz/4 tbsps Dijon mustard
60g/2oz/4 tbsps honey
60g/2oz/4 tbsps Worcestershire sauce

VEGETABLE ACCOMPANIMENT
225g/8oz salsify, peeled and cut into
    7.5cm/3 inch pieces
3 carrots, peeled and cut to the same size
    as the salsify
½ a celeriac root, peeled and cut into
    strips
15ml/1 tbsp chopped parsley
15ml/1 tbsp fresh rosemary leaves
60ml/4 tbsps double/heavy cream

Mix together the mustard, honey, Worcestershire sauce and veal. Heat a browning dish according to the manufacturer's directions and melt the butter. When foaming, add the veal in small batches, pressing down firmly on one side, turning over and pressing down again to seal both sides. Cook in 2 batches. Cook on HIGH for 5 minutes. Add the mushrooms and cook 1 minute on HIGH, cover and keep them warm. Combine the meat juices with all of the vegetables and toss well to coat. Add the herbs and salt and pepper and microwave, uncovered, on HIGH for 2 minutes. Cover and continue cooking on HIGH for 6 minutes or until the salsify is tender. Stir in the cream. Reheat the veal for 1-2 minutes on HIGH and serve with the vegetables.

Petits Vacherins

PREPARATION TIME: 20 minutes

MICROWAVE COOKING TIME:
6 minutes

SERVES: 6 people

MERINGUES
1 egg white
450g/1lb/4 cups icing/powdered sugar
45g/1½ oz/approximately ¼ cup finely
    chopped walnuts

SAUCE
340g/12oz raspberries
Lemon juice to taste
Icing/powdered sugar to taste

TOPPING
180ml/6 fl oz/¾ cup whipping cream
Walnut halves
Reserved raspberries

To make the meringues, put the egg white into a bowl and whisk lightly with a fork. Add enough of the icing/powdered sugar, sifted, to give a firm, pliable dough. It may not be necessary to add all the sugar. Keep the mixture covered while shaping the meringues. Put out a portion on a surface dusted with more icing/powdered sugar and form a sausage about the thickness of a little finger. Cut into 2.5cm/1 inch pieces and place well apart on greaseproof/wax paper on a plate or microwave baking sheet. Cook for about 1 minute or until dry and crisp. Reserve 6-12 raspberries for decoration and put the rest into a food processor or blender with the lemon juice. Purée until smooth and add sugar to taste. Process again to mix the sugar and sieve the sauce to remove the seeds. Divide the sauce equally among 6 dessert plates and place a meringue on top of the sauce on each plate. Crush 6 of the meringues and set aside. Any remaining meringues may be frozen or stored in an airtight container. Whip the cream and pipe on top of each meringue. Sprinkle with the reserved crushed meringue and decorate with walnut halves and the reserved raspberries.

MENU 5

Oeufs en Croustade

PREPARATION TIME: 30 minutes

MICROWAVE COOKING TIME:
22-24 minutes

SERVES: 6 people

12 slices wholemeal/whole-wheat bread,
  crusts removed
90g/3oz/6 tbsps butter

FILLING
120g/4oz mushrooms, finely chopped
1 shallot, finely chopped
10ml/2 tsps butter or margarine
10ml/2 tsps flour
15ml/1 tbsp sherry
60ml/4 tbsps single/light cream
12 quail eggs

SAUCE
15g/½ oz/1 tbsp butter or margarine
15g/½ oz/1 tbsp flour
140ml/¼ pint/½ cup milk
5ml/1 tsp chopped parsley
1 small cap pimento, finely chopped
Salt and pepper
Paprika

Roll the slices of bread to flatten. Cut into 7.5cm/3 inch rounds with a pastry cutter. Melt the butter for 30 seconds on HIGH and brush over both sides of the bread rounds. Mould into small ramekins/custard cups and cook for 3 minutes on HIGH until crisp. Remove from the ramekins/custard cups and place on a serving plate. Combine the mushrooms, shallot and butter for the filling in a small bowl and heat for 2-3 minutes on HIGH, or until the shallot is soft and the mushrooms are cooked. Stir in the flour and add the sherry and cream. Season lightly with salt and pepper and cook on HIGH for 2-3 minutes or until thickened. Allow to cool slightly. Melt the butter for the sauce for 30 seconds on HIGH and stir in the flour. Beat in the milk gradually until smooth and cook for 2-3 minutes on HIGH, or until thickened. Add the parsley and the pimento, season lightly with salt and pepper and set aside, with cling film/plastic wrap pressed directly over the sauce. Bring water in a shallow dish to the boil with 5ml/1 tsp vinegar and a pinch of salt. This should take about 8 minutes. Carefully break each quail egg onto a saucer and gently lower the egg into the water. Return to the oven and cook on HIGH for 30 seconds-1 minute or until nearly set. Leave to stand for 1-2 minutes to complete cooking. Eggs may be cooked in advance and kept in cold water. Place the mushroom mixture in the bottom of each tartlet shell. Drain the quail eggs and place 1 egg in each tartlet. Spoon over the sauce and dust lightly with paprika. Arrange the tartlets in a circle on a serving dish and heat through for 1-2 minutes on MEDIUM. Serve immediately.

Quail with Garlic and Green Olives

PREPARATION TIME: 30 minutes

MICROWAVE COOKING TIME:
23-34 minutes

SERVES: 6 people

6 quail
60g/2oz/4 tbsps butter or margarine
6 cloves garlic
280ml/½ pint/1 cup brown stock
140ml/¼ pint/½ cup dry white wine
25ml/1½ tbsps cornflour/cornstarch
2.5ml/½ tsp thyme
15ml/1 tbsp chopped parsley
Salt and pepper
18 large green olives, pitted and quartered
5ml/1 tsp Dijon mustard
Salt and pepper

POMMES PAILLASSON
60g/2oz/4 tbsps butter or margarine
450g/1lb potatoes, peeled and coarsely grated
Salt and pepper

First prepare the potatoes. Melt the butter in a round, glass dish for 1½ minutes on HIGH. Layer in the grated potatoes, pressing down well and seasoning in between each layer. Loosely cover the dish with cling film/plastic wrap and cook on HIGH for 10-15 minutes. Set aside while preparing the quail. Heat a browning dish according to the manufacturer's directions. Melt the butter and when foaming brown the quail, 2 at a time, on HIGH for 2-3 minutes. Combine all the remaining ingredients except the olives in a casserole dish and add the quail and the juices from the browning dish. Cover and cook on HIGH for a further 6-8 minutes. Stir the sauce occasionally while the quail are cooking. To serve, turn out the potatoes onto a heatproof serving dish and brown the top under a preheated grill/broiler. Remove the quail from the sauce and trim them if necessary. Arrange the quail on top of the potato cake, cover and keep warm. Purée the sauce in a food processor or blender until the garlic is completely broken down. Sieve if desired and add the olives. Season with salt and pepper and reheat the sauce on HIGH for 1-2 minutes. Spoon some of the sauce over the quail to serve and serve the rest of the sauce separately. Serve with a green vegetable or carrots in parsley butter.

Chocolate Orange Mousse

PREPARATION TIME: 20 minutes

MICROWAVE COOKING TIME:
4-5 minutes

SERVES: 6 people

180g/6oz plain/semi-sweet chocolate
280ml/½ pint/1 cup double/heavy cream
1 egg
Grated rind of half an orange
10ml/2 tsps orange juice

DECORATION
Orange rind cut into thin strips
140ml/¼ pint/½ cup double/heavy cream, whipped

Menu 5: Oeufs en Croustade (below), Quail with Garlic and Green Olives (bottom) and Chocolate Orange Mousse (far right).

Chop the chocolate into small pieces and combine with the cream. Heat on HIGH for 2-3 minutes, stirring frequently until the chocolate has melted and the mixture is smooth. Beat the egg with the orange rind and juice and gradually beat in the chocolate mixture. Pour into 6 individual dessert dishes and heat for 1 minute on HIGH to thicken. Chill until set. To serve, whip the remaining cream and pipe 1 rosette on top of each serving dish. Place the strips of orange rind in a small bowl with 60ml/4 tbsps water and heat for 1 minute on HIGH to soften. Drain and rinse under cold water and pat dry. Sprinkle on top of the mousse to serve.

MENU 6

Avocado and Chicken Livers

PREPARATION TIME: 25 minutes

MICROWAVE COOKING TIME: 4½-5½ minutes

SERVES: 6 people

2 ripe avocados
225g/8oz chicken livers
30ml/1oz/2 tbsps butter or margarine
1 shallot, finely chopped
15ml/1 tbsp sherry
4-6 tomatoes, peeled, seeded and thinly sliced

DRESSING
120ml/8 tbsps oil
Juice of 1 small lemon
10ml/2 tsps chopped fresh herbs
Pinch sugar
Salt and pepper
1 head curly endive

Heat a browning dish according to the manufacturer's instructions. Pick over the chicken livers and trim away any discoloured parts. Melt the butter in the browning dish and add the chicken livers, tossing to coat well. Add the shallot and cook on HIGH for 4-5 minutes, or until the shallot is softened and the livers are just barely pink inside. Pour over the sherry and set aside. Cut the avocados in half and remove the stones. Peel and cut each avocado half into thin slices. Combine all the dressing ingredients and mix with the tomatoes. Arrange a bed of curly endive on each serving plate and place the avocados on top so that the slices form a fan. Spoon over the dressing. Slice the chicken livers thinly and place a portion at the bottom of each avocado fan along with some tomato slices. Loosely cover the dishes and reheat for 30 seconds on HIGH before serving.

Monkfish Medallions Paprika

PREPARATION TIME: 25 minutes

MICROWAVE COOKING TIME: 16-19 minutes

SERVES: 6 people

450g/1lb monkfish tails, skinned and cut into 1.25cm/½ inch slices
90ml/6 tbsps white wine
1 red pepper, seeded and sliced
140ml/¼ pint/½ cup double/heavy cream
15ml/1 tbsp paprika
15ml/1 tbsp cornflour/cornstarch
Salt and pepper
225g/8oz fresh pasta
570ml/1 pint/2 cups boiling water
15ml/1 tbsp oil
Pinch salt

Place the sliced monkfish and the wine in a shallow dish and cover loosely with cling film/plastic wrap. Cook on HIGH for 4 minutes. Place the red pepper in a deep bowl, cover loosely and cook on HIGH for 1-2 minutes to soften. Add the double/heavy cream and paprika and cook on HIGH for 2-3 minutes. Mix the cornflour/cornstarch with the cooking liquid from the fish and add the cream and pepper. Add a pinch of salt and pepper to taste and cook on HIGH for a further 2-3 minutes or until thickened. Cover and set aside while preparing the pasta. Pour the boiling water into a deep bowl, add a pinch of salt and the pasta. Loosely cover and cook on HIGH for 6 minutes. Leave to stand for 3 minutes before draining. Place the pasta in a serving dish and arrange the monkfish slices on top. Pour over the sauce to serve. If necessary, reheat on HIGH for 1-2 minutes.

Oeufs à la Neige

PREPARATION TIME: 25 minutes

MICROWAVE COOKING TIME: 23-26 minutes

SERVES: 6 people

MERINGUE
2 egg whites
45g/3 tbsps sugar
2 drops vanilla essence/extract

ORANGE CUSTARD
430ml/¾ pint/1½ cups milk
Grated rind of ½ an orange
15g/1 tbsp sugar
4 egg yolks
2.5ml/½ tsp cornflour/cornstarch

CARAMEL TOPPING
90g/6 tbsps sugar
90ml/6 tbsps water

Menu 6: Oeufs à la Neige (top), Monkfish Medallions Paprika (centre) and Avocado and Chicken Livers (bottom).

To make the meringues, whisk the egg whites until stiff but not dry. Add the sugar gradually, whisking continuously until the meringue is stiff, smooth and shiny. Fill a large, shallow dish with hot water. Shape the meringue with 2 damp tablespoons into egg shapes and slide them carefully onto the hot water. Cook on LOW or DEFROST for 2-3 minutes. Turn the meringues over and cook again on LOW or DEFROST for a further 2-3 minutes.

Heat the milk and the orange rind for the custard on HIGH for 2 minutes. Beat the sugar, egg yolks and cornflour/cornstarch until light, and gradually pour on the milk, beating constantly. Cook the custard on LOW or DEFROST for about 12 minutes, stirring every 30 seconds. Remove the custard when it coats the back of a spoon. Pour into a large serving dish or individual dishes and chill. Carefully float the meringues on top of the custard. To prepare the caramel topping, combine the sugar and water in a small, deep bowl and cook on HIGH for 5-6 minutes until golden. Do not allow the syrup to become too dark as it will continue to cook after it is removed from the oven. Dip the caramel bowl into another bowl of cold water to stop the cooking and to thicken the caramel slightly. Using a fork, drizzle the caramel over the meringues on top of the custard and allow it to set before serving.

MENU 7

Watercress Soup

PREPARATION TIME: 20 minutes

MICROWAVE COOKING TIME: 14-17 minutes

SERVES: 6 people

4 medium-sized potatoes, peeled and
    thinly sliced
1 small onion, finely chopped
30g/1oz/2 tbsps butter or margarine
1 litre/1¼ pints/3½ cups vegetable or
    chicken stock
1 bay leaf
Salt and pepper
2 bunches watercress, well washed and
    thick stems removed
140ml/¼ pint/½ cup double/heavy
    cream
Nutmeg

GARNISH
Reserved small watercress leaves

Place the potatoes, onion and butter into a large, deep bowl and loosely cover with cling film/plastic wrap. Cook on HIGH for 4-6 minutes or until the potatoes and onions are beginning to soften. Pour on the stock and add the bay leaf, salt and pepper. Re-cover the bowl and cook a further 8 minutes on HIGH or until the stock just comes to the boil. Allow to cool slightly and pour into a food processor or blender. Reserve 6 small sprigs of watercress for garnish and roughly chop the rest.

Place the watercress in the blender or food processor with the soup and purée until smooth. The soup should be lightly flecked with green. Add the cream to the soup and adjust the seasoning. Add a pinch of nutmeg and reheat on HIGH 2-3 minutes before serving. Garnish with the small watercress leaves.

Plié a l'Indienne

PREPARATION TIME: 25 minutes

MICROWAVE COOKING TIME: 9½ minutes

SERVES: 6 people

12 plaice/flounder fillets
1 bay leaf
1 slice onion
6 black peppercorns
250ml/7 fl oz/scant 1 cup water
30g/1oz/2 tbsps butter or margarine
25g/1½ tbsps flour
7.5-15ml/½-1 tbsp mild curry powder
5ml/1 tsp turmeric
Salt and pepper
60ml/4 tbsps single/light cream
1 small can pineapple pieces

GARNISH
Toasted almonds
Desiccated coconut

Place the fish in a shallow dish with the bay leaf, onion slice, peppercorns and water. Loosely cover with cling film/plastic wrap and cook on HIGH for 4 minutes. Leave to stand while preparing the sauce. Melt the butter for 30 seconds on HIGH and stir in the flour. Strain on the fish cooking liquid and add the curry powder, turmeric and salt and pepper. Cook on HIGH for 5 minutes. Stir in the cream and drained pineapple, cover and set aside. Place the fish in a serving dish or on individual plates and coat with the sauce. Sprinkle with toasted almonds and desiccated coconut. Serve with rice.

Almond Float with Fresh Fruit

PREPARATION TIME: 25 minutes

MICROWAVE COOKING TIME: 13-15 minutes

SERVES: 6 people

15g/1 tbsp gelatine
60ml/4 tbsps cold water
140ml/¼ pint/½ cup milk
15ml/1 tbsp sugar
1.25ml/½ tsp almond essence/extract
Few drops red food colouring (optional)

Menu 7: Almond Float with Fresh Fruit (top), Plié a l'Indienne (centre) and Watercress Soup (bottom).

Assortment of fruits such as lychees,
  peeled, kiwi fruit, peeled and sliced, star
  fruit, thinly sliced, kumquats, thinly
  sliced, papayas, peeled, seeded and
  thinly sliced or cut into cubes, melon,
  peeled, seeded and thinly sliced or cut
  into cubes

SYRUP
120g/4oz/½ cup sugar
280ml/½ pint/1 cup water
Almond essence/extract or amaretto
  (almond liqueur)

Sprinkle the gelatine over the water
in a small bowl or cup and leave to
soften for 5 minutes. Melt on HIGH
for 15-20 seconds or until clear. Mix
the milk with an equal amount of
water and add the sugar. Heat for 2-3
minutes on HIGH to dissolve the
sugar. Allow to cool and stir in the
gelatine and the almond essence/
extract and colouring if using, and
pour into a shallow, rectangular dish.
Chill in the refrigerator until set.
Meanwhile, prepare the syrup.
Combine the water and sugar in a
deep bowl and stir well. Cook on
HIGH for 8-10 minutes or until the
sugar is completely dissolved and the
syrup is boiling. Do not allow the
syrup to brown. Check carefully, it
may be necessary to remove the
syrup from the oven before the end
of cooking time. Leave to cool
completely and add the almond
essence/extract or amaretto. Chill
the syrup completely and, when the
almond float is set and the syrup is
cold, prepare the fruit as directed.
Cut the almond float into diamond
shapes about 7.5cm/3 inches in
length. Place 2 diamond shapes on
each of 6 serving plates and arrange
an assortment of fruit around them.
Spoon over the syrup to serve.

MENU 8

French Beans, Pâté and Mushrooms

PREPARATION TIME: 20 minutes
MICROWAVE COOKING TIME: 9½-11 minutes
SERVES: 6 people

450g/1lb young French/green beans
225g/8oz mushrooms
120g/4oz firm pâté

DRESSING
60ml/4 tbsps oil
1 clove garlic, crushed
10ml/2 tsps chopped chives
5ml/1 tsp chopped parsley
25ml/1½ tsps white wine vinegar
Salt and pepper

Cook the French/green beans in
30ml/2 tbsps salted water for 6
minutes on HIGH. Stir occasionally
and leave to stand for 1-2 minutes.
The beans should still be crisp.
While the beans are standing,
combine the mushrooms with half of
the measured oil from the dressing in
a small bowl and cook on HIGH for
1-2 minutes or until just softened.
Slice the pâté into thin strips or cut
into small cubes. Combine the
remaining dressing ingredients with
the mushrooms and toss with the
French/green beans. Add the pâté
and mix carefully. Heat through on
HIGH for 30 seconds-1 minute
before serving. Pile the mixture onto
serving plates lined with lettuce
leaves if desired.

Sole d'Epinard

PREPARATION TIME: 30 minutes
MICROWAVE COOKING TIME: 14-17 minutes
SERVES: 6 people

FILLING
225g/8oz fresh spinach, stems removed
  and well washed
Salt and pepper
Nutmeg
3 slices white bread, crusts removed and
  made into crumbs
1 egg white
30ml/2 tbsps double/heavy cream

6 double fillets of sole
60ml/4 tbsps dry white wine

SAUCE
30g/1oz/2 tbsps butter
30g/1oz/2 tbsps flour
280ml/½ pint/1 cup milk
Juice and rind of 1 lemon
Salt and pepper

TOPPING
Parmesan cheese, grated
Dry breadcrumbs

GARNISH
Lemon slices

Cook the spinach for 4 minutes on
HIGH in a roasting bag or casserole,
well covered. Drain and chop in a
food processor with the salt and
pepper, nutmeg and breadcrumbs.
Add the egg white and process once
or twice to mix. Stir in the cream by
hand. Spread evenly over the fish
fillets and fold or roll up. Place fish in
a dish in a circle with the wine and
cover with cling film/plastic wrap.
Cook on HIGH for 4-5 minutes.
Melt the butter for 30 seconds on
HIGH and add the flour. Strain in
the cooking liquid from the fish, add
the milk and beat well. Cook on
HIGH 3-5 minutes until thickened.
Add the lemon rind and juice, salt
and pepper. Arrange the sole in a
serving dish and pour over the sauce.
Mix the Parmesan cheese and the
breadcrumbs together and sprinkle
over the top. Brown under a
preheated grill/broiler or cook a

**Menu 8: Tartelettes aux Fruits (top),
Sole d'Epinard (centre) and French
Beans, Pâté and Mushrooms
(bottom).**

further 2 minutes on HIGH. Garnish with lemon slices. Serve with boiled potatoes or rice.

Tartelettes aux Fruits

PREPARATION TIME: 40 minutes	
MICROWAVE COOKING TIME: 5½-8 minutes	
SERVES: 6 people	

PASTRY
120g/4oz/1 cup plain/all-purpose flour
*30g/2 tbsps toasted ground hazelnuts or
   almonds*
75g/2½ oz/5 tbsps butter or margarine
10ml/2 tsps sugar
1 egg yolk

FILLING
280ml/½ pint/1 cup milk
2 egg yolks
60g/4 tbsps sugar
30g/2 tbsps cornflour/cornstarch
1.25ml/¼ tsp almond essence/extract

TOPPING
*Selection of fresh fruit such as white or
   black grapes, strawberries, satsumas,
   apricots, cherries or kiwi fruit*

GLAZE
Apricot jam
Redcurrant jelly

Rub the fat and flour for the pastry together until the mixture resembles fine breadcrumbs. Add the sugar and nuts and stir in the egg yolk. Knead lightly, wrap in cling film/plastic wrap and chill in the refrigerator for 30 minutes. Alternatively, prepare the pastry in a food processor, taking care not to over-mix. Roll the pastry out thinly on a floured board and cut into 12 rounds about 5cm/2 inches in diameter. Use the pastry to line microwave bun/muffin trays or small ramekins/custard cups. Prick the bases with a fork and cook on HIGH for 3 minutes. Cook in two batches of 6. Allow the pastry to cool slightly in the baking dishes and then transfer to a wire rack to cool completely. To make the filling, heat the milk for 1-2 minutes on HIGH, or until boiling. Beat the egg yolks, sugar cornflour/ cornstarch and almond essence/ extract together until light. Gradually pour on the milk, beating well. Return to the microwave oven and cook on HIGH for 1-2 minutes, stirring every 15 seconds until thick and smooth. Place greaseproof/wax paper directly over the top of the filling to allow it to cool without forming a skin. When the filling is nearly cool, spoon in equal amounts into each pastry shell. Cut the grapes in half and remove the seeds. Place them cut side down on top of the filling or cut into quarters and arrange in attractive patterns. Arrange the other fruit as desired, making sure that all the pith is removed from the satsuma segments. Melt the apricot jam and the redcurrant jelly in two separate bowls for 30 seconds to 1 minute on HIGH. Sieve both and use the apricot jam for the light coloured fruit and the redcurrant jelly for the red fruit. Brush the glazes on the fruit while the glaze is still warm. Allow the glaze to set before serving.

MENU 9

Mangetout and King Prawns

PREPARATION TIME: 25 minutes	
MICROWAVE COOKING TIME: 3-4 minutes	
SERVES: 6 people	

225g/8oz mangetout/pea pods
*180g/6oz king prawns/jumbo shrimp,
   cooked and shelled*

**Menu 9: Marrons en Chemise
(top left) Noisettes d'Agneau
Maltaise (top right) and Mangetout
and King Prawns (bottom).**

2 spring/green onions, shredded or thinly
    sliced
4-6 water chestnuts, thinly sliced

DRESSING
60ml/4 tbsps oil
Dash sesame oil
5ml/1 tsp grated fresh ginger
½ clove garlic, crushed
Juice and grated rind of half a lemon
Salt and pepper

Top and tail the mangetout/pea pods
and place in a bowl or casserole with
30ml/2 tbsps salted water. Cover
loosely and cook on HIGH for 1-2
minutes. Set aside while preparing
the other ingredients. Slice the water
chestnuts thinly and slice the king
prawns/jumbo shrimp in half
through the middle. Heat the oil with
the sesame oil, ginger and garlic on
HIGH for 1 minute. Allow to cool
and combine with the remaining
dressing ingredients. Drain the
mangetout/pea pods and combine
with the prawns/shrimp, water
chestnuts and spring/green onions.
Mix with the dressing ingredients and
place on serving dishes. Reheat
through on HIGH for 1 minute
before serving.

Noisettes d'Agneau Maltaise

PREPARATION TIME: 30 minutes

MICROWAVE COOKING TIME:
26-32 minutes

SERVES: 6 people

6 noisettes of lamb cut from the best end,
    about 3.75cm/1½ inch thick
Oil

SAUCE MALTAISE
2 egg yolks
120g/4oz/½ cup butter
Salt and pepper
Grated rind of ½ a blood orange

POMMES DUCHESSE
675g/1½ lbs potatoes, peeled and cut into
    even-sized pieces
Salt and pepper
30g/1oz/2 tbsps butter
30-45ml/2-4 tbsps hot milk

1 large egg, beaten
Paprika

First prepare the potatoes. Place
them in a large bowl with a pinch of
salt and 60ml/4 tbsps water. Cover
with pierced cling film/plastic wrap
and cook on HIGH for 5-10 minutes.
Leave to stand for 5 minutes. Mash
until smooth and then beat in the
butter and pepper. Beat in the hot
milk until smooth. Allow to cool
slightly and then beat in the egg,
reserving about half. Mix very well
and fill a piping/pastry bag fitted
with a rosette nozzle/tube. Pipe
swirls of potato onto a plate covered
with greaseproof/wax paper. Chill
thoroughly. Heat a browning dish
according to the manufacturer's
directions. Lightly oil the surface and
cook the noisettes 2 or 3 at a time,
pressing them down against the hot
browning dish on both sides to seal.
Cook the noisettes on HIGH for
about 7 minutes. Cover and keep
warm while preparing the sauce. Melt
the butter for 2 minutes on HIGH in
a large glass measure. Beat the egg
yolks together with orange rind. Add
a pinch of salt and white pepper and
gradually beat into the hot butter.
Cook on MEDIUM for 1 minute,
whisking after 15 seconds and at 15
second intervals thereafter. If the
sauce begins to curdle, dip the glass
measure into a bowl of iced water to
stop the cooking and whisk well.
Continue cooking until the sauce
thickens. Cover the sauce and set
aside. To finish the potatoes, brush
with additional beaten egg mixed
with a pinch of salt and sprinkle
lightly with paprika. Cook on HIGH
for 3-4 minutes until piping hot.
Brown under a preheated grill/
broiler if desired. Reheat the
noisettes for 1-2 minutes on HIGH if
necessary and place on a serving dish,
removing the string around each.
Spoon over some of the sauce and
garnish with the segmented orange if
desired. Place a swirl of potato on
each plate and serve immediately.

Marrons en Chemise

PREPARATION TIME: 30 minutes

MICROWAVE COOKING TIME:
5-7 minutes

SERVES: 6 people

WHITE CHOCOLATE MOUSSE
280ml/½ pint/1 cup milk
120g/4oz white chocolate, roughly
    chopped
2 egg yolks, 1 white reserved
30g/2 tbsps sugar
45ml/3 tbsps water
15g/1 tbsp gelatine
140ml/¼ pint/½ cup whipping cream

150g/5oz/approximately 1 cup crème de
    marron (sweetened chestnut spread)

DECORATION
60-90g/2-3oz/2-3 squares plain/semi-
sweet chocolate

Heat the milk for 2-3 minutes on
HIGH with the chopped white
chocolate. Beat the egg yolks and the
sugar together until light. Gradually
pour on the milk, stirring constantly.
Return to the oven and cook on
HIGH for 2-3 minutes, stirring every
15 seconds until the mixture coats
the back of a spoon. Allow to cool.
Meanwhile, sprinkle the gelatine on
top of the water in a small bowl.
Allow to stand for 5-10 minutes to
soften and then melt on HIGH for
20-30 seconds. Pour into the cooled
custard and set the bowl in another
bowl of iced water. Allow to cool
completely and stir frequently to
help the gelatine to set evenly.
Meanwhile, whip the cream and the
egg white and fold into the custard
when the gelatine is nearly set. Spoon
the crème de marron into the bottom
of each of 6 small dessert dishes. Pour
the white chocolate mousse on top
to cover before the mousse sets
completely. Chill in the refrigerator
until firm. To decorate, melt the
chocolate for 20-30 seconds on
HIGH, stirring frequently. Put into a
small piping/pastry bag fitted with a
writing nozzle/tube. Pipe out a lacy
design on top of the white chocolate
mousse and let the chocolate set
before serving. Mousse may be
prepared and assembled the day
before serving. Decorate with
chocolate no more than 2 hours in
advance.

MENU 10

Tomato Farcis

PREPARATION TIME: 25 minutes

MICROWAVE COOKING TIME:
9-12 minutes

SERVES: 6 people

6 large tomatoes, peeled

FILLING
180g/6oz low fat soft cheese
90g/3oz cooked ham, finely chopped
1 clove garlic, crushed
15ml/1 tbsp chopped parsley
10ml/2 tsps chopped fresh thyme or
    2.5ml/½ tsp dried thyme

GARNISH
Whole chives

ACCOMPANIMENT
Hot butter toast or melba toast

To peel the tomatoes, place 1150ml/
2 pints/4 cups water in a large bowl,
cover with cling film/plastic wrap
and microwave on HIGH for 8-11
minutes or until boiling. Place 2 of
the tomatoes in the water and leave
to stand for 1-1½ minutes. Remove
the tomatoes to another bowl of cold
water and bring the hot water back
to the boil. Repeat with the
remaining 4 tomatoes. The skin
should peel off easily. On the
rounded end of the tomato, cut a
slice about 1.25cm/½ inch. Scoop
out the pulp, sieve and set aside the
juice. Combine the tomato juice with
the filling ingredients and spoon into
the tomatoes. Set the tops on at an
angle and place the tomatoes in a
circle on a plate. Heat on HIGH for
1 minute and place on individual
serving plates. Garnish the plates
with whole fresh chives and serve
with the toast.

Scallops aux Herbes

PREPARATION TIME: 25 minutes

MICROWAVE COOKING TIME:
23-24 minutes plus standing time

SERVES: 6 people

18-24 scallops with roes attached
90ml/6 tbsps dry white wine
1 bay leaf

SAUCE
180ml/6 fl oz/¾ cup double/heavy
    cream
45ml/3 tbsps chopped mixed herbs such
    as tarragon, chives, chervil or marjoram
Salt and pepper
Squeeze lemon juice

WILD RICE PILAF
120g/4oz/½ cup long grain rice
120g/4oz/½ cup wild rice
60g/2oz/½ cup chopped walnuts
Salt and pepper

Place the scallops in a shallow dish
with the white wine and bay leaf.
Cover and cook on MEDIUM for
3 minutes. Leave to stand while
preparing the remaining ingredients.
Boil the cream for 5 minutes on
HIGH. Add 30ml/2 tbsps of the
cooking liquid from the scallops and
cook a further 2-3 minutes on HIGH.
Stir in the herbs, salt, pepper and
lemon juice. To cook the rice, place in
a casserole with 570ml/1 pint/2 cups
boiling, salted water. Cook on HIGH
for 12 minutes and leave to stand
5-10 minutes. Drain any water that is
not absorbed and add the walnuts.
Reheat on HIGH for 2 minutes. Add
the scallops to the sauce and reheat
on HIGH for 1 minute. Serve the
scallops on a bed of rice.

Petites Galettes Normandes

PREPARATION TIME: 30 minutes

MICROWAVE COOKING TIME:
10-11 minutes plus standing time

SERVES: 6 people

PASTRY
120g/4oz/1 cup plain/all-purpose flour
5ml/1 tsp ground allspice

60g/2oz/4 tbsps butter or margarine
10ml/2 tsps brown sugar
1 egg yolk

FILLING
450g/1lb dessert apples, peeled, cored and
    sliced
2.5ml/½ tsp ground cinnamon
30ml/2 tbsps apricot jam
280ml/½ pint/1 cup double/heavy
    cream, whipped

TO DECORATE
6 browned hazelnuts

To make the pastry, sift the flour with
the sugar and the allspice and rub in
the butter until the mixture
resembles fine breadcrumbs. Add the
egg yolk and mix to a soft dough.
Knead lightly and wrap in cling film/
plastic wrap and chill in the
refrigerator for 30 minutes.
Alternatively, make the pastry in a
food processor. Roll the pastry out
thinly and cut into 12 rounds, 6 at
7.5cm/3 inches and 6 at 5cm/
2 inches diameter. Place the rounds
on a plate or microwave baking sheet
and cook on HIGH for 3 minutes.
Cook the pastry in 2 batches. Allow
to cool slightly on the dish or baking
sheet and then transfer to a wire rack
to cool. Combine the apples,
cinnamon and apricot jam in a
casserole, cover and cook on HIGH
for 4-5 minutes. Leave to stand for
5 minutes, uncovered, and leave to
cool. Place a large round of pastry on
a serving plate and top with some of
the apple filling. Whip the cream
until soft peaks form and pipe or
spoon on top of the apple. Place the
smaller round of pastry on top of the
cream and pipe a rosette on top.
Decorate the rosette with a hazelnut
and sprinkle lightly with icing/
powdered sugar if desired.

**Overleaf: Menu 10 – Tomato Farcis
(left), Scallops aux Herbes (centre)
and Petites Galettes Normandes
(right).**

MENU 11

Spinach Mousse with Tomato Tarragon Sauce

PREPARATION TIME: 25 minutes

MICROWAVE COOKING TIME: 18-22 minutes plus standing time

SERVES: 6 people

120ml/4 fl oz/scant ½ cup whipping cream
½ clove garlic, crushed
450g/1lb fresh spinach, stems removed and leaves well washed
2 eggs
Salt and pepper
Grated nutmeg

SAUCE
400g/14oz canned plum tomatoes
1 shallot, roughly chopped
3 sprigs fresh tarragon or 10ml/2 tsps dried tarragon leaves
Salt and pepper
Pinch sugar
10ml/2 tsps tomato purée/paste
15ml/1 tbsp white wine or tarragon vinegar

GARNISH
3 tomatoes, peeled, seeded and cut into small dice

To prepare the spinach mousse, place the spinach in a roasting bag and tie loosely with string. Cook on HIGH for 4-5 minutes or until wilted. Leave to stand for 1-2 minutes and drain if necessary. Combine in a food processor with the garlic, eggs, salt, pepper and nutmeg. Blend until a smooth purée. Stir in the cream by hand. Grease 6 small ramekins/custard cups lightly with butter and place a round of greaseproof/wax paper in the bottom. Divide the mixture between the ramekins/custard cups and cook in a shallow dish of hot water to come halfway up the sides of the ramekins/custard cups. Loosely cover the dish and cook on HIGH for 5-6 minutes. The mousses should feel firm when lightly pressed and should rise slightly in the dishes. Set aside while preparing the sauce. Combine all the sauce ingredients except the vinegar in a deep bowl and loosely cover. Cook

on HIGH for 8-10 minutes, until boiling rapidly. Allow to stand for 3-5 minutes and sieve or purée in a food processor. Push through a strainer to remove the seeds and stir in the vinegar. Place an equal portion of the sauce on each of 6 serving dishes and turn out the spinach mousses on top. Reheat 1 minute on HIGH. Place a spoonful of the tomato dice on top of each mousse and serve immediately.

Beef Stroganoff

PREPARATION TIME: 25 minutes

MICROWAVE COOKING TIME: 14½ minutes

SERVES: 6 people

60g/2oz/4 tbsps butter or margarine
900g/2lbs rump or sirloin steak, trimmed and cut into thin strips
225g/8oz mushrooms, sliced if large
1 clove garlic, crushed
30g/1oz/2 tbsps flour
60ml/4 tbsps brown stock
60ml/4 tbsps brandy or sherry
Salt and pepper
140ml/¼ pint/½ cup sour cream or whole milk yogurt
60ml/4 tbsps snipped chives

Heat a browning dish according to the manufacturer's directions. Melt the butter and, when foaming, brown the meat in three or four batches. Pour the contents of the browning dish into a casserole and sprinkle over the flour. Gradually stir in the stock and the brandy or sherry. Add salt and pepper to taste and cook on HIGH for 4 minutes. Add the mushrooms and cook for a further 4 minutes, covered. Add salt and pepper to taste and stir in the chives. Gently stir in the sour cream and cook for 30 seconds on HIGH. Serve with noodles.

Kissel

PREPARATION TIME: 20 minutes

MICROWAVE COOKING TIME: 9-11 minutes

SERVES: 6 people

120g/4oz blackcurrants, canned or frozen
120g/4oz redcurrants, canned or frozen
120g/4oz canned or frozen black cherries, pitted
60g/4 tbsps sugar
60ml/4 tbsps water
Grated rind and juice of 1 orange
1 cinnamon stick
120g/4oz raspberries, fresh or frozen
120g/4oz strawberries, fresh or frozen
15g/1 tbsp arrowroot or cornflour/cornstarch mixed with 60ml/4 tbsps brandy

TOPPING
140ml/¼ pint/½ cup double/heavy cream, whipped
140ml/¼ pint/½ cup natural yogurt or sour cream
15g/1 tbsp icing/powdered sugar
Grated nutmeg

Place the blackcurrants, redcurrants and cherries in a deep bowl along with their juices. Add the sugar, water, grated rind and juice of the orange and cinnamon stick. Cover with pierced cling film/plastic wrap and cook on HIGH for 7-8 minutes or until boiling. Strain, reserving the syrup. Place the fruit in another bowl with the strawberries and raspberries. Mix the arrowroot or cornflour/cornstarch with the brandy, add to the reserved syrup and cook, about 2-3 minutes on HIGH until thickened and clear. Remove the cinnamon stick and pour over the fruit. Stir well and leave to cool slightly. To serve, spoon the fruit mixture into glasses or dessert dishes. Whip the cream lightly and fold in the icing/powdered sugar and sour cream or natural yogurt. Top each serving with some of the cream and sprinkle on nutmeg to serve.

Menu 11: Kissel (top), Beef Stroganoff (centre) and Spinach Mousse with Tomato Tarragon Sauce (bottom).

MENU 12

Coquilles aux Poissons Fumé

PREPARATION TIME: 25 minutes

MICROWAVE COOKING TIME: 22-30 minutes

SERVES: 6 people

340g/¾ lb smoked haddock fillets
340g/¾ lb smoked cod fillets
140ml/¼ pint/½ cup dry white wine
1 bay leaf
3 parsley stalks

SAUCE
1 shallot, finely chopped
½ clove garlic, chopped
140ml/¼ pint/½ cup dry white wine
140ml/¼ pint/½ cup cooking liquid from the fish
30g/1oz/2 tbsps butter or margarine
30g/1oz/2 tbsps flour
Pinch turmeric
25ml/½ tsp dill seed
140ml/¼ pint/½ cup double/heavy cream
Squeeze lemon juice
Salt and pepper

GARNISH
Sprigs of fresh dill
60g/2oz smoked salmon, cut into thin strips

Cut the fish into 2.5cm/1 inch pieces, place in a shallow casserole, pour over the wine and add the parsley and bay leaf. Loosely cover and cook on HIGH for 1-2 minutes. Leave to stand, covered, while preparing the remaining ingredients. For the sauce, put the shallots, garlic, wine, turmeric and dill seed into a small, deep bowl or glass measure. Cook on HIGH for 8-10 minutes, or until boiling. Allow to boil another 2-3 minutes to reduce slightly. Strain the liquid and reserve. Melt the butter in a small casserole for 30 seconds on HIGH and stir in the flour. Pour in the reduced wine mixture and strain on the required amount of fish cooking liquid. Stir well and cook on HIGH for 4-5 minutes, or until thickened. Pour the cream into a deep bowl or glass measure and cook on HIGH for 6-8 minutes to reduce. Pour into the sauce and blend well. Season with salt and pepper. Divide the haddock and cod among 6 shells or shell shaped dishes. Pour over the sauce, loosely cover the dishes and reheat on HIGH for 1-2 minutes. Garnish the dishes with strips of smoked salmon and sprigs of fresh dill.

Lamb Poivrade

PREPARATION TIME: 35 minutes

MICROWAVE COOKING TIME: 26-30 minutes

SERVES: 6 people

4 best end necks of lamb

SAUCE
30g/1oz/2 tbsps butter or margarine
30g/1oz/2 tbsps flour
1 onion, finely chopped
1 clove garlic, crushed
280ml/½ pint/1 cup rich brown stock
60ml/4 tbsps dry white wine
5ml/1 tsp tomato purée/paste
1 bay leaf
1 sprig thyme
Salt
15ml/1 tbsp green peppercorns, slightly crushed (drained and rinsed if packed in brine)

POMMES DAUPHINOISE
60g/2oz/4 tbsps butter or margarine
1 clove garlic, peeled
450g/1lb potatoes, peeled and thinly sliced
140ml/¼ pint/½ cup single/light cream
1 egg, beaten
Salt and pepper
Grated nutmeg
60g/2oz/½ cup grated Gruyère cheese

First prepare the potatoes. Melt the butter in a round dish or casserole with the garlic for 1½ minutes on HIGH. Remove the garlic clove and arrange the potatoes in neat layers, seasoning with salt, pepper and nutmeg in between each layer. Cover the dish with cling film/plastic wrap and cook on HIGH for 9 minutes. Remove the dish from the oven. Whisk the cream and the egg together and pour evenly over the potatoes, shaking the dish gently to allow it to seep down the sides to the bottom. Re-cover and cook on HIGH for 6 minutes more. Uncover the dish, sprinkle the cheese over the top and leave to stand while preparing the lamb. Trim away the bones and all the fat from each best end neck of lamb until only the eye of the meat remains. Slice into 1.25cm/½ inch thick slices. Heat a browning dish according to the manufacturer's directions and lightly grease with oil. Press the slices of lamb down firmly on one side and turn over and press again to seal both sides. Cook in several batches. Set aside, covered, while preparing the sauce. Put the remaining butter in the browning dish and add the onion and flour. Cook on HIGH for 3-4 minutes or until the onion and the flour are beginning to brown. Deglaze the browning dish with some of the stock and pour the contents into a casserole dish. Add the remaining stock, white wine, tomato purée/paste, bay leaf and sprig of thyme. Season with salt and cook on HIGH 3-5 minutes or until thickened. If desired, a few drops of gravy browning may be added to make the sauce darker. Add the peppercorns and the lamb and stir well. Cover and cook on HIGH for 3 minutes to heat through and finish cooking the lamb. Reheat the potatoes for 1-2 minutes on HIGH. Brown under a preheated grill/broiler and cut into even-sized portions. Serve with the Lamb Poivrade and lightly cooked mangetout/pea pods.

Menu 12: Pêches Melba (top left), Pommes Dauphinoise (top right) Lamb Poivrade (centre) and Coquilles aux Poissons Fumé (bottom).

Pêches Melba

PREPARATION TIME: 25 minutes
MICROWAVE COOKING TIME: 10-14 minutes
SERVES: 6 people

570ml/1 pint/2 cups vanilla ice cream
6 ripe peaches
225g/8oz raspberries, fresh or frozen
10ml/2 tsps lemon juice
Icing/powdered sugar to taste
60ml/4 tbsps raspberry liqueur
Ground blanched almonds

Place the vanilla ice cream in a bowl and soften for 20-30 seconds on HIGH. Place in a piping bag and quickly pipe the ice cream in swirls into 6 individual dishes, filling them halfway. Freeze the dishes until the ice cream is firm. Meanwhile, place 1150ml/2 pints/4 cups water in a large bowl. Cover with cling film/plastic wrap and heat on HIGH for 8-11 minutes or until boiling. Place 3 of the peaches in the water and allow to stand for 1-2 minutes. Remove the fruit to a bowl of cold water and then peel. Return the bowl to the oven and reboil the water. Repeat with the remaining 3 peaches. To prepare the sauce, combine the raspberries and lemon juice in a deep bowl and cook on HIGH for 2-3 minutes. Place in a food processor or liquidizer and purée until smooth. Add icing/powdered sugar to taste and process once or twice to mix well. Strain out the seeds and push as much of the purée through the sieve as possible. Stir in the raspberry liqueur and set the sauce aside. Soften the ice cream at room temperature for 15 minutes. To serve, place a peach on top of the ice cream in each dish and spoon over some of the raspberry sauce. Sprinkle the top of the peaches with some of the blanched ground almonds. Serve the remaining sauce separately.

MENU 13

Consommé Valentine

PREPARATION TIME: 20 minutes
MICROWAVE COOKING TIME: 10-11 minutes
SERVES: 6 people

1 large carrot, thinly sliced
1-2 turnips, depending upon size, peeled and thinly sliced
15ml/1 tbsp chopped chervil or parsley
1150ml/2 pints/4 cups canned or freshly prepared chicken or beef consommé
60ml/4 tbsps sherry

Cut each slice of carrot and turnip into a heart shape with a small pastry/cookie cutter. Place the carrots and turnips in separate bowls with 15ml/1 tbsp water in each. Loosely cover the bowls with cling film/plastic wrap and cook on HIGH for 2-3 minutes. Leave to stand while reheating the consommé. Pour the consommé into a microwave proof soup tureen or individual bowls and add the sherry and chervil or parsley. Cover loosely and cook on HIGH for 8 minutes for the soup tureen or 2-3 minutes for individual bowls. Halfway through the reheating time, add the drained carrot and turnip hearts. Serve hot.

Poulet au Concombres

PREPARATION TIME: 30 minutes
MICROWAVE COOKING TIME: 20-28 minutes
SERVES: 6 people

6 chicken breasts, skinned and boned
200ml/7 fl oz/scant 1 cup chicken stock
1 small cucumber, seeded and cut into thin strips, but not peeled
30g/1oz/2 tbsps butter or margarine
25g/1½ tbsps flour
Salt and pepper
180ml/6 fl oz/¾ cup single/light cream
30ml/2 tbsps chopped fresh dill or 15ml/1 tbsp dried dill weed

GARNISH
Whole sprigs of fresh dill

Place the chicken breasts in a dish in a circle and pour over the chicken stock. Cover with pierced cling film/plastic wrap and cook on HIGH for 15-20 minutes or until the juices from the chicken run clear. If desired, cut the chicken breasts into thin strips. Alternatively, leave whole if they have retained their shape. Melt the butter for 30 seconds on HIGH and stir in the flour. Strain on the cooking liquid from the chicken and add the cream. Season with salt and pepper and add the chopped dill. Cook on HIGH for 3-5 minutes, stirring occasionally until thickened. Place the chicken in a serving dish with the cucumber strips, loosely cover and reheat on HIGH for 2-3 minutes. Pour over the sauce to serve. Garnish with fresh dill.

Pavlova

PREPARATION TIME: 30 minutes
MICROWAVE COOKING TIME: 3 minutes
SERVES: 6 people

6 egg whites
340g/12oz/1½ cups sugar
1.25ml/¼ tsp vanilla essence/extract
10ml/2 tsps cornflour/cornstarch
5ml/1 tsp white distilled vinegar
60g/2oz/½ cup toasted flaked/sliced almonds

Menu 13: Pavlova (top), Consommé Valentine (centre) and Poulet au Concombres (bottom).

FILLING

1 small pineapple, peeled, cored and cut into pieces or 225g/8oz canned pineapple pieces, drained
2 kiwi fruit, peeled and sliced
1 passion fruit
120g/4oz fresh strawberries (if available) or 2 oranges, peeled and segmented
280ml/½ pint/1 cup whipping cream
Icing/powdered sugar

Beat the egg whites until stiff peaks form. Add the sugar, a spoonful at a time, beating well in between each addition, until the meringue is stiff and glossy. Fold in the vanilla, vinegar and cornflour/cornstarch. Spread the meringue in a circle on the plate or serving dish and make a deep well in the centre. Do not spread to the edge of the plate. Sprinkle with the toasted almonds and cook on HIGH for 3 minutes. Allow to cool completely. Mix half the fruit with half the cream and fill the well in the centre of the pavlova. Reserve the passion fruit for the top. Spoon or pipe the remaining cream into the centre of the pavlova and decorate the top with the remaining fruit, scooping out the seeds and pulp from the passion fruit to drizzle on top as a sauce. Sprinkle lightly with icing/powdered sugar and chill before serving.

MENU 14

Artichokes with Orange Mousseline Sauce

PREPARATION TIME: 30 minutes

MICROWAVE COOKING TIME: 17½-23 minutes

SERVES: 6 people

6 medium globe artichokes
140ml/¼ pint/½ cup salted water
30ml/2 tbsps lemon juice
1 bay leaf

SAUCE
120g/4oz/½ cup butter
15ml/1 tbsp orange juice
15ml/1 tbsp lemon juice
2 egg yolks
5ml/1 tsp chopped tarragon
Salt and pepper
60ml/4 tbsps whipped cream

Wash the artichokes and trim off the stems and the lower leaves. Trim the pointed ends off all the leaves and place the artichokes in a large casserole or bowl with the salted water, lemon juice and bay leaf. Cook on HIGH for 15-20 minutes, turning the dish or re-arranging the artichokes twice during cooking. To test if the artichokes are cooked, pull one of the leaves from the bottom, it should come away easily. Drain the artichokes upside down on paper towels and leave to cool. To prepare the sauce, heat the butter in a glass measure for 2 minutes on HIGH. Beat the egg yolks and the orange and lemon juice together with salt and pepper and tarragon. Gradually whisk the egg yolks into the butter. Cook on MEDIUM for 1 minute, whisking well after 15 seconds. Do not allow the sauce to boil. If the sauce looks curdled, dip the glass measure into a bowl of iced water and whisk well. Continue heating until the sauce thickens. Allow to cool slightly and fold in the whipped cream. Carefully separate the centre leaves on the artichoke and, using a teaspoon, remove the thistle-like choke from the inside. Reshape the artichoke and place 1 on each serving plate. Reheat on HIGH for 30 seconds-1 minute and serve with the mousseline sauce.

Stuffed Trout

PREPARATION TIME: 35 minutes

MICROWAVE COOKING TIME: 39-44 minutes

SERVES: 6 people

6 even-sized rainbow trout, boned

FILLING
180g/6oz crabmeat
15ml/1 tbsp snipped chives
225g/8oz/1 package low fat soft cheese
5 slices bread, crusts removed made into crumbs
Cayenne pepper
Salt
90g/3oz/6 tbsps butter
Juice of half a lemon
30ml/2 tbsps chopped parsley

GARNISH
Lemon slices

NEW POTATOES
450g/1lb new potatoes, scrubbed but not peeled
280ml/½ pint/1 cup water
Salt
45ml/1½ oz/3 tbsps butter or margarine

Ask the fishmonger to bone the trout. Mix the filling ingredients together and stuff each trout. Cover the heads and tails with foil and place the trout, three at a time, in a shallow dish. Cover with cling film/plastic wrap and cook 12 minutes on HIGH. Set the trout aside while cooking the remaining fish. In a deep bowl, microwave the butter for 2 minutes on HIGH until lightly brown. Add the lemon juice and parsley and set aside. To cook the potatoes, place them in a casserole dish with salt and water. Cover and cook on HIGH for 10-14 minutes. Drain and reheat with the butter 1-2 minutes. Leave to stand, covered. Reheat the fish for 2 minutes on HIGH and pour over the butter to serve. Garnish with lemon slices.

Menu 14: Artichokes with Orange Mousseline Sauce (top left), Flummery (top right) and Stuffed Trout (bottom).

Flummery

PREPARATION TIME: 30 minutes

MICROWAVE COOKING TIME: 9-10 minutes

SERVES: 6 people

30g/1oz/2 tbsps butter or margarine
120g/4oz/1 cup porridge oats
570ml/1 pint milk
30g/2 tbsps cornflour/cornstarch
15ml/1 tbsp gelatine
45ml/3 tbsps water
30-45ml/2-3 tbsps honey
45ml/3 tbsps Scotch or malt whisky
140ml/¼ pint/½ cup double/heavy
   cream

120g/4oz berries such as blackberries,
   blackcurrants, blueberries or
   strawberries

Melt the butter for the topping on HIGH for 30 seconds and stir in the oats. Cook for a further 3 minutes on HIGH, stirring occasionally, until the oats are evenly browned. Set aside. Mix the milk and the cornflour/cornstarch together in a deep bowl and cook on HIGH for 5-6 minutes, stirring every minute until the mixture thickens. Allow to cool, covered with greaseproof/wax paper to prevent a skin from forming. Sprinkle the gelatine over the water and allow to soak for 5 minutes.

Cook on HIGH for 15-20 seconds to dissolve. Stir the gelatine, honey and whisky into the thickened milk mixture. Whip the cream until soft peaks form and fold into the mixture. Taste the berries and sweeten with more honey if desired. Place some of the berries in the bottom of a glass dessert dish and sprinkle over some of the topping. Spoon in flummery mixture and continue alternating with the oats, fruit and mixture for the 6 dishes. Finish with a layer of oats and a few pieces of fruit. Serve cold.

MENU 15

Cream of Smoked Salmon Soup

PREPARATION TIME: 15 minutes

MICROWAVE COOKING TIME: 11-14 minutes

SERVES: 6 people

340g/¾ lb whitefish, skinned, boned and
   cut into 2.5cm/1 inch chunks
250g/9oz smoked salmon, cut into
   2.5cm/1 inch pieces, with 6 thin strips
   reserved for garnish
45g/1½ oz/3 tbsps butter or margarine
45g/1½ oz/3 tbsps flour
140ml/¼ pint/½ cup dry white wine
1 litre/1¾ pints/3½ cups milk
140ml/¼ pint/½ cup double/heavy
   cream
Freshly ground white pepper
5ml/1 tsp tomato purée/paste (optional)

GARNISH
Sour cream
Chopped chives

Combine the whitefish and smoked salmon with the white wine in a large, deep bowl. Cover and cook on HIGH for 2-3 minutes. Leave to stand for 1-2 minutes before spooning into a food processor or blender. Add the milk and purée

until smooth. Rinse out the bowl and melt the butter for 1 minute on HIGH. Stir in the flour and gradually pour in the milk and fish mixture. Heat for 3-5 minutes on HIGH, or until thickened. Add the pepper and the cream and reheat a further 5 minutes on HIGH. If the colour of the soup is too pale, add 5ml/1 tsp tomato purée/paste. Garnish with sour cream, chopped chives and the reserved strips of smoked salmon.

Fillet Steaks Rossini

PREPARATION TIME: 20 minutes

MICROWAVE COOKING TIME: 14-18 minutes

SERVES: 6 people

MADEIRA SAUCE
30g/1oz/2 tbsps butter
30g/1oz/2 tbsps flour
1 small onion, finely chopped
280ml/½ pint/1 cup rich brown stock
60ml/4 tbsps Madeira or sherry
2.5ml/½ tsp tomato purée/paste
1 bay leaf
Salt and pepper
Gravy browning (optional)

6 fillet steaks/filet mignons
30g/1oz/2 tbsps butter or margarine

GARNISH
90g/3oz firm pâté
6 mushroom caps, fluted if desired

Heat a browning dish according to the manufacturer's directions and add the butter for the Madeira sauce. Add the onion and the flour and cook on HIGH, stirring frequently, until the flour and the onions brown lightly – this should take about 5 minutes. Deglaze the browning dish with some of the brown stock and spoon the contents into a deep bowl. Add the remaining stock and the bay leaf. Cook on HIGH for 3-5 minutes or until thickened. Strain into a clean bowl and discard the onions and bay leaf. Add the Madeira, tomato purée/paste, salt and pepper and gravy browning, if using. Cover the sauce and set it aside. Clean the browning dish and reheat. Add the butter for the steaks and, when foaming, place three fillet steaks on the browning dish and press down firmly. Turn over and press again to seal both sides. Cook the steaks on HIGH for 4 minutes. Repeat with the remaining fillet steaks. Place all the steaks on individual serving dishes. Top each with a round, thin slice of pâté, cover well and keep warm. Add the mushrooms to the browning dish and cook for 1-2 minutes on HIGH, stirring occasionally. Place 1 mushroom on top of each slice of pâté and re-cover the meat. Reheat the Madeira sauce on HIGH for 1-2 minutes and spoon some over each fillet steak. Serve the remaining sauce separately. Serve with an accompaniment of French/green beans cooked with thinly sliced red peppers.

Raspberry Sorbet in Chocolate Cups

PREPARATION TIME: 35 minutes

MICROWAVE COOKING TIME: 6 minutes

SERVES: 6 people

RASPBERRY SORBET
225g/8oz fresh or frozen raspberries
90g/3oz/¾ cup sugar
30ml/2 tbsps lemon juice
1 egg white, stiffly beaten

CHOCOLATE CUPS
90g/3oz/3 squares plain/semi-sweet chocolate
7.5ml/1½ tsps vegetable shortening

TO SERVE
90ml/6 tbsps raspberry liqueur
12 whole raspberries
Mint leaves

If using frozen raspberries, thaw on DEFROST for about 1-2 minutes. Purée the fruit in a food processor or blender and sieve to remove the seeds. Combine the sugar with 140ml/¼ pint/½ cup water in a deep bowl or glass measure. Heat on HIGH for 4 minutes, stirring every minute. Allow the syrup to cool and add the lemon juice. Stir in the fruit purée and pour the mixture into a freezer container. Freeze until the mixture is slushy, return to the food processor and beat until smooth. Return to the freezer and freeze again until almost solid. Take out the mixture and process again in the

Menu 15: Raspberry Sorbet in Chocolate Cups (top), Fillet Steaks Rossini (centre) and Cream of Smoked Salmon Soup (bottom).

food processor or blender, adding the stiffly beaten egg white. Return to the freezer until firm. To make the chocolate cups, combine the chocolate in a small bowl with the vegetable shortening and cook on HIGH for 2-2½ minutes until melted. Stir frequently while melting. Use a double layer of paper cases/cup cake liners and fill 6 cases with an equal

amount of chocolate. Tilt case to coat the sides within 5mm/¼ inch of the top. Continue to tilt to form a thick chocolate layer. Alternatively, brush on the chocolate with a pastry brush. Chill until set. Thirty minutes before serving, remove the sorbet from the freezer to allow it to soften. Alternatively, heat the container on HIGH for 20 seconds to soften. Carefully peel away the paper from the chocolate cups and place 1 on each serving plate. Fill with 1 scoop of sorbet and pour a spoonful of raspberry liqueur over the sorbet. Garnish with fresh raspberries and mint leaves.

Brunch

Apricot Cheesecake

PREPARATION TIME: 40 minutes
MICROWAVE COOKING TIME:
12-17 minutes
SERVES: 8 people

BASE
120g/4oz/1 cup plain/all-purpose flour, sifted
Pinch salt
30g/1oz/2 tbsps butter or margarine
10g/2 tsps fresh yeast
10ml/2 tsps sugar
1 egg, separated

FILLING AND TOPPING
225g/8oz cream or curd cheese
30g/2 tbsps sugar
Grated rind of 1 lemon
60ml/4 tbsps single/light cream
1 egg, separated
450g/1lb fresh or canned apricots, halved and stoned
Demerara sugar

Sift the flour and salt and rub in the butter by hand or with a food processor. Mix the yeast with 15ml/1 tbsp warm water and the sugar. Beat the egg yolk and add to the flour with the yeast. Mix together to form a smooth dough by hand or with a food processor and then knead for about 10 minutes, by hand on a lightly-floured surface. Roll the dough out to line a 23cm/9 inch round dish. Trim the edges and cover the dish with cling film/plastic wrap. Heat on HIGH for 15 seconds and then leave to rise for about 30 minutes or until a finger mark stays when the dough is lightly pressed. Cook on HIGH for 3-4 minutes, turning the dish occasionally. Leave to cool in the dish. To prepare the filling, mix the cheese, sugar, lemon rind, cream and the egg yolk together until smooth. Whisk both the egg whites until stiff but not dry and fold into the cheese mixture. Chop half of the apricots and arrange them over the dough base. Spoon the cheese mixture over the apricots and arrange the remaining apricot halves over the top of the cheese. Cook on HIGH for 4-5 minutes or until just beginning to set. Sprinkle with the demerara sugar and continue cooking for 5-8 minutes until the centre is set. Turn the dish occasionally while the cheesecake is cooking. The top may be browned under a preheated grill/broiler before serving if desired.

Red Fruit Compôte

PREPARATION TIME: 20 minutes
MICROWAVE COOKING TIME:
7-8 minutes
SERVES: 8 people

900g/2lbs of the following fruits: cranberries; redcurrants, topped and tailed; cherries, fresh or canned, pitted; plums, halved and stoned; strawberries; raspberries.
120g/4oz/½ cup sugar
30g/2 tbsps cornflour/cornstarch
140ml/¼ pint/½ cup orange juice

TOPPING
Natural yogurt
Ground cinnamon

Combine the cranberries, redcurrants and plums with sugar in a large, deep bowl. Cover and cook on HIGH for 3 minutes. If the cherries are fresh, add them with the cranberries, redcurrants and plums. If canned cherries are used, add them and their juice to the cooked fruit. Combine the cornflour/cornstarch and the orange juice in a small, deep bowl or a glass measure. Strain on 140ml/¼ pint/½ cup of the cooked fruit juice and stir well. Cook on HIGH 4-5 minutes, or until thickened. Fold carefully into the cooked fruit and allow the mixture to cool. When completely cooled add the strawberries and raspberries and chill before serving. Serve topped with natural yogurt sprinkled with cinnamon.

Red Flannel Hash

PREPARATION TIME: 20 minutes
MICROWAVE COOKING TIME:
19-22 minutes
SERVES: 8 people

6 potatoes, peeled and cut into small dice
900g/2lbs corned beef
1 onion, finely chopped
4 cooked beetroot/beets, peeled and diced
Salt and pepper
30ml/2 tbsps Worcestershire sauce
Dash tabasco
45g/1½ oz/3 tbsps butter or margarine
Chopped parsley

Place the potatoes in a large bowl with 90ml/6 tbsps water. Cover with cling film/plastic wrap and cook on HIGH for 5 minutes. Cut the corned beef roughly and drain the potatoes. Mix with the onions, beetroot/beets and seasonings. Place the mixture

Facing page: Apricot Cheesecake (top) and Red Fruit Compôte (bottom).

remaining butter in a casserole for 30 seconds on HIGH and add the onion. Cook for 1-2 minutes to soften slightly and stir in the flour. Gradually stir in the stock and sherry. Add the thyme and tomato purée/ paste, spoon in the kidneys and mushrooms, scraping the browning dish to remove the meat juices. Add a pinch of salt and pepper and cover the casserole. Cook on HIGH for 3 minutes. Stir well and cook a further 2 minutes on HIGH or until the kidneys are just tender. Stir in the cream and sprinkle with chopped parsley. Serve on, or surrounded by, triangles of hot, buttered toast, with the crusts removed.

Oeufs Florentine

PREPARATION TIME: 20 minutes

MICROWAVE COOKING TIME: 11½-13 minutes

SERVES: 4 people

450g/1lb fresh spinach
4 eggs

SAUCE
120g/4oz butter
Juice of ½ a lemon
Pinch cayenne pepper
Pinch dry mustard
2 egg yolks
Salt and pepper
Paprika

Wash the spinach well and remove any thick stalks. Place in a roasting bag and tie loosely with string. Cook on HIGH for 5-6 minutes, drain if necessary before using. To poach the eggs, pour 90ml/6 tbsps of hot water and a few drops of vinegar into each of 4 small dishes. Microwave on HIGH for about 1-2 minutes to bring to the boil. Break an egg into each dish and pierce the yolk with a skewer. Arrange the dishes in a circle and cook on HIGH for 2½-3

into a shallow dish or individual dishes and dot the top with butter or margarine. Cook on HIGH for 9-12 minutes. Leave to stand for 5 minutes before serving sprinkled with chopped parsley. Poached eggs may be served on top.

Sherried Kidneys and Mushrooms

PREPARATION TIME: 15 minutes

MICROWAVE COOKING TIME: 18 minutes

SERVES: 8 people

4-6 veal kidneys, cored and cut into small pieces

225g/8oz even-sized mushrooms, left whole
1 onion, finely chopped
45g/1½ oz/3 tbsps butter or margarine
45g/1½ oz/3 tbsps flour
1 clove garlic, crushed
280ml/½ pint/1 cup brown stock
140ml/¼ pint/½ cup dry sherry
1.25ml/¼ tsp thyme
15ml/1 tbsp tomato purée/paste
45ml/3 tbsps double/heavy cream
Chopped parsley
Toast

Heat a browning dish according to the manufacturer's directions. Melt 15g/1 tbsp of the butter and, when foaming, place in the kidneys and mushrooms. Cook for 3 minutes on HIGH, in two batches. Melt the

This page: Oeufs Florentine. Facing page: Red Flannel Hash (top) and Sherried Kidneys and Mushrooms (bottom).

minutes. Alternatively, cook on MEDIUM for 3-3¼ minutes. Allow the eggs to stand in the water for 30 seconds-1 minute before removing. If preparing the eggs in advance, place cooked eggs in a dish of cold water and keep until needed. To prepare the sauce, place the butter in a large, glass measure and heat on HIGH for 1½-2 minutes. Mix the lemon juice with the cayenne pepper, mustard and egg yolks and beat into the hot butter. Beat well and then add salt and pepper to taste. Cook on MEDIUM for 1 minute. Whisk the sauce thoroughly after 15 seconds and then continue cooking for another 15 seconds. Do not allow the sauce to boil. If the sauce begins to curdle, dip the glass measure into a bowl of cold water to stop the cooking. Whisk well and continue cooking until the sauce thickens. Season the spinach with salt and pepper and some grated nutmeg, if desired. Divide the spinach between 4 serving dishes. Spread it out evenly, leaving a slight well in the centre. Drain the poached eggs and place 1 egg in each dish. Cover the dishes and reheat on HIGH for 30 seconds. Pour over the sauce and serve immediately. To double the recipe, increase cooking time by half as much again.

Kedgeree

PREPARATION TIME: 25 minutes

MICROWAVE COOKING TIME: 27-32 minutes plus standing time

SERVES: 8 people

450g/1lb smoked haddock or cod
225g/8oz/1 cup long grain rice
10ml/2 tsps oil
180g/6oz cooked, peeled prawns/shrimp
2 hard-boiled eggs
5-10ml/1-2 tsps mild curry powder
180ml/6 fl oz/¾ cup single cream
Chopped parsley
Nutmeg

Place the fish in a covered casserole and cook on HIGH for 10-12 minutes. Flake the fish and discard the skin and bones. Place the rice in a

large, deep bowl with 570ml/1 pint/2 cups boiling water, a pinch of salt and the oil. Cover with cling film/plastic wrap and cook on HIGH for 12 minutes, stirring halfway through to separate the grains. Leave to stand for 7 minutes. Drain if all the water has not been absorbed. Stir in the flaked fish and prawns/shrimp and leave covered. Place the curry powder and the cream in a glass measure or a small, deep bowl. Cook on HIGH for 3-5 minutes or until almost boiling. Chop 1 of the hard-boiled eggs and add it to the rice and fish

This page: Kedgeree. Facing page: Scones (top) and Shortbread (bottom).

with the cream. Stir gently and spoon into a serving dish. Garnish the top with the remaining hard-boiled egg sliced, chopped or cut into eighths. Sprinkle over chopped parsley and paprika before serving. If necessary, reheat the kedgeree for 2-3 minutes on HIGH before garnishing with the hard-boiled egg.

MICROWAVE ENTERTAINING

Treats for Tea

Shortbread

PREPARATION TIME: 15 minutes

MICROWAVE COOKING TIME:
4½-6 minutes

MAKES: 10

120g/4oz/½ cup butter or margarine
60g/4 tbsps sugar
120g/4oz/1 cup plain/all-purpose flour
60g/2oz/4 tbsps rice flour
Pinch salt
120g/4oz plain/semi-sweet chocolate

Put the flour into a bowl with the rice flour and a pinch of salt. Rub in the butter or margarine until the mixture resembles fine breadcrumbs. Stir in half the sugar and knead the ingredients together lightly to form a dough. Line an 18cm/7 inch flan dish with greaseproof/wax paper. Alternatively, line the whole dish with cling film/plastic wrap. Press in the prepared shortbread mixture and smooth the top. Mark into 10 wedges and prick well with a fork. Cook on HIGH for 3-4 minutes. Sprinkle with the remaining sugar and allow to cool slightly. Cut through the markings in the wedges, remove from the dish and allow to cool on a wire rack. Melt the chocolate for 1½-2 minutes on MEDIUM, stirring until smooth. Holding the pointed end of each wedge of shortbread, place in the chocolate to coat about 5cm/ 2 inches or drizzle over the chocolate. Allow the chocolate to set and cool completely before serving.

Scones

PREPARATION TIME: 15 minutes

MICROWAVE COOKING TIME:
2-3½ minutes

MAKES: 9

120g/4oz/1 cup wholemeal/whole-
wheat flour
7.5ml/1½ tsps baking powder
Pinch salt
30g/1oz/2 tbsps butter or margarine

60g/½ cup sultanas/golden raisins
90ml/6 tbsps milk

Sift the flour, baking powder and a pinch of salt into a mixing bowl. Return the bran to the bowl. Cut in the butter or margarine until the mixture resembles fine breadcrumbs. This may be done in a food processor or by hand. Stir in the sultanas/golden raisins by hand and add the milk, gradually, until the dough comes together. It may not be necessary to add all the milk. Knead the dough lightly and turn it out onto a floured surface. Roll out to a thickness of 1.25-2.5cm/½-1 inch. Using a 5cm/2 inch round pastry cutter, cut the dough into approximately 9 rounds. The dough may also be cut into squares. Sprinkle each scone lightly with a mixture of sugar and cinnamon and place close together around the edge of a 23cm/9 inch round dish or microwave baking tray. Cook on HIGH for 2-3½ minutes or until the scones spring back lightly when touched. If necessary, rearrange the scones several times during cooking. Serve warm with jam and cream or butter.

Dundee Cake

PREPARATION TIME: 20 minutes

MICROWAVE COOKING TIME:
41-47 minutes plus standing time

MAKES: 1 cake

180g/6oz/¾ cup butter or margarine
180g/6oz/¾ cup dark brown sugar
3 eggs, lightly beaten
30ml/2 tbsps treacle/molasses
30ml/2 tbsps whisky
225g/8oz/2 cups plain/all-purpose flour
25g/1½ tbsps baking powder
15ml/1 tbsp allspice
60g/2oz/½ cup chopped almonds
60g/2oz/½ cup glacé/candied cherries, chopped
675g/1½ lbs/4½ cups mixed dried fruit (raisins, sultanas/golden raisins, currants, candied peel)

DECORATION
Apricot jam
Blanched split/halved almonds
Glacé cherries, halved

Soften the butter or margarine in a large bowl for 10-20 seconds on HIGH. Gradually beat in the sugar until light and fluffy. Beat in the eggs, one at a time, and add the treacle/molasses and whisky. Beat until smooth and then sift in the flour,

baking powder and spice. Carefully fold into the cream mixture and add the fruit, nuts and cherries. Use an 18cm/7 inch straight-sided deep baking dish, lightly greased and lined with greaseproof/wax paper. Spoon the prepared cake mixture into the dish and cook on LOW or DEFROST for 40-45 minutes. Leave to stand for 5 minutes before removing from the dish to cool on a wire rack. Melt the apricot jam for 1-2 minutes on HIGH, stir and sieve. Brush a thin layer of jam over the top of the cake while it is still warm and decorate with the almond and glacé cherries before the jam sets completely. Leave to cool completely before serving.

Orange Cake

PREPARATION TIME: 25 minutes

MICROWAVE COOKING TIME:
7½ minutes plus standing time

MAKES: 1 cake

180g/6oz/¾ cup butter or margarine
180g/6oz/¾ cup sugar
3 eggs
Grated rind of 2 oranges
180g/6oz/1½ cups plain/all-purpose flour
10ml/2 tsps baking powder
Orange juice or milk

ORANGE ICING/FROSTING
225g/8oz/2 cups sifted icing/powdered sugar
Juice of 1 orange made up to 60-75ml/4-5 tbsps with water
Rind of 1 orange cut into thin strips

Lightly grease the base and sides of an 18cm/7 inch diameter deep cake dish. Line the base with a circle of nonstick paper. Soften the butter or margarine for 30 seconds on HIGH in a large bowl. Mix in the sugar and, when light and fluffy, gradually beat in the eggs. Add the grated rind while beating in the eggs. Sift the flour and the baking powder together and fold into the mixture. Add enough orange juice or milk to bring the mixture to a thick dropping consistency. Spoon the mixture into the prepared dish

and smooth down the top. Cook on HIGH for 6 minutes. Leave the cake to stand in its dish on a flat surface for 5 minutes and then loosen the sides. Turn the cake out onto a wire rack set over a tray. For the icing/frosting, place the orange juice and water, if using, in a deep bowl with the strips of orange rind. Cook on HIGH for 1 minute to soften the orange rind and to heat the liquid. Sift in about ¾ of the icing/powdered sugar and stir to mix. The icing/frosting should coat the back of a spoon and slowly run off if it is thick enough. Add remaining sugar if necessary or thin down with more hot water. When the cake is completely cool, pour the icing/frosting onto the top and ease down the sides with a palette knife/spatula. Allow to set completely before serving.

Apricot Nut Loaf

PREPARATION TIME: 20 minutes

MICROWAVE COOKING TIME:
4-5 minutes

MAKES: 1 loaf

120g/4oz dried apricots, chopped
140ml/¼ pint/½ cup water
75g/2½ oz/5 tbsps margarine
75g/2½ oz/5 tbsps light brown sugar
120g/4oz/1 cup plain/all-purpose flour
7.5ml/1½ tsps baking powder
1.25ml/¼ tsp mixed spice or ground allspice
1.25ml/¼ tsp cinnamon
1 egg, slightly beaten
10ml/2 tsps golden syrup
45ml/3 tbsps milk
60g/2oz/½ cup chopped almonds or walnuts

Combine the apricots and water in a small bowl and cover loosely. Heat on HIGH for 2 minutes and leave to stand for 30 minutes. Combine the remaining ingredients except the nuts and mix well. Drain the apricots and reserve the juice. Stir the nuts and apricots into the loaf mixture, adding

Facing page: Dundee Cake.

enough of the reserved apricot juice to bring to a soft dropping consistency. Line a loaf dish with greaseproof/wax paper and spoon in the loaf mixture. Microwave on HIGH for 4 minutes. Reduce the setting to LOW and continue cooking for 8-9 minutes. Stand for 5 minutes before removing from the dish. When cool, sprinkle the top with icing/powdered sugar.

Chocolate Walnut Layer Cake

PREPARATION TIME: 25 minutes

MICROWAVE COOKING TIME:
11½-14 minutes plus standing time

MAKES: 1 cake

CHOCOLATE CAKE
225g/8oz/1 cup butter or margarine
250g/9oz/1⅛ cups brown sugar
140ml/4 fl oz/½ cup vegetable oil
4 eggs
180g/6oz/1½ cups plain/all-purpose
*   flour*
10ml/2 tsps baking powder
60g/4 tbsps cocoa

FILLING
45g/3 tbsps butter or margarine
60g/2oz/½ cup walnuts, finely chopped
30ml/2 tbsps single/light cream or
*   evaporated milk*
225g/8oz/2 cups icing/powdered sugar
2.5ml/½ tsp rum essence/extract

TOPPING
120g/4oz plain/semi-sweet chocolate
Walnut halves
Icing/powdered sugar

Line a 17.5cm/7 inch microwave cake dish with cling film/plastic wrap or place a greaseproof/wax paper circle in the bottom of a greased dish. Place the butter or margarine in a deep bowl and microwave on HIGH for 10-20 seconds to soften. Using an electric mixer, add the sugar and the oil gradually, making sure the sugar is well blended and the mixture is light and fluffy. When the sugar is no longer grainy, gradually beat in the eggs. If the mixture begins to curdle, add a little flour and whisk again. Put

the remaining flour with the baking powder and cocoa and fold into the cream mixture. Pour the mixture into the baking dish and cook on HIGH for 7 minutes. Leave to cool on a flat surface in the dish for 5-10 minutes and then remove to a cooling rack. While the cake cools, prepare the filling. Microwave the butter or margarine in a small mixing bowl on HIGH for about 1 minute or until melted. Stir in the walnuts and heat a further 2-4 minutes on HIGH until the butter and the nuts are light brown. Stir every 2 minutes. Sift in the icing/powdered sugar and beat well. Gradually add the cream until the filling is of spreading consistency. Add the rum essence/extract and set aside. Cut the cake horizontally into 3 layers and sandwich with the

This page: Apricot Nut Loaf (top) and Orange Cake (bottom). Facing page: Chocolate Walnut Layer Cake.

walnut filling. Break up the chocolate for the topping and put it into a small bowl. Microwave on MEDIUM for 1½-2 minutes, stirring often until the chocolate is spreadable. Using a palette knife/spatula, spread the chocolate onto the top of the cake. Toss the walnuts into the icing/powdered sugar to coat lightly. Shake off the excess sugar and, when the chocolate topping is nearly set, arrange the walnuts around the outside edge of the cake. Allow the chocolate to set completely before cutting to serve.

Cocktail Savouries

Prawns/Shrimp on Horseback

PREPARATION TIME: 30 minutes

MICROWAVE COOKING TIME:
7-8 minutes

MAKES: 16

8 slices bacon/smoked streaky bacon,
  rinds and bones removed
16 large uncooked prawns/shrimp, peeled
  but tail ends left on
1 large green pepper, seeded and cut into
  16 even-sized pieces
16 anchovy fillets, soaked in 60ml/4 tbsps
  milk
60ml/4 tbsps lemon juice
Dash tabasco
16 whole chives (optional)

Precook the bacon on a microwave
roasting rack or on a plate with paper
towels. Place two layers of paper
towels on a plate and arrange 4 slices
of bacon on the towel; cover with
another sheet of paper towel.
Arrange another 4 slices on top and
cover with another towel. If using a
microwave roasting rack place the
strips of bacon in an even layer. Cook
on HIGH for 4 minutes, or until the
bacon is slightly brown but not
completely cooked. Meanwhile, drain
the anchovies, rinse in cold water
and pat dry. Place a prawn/shrimp on
top of each slice of pepper and wrap
an anchovy around the middle.
Sprinkle with lemon juice and a dash
of tabasco. Cut the bacon strips in
half and wrap one half around each
prawn/shrimp. If using chives, soften
for 15 seconds on HIGH in a small
dish of water. Drain and tie up each
prawn/shrimp roll. Alternatively,
secure with cocktail sticks/wooden
picks. Place the prawns/shrimp on a
plate or in a microwave baking dish.
Cook on HIGH for 3-4 minutes or
until the prawns/shrimp are cooked.

Sweet and Sour Sausages

PREPARATION TIME: 25 minutes

MICROWAVE COOKING TIME:
6-10 minutes plus standing time

SERVES: 6-8 people

450g/1lb chipolatas/pork sausages
30ml/2 tbsps oil
225g/8oz canned pineapple pieces/
  chunks, drained and juice reserved
1 large or 2 small green peppers, seeded
  and cut into 2.5cm/1 inch pieces
225g/8oz cherry tomatoes (if
  unavailable, substitute 1 large or 2
  small sweet red peppers, seeded and cut
  into 2.5cm/1 inch pieces

SAUCE
15ml/1 tbsp cornflour/cornstarch
30ml/2 tbsps brown sugar
1.25ml/¼ tsp ground ginger
1 clove garlic, crushed
15ml/1 tbsp tomato ketchup
15ml/1 tbsp soy sauce
Reserved pineapple juice

Heat a browning dish according to
the manufacturer's directions. Prick
the sausage skins all over with a fork.
When the browning dish is hot, add
the oil and the sausages and cook for
3 minutes on HIGH, turning
frequently to brown evenly. Drain
the sausages on paper towels and cut
them into 2.5cm/1 inch pieces.
Combine all the sauce ingredients,
stirring in the reserved pineapple
juice gradually. Combine the sauce
with all the other ingredients, except
tomatoes, in a casserole dish and
cook on HIGH for 3-7 minutes or
until the sauce is thickened, stirring
carefully two or three times. Add
tomatoes and leave to stand 1-2
minutes. Provide cocktail sticks/
wooden picks for serving.

Chicken Satays with Peppers

PREPARATION TIME: 25 minutes
plus marinating time

MICROWAVE COOKING TIME:
11-15 minutes

SERVES: 6-8 people

4 chicken breasts, skinned and boned
3 small peppers, red, green and yellow

MARINADE
60ml/4 tbsps oil
Grated rind and juice of 1 lime
5ml/1 tsp dry mustard powder
15ml/1 tbsp light soy sauce
1 clove garlic, crushed

BASTING SAUCE
1 shallot, finely chopped
1 clove garlic, crushed
15ml/1 tbsp tomato purée/paste
½ chili pepper, finely chopped
60ml/4 tbsps chicken stock
15ml/1 tbsp soy sauce
30ml/2 tbsps smooth peanut butter

GARNISH
Lime wedges

**Facing page: Sweet and Sour
Sausages.**

Lamb and Mint Meatballs

PREPARATION TIME: 20 minutes

MICROWAVE COOKING TIME: 8 minutes

SERVES: 6-8 people

450g/1lb minced/ground lamb
1 medium onion, roughly chopped
1.25ml/¼ tsp ground allspice
Salt and pepper
10ml/2 tsps chopped fresh mint
10ml/2 tsps chopped fresh parsley
4 slices bread, crusts removed
Water
Fresh mint leaves, as large as possible

GARNISH
Lemon twists

Chop the onion in a food processor until fine. Add the lamb, allspice, salt, pepper, chopped mint, chopped parsley and the bread slices, torn into small pieces. Process again to mix, but do not overwork the meat. Add about 60ml/4 tbsps water and process again briefly. The mixture should be very moist but still hold together. Use more water if necessary. Pat the mixture into 2.5cm/1 inch balls. Wrap each meatball in a mint leaf. Place the meatballs on a microwave baking sheet or in a shallow dish. Place the ends of the mint leaves on the bottom. Cook on HIGH for 5 minutes. Turn over and reposition the meatballs and cook a further 3 minutes on HIGH or until fully cooked. Garnish serving dish with lemon twists.

Cut the chicken breasts into 2.5cm/ 1 inch pieces. Seed the pepper and cut them into pieces the same size as the chicken. Thread three pieces of chicken and three pieces of pepper, alternating the colours, onto small wooden skewers. Place them in a shallow microwave ovenproof dish. Mix together the marinade ingredients and pour over the satays. Cover with cling film/plastic wrap and leave to stand for 2 hours or overnight in the refrigerator. Turn the satays often to coat them evenly. Place all the sauce ingredients in a blender or food processor and purée until smooth. Pour into a small bowl and cook on HIGH for 5-6 minutes, until boiling, stirring frequently. Heat

This page: Prawns/Shrimp on Horseback. Facing page: Chicken Satays with Peppers (top) and Lamb and Mint Meatballs (bottom).

a browning dish according to the manufacturer's directions and when hot place the satays on the dish, turning to lightly brown all sides. Cook in the browning dish or on a microwave oven rack for 5-7 minutes, turning frequently and basting with the sauce. Combine any remaining sauce with the remaining marinade and reheat on HIGH for 1-2 minutes. Before serving, brush the satays lightly with sauce and serve the remaining sauce separately.

Hot Salmon and Horseradish Pinwheels

PREPARATION TIME: 25 minutes

MICROWAVE COOKING TIME: 1-2 minutes 20 seconds

SERVES: 6-8 people

225g/8oz smoked salmon, thinly sliced
225g/8oz cream, curd or low fat soft cheese
15ml/1 tbsp prepared horseradish sauce
10ml/2 tsps chopped fresh or dried dill

1 medium-sized cucumber, cut into 1.25cm/½ inch thick rounds

Place slices of smoked salmon on separate sheets of cling film/plastic wrap. Soften the cheese for 20 seconds on HIGH and mix with the horseradish and dill. Divide the cheese mixture among all the slices of smoked salmon and spread evenly. Roll-up the salmon Swiss roll/jelly roll fashion and wrap tightly in the cling film/plastic wrap. Place in the freezer until well chilled and firm, but not frozen. Score the skin of the cucumber, lengthwise, with the prongs of a fork, if desired. Slice the cucumber and sprinkle lightly with salt. Leave to drain on paper towels for 30 minutes. Rinse well and pat dry. Slice the salmon rolls crosswise into 6mm/¼ inch slices. Place one slice on each slice of cucumber and arrange in a circle on a plate or microwave baking sheet. Heat for 1-2 minutes on HIGH before serving.

This page: Hot Salmon and Horseradish Pinwheels. Facing page: Pâté en Gelée.

MICROWAVE ENTERTAINING

Buffet

Pâte en Gelée

PREPARATION TIME: 25 minutes
plus chilling time

MICROWAVE COOKING TIME:
27-30 minutes

SERVES: 8-10 people

225g/8oz bacon/rindless streaky bacon
450g/1lb coarsely minced/ground pork
225g/8oz minced/ground veal
225g/8oz pig/pork liver, skinned
1 clove garlic, crushed
1.25ml/¼ tsp ground allspice
30g/2 tbsps aspic powder
1.25ml/¼ tsp ground nutmeg
1.25ml/¼ tsp ground ginger
570ml/1 pint/2 cups water and white
* wine mixed half and half*
2.5ml/½ tsp thyme
10ml/1 tsp chopped parsley
Salt and pepper
140ml/¼ pint/½ cup double/heavy
* cream*
30ml/2 tbsps brandy
150g/5oz thick-cut gammon or ham
2 bay leaves

DECORATION
Fresh herbs
Capers
Green peppercorns

Stretch the bacon with the back of a knife and use it to line a 1.7 litre/ 3 pint/6 cup glass loaf dish. Combine the minced/ground meats, liver, garlic, spices, herbs, salt and pepper in a food processor and work to chop roughly. Add the cream and the brandy and process once or twice to mix. Cut the ham or gammon into strips and set aside. Place ⅓ of the meat mixture into the lined terrine and spread smoothly. Place a layer of ham or gammon on top and then cover with a layer of meat. Repeat with the remaining gammon and meat mixture, smooth down the top and fold any overlapping strips of bacon. Place 2 bay leaves on the top and cover the dish with cling film/ plastic wrap. Cook on MEDIUM for 12 minutes. Allow the pâté to rest for 5 minutes. Cook on MEDIUM for a further 20 minutes. Cover the top of the pâté with foil and weight down. Chill for at least 2-4 hours or overnight. To serve, prepare aspic as for the Salmon in Aspic. Slice the pâté in 5mm/¼ inch slices and place them on a cooling rack. Decorate the slices with small sprigs of fresh herbs, capers, green peppercorns or pimento. Pour a small amount of nearly set aspic over the top of the decoration to set it. When the aspic is completely set, coat the whole slice of pâté with a thin layer of nearly set aspic. Allow to set and then arrange on a serving plate slightly overlapping. Put any remaining aspic in a tray, turn out when set and cut into cubes or chop roughly. Pile the aspic in the middle of the pâté slices to serve.

Salmon in Aspic

PREPARATION TIME: 35 minutes

MICROWAVE COOKING TIME: 32-39 minutes

SERVES: 8-10 people

1.25kg/3¼ lbs whole salmon or salmon trout
Whole dill or fennel
Oil for brushing
30g/2 tbsps aspic powder
570ml/1 pint/2 cups water and white wine mixed half and half
Fresh herbs for decoration
Pimento
Lemon or lime slices
Fresh bay leaves

Rinse the salmon and dry well. Trim off the fins and brush the skin lightly with oil. Place dill or fennel inside the fish for extra flavour. Cover the head and tail with foil and cover the foil with a double thickness of cling film/ plastic wrap. Make a steam hole with a sharp knife on either side of the dorsal fin. Curve the fish to fit the turntable and then loosely tie the head to the tail with a slip knot. Cook on LOW or DEFROST for 26-29 minutes. Remove the string, cling film/plastic wrap and foil halfway through cooking time. To test if the salmon is cooked, insert a sharp knife into one of the steam holes at the dorsal fin. The blade should pass easily through the fish if it is fully cooked. Allow the fish to cool slightly and then peel away the skin using a filleting knife or a table knife. Cover the fish loosely with cling film/plastic wrap and allow to cool completely. Remove the herbs from inside the fish and discard them. Place the fish on a serving dish while preparing the aspic and decorations. Bring the water and wine to the boil in a deep bowl or glass measure. This should take about 4-6 minutes. Stir in the aspic powder and heat 1-2 minutes on HIGH to dissolve it completely. Place the bowl or glass measure into a bowl of iced water and allow the aspic to cool completely, until almost set. Brush a thin layer of the aspic over the salmon and allow it to set. To re-use the aspic, melt 1-2 minutes on HIGH and stir gently. Allow to thicken slightly again in iced water and spoon a thin layer over the salmon. When almost set, decorate with small sprigs of fresh herbs, lemon slices, bay leaves and pimento. Reheat the aspic once more and thicken it again over ice. Carefully spoon the thickened aspic over the decorations and leave to set completely. Pour the remaining aspic into a shallow pan and set in the refrigerator. Remove the set aspic and turn out onto a dampened cutting board. Cut into small cubes or chop roughly. Use to decorate serving dish for the salmon along with small bunches of fresh herbs and lemon slices.

Salad Singapore

PREPARATION TIME: 25 minutes plus marinating time

MICROWAVE COOKING TIME: 10-15 minutes

SERVES: 6-8 people

1 1.5kg/3¼ lb chicken
5ml/1 tsp freshly ground black pepper
5ml/1 tsp ground mustard
5ml/1 tsp ground ginger
1 clove garlic, crushed
2.5ml/½ tsp ground turmeric
5ml/1 tsp mild curry powder
30ml/2 tbsps vegetable oil
60g/4 tbsps raw peanuts
225g/8oz courgettes/zucchini, sliced diagonally
1 red pepper, seeded and shredded
225g/8oz mangetout/pea pods
1 medium-sized cucumber
30g/2 tbsps desiccated coconut

Skin and bone the chicken and cut the meat into shreds. Mix all the spices together and toss with the chicken. Allow to stand in the refrigerator for at least 2 hours. Heat a browning dish according to the manufacturer's directions and add the oil. Add the peanuts and cook on HIGH for 2-3 minutes, stirring frequently until lightly browned. Remove the peanuts with a draining spoon and add the courgettes/ zucchini, red pepper and mangetout/ pea pods to the browning dish. Return to the microwave oven and cook on HIGH for 2 minutes. Place in a serving dish and keep warm. If necessary, add another 15ml/1 tbsp oil to the browning dish and reheat. Add the chicken and cook in small batches for 5-7 minutes on HIGH. Cut the cucumber into thin strips and add to the vegetables in the serving dish. Add the chicken and the peanuts and toss thoroughly. Sprinkle over the desiccated coconut and reheat for 1-2 minutes on HIGH if desired before serving. May also be served cold.

Potato, Cucumber and Dill Salad

PREPARATION TIME: 20 minutes

MICROWAVE COOKING TIME: 16-22 minutes

SERVES: 6-8 people

450g/1lb even-sized small new potatoes, scrubbed
3 sprigs dill
Salt
1 cucumber, cut into 2.5cm/1 inch chunks

DRESSING
1 whole egg and 1 egg yolk
½ pint oil
30ml/2 tbsps chopped fresh dill or 15ml/ 1 tbsp dried dill
15ml/1 tbsp mild mustard
15ml/1 tbsp white wine vinegar
1 spring/green onion, finely chopped

GARNISH
Sprigs of fresh dill

Facing page: Salmon in Aspic.

Put the potatoes into a large bowl with the dill and salt. Pour over enough boiling water to cover. Cover the bowl with pierced cling film/ plastic wrap and cook on HIGH for 15-20 minutes or until the potatoes are tender. Do not allow the potatoes to boil too rapidly. Reduce the setting to MEDIUM if necessary. Drain and leave the potatoes to cool. Prepare the dressing in a food processor. Combine the eggs with all the remaining ingredients except the oil. With the machine running, gradually pour the oil through the feed tube in a thin, steady stream.

This page: Boeuf Niçoise. Facing page: Cheesecake (top) and Chocolate Truffle Cake (bottom).

Add salt and pepper to taste. Place the chunks of cucumber in a casserole with 60ml/4 tbsps water. Cook on HIGH for 1-2 minutes to blanch. Rinse immediately under cold water and leave to dry. Combine the potatoes and the cucumbers in a bowl with the dressing. Transfer to a serving dish and garnish with sprigs of fresh dill.

Chocolate Truffle Cake

PREPARATION TIME: 20 minutes

MICROWAVE COOKING TIME: 7 minutes

SERVES: 8-10 people

340g/12oz plain/semi-sweet chocolate
120g/4oz/½ cup butter
60ml/4 tbsps brandy or rum
2 eggs
225g/8oz/2 cups digestive biscuits/ graham crackers, crushed
60g/2oz/½ cup chopped blanched almonds

280ml/½ pint/1 cup whipped cream
Chocolate curls

Melt the chocolate and butter together on MEDIUM for 5 minutes. Beat in the eggs and heat a further 2 minutes on MEDIUM, stirring twice to thicken the eggs. Stir in the brandy, biscuits and chopped almonds. Spread into a 17cm/7 inch springform or removable base pan. Chill overnight until firm. Transfer to a serving dish and pile the cream on top. Decorate the top with chocolate curls. To prepare chocolate curls, take a thick block of plain/semi-sweet chocolate and microwave on MEDIUM LOW for 30-60 seconds or until the chocolate is just barely warm. Turn the chocolate once or twice while heating. To form the curls, draw a swivel vegetable peeler towards you across the edge of the chocolate in a continuous, even motion. Chocolate curls may be kept in an airtight container.

Cheesecake

PREPARATION TIME: 30 minutes

MICROWAVE COOKING TIME: 14-25½ minutes

SERVES: 6-8 people

FILLING
450g/1lb cream cheese
150g/5oz/⅔ cup sugar
Pinch salt
90ml/3 fl oz/⅓ cup single/light cream
Rind and juice of ½ lemon
Pinch ground coriander
4 eggs

CRUST
60g/2oz/4 tbsps butter or margarine
8-10 digestive biscuits/¾ cup graham
   crackers, crushed
30ml/2 tbsps sugar

TOPPING
1 kiwi fruit, peeled and thinly sliced
2-3 satsumas, pith carefully removed
120g/4oz fresh strawberries, washed and
   halved or raspberries (if strawberries or
   raspberries are unavailable, use black/
   purple grapes, halved and seeded)
Green seedless grapes, halved
Apricot jam

Place the cream cheese in a bowl and microwave on MEDIUM for 1 minute or until softened. Beat in the sugar, salt, cream and lemon rind. Gradually blend in the lemon juice and eggs. Cook on HIGH for 4-7 minutes, stirring very well every 2 minutes. Line the bottom of a 22.5cm/9 inch round baking dish with a circle of greaseproof/wax paper. Pour in the cream cheese mixture and cook on MEDIUM for 7-15 minutes or until almost set. Meanwhile prepare the crust. Mix the crushed digestive biscuits/ graham crackers in a food processor or blender with the sugar. Work until fine. Melt the butter for 1½-2 minutes on HIGH. With the machine running, pour in the butter to mix with the crmbs. When the cheese filling is nearly set, carefully spoon over the crumb crust. Press down lightly and cook on HIGH for 1½ minutes. Allow the cheesecake to cool in the dish and then refrigerate overnight. To decorate, loosen the cheesecake from the sides of the dish and turn out onto a serving plate. Carefully peel away the disc of paper from the top. Arrange the various prepared fruits in circles on top of the cheesecake. Melt the apricot jam for 1 minute on HIGH and strain. Brush the fruit with a light layer of warm glaze, making sure that all the fruit is covered completely. Allow the glaze to set before serving.

Boeuf Niçoise

PREPARATION TIME: 30 minutes plus chilling time

MICROWAVE COOKING TIME: 23-31 minutes

SERVES: 8-10 people

450g/1lb fillet of beef/beef tenderloin

SALAD
1 head cauliflower, trimmed into flowerets
225g/8oz broccoli, trimmed into flowerets
225g/8oz French/green beans, trimmed
8 tomatoes, peeled and quartered
60g/½ cup black olives, stoned

DRESSING
120ml/4oz olive oil
30ml/2 tbsps white wine vinegar
10ml/2 tsps Dijon mustard
10ml/2 tsps chopped fresh basil
5ml/1 tsp chopped fresh parsley
Salt and pepper

Place the meat on a microwave roasting rack with the thinner portion of the meat tucked under for an even shape. Tie with string to keep the shape. Wrap the ends of the beef with foil, shiny side down, and cook on HIGH for 3 minutes. Remove the foil from the beef and reduce the power to MEDIUM. Cook a further 5-8 minutes longer, turning the beef over once. Allow to stand until cool. The meat should be rare. If desired, brush the beef lightly with gravy browning before beginning to cook. Bring 1150ml/ 2 pints/4 cups water to the boil in a large glass bowl for 8-11 minutes on HIGH. Drop in 4 tomatoes and leave for 5 seconds. Remove to a bowl of iced water and reboil the water. Repeat with a further 4 tomatoes. Skin the tomatoes, quarter them and set them aside. Place the cauliflower flowerets in a casserole dish with

This page: Salad Singapore (top) and Potato, Cucumber and Dill Salad (bottom). Facing page: Raspberry Ripple Cake.

60ml/4 tbsps water and a pinch of salt. Cover the dish and cook on HIGH for 4-5 minutes. Place the broccoli flowerets in the water after 2 minutes of cooking time. Drain the vegetables and rinse under cold water to stop the cooking. Cook the beans in a casserole dish with 90ml/6 tbsps water. Cover the dish and cook on

HIGH for 3-4 minutes. Rinse the beans under cold water to stop the cooking and leave them to drain with the cauliflower and the broccoli. Mix the dressing ingredients together in a large bowl and when the vegetables are dry add them to the dressing along with the tomatoes and the olives. Toss the vegetables to coat, then leave in the refrigerator for 1 hour to marinate. To assemble the salad, slice the beef thinly and arrange on a serving plate in a semi-circle with the slices overlapping. Using a draining spoon, pile the vegetable salad onto the plate. Pour some of the remaining dressing over the meat before serving.

MICROWAVE ENTERTAINING

A Children's Party

Raspberry Ripple Cake

PREPARATION TIME: 2 minutes

MICROWAVE COOKING TIME:
11-13 minutes

MAKES: 1 cake

180g/6oz/¾ cup butter or margarine
180g/6oz/¾ cup sugar
3 eggs, lightly beaten
180g/6oz/1½ cups plain/all-purpose
  flour
Salt
10ml/2 tsps baking powder
45ml/3 tbsps seedless raspberry jam
30ml/2 tbsps hot water (optional)
Few drops red food colouring

ICING/FROSTING
45ml/3 tbsps seedless raspberry jam
450g/1lb/4 cups icing/powdered sugar
Hot water

Heat butter or margarine for 1 minute on HIGH to soften. Beat until creamy, and gradually beat in the sugar until light and fluffy. Gradually beat in the eggs until the mixture is mousse-like and all the eggs have been incorporated. Sift in the flour with a pinch of salt and the baking powder. Fold the dry ingredients into the butter, sugar and eggs. Divide the mixture into two bowls and add the raspberry jam and red food colouring to half the mixture. Stir thoroughly. Add hot water to the plain half as necessary to bring the mixture to soft dropping consistency. Line a round or decorative microwave cake dish with cling film/plastic wrap. Fill with spoonfuls of the two mixtures, alternating the colours. Draw a knife or spatula through the mixtures to marble the two colours. Cook for 6-8 minutes on HIGH, turning the dish occasionally if it is not a round shape. If the corners of the cake appear to be overcooking, cover with foil if your oven manufacturer allows its use. Leave in the dish for 5 minutes before turning out to cool. Soften the jam for the icing/frosting for 20 seconds on HIGH and beat until smooth. Fill a piping/pastry bag fitted with a small writing nozzle/tube with the jam. Heat about 280ml/½ pint/1 cup water on HIGH for 4-5 minutes. Sift in the icing/powdered sugar gradually, beating until the icing/frosting coats the back of a spoon but runs off slowly. It may not be necessary to add all the sugar.

Pour over the cake, using a palette knife/spatula to help spread the icing. Pipe thin lines of jam over the cake before the icing/frosting sets completely. Quickly swirl the jam through the icing/frosting with a skewer and allow to set completely before cutting to serve.

Chocolate Marshmallow Turtles

PREPARATION TIME: 15 minutes

MICROWAVE COOKING TIME: 2 minutes 15 seconds-4½ minutes

MAKES: 12

48 shelled pecans
12 marshmallows
120g/4oz/½ cup chocolate chips
15g/1 tbsp vegetable shortening

Put the pecans in groups of 4 on a microwave baking sheet lined with nonstick paper. Place a marshmallow on top of the pecans. Microwave on HIGH for 15-30 seconds or until the marshmallows just start to puff. Place the chocolate chips and the vegetable shortening in a small bowl. Microwave on MEDIUM for 2-4 minutes, stirring frequently until the chocolate melts. Spoon over the top of each turtle to cover the marshmallow. Leave to set completely before serving.

Chocolate Squares

PREPARATION TIME: 30 minutes

MICROWAVE COOKING TIME: 5 minutes

MAKES: 16

60g/2oz/4 tbsps butter or margarine
180g/6oz plain/semi-sweet chocolate
30ml/2 tbsps golden syrup or honey
225g/8oz/2 cups digestive biscuits/
  graham crackers, crushed
Coloured glacé cherries

Place the butter or margarine, chocolate and syrup or honey in a small, deep bowl and heat on MEDIUM for 5 minutes, stirring

occasionally until the chocolate melts. Stir in the biscuit crumbs and mix thoroughly. Grease a shallow 18cm/7 inch square pan and spoon in the chocolate mixture. Smooth the top and mark into squares with a sharp knife. Cut the glacé cherries in half and put a half on top of each square, alternating the colours. Leave to set completely and then cut into squares to serve.

Granola Bars

PREPARATION TIME: 15 minutes

MICROWAVE COOKING TIME: 7-8 minutes

MAKES: 12

675g/1½ lbs/6 cups toasted muesli/fruit
  and nut granola

120g/4oz/½ cup butter or margarine
120g/4oz/½ cup dark brown sugar
Pinch salt
2 eggs, beaten
Few drops vanilla essence/extract

Place the butter or margarine in a glass measure and microwave for 45 seconds-1 minute on HIGH. Combine the brown sugar, salt, eggs and flavouring in a large bowl and gradually beat in the melted butter. Add the granola and stir to coat well. Lightly grease a 30 x 20cm/12 x 8 inch baking dish and press in the mixture. Cook on HIGH for 6-8 minutes or until just firm to the touch. If the corners of the mixture seem to be cooking before the centre, place foil across all 4 corners and continue cooking. Press the mixture with a palette knife/spatula every few minutes to smooth down. Before allowing to cool, cut the mixture into 12 bars. Allow to cool completely before removing from the dish.

Animal Crackers

PREPARATION TIME: 20 minutes

MICROWAVE COOKING TIME: 2-4 minutes

MAKES: 24

120g/4oz/1 cup plain/all-purpose flour
60g/2oz/½ cup wholemeal/whole-wheat flour
30g/2 tbsps sugar
2.5ml/½ tsp bicarbonate of soda
1.25ml/¼ tsp salt
1.25ml/¼ tsp ground cinnamon
60g/4 tbsps vegetable shortening
15g/1 tbsp butter or margarine
30ml/2 tbsps water

15ml/1 tbsp honey
15ml/1 tbsp treacle/molasses
Few drops vanilla essence/extract

Sift the flours with the sugar, bicarbonate of soda, salt and cinnamon into a deep bowl. Return the bran to the bowl. Cut in the vegetable shortening and butter or margarine until the particles are the size of small peas. This may also be done in a food processor. Combine the water, honey, treacle/molasses and vanilla in a small bowl. Mix with the dry ingredients, tossing and mashing with a fork until the particles cling together. Form into a ball, cover with cling film/plastic wrap and refrigerate at least 1 hour. Divide the dough in half and roll out to 5mm/¼ inch thickness on a well-floured surface. Flour the rolling pin frequently while rolling out. Cut the

Facing page: Animal Crackers (top) and Chocolate Marshmallow Turtles (bottom). This page: Granola Bars (top), and Chocolate Squares (bottom).

dough with animal shaped biscuit/cookie cutters. Prick lightly with a fork and transfer to a plate or microwave baking sheet lined with nonstick/wax paper. Cook 12 cookies at a time arranged in a circle around the edge of the plate or baking sheet. Cook on HIGH for 1-2 minutes or until the surface of the dough is dry and firm to touch. Cool on a wire rack. Sprinkle lightly with icing/powdered sugar or decorate with melted chocolate or coloured icings/frostings.

INDEX

Dep. Leg. B-4191-88